READINGS ON HOW THE WORLD WORKS

Current Issues in International Relations

Russell Bova
Dickinson College

Longman

New York   San Francisco   Boston
London   Toronto   Sydney   Tokyo   Singapore   Madrid
Mexico City   Munich   Paris   Cape Town   Hong Kong   Montrea

Acquisitions Editor: Vik Mukhija
Marketing Manager: Lindsey Prudhomme
Production Manager: Denise Phillip
Project Coordination, Text Design, and Electronic Page Makeup: Electronic Publishing
    Services Inc., NYC
Cover Design Manager: Wendy Ann Fredericks
Cover Photo: Photodisc Photography/Veer
Photo Researcher: Jody Potter
Senior Manufacturing Buyer: Dennis J. Para

For permission to use copyrighted material, grateful acknowledgment is made to the copyright
holders credited throughout the book, which are hereby made part of this copyright page.

Library of Congress Cataloging-in-Publication Data

Bova, Russell, 1955-
    Readings on how the world works : current issues in international relations / Russell Bova.
        p.   cm.
    Includes bibliographical references.
    ISBN-13:   978-0-321-40999-7
    ISBN-10:   0-321-40999-X
 1.   International relations—Textbooks.   I. Title.
    JZ1242.B69 2010
    327—dc22

                                                                                2008054014

Longman
is an imprint of

www.pearsonhighered.com

ISBN 13: 978-0-321-40999-7
ISBN 10:   0-321-40999-X

BRIEF CONTENTS

DETAILED CONTENTS

PREFACE

We are living in an era of profound change in world politics. Over the past two decades we have witnessed, to note just a few of the most dramatic events, the fall of the Berlin wall, the disintegration of the USSR, terror attacks in the United States, the rise of China as a global economic power, two wars in the Persian Gulf, and a global financial crisis. At a larger level, we have experienced the decline of communism, the acceleration of economic globalization, and a shift in the global distribution of economic, political, and military power from the West to Asia. These events, and the more fundamental changes that are both their cause and effect, have had a significant impact on the field of international relations. The once dominant realist paradigm has faced renewed criticism from old challengers (liberalism and neo-Marxism) as well as from newer (at least to international relations theory) paradigms such as constructivism and feminism.

In the face of these changes in both the world and study of international relations, scholars, perhaps less than ever, can be said to speak with one voice. Thus, it is essential that students be exposed to a range of voices, coming from a variety of theoretical perspectives, on how the world works. *Readings on How the World Works* provides that variety. Like the accompanying survey text, *How the World Works,* this collection of readings provides perspectives on international relations that provide ammunition to both realists and their critics. It is intended for use in introductory and advanced courses in international relations and world politics. The organization and chapter titles found in the reader mirror those of the survey, and the selections were chosen with the content of that text in mind. To help students link concepts covered in the main text, the selections in this reader are referenced in boxes inserted in the margins of *How the World Works*. At the same time, this reader covers the range of topics typically addressed in world politics courses, and it could be assigned in combination with any standard international relations textbook. It could also serve alone or supplemented by other readings or short topical paperbacks as the backbone of a course in which no survey text is adopted.

FEATURES

Selecting 36 readings to include from the thousands available is a challenge. At the most basic level, the choice faced was one that instructors continually confront in assigning supplementary readings to their students—whether to lean toward theory or issues. While students typically want to read about current issues, instructors want to develop a theoretical sophistication that will outlast newspaper headlines. The assumption underlying the selections included here is that to get beginning students of international relations to think theoretically and to appreciate the relevance of theory requires the presentation of theory in an issue-oriented context. Abstract theoretical discussions that might be intriguing to scholars are largely meaningless to students not yet in possession of basic information about the world in which they live. For example, it is hard to imagine a student who lacks an understanding of the structure and record of the United Nations appreciating and learning much from an abstract discussion of realism vs. liberal institutionalism.

Thus, the goal was to include readings that work simultaneously to engage students (what students want) and to elevate their level of theoretical sophistication in thinking about world politics (what teachers want). To that end, the readings selected for inclusion are intended to help students bridge the gap between theory and issues. They are of two types:

1. Readings that explicitly extend discussion of the main macro-level paradigms or theoretical perspectives on world politics. Chapter 1 includes pieces from well-known proponents of some of the major contending perspectives. Most of the other chapters also include one such selection, and they help put the other more issue-oriented readings included in each chapter into their proper theoretical context. In selecting these readings, special care was made to include those that would be accessible to undergraduates taking their first world politics course. In most cases, they were selected because they not only discuss large theoretical concepts, but also apply them to contemporary issues.

2. Readings that enrich and deepen student understanding of specific micro-level issues and controversies in world politics. The readings of this second type are what might be categorized as applied theory. However, in all cases, selections were included not only for the information and insight on specific issues, but also because they speak, directly or indirectly, to the larger theoretical debate among realists, liberals, constructivists, feminists, and neo-Marxists over "how the world works" on a grand scale. To achieve this goal, individual readings do not necessarily display an overt theoretical perspective (though many of those included do). A reading that casts doubt on the effectiveness of global human rights efforts might be useful ammunition for realists without ever mentioning the word *realism*. In contrast, a reading that makes the case for the significance of the United Nations or international law could contribute to the case for "liberal institutionalist" approaches to world politics.

To help students understand the larger significance of what they are reading and to help them make the connection between theory and issues, the reader includes the following pedagogical aids.

- **Chapter Introductions.** Each chapter of the reader begins with a brief introduction to the general themes found in the readings for that chapter. That introduction gives a sense of the general purposes and goals of the chapter as a whole.

● **Reading Headnotes.** Realistically, students may not refer to the general chapter introduction before completing each reading assignment, and instructors who adopt this reader, especially those who do not use my accompanying text, are likely to skip around in assigning readings. Thus, each individual reading begins with a one-paragraph introduction which sets up that reading for the student and puts it into some context. In each case, the introduction raises three questions that the student should keep in mind as he or she reads the selection.

SUPPLEMENTS

Longman is pleased to offer several resources to qualified adopters of *Readings on How the World Works* and their students that will make teaching and learning from this book even more effective and enjoyable.

FOR INSTRUCTORS

MyPoliSciKit Video Case Studies for International Relations and Comparative Politics. This DVD series contains video clips featured in the MyPoliSciKit case studies for this and other Longman political science titles. Featuring video from major news sources and providing reporting and insight on recent world affairs, this DVD helps instructors integrate current events into their courses by letting them use the clips as lecture launchers or discussion starters.

FOR STUDENTS

Longman Atlas of World Issues (0-321-22465-5). Introduced and selected by Robert J. Art of Brandeis University and excerpted from the acclaimed Penguin Atlas Series, the *Longman Atlas of World Issues* is designed to help students understand the geography and major issues facing the world today, such as terrorism, debt, and HIV/AIDS. These thematic, full-color maps examine forces shaping politics today at a global level. Explanatory information accompanies each map to help students better grasp the concepts being shown and how they affect our world today. Available at no additional charge when packaged with this book.

New Signet World Atlas (0-451-19732-1). From Penguin Putnam, this pocket-sized yet detailed reference features 96 pages of full-color maps plus statistics, key data, and much more. Available at a discount when packaged with this book.

The Penguin Dictionary of International Relations (0-140-51397-3). This indispensable reference by Graham Evans and Jeffrey Newnham includes hundreds of cross-referenced entries on the enduring and emerging theories, concepts, and events that are shaping the academic discipline of international relations and today's world politics. Available at a discount when packaged with this book.

Research and Writing in International Relations (0-321-27766-X). Written by Laura Roselle and Sharon Spray of Elon University, this brief and affordable guide provides the basic step-by-step process and essential resources that are needed to write political science papers that go beyond simple description and into more systematic and sophisticated inquiry. This text focuses on the key areas in which students need the most help: finding a topic, developing a question, reviewing literature, designing research, analyzing findings, and last, actually writing the paper. Available at a discount when packaged with this book.

Study Card for International Relations (0-321-29231-6). Packed with useful information, Allyn & Bacon/Longman's Study Cards make studying easier, more efficient, and more enjoyable. Course information is distilled down to the basics, helping students quickly master the fundamentals, review a subject for under-standing, or prepare for an exam. Because they're laminated for durability, students can keep these Study Cards for years to come and pull them out whenever they need a quick review. Available at no additional charge when packaged with this book.

Careers in Political Science (0-321-11337-3). Offering insider advice and prac-tical tips on how to make the most of a political science degree, this booklet by Joel Clark of George Mason University shows students the tremendous potential such a degree offers and guides them through: deciding whether political science is right for them; the different career options available; job requirements and skill sets; how to apply, interview, and compete for jobs after graduation; and much more. Available at a discount when packaged with this book.

ACKNOWLEDGMENTS

Many people contributed to this book of readings. The team at Longman, spear-headed by Vikram Mukhija, helped me refine my selections and make tough choices from the much larger list under original consideration. Students in my international relations classes unknowingly helped in the process by reacting positively to some readings and negatively to others that I have used in my classes in recent semesters. Reviewers of this reader—Nozar Alaolmolki, Hiram College; Kristian Alexander, University of Utah; Vincent Auger, Western Illinois University; William Batkay, Montclair State University; Eric Cox, Texas Christian University; Richard Chadwick, University of Hawaii, Manoa; John Dietrich, Bryant University; Vittorio Nicholas Galasso, University of Delaware; Stephanie Hallock, Harford Community College; Maia Hallward, Kennesaw State University; James Hentz, Virginia Military Institute; Nathan Jensen, Washington University in St. Louis; Michael Koch, Texas A&M University; William Lahneman; Towson University; Keith Lepak, Youngstown State

University; Kristina Mani, Oberlin College; Scott Nelson, Virginia Tech; Laura Neack, Miami University; Mark Schroeder, University of Kentucky; Johanes Sulaiman, Ohio State University; Eugene Tadie, George Mason University; James Toole; Indiana University-Purdue; Julie Webber, Illinois State University; and Andrew Yeo, Catholic University—also made some useful suggestions and alerted me to possibilities that I otherwise might not have considered. Susan Messer helped me clean up and sharpen the writing in the chapter and individual article introductions. My wife, Candace L. Bova, and my three daughters—Laura, Samantha, and Alexandra—did not make any suggestions for readings to include. But in their own way they provided the most important contributions of all—love, support, and a larger sense of life's purpose.

—*Russell Bova*

CHAPTER 1

HOW TO THINK ABOUT WORLD POLITICS
Realism and Its Critics

To understand and make sense of the rush of empirical events that make up the day-to-day practice of international relations and world politics, scholars tend to view the world through larger theoretical frameworks. Those frameworks (variously referred to as *perspectives, approaches,* or *paradigms*) have the virtue of taking the complexity of the world and reducing it to a set of core assumptions that make the twists and turns of daily events more comprehensible. In so doing, however, scholars must inevitably simplify reality, and as a result, they disagree sharply over which theoretical approach best captures and explains how the world really works.

For much of the post–World War II era, the dominant paradigm was realism. The pessimism inherent in the realist perspective seemed to many an appropriate lens through which to view a pessimistic century characterized by two world wars, countless smaller wars, violent revolutions, the development of nuclear weapons, and a decades-long Cold War that threatened to turn hot at any time. The end of the Cold War, however, provided fuel to a growing dissatisfaction with realism among many scholars who saw it as increasingly unable to explain trends in the late twentieth-century world.

The readings included in this chapter aim at deepening your understanding of these contending approaches to analyzing international relations in the early twenty-first century. They include representative selections of well-known scholars from the realist, liberal, constructivist, and feminist paradigms. After reading these selections, you should have a good understanding of the essential differences among the various approaches and be in a position to form at least some preliminary impressions of the explanatory value of each. Those first impressions will, of course, be challenged and tested as you read further into this volume and as you explore more specific issues and topics in the study of international relations.

THE TRAGEDY OF GREAT POWER POLITICS

John J. Mearsheimer

Mearsheimer is one of the best-known contemporary proponents of the realist approach to international relations. In this reading, adapted from his widely read 2001 book, he summarizes his view. As you read this selection, ask yourself:

❋ What are the essential assumptions of the realist perspective?

❋ What are the sub-types of realism that he discusses, and how do they differ?

❋ Why do Americans, according to Mearsheimer, dislike realism?

Many in the West seem to believe that "perpetual peace" among the great powers is finally at hand. The end of the Cold War, so the argument goes, marked a sea change in how great powers interact with one another. We have entered a world in which there is little chance that the major powers will engage each other in security competition, much less war, which has become an obsolescent enterprise. In the words of one famous author, the end of the Cold War has brought us to the "the end of history."[1]

This perspective suggests that great powers no longer view each other as potential military rivals, but instead as members of a family of nations, members of what is sometimes called the "international community." The prospects for cooperation are abundant in this promising new world, a world which is likely to bring increased prosperity and peace to all the great powers. Even a few adherents of realism, a school of thought that has historically held pessimistic views about the prospects for peace among the great powers, appear to have bought into the reigning optimism, as reflected in an article from the mid-1990s titled "Realists as Optimists."[2]

Alas, the claim that security competition and war between the great powers have been purged from the international system is wrong. Indeed, there is much evidence that the promise of everlasting peace among the great powers was stillborn. Consider, for example, that even though the Soviet threat has disappeared, the United States still maintains about one hundred thousand troops in Europe and roughly the same number in Northeast Asia. It does so because it recognizes that dangerous rivalries would probably emerge among the major powers in these regions if U.S. troops were withdrawn. Moreover, almost every European state, including the United Kingdom and France, still harbors deep-seated, albeit muted, fears that a Germany unchecked by American power might behave aggressively; fear of Japan in Northeast Asia is probably even more profound, and it is certainly more frequently expressed. Finally, the possibility of a clash between China and the United States over Taiwan is hardly remote. This is not to say that such a war is likely, but the possibility reminds us that the threat of great-power war has not disappeared.

The sad fact is that international politics has always been a ruthless and dangerous business, and it is likely to remain that way. Although the intensity of their competition waxes and wanes, great powers fear each other and always compete with each other for power. The overriding goal of each state is to maximize its share of world power, which means gaining power at the expense of other states. But great powers do not merely strive to be the strongest of all the great powers, although that is a welcome outcome. Their ultimate aim is to be the hegemon—that is, the only great power in the system.

There are no status quo powers in the international system, save for the occasional hegemon that wants to maintain its dominating position over potential rivals. Great powers are rarely content with the current distribution of power; on the contrary, they face a constant incentive to change it in their favor. They almost always have revisionist intentions, and they will use force to alter the balance of power if they think it can be done at a reasonable price.[3] At times, the costs and risks of trying to shift the balance of power are too great, forcing great powers to wait for more favorable circumstances. But the desire for more power does not go away, unless a state achieves the ultimate goal of hegemony. Since no state is likely to achieve global hegemony, however, the world is condemned to perpetual great-power competition.

This unrelenting pursuit of power means that great powers are inclined to look for opportunities to alter the distribution of world power in their favor. They will seize these opportunities if they have the necessary capability. Simply put, great powers are primed for offense. But not only does a great power seek to gain power at the expense of other states, it also tries to thwart rivals bent on gaining power at its expense. Thus, a great power will defend the balance of power when looming change favors another state, and it will try to undermine the balance when the direction of change is in its own favor.

Why do great powers behave this way? My answer is that the structure of the international system forces states which seek only to be secure nonetheless to act aggressively toward each other. Three features of the international system combine to cause states to fear one another: 1) the absence of a central authority that sits above states and can protect them from each other, 2) the fact that states always have some offensive military capability, and 3) the fact that states can never be certain about other states' intentions. Given this fear—which can never be wholly eliminated—states recognize that the more powerful they are relative to their rivals, the better their chances of survival. Indeed, the best guarantee of survival is to be a hegemon, because no other state can seriously threaten such a mighty power.

This situation, which no one consciously designed or intended, is genuinely tragic. Great powers that have no reason to fight each other—that are merely concerned with their own survival—nevertheless have little choice but to pursue power and to seek to dominate the other states in the system. This dilemma is captured in brutally frank comments that Prussian statesman Otto von Bismarck made during the early 1860s, when it appeared that Poland, which was not an independent state at the time, might regain its sovereignty. "Restoring the Kingdom of Poland in any shape or form is tantamount to creating an ally for any enemy that chooses to attack us," he believed, and therefore he advocated that Prussia should "smash those Poles till, losing all hope, they lie down and die; I have every sympathy for their situation, but if we wish to survive we have no choice but to wipe them out."[4]

Although it is depressing to realize that great powers might think and act this way, it behooves us to see the world as it is, not as we would like it to be. For example, one of the key foreign policy issues facing the United States is the question of how China will behave if its rapid economic growth continues and effectively turns China into a giant Hong Kong. Many Americans believe that if China is democratic and enmeshed in the global capitalist system, it will not act aggressively; instead it will be content with the status quo in Northeast Asia. According to this logic, the United States should engage China in order to promote the latter's integration into the world economy, a policy that also seeks to encourage China's transition to democracy. If engagement succeeds, the United States can work with a wealthy and democratic China to promote peace around the globe.

Unfortunately, a policy of engagement is doomed to fail. If China becomes an economic powerhouse it will almost certainly translate its economic might into military might and make a run at dominating Northeast Asia. Whether China is democratic and deeply enmeshed in the global economy or autocratic and autarkic will have little effect on its behavior, because democracies care about security as much as non-democracies do, and hegemony is the best way for any state to guarantee its own survival. Of course, neither its neighbors nor the United States would stand idly by while China gained increasing increments of power. Instead, they would seek to contain China, probably by trying to form a balancing coalition. The result would be an intense security competition between China and its rivals, with the ever-present danger of great-power war hanging over them. In short, China and the United States are destined to be adversaries as China's power grows. . . .

LIBERALISM VS. REALISM

Liberalism and realism are the two bodies of theory which hold places of privilege on the theoretical menu of international relations. Most of the great intellectual battles among international relations scholars take place either across the divide between realism and liberalism, or within those paradigms.[5] To illustrate this point, consider the three most influential realist works of the twentieth century:

1. E. H. Carr's *The Twenty Years' Crisis, 1919–1939,* which was published in the United Kingdom shortly after World War II started in Europe (1939) and is still widely read today.
2. Hans Morgenthau's *Politics among Nations,* which was first published in the United States in the early days of the Cold War (1948) and dominated the field of international relations for at least the next two decades.
3. Kenneth Waltz's *Theory of International Politics,* which has dominated the field since it first appeared during the latter part of the Cold War (1979).[6]

All three of these realist giants critique some aspect of liberalism in their writings. For example, both Carr and Waltz take issue with the liberal claim that economic interdependence enhances the prospects for peace.[7] More generally, Carr and Morgenthau frequently criticize liberals for holding utopian views of politics which, if followed, would lead states to disaster. At the same time, these realists also disagree about a number of important issues. Waltz, for example, challenges Morgenthau's claim that multipolar systems are more stable than bipolar systems.[8] Furthermore, whereas Morgenthau argues that states strive to gain power because they have an innate desire for power, Waltz maintains that the structure of the international system forces states to pursue power to enhance their prospects for survival. These examples are just a small sample of the differences among realist thinkers.[9]

Let us now look more closely at liberalism and realism, focusing first on the core beliefs shared by the theories in each paradigm, and second on the differences among specific liberal and realist theories.

Liberalism

The liberal tradition has its roots in the Enlightenment, that period in eighteenth-century Europe when intellectuals and political leaders had a powerful sense that reason could be employed to make the world a better place.[10] Accordingly, liberals tend to be hopeful about the prospects of making the world safer and more peaceful. Most liberals believe that it is possible to substantially reduce the scourge of war and to increase international prosperity. For this reason, liberal theories are sometimes labelled "utopian" or "idealist."

Liberalism's optimistic view of international politics is based on three core beliefs, which are common to almost all of the theories in the paradigm. First, liberals consider states to be the main actors in international politics. Second they emphasize that the internal characteristics of states vary considerably, and that these differences have profound effects on state behavior.[11] Furthermore, liberal theorists often believe that some internal arrangements (e.g., democracy) are inherently preferable to others (e.g., dictatorship). For liberals, therefore, there are "good" and "bad" states in the international system. Good states pursue cooperative policies and hardly ever start wars on their own, whereas bad states cause conflicts with other states and are prone to use force to get their way.[12] Thus, the key to peace is to populate the world with good states.

Third, liberals believe that calculations about power matter little for explaining the behavior of good states. Other kinds of political and economic calculations matter more, although the form of those calculations varies from theory to theory, as will become apparent below. Bad states might be motivated by the desire to gain power at the expense of other states, but that is only because they are misguided. In an ideal world, where there are only good states, power would be largely irrelevant.

Among the various theories found under the big tent of liberalism, the three main ones mentioned earlier are particularly influential. The first argues that high levels of economic interdependence among states make them unlikely to fight each other.[13] The taproot of stability, according to this theory, is the creation and maintenance of a liberal economic order that allows for free economic exchange among states. Such an order makes states more prosperous, thereby bolstering peace, because prosperous states are more economically satisfied and satisfied states are more peaceful. Many wars are waged to gain or preserve wealth, but states have much less motive to initiate war if they are already wealthy. Furthermore, wealthy states with interdependent economies stand to become less prosperous if they fight each other, since they are biting the hand that feeds them. Once states establish extensive economic ties, in short, they avoid war and can concentrate instead on accumulating wealth.

The second, democratic peace theory, claims that democracies do not go to war against other democracies.[14] Thus, a world containing only democratic states would be a world without war. The argument here is not that democracies are less warlike than non-democracies, but rather that democracies do not fight among themselves. There are a variety of explanations for the democratic peace, but little agreement as to which one is correct. Liberal thinkers do agree, however, that democratic peace theory offers a direct challenge to realism and provides a powerful recipe for peace.

Finally, some liberals maintain that international institutions enhance the prospects for cooperation among states and thus significantly reduce the likelihood of war.[15] Institutions are not independent political entities that sit above states and force them to behave in acceptable ways. Instead, institutions are sets of rules that stipulate the ways in which states should cooperate and compete with each other. They prescribe acceptable forms of state behavior and proscribe unacceptable kinds of behavior. These rules are not imposed on states by some leviathan, but are negotiated by states, which agree to abide by the rules they created because it is in their interest to do so. Liberals claim that these institutions or rules can fundamentally change state behavior. Institutions, so the argument goes, can discourage states from calculating self-interest on the basis of how their every move affects their relative power position, and thus they push states away from war and promote peace.

Realism

In contrast to liberals, realists are pessimists when it comes to international politics. Realists agree that creating a peaceful world would be desirable, but they see no easy way to escape the harsh world of security competition and war. Creating a peaceful world is surely an attractive idea, but it is not a practical one. "Realism," as Carr notes, "tends to emphasize the irresistible strength of existing forces and the inevitable character of existing tendencies, and to insist that the highest wisdom lies in accepting, and adapting oneself to these forces and these tendencies."[16]

This gloomy view of international relations is based on three core beliefs. First, realists, like liberals, treat states as the principal actors in world politics. Realists focus mainly on great powers, however, because these states dominate and shape international politics and they also cause the deadliest wars. Second, realists believe that the behavior of great powers is influenced mainly by their external environment, not by their internal characteristics. The structure of the international system, which all states must deal with, largely shapes their foreign policies. Realists tend not to draw sharp distinctions between "good" and "bad" states, because all

great powers act according to the same logic regardless of their culture, political system, or who runs the government.[17] It is therefore difficult to discriminate among states, save for differences in relative power. In essence, great powers are like billiard balls that vary only in size.[18]

Third, realists hold that calculations about power dominate states' thinking, and that states compete for power among themselves. That competition sometimes necessitates going to war, which is considered an acceptable instrument of statecraft. To quote Carl von Clausewitz, the nineteenth-century military strategist, war is a continuation of politics by other means.[19] Finally, a zero-sum quality characterizes that competition, sometimes making it intense and unforgiving. States may cooperate with each other on occasion, but at root they have conflicting interests.

Although there are many realist theories dealing with different aspects of power, two of them stand above the others: human nature realism, which is laid out in Morgenthau's *Politics among Nations,* and defensive realism, which is presented mainly in Waltz's *Theory of International Politics.* What sets these works apart from those of other realists and makes them both important and controversial is that they provide answers to the two foundational questions described above. Specifically, they explain why states pursue power—that is, they have a story to tell about the *causes* of security competition—and each offers an argument about how much power a state is likely to want.

Some other famous realist thinkers concentrate on making the case that great powers care deeply about power, but they do not attempt to explain why states compete for power or what level of power states deem satisfactory. In essence, they provide a general defense of the realist approach, but they do not offer their own theory of international politics. The works of

Carr and American diplomat George Kennan fit this description. In his seminal realist tract, *The Twenty Years' Crisis,* Carr criticizes liberalism at length and argues that states are motivated principally by power considerations. Nevertheless, he says little about why states care about power or how much power they want.[20] Bluntly put, there is no theory in his book. The same basic pattern obtains in Kennan's well-known book *American Diplomacy 1900–1950.*[21] Morgenthau and Waltz, on the other hand, offer their own theories of international relations, which is why they have dominated the discourse about world politics for the past fifty years.

Human nature realism, which is sometimes called "classical realism," dominated the study of international relations from the late 1940s, when Morgenthau's writings began attracting a large audience, until the early 1970s.[22] It is based on the simple assumption that states are led by human beings who have a "will to power" hardwired into them at birth.[23] That is, states have an insatiable appetite for power, or what Morgenthau calls "a limitless lust for power," which means that they constantly look for opportunities to take the offensive and dominate other states.[24] All states come with an *"animus dominandi,"* so there is no basis for discriminating among more aggressive and less aggressive states, and there certainly should be no room in the theory for status quo states.[25] Human nature realists recognize that international anarchy—the absence of a governing authority over the great powers—causes states to worry about the balance of power. But that structural constraint is treated as a second-order cause of state behavior. The principal driving force in international politics is the will to power inherent in every state in the system, and it pushes each of them to strive for supremacy.

Defensive realism, which is frequently referred to as "structural realism," came on the scene in the late 1970s with the appearance of

Waltz's *Theory of International Politics.*[26] Unlike Morgenthau, Waltz does not assume that great powers are inherently aggressive because they are infused with a will to power; instead he starts by assuming that states merely aim to survive. Above all else, they seek security. Nevertheless, he maintains that the structure of the international system forces great powers to pay careful attention to the balance of power. In particular, anarchy forces security-seeking states to compete with each other for power, because power is the best means to survival. Whereas human nature is the deep cause of security competition in Morgenthau's theory, anarchy plays that role in Waltz's theory.[27]

Waltz does not emphasize, however, that the international system provides great powers with good reasons to act offensively to gain power. Instead, he appears to make the opposite case: that anarchy encourages states to behave defensively and to maintain rather than upset the balance of power. "The first concern of states," he writes, is "to maintain their position in the system."[28] There seems to be, as international relations theorist Randall Schweller notes, a "status quo bias" in Waltz's theory.[29]

Waltz recognizes that states have incentives to gain power at their rivals' expense and that it makes good strategic sense to act on that motive when the time is right. But he does not develop that line of argument in any detail. On the contrary, he emphasizes that when great powers behave aggressively, the potential victims usually balance against the aggressor and thwart its efforts to gain power.[30] For Waltz, in short, balancing checkmates offense.[31] Furthermore, he stresses that great powers must be careful not to acquire too much power, because "excessive strength" is likely to cause other states to join forces against them, thereby leaving them worse off than they would have been had they refrained from seeking additional increments of power.[32]

Waltz's views on the causes of war further reflect his theory's status quo bias. There are no profound or deep causes of war in his theory. In particular, he does not suggest that there might be important benefits to be gained from war. In fact, he says little about the causes of war, other than to argue that wars are largely the result of uncertainty and miscalculation. In other words, if states knew better, they would not start wars.

Robert Jervis, Jack Snyder, and Stephen Van Evera buttress the defensive realists' case by focusing attention on a structural concept known as the offense-defense balance.[33] They maintain that military power at any point in time can be categorized as favoring either offense or defense. If defense has a clear advantage over offense, and conquest is therefore difficult, great powers will have little incentive to use force to gain power and will concentrate instead on protecting what they have. When defense has the advantage, protecting what you have should be a relatively easy task. Alternatively, if offense is easier, states will be sorely tempted to try conquering each other, and there will be a lot of war in the system. Defensive realists argue, however, that the offense-defense balance is usually heavily tilted toward defense, thus making conquest extremely difficult.[34] In sum, efficient balancing coupled with the natural advantages of defense over offense should discourage great powers from pursuing aggressive strategies and instead make them "defensive positionalists."[35]

My theory of offensive realism is also a structural theory of international politics. As with defensive realism, my theory sees great powers as concerned mainly with figuring out how to survive in a world where there is no agency to protect them from each other; they quickly realize that power is the key to their survival. Offensive realism parts company with defensive realism over the question of how much power states want. For defensive realists, the international structure provides states with little incentive to seek additional increments of power; instead it pushes them to maintain the existing balance of power. Preserving power, rather than increasing it, is the main goal of states. Offensive realists, on the other hand, believe that status quo powers are rarely found in world politics, because the international system creates powerful incentives for states to look for opportunities to gain power at the expense of rivals, and to take advantage of those situations when the benefits outweigh the costs. A state's ultimate goal is to be the hegemon in the system.[36]

It should be apparent that both offensive realism and human nature realism portray great powers as relentlessly seeking power. The key difference between the two perspectives is that offensive realists reject Morgenthau's claim that states are naturally endowed with Type A personalities. On the contrary, they believe that the international system forces great powers to maximize their relative power because that is the optimal way to maximize their security. In other words, survival mandates aggressive behavior. Great powers behave aggressively not because they want to or because they possess some inner drive to dominate, but because they have to seek more power if they want to maximize their odds of survival. (Table 1.1 summarizes how the main realist theories answer the foundational questions described above.)

No article or book makes the case for offensive realism in the sophisticated ways that Morgenthau does for human nature realism and Waltz and others do for defensive realism. For sure, some realists have argued that the system gives great powers good reasons to act aggressively. Probably the best brief for offensive realism is a short, obscure book written during World War I by G. Lowes Dickinson, a British academic who was an early advocate of the League of Nations.[37] In *The European Anarchy,*

TABLE 1.1 The Major Realist Theories

	Human Nature Realism	Defensive Realism	Offensive Realism
What causes states to compete for power?	Lust for power inherent in states	Structure of the system	Structure of the system
How much power do states want?	All they can get. States maximize relative power, with hegemony as their ultimate goal.	Not much more than what they have. States concentrate on maintaining the balance of power.	All they can get. States maximize relative power, with hegemony as their ultimate goal.

he argues that the root cause of World War I "was not Germany nor any other power. The real culprit was the European anarchy," which created powerful incentives for states "to acquire supremacy over the others for motives at once of security and domination."[38] Nevertheless, neither Dickinson nor anyone else makes a comprehensive case for offensive realism.[39] . . .

POWER POLITICS IN LIBERAL AMERICA

Whatever merits realism may have as an explanation for real-world politics and as a guide for formulating foreign policy, it is not a popular school of thought in the West. Realism's central message—that it makes good sense for states to selfishly pursue power—does not have broad appeal. It is difficult to imagine a modern political leader openly asking the public to fight and die to improve the balance of power. No European or American leader did so during either world war or the Cold War. Most people prefer to think of fights between their own state and rival states as clashes between good and evil, where they are on the side of the angels and their opponents are aligned with the devil. Thus, leaders tend to portray war as a moral crusade or an ideological contest, rather than as a struggle for power. Realism is a hard sell.

Americans appear to have an especially intense antipathy toward balance-of-power thinking.

The rhetoric of twentieth-century presidents, for example, is filled with examples of realism bashing. Woodrow Wilson is probably the most well-known example of this tendency, because of his eloquent campaign against balance-of-power politics during and immediately after World War I.[40] Yet Wilson is hardly unique, and his successors have frequently echoed his views. In the final year of World War II, for example, Franklin Delano Roosevelt declared, "In the future world the misuse of power as implied in the term 'power politics' must not be the controlling factor in international relations."[41] More recently, Bill Clinton offered a strikingly similar view, proclaiming that "in a world where freedom, not tyranny, is on the march, the cynical calculus of pure power politics simply does not compute. It is ill-suited to a new era."[42] He sounded the same theme when defending NATO expansion in 1997, arguing that the charge that this policy might isolate Russia was based on the mistaken belief "that the great power territorial politics of the 20th century will dominate the 21st century." Instead, Clinton emphasized his belief that "enlightened self-interest, as well as shared values, will compel countries to define their greatness in more constructive ways . . . and will compel us to cooperate."[43]

Why Americans Dislike Realism

Americans tend to be hostile to realism because it clashes with their basic values. Realism stands opposed to Americans' views of both themselves and the wider world.[44] In particular, realism is at odds with the deep-seated sense of optimism and moralism that pervades much of American society. Liberalism, on the other hand, fits neatly with those values. Not surprisingly, foreign policy discourse in the United States often sounds as if it has been lifted right out of a Liberalism 101 lecture.

Americans are basically optimists.[45] They regard progress in politics, whether at the national or the international level, as both desirable and possible. As the French author Alexis de Tocqueville observed long ago, Americans believe that "man is endowed with an indefinite faculty of improvement."[46] Realism, by contrast, offers a pessimistic perspective on international politics. It depicts a world rife with security competition and war, and holds out little promise of an "escape from the evil of power, regardless of what one does."[47] Such pessimism is at odds with the powerful American belief that with time and effort, reasonable individuals can cooperate to solve important social problems.[48] Liberalism offers a more hopeful perspective on world politics, and Americans naturally find it more attractive than the gloomy specter drawn by realism.

Americans are also prone to believe that morality should play an important role in politics. As the prominent sociologist Seymour Martin Lipset writes, "Americans are utopian moralists who press hard to institutionalize virtue, to destroy evil people, and eliminate wicked institutions and practices."[49] This perspective clashes with the realist belief that war is an intrinsic element of life in the international system. Most Americans tend to think of war as a hideous enterprise that should ultimately be abolished from the face of the Earth. It might justifiably be used for lofty liberal goals like fighting tyranny or spreading democracy, but it is morally incorrect to fight wars merely to change or preserve the balance of power. This makes the Clausewitzian conception of warfare anathema to most Americans.[50]

The American proclivity for moralizing also conflicts with the fact that realists tend not to distinguish between good and bad states, but instead discriminate between states largely on the basis of their relative power capabilities. A purely realist interpretation of the Cold War, for example, allows for no meaningful difference in the motives behind American and Soviet behavior during that conflict. According to realist theory, both sides were driven by their concerns about the balance of power, and each did what it could to maximize its relative power. Most Americans would recoil at this interpretation of the Cold War, however, because they believe the United States was motivated by good intentions while the Soviet Union was not.

Liberal theorists do distinguish between good and bad states, of course, and they usually identify liberal democracies with market economies as the most worthy. Not surprisingly, Americans tend to like this perspective, because it identifies the United States as a benevolent force in world politics and portrays its real and potential rivals as misguided or malevolent troublemakers. Predictably, this line of thinking fueled the euphoria that attended the downfall of the Soviet Union and the end of the Cold War. When the "evil empire" collapsed, many Americans (and Europeans) concluded that democracy would spread across the globe and that world peace would soon break out. This optimism was based largely on the belief that democratic America is a virtuous state. If other states emulated the United States, therefore, the world would be populated by good states, and this development could only mean the end of international conflict.

Rhetoric vs. Practice

Because Americans dislike realpolitik, public discourse about foreign policy in the United

States is usually couched in the language of liberalism. Hence the pronouncements of the policy elites are heavily flavored with optimism and moralism. American academics are especially good at promoting liberal thinking in the marketplace of ideas. Behind closed doors, however, the elites who make national security policy speak mostly the language of power, not that of principle, and the United States acts in the international system according to the dictates of realist logic.[51] In essence, a discernible gap separates public rhetoric from the actual conduct of American foreign policy.

Prominent realists have often criticized U.S. diplomacy on the grounds that it is too idealistic and have complained that American leaders pay insufficient attention to the balance of power. For example, Kennan wrote in 1951, "I see the most serious fault of our past policy formulation to lie in something that I might call the legalistic-moralistic approach to international problems. This approach runs like a red skein through our foreign policy of the last fifty years."[52] According to this line of argument, there is no real gap between American's liberal rhetoric and its foreign policy behavior, because the United States practices what it preaches. But this claim is wrong, as I will argue at length below. American foreign policy has usually been guided by realist logic, although the public pronouncements of its leaders might lead one to think otherwise.

It should be obvious to intelligent observers that the United States speaks one way and acts another. In fact, policymakers in other states have always remarked about this tendency in American foreign policy. As long ago as 1939, for example, Carr pointed out that states on the European continent regard the English-speaking peoples as "masters in the art of concealing their selfish national interests in the guise of the general good," adding that "this kind of hypocrisy is

a special and characteristic peculiarity of the Anglo-Saxon mind."[53]

Still, the gap between rhetoric and reality usually goes unnoticed in the United States itself. Two factors account for this phenomenon. First, realist policies sometimes coincide with the dictates of liberalism, in which case there is no conflict between the pursuit of power and the pursuit of principle. Under these circumstances, realist policies can be justified with liberal rhetoric without having to discuss the underlying power realities. This coincidence makes for an easy sell. For example, the United States fought against fascism in World War II and communism in the Cold War for largely realist reasons. But both of those fights were also consistent with liberal principles, and thus policymakers had little trouble selling them to the public as ideological conflicts.

Second, when power considerations force the United States to act in ways that conflict with liberal principles, "spin doctors" appear and tell a story that accords with liberal ideals.[54] For example, in the late nineteenth century, American elites generally considered Germany to be a progressive constitutional state worthy of emulation. But the American view of Germany changed in the decade before World War I, as relations between the two states deteriorated. By the time the United States declared war on Germany in April 1917, Americans had come to see Germany as more autocratic and militaristic than its European rivals.

Similarly, during the late 1930s, many Americans saw the Soviet Union as an evil state, partly in response to Josef Stalin's murderous internal policies and his infamous alliance with Nazi Germany in August 1939. Nevertheless, when the United States joined forces with the Soviet Union in late 1941 to fight against the Third Reich, the U.S. government began a massive public relations campaign to clean up the image of America's new ally and make it compatible with liberal ideals. The Soviet Union was now portrayed as a proto-democracy, and Stalin became "Uncle Joe."

How is it possible to get away with this contradiction between rhetoric and policy? Most Americans readily accept these rationalizations because liberalism is so deeply rooted in their culture. As a result, they find it easy to believe that they are acting according to cherished principles, rather than cold and calculated power considerations.[55]. . .

NOTES

1. The phrase "perpetual peace" was made famous by Immanuel Kant. See his "Perpetual Peace," in Hans Reiss, ed., *Kant's Political Writings*, trans. H. B. Nisbet (Cambridge: Cambridge University Press, 1970), pp. 93–130. Also see John Mueller, *Retreat from Doomsday: The Obsolescence of Major War* (New York: Basic Books, 1989); Michael Mandelbaum, "Is Major War Obsolete?" *Survival* 40, No. 4 (Winter 1998–99), pp. 20–38; and Francis Fukuyama, "The End of History?" *The National Interest*, No. 16 (Summer 1989), pp. 3–18, which was the basis of Francis Fukuyama, *The End of History and the Last Man* (New York: Free Press, 1992).

2. Charles L. Glaser, "Realists as Optimists: Cooperation as Self-Help," *International Security* 19, No. 3 (Winter 1994–95), pp. 50–90.

3. The balance of power is a concept that has a variety of meanings. See Inis L. Claude, Jr., *Power and International Relations* (New York: Random House, 1962), chap. 2; and Ernst B. Haas, "The Balance of Power: Prescription, Concept, or Propaganda?" *World Politics* 5, No. 4 (July 1953), pp. 442–77. I use it to mean the actual distribution of military assets among the great powers in the system.

4. Quoted in Lothar Gall, *Bismarck: The White Revolutionary*, vol. 1, 1851–1871, trans. J. A. Underwood (London: Unwin Hyman, 1986), p. 59.

5. This point is made clear in Michael W. Doyle, *Ways of War and Peace: Realism, Liberalism, and Socialism* (New York: Norton, 1997); and Brian C. Schmidt, *The Political Discourse of Anarchy: A Disciplinary History of International Relations* (Albany: State University of New York Press, 1998).

6. E. H. Carr, *The Twenty Years' Crisis, 1919–1939: An Introduction to the Study of International Relations*, 2d ed. (London: Macmillan, 1962; the first edition was published in 1939); Hans Morgenthau, *Politics among Nations: The Struggle for Power and Peace*, 5th ed. (New York: Knopf, 1973; the first edition was published in 1948); and Waltz, *Theory of International Politics* (Reading MA; Addison-Wesley, 1979).

7. Carr, *Twenty Years' Crisis*, chap. 4; Kenneth Waltz, "The Myth of National Interdependence," in Charles P. Kindelberger, ed., *The International Corporation* (Cambridge, MA: MIT Press, 1970), pp. 205–223; and Waltz, *Theory of International Politics*, chap. 7.

8. See Morgenthau, *Politics among Nations*, chaps. 14, 21; and Kenneth N. Waltz, "The Stability of a Bipolar World," *Daedalus* 93, No. 3 (Summer 1964), pp. 881–909.

9. For further evidence of those differences, see *Security Studies* 5, No. 2 (Winter 1995–96, special issue on "Roots of Realism," ed. Benjamin Frankel); and *Security Studies* 5, No. 3 (Spring 1996, special issue on "Realism: Restatements and Renewal," ed. Benjamin Frankel).

10. See F. H. Hinsley, *Power and the Pursuit of Peace: Theory and Practice in the History of Relations between States* (Cambridge: Cambridge University Press, 1967), pt. I; Torbjorn L. Knutsen, *A History of International Relations Theory: An Introduction* (New York: Manchester University Press, 1992), chap. 5; and F. Parkinson, *The Philosophy of International Relations: A Study in the History of Thought* (Beverly Hills, CA: Sage Publications, 1977), chap. 4.

11. See Andrew Moravcsik, "Taking Preferences Seriously: A Liberal Theory of International Politics," *International Organization* 51, No. 4 (Autumn 1997), pp. 513–53.

12. See Michael Howard, *War and the Liberal Conscience* (New Brunswick, NJ: Rutgers University Press, 1978).

13. See *inter alia* Norman Angell, *The Great Illusion: A Study of the Relation of Military Power in Nations to Their Economic and Social Advantage*, 3d rev. and enl. ed. (New York: G. P. Putnam's, 1912); Thomas L. Friedman, *The Lexus and the Olive Tree: Understanding Globalization* (New York: Farrar, Straus and Giroux, 1999); Edward D. Mansfield, *Power, Trade, and War* (Princeton, NJ: Princeton

University Press, 1994); Susan M. McMillan, "Interdependence and Conflict," *Mershon International Studies Review* 41, Suppl. 1 (May 1997), pp. 33–58; and Richard Rosecrance, *The Rise of the Trading State: Commerce and Conquest in the Modern World* (New York: Basic Books, 1986).

14. Among the key works on democratic peace theory are Michael E. Brown, Sean M. Lynn-Jones, and Steven E. Miller, eds., *Debating the Democratic Peace* (Cambridge, MA: MIT Press, 1996), pts. I and III; Michael Doyle, "Liberalism and World Politics," *American Political Science Review* 80, No. 4 (December 1986), pp. 1151–69; Fukuyama, "End of History?"; John M. Owen IV, *Liberal Peace, Liberal War: American Politics and International Security* (Ithaca, NY: Cornell University Press, 1997); James L. Ray, *Democracy and International Conflict: An Evaluation of the Democratic Peace Proposition* (Columbia: University of South Carolina Press, 1995); and Bruce Russett, *Grasping the Democratic Peace: Principles for a Post–Cold War World* (Princeton, NJ: Princeton University Press, 1993). Some scholars argue that democracies are more peaceful than non-democracies, regardless of the regime type of their adversary. But the evidence for this proposition is weak; stronger evidence exists for the claim that the pacific effects of democracy are limited to relations between democratic states.

15. See *inter alia* David A. Baldwin, ed., *Neorealism and Neoliberalism: The Contemporary Debate* (New York: Columbia University Press, 1993); Robert O. Keohane, *After Hegemony: Cooperation and Discord in the World Political Economy* (Princeton, NJ: Princeton University Press, 1984); *International Organization* 36, No. 2 (Spring 1982, special issue on "International Regimes," ed. Stephen D. Krasner); Lisa L. Martin and Beth A. Simmons, "Theories and Empirical Studies of International Institutions," *International Organization* 52, No. 4 (Autumn 1998), pp. 729–57; and John G. Ruggie, *Constructing the World Polity: Essays on International Institutionalization* (New York: Routledge, 1998), chaps. 8–10. Regimes and international law are synonymous with institutions, since all are essentially rules that states negotiate among themselves.

16. Carr, *Twenty Years' Crisis,* p. 10.

17. Although realists believe that the international system allows for little variation in the external conduct of great powers, they recognize that there are sometimes profound differences in how governments deal with their own people. For example, although the Soviet Union and the United States behaved similarly toward each other during the Cold War, there is no question that the leaders of each superpower treated their citizens in fundamentally different ways. Thus, one can rather easily distinguish between good and bad states when assessing internal conduct. Such distinctions, however, tell us relatively little about international politics.

18. Morgenthau is something of an exception regarding this second belief. Like other realists, he does not distinguish between good and bad states, and he clearly recognizes that external environment shapes state behavior. However, the desire for power, which he sees as the main driving force behind state behavior, is an internal characteristic of states.

19. Carl von Clausewitz, *On War,* trans. and ed. Michael Howard and Peter Paret (Princeton, NJ: Princeton University Press, 1976), esp. books 1, 8. Also see Richard K. Betts, "Should Strategic Studies Survive?" *World Politics* 50, No. 1 (October 1997), pp. 7–33, esp. p. 8; and Michael I. Handel, *Masters of War: Classical Strategic Thought,* 3d ed. (London: Frank Cass, 2001).

20. Michael J. Smith notes in *Realist Thought from Weber to Kissinger* (Baton Rouge: Louisiana State University Press, 1986) that Carr does not "explain why politics always involves power, an explanation vital to any attempt to channel the exercise of power along lines compatible with an ordered social existence. Is a lust for power basic to human nature—the view of Niebuhr and Morgenthau— . . . [or] is it the result of a security dilemma?" (p. 93).

21. George F. Kennan, *American Diplomacy, 1900–1950* (Chicago: University of Chicago Press, 1951). Smith writes, "Kennan nowhere offers a systematic explanation of his approach to international politics or of his political philosophy in general: he is a diplomat turned historian, not a theologian or a political theorist, and he is concerned neither to propound a doctrine of human nature nor to set forth the recurring truths of international politics in a quasi-doctrinal way." Smith, *Realist Thought,* p. 166.

22. Human nature realism lost much of its appeal in the early 1970s for a variety of reasons. The backlash against the Vietnam War surely contributed to its demise, since any theory that saw the pursuit

of military power as inevitable was likely to be unpopular on university campuses by 1970. [Ironically, Morgenthau was an early and vocal critic of the Vietnam War. See Hans J. Morgenthau, *Vietnam and the United States* (Washington, DC: Public Affairs, 1965); and "Bernard Johnson's Interview with Hans J. Morgenthau," in Kenneth Thompson and Robert J. Myers, eds., *Truth and Tragedy: A Tribute to Hans J. Morgenthau* (New Brunswick, NJ: Transaction Books, 1984), pp. 382–84.] Furthermore, the collapse of the Bretton Woods system in 1971, the oil shock of 1973, and the growing power of multinational corporations (MNCs) led many to think that economic issues had become more important than security issues, and that realism, especially Morgenthau's brand, had little to say about questions of international political economy. Some even argued in the early 1970s that MNCs and other transnational forces were threatening the integrity of the state itself. "Sovereignty at bay" was a widely used phrase at the time. Finally, human nature realism was essentially a philosophical theory that was out of sync with the behavioral revolution that was overwhelming the study of international politics in the early 1970s. Morgenthau intensely disliked modern social science theories, but he was badly outnumbered in this war of ideas and his theory lost much of its legitimacy. For Morgenthau's views on social science, see Hans J. Morgenthau, *Scientific Man vs. Power Politics* (Chicago: University of Chicago Press, 1946). For a recent but rare example of human nature realism, see Samuel P. Huntington, "Why International Primacy Matters," *International Security* 17, No. 4 (Spring 1993), pp. 68–71. Also see Bradley A. Thayer, "Bringing in Darwin: Evolutionary Theory, Realism, and International Politics," *International Security* 25, No. 2 (Fall 2000), pp. 124–51.

23. See Morgenthau, *Politics among Nations;* and Morgenthau, *Scientific Man.* Although Morgenthau is the most famous human nature realist, Reinhold Niebuhr was also a major intellectual force in this school of thought. See Niebuhr's *Moral Man and Immoral Society* (New York: Scribner's, 1932). Friedrich Meinecke made the case for human nature realism at considerable length well before Morgenthau began publishing his views on international politics in the mid-1940s. See Meinecke's *Machiavellism: The Doctrine of Raison d'Etat and Its Place in Modern History*, trans. Douglas Scott

(Boulder, CO: Westview, 1984), which was originally published in Germany in 1924 but was not published in English until 1957. Morgenthau, who was educated in Germany, was familiar with *Machiavellism*, according to his former student Kenneth W. Thompson. Correspondence with author, August 9, 1999. Also see Christoph Frei, *Hans J. Morgenthau: An Intellectual Biography* (Baton Rouge: Louisiana State University Press, 2001), pp. 207–26.

24. Morgenthau, *Scientific Man,* p. 194. Also see Morgenthau, *Politics among Nations,* p. 208.

25. Morgenthau, *Scientific Man,* p. 192. Despite his claim that "the desire to attain a maximum of power is universal" (*Politics among Nations,* p. 208), Morgenthau distinguishes between status quo and revisionist powers in his writings. *Politics among Nations,* pp. 40–44, 64–73. But there is an obvious problem here: if all states have a "limitless aspiration for power" (*Politics among Nations,* p. 208), how can there be status quo powers in the world? Moreover, although Morgenthau emphasizes that the drive for power is located in human nature, he also recognizes that the structure of the international system creates powerful incentives for states to pursue offense. He writes, for example, "Since . . . all nations live in constant fear lest their rivals deprive them, at the first opportune moment, of their power position, all nations have a vital interest in anticipating such a development and doing unto the others what they do not want the others to do unto them" (*Politics among Nations,* p. 208). However, if all states have a vital interest in taking advantage of each other whenever the opportunity presents itself, how can there be status quo powers in the system? Indeed, this incentive structure would seem to leave no room for satiated powers. Again, Morgenthau provides no explanation for this apparent contradiction. Arnold Wolfers notes this same problem in Morgenthau's work. See Wolfers's *Discord and Collaboration: Essays on International Politics* (Baltimore, MD: Johns Hopkins University Press, 1962), pp. 84–86.

26. Waltz's other key works on realism include *Man, the State, and War: A Theoretical Analysis* (New York: Columbia University Press, 1959); "Theory of International Relations," in Fred I. Greenstein and Nelson W. Polsby, eds., *The Handbook of Political Science,* vol. 8, *International Politics* (Reading, MA: Addison-Wesley, 1975), pp. 1–85; "The Origins of War in Neorealist Theory," in Robert I. Rotberg and

Theodore K. Rabb, eds., *The Origin and Prevention of Major Wars* (Cambridge: Cambridge University Press, 1989), pp. 39–52; and "Reflections on *Theory of International Politics:* A Response to My Critics," in Robert Keohane, ed., *Neorealism and Its Critics* (New York: Columbia University Press, 1986), pp. 322–45. Unlike Morgenthau's *Politics among Nations,* Waltz's *Theory of International Politics* clearly qualifies as a work of modern social science (esp. its chap. 1).

27. Structural theories emphasize that the configuration of the international system sharply constrains the behavior of the great powers and forces them to act in similar ways. Thus, we should expect to find common patterns of great-power behavior in anarchic systems. Nevertheless, anarchic systems themselves can be configured differently, depending on the number of great powers and how power is distributed among them. As discussed in subsequent chapters, those structural differences sometimes cause important variations in state behavior.

28. Waltz, *Theory of International Politics,* p. 126. Also see ibid., pp. 118, 127; and Joseph M. Grieco, "Anarchy and the Limits of Cooperation: A Realist Critique of the Newest Liberal Institutionalism," *International Organization* 42, No. 3 (Summer 1988), pp. 485–507, which builds directly on Waltz's claim that states are mainly concerned with preserving their share of world power.

29. Randall L. Schweller, "Neorealism's Status-Quo Bias: What Security Dilemma?" *Security Studies* 5, No. 3 (Spring 1996, special issue), pp. 90–121. Also see Keith L. Shimko, "Realism, Neorealism, and American Liberalism," *Review of Politics* 54, No. 2 (Spring 1992), pp. 281–301.

30. Waltz, *Theory of International Politics,* chaps. 6, 8. The other key work emphasizing that states have a powerful tendency to balance against aggressors is Stephen M. Walt, *The Origins of Alliances* (Ithaca, NY: Cornell University Press, 1987).

31. See Waltz, *Theory of International Politics,* chap. 8; and Waltz, "Origins of War."

32. Waltz, "Origins of War," p. 40.

33. The key works include Robert Jervis, "Cooperation under the Security Dilemma," *World Politics* 30, No. 2 (January 1978), pp. 167–214; Jack L. Snyder, *Myths of Empire: Domestic Politics and International Ambition* (Ithaca, NY: Cornell University Press, 1991), esp. chaps. 1–2; and Van Evera, *Causes of War,* esp. chap. 6. Also see Glaser, "Realists as Optimists";

and Robert Powell, *In the Shadow of Power: States and Strategies in International Politics* (Princeton, NJ: Princeton University Press, 1999), esp. chap. 3. George Quester's *Offense and Defense in the International System* (New York: Wiley, 1977) is an important book on the offense-defense balance, although he is generally not considered a defensive realist. For an overview of the literature on the subject, see Sean M. Lynn-Jones, "Offense-Defense Theory and Its Critics," *Security Studies* 4, No. 4 (Summer 1995), pp. 660–91.

34. Jervis has a more qualified view on this point than either Snyder or Van Evera. See Snyder, *Myths of Empire,* pp. 22–24; Van Evera, *Causes of War,* pp. 118, 191, 255.

35. Grieco, "Anarchy and the Limits of Cooperation," p. 500.

36. Some defensive realists emphasize that great powers seek to maximize security, not relative power. "The ultimate concern of states," Waltz writes, "is not for power but for security." Waltz, "Origins of War," p. 40. There is no question that great powers maximize security, but that claim by itself is vague and provides little insight into actual state behavior. The important question is, How do states maximize security? My answer: By maximizing their share of world power. Defensive realists' answer: By preserving the existing balance of power. Snyder puts the point well in *Myths of Empire* when he writes that both offensive and defensive realists "accept that security is normally the strongest motivation of states in international anarchy, but they have opposite views about the most effective way to achieve it" (pp. 11–12).

37. G. Lowes Dickinson, *The European Anarchy* (New York: Macmillan, 1916). Also see G. Lowes Dickinson, *The International Anarchy, 1904–1914* (New York: Century Company, 1926), esp. chap. 1.

38. Dickinson, *European Anarchy,* pp. 14, 101.

39. Eric Labs, Nicholas Spykman, and Martin Wight also make the case for offensive realism in their writings, although none lays the theory out in any detail. See Eric J. Labs, "Offensive Realism and Why States Expand Their War Aims," *Security Studies* 6, No. 4, pp. 1–49; Nicholas J. Spykman, *America's Strategy in World Politics: The United States and the Balance of Power* (New York: Harcourt, Brace, 1942), introduction and chap. 1; and Martin Wight, *Power Politics,* eds. Hedley Bull and Carsten Holbraad (New York: Holmes and

Meier, 1978), chaps. 2, 3, 9, 14, 15. One also catches glimpses of the theory in Herbert Butterfield, *Christianity and History* (New York: Scribner's, 1950), pp. 89–91; Dale C. Copeland, *The Origins of Major War* (Ithaca, NY: Cornell University Press, 2000), passim; Robert Gilpin, *War and Change in World Politics* (Cambridge: Cambridge University Press, 1981), pp. 87–88; John H. Herz, "Idealist Internationalism and the Security Dilemma," *World Politics* 2, No. 2 (January 1950), p. 157; John H. Herz, *Political Realism and Political Idealism* (Chicago: University of Chicago Press, 1951), pp. 14–15, 23–25, 206; A.F.K. Organski, *World Politics*, 2d ed. (New York: Knopf, 1968), pp. 274, 279, 298; Frederick L. Schuman, *International Politics: An Introduction to the Western State System* (New York: McGraw-Hill, 1933), pp. 512–19; and Fareed Zakaria, *From Wealth to Power: The Unusual Origins of America's World Role* (Princeton, NJ: Princeton University Press, 1998), passim. Finally, aspects of Randall Schweller's important work are consistent with offensive realism. See Schweller, "Neorealism's Status-Quo Bias"; Randall L. Schweller, "Bandwagoning for Profit: Bringing the Revisionist State Back In," *International Security* 19, No. 1 (Summer 1994), pp. 72–107; and Randall L. Schweller, *Deadly Imbalances: Tripolarity and Hitler's Strategy of World Conquest* (New York: Columbia University Press, 1998). However, as Gideon Rose makes clear, it is difficult to classify Schweller as an offensive realist. See Gideon Rose, "Neoclassical Realism and Theories of Foreign Policy," *World Politics* 51, No. 1 (October 1998), pp. 144–72.

40. See Inis L. Claude, *Power and International Relations* (New York: Random House, 1962); August Heckscher, ed., *The Politics of Woodrow Wilson: Selections from His Speeches and Writings* (New York: Harper, 1956); and James Brown Scott, ed., *President Wilson's Foreign Policy: Messages, Addresses, Papers* (Oxford: Oxford University Press, 1918).

41. Quoted in Wight, *Power Politics*, p. 29.

42. William J. Clinton, "American Foreign Policy and the Democratic Ideal," campaign speech, Pabst Theater, Milwaukee, WI, October 1, 1992.

43. "In Clinton's Words: 'Building Lines of Partnership and Bridges to the Future,' " *New York Times*, July 10, 1997.

44. See Shimko, "Realism, Neorealism, and American Liberalism."

45. See Seymour Martin Lipset, *American Exceptionalism: A Double-Edged Sword* (New York: Norton, 1996), pp. 51–52, 237. Also see Gabriel A. Almond, *The American People and Foreign Policy* (New York: Praeger, 1968), pp. 50–51.

46. Alexis de Tocqueville, *Democracy in America*, vol. II, trans. Henry Reeve (New York: Schocken Books, 1972), p. 38.

47. Morgenthau, *Scientific Man*, p. 201.

48. See Reinhold Niebuhr, *The Children of Light and the Children of Darkness: A Vindication of Democracy and a Critique of Its Traditional Defense* (New York: Scribner's, 1944), esp. pp. 153–90.

49. Lipset, *American Exceptionalism*, p. 63.

50. See Samuel P. Huntington, *The Soldier and the State: The Theory and Practice of Civil-Military Relations* (Cambridge, MA: Harvard University Press, 1957).

51. For example, it is apparent from archival-based studies of the early Cold War that American policymakers thought largely in terms of power politics, not ideology, when dealing with the Soviet Union. See H. W. Brands, *The Specter of Neutralism: The United States and the Emergence of the Third World, 1947–1960* (New York: Columbia University Press, 1989); Thomas J. Christensen, *Useful Adversaries: Grand Strategy, Domestic Mobilization, and Sino-American Conflict, 1947–1958* (Princeton, NJ: Princeton University Press, 1996); Melvyn P. Leffler, *A Preponderance of Power: National Security, the Truman Administration, and the Cold War* (Stanford, CA: Stanford University Press, 1992); and Trachtenberg, *Constructed Peace*. Also see Keith Wilson, "British Power in the European Balance, 1906–14," in David Dilks, ed., *Retreat from Power: Studies in Britain's Foreign Policy of the Twentieth Century*, vol. 1, *1906–1939* (London: Macmillan, 1981), pp. 21–41, which describes how British policymakers "constantly and consistently employed the concept of the balance of power" (p. 22) in private but employed more idealistic rhetoric in their public utterances.

52. Kennan, *American Diplomacy*, p. 82. For examples of other realists emphasizing this theme, see Walter Lippmann, *U.S. Foreign Policy: Shield of the Republic* (Boston: Little, Brown, 1943); Hans Morgenthau, *In Defense of the National Interest: A Critical Examination of American Foreign Policy*

(New York: Knopf, 1951); Norman A. Graebner, *America as a World Power: A Realist Appraisal from Wilson to Reagan* (Wilmington, DE: Scholarly Resources, 1984); and Norman A. Graebner, *Cold War Diplomacy: American Foreign Policy, 1945–1975,* 2d ed. (New York: Van Nostrand, 1977).

53. Carr, *Twenty Years' Crisis,* p. 79. For evidence that this kind of hypocrisy is not limited to Anglo-Saxons, see Markus Fischer, "Feudal Europe, 800–1300: Communal Discourse and Conflictual Practices," *International Organization* 46, No. 2 (Spring 1992), pp. 427–66.

54. The key work on this subject is Ido Oren, "The Subjectivity of the 'Democratic' Peace: Changing U.S. Perceptions of Imperial Germany," *International Security* 20, No. 2 (Fall 1995), pp. 147–84. For additional evidence on the examples discussed in this paragraph and the next, see Konrad H. Jarausch, "Huns, Krauts, or Good Germans? The German Image in America, 1800–1980," in James F. Harris, ed., *German-American Interrelations: Heritage and Challenge* (Tubingen: Tubingen University Press,

1985), pp. 145–59; Frank Trommler, "Inventing the Enemy: German-American Cultural Relations, 1900–1917," in Hans-Jurgen Schroder, ed., *Confrontation and Cooperation: Germany and the United States in the Era of World War I, 1900–1924* (Providence, RI: Berg Publishers, 1993), pp. 99–125; and John L. Gaddis, *The United States and the Origins of the Cold War, 1941–1947* (New York: Columbia University Press, 1972), chap. 2. For discussions of how British policymakers worked to clean up Russia's image during both world wars, see Keith Neilson, *Britain and the Last Tsar: British Policy and Russia, 1894–1917* (Oxford: Clarendon, 1995), pp. 342-43; and P.M.H. Bell, *John Bull and the Bear: British Public Opinion, Foreign Policy and the Soviet Union, 1941–1945* (London: Edward Arnold, 1990).

55. The classic statement on the profound impact of liberal ideas on American thinking is Louis Hartz, *The Liberal Tradition in America: An Interpretation of American Political Thought since the Revolution* (New York: Harcourt, Brace and World, 1955).

INTERNATIONAL SYSTEMS: VICIOUS CIRCLES AND VIRTUOUS CIRCLES

Bruce Russett and John Oneal

For many decades, the most prominent challenger to realism was liberalism, and this selection from Russett and Oneal provides a useful summary of the liberal perspective. The authors suggest that the "vicious circles" of world politics that realists anticipate as leading to war and conflict can be replaced by "virtuous circles" within which cooperation and peace might be generated and maintained. As you read this selection, ask yourself:

◉ How does the experience of Europe after World War II illustrate, for Russett and Oneal, the promise of the liberal perspective?

◉ What are the three elements of the "Kantian triangle," and how does each contribute to cooperation and peace?

◉ How do the elements of this Kantian triangle interact with and reinforce one another?

ANARCHY AS A POTENTIALLY VICIOUS CIRCLE

. . . "Realist" theories of world politics emphasize that because there is no supranational government, the international system has the characteristics Thomas Hobbes attributed, in the seventeenth century, to a country undergoing civil war. (Hobbes wrote his book *Leviathan* right after a bitter civil war between royalists and republicans in Britain.) To Hobbes, chaos was the greatest danger: a war of all against all. An additional danger is the potential for strong states to establish hegemony over others in the international system. According to realist theories, for these reasons, states must always be vigilant. They must be prepared to act vigorously to confront emerging powers controlled by ambitious, aggressive leaders. Preferably they must act preventively, before the emerging power becomes too great. Consequently, military strategy may have a hair trigger. And states may feel obliged to react against emerging powers regardless of the others' intentions; for if the power of a potential adversary becomes too great and what seemed originally to be (or in fact was) limited ambition turns out to be something more, a challenge to a state's sovereignty could only be beaten back at great cost, or possibly not at all. The necessity for vigilance is especially great in periods when military technology and organizational doctrine are evolving rapidly or seem to favor the offense over the defense. If by quick and powerful invasion (like Hitler's blitzkrieg early in World War II) an attacker can overwhelm defenders, then even a defensive-minded state may feel obliged to strike first just to protect itself. It may not feel able to afford the luxury of waiting to figure out whether its opponent's intentions are, like its own, merely defensive.

Here then is an example of a potentially vicious circle, a series of strategic interactions within a Hobbesian system that magnify hostility and end in war—even though neither state originally intended it. The danger in international politics is that reasonable, defensive behavior can lead to a self-perpetuating downward spiral of action and reaction that produces an outcome no one desired. One state's military capabilities are seen to threaten another state, whether or not that is the intention. Indeed military leaders are trained to focus on the capabilities, not the intentions, of other states and to plan for the worst case because intentions can change. Frequently states regard their own intentions as clear and defensive and, to be prudent, regard their capabilities as relatively weak. But at the same time, they fear their adversaries are strong and expansionist. This was so in the crisis that produced World War I (Holsti 1972). The security dilemma may merely drive an escalating arms race or the competition for spheres of influence, but growing military capabilities, reduced diplomatic and economic contacts, and increasing distrust can end in a catastrophic war (Choucri and North 1975). Indeed, those who counsel a "realistic" strategy of military preparedness and constant vigilance because of the dangers of international politics may create a self-fulfilling prophecy (Smith 1986, 48). Of course, realists do not believe that war is equally probable with everyone, and states do not always assume the worst is likely to happen (Brooks 1997); but the Westphalian system is vulnerable to vicious circles. . . .

THE CREATION OF VIRTUOUS CIRCLES

There are also virtuous circles in world politics. Much of international relations involves peaceful interactions that are not seen as threatening but rather as mutually beneficial. These benefits can increase over time and expand in scope.

What began as a vicious circle can sometimes be broken by deliberate policy and turned into a virtuous circle. Perhaps the most prominent case of such a reversal occurred in Western Europe after World War II. With tens of millions dead, their economies in shambles, and cities in ashes, the new European leaders consciously decided to break the old pattern of hostility and war. Those leaders, including Konrad Adenauer, Alcide de Gasperi, Jean Monnet, and Robert Schuman, did not make the change all at once simply by an act of will. Rather, they set up an intricate system of political, economic, and social institutions designed to reinforce one another, creating a set of virtuous circles that would both directly and indirectly promote peaceful relations. This system depended upon three elements that are key to "liberal" theories of international relations.

First was the *promotion of democracy*. The post–World War II European leaders believed that the breakdown of democracy had played a key role in destroying peace. Dictators had been aggressively expansionist, and World War II could readily be blamed on authoritarian or totalitarian states, especially Germany, Japan, and Italy. Even World War I could plausibly be blamed on the ambitions or incompetence of authoritarian rulers in Austria-Hungary, Germany, and Russia. The initial task, therefore, was to establish stable democratic institutions throughout Europe and to root out old nationalist and authoritarian ideologies. In this the victors were aided by the total defeat and discrediting of the old authoritarian leaders (some of whom were executed for war crimes) and by institutional changes put in place by the Allied occupation of western Germany.

The second element in establishing a virtuous circle was the *bolstering of national economies*. European leaders realized that authoritarian governments had arisen in large part because of the breakdown of the world economy in the 1930s and the poverty induced by depression. During the course of the depression, most governments tried to protect their own citizens' income by restricting trade; it seemed better to preserve jobs at home than to import goods produced by foreign workers. In its extreme form, this kind of economic policy leads to economic isolation, or autarky. Autarky has a basis in eighteenth-century doctrines and practices of mercantilism, which were intended to strengthen a state's security by promoting exports, controlling and discouraging imports, and producing an inflow of gold and foreign currency that the state could tap to build its power. The Soviet Union practiced a modern version of this extreme policy in its quest to construct an independent military and industrial base, and in various periods, so, too, did China and some other poor countries.

Even less extreme mercantilistic practices can turn into the kind of competitive imposition of tariffs and other trade barriers characteristic of the "beggar my neighbor" policies of the Great Depression (Kindleberger 1973). One of the countries hardest hit by this vicious circle of economic policies was Germany. The Weimar Republic, established in 1918 after the forced abdication of Kaiser Wilhelm, was distrusted by supporters of the old autocratic system. Only slowly recovering from World War I, Germany was especially damaged by the drop in global prosperity and trade of the early 1930s. Millions of Germans, impoverished by unemployment and inflation, turned away from democracy. They became ready to accept drastic action by Hitler, who promised to restore prosperity and their country's glory. After World War II, Europe's new leaders understood that real prosperity, and an approach toward American living standards, would require the efficiencies and economies of scale made possible by a market bigger than that of any one European country. The economies of Europe were relatively small, at least as compared with the United States, especially after the destructiveness of the war. Adenauer, de Gasperi, Monnet, and Schuman believed that democracy must rest on a foundation of prosperity and that the economic well-being of each of their countries depended on stable, cooperative economic relations among themselves and with others.

To this the leaders of the new Europe added a further insight. A complex network of economic interdependence would not only underpin democracy, thereby indirectly contributing to peace, it would also strengthen peace directly. Businessmen, companies, and workers with strong economic interests in other countries would naturally oppose war with those countries. If they were dependent on other countries for markets, for vital raw materials and other supplies, they would resist any policy or movement that threatened to break those economic ties. If international investment could be encouraged, capitalists would resist war, because to permit their country to attack another would risk the destruction of factories they owned in that other country. War would be economically irrational: those with important economic interests would suffer from war, and so they would use their political power to oppose policies that might lead to it. Consequently, European leaders in the late 1940s planned to open their markets to trade and investment with one another. They expected this to lead to stable economic relations, prosperity, and peace.

These efforts at economic integration began with the industries—coal and steel—then considered most important to an industrialized economy and especially to its war potential. In 1951, European leaders formed a new institution, the European Coal and Steel Community, designed to create a common market in these vital commodities, to facilitate investment across national borders and to insure that Germany could not again turn its heavy industries into a war machine. This was followed by a similar plan for the nuclear industry (Euratom) and others. Despite some concerns that a united Europe might become an economic and political rival to the United States, American policy makers encouraged this program of economic integration. Indeed, the United States insisted that its aid for European recovery from World War II, provided through the Marshall Plan, be coordinated by a new organization, the Organization for European Economic Cooperation. This ultimately became a global organization, the Organization for Economic Cooperation and Development (OECD), with members around the world, including a number of newly industrialized countries.

Thus emerged the third element in establishing a virtuous circle in Europe after World War II: the *construction of a thick web of international institutions,* based on the belief that trade and other forms of economic interchange would not develop unless there were organizations empowered to promote cooperation and to make rules that encouraged and protected that cooperation. European leaders therefore created international institutions that would promote freer trade in goods and services. As they did so, it became apparent that all the benefits of a free trade area could not be achieved if member states had radically different labor or social policies. True economic interdependence meant dismantling the regulatory barriers to free movement not just of goods but of services, capital, and workers, too. Travel and even immigration, for example, had to be freed of old restrictions. With the old regulations eliminated, then the legal gaps had to be filled by writing new regulations based on common principles. Common environmental policies and health standards were necessary if producers in countries with lax standards were not to have a market advantage over those in countries with strict controls. Economic policies had to be coordinated, and fluctuations in the relative value of national currencies brought under control. Therefore, one form of economic liberalization led almost inevitably to others in related areas of activity. This process is called "spillover": institutions built to fulfill particular needs or functions create the necessity for cooperation in other, related areas of society. Theorists of economic integration had foreseen that this would occur (Mitrany 1966; Haas 1958; Lindberg 1963): the European Common Market, once established, became the European Community and ultimately the European Union. At each stage of development the institutions assumed much broader functions. The process and institutionalization of integration was so successful that other countries wanted to join. . . .

This move toward European integration was begun during the cold war, when the security of Europe depended to a substantial degree upon the strategic protection of the United States and the United States was eager to see its allies more integrated and therefore stronger. Thus Western concerns regarding the global balance of power surely helped propel this process. It is also true, however, that this integration has expanded beyond the initial cold war allies, has become deeper than originally envisioned by most, and has outlasted the cold war. European economic interdependence and its political and economic integration did not depend on cold war imperatives. The European experience of the late twentieth century shows that it is possible to establish virtuous circles that solidify peaceful relations even while states retain many of their traditional Westphalian characteristics. . . .

BACKGROUND AND LEGACY OF THE EUROPEAN ACHIEVEMENT

The post–World War II leaders of Europe were not the first to recognize that these three key elements—democracy, economic interdependence, and international institutions—had great potential to create a system of virtuous circles supporting each other and, together, underpinning peace between states. A number of eighteenth-century writers had theorized about the conditions that would produce a stable long-term peace. The most famous of these writers was Immanuel Kant, whose 1795 essay, *Perpetual Peace,* is still widely cited. Kant thought peace could be rooted in relations between states governed by three principles of conflict resolution. One is what he called "republican constitutions," which in the present era we interpret as *representative democracy,* with freedom, legal equality of subjects, and the separation of governmental powers. An understanding of the legitimate rights of all citizens and republics in turn creates, in Kant's view, a moral foundation upon which a "pacific union" can be established by treaty in *international law and organization.* Finally, what he called "cosmopolitan law," embodied in *commerce and free trade,* creates transnational ties of material incentives that encourage accommodation rather than conflict. Kant's vision was remarkably perspicacious for a time when he could have little practical experience with key parts of it. There were very few democracies in the world in the late 1700s and no international organizations as we now know them. . . .

Other classical writers stressed various elements of the same vision. There have been advocates of free trade for several centuries and from many countries. Their position came to be expressed most powerfully in the eighteenth and nineteenth century in Britain. Adam Smith linked free trade to both prosperity and peace in his famous book *The Wealth of Nations,* which was published in 1776. Later, Richard Cobden, a manufacturer and parliamentary leader, further developed this argument, suggesting that trade would both strengthen economic interests with a stake in avoiding the disruptions caused by war and serve as an instrument of communication to promote understanding between countries. . . . Hugo Grotius, a Dutch contemporary of Hobbes, was an early advocate of the pacific benefits of international law, which he believed could ameliorate conflict not only directly but also by providing a basis for the promotion of trade and a sense of community among states.

In the modern era, Woodrow Wilson expressed Kant's three principles in the Fourteen Points he laid out as the basis for a more peaceful world after World War I. Wilson did not explicitly invoke the need for universal democracy, since not all of America's wartime allies were democratic. But his meaning is clear if one considers the domestic political conditions necessary for his first point: "Open covenants of peace, openly arrived at, after which there shall be no private international understandings of any kind but diplomacy shall proceed always frankly and in the public view." Point three echoed Kant's notion of "cosmopolitan law" in demanding "removal, so far as possible, of all economic barriers and the establishment of an equality of trade conditions among all the nations consenting to the peace and associating themselves for its maintenance." The fourteenth point expressed his vision of a "pacific union": "A general association of nations must be formed under specific covenants for the purpose of affording mutual guarantees of political independence and territorial integrity to great and small states alike." He made this last the basis for the League of Nations.

In 1945, the founders of the United Nations were certainly realistic about the necessity of pursuing power politics in a dangerous world, but many also shared a commitment to incorporating Wilson's principles into their plans (Ikenberry 1996). These principles are clearly evident in the structure of the UN, with major units devoted to peace and security (notably the Security Council and the mediation activities of the secretary general), economic development and interdependence (especially the UN Development Programme, the Economic and Social Council, and UN-associated institutions such as the International Monetary Fund, the World Bank, and the World Trade Organization), and, following the Universal Declaration of Human Rights in 1948, human rights (UN High Commissioners for Human Rights and for Refugees, the Council on Human Rights, and the new International Criminal Court). Many of these institutions have developed their powers over the years, but they are not nearly as extensive as those of the European Union.

Europeans had learned from their historical experience, particularly the world wars of the twentieth century, what needed to change. They were aided in their efforts to reshape the regional interstate system by having begun from a greater degree of cultural and political homogeneity and a higher level of economic development than those which characterize most other parts of the world. Nevertheless, while Europe has advanced furthest in establishing the three Kantian principles, other areas of the world have also achieved substantial success but with less development of intergovernmental organizations. The United States, Canada, and increasingly Mexico constitute one such area; cooperation among the Nordic states another; and Japan's relations with the United States and other industrialized democracies both in Europe and the Pacific yet another. (Like Germany,

Japan drastically changed its domestic and international policies following its World War II debacle. Japan, again like Germany, had some precedent in its history for this transformation: its period of Taisho democracy in the 1920s was marked by parliamentary politics and a wide franchise, and cooperative economic and political engagement with the world.) States within these three areas abide by Kantian principles and refrain from power politics.

Others have made efforts to break out of the vicious circle of fear, hostility, and war. Mikhail Gorbachev, the last president of the Soviet Union, deserves significant credit for ending the period of East-West hostility. Gorbachev was certainly not alone in bringing an end to the cold war, and his reasons surely were rooted in his understanding of what was best for his country and his own ruling group. Nor did he understand the full impact his policies would have, leading as they did to the political and economic collapse of the Soviet Union and the end of power for himself and most of those around him. Yet his actions changed the destructive pattern of relations in which the Soviet Union had become mired. As important as anything else, Gorbachev and his advisers accepted the idea that there are "universal interests and values" (Brown 1996, chap. 7; Wohlforth 1993, chap. 9). In this, they may well have been inspired by the success of Western Europe in establishing peace and prosperity based on the three principles discussed above.

Understanding the implications of democracy, economic interdependence, and international organizations may help us understand the end of the cold war: not simply why it ended, but why it ended prior to the drastic change in the bipolar distribution of power, and why it ended peacefully. In November 1988, British prime minister Margaret Thatcher proclaimed, "The cold war is over." By the spring of 1989 the U.S. State Department stopped referring to the Soviet Union as an enemy of the United States. The fundamental patterns of East-West behavior had changed, on both sides, beginning even before the razing of the Berlin Wall in November 1989, the unification of Germany in October 1990, and the dissolution of the Warsaw Pact in July 1991. Even after these events, the military power of the Soviet Union remained largely intact until the dissolution of the USSR on the last day of December 1991. None of these events was resisted violently by Soviet leaders.

Some of the actions that led to the end of the cold war were initiated by the West, and the West in time also reciprocated Soviet initiatives. Nevertheless, Gorbachev's policies of glasnost (openness) and perestroika (restructuring) were key to the unfolding of events. He instituted substantial political liberalization and movement toward democracy in the Soviet Union, with consequent improvements in free expression and the treatment of dissidents. Though his reforms fell short of full democracy, they were the beginning of a process of democratization, a major step in the journey away from authoritarianism. Notably, Gorbachev also permitted the process of liberalization to develop in the East European satellites, not just at home.

The Soviet and East European economies were in dire shape; they had been stagnant or in decline for a decade. In the early Stalinist years of the cold war they had been very autarkic, with most trade limited to the Communist bloc. Slowly they opened to the West, but the reform was insufficient. Gorbachev decided that imminent collapse of these economies could only be avoided by seeking economic interdependence with the West. This would allow the Soviet bloc access to Western markets, goods, technology, and capital. To get these, Soviet military and diplomatic behavior toward the West had to become markedly less antagonistic.

Gorbachev and the "new thinkers" around him also showed greatly increased interest in international organizations. In the late 1980s, perhaps anticipating political instability in parts of the empire they could no longer afford to maintain (outposts in Africa, Asia, Latin America, and even Eastern Europe), Soviet foreign policy leaders took a number of initiatives to revitalize the United Nations and considered innovative ways, including greater use of the International Court of Justice (Rosenne 1995, 258), by which it might be strengthened. When, after Iraq's aggression against Kuwait in 1990, the United States chose to work with and through the UN to legitimate American military actions, Gorbachev was supportive. Some other experiences of the Soviet Union's involvement with international organizations were unanticipated. The Conference on Security and Cooperation in Europe (CSCE, later the Organization for Security and Cooperation in Europe) and the human rights accords of the Helsinki agreements of 1975 were important for legitimating dissent in the Soviet Union and Eastern Europe. The Soviet Union did not repudiate these agreements and even came to see the CSCE as a potential bulwark for a new kind of political stability (Adler 1998).

One other world leader who has appreciated the importance of the Kantian principles and their interrelatedness should be acknowledged. Boutros Boutros-Ghali (1993, paragraphs 10–12), who was secretary general of the United Nations from 1992 to 1996, declared that the United Nations needed to support three interlinked efforts:

> The real development of a State must be based on the participation of its population; that requires human rights and democracy. . . . Without

peace, there can be no development and there can be no democracy. Without development, the basis for democracy will be lacking and societies will tend to fall into conflict. And without democracy, no sustainable development can occur; without such development peace cannot long be maintained. And so it has become evident that three great concepts and priorities are interlinked, and they must be addressed at every level of human society.

A COMPLEX SYSTEM OF INTERACTIONS SUPPORTING PEACE

The view of international politics as potentially cooperative, at least among large numbers of states, is by no means universally held. The Westphalian system is a European construction, and key realist thinkers such as Machiavelli and Hobbes wrote around the time of its origin, in the sixteenth and seventeenth centuries. Not only were the states of that era ruled by autocrats, but most were fairly self-sufficient economically rather than interdependent, international law was little developed, and international organizations were virtually nonexistent. (Grotius and Kant are interesting exceptions; both lived in small trading states, and the Dutch Republic where Grotius lived was relatively liberal.) These characteristics remained true of the international system up to the nineteenth century. (Cobden and the British liberals lived in a trading state that was democratic, but the popular control of government was still limited: only men with property had the right to vote, for example.)

Even in the twentieth century, the spread of the Kantian principles was limited. The colonial systems established by the European powers remained in place until after the end of World War II, and the colonies were, of course, not democratically governed. Nor were they allowed to develop interdependent economic relations or participate in international organizations. Understandably, leaders of countries outside the West are now vigorous defenders of the concepts of state sovereignty and nonintervention. Moreover, early Asian theorists who wrote in periods of political independence—such as Kautilya in India and Sun Szu in China, both in the fourth century B.C.—observed Asian interstate systems that were very like the Westphalian system that later developed in Europe. Their rulers were autocrats, controlling substantially self-sufficient states, essentially unconstrained by concepts of international law. The Communist tradition of Marx, Lenin, and Mao Zedong—still represented in somewhat weakened form in China, North Korea, Cuba, and Vietnam—constitutes another overlay of beliefs about the inherently conflictual and dangerous character of international relations. Even now, democracies live close to autocracies in Asia, where economic interdependence has become significant only recently and the network of international organizations is less dense than in Europe or even Latin America. It is therefore hardly surprising that, to this day, many Asian leaders adhere more to realist views than to liberal ones. Still, we have seen how, in a variety of historical times and circumstances, some political leaders have tried to reverse vicious circles with a new pattern of behavior drawing upon mutually reinforcing influences for peace. Contemporary Germany and Japan, for instance, having experienced disastrous consequences from abiding by the principles of realpolitik, now largely follow liberal policies (Maull 1990–91). . . .

THE KANTIAN TRIANGLE

A simple diagram helps in visualizing the three elements of the Kantian system and the virtuous circles connecting them. . . .

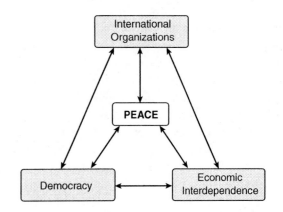

This schematic representation is a roadmap. . . . First, notice the arrows running toward peace from each of the three points of the triangle. The one from the lower left (democracy) represents the widespread understanding that democracies rarely fight each other. As we will see, not only do democracies virtually never wage war on other democracies, they are also much less likely than other kinds of states to have serious military disputes or skirmishes with each other. Democracies are also more peaceful in general than are authoritarian political systems, although this proposition is more controversial and the evidence more mixed. . . .

The arrow from the lower right (economic interdependence) represents the proposition that economically important trade and investment limit the likelihood that a state will use force against its commercial partner. It draws on the theoretical tradition in support of free trade strongly advanced by Smith, Cobden, and the other British liberals. It also finds strong support in recent evidence. Critics of the argument that democracies are less likely to fight each other do not contend that democracies are *more* likely to fight each other; at most, they maintain that democracies act in the same ways autocracies do, that the character of a state's political system is irrelevant in an anarchic international system. Critics of the argument that interdependence increases the chances for peace, on the other hand, sometimes do take the stronger position that trade can increase military conflict. Others maintain that economic relations, like domestic politics, do not much influence the probability that military force will be used. They claim that states fight over other issues, territory or access to resources, for example. In our view, the critical perspective on economic interdependence, in either its strong or weaker form, is not supported by the evidence. . . .

Finally, the arrow from the top (international organizations) to the center (peace) signifies that international organizations also make a direct contribution to preventing and resolving conflicts between countries. This proposition implies that the more international organizations to which two states belong together, the less likely they will be to fight one another or even to threaten the use of military force. International organizations may reduce the likelihood of conflict in various ways. They may directly coerce and restrain those who break the peace, serve as agents of mediation and arbitration, or reduce uncertainty in negotiations by conveying information. They may encourage states to expand their conception of the interests at stake, promoting more inclusive and longer-term thinking; shape general norms and principles of appropriate behavior; or encourage empathy and mutual identification among peoples. Different organizations concentrate on different activities. . . .

In addition to these three arrows, there are separate arrows returning to each of the corners from the center. The reciprocal effects represented by these arrows are important in understanding the international system. Democracy is easier to sustain in a peaceful environment. States involved in serious protracted conflict or militarized rivalries with other states are likely to have bigger military establishments, to restrict public information about key government activities, and to limit public criticism of those activities. In more extreme forms, external threats become reasons or justifications for suspending normal civil liberties, elections, and constitutional government. On the other hand, if the states relevant to democracies' security become themselves more democratic, the democracies will reduce their military expenditure and get involved in fewer conflicts, as the end of the cold war indicates (Maoz 1996). . . .

Trade is discouraged by international conflict and especially by war. States do not look kindly on their citizens who try to profit from commercial relations with a national adversary. Economic sanctions are a common tool of policy in dealing with hostile nations, either as an alternative or as a supplement to military means. During the cold war, the Soviet Union tried to maintain a high degree of autarky so as not to have its military capabilities dependent on the West. Western states, in turn, developed a system for restricting the sale of weapons and a wide range of military-related technology that could strengthen their adversary. Private traders are naturally reluctant to trade with, or invest in, countries with which political relations may at any time be violently disrupted.

International organizations sometimes are created to reduce or manage tensions between adversarial states. These organizations may seek to strengthen uncertain or ambivalent political relations, perhaps by encouraging arms control or by becoming involved in crisis management. The United Nations is an obvious example, organized with the full knowledge that peaceful relations among its members, especially the great powers, could not be taken for granted. Most IGOs, however, depend on reasonably peaceful relations among their members to be effective. They are devoted to promoting international cooperation in a wide range of activities, including diplomacy, trade and investment, health and education, and human rights, as well as mundane things such as postal services, the standardization of weights and measures, etc. They are most often formed when a certain level of peace seems probable.

These reverse arrows, or "feedback loops," create the potential for the virtuous circles we want to emphasize. But there are also arrows along the sides of the triangle. . . . For example, that democracies are more likely to trade with one another, partly because, confident in peaceful relations, they do not feel that the economic benefits that accrue from trade will strengthen a state likely to become an adversary. They do not have such assurance with authoritarian states, as was the case during the cold war. Interdependence in turn may induce a certain externally supported pluralism that encourages democracy. Democracies are more likely than authoritarian states to form and to join many international organizations, and international organizations (such as organs of the EU and parts of the contemporary UN) may overtly support and strengthen democratic governments. For example, countries that hope to join the European Union in order to benefit from economic interdependence must first meet EU standards for political democracy. Finally, IGOs may be formed specifically for the purpose of promoting international trade and finance, embedding free trade in a structure of liberal international institutions to promote an integrated world market-based economy (Gardner 1980; Ruggie 1982; Murphy 1994). In turn, a high level of interdependence among states is likely to create a need for institutions to manage and stabilize their commercial relations; the World Trade Organization, for example, plays an important role in arbitrating disputes over fair trading practices.

We should also say something about the nongovernmental influences on world affairs that are not represented in our diagram. . . . Our focus here is on relations between states, and so we might risk overemphasizing the role of states or organizations formed by states as their agents. That would be a serious error. Peace between states is also a result of actions taken by transnational actors or international nongovernmental organizations, such as multinational corporations, churches, international labor unions, charitable organizations, and a wide variety of other groups, of which there are thousands in the contemporary world. These INGOs may promote democracy or attempt to influence the policies of democracies, foster cultural exchange, encourage interdependence, or support the activities of IGOs. Individuals, too, can make a difference. The Swedish industrialist Alfred Nobel did so by funding the peace prize that bears his name; so, too, have many of the winners of that prize over the years. But one need not do something so grand to affect international relations and promote peace. Studying abroad and culturally sensitive tourism count, too.

Not all of the arrows in our diagram are equally important. Some of our hypotheses may even prove to be unfounded. But if most or even many of them are true . . . there is a basis for a dynamic international system that is able to perpetuate and enhance itself. Peace between states . . . would comprise a key product of, but also an ingredient in, this Kantian system of virtuous circles. In such a complex, dynamic system, it is inherently difficult to identify one or two single "causes" and say that they are key. Particular relationships cannot readily be plucked out and considered in isolation from the others. Nevertheless, we attempt to identify those that affect most powerfully the prospects for peace. . . .

Different instruments will be available in different historical and regional contexts, so we need to consider when, where, and how they operate. In Europe after World War II, the most effective entry point in creating a virtuous circle may have been through promoting economic interdependence. In South America in the last decade or so, the effective entry point was probably the revival of democracy. Under military dictatorships, Argentina, Brazil, and Chile conducted an arms race in conventional weapons, especially in ships and aircraft. Argentina and Chile had serious border disputes that could readily have erupted into war, and the Argentine military actually seems to have wanted war in the 1970s and early 1980s. Argentina and Brazil were involved in a scarcely covert race to gain nuclear arms. All that changed, however, after the Argentine military regime was overthrown in 1983. This development was followed later in the decade by the restoration of civilian governments in Brazil and Chile. Between 1985 and 1994 Argentina's military budget fell from 3.8 percent of its gross national product to only 1.7 percent. Brazil decreased its military expenditures from 1.7 to 1.2 percent from 1990 to 1994. Argentina and Chile settled their border disputes with arbitration by the pope. Argentina and Brazil ratified the Nuclear Non-Proliferation Treaty and became fully compliant with the Treaty of Tlateloco, which established a regional nuclear nonproliferation regime in Latin America. They abandoned their nuclear weapons programs. In 1991, Argentina, Brazil, Paraguay, and Uruguay formed a regional trading market (Mercosur), and trade among the largest economies (including Chile) grew by 50 percent between 1991 and 1994. Thus the establishment of democratic governments in these countries was a sufficient condition for peace among them (Kacowicz 1998, chap. 3; also Hurrell 1998). Some of them had experienced peace for periods even under

dictatorships. Yet conditions in the 1990s became much more cooperative, warmer than just a "negative peace" of no overt conflict, and a return to authoritarian government would put severe strains on their international relations. One means to prevent this is the provision of Mercosur that requires member governments to be democracies.

In contemporary East Asia, a region that is still far short of a generalized system of virtuous circles and where there are only a minority of stable democracies, the most effective entry point for the promotion of peace may again be through continuing growth in economic interdependence. North Korea, while holding tightly to its authoritarian political system, seems to be inching toward partially opening its closed economy. China, though hardly democratic, now has a ratio of foreign trade to GDP higher than Japan's and has come far toward a more open economy and better integration into global economic institutions. All the Kantian elements of change remain severely restricted in China, but major improvements have occurred. The strength of internal forces with an interest in maintaining and extending political and economic reforms and constructive engagement in world affairs suggests this is likely to continue. Still, it is possible to imagine circumstances—an economic slump, internal political unrest, or a deterioration of relations with the West—that could halt or even reverse this trend.

The downside is that, like vicious circles, virtuous circles can sometimes be interrupted or broken. Hobbesian thinking emphasizes the danger of vicious circles of military threats and the impossibility of breaking out of them. The first efforts to build a global system of peace based on Wilson's version of Kant's vision failed. They were imperfectly instituted, as the United States refused to join the League of Nations. International trade took a dive in the

Great Depression, spreading misery rather than prosperity. A really deep and sustained economic downturn is probably the primary threat to a Kantian system. Newly established democracy proved fragile in much of Europe, Japan, and elsewhere. The Weimar Republic collapsed and gave way to Hitler, and Taisho democracy fell to Japanese militarism. The League of Nations collapsed, and the world was once again at war. . . .

The revived Kantian vision emphasizes the *possibility* of changing international politics, especially with the peaceful end of the cold war, from one dominated by vicious circles into something more constructive. The next century of world politics may build on the achievements of the past century, or it may see them reversed. A collapse of the world economy, a war triggered by an aggressive dictatorship, or a global environmental catastrophe could cause a collapse in the system that was so painfully constructed on the desolation of two world wars and a third, nuclear, near miss. Once broken, the same relationships in reverse could lead to a negative spiral: declining trade, failed democracies, further wars, and impotent international organizations. This would no longer be a Kantian system but would represent a return to a Hobbesian system of insecurity, economic decline, and war. Proponents of peace may be able to relax periodically, but they can never sleep. Every good thing must be re-won each day.

REFERENCES

Adler, Emanuel. 1998. Seeds of Peaceful Change: The OSCE as a Pluralistic Security Community–Building Organization. In *Security Communities in Comparative Perspective,* edited by Emanuel Adler and Michael N. Barnett. Cambridge: Cambridge University Press.

Boutros-Ghali, Boutros. 1993. *Report on the Work of the Organization from the Forty-Seventh to the Forty-Eighth Session of the General Assembly.* New York: United Nations.

Brooks, Stephen G. 1997. Dueling Realisms. *International Organization* 51 (3): 445–78.

Brown, Archie. 1996. *The Gorbachev Factor.* Oxford: Oxford University Press.

Choucri, Nazli, and Robert North. 1975. *Nations in Conflict: National Growth and International Violence.* New York: Freeman.

Gardner, Richard. 1980. *Sterling Dollar Diplomacy in Current Perspective* New York: Columbia University Press.

Haas, Ernst. 1958. *The Uniting of Europe.* Stanford, CA: Stanford University Press.

Holsti, Ole. 1972. *Crisis Escalation War.* Montreal: McGill University Press.

Hurrell, Andrew. 1998. An Emerging Security Community in South America? In *Security Communities,* edited by Emmanuel Adler and Michael Barnett. Cambridge: Cambridge Community Press.

Ikenberry, G. John. 1996. The Myth of Post–Cold War Chaos. *Foreign Affairs* 75 (3): 79–91.

Kacowicz, Arie M. 1998. *Zones of Peace in the Third World: South America and West Africa in Comparative Perspective.* Albany: State University of New York Press.

Kindleberger, Charles. 1973. *The World in Depression, 1929–1939.* Berkeley: University of California Press.

Lindberg, Leon. 1963. *The Political Dynamics of European Economic Integration.* Stanford, CA: Stanford University Press.

Maoz, Zeev. 1996. *Domestic Sources of Global Change.* Ann Arbor: University of Michigan Press.

Maull, Hanns. 1990–91. Germany and Japan: The New Civilian Powers. *Foreign Affairs* 69 (5): 91–106.

Mitrany, David. 1966. *A Working Peace System.* Pittsburgh, PA: Quadrangle.

Murphy, Craig. 1994. *International Organizations and Industrial Change: Global Governance since 1850.* New York: Oxford University Press.

Rosenne, Shabtai. 1995. *The World Court and How It Works.* 5th ed. Dordrecht: Martinus Nijhoff.

Ruggie, John Gerard. 1982. International Regimes, Transactions, and Change: Embedded Liberalism in the Postwar Economic Order. *International Organization* 36 (2): 379–416.

Smith, Michael J. 1986. *Realist Thought from Weber to Kissinger.* Baton Rouge: Lousiana State University Press.

Wohlforth, William. 1993. *The Elusive Balance.* Ithaca, NY: Cornell University Press.

CONSTRUCTING INTERNATIONAL POLITICS

Alexander Wendt

In the 1990s, following the end of the Cold War, *constructivism* emerged as a new challenger to both the liberal and, especially, the realist approaches in international relations. Wendt has been at the forefront of this constructivist movement. In this piece he directly challenges John Mearsheimer and his realist view of the world; Wendt is reacting to an article by Mearsheimer that is not included in this volume. As you read this selection, ask yourself:

- Is there anything about realism that Wendt and constructivists would accept?
- What is it about realism that he rejects?
- How do constructivists differ from liberals in their critique of realism?

ASSUMPTIONS

I share Mearsheimer's "realist" assumptions: that international politics is anarchic, and that states have offensive capabilities, cannot be 100 percent certain about others' intentions, wish to survive, and are rational. We even share two more: a commitment to states as units of analysis, and to the importance of systemic or "third image" theorizing.

The last bears emphasis, for in juxtaposing "structure" to "discourse" and in emphasizing the role of individuals in "critical theory," Mearsheimer obscures the fact that constructivists are structuralists. Indeed, one of our main objections to neorealism is that it is not structural enough: that adopting the individualistic metaphors of micro-economics restricts the effects of structures to state behavior, ignoring how they might also constitute state identities and interests.[1] Constructivists think that state interests are in important part constructed by systemic structures, not exogenous to them; this leads to a sociological rather than micro-economic structuralism.

Where neorealist and constructivist structuralisms really differ, however, is in their assumptions about what structure is made of. Neorealists think it is made only of a distribution of material capabilities, whereas constructivists think it is also made of social relationships. Social structures have three elements: shared knowledge, material resources, and practices.[2]

First, social structures are defined, in part, by shared understandings, expectations, or knowledge. These constitute the actors in a situation and the nature of their relationships, whether cooperative or conflictual. A *security dilemma*, for example, is a social structure composed of intersubjective understandings in which states are so distrustful that they make worst-case assumptions about each others' intentions, and as a result define their interests in self-help terms. A *security community* is a different social structure, one composed of shared knowledge in which states trust one another to resolve disputes without war.[3] This dependence of social structure on ideas is the sense in which constructivism has an

Alexander Wendt, excerpt from "Constructing International Politics," *International Security*, 20:1, Summer 1995, pp. 71–81. © 1995 by the President and Fellows of Harvard College and the Massachussetts Institute of Technology. Reprinted by permission of MIT Press Journals.

idealist (or "idea-ist") view of structure. What makes these ideas (and thus structure) "social," however, is their intersubjective quality. In other words, sociality (in contrast to "materiality," in the sense of brute physical capabilities), is about shared knowledge.

Second, social structures include material resources like gold and tanks. In contrast to neo-realists' desocialized view of such capabilities, constructivists argue that material resources only acquire meaning for human action through the structure of shared knowledge in which they are embedded.[4] For example, 500 British nuclear weapons are less threatening to the United States than 5 North Korean nuclear weapons, because the British are friends of the United States and the North Koreans are not, and amity or enmity is a function of shared understandings. As students of world politics, neorealists would probably not disagree, but as theorists the example poses a big problem, since it completely eludes their materialist definition of structure. Material capabilities as such explain nothing; their effects presuppose structures of shared knowledge, which vary and which are not reducible to capabilities. Constructivism is therefore compatible with changes in material power affecting social relations, as long as those effects can be shown to presuppose still deeper social relations.

Third, social structures exist, not in actors' heads nor in material capabilities, but in practices. Social structure exists only in process. The Cold War was a structure of shared knowledge that governed great power relations for forty years, but once they stopped acting on this basis, it was "over."

In sum, social structures are real and objective, not "just talk." But this objectivity depends on shared knowledge, and in that sense social life is "ideas all the way down" (until you get to biology and natural resources). Thus, to ask "when do ideas, as opposed to power and interest, matter?" is to ask the wrong question. Ideas always matter, since power and interest do not have effects apart from the shared knowledge that constitutes them as such.[5] The real question, as Mearsheimer notes, is why does one social structure exist, like self-help (in which power and self-interest determine behavior), rather than another, like collective security (in which they do not).

The explanatory as opposed to normative character of this question bears emphasis. Constructivists have a normative interest in promoting social change, but they pursue this by trying to explain how seemingly natural social structures, like self-help or the Cold War, are effects of practice (this is the "critical" side of critical theory). This makes me wonder about Mearsheimer's repeated references to critical theorists' "goals," "aims," and "hopes" to make peace and love prevail on Earth. Even if we all had such hopes (which I doubt), and even if these were ethically wrong they are beside the point in evaluating critical theories of world politics. If critical theories fail, this will be because they do not explain how the world works, not because of their values. Emphasizing the latter recalls the old realist tactic of portraying opponents as utopians more concerned with how the world ought to be than how it is. Critical theorists have normative commitments, just as neorealists do, but we are also simply trying to explain the world. . . .

EXPLAINING WAR AND PEACE

Mearsheimer frames the debate between realists and critical theorists as one between a theory of war and a theory of peace. This is a fundamental mistake. Social construction talk is like game theory talk: analytically neutral between conflict and cooperation.[6] Critical theory does not predict peace.[7] War no more disproves critical theory than peace disproves realism. The confusion stems from conflating description and explanation.

The descriptive issue is the extent to which states engage in practices of *realpolitik* (warfare, balancing, relative-gains seeking) versus accepting the rule of law and institutional constraints on their autonomy. States sometimes do engage in power politics, but this hardly describes all of the past 1300 years, and even less today, when most states follow most international law most of the time,[8] and when war and security dilemmas are the exception rather than the rule, Great Powers no longer tend to conquer small ones, and free trade is expanding rather than contracting.[9] The relative frequency of *realpolitik,* however, has nothing to do with "realism." Realism should be seen as an explanation of *realpolitik,* not a description of it. Conflating the two makes it impossible to tell how well the one explains the other, and leads to the tautology that war makes realism true. Realism does not have a monopoly on the ugly and brutal side of international life. Even if we agree on a *realpolitik* description, we can reject a realist explanation.

The explanatory issue is *why* states engage in war or peace. Mearsheimer's portrayal of constructivist "causal logic" on this issue is about 30 percent right. The logic has two elements, structure and agency. On the one hand, constructivist theorizing tries to show how the social structure of a system makes actions possible by constituting actors with certain identities and interests, and material capabilities with certain meanings. Missing from Mearsheimer's account is the constructivist emphasis on how agency and interaction produce and reproduce structures of shared knowledge over time. Since it is not possible here to discuss the various dynamics through which this process takes place,[10] let me illustrate instead. And since Mearsheimer does not offer a neorealist explanation for inter-state

cooperation, conceding that terrain to institutionalists, let me focus on the "hard case" of why states sometimes get into security dilemmas and war, that is, why they sometimes engage in *realpolitik* behavior.

In "Anarchy is What States Make of It" I argued that such behavior is a self-fulfilling prophecy,[11] and that this is due to both agency and social structure. Thus, on the agency side, what states do to each other affects the social structure in which they are embedded, by a logic of reciprocity. If they militarize, others will be threatened and arm themselves, creating security dilemmas in terms of which they will define egoistic identities and interests. But if they engage in policies of reassurance, as the Soviets did in the late 1980s, this will have a different effect on the structure of shared knowledge, moving it toward a security community. The depth of interdependence is a factor here, as is the role of revisionist states, whose actions are likely to be especially threatening. However, on the structural side, the ability of revisionist states to create a war of all against all depends on the structure of shared knowledge into which they enter. If past interactions have created a structure in which status quo states are divided or naive, revisionists will prosper and the system will tend toward a Hobbesian world in which power and self-interest rule. In contrast, if past interactions have created a structure in which status quo states trust and identify with each other, predators are more likely to face collective security responses like the Gulf War.[12] *History matters.* Security dilemmas are not acts of God: they are effects of practice. This does not mean that once created they can necessarily be escaped (they are, after all, "dilemmas"), but it puts the causal locus in the right place.

Contrast this explanation of power politics with the "poverty of neorealism."[13] Mearsheimer thinks it significant that in anarchy, states cannot be 100 percent certain that others will not attack. Yet even in domestic society, I cannot be certain that I will be safe walking to class. There are no guarantees in life, domestic or international, but the fact that in anarchy war is possible does not mean "it may at any moment occur."[14] Indeed, it may be quite unlikely, as it is in most interactions today. Possibility is not probability. Anarchy as such is not a structural cause of anything. What matters is its social structure, which varies across anarchies. An anarchy of friends differs from one of enemies, one of self-help from one of collective security, and these are all constituted by structures of shared knowledge. Mearsheimer does not provide an argument for why this is wrong; he simply asserts that it is.

Other realist explanations for power politics fare somewhat better. Although neorealists want to eschew arguments from human nature, even they would agree that to the extent human-beings-in-groups are prone to fear and competition, it may predispose them to war.[15] However, this factor faces countervailing dynamics of interdependence and collective identity formation, which sometimes overcome it. The distribution of material capabilities also matters, especially if offense is dominant, and military build-ups will of course concern other states. Again, however, the meaning of power depends on the underlying structure of shared knowledge. A British build-up will be less threatening to the United States than a North Korean one, and build-ups are less likely to occur in a security community than in a security dilemma.

In order to get from anarchy and material forces to power politics and war, therefore, neorealists have been forced to make additional, *ad hoc* assumptions about the social structure of the international system. We see this in Mearsheimer's interest in "hyper-nationalism," Stephen Walt's emphasis on ideology in the "balance of threat," Randall Schweller's focus on the status quo–revisionist distinction and, as I argued in my "Anarchy" piece, in Waltz's assumption that anarchies are self-help systems.[16] Incorporating these assumptions generates more explanatory power, but how? In these cases the crucial causal work is done by social, not material, factors. This is the core of a constructivist view of structure, not a neorealist one.

The problem becomes even more acute when neorealists try to explain the relative absence of inter-state war in today's world. If anarchy is so determining, why are there not more Bosnias? Why are weak states not getting killed off left and right? It stretches credulity to think that the peace between Norway and Sweden, or the United States and Canada, or Nigeria and Benin are all due to material balancing. Mearsheimer says cooperation is possible when core interests are not threatened and that "some states are especially friendly for historical or ideological reasons." But this totally begs the question of why in an ostensibly "realist" world states do not find their interests continually threatened by others, and the question of how they might become friends. Perhaps Mearsheimer would say that most states today are status quo and sovereign.[17] But again this begs the question. What is sovereignty if not an institution of mutual recognition and non-intervention? And is not being "status quo" related to the internalization of this institution in state interests? David Strang has argued that those states recognized as sovereign have better survival prospects in anarchy than those that are not.[18] Far from challenging this argument, Mearsheimer presupposes it.

Neorealists' growing reliance on social factors to do their explanatory work suggests that if ever there were a candidate for a degenerating research program in IR theory, this is it.[19] The progressive response (in the Lakatosian sense) would be to return to realism's materialist roots by showing that the background understandings that give capabilities meaning are caused by still deeper material conditions, or that capabilities have intrinsic meaning that cannot be ignored. To show that the material base determines international superstructure, in other words, realists should be purging their theory of social content, not adding it as they are doing.[20] And anti-realists, in turn, should be trying to show how the causal powers of material facts presuppose social content, not trying to show that institutions explain additional variance beyond that explained by the distribution of power and interest, as if the latter were a privileged pre-social baseline.

RESPONSIBILITY

[Mearsheimer] . . . links neorealism and its rivals to the ethical responsibilities of foreign policy-makers. These responsibilities depend in part on how much it is possible to change the structure of shared knowledge within anarchy. If such change is impossible, then Mearsheimer is right that it would be irresponsible for those charged with national security to pursue it. On the other hand, if it *is* possible, then it would be irresponsible to pursue policies that perpetuate destructive old orders, especially if we care about the well-being of future generations.

To say that structures are socially constructed is no guarantee that they can be changed.[21] Sometimes social structures so constrain action that transformative strategies are impossible. This goes back to the collective nature of social structures; structural change depends on changing a system of expectations that may be mutually reinforcing. A key issue in determining policymakers' responsibilities, therefore, is how much "slack" a social structure contains. Neorealists think there is little slack in the system, and thus states that deviate from power politics will

get punished or killed by the "logic" of anarchy. Institutionalists think such dangers have been greatly reduced by institutions such as sovereignty and the democratic peace, and that there is therefore more possibility for peaceful change.

The example of Gorbachev is instructive in this respect, since the Cold War was a highly conflictual social structure. I agree with Mearsheimer that Soviet nuclear forces gave Gorbachev a margin of safety for his policies. Yet someone else in his place might have found a more aggressive solution to a decline in power. What is so important about the Gorbachev regime is that it had the courage to see how the Soviets' own practices sustained the Cold War, and to undertake a reassessment of Western intentions. This is exactly what a constructivist would do, but not a neorealist, who would eschew attention to such social factors as naive and as mere superstructure. Indeed, what is so striking about neorealism is its total neglect of the explanatory role of state practice.[22] It does not seem to matter what states do: Brezhnev, Gorbachev, Zhirinovsky, what difference does it make? The logic of anarchy will always bring us back to square one. This is a disturbing attitude if *realpolitik* causes the very conditions to which it is a response; to the extent that realism counsels *realpolitik*, therefore, it is part of the problem. Mearsheimer says critical theorists are "intolerant" of realists for this reason. The ironies of this suggestion aside, what matters is getting policymakers to accept responsibility for solving conflicts rather than simply managing or exploiting them. If neorealism can move us in that direction, then it should, but as I see it, neorealist ethics come down to "*sauve qui peut.*". . .

NOTES

1. "Constitute" is an important term in critical theory, with a special meaning that is not captured by related terms like "comprise," "consist of," or "cause." To

say that "X [for example, a social structure] constitutes Y [for example, an agent]," is to say that the properties of those agents are made possible by, and would not exist in the absence of, the structure by which they are "constituted." A constitutive relationship establishes a conceptually necessary or logical connection between X and Y, in contrast to the contingent connection between independently existing entities that is established by causal relationships.

The identity-behavior distinction is partly captured by Robert Powell's distinction between preferences over outcomes and preferences over strategies; Robert Powell, "Anarchy in International Relations Theory," *International Organization,* Vol. 48, No. 2 (Spring 1994), pp. 313–344. The main exception to the mainstream neglect of structural effects on state identity is Kenneth Waltz's argument that anarchy produces "like units"; Kenneth Waltz, *Theory of International Politics* (Reading, Mass.: Addison-Wesley, 1979), pp. 74–77. Constructivists think there are more possibilities than this; see Alexander Wendt, "Anarchy is What States Make of It: The Social Construction of Power Politics," *International Organization,* Vol. 46, No. 2 (Spring 1992), pp. 391–425.

2. What follows could also serve as a rough definition of "discourse."

3. See Karl Deutsch, et al., *Political Community and the North Atlantic Area* (Princeton: Princeton University Press, 1957).

4. For a good general discussion of this point, see Douglas Porpora, "Cultural Rules and Material Relations," *Sociological Theory,* Vol. 11, No. 2 (July 1993), pp. 212–229.

5. On the social content of interests, see Roy D' Andrade and Claudia Strauss, eds., *Human Motives and Cultural Models* (Cambridge: Cambridge University Press, 1992).

6. On the social basis of conflict, see Georg Simmel, *Conflict and the Web of Group Affiliations* (Glencoe, Ill.: Free Press, 1955). This is also why I prefer to avoid the term "institutionalism," since it associates sociality with peace and cooperation.

7. Fischer's suggestion that critical theory predicts cooperation in feudal Europe is based on a failure to understand the full implications of this point; see Fischer, "Feudal Europe, 800–1300."

8. See Louis Henkin, *How Nations Behave* (New York: Council on Foreign Relations, 1979), p. 47.

9. On the inadequacy of "realist" descriptions of international politics, see Paul Schroeder, "Historical

Reality vs. Neo-realist Theory," *International Security,* Vol. 19, No. 1 (Summer 1994), pp. 108–148.

10. For a start, see Alexander Wendt, "Collective Identity Formation," and Emanuel Adler, "Cognitive Evolution," in Emanuel Adler and Beverly Crawford, eds., *Progress in Postwar International Relations* (New York: Columbia University Press, 1991), pp. 43–88. The best introduction to processes of social construction remains Peter Berger and Thomas Luckmann, *The Social Construction of Reality* (New York: Anchor Books, 1966).

11. A similar argument is developed in John Vasquez, *The War Puzzle* (Cambridge: Cambridge University Press, 1993).

12. On the role of collective identity in facilitating collective security, see Wendt, "Collective Identity Formation."

13. Richard Ashley, "The Poverty of Neorealism," *International Organization,* Vol. 38, No. 2 (Spring 1984), pp. 225–286.

14. Kenneth Waltz, *Man, the State, and War* (New York: Columbia University Press, 1959), p. 232.

15. For a good argument to this effect, see Jonathan Mercer, "Anarchy and Identity," *International Organization,* Vol. 49, No. 2 (Spring 1995).

16. John J. Mearsheimer, "Back to the Future," *International Security,* Vol. 15, No. 1 (Summer 1990), pp. 5–56; Stephen Walt, *The Origins of Alliances* (Ithaca: Cornell University Press, 1987); Randall Schweller, "Tripolarity and the Second World War," *International Studies Quarterly,* Vol. 37, No. 1 (March 1993), pp. 73–103; and Wendt, "Anarchy is What States Make of It."

17. Mearsheimer and Waltz both assume sovereignty, without acknowledging its institutional character; see Mearsheimer, "False Promise," p. 11, and Waltz, *Theory of International Politics,* pp. 95–96.

18. David Strang, "Anomaly and Commonplace in European Political Expansion," *International Organization,* Vol. 45, No. 2 (Spring 1991), pp. 143–162.

19. "Degenerating" problem shifts are adjustments to a theory that are *ad hoc,* while "progressive" shifts are those that have a principled basis in its hard core assumptions. See Imre Lakatos, "Falsification and the Methodology of Scientific Research Programmes," in Lakatos and Alan Musgrave, eds., *Criticism and the Growth of Knowledge* (Cambridge: Cambridge University Press, 1970), pp. 91–196.

20. The significance of Dan Deudney's work lies partly in his appreciation of this point; see Dan Deudney,

"Dividing Realism: Structural Realism versus Security Materialism on Nuclear Security and Proliferation," *Security Studies*, Vol. 1, Nos. 2 and 3 (1993), pp. 7–37.

21. Hence, *contra* Mearsheimer, there is nothing problematic about the fact that critical theorists do not make predictions about the future. What happens in the future depends on what actors do with the structures they have made in the past.

22. This is not true of classical realists; for a sympathetic discussion of the latter from a critical standpoint, see Richard Ashley, "Political Realism and Human Interests," *International Studies Quarterly*, Vol. 25, No. 2 (June 1981), pp. 204–237.

SEARCHING FOR THE PRINCESS?

J. Ann Tickner

In recent decades, feminist perspectives on international relations have become increasingly important in the debates over international relations theory. Tickner is one of the most prominent representatives of a diverse group of feminist international relations scholars who disagree among themselves on many issues. In this reading, she summarizes some of the essential and most widely shared components of the feminist perspective. As you read this article, ask yourself:

※ What do feminists mean when they suggest that the field of international relations is "highly gendered"?

※ What "foundational myths" of the field does she single out for criticism?

※ What is the meaning behind the title of this article?

Princesses are scarce both in the discipline of international relations and in the realm of international politics. Princes, however, abound. For example, Machiavelli's Prince is enshrined in the canons of the field: The Prince tells us how states and their princes ought to behave if their foreign policies are to be successful. Machiavelli warns us that the way to lose one's state is to neglect the art of war: the prince must demonstrate courage, sobriety, and strength, for the only enduring methods of defense are those based on one's own action. Yet, as princes strive for power and control, dangers in the guise of Fortuna abound: random events that Machiavelli compares to violent rivers, which show their unpredictability and destructive capacities when there is no well-regulated power to resist them.

There are no princesses in Machiavelli's text, but Fortuna is described as a woman whom it is necessary to beat and coerce into submission. In contemporary international relations, dangers similar to Machiavelli's Fortuna are found in the realm of anarchy—spaces outside the sovereign state where force is the ultimate arbiter of disputes. Anarchy is frequently compared to Thomas Hobbes's pre-contractual state

J. Ann Tickner, "Searching for the Princess?" *Harvard International Review* 21:4, Fall 1999, pp. 44–48. Reprinted by permission of Harvard International Review.

An expanded version of this article was given as the keynote address at a conference, "Feminist Theory and Gender Perspectives in World Politics." Ohio University, May 18–20, 1995.

of nature where men exist in a state of war. For Hobbes the solution was the mighty Leviathan, a prince endowed with the sovereign power necessary for subduing dangerous environments. For scholars of contemporary international relations, possible solutions to the dangers of international anarchy can be found in either a hierarchy of states or a balance of power.

I will come back to the gendered implications of these representations of the anarchy-order distinction and the policies necessary for state survival later. I will now proceed to a brief review of the development of the discipline of international relations: then I will offer some thoughts as to why the field has been so resistant to gender analysis and what we are likely to see when we look at the field through feminist lenses. Finally, I will ask whether the future task of feminist perspectives on international relations should include looking for princesses.

EVOLUTION OF GLOBAL POLITICS

In its formative years, the discipline of international relations was concerned with the prevention of war through the development of international institutions. Woodrow Wilson's belief in democracy as a model for the conduct of diplomacy was epitomized in his Fourteen Points put forward near the end of World War I. However, in 1939, the hopes for the restraining influence of international law and democracy were shattered by another more terrible war. Kantian internationalists were replaced by self-named realists who, like Machiavelli's Prince, advised that only through power projection, military preparedness, and self-help could state survival be assured. Realists labeled their predecessors, idealists—in their view, misguided individuals who believed in the possibility of human improvement and law-governed behavior

in the international system. It is interesting to note that one can map gender distinctions onto this realist-idealist debate of the 1940s and 1950s, with realists attributing stereotypical characteristics of women, such as "unrealistic" and "naive," to the idealists.

The expansionary policies of European dictators caused the early realists to question the importance of morality and ideology in state behavior and thus motivated their support for universal objective laws. As realism evolved, the belief that models based on the natural sciences could reveal objective and universal laws capable of explaining state behavior became more entrenched. The popularity of rational choice theory, which remains the dominant approach to international theorizing today, reveals how strongly international relations theory has been influenced by the realists.

It was not until the 1980s that the theoretical consensus, centered on a commitment to the possibilities of positivist science, began to break down. Critical scholars proclaimed a "third debate," which evidenced a shift from mechanistic causal explanations to a greater interest in historically contingent interpretive theories. Besides challenging the epistemological foundations of the field, critics began to question the neutrality of realist theories. Contemporary feminist perspectives on international relations began to take hold during this disciplinary ferment of the 1980s; yet, the task of bringing feminist perspectives to a field that has been so resistant to gender analysis has not been easy.

GENDER & INTERNATIONAL AFFAIRS

When feminists began their gender-based analyses of the discipline in the late 1980s, they asserted that the field of international relations was highly gendered rather than gender neutral.

Its theories were based on foundational stories by androcentric authors, such as Machiavelli and Hobbes. From the very beginning, political science and international relations have been inhospitable to gender studies.

The first reason, though obvious, is also the most intractable. Diplomatic practices and the art of war are the business of princes; princesses belong on pedestals in private spaces, guardians of a morality that is unsuitable and even dangerous in the world of *realpolitik*. In spite of the visibility of Madeleine Albright, there are still relatively few women in the top ranks of the foreign service. In academic international relations, there are few women in the sub-field of national security. As Donald Regan, President Ronald Reagan's National Security Adviser, proclaimed in 1985, "Women are not going to understand missile throw-weights or what is happening in Afghanistan . . . most women would rather read the human interest stuff."

At least we can agree with Regan that the "human interest stuff" has not been the business of international relations scholarship. In neo-realism—a more parsimonious and "scientific" devolution from classical realism—human beings have disappeared altogether. This point leads to the second reason why the discipline is inhospitable terrain for feminist perspectives. In their search for mechanistic laws, international relations theorists have typically preferred explanatory theories that favor a structurally determined level of analysis; the international system is a world in which, as political theorist Jean Elshtain observes, "No children are ever born, and nobody ever dies. . . . There are states, and they are what is." Rational choice theory, modeled on the behavior of firms in the marketplace, has further reinforced this depersonalization of state behavior. Explanations that focus on social relations, a space where gender relations could be analyzed, are considered reductionist

and, therefore, unable to shed much light on the behavior of states in the international system.

My third reason for the inhospitality of international relations to feminist perspectives has to do with what Martin Wight called the intellectual and moral poverty of its theories. Given that all individuals must be citizens of sovereign states, the state remains the consummation of political experience according to Wight; outside the state lies only the realm of necessity where progress is impossible and theory can only be what international theorist Andrew Linklater, has called a theory of estrangement. Given that women's historical relationship to the state has been marginal in most societies, feminist perspectives do not fit comfortably within these state boundaries in which political life has been situated. Largely excluded from the realm of policy making, women's "foreign relations" have generally taken place across the borders of civil society.

FEMINIST LENSES

It is important to note that feminists engaged in re-visioning international relations are not going out and looking for princesses. Efforts to integrate women and to consider them equal to men tend to reinforce existing gender stereotypes. In the tough world of international politics, successful women leaders must often assume masculine roles and personalities. Conversely, if we go looking for women working in "women's spheres" such as peace groups, it only reinforces the socially constructed boundaries between activities deemed appropriate for women and men. We must search deeper to find ways in which gender hierarchies serve to reinforce these socially constructed boundaries which perpetuate inequalities between women and men. Similarly, we cannot hope to build a comprehensive understanding of the behavior of states in the international system unless we include gender as a category of analysis.

Feminist scholars of international relations use gender sensitive lenses to challenge the foundations of the discipline through four main ways; feminists question the heroic model of science which has been so central to the discipline; they critique its foundational myths; they challenge some of the core concepts of the field; and they rewrite women's experiences within these new conceptual frameworks.

THE HEROIC MODEL OF SCIENCE

Besides the state of nature discussed earlier, another important legacy of Hobbes for contemporary international relations has been the strong commitment to the "heroic" model of science, the notion that the world can be discovered through mechanistic laws of nature. Feminist theorist Spike Peterson claims that the scientific revolution of the 17th century marked a shift in our understanding of "the world" and the position of "man" within it. Beginning in the 17th century, scientific reasoning was explicitly constructed as "male" and promoted as superior to and exclusive of that which was marked as "female." Man, the knower, was identified with science and reason; women were associated with emotion and irrationality.

The claim that women have been absent from the construction of knowledge has been particularly true in the discipline of international relations. As mentioned earlier, realism and neorealism claim to have developed a "science" of international politics whereby the behavior of states in the international system can be explained in terms of universal, objective laws.

Feminists writing about international relations have suggested that international relations draws on experiences more typical of men than

women under the guise of objectivity. For example, rational choice theorists' explanations of the instrumentally competitive behavior of states in an anarchical international system parallel the self-interested behavior historically associated with men as actors in the marketplace. Favorable attributes of states, such as independence, strength, autonomy, and self-help, resemble the characteristics of the sovereign man, the defining figure of the heroic model. Feminists, who attempt to unsettle this model of science, are particularly critical of dichotomies associated with this way of thinking. Thus, feminist critiques of the foundational myths of the discipline have been especially concerned with challenging the boundaries, such as those between anarchy and order.

FOUNDATIONAL MYTHS

When women are absent from foundational theories, established gender biases extend into contemporary international theory. The two theorists mentioned earlier, Hobbes and Machiavelli, have constructed some traditional stories of international politics. Although Hobbes's description of human behavior in the state of nature refers explicitly to that of adult males, contemporary realism has taken this behavior as constitutive of human nature as a whole. Such analogies have appealed to international relations' gloomy picture of the unsocialized behavior of states in an international system of anarchy. But as feminists remind us, if life was to go on for more than one generation in the state of nature, other more cooperative activities, such as child rearing, must have also taken place. Bringing this assumption to contemporary international politics, we might conclude that states are engaged in cooperative as well as competitive activities.

Returning to Machiavelli, we find danger not in the unsocialized behavior of men in the state of nature, but in the wild spaces inhabited by the capricious goddess Fortuna. The feminization of dangerous spaces outside the territory of the state has been a metaphor frequently called upon to justify defense budgets or the policies of expansionary states. Feminist theorist Cynthia Enloe describes pictures of native women on postcards sent home from Africa and Asia in the early part of this century, which depicted appealing images, while making clear that these alien societies needed the civilizing government that only whites could bestow. Former colonial states and their leaders have frequently been portrayed as emotional and unpredictable, characteristics also associated with women.

This discourse, which associates danger with those on the outside, is frequently framed in gendered terms. Feminists have suggested that, in today's world of advanced technologies, overly militaristic definitions of security may actually decrease the security of both women and men, directly due to the likely level of destruction should war break out, and indirectly as it decreases resources for other uses.

CHALLENGING THE CORE CONCEPTS

Security, power, and sovereignty are some of the key concepts in international relations that contemporary feminist approaches are re-examining. Complementing my emphasis on princes and princesses, I shall focus on some feminist reformulations of the state.

The modern state was created as an instrument for increasing the capacity of princes to wage war. States in 16th and 17th century Europe were identified with the sovereign king. In 17th century Europe, war brought adventure and reputation to kings and princes. Fame, wealth, and women were prizes to be won in battle. For the typical prince, war was a means to reputation and glory. Hobbes's depiction of the Leviathan, a man in armor carrying a sword, serves as a visual representation of this early form of sovereign authority. International relations were relations between kings and princes whose foreign policymaking was conducted in isolation from their populations.

With the advent of republican forms of government in the 18th and 19th centuries, the state became associated with the will of the people rather than the crown. Yet the identity of the "people" was limited: in no state were women incorporated into republican forms of government on equal footing with men. Even today, when women have achieved formal equality in many states, this historical legacy still inhibits women's voices in foreign policymaking. In contemporary neo-realism, where states' identities are hidden behind the unitary actor model, the characteristics that neo-realists attribute to states are quite similar to masculine images of sovereignty. Feminists are asking whether these masculine representations have any effect on the foreign policies of states.

RECOVERING WOMEN'S EXPERIENCES

Once feminist perspectives have exposed the gendered construction of international theory and the diplomatic practices of states, women's experiences can help us to understand how these hierarchies are created and sustained. In *Bananas, Beaches, and Bases,* Cynthia Enloe takes us behind the scenes to find out what women in international relations do: she tells us that women's experiences of war, marriage, trade, travel and factory work have generally been relegated to the human interest columns. Yet, women working as secretaries and low-paid workers in export processing zones, as domestic servants often forced to work abroad to support their families, and as unpaid wives of diplomats who perform crucial functions in the running of embassies, are all necessary to foreign policy-making and to the efficiency of the global market. By performing roles that have come to be seen as "natural" ones for women, these women and many more are providing the labor that sustains the power structures of states and markets.

FINDING THE PRINCESS?

By way of conclusion, I should like to return to my original question: should we be searching for the princess, a figure who can serve as an alternative model to Machiavelli's Prince for the way states should conduct their foreign policies? I do not believe so; international relations feminists are not searching for another totalizing concept within which to frame our understanding and prescriptions for state behavior. Instead, let me propose the adoption of Fortuna, the unpredictable goddess who tolerates ambiguity and uncertainty, a position which certain scholars have suggested may not be far from Machiavelli's own.

Tolerating uncertainty may be necessary if, as feminist perspectives suggest, we must chart new courses rather than try to fit women's encounters with international relations into existing frameworks. Unless we recognize gender as a category of analysis, we cannot understand how gender relations of inequality act to exclude women from the business of foreign policymaking and ensure that they are located disproportionately at the bottom of the socio-economic scale in all societies.

Should we then give up on theory? My answer to this question is also negative. I share the views of many contemporary feminists that developing causal explanations modeled on the natural sciences is inappropriate in the social sciences due to the impossibility of separating human intentions and human interests from our knowledge construction. But we must continue to strive for a deeper and more systematic understanding of the political, social and economic relations, including gender relations, which inform the behavior of states.

Therefore, while acknowledging the impossibility of representing all the world's multiple realities in terms of one universal truth, feminists are seeking theories which offer us what feminist theorist Donna Haraway calls a reliable account of things, . . . an earth-wide network of connections, including the ability partially to translate knowledges among very different—and power-differentiated—communities." Haraway argues for what she calls "embodied objectivity" or "situated knowledge." Situated knowledge does not mean relativism, but rather, shared conversations leading to "better accounts of the world."

Princes and princesses belong to the elite world of an aristocracy that has begun to fade. Democratic politics grows out of local knowledge, the kind of knowledge that emerges from feminist theories' emphasis on diversity, contextuality and contingency. Searching for understanding through shared conversations can help us envision, not a world of princes and their principalities, but a democratic global political arena that allows new voices to be heard and is less constrained by socially constructed boundaries.

CHAPTER 2

HISTORICAL PERSPECTIVES
Continuity and Change in World Politics

For a student of world politics, examining the history of international relations is useful for developing both better theory and better policy. For international relations theorists, history provides a vast laboratory of events, policies, and behaviors that can be used to test our theoretical understanding of how the world works. Do countries really balance the power of one another, as realists suggest? Does democracy really lead to peace, as liberals argue? The use of historical evidence to address such theoretical questions provides a pool of data that an exclusive focus on current events—the outcome of which often remains uncertain—cannot provide. At the same time, an understanding of the past can also be useful in formulating contemporary foreign policy. As the author George Santayana once wrote, "Those who cannot remember the past are condemned to repeat it." The implication is that knowing something about the past informs one in a way that helps one to avoid repeating mistakes in judgment, interpretation, and policy.

The two readings in this chapter focus on how the study of history and the application of its lessons can inform our understanding of the contemporary world. The selection by historian Paul Schroeder is an excerpt from an article in which he attempts to use his knowledge of history to test certain assumptions of the structural realist (neorealist) paradigm and see how well those assumptions reflect the actual behavior of states across time. Thus, his concern is largely with how history can contribute to the development and assessment of international relations theory. The article by Jeffrey Record focuses more directly on how history, and especially arguments by historical analogy, is used in the formulation and promotion of contemporary foreign policy. As he notes, two different historical analogies have been frequently applied to the U.S. war in Iraq. The 1938 Munich analogy is often applied by those supporting the U.S. decision to invade as a lesson in the dangers of appeasing dictators. The Vietnam War analogy is often cited by opponents of the Iraq war as a lesson in the dangers of getting bogged down in unwinnable wars. In examining those cases he considers not only how history can be used but also misused by policy makers.

HISTORICAL REALITY VS. NEO-REALIST THEORY

Paul Schroeder

This selection is an excerpt from a much longer article in which historian Paul Schroeder uses his knowledge of history to test certain generalizations made by structural realists. In this excerpt, the question is whether states really engage in self-help and balancing of power when faced with external threats to their security. As you read this excerpt, ask yourself:

⚜ How and why would realists predict that states will act when faced with external threats?

⚜ In what ways does the historical record according to Schroeder contradict those realist expectations?

⚜ Is the evidence he cites sufficient to prove realists wrong?

Realism has been for some time the reigning tradition in international theory and remains a major current in it.[1] The neo-realism or structural realism developed in Kenneth N. Waltz's *Theory of International Politics* is generally considered a major advance on the classical version of Hans Morgenthau and others. The central argument is that the broad outcomes of international politics derive more from the structural constraints of the states system than from unit behavior. The theory proceeds in a series of logical inferences from the fundamental postulate of a states system in which all units are autonomous, so that the system is structured by anarchy rather than hierarchy; to the primacy of survival, security, and independence for each unit wishing to remain part of the system; to the mandate of self-help this need imposes upon each unit; and to a resultant competition between units which produces a recurrent pattern of various balances of power.

Much current debate over neo-realism centers on what implications the end of the Cold War might have for realist theory, in terms of its ability both to explain this particular outcome and to prescribe future policy.[2] This essay will not, however, discuss how neo-realist theory fits recent and current history. Instead it takes up a question seldom if ever discussed, yet clearly important for international historians and arguably also for international relations theorists, namely, whether neo-realist theory is adequate and useful as an explanatory framework for the history of international politics in general, over the whole Westphalian era from 1648 to 1945, the period in which the validity of a realist paradigm of some sort is widely accepted even by non-realists.[3]. . .

A HISTORIAN'S VIEW OF THE NEO-REALIST HISTORICAL WORLD

Some facts in the history of international politics seem to hold broadly for the modern European states system through much of its existence. . . . It is generally true, though not at all uniformly so, that states in the modern era, regardless of their ideology, domestic structure, individual aims, etc., have claimed exclusive sovereignty over their territory and the sole right to the legitimate use of force within it, have set a high value on

Paul Schroeder, excerpt from "Historical Reality vs. Neo-Realist Theory," *International Security,* 19:1, Summer 1994, pp. 108–148. © 1994 by the President and the Fellows of Harvard College and the Massachussetts Institute of Technology. Reprinted by permission of MIT Press Journals.

their independence and security, have upheld their right to use force in self-defense, have tried to provide means for their defense, and have conducted foreign policy with an eye to maintaining their security and independence. This is obvious and familiar. Nevertheless, the more one examines . . . historical generalizations about the conduct of international politics throughout history with the aid of the historian's knowledge of the actual course of history, the more doubtful—in fact, strange—these generalizations become.

Self-Help: Theory Confronts Practice

Do all states, or virtually all, or all that really count, actually resort to self-help in the face of threats to their security and independence? Though Waltz does not clearly define self-help or describe its practice, one may reasonably infer, given the link frequently drawn between self-help and the balance of power, and given Waltz's insistence on the primacy of power and the structural role of the potential and actual use of force in international politics, that self-help means, at least generally and primarily, the potential or actual use of a state's own power along with that of other units for the purposes of compellence, deterrence, and other modes of controlling the actions of one's opponents. By Waltz's rules for testing theories, neo-realist theory should correctly predict or confirm this kind of conduct in international politics throughout history, and Waltz clearly believes it does so. . . .

I do not. I cannot construct a history of the European states system from 1648 to 1945 based on the generalization that most unit actors within that system responded to crucial threats to their security and independence by resorting to self-help, as defined above. In the majority of instances this just did not happen. In each major period in these three centuries, most unit actors tried if they possibly could to protect their vital interests in other ways. (This includes great powers as well as smaller ones, undermining the neo-realist argument that weaker states are more inclined to bandwagon than stronger ones, as discussed below.) The reasons are clear. For one thing, most states, most of the time, could not afford a strategy of self-help of this kind. They were like landowners with valuable property which they knew they could not possibly insure, first because insurance premiums were ruinously expensive, second because against the most devastating dangers no insurance policy was available at any price, and third because the very attempt on their part to take out an insurance policy would encourage robbers to attack them.[4] Hence the insurance policies they took out and maintained in the form of armed forces, alliances, and diplomacy were mostly intended to protect against minor risks and to deter casual attacks or vandalism, with the full knowledge that if something more serious threatened, another recourse would be necessary.

Other strategies were available and often tried. One commonly employed was *hiding* from threats. This could take various forms: simply ignoring the threat or declaring neutrality in a general crisis, possibly approaching other states on one or both sides of a quarrel to get them to guarantee one's safety; trying to withdraw into isolation; assuming a purely defensive position in the hope that the storm would blow over; or, usually as a later or last resort, seeking protection from some other power or powers in exchange for diplomatic services, friendship, or non-military support, without joining that power or powers as an ally or committing itself to any use of force on its part.[5] A strategy less common, but far from unusual or unknown, was *transcending,* i.e., attempting to surmount international anarchy and go beyond the normal limits of conflictual politics: to solve the problem, end the threat, and prevent its recurrence through some institutional arrangement involving an international consensus or formal agreement on norms, rules, and procedures for these purposes. Efforts of this kind were made in every era of these centuries. Another strategy was *bandwagoning,* i.e., joining the stronger side for the sake of protection and payoffs, even if this meant insecurity *vis-à-vis* the protecting power and a certain sacrifice of independence. . . . I see bandwagoning as historically more common than balancing, particularly by smaller powers. Finally comes the strategy which, according to Waltz and others, is dominant and structural in international politics: *self-help* in the form of balancing against an actual or potential hegemon. Once again, contrary to the view of many scholars including historians, I see this as having been relatively rare, and often a fallback policy or last resort.[6]

A concrete example illustrating these different strategies in practice is the crisis in Germany (the Holy Roman Empire or Reich) caused by the Austrian Emperor Joseph II's attempt in 1785 to carry through the exchange of the Austrian Netherlands (Belgium) for Bavaria.[7] Almost all German states and principalities saw this move as a threat to the German "balance"—by which they meant not simply the balance of power between the German great powers, Austria and Prussia, and their respective clients, but even more importantly for some states, the balance provided by the Reich constitution between the sovereign powers of Germany's various states and the limits to individual state power and guarantees of corporate "liberties" (i.e., privileges) within those states. The reason the proposed move would threaten the independence and security of the Reich and its members was not just that it would strengthen Austria, but also and mainly that it would damage the Reich as a legal order guaranteeing the liberties of all its members (another indication of the ways in which a purely power-political view of international politics is too crude to capture vital elements of the process).[8] Many units hid from the threat, i.e., simply ignored the issue or remained neutral, even though they knew the outcome might affect them critically. Some balanced against it. Prussia and Hanover, old rivals, joined to exploit an idea already current, that of forming a Protestant League of Princes to check the Catholic Emperor and his ecclesiastical princely clients.[9] Some began by hiding out, then saw that Emperor Joseph would lose his nerve, and bandwagoned to the winning Prussian side. But some also tried to transcend; that is, certain lesser princes attempted to form a union of smaller states not to stop Prussia or Austria by force (which they knew was beyond their resources) or to balance with either great power or against both, but to rise above the quarrel, reviving and reforming the institutions and constitution of the Empire so as to provide guarantees for everyone's territorial rights, and a machinery for the arbitration of future disputes.[10]

This kind of scenario, in which different states perceiving the same threat or similar ones adopted differing strategies to meet them, is seen in almost every major crisis throughout the centuries in question. For this reason alone, neo-realist theory cannot accommodate the history of international politics as I know it; too many facts and insights vital for explaining broad developments and results do not pass through its prism. . . .

I can back the assertion that neorealism is incorrect in its claims for the repetitiveness of strategy and the prevalence of balancing in international politics, with brief examples of how the various competing strategies were used in the face of threat in four major periods of war: the French revolutionary and Napoleonic wars (1792–1815), the Crimean War (1853–56), the First World War (1914–18), and the Second

World War (1939–45). These make a *prima facie* case against Waltz's generalizations.

French Revolutionary and Napoleonic Wars The French revolutionary and Napoleonic wars are often considered a classic case of balancing, with allied coalitions repeatedly being formed to defeat France's bid for hegemony and restore the balance of power. However, this view will not stand examination. The First Coalition (1792–97) was formed against France at a time when, though it provoked the coalition into being and started the war by its aggressive behavior and ideology, France was militarily extremely weak and vulnerable and had lost all its allies and political influence in Europe. Austria and Prussia (or at least most of their leaders) expected to win the war easily; the smaller states, if they could not hide from the conflict, gravitated toward the apparently overwhelmingly superior allied coalition, which included Spain, Piedmont, Tuscany, Naples, and various German states, soon joined in early 1793 by Great Britain. Once France's real revolutionary power became apparent from late 1793 on, states began hiding by leaving the coalition (Prussia, Tuscany, and some German states) or bandwagoning by joining France, as Spain did.[11] The same thing happened to the Second Coalition (1798–1801): states hid or bandwagoned to the allied side so long as it was winning, to mid-1799, and then bandwagoned to France's side from late 1799 on. Even Russia, a main founder of the Second Coalition, did so.[12] In every succeeding war from late 1799 to mid-1813, despite the fact that France under Napoleon had become by far both the most powerful Continental state and the most ambitious and insatiable one, the French-led coalition was always larger and stronger than its counterpart; more states always bandwagoned than balanced. In several instances Napoleon was able to organize most of Europe for war

against a single isolated foe (Britain in 1803 and 1807, Prussia in 1806, Spain in 1808, Austria in 1809, Russia in 1812). In short, the main response to Napoleonic hegemony and imperialism by European states, large and small alike, was not balancing but either hiding or bandwagoning. (There were also attempts to transcend, mainly in the form of trying to transform French conquest and domination into a new federal order for Germany and Europe, but these proved futile in the face of Napoleon's militarism.) Besides the smaller, weaker states who bandwagoned as Napoleon's satellites, many of them willingly and profitably, every major power in Europe except Great Britain—Prussia, Austria, Russia, Spain—bandwagoned as France's active ally for a considerable period. Wars continued to break out mainly not because European states tried to balance against France as a hegemonic power, but because Napoleon's ambition and lawless conduct frustrated their repeated efforts to hide or bandwagon. This happened to Prussia from 1795 to 1806 and from 1807 to 1810, Spain from 1795 to 1808, Austria in 1806–08 and 1809–13, and Russia in 1807–12.[13] Even after Napoleon's disastrous defeat in Russia in 1812, the Continental coalition that Russia and Prussia formed in early 1813 to "balance" against France was smaller than the coalition Napoleon reformed from his allies and satellites, and was initially defeated by it. Only after the failure of Austria's attempt to transcend the crisis, by mediating a negotiated peace in the summer of 1813, did Austria join the coalition (for purposes of controlling and ending rather than winning the war), and only after the decisive defeat of Napoleon's army at Leipzig in October 1813 did his coalition break up, with smaller states bandwagoning to the winning allied side.[14]

The Crimean War The Crimean War, originally seen by most Britons and still viewed by some historians as a case of "balancing" against Russian domination of Europe, actually began with a clearly superior allied coalition (Britain, France, and the Ottoman Empire) facing a Russia diplomatically isolated, politically and militarily threatened, aware of its peril, and looking for an honorable retreat. No neutral state in Europe therefore considered Russia a military threat at that time. Even Austria, which had a general fear of Russian domination of the Balkans, recognized that this danger was for the moment allayed, and tried hard to prevent the war. Most German states, including Prussia, considered the Anglo-French coalition a greater military and political threat to their security and interests. Yet Sardinia-Piedmont joined the dominant coalition militarily, Austria did so politically, and even Prussia and the German Confederation, although sympathetic to Russia and wanting only to hide from the conflict, were dragged into helping force Russia to admit defeat and accept an imposed settlement. In short, some states, great and small, bandwagoned; others tried to hide and then bandwagoned; still others, like Sweden, Denmark, and the Low Countries, remained in hiding; none balanced against Anglo-French domination. Once again, moreover, there was a major effort to transcend: Austria's attempt to stop the war short of victory by a negotiated settlement intended to produce a new concert and a permanent solution to the Eastern question.[15]

The First World War The distinction between balancing and bandwagoning becomes especially difficult to draw in the First World War. It is possible, though far from clear, that initially both sides were balancing against the other's threat rather than bidding for hegemony. However, the distinction between aiming for balance or hegemony, always problematic, becomes virtually meaningless here, since, once

engaged in war, both sides could envision security only through clear military supremacy, and both fought for imperialist goals designed to insure it.[16] Moreover, other states plainly preferred either to hide (Spain, Holland, Denmark, Sweden, Switzerland) or to bandwagon with the victor so as to defeat their particular enemies and make gains at their expense (Turkey, Bulgaria, Italy, Rumania, Greece, Japan, and China). As things turned out, only two powers joined the smaller and putatively weaker Central Powers (Bulgaria and Turkey, both under a degree of duress); more joined the larger allied one (Italy, Rumania, Greece, Japan, China, the United States, and all the British Dominions). Certain of these, especially Italy and Rumania, explicitly tried to bandwagon with the victorious side at the right moment to share the spoils. Moreover, one cannot overlook attempts by neutrals (the Papal State, Sweden, Switzerland, the United States) and even certain belligerents (Austria-Hungary and the Russian Provisional Government in 1917) to transcend the conflict by promoting a negotiated peace.[17]

World War Two The pattern is a bit clearer in World War Two in Europe. Even before the war, Germany's growing power and political success promoted extensive hiding and bandwagoning in Western and Eastern Europe. Belgium dropped its ties to France in 1936 and reverted to neutrality; Holland, Denmark, and Norway not only remained ostentatiously neutral but declined even to arm for self-defense before they were overrun. Chamberlain's appeasement policy was certainly not balancing, but an attempt at a British partnership with Germany for peace; Daladier's abandonment of Czechoslovakia can be seen as France's attempt to avoid war by hiding. The Little Entente of Czechoslovakia, Rumania, and Yugoslavia, a potential instrument for balancing against Germany, fell apart even before Munich;

the French-Czech-Russian alliance collapsed at Munich; and Poland and Hungary joined with Germany in despoiling Czechoslovakia. Italy, despite Mussolini's and Ciano's fears of Germany, moved decisively to Hitler's side in May 1939, and the Soviet Union followed in August. The Poles, although standing firm against German demands and accepting a British guarantee, steadfastly refused to join a balancing alliance with Russia against Germany and essentially pinned their hopes of salvation on hiding in independent neutrality. After France's defeat, the Vichy regime tried to bandwagon with Hitler's Germany. Hungary, Bulgaria, and Rumania joined his camp, while Yugoslavia's apparent reversal of its decision to do so in March 1941 was actually a purely domestic political coup. Even neutrals (Sweden, Turkey, Switzerland, Spain) leaned toward Germany so long as the tide of war was going Hitler's way. Once the tide of battle turned in 1941–42, however, states began bandwagoning with Hitler's enemies, many joining the "United Nations." Even Franco's Spain and Perón's Argentina finally leaned toward the Allies (although Spain felt a threat from Britain and Argentina from the United States), while Fascist Italy did an eighteenth-century *volte-face* and joined them as a co-belligerent.

Even if one allows considerable room for differences of interpretation of these well-known developments, neo-realist generalizations about the repetitiveness of strategy and the prevalence of balancing in international politics do not withstand historical scrutiny.

The neo-realist answer is likely to be that regardless of all the supposed variations in unit behavior, neo-realism still explains and predicts the broad patterns of behavior and overall outcomes of international history. Hiding, transcending, and bandwagoning are all just different forms and strategies of self-help; and in the last analysis, bids for hegemony are defeated, and new

balances of power do emerge. The historian's preliminary reply would be, first, to ask what serious content remains to the concept of self-help if it includes strategies so diverse and even contradictory as these. Indeed, what becomes of the structural constraints of anarchy if they are elastic enough to allow some of the behaviors involved in transcending? Second, it is far from obvious that in the long run bids for hegemony always fail and new balances emerge. Finally, if these central generalizations of neo-realist theory do not hold, what use is it to the historian? What does it really explain and predict? . . .

NOTES

1. The central work is Kenneth N. Waltz, *Theory of International Politics* (Reading, Mass.: Addison-Wesley, 1979).

2. For current neo-realist arguments, see John Mearsheimer, "Back to the Future: Instability in Europe After the Cold War," *International Security*, Vol. 15, No. 1 (Summer 1990), pp. 5–55; Christopher Layne, "The Unipolar Illusion: Why New Great Powers Will Rise," *International Security*, Vol. 17, No. 4 (Spring 1993), pp. 5–51; and Kenneth N. Waltz, "The Emerging Structure of International Politics," *International Security*, Vol. 18, No. 2 (Fall 1993), pp. 44–79. Layne's argument is analyzed more closely below.

3. It is striking, for example, that a strong opponent of realism, Bruce Russett, seems to accept the validity of the realist paradigm for this period in writing: "It may be possible in part to supersede the 'realist' principles (anarchy, the security dilemma of states) that have dominated practice to the exclusion of 'liberal' or 'idealist' ones since at least the seventeenth century." Russett, *Grasping the Democratic Peace* (Princeton, N.J.: Princeton University Press, 1993), p. 24.

4. A classic example of this can be seen in the origins of the War of the Austrian Succession in 1740. The Habsburg monarch and German Emperor Charles VI had devoted years of costly diplomacy to trying to insure the rights of his daughter Maria Theresa to inherit his Austrian lands against any challenge to the succession on his death, by getting all interested powers including Prussia formally to endorse the

so-called Pragmatic Sanction of her title. Frederick II of Prussia, seeing Charles rely on this insurance policy, and knowing that others were likely also to disregard their obligations under it, immediately seized Austrian Silesia when he and Maria Theresa acceded to their thrones in 1740, and France and Bavaria quickly joined in the attack on Austria. For the historical details, see on the French and European side especially Paul Vaucher, *Robert Walpole et la politique de Fleury (1731–1742)* (Paris: Plon-Nourrit, 1924); on the Austrian, Max Braubach, *Versailles und Wien von Ludwing XIV bis Kaunitz* (Bonn: L. Röhrschild, 1952)

5. What I here call "hiding" may be related to "buckpassing"; see Thomas J. Christensen and Jack Snyder, "Chain Gangs and Passed Bucks: Predicting Alliance Patterns in Multipolarity," *International Organization,* Vol. 44, No. 2 (Spring 1990), pp. 137–168. Hiding, however, would seem to be broader in scope, often involving not just an effort to pass the costs of international politics to someone else, or to avoid any active participation in it, but a search for some method of handling the threat apart from being drawn into the power-political fray, often by a very active foreign policy. "Hiding" may therefore be somewhat misleading as a blanket term for all these forms of conduct, but I can think of no more satisfactory one.

6. This list of the ways states have reacted to international crises and threats or tried to use them is not proposed as exhaustive. It was common, for example, to try to exploit threats, i.e., use them to gain some particular advantage for one's own state, often at the expense of another state than the one posing the threat. This strategy, however, seems impossible to characterize as a particular response to threats, since it always or almost always plays into attempts to balance or bandwagon, and frequently is involved in attempts to hide and transcend as well. Thus it would seem characteristic of competitive power politics in general, and not a particular mode of response to threats within it.

7. Good discussions are in K.O. von Aretin, *Heiliges Römisches Reich 1776–1806,* 2 vols. (Wiesbaden: F. Steiner, 1967); and Max Braubach, *Maria Theresias jüngster Sohn Max Franz, letzter Kurfürst von Köln* (Vienna: Herold, 1961).

8. Aretin, *Heiliges Römisches Reich,* repeatedly stresses this theme, but it is also generally recognized by students of the constitutional history of the Empire. See for example John C. Gagliardo, *Reich and Nation: The Holy Roman Empire as Idea and Reality, 1763–1806* (Bloomington: Indiana University Press, 1980); Jean-François Noël, *Le Saint Empire* (Paris: Presses Universitaires de France, 1976). This tension between balance of power and balance of rights, *Machtordnung* and *Rechtsordnung,* prominent especially in the old regime but important in all eras, tends to be blurred or erased by the neo-realist approach.

9. T.C.W. Blanning, "George III and the Fürstenbund," *Historical Journal,* Vol. 20, No. 2 (June 1977), pp. 311–344.

10. For evidence that this kind of transcending was not an uncommon occurrence, but a frequent feature of Imperial politics, see K.O. von Aretin, ed., *Der Kurfürst von Mainz und die Kreisassoziationen 1648–1746* (Wiesbaden: F. Steiner, 1975).

11. I draw here on the account in my *Transformation of European Politics,* chap. 3; but see also T.C.W. Blanning, *The Origins of the French Revolutionary Wars* (London: Longman's, 1986).

12. Paul W. Schroeder, "The Collapse of the Second Coalition," *Journal of Modern History,* Vol. 59, No. 2 (June 1987), pp. 244–290.

13. For a brief survey of the evidence, see Paul W. Schroeder, "Napoleon's Foreign Policy: A Criminal Enterprise," *Journal of Military History,* Vol. 54, No. 2 (April 1990), pp. 147–162.

14. Again, this is shown in detail in my *Transformation of European Politics,* chaps. 5–8, 10–12.

15. See Paul W. Schroeder, *Austria, Great Britain and the Crimean War* (Ithaca, N.Y.: Cornell University Press, 1972); Winfried Baumgart, *Der Frieden von Paris 1856* (Wiesbaden: F. Steiner, 1972); Ann Pottinger Saab, *Origins of the Crimean Alliance* (Charlottesville: University of Virginia Press, 1977); and Norman Rich, *Why the Crimean War?* (Hanover, N.H.: University Press of New England, 1985).

16. A brilliant recent study proving this with massive evidence, especially for the Allied side, is G.-H. Soutou, *L'Or et le Sang: les buts de guerre économiques de la Première Guerre mondiale* (Paris: Fayard, 1989).

17. The literature here is too massive to summarize; a good recent overview is David Stevenson, *The First World War and International Politics* (Oxford: Clarendon, 1988).

THE USE AND ABUSE OF HISTORY: MUNICH, VIETNAM AND IRAQ

Jeffrey Record

In this article, Jeffrey Record considers the role and utility of reasoning by historical analogy as it is often employed by policy makers. In particular, he examines the utility of the Munich and Vietnam analogies as applied to the ongoing debate over the U.S. decision to invade Iraq in 2003. As you read his analysis, ask yourself:

- To what extent does the Munich analogy usefully help us understand the situation faced in Iraq prior to the invasion?
- To what extent does the Vietnam analogy usefully help us understand the situation in Iraq since the invasion?
- In general, should we be comforted or alarmed when policy makers seek to make policy based on the lessons of history?

During the run-up to America's second war against Iraq in 2003, proponents and opponents of war trotted out the historical analogies of Munich and Vietnam to justify their positions. These arguments by analogy were familar and predictable—Munich has been invoked in debates over presidential use of force since the outbreak of the Korean War in 1950, augmented by the Vietnam analogy since the 1960s.

Proponents of the Iraq War cited the consequences of the democracies' appeasement of the burgeoning Nazi menace during the 1930s and claimed that war was necessary to remove Iraqi President Saddam Hussein before he obtained nuclear weapons with which he would threaten and even attack the United States. Munich's lesson was to move early and decisively against rising threats. The Second World War could have been avoided had the democracies been prepared to fight for Czechoslovakia in 1938; instead, they handed over vital chunks of Czech territory to Hitler, whetting his appetite for more. Thus military action against a pre-nuclear

Saddam in 2003 would be much easier and less risky than war with a nuclear Saddam later on. War with Saddam was inevitable, as it was with Hitler, so it was better to have it now on more favourable terms. 'Time is not on our side', declared President George W. Bush in his January 2002 State of the Union Address. 'I will not wait on events while dangers gather. I will not stand by as peril draws closer and closer. The United States of America will not permit the world's most dangerous regimes to threaten us with the world's most dangerous weapons.'[1]

Opponents and sceptics of the war argued that Saddam Hussein posed no credible threat to US security worth a war, and that a US invasion of Iraq risked stumbling into a Vietnam-like quagmire. As in Vietnam, US forces in Iraq could be sucked into a protracted, indecisive war while attempting to create an Iraqi state of sufficient political legitimacy and military competence to survive after American combat forces departed. That the United States failed to create a viable South Vietnamese state after 20 years and

Jeffrey Record, excerpt from "The Use and Abuse of History: Munich, Vietnam and Iraq," *Survival* 49:1, Spring 2007. Reprinted by permission of the publisher Taylor & Francis Ltd, http://www.tandf.co.uk/journals.

billions of dollars argued strongly against success in Iraq, where the United States faced significant disadvantages compared to Vietnam. . . .

THE SHADOW OF MUNICH

Decision-makers and their critics employ reasoning by historical analogy to interpret new events as well as deploying historical analogies to mobilise public opinion.[2] Presidential decisions to use or not use force in a crisis are of course influenced by myriad factors, including personality, professional military advice, the presence or absence of prior obligations, perceived stakes, anticipated enemy responses and domestic political considerations. But they also can be, and often are, influenced by ideas in the form of goals sought (e.g., a global democratic peace) or 'lessons learned' from past historical experience (e.g., appeasing aggression only invites more of it). As Woodrow Wilson went to war in Europe to make the world safe for democracy, so too did Harry Truman and Lyndon Johnson go to war in Asia because they believed the experience of Munich left them no choice. Indeed, presidents from Truman to George W. Bush repeatedly found themselves in crises in which they concluded that military inaction risked appeasing an aggressive threat, and then went on to mobilise public support for subsequent use of force by invoking the Munich analogy.

The analogy informed every major threatened or actual US use of force during the first two decades of the Cold War as well as the decisions to attack Iraq in 1991 and 2003. Munich conditioned the thinking of every Cold War administration from Truman to George H.W. Bush. For Truman, the analogy dictated intervention in Korea: 'Communism was acting in Korea just as Hitler and the Japanese had acted ten, fifteen, twenty years earlier'.[3] A year after the Korean War ended, President Dwight Eisenhower, citing

the 'domino effects' of a communist victory in French Indochina on the rest of Southeast Asia, invoked Munich in an appeal for Anglo-American military action: 'we failed to halt Hirohito, Mussolini and Hitler by not acting in unity and in time . . . May it not be that [we] have learned something from that lesson?'[4] President John F. Kennedy invoked the Munich analogy during the Cuban Missile Crisis, warning that the '1930s taught us a clear lesson: aggressive conduct, if allowed to go unchecked, ultimately leads to war'.[5]

Munich indisputably propelled the United States into Vietnam. President Johnson told his secretary of defense, Robert McNamara, that if the United States pulled out of Vietnam, 'the dominoes would fall and a part of the world would go Communist'.[6] Johnson later told historian Doris Kearns that 'everything I knew about history told me that if I got out of Vietnam and let Ho Chi Minh run through the streets of Saigon, then I'd be doing exactly what Chamberlain did . . . I'd be giving a fat reward to aggression'.[7] Richard Nixon's administration also believed Munich applied to Vietnam. In his memoirs, Nixon approvingly quoted Churchill's condemnation of the 1938 Munich agreement and then went on to conclude that 'what had been true of the betrayal of Czechoslovakia to Hitler in 1938 was no less true of the betrayal of South Vietnam to the communists advocated by many in 1965'.[8]

Reagan saw in the Soviet Union a replay of the challenges the democracies faced in the 1930s and invoked the Munich analogy to justify a major US military buildup as well as intervention in Grenada and possible intervention in Nicaragua. 'One of the great tragedies of this century', he said in a 1983 speech, 'was that it was only after the balance of power was allowed to erode and a ruthless adversary, Adolf Hitler, deliberately weighed the risks and decided to strike that the importance of a strong defense was realized'.[9] Similarly, G.H.W. Bush saw in Saddam Hussein an Arab Hitler whose aggression against Kuwait, if unchecked, would lead to further aggression in the Persian Gulf. In announcing the dispatch of US forces to Saudi Arabia in response to Saddam Hussein's conquest of Kuwait, he declared, 'if history teaches us anything, it is that we must resist aggression or it will destroy our freedoms. Appeasement does not work. As was the case in the 1930s, we see in Saddam Hussein an aggressive dictator threatening his neighbors.'[10]

THE SHADE OF VIETNAM

US defeat in Vietnam temporarily discredited the Munich analogy, which Johnson and Secretary of State Dean Rusk had invoked ad nauseum to convince the American electorate that the United States had to intervene in Vietnam. There was, as it turned out, no analogy between Ho Chi Minh and Hitler, North Vietnam and Nazi Germany, and Southeast Asia of the 1960s and Europe of the 1930s. What US defeat in Vietnam did provide was another powerful analogy that influenced subsequent presidential use of force decisions. If Munich argues for early and decisive military action against aggressors, the experience of Vietnam cautions against military intervention in circumstances where both the strength of security interests and the decisiveness of conventional military superiority are questionable. Vietnam warns against intervention in politically messy Third-World conflicts, especially those fueled by nationalism and waged asymmetrically. As Christopher Hemmer succinctly puts it, 'a policy maker who interprets a challenge from abroad as similar to the challenge posed by Hitler in the 1930s is far more likely to favor an activist policy than one who interprets a challenge from abroad as similar to the one posed by Vietnam in the 1960s'.[11]

Vietnam bred a profound aversion to the use of force as well as a tendency, when the use of force appeared unavoidable, to use the minimum believed necessary to accomplish the objective.[12] Indeed, President Ronald Reagan decried what he called the 'post-Vietnam syndrome', or 'the resistance of many in Congress to the use of force abroad for any reason, because of our nation's experience in Vietnam'.[13]

In President Bill Clinton's case, the Executive Branch rather than Congress was spooked about using force. The first administration headed by a Vietnam-War-generation president seemed paralysed in the face of Serbian aggression and atrocities in the former Yugoslavia. When it finally acted in Bosnia and later in Kosovo, it did so in a manner (sole reliance on air power) that minimised the risk of casualties even at the cost of mission accomplishment.

If the Munich analogy has been associated with official decisions to use force, the Vietnam analogy, reinforced by failed US interventions in civil wars in Lebanon in 1982 and Somalia in 1993, has been popular among opponents of military intervention. Indeed, the Vietnam War's chilling effect on US willingness to use force was enshrined in the Weinberger Doctrine enunciated in 1984 and its subsequent corollary, proclaimed by Colin Powell when he was chairman of the Joint Chiefs of Staff. Weinberger's six 'tests' for using force and Powell's insistence on 'overwhelming force' reflect the professional military's 'take' on the lessons of Vietnam.

'Risking another Vietnam' can be a powerful argument against military action. Opponents of US intervention in Lebanon and Central America in the 1980s, and in Bosnia and Kosovo in the 1990s, warned of another Vietnam. Indeed, the Clinton administration refused to employ US ground combat forces in the Balkans for fear of being drawn into a protracted bloody war. And during the run-up to the 1991 Gulf War,

G.H.W. Bush also felt it necessary to reassure the American people *Operation Desert Storm* did not entail any significant risk of an Arab Vietnam because the United States had no intention of involving itself in postwar Iraq's internal affairs. The United States simply wished to liberate Kuwait, not march on to Baghdad to install a new regime in Iraq. At the conclusion of *Desert Storm,* then Secretary of Defense Dick Cheney prophetically defended the decision to limit the war:

> If you're to go in and try to topple Saddam Hussein, you have to go to Baghdad. Once you've got Baghdad, it's not clear what you do with it. It's not clear what kind of government you would put in place of the one that's currently there now. Is it going to be a Shia regime, a Sunni regime or a Kurdish regime? Or one that tilts toward the Ba'athists, or one that tilts toward the Islamic fundamentalists? How much credibility is that government going to have if it's set up by the United States military when it's there? How long does the United States military have to stay to protect the people that sign on for that government, and what happens to it once we leave?[14]

Twelve years later, the G.W. Bush administration and its supporters rejected any suggestion that a second war with Iraq, this one involving a march to Baghdad to change the regime, risked another Vietnam. Even a year into the unexpected insurgency the United States encountered in Iraq, the president emphatically denied any comparison. In his 13 April 2004 press conference, a reporter, noting that 'some people are comparing Iraq to Vietnam and talking about a quagmire', asked Bush 'how do you answer the Vietnam comparison?' The president replied: 'I think the analogy is false'.[15]

SPOTLIGHT ON IRAQ

In the run-up to *Operation Iraqi Freedom,* war proponents focused not on the risks of another Vietnam, but rather on the necessity for war, citing the lessons of Munich. Argued neo-conservative Richard Perle, the influential chairman of the Defense Policy Board, in an August 2002 interview:

> [An] action to remove Saddam could precipitate the very thing we are most anxious to prevent: his use of chemical and biological weapons. But the danger that springs from his capabilities will only grow as he expands his arsenal. A preemptive strike against Hitler at the time of Munich would have meant an immediate war, as opposed to the one that came later. Later was much worse.[16]

In that same month, Secretary of Defense Donald Rumsfeld, in a television interview, opined, 'think of all the countries that said, "well, we don't have enough evidence". *Mein Kampf* had been written. Hitler had indicated what he intended to do. Maybe he won't attack us. . . . Well, there are millions of dead because of [those] miscalculations.' Later, he added, 'maybe Winston Churchill was right. Maybe that lone voice expressing concern about what was happening was right.'[17] Bush, in his 'ultimatum' speech of 17 March 2003, pointedly noted that in 'the twentieth century, some chose to appease murderous dictators, whose threats were allowed to grow into genocide and global war'.

In facing Saddam Hussein, the Bush administration and the neo-conservatives who provided the intellectual foundation of the administration's post-11 September 2001 foreign policy claimed the United States was facing a Hitlerian threat requiring a Churchillian response.[18]

Was it? Did the Munich analogy usefully inform the public debate on the nature of the Iraqi threat, or was it, as Second World War historian Gerhard Weinberg contends, 'deployed in a shallow way to intimidate political foes as much as to threaten enemies who mean us actual harm'?[19] And what of the aftermath of Saddam Hussein's fall? Does the course of events in post-Ba'athist Iraq bear meaningful resemblance to the US experience in Vietnam, or has the use of that analogy, too, been a cynical ploy by political adversaries of the Bush administration?

There are some obvious similarities between Saddam Hussein and Adolf Hitler. Both were brutal dictators with agendas of conquest. Both operated in regions of indisputable strategic importance, and both committed aggression against their neighbours. Both also fatally miscalculated the will and capacity of key enemies.

That said, the differences overwhelm the similarities. Hitler presided over the most powerful military–industrial state in Europe, and it took the combined might of the United States, the Soviet Union and the British Empire to bring him down, and even then only after four years of bloody military operations not witnessed on a comparable scale before or since. In contrast, the coalition conquered Saddam Hussein's Iraq in three weeks at a cost of less than 200 dead.

Moreover, not until 1939 was any serious attempt made to deter Hitler from violating the provisions of the Versailles Treaty, including his rearming Germany, remilitarising the Rhineland, annexing Austria and gobbling up the German-speaking areas of Czechoslovakia. By the time Hitler decided to invade Poland, he had good reason to believe the British and the French would roll over yet again, as they had at Munich.

Saddam Hussein, in contrast, was effectively deterred from territorial aggression from the end of the Gulf War in 1991 onward by the fact of the Gulf War itself and by subsequently threatened and actual US military action. Unlike Hitler, Saddam Hussein lived in a region militarily dominated by a hostile superpower—precisely the reverse of Hitler's domination of Europe by the summer of 1940.

The Munich Agreement gave away sovereign territory of a democracy to an incorrigible aggressor. Iraq after the Gulf War was given nothing but harsh punishment in the form of military and economic sanctions, bombing attacks and strict limitations on its sovereignty. Its conventional military power and economy collapsed. For proponents of a second war with Iraq to argue that not taking decisive military action against Saddam Hussein was tantamount to appeasement was thus to completely distort the meaning of the Munich analogy. Hitler was neither weak nor deterred; Saddam was nothing but weak and deterred. He wasn't going anywhere, across either an international border or the nuclear threshold.

We now know, of course, that Iraq had no chemical and biological weapons, and even before the second war with Iraq there was considerable evidence that Saddam had no credible nuclear-weapons programme.[20] But the political scandal that erupted over the failure to find nuclear, chemical or biological weapons[21] misses the point: even had Saddam acquired nuclear weapons, there is no convincing reason to believe that he could not have been deterred from using them. Unlike suicide bombers, Saddam Hussein always loved himself more than he hated the United States, and he presided over a state rather than a shadowy terrorist organisation, which meant that he had assets that could be held hostage. Is it sheer coincidence that he was always careful not to employ what chemical weapons he did possess against enemies capable of nuclear retaliation (e.g., the United States and Israel in the Gulf War)?

Moreover, the notion that he was itching to hand over nuclear, chemical or biological weapons to al-Qaeda was always farfetched. As paranoid as Stalin, Saddam Hussein profoundly mistrusted Osama bin Laden (the feeling was mutual), and he was not about to transfer the very weapons that made him a feared international actor to an organisation he could not control. Nor could he have had much confidence that he could a transfer such weapons without detection or avoid US retaliation in the event of their use. In fact, according to the 9/11 Commission, there is 'no evidence that . . . earlier contacts' between Saddam and al-Qaeda 'ever developed into a collaborative operational relationship',[22] a judgement echoed by Rumsfeld, who in early October 2004 declared that 'there is no strong, hard evidence' linking Saddam Hussein and al-Qaeda.[23]

By autumn 2002, Saddam Hussein, far from being a rising menace to the United States, was so desperate to avoid war with the United States that he permitted the return to Iraq of unfettered UN inspections that, had they been permitted to take their course, would inevitably have exposed his 'grave and gathering' WMD 'threat' for the Potemkin village it actually was.

Of course, the Munich analogy was not the only argument for going to war against Iraq. There was always a moral case for removing the unusually cruel Iraqi dictator. But it was the postulated security threat to the United States—an undeterrable Arab Hitler going nuclear—upon which the war was sold to Congress and the public.

In sum, the Munich analogy had no more bearing on Saddam Hussein's Iraq in 2002–03 than it did on Ho Chi Minh's North Vietnam in 1964–65. Indeed, given the rarity of genuine Hitlerian threats—agendas of regional, even global, conquest married to the military superi-

ority to act on them—the Munich analogy has been misused far more often than used accurately to depict a security threat.[24]

But what of the Vietnam analogy? Numerous commentators have identified surface commonalities: a protracted insurgent war, insistent official optimism and reluctance to concede errors of judgement, lack of support from key allies, faulty intelligence, rising casualties and falling presidential poll numbers.[25] Clearly, expectations of a quick and clean military win, followed by rapid transfer of political authority to a popularly acclaimed government of returned exiles that would permit a fast drawdown of US forces, did not materialise. However, even the most vocal critics of the Bush administration's Iraq policies cannot ignore profound differences separating Iraq and Vietnam, especially in the strategic and military realms.

For starters, the US strategic objective in Iraq is much more ambitious than the objective in Vietnam. In Vietnam the aim was regime preservation; the United States sought to preserve the status quo by saving the non-communist government of South Vietnam from a communist takeover by the North. In Iraq the United States has sought to overthrow the status quo by regime change culminating in the establishment of a democracy. This means, if Washington adheres to its objective of democracy in Iraq, that the course ahead in that country could be more challenging and difficult than the road it sought to travel in Vietnam, where it accepted authoritarian rule in the south.

Next, consider the differences in the duration and scale of the fighting. The United States conducted major combat operations in Vietnam for eight years (1965–73), including a massive air war against North Vietnam that had no equivalent in Iraq, with US forces peaking at 543,000 troops in 1969. The fighting in Iraq, beginning with large-scale conventional warfare in March

2003 and morphing quickly thereafter into counter-insurgent operations, is in its fourth year, with US forces peaking at 175,000 in the aftermath of the invasion and then settling down to about 140,000. In Vietnam, the war evolved in exactly the opposite direction, from an insurgency to conventional warfare. There is no comparison between the size of forces committed. In Vietnam, in addition to US forces, South Vietnam and third-country allies eventually fielded over 1,000,000 troops. In South Vietnam alone, enemy forces, comprising North Vietnamese Army regulars and Viet Cong, numbered between 250,000 and 300,000. In contrast, estimates of Iraqi insurgents have ranged from 5,000 to 40,000.[26]

Nor is there any comparison on the critical matter of US casualties. During the eight years of major US military operations in Vietnam, the United States suffered a total of 55,750 dead and 292,000 wounded, which translates into loss rates of 6,968 dead and 36,600 wounded per year, 134 and 703 per week, and 19 and 100 per day. In contrast, by late October 2006, US losses since the initiation of *Operation Iraqi Freedom* totaled 2,809 dead and 20,687 wounded, or an average of 777 dead and 5,737 wounded per year, 15 and 110 per week, and 2+ and 16 per day.[27] (Communist manpower losses in Vietnam totaled 1,100,000 military dead, or 5% of the communist population base.[28])

The United States also fought in Vietnam at considerable strategic disadvantage. North Vietnam enjoyed massive Soviet and Chinese military assistance, and the United States abjured a ground invasion of North Vietnam and limited its aerial operations against that country for fear of provoking direct Chinese intervention. In Vietnamese communist forces the United States also faced a numerically large, centrally directed, highly skilled and superbly motivated enemy that had spent 20 years perfecting a style of warfare that pitted communist strengths against US political and military weaknesses. In contrast, the relatively small Iraqi insurgency is a disparate mélange of resistance groups—Ba'athist remnants, foreign jihadists and ordinary Iraqis whose nationalism has been awakened by the humiliation and pain of foreign military occupation—with neither a tested operational doctrine nor a common political agenda.

The communists coerced the United States out of South Vietnam by decisively altering American calculations of the costs and benefits of remaining in the war. Such a coerced withdrawal appears to be the objective of the Iraqi insurgency, and although the insurgents enjoy neither external Great Power military assistance nor large geographical sanctuaries, they have a number of advantages they can pit against US weaknesses.[29]

The war in Iraq will be decided at the level of insurgency and counter-insurgency, because the Iraqi insurgency lacks the numbers and external assistance to transform the war into a conventional military struggle, as the communists did in Vietnam.[30] Yet the US success in crippling the insurgent component of the communist threat by 1970–71 may not be repeatable in Iraq. Insurgency in South Vietnam was rooted in peasant social grievances and poverty which meant that a successful counter-insurgency had to contain large political and economic carrots as well as military sticks. And those carrots were forthcoming in the form of US-financed massive land reform and the generation of rapid increases in rural living standards via such initiatives as infrastructure modernisation and spectacular increases in agricultural productivity. The United States invested billions of dollars in these projects, which were administered by hundreds of American civil-military advisory teams operating at the provincial and district levels throughout the country. By 1972, the insurgency in the south (as opposed to conventional military operations mounted by North Vietnamese regulars) was a mere fraction of its peak strength and vitality.

In Iraq, the principal insurgent grievance seems to be the continued American force presence, and nothing short of a highly unlikely US withdrawal will satisfy that grievance. Suppression of the Iraqi insurgency, short of a grand political bargain that reconciles the Sunni Arab community to Shia governance of Iraq, will therefore require brute force; yet sole reliance on harsh military action, such as aerial bombardment of suspected targets in urban areas, risks generating more insurgent recruits than it eliminates. And there is the question of whether sufficient US force is available to pacify the insurgent areas of Iraq. Ambassador L. Paul 'Jerry' Bremer, who administered the US-led occupation government (the Coalition Provisional Authority), declared in autumn 2004 that 'we never had enough troops on the ground in Iraq' to stop the early looting and seize control of the 'Sunni triangle'.[31] (US force sufficiency was not a major issue in the Vietnam War; President Johnson granted all of General Westmoreland's troop requests.[32])

On the military side of the ledger, then, the differences between the Vietnam War and the continuing war in Iraq greatly outnumber the similarities. It is rather on the political side where the success or failure of the United States in Iraq may have analogues to the US experience in Vietnam—specifically, the American failure to construct a politically and militarily viable state in South Vietnam, and the collapse over time of domestic political support for the war.

During the 20-year life of the Republic of Vietnam (1955–75), the United States invested enormous resources in creating a politically legitimate and militarily competitive state capable of thwarting the communist threat. It fostered and funded the creation of political institutions, administrative structures and military forces for

the purpose of establishing and protecting a non-communist political and economic order in the south that could offer a viable alternative to the communist order in the north. In the end, however, the Republic of Vietnam disintegrated. The obvious reason is the success of the communist invasion of 1975. But this raises the question of why the South Vietnamese army, numerically strong and well equipped, collapsed in less than two months, with officers abandoning their men.

It is easy to blame the United States: it unilaterally withdrew its military forces, leaving North Vietnamese forces in place in South Vietnam; and when North Vietnam attacked in 1975, Washington did little to assist Saigon. But the Republic of Vietnam was crippled from the start by three critical weaknesses that no amount of American intervention could offset: professional military inferiority, rampant corruption and lack of political legitimacy.[33] The Nixon administration's attempt to Vietnamise the war failed because no amount of additional divisions, training and equipment could compensate for a military leadership selected on the basis of political loyalty, permeated by corruption, penetrated by communist agents and callous to the cares and concerns of the troops it commanded. There was simply no contest between the integrity and professional military competence and combativeness of the communist military leadership and their South Vietnamese counterparts. Stuart Herrington, in his assessment of South Vietnam's final years, argues that venality was so pervasive that purging the corrupt would have 'decimated the officer corps. . . . To have attempted to cut out the cancer would have killed the patient.'[34]

The Republic of Vietnam was unsustainable because it failed to achieve the measure of political legitimacy necessary to compete with the communists. The leading American historian of Vietnamese communism argues persuasively that the most important factor underlying the defeat of the South was the Communist Party's 'successful effort to persuade millions of Vietnamese in both North and South that it was the sole legitimate representative of Vietnamese nationalism and national independence', a success personified in the charismatic Ho Chi Minh, whose personality, 'embodying the qualities of virtue, integrity, dedication, and revolutionary asceticism, transcended issues of party and ideology and came to represent . . . the struggle for independence and self-realization of the Vietnamese nation'.[35]

In Vietnam, anti-communism was always burdened by its initial association with detested French rule (many military leaders in the south, including Nguyen Cao Ky and Nguyen van Thieu, had fought on the French side during the first Indochinese War) and by its antipathy to the powerful nationalist sentiment mobilised by Ho Chi Minh against both the French and their American successors. And as the Americans began flooding the country with troops and dollars, taking over the war from the South Vietnamese, it became increasingly difficult for the Saigon government to advertise itself as anything other than a Vietnamese political front for American power and purpose. 'By its own efforts, Hanoi cannot force the withdrawal of American forces from South Vietnam', noted Henry Kissinger in 1969. 'Unfortunately, our military strength has no political corollary; we have been unable to . . . create a political structure that could survive military opposition from Hanoi after we withdraw.'[36]

This is precisely the dilemma the United States may be facing in Iraq. There, as in Vietnam, political success will require creation of a government regarded as legitimate by the great majority of the people as well as security forces capable of protecting the new political order.[37] In Iraq, the United States started virtually from scratch because no real government or security forces existed. Moreover, any government the United States fosters in Iraq will be tainted in the eyes of many Iraqis by virtue of its American association, especially if the security situation continues to require a large and highly visible US military presence. Chances of success are further complicated by an obstacle the United States did not face in Vietnam: a society deeply divided along ethnic, religious and tribal lines.[38]. . .

The United States faces a difficult dilemma in Iraq: though its continued military presence in that country threatens to delegitimise a new Iraqi government, a premature and abrupt withdrawal would create a security vacuum encouraging civil war. Moreover, the new Iraqi army the United States is rushing to create may not offer an effective substitute for US forces. The failure of Vietnamisation 30 years ago underscores the reality that even a large and well-armed surrogate army counts for little if it is poorly led and motivated.

These judgements do not mean that the United States is condemned to repeat in Iraq its failed state-building effort in South Vietnam; the enemy in Vietnam was much more powerful than the enemy in Iraq, and the strategic value of South Vietnam pales in comparison to that of Iraq. But the legitimacy challenge in Iraq today is essentially the same legitimacy challenge confronted in South Vietnam.

So, too, is the influence of domestic public opinion on US policy stamina. The United States, after years of fighting, abandoned its central war aim in Vietnam and subsequently Vietnam itself because the war effort became unsustainable at home. Though the United States was militarily unbeatable in Vietnam, it lacked the political stakes in the war that the communists had. In the end, the Vietnam War boiled down to a contest of political wills, and the communists had the stronger. As Rusk acknowledged after the war, 'I made two mistakes with respect to Vietnam. First, I overestimated the patience of the American people, and second, I underestimated the tenacity of the North Vietnamese.'[39]

Years of escalating combat, mounting American casualties and no convincing progress toward the satisfaction of the US objective in Vietnam slowly undermined public and congressional support for the war. Even before the watershed Tet Offensive, public opinion was turning against the war. A Gallup poll taken in July 1967 revealed that 52% of Americans disapproved of the administration's handling of the war (only 34% approved). A month later, another Gallup poll found, for the first time since the war began, that a majority of Americans (53%) believed that it had been a mistake to send US troops to Vietnam.[40] By March 1969, a year after the Tet Offensive and four years after deployment of US ground combat forces to Vietnam, US battle deaths equalled those of the highly unpopular Korean War, and nearly two out of three Americans polled said they would have opposed US entry into the war had they known what it would cost in American lives.[41] It is little wonder that Nixon, seeking to reduce US casualty rates, began unilaterally withdrawing US troops from Vietnam even though he clearly understood that a shrinking US presence reduced his bargaining leverage with the communists.

What is the relationship among casualties, prospects for victory in Iraq and public support for the US war effort there? The administration anticipated a quick and clean military victory in Iraq and led the American people to believe it would happen. The Ba'athist regime's unexpectedly abrupt and total administrative collapse created a security vacuum throughout Iraq that US forces were unable to fill. An unexpected insurgency emerged that continues to inflict casualties on US forces and damage on reconstruction targets and to impede greatly efforts to create a politically stable democratic order in Iraq. Failure to discover any nuclear, biological or chemical weapons in Iraq or uncover any convincing evidence of a collaborative operational relationship between Saddam Hussein and al-Qaeda has undermined the two primary arguments for the war. Public attitudes toward the decision to invade Iraq and the administration's handling of the situation since then have shown downward trends. The 2006 congressional elections were widely regarded as a referendum on the Iraq War, and as the elections approached, multiple polls revealed that a growing majority of Americans believed the war to have been a mistake and that the administration was mishandling the war.

Will the United States fail in Iraq as it did in Vietnam? It is important to recognise perhaps the most important difference between the Vietnam War and the current conflict in Iraq: the former is a finished event, whereas the latter is an event in progress. We know what happened to Vietnam and US policies there in the 1960s and 1970s; in contrast, the ultimate fate of Iraq and US policy objectives in that country remains to be seen. But the lesson of Vietnam better informs America's dilemmas and challenges in post-Ba'athist Iraq than the lesson of Munich did for the decision to invade in the first place.

NOTES

1. George W. Bush, State of the Union Address, 29 January 2002, excerpted in *We Will Prevail: President George W. Bush on War, Terrorism, and Freedom* (New York: Continuum, 2003), p. 108.
2. There is a large and growing literature on reasoning by historical analogy. In addition to my own *Making War, Thinking History: Munich, Vietnam, and Presidential Uses of Force from Korea to Kosovo* (Annapolis, MD: Naval Institute Press, 2002), see, for examples, Ernest R. May, *'Lessons' of the Past:*

The Use and Misuse of History in American Foreign Policy (New York: Oxford University Press, 1973); Robert Jervis, *Perception and Misperception in International Politics* (Princeton, NJ: Princeton University Press, 1976), pp. 217–82; Yuen Foong Khong, *Analogies at War: Korea, Dien Bien Phu and the Vietnam Decisions of 1965* (Princeton, NJ: Princeton University Press, 1992); Richard E. Neustadt and Ernest R. May, *Thinking In Time: The Use of History for Decision Makers* (New York: The Free Press, 1986); and Christopher Hemmer, *Which Lessons Matter? American Foreign Policy Decision Making, 1979–1987* (Albany, NY: State University of New York Press, 2000).

3. Harry S. Truman, *Memoirs*, vol. 2, *Years of Trial and Hope, 1946–1952* (Garden City, NY: Doubleday, 1956), p. 335.

4. Eisenhower letter to Winston Churchill, 1954, excerpted in Robert J. MacMahon (ed.), *Major Problems in the History of the Vietnam War*, 2nd ed. (Lexington, MA: D.C. Heath, 1995), p. 373.

5. Quoted in Theodore C. Sorenson, *Kennedy* (New York: Harper and Row, 1965), p. 703.

6. Quoted in Michael Beschloss (ed.), *Taking Charge: The Johnson White House Tapes, 1963–1964* (New York: Simon and Schuster, 1997), p. 248.

7. Doris Kearns, *Lyndon Johnson and the American Dream* (New York: Harper and Row, 1976), p. 252.

8. Richard Nixon, *The Memoirs of Richard Nixon* (New York: Grosset and Dunlap, 1978), pp. 269–70.

9. Radio address to the nation on defence spending, 19 February 1983, in Ronald Reagan, *Public Papers of the Presidents of the United States: Ronald Reagan, 1983*, vol. 1, p. 258.

10. Address to nation announcing the deployment of United States armed forces to Saudi Arabia, 8 August 1990, in George Bush, *Public Papers of the Presidents of the United States: George Bush, 1990*, vol. 2, p. 1,108.

11. Christopher Hemmer, 'Unipolarity, the Lessons of September 11th, Iraq, and the American Pendulum', unpublished draft, 30 June 2004, p. 13.

12. Unlike the perceived lesson of Munich, which reflects a unanimous interpretation given to the events in 1938, the lesson of Vietnam can be either avoidance of intervention or intervention with overwhelming force and a determination to win. See discussion of the Weinberger Doctrine below.

13. Ronald Reagan, *An American Life* (New York: Simon and Schuster, 1990), p. 456.

14. 'Interview with Now-Vice President Richard Cheney', *New York Times*, 13 April 1991, reprinted in *The Nation*, 11 November 2002, p. 24.

15. 'President Addresses the Nation in Prime Time Press Conference', 13 April 2004, http://www.whitehouse.gov/news/releases/2004/04/print/2004041320.html.

16. Reprinted in 'Rhetoric Starts Here', *Washington Post*, 11 November 2002.

17. Quoted in Gwynne Dyer, 'Laying on that Old Munich Smear', *Toronto Star*, 2 September 2002.

18. In his address to the 2004 Republican National Convention, former New York mayor Rudy Giuliani compared Bush to Churchill: 'Winston Churchill saw the dangers of Hitler when his opponents and much of the press characterized him as a warmongering gadfly. George W. Bush sees world terrorism for the evil it is and he will remain consistent to the purpose of defeating it while working to make us ever safer at home.' Alec Russell, ' "Mayor of America" Compares Bush to Churchill', http://www.telegraph.co.uk/news/main.jhtml?xml=/news/2004/08/31/wus31.xml.

19. Gerhard L. Weinberg, 'No Road from Munich to Iraq', *Washington Post*, 3 November 2002.

20. Joseph Cirincione et al., *WMD in Iraq: Evidence and Implications* (Washington DC: Carnegie Endowment for International Peace, 2004); and David Barstow et al., 'How the White House Embraced Disputed Arms Intelligence', *New York Times*, 3 October 2004.

21. See 'Iraq Weapons Report Becomes Political Fodder'.

22. *Final Report of the National Commission on Terrorist Attacks Upon the United States* (New York: W.W. Norton and Company, 2004), p. 66.

23. Thom Shanker, 'Rumsfeld Sees Lack of Proof for Qaeda–Hussein Link', *New York Times*, 5 October 2004.

24. See Cirincione et al., *WMD in Iraq*; Michael E. O'Hanlon, 'Iraq's Threat to U.S. Exaggerated', *Baltimore Sun*, 26 September 2002; John Prados, *Hoodwinked: The Documents That Reveal How Bush Sold Us a War* (New York: New Press, 2004); and Hans Blix, *Disarming Iraq* (New York: Pantheon, 2004).

25. See, for examples, William S. Turley, 'Apples and Oranges are Both Fruit, But . . .', *YaleGlobal*, 24 October 2003, http://yaleglobal.edu/display.article?id=2677; Joseph L. Galloway, 'Iraq No Vietnam, But There Are Parallels', 19 November 2003, http://www.military.com/NewContent/0,13190,

Galloway_111903,00.html; Robert G. Kaiser, 'Iraq Isn't Vietnam, But They Rhyme', *Washington Post,* 28 December 2003; Ted Galen Carpenter, 'Iraq 2004, Vietnam 1964', 27 April 2004, http://www.cato.org/cgi-bin/scripts/printtech.cgi/dailys/04-27-04.html; and William Greider, 'Iraq as Vietnam', *The Nation,* 3 May 2004, p. 5.

26. Andrew J. Bacevich, 'Hour of the Generals', *The American Conservative,* 30 August 2004; Adriana Lins De Albuquerque, Michael O'Hanlon and Amy Unikewicz, 'The State of Iraq: An Update', *New York Times,* 21 February 2005; and Tom Lasseter and Jonathan S. Landay, 'U.S. in Danger of Losing the War', *Detroit Free Press,* 22 January 2005.

27. Figures for both wars include battle and non-battle deaths. Figures for Vietnam are calculated from data appearing in Harry G. Summers, Jr, *Vietnam War Almanac* (New York: Facts on File Publications, 1985), p. 113, and David L. Anderson, *The Columbia Guide to the Vietnam War* (New York: Columbia University Press, 2002), p. 290. Figures on Iraq are calculated from data appearing daily on the website Iraq Coalition Casualties, http://icasualties.org/oif/.

28. Spencer C. Tucker (ed.), *Encyclopedia of the Vietnam War: A Political, Social, and Military History* (New York: Oxford University Press, 1998), p. 64; and Jeffrey Record and W. Andrew Terrill, *Iraq and Vietnam: Differences, Similarities, and Insights* (Carlisle, PA: Strategic Studies Institute, US Army War College, 2004), p. 13.

29. For an informed yet succinct assessment of the strengths and weaknesses of the insurgency and the coalition, see Thomas X. Hammes, *The Sling and the Stone: On War in the 21st Century* (St Paul, MN: Zenith Press, 2004), pp. 183–8.

30. The 'conventionalisation' of the communist military threat in Vietnam followed an insurgent phase of the war, culminating in the Tet Offensive, that forced a shift in the US war aim from defeating the communist threat in South Vietnam to finding an 'honourable' way out of Vietnam.

31. Robin Wright and Thomas E. Ricks, 'Bremer Criticizes Troop Levels', *Washington Post,* 5 October 2004.

32. It was not Westmoreland, but rather Joint Chiefs of Staff Chairman General Earl Wheeler through Westmoreland, who, in the wake of the Tet Offensive, generated a request for 206.000 additional troops. Westmoreland regarded the Tet Offensive as a major defeat for the communists and did not believe additional US force deployments to Vietnam were necessary. Wheeler sought to use Tet to compel Johnson to mobilise the army's reserve components and talked Westmoreland into asking for more troops. Johnson refused. See Jeffrey Record, *The Wrong War: Why We Lost in Vietnam* (Annapolis, MD: Naval Institute Press, 1998), pp. 166–7.

33. *Ibid.,* pp. 122–40.

34. Stuart A. Herrington, *Peace With Honor? An American Reports on Vietnam, 1973–1975* (Novato, CA: Presidio Press, 1983), p. 40.

35. William J. Duiker, *The Communist Road to Power in Vietnam,* 2nd ed. (Boulder, CO: Westview Press), pp. 350, 359.

36. Henry A. Kissinger, 'The Vietnam Negotiations', *Foreign Affairs,* vol. 47, 1969, p. 230.

37. See Faleh A. Jabar, *Postconflict Iraq: A Race for Stability, Reconstruction, and Legitimacy* (Washington DC: United States Institute of Peace, May 2004), and Toby Dodge, 'A Sovereign Iraq?', *Survival,* vol. 46, no. 3, Autumn 2004, pp. 39–58.

38. See W. Andrew Terrill, *Nationalism, Sectarianism, and the Future of the U.S. Presence in Post-Saddam Iraq* (Carlisle, PA: Strategic Studies Institute, U.S. Army War College, 2003).

39. Dean Rusk, with Richard Rusk and Daniel S. Papp, *As I Saw It* (New York: W.W. Norton, 1990), p. 497.

40. Joseph Carroll, 'The Iraq–Vietnam Comparison', The Gallup Poll Tuesday Briefing, 15 June 2002, http://www.galluppoll.com/content/?CI=11998.

41. Eric V. Larson, *Casualties and Consensus: The Role of Casualties in Domestic Support for U.S. Military Operations* (Santa Monica, CA: Rand Corporation, 1996), pp. 27–9.

CHAPTER 3

LEVELS OF ANALYSIS
The Making of Foreign Policy

The realist view of foreign policy decision making is based on three assumptions: (1) states are unitary actors driven by a clear, consistent, and objectively derived conception of the national interest; (2) states are rational actors whose policies clearly and consistently link ends and means; and (3) states are primarily influenced in the shaping of foreign policy by the structure of the international system (the international level of analysis). All three of those assumptions, however, have been challenged by critics who have argued that: (1) states are composed of multiple actors and decision makers with divergent interests, (2) decision making often falls short of realist expectations of rationality, and (3) domestic factors (the domestic level of analysis) and the individual qualities of leaders (the individual level of analysis) also play an important role in shaping the foreign behavior of states.

The readings in this chapter begin with Scott Sagan's analysis of the reasons why states either do or do not seek to acquire nuclear weapons. This piece is included less for its substantive topic (though in reading it you will learn much about nuclear proliferation), than for its explicit attempt to explain the issue of nuclear proliferation via different models operating at different levels of analysis. The other selections focus on the analysis of domestic sources of foreign policy. In its own way, each reading addresses one or more of the theoretical assumptions outlined above. Included are articles on the impact on foreign policy of public opinion, organized lobbies, and bureaucratic interests. All of the selections after the Sagan piece look at these larger theoretical issues in the context of U.S. policy making vis-à-vis the Iraq War and the Middle East, thus providing a common empirical grounding within which to examine the larger theoretical issues.

In reading the selections in this chapter, you should keep in mind the question of how the evidence and analysis in each is related to the larger theoretical assumptions noted above. Based on that evidence, do realist assumptions along these lines do more, in your view, to clarify or mislead us in our understanding of the sources and processes of foreign policy making?

THE CAUSES OF NUCLEAR PROLIFERATION

Scott D. Sagan

In this article, Sagan considers both why some states seek to acquire nuclear weapons and why others do not. In so doing, he compares three competing models: the "security model," the "domestic politics model," and the "norms model." As you read this article, ask yourself:

- Which levels of analysis are represented in his three models?
- Without mentioning "constructivism" by name, which model is most "constructivist" in its approach?
- What level of analysis is not represented in Sagan's article and how might it be integrated in the discussion of nuclear proliferation?

Why do states build nuclear weapons? Many policymakers and scholars believe that there is a simple answer: states seek to develop nuclear weapons if they face security threats that cannot be met by alternative means; if they do not face such threats, they will willingly remain nonnuclear states. This belief—the "security model" of proliferation—is dangerously misleading, for nuclear weapons programs also serve objectives other than national security; they are key issues in domestic politics and bureaucratic struggles and important symbols of modernity and national identity. When United States policy focuses exclusively on the security model, it ignores nonproliferation tools and strategies that can address these other sources of the demand for nuclear weapons. . . .

PROLIFERATION AS A STRATEGIC CHAIN REACTION

According to neorealist theory, a state can balance against a nuclear rival in one of two ways.[1] First, a state can form an alliance with another nuclear power by relying on extended deterrence commitments. This is usually the cheapest option available, but the policy raises questions about credibility, since the nuclear power would fear retaliation if it responded to an attack on its ally. The second option is for a state to pursue a form of internal balancing by developing its own nuclear weapons as an ultimate guarantee of state survival.

According to this realist security model, the basic history of proliferation can be easily outlined as a strategic chain reaction. During World War II, none of the major belligerents was certain that the development of nuclear weapons was possible, but all knew that other states could soon be working on a bomb. The United States developed atomic weapons first, not because it had any greater demand for the bomb, but because it had invested more heavily in the program and made the right technological and organizational choices. After August 1945, the Soviet Union's program was reinvigorated because Hiroshima and Nagasaki served as demonstrations that nuclear weapons were technically possible and the emerging cold war meant that a Soviet bomb was a strategic imperative.

Once the Soviet Union developed nuclear weapons, Britain and France sought their own capability to counter the threat because of the

Scott D. Sagan, excerpt from "The Causes of Nuclear Proliferation." Reprinted with permission from *Current History* Magazine 96:609, April 1997. © 2007 Current History, Inc.

resulting reduction in the credibility of the United States nuclear guarantee to NATO. China developed the bomb because the United States threatened to use nuclear weapons at the end of the Korean War and during the Taiwan Strait crises in the 1950s, and because of the emergence of Sino-Soviet tensions in the 1960s. After China developed the bomb in 1964, India, which had fought a war with China in 1962, responded with its "peaceful nuclear explosion" of May 1974. After the Indian detonation, it was inevitable that leaders in Islamabad would decide that Pakistan, too, needed a nuclear deterrent.

Looking toward the future, the security model leads one to fear that new states will respond to emerging or potential regional threats by developing their own nuclear deterrent. Two central policy prescriptions are thereby produced. First, since alliance guarantees with a nuclear power are the main alternative method for gaining some degree of nuclear security, a key nonproliferation tool is maintaining United States extended deterrence commitments to allies in Europe and Asia, including some form of continued United States nuclear first-use policy. In Asia, this highlights the need for a strong United States military commitment to Japan and South Korea; in Europe, it suggests that it is important to continue stationing nuclear weapons in Germany and to maintain NATO's traditional "flexible response" military doctrine, under which nuclear weapons may be used if conventional defense fails.

Second, the Nuclear Non-Proliferation Treaty (NPT) is needed to permit nonnuclear states to overcome a collective action problem: latent nuclear states might refrain from proliferation if the treaty provides increased confidence that their neighbors will follow suit. It follows, therefore, that other elements of the NPT regime are far less important; specifically, the commitments that the United States has made under Article VI of the treaty—that the nuclear powers

will pursue "negotiations in good faith on measures relating to cessation of the nuclear arms race at an early date and to nuclear disarmament"—are seen as mere sops to public opinion in nonnuclear countries. The degree to which the nuclear states follow through on Article VI commitments will not significantly influence the actual behavior of nonnuclear states, since it will not change their basic security calculation.

DOMESTIC SOURCES OF PROLIFERATION

A second approach to understanding proliferation focuses on the domestic actors who encourage or discourage governments from pursuing the bomb. Whether or not the acquisition of nuclear weapons serves the national security interests of a state, it can serve the parochial interests of such actors as the nuclear energy establishment (officials in state-run laboratories as well as private reactor facilities); important units within the professional military (often within the air force, though sometimes in navy bureaucracies interested in nuclear propulsion); and politicians in states in which individual parties or the mass public strongly favor nuclear weapons acquisition. When such actors form coalitions that are strong enough to control the government's decision-making process—either through their direct political power or indirectly through their control of information—nuclear weapons programs are likely to thrive.

From this perspective, nuclear weapons programs are solutions looking for a problem to justify their existence. Potential threats to a state's security may certainly exist, but these threats are seen as malleable and subject to interpretation, and can produce different responses. External security threats are therefore not the central cause of weapons decisions: they are merely windows of opportunity for parochial interests.

The historical case of proliferation that most strongly fits the domestic politics model is the Indian government's 1974 decision to test a peaceful nuclear explosive and subsequently to develop a significant larger nuclear weapons capability. Contrary to the neorealist account outlined earlier, there was no consensus among officials in New Delhi that it was necessary to have a nuclear deterrent after the 1964 Chinese nuclear test. If that had been the case, one of two events would have occurred. First, given the relatively advanced state of Indian nuclear energy research at the time, an Indian nuclear weapon would have been tested in the mid- to late 1960s. Second, leaders in New Delhi would have made a concerted effort to acquire nuclear guarantees from the United States or other nuclear powers; instead, Indian officials only reluctantly entered into discussions of security assurances, refused to consider foreign bases in India to support a nuclear commitment, and publicly questioned whether any guarantee could be credible.

Instead of a united Indian effort to acquire a deterrent, the Chinese test produced a prolonged bureaucratic battle inside the political elite and nuclear energy establishment. After the Chinese test, for example, Prime Minister Lal Bhadur Shastri argued against developing an Indian arsenal, in part because the estimated costs (between $42 million and $84 million) were deemed excessive; Homi Bhabba, the head of the Atomic Energy Commission, however, lobbied for the development of nuclear weapons capability, claiming that India could manufacture 50 atomic bombs for less than $21 million. A compromise policy was the result of this deep disagreement: pro-bomb nuclear scientists could conduct research and make technical preparations for future contingencies, but they could not develop complete nuclear weapons to be tested.

Although firm evidence on why Prime Minister Indira Gandhi reversed this policy and gave approval for the nuclear test in 1974 is not available, a number of points suggest that addressing changing domestic political concerns—rather than countering international security threats—was her primary motivation. Senior defense and foreign affairs officials were not extensively involved in the decision to prepare the nuclear device, nor in the final decision to test it. At a minimum, this suggests that security arguments were not thoroughly analyzed before the test. Moreover, the subsequent absence of a systematic program for nuclear weapons or peaceful nuclear explosions development and testing suggests that the decision was made quickly and focused more on immediate political concerns (such as shoring up the government's sagging domestic support) than on longer-term security or energy interests. Indeed, public support for the Gandhi government had fallen to an all-time low during the months preceding the nuclear weapons test because of a severe domestic recession and the disruption caused by India's first nationwide railway strike. Gandhi used the test to defuse an issue about which she had been criticized by her more hawkish domestic opponents.

The ambiguity of Indian nuclear weapons policy since the 1974 test appears less like the product of a strategy of nuclear ambiguity and more like a post-hoc doctrine used to justify capabilities developed for other reasons. From this perspective, the subsequent building of greater nuclear weapons capabilities is not a proud symbol of the success of an Indian national security program. Instead, it is a symbol of the failure of the Indian civilian nuclear power industry, which has been forced to form an alliance with the pro-bomb lobby to justify its existence and funding after its failure to avoid cost overruns and prevent safety problems in domestic energy programs.

A focus on domestic politics also provides a different prediction about the future. If India starts to test new nuclear weapons and deploys them in the field, it will not be the result of new Chinese or Pakistani military threats to Indian security—it will be the result of the domestic weakness of a coalition government in New Delhi that could flout the international nonproliferation regime and test weapons to increase its standing in public opinion polls and to defend itself against common criticisms emanating from the opposition Hindu nationalist parties.

A NEW SET OF NONPROLIFERATION TOOLS

A domestic politics approach suggests that the United States needs to develop a broader set of nonproliferation tools. For example, United States and international financial institutions are increasingly demanding cuts in military expenditures as part of conditionality packages for aid recipients; future efforts to develop more conditionality linkages to nuclear programs—such as deducting the estimated budget of any suspect research and development program from loans to a country—could heighten domestic opposition to nuclear programs. Providing technical information and intellectual ammunition to domestic actors by encouraging more accurate estimates of the economic and environmental costs of nuclear weapons programs and highlighting the risks of nuclear accidents could bring new members into antiproliferation coalitions. In addition, efforts to encourage strict civilian control of the military through educational and organizational reforms could be productive, especially in states in which the military has the capability to create secret nuclear programs (as in Brazil in the 1980s) to serve their parochial interests.

To the degree that professional military organizations are instrumental, encouraging their involvement in other military activities (such as Pakistani participation in peacekeeping operations or the Argentine navy's role in the Persian Gulf) could decrease their support for nuclear weapons programs; to the degree that the key actors are laboratory officials and scientists, assistance in nonnuclear weapons research and development programs (as in the current Russian-American lab-to-lab programs) could decrease personal and organizational incentives for nuclear weapons research.

Finally, the nuclear powers' commitment under Article VI of the NPT to work for disarmament is important because of the impact that it can have on domestic discussions in nonnuclear states. In future debates in potential proliferants, the arguments of antinuclear actors—that nuclear weapons programs do not serve the interests of their states—can be more easily countered by pro-bomb actors whenever they can point to specific actions of the nuclear powers, such as refusing to negotiate "deep cuts" in arms control agreements or continuing to maintain nuclear first-use doctrines, that highlight their reliance on nuclear deterrence.

NUCLEAR WEAPONS AND THE THOROUGHLY MODERN STATE

A third explanation of nuclear proliferation focuses on international norms on weapons acquisition. According to this perspective, state behavior is determined not by leaders' cold calculations about national security or parochial domestic interests but, rather, by deeper norms and shared beliefs about what international actions are legitimate and modern. Military arsenals can be envisioned as serving symbolic functions similar to flags, airlines, and Olympic teams. They are part of an international norm concerning what it means to be a modern and legitimate state.

The symbolic meaning of an international action is often contested at first, and the resulting norms may be spread by power and coercion, not by the strength of ideas alone. Still, once created, such international norms can take on a life of their own. For example, existing norms in the NPT against nuclear weapons acquisition were in large part created by the most powerful states in the international system to serve their narrow political interests. Yet, once that effort was successful, these norms shaped states' identities and expectations; even powerful actors have become constrained by the norms they have created.

The history of nuclear proliferation is particularly interesting in this regard because there appears to be a major discontinuity emerging as a result of the NPT. The NPT appears to have shifted the norm concerning what acts grant prestige and represent modernity from the 1960s notion of joining "the nuclear club" to the 1990s concept of joining "the club of the nations adhering to the NPT." These arguments are best supported by contrasting two cases: France in the 1950s and Ukraine in the 1990s.

The French decision to build nuclear weapons is best explained if one focuses on French leaders' perceptions of the bomb's symbolic significance. France emerged from World War II a liberated victor whose military capabilities and international standing were not at all comparable to its prewar power and status. The governments of the Fourth and Fifth Republics vigorously explored how to return France to its historical great power status. The initial French effort focused on its overseas empire, yet that source of *grandeur* diminished greatly in the anti-colonial fervor of the 1950s.

After 1958, the Algerian crisis contributed to President Charles de Gaulle's obsession with nuclear weapons as the remaining symbol of French greatness. Indeed, de Gaulle was not terribly concerned about whether French nuclear forces could provide adequate deterrence against the Soviet military threat: during both the 1958 Berlin crisis and the 1962 Cuban crisis, for example, he expressed great confidence that the Soviet Union would not risk an attack on NATO Europe. Instead, the atomic bomb was a dramatic symbol of independence; it was needed for France to continue to be seen, by itself and others, as a great power.

When the French nuclear weapons arsenal is viewed in this way, a number of otherwise puzzling aspects of the history of French atomic policy become more understandable. For example, the repeated Gaullist declarations that French nuclear weapons should have worldwide capabilities and must be aimed in all directions (*"tous azimuts"*) are seen not as the product of security threats that came from everywhere, but rather the result of a policy logically consistent with global *grandeur* and independence. Similarly, the profound French reluctance to stop nuclear testing in the mid-1990s is seen as being produced, less by concerns for weapons modernization or warhead safety, and more because weapons tests were perceived by the Paris government as potent symbols of French identity and status.

Contrast the French proliferation decisions of the 1950s and the Ukrainian decision to give up its weapons in 1994. Ukraine's decision is puzzling for neorealists since the history of Russian expansionist behavior and continuing tensions over the Crimea should have led Kiev to hold onto its inherited nuclear arsenal. The disarmament decision is also puzzling from a domestic politics perspective since public opinion polls in Ukraine showed rapidly growing support for keeping nuclear weapons in 1992 and 1993. Prime Minister (later President) Leonid Kuchma and other senior political leaders came from the missile-building industry and would not have been expected to take an antinuclear position.

Ukraine's decision is more easily understood when one focuses on the role played by

NPT norms. Although Ukrainian officials continued to be interested in enhancing the state's international prestige, the NPT regime created a history in which the most recent examples of new or potential nuclear powers were so-called rogue states such as North Korea, Iran, and Iraq. This was hardly a nuclear club whose new members would receive international prestige. At the same time, the ability to present strong international pressures for disarmament were critically influenced by the existence of the NPT norm; without the norm, threats to eliminate economic aid and suspend political ties would be less credible, since individual states would be more likely to defect from an agreement. Last, the Kiev government and the Ukrainian public could more easily accept the economic inducements for weapons destruction, offered by the United States and others, under the belief that such funds were enabling Ukraine to keep an international commitment, rather than being seen as the crass purchase of Ukrainian weapons by foreign governments.

To the degree that these norms remain influential, it will be important for the United States and other nuclear powers to adjust their nuclear weapons doctrines and arms control policies. This will be difficult, because some of the policy changes that would support the emerging norms against nuclear weapons contradict policy recommendations derived from other models. For example, focusing on NPT norms raises concerns about how existing United States nuclear first-use doctrine influences potential proliferators' perceptions of the legitimacy of nuclear weapons possession and use. To the degree that first-use policies create beliefs that nuclear threats are what strong powers issue, they will become desired symbols for states that aspire to that status. Similarly, the norms perspective suggests that current United States declaratory statements threatening the use of nuclear weapons to deter biological or chemical weapons use would have a negative impact on the nonproliferation regime. How can the United States convince other states that they should not build nuclear weapons to deter neighbors with chemical or biological weapons if the greatest conventional power in the world still thinks that it needs nuclear weapons for that purpose?

Other policy initiatives are less problematic. In specific cases when norms concerning prestige are important for states, the United States could support a future initiative to make UN Security Council membership for Japan, Germany, and India conditional on their permanent nonnuclear status under the NPT. This perspective also suggests that it is important for the United States to reaffirm its NPT commitments to complete disarmament, since backsliding from Article VI could encourage nonnuclear states to envision nuclear weapons as granting legitimacy and prestige for a long time into the future.

POLICY CONUNDRUMS

The history of weapons decisions suggests that nuclear proliferation (and conversely, nuclear restraint) has occurred in the past, and can occur in the future, for more than one reason; different historical cases are best explained by different causal models. If this argument is correct, it poses difficult challenges for international nonproliferation policy; no single policy is likely to be sufficient to ameliorate all future proliferation problems, and actions that help address one proliferation danger might well exacerbate another. Most important, a security-oriented strategy of maintaining a major role for United States nuclear guarantees to restrain proliferation among its allies will eventually create strong tensions with a norms-oriented strategy seeking to delegitimize nuclear weapons use and acquisition. United States decision makers will eventually have to choose between the difficult nonproliferation task of weaning allies away from nuclear guarantees without producing new nuclear states, and the equally difficult task of maintaining a norm against nuclear proliferation without the United States facing its logical final consequence.

NOTE

1. See Scott D. Sagan and Kenneth N. Waltz, *The Spread of Nuclear Weapons: A Debate* (New York: W. W. Norton, 1995).

THE WAR OVER ISRAEL'S INFLUENCE

John J. Mearsheimer and Stephen M. Walt with responses by Dennis Ross and Zbigniew Brzezinski

This selection begins with a brief summary by Mearsheimer and Walt of their controversial thesis that U.S. policy in the Mid-East is dominated by the influence of the pro-Israel lobby. It is followed by two brief responses. As you read these selections, ask yourself:

- What is the basis of Mearsheimer and Walt's claim about the influence of the Israel lobby?
- How do the two responses differ in their reaction to the Mearsheimer and Walt thesis?
- Why have some critics argued that Mearsheimer and Walt's argument on this issue is inconsistent with their long-established status as international relations realists?

UNRESTRICTED ACCESS

**What the Israel lobby wants,
it too often gets.**

by John J. Mearsheimer and Stephen M. Walt
America's relationship with Israel is difficult to discuss openly in the United States. In March, we published an article in the *London Review of Books* titled "The Israel Lobby," based on a working paper which we posted on the faculty Web site at Harvard's John F. Kennedy School of Government. Our goal was to break the taboo and to generate a candid discussion of U.S. support for Israel, because it

has far-reaching consequences for Americans and others around the world. What followed was a barrage of responses—some constructive, some not.

Every year, the United States gives Israel a level of support that far exceeds what it provides to other states. Although Israel is now an industrial power with a per-capita GDP roughly equal to Spain's or South Korea's, it still receives about $3 billion in U.S. aid each year— that is, roughly $500 per Israeli citizen. Israel also gets a variety of other special deals and consistent diplomatic support. We believe that this generosity cannot be fully explained on either strategic or moral grounds. Israel may have been a strategic asset during the Cold War, but it is a strategic burden in the war on terror and the broader U.S. effort to deal with rogue states. The moral rationale for unconditional U.S. support is undermined by Israel's treatment of the Palestinians and its unwillingness to offer them a viable state. We believe there is a strong moral case for Israel's existence, but that existence is not at risk. Palestinian extremists and Iranian President Mahmoud Ahmadinejad may dream of wiping Israel "off the map," but fortunately neither has the ability to make that dream a reality.

The "special relationship" with Israel, we argue, is due largely to the activities of the Israel lobby—a loose coalition of individuals and organizations who openly work to push U.S. foreign policy in a pro-Israel direction. The lobby is not synonymous with Jewish Americans, because many of them do not support its positions, and some groups that work on Israel's behalf (Christian evangelicals, for example) are not Jewish. The lobby has no central leadership. It is not a cabal or a conspiracy. These organizations are simply engaged in interest-group politics, a legitimate activity in the American political system. These organizations believe their efforts advance both American and Israeli interests. We do not.

We described how the Israel lobby fosters support within the U.S. Congress and the executive branch, and how it shapes public discourse so that Israel's actions are perceived sympathetically by the American public. Groups in the lobby direct campaign contributions to encourage politicians to adopt pro-Israel positions. They write articles, letters, and op-eds defending Israel's actions, and they go to great lengths to discredit or marginalize anyone who criticizes U.S. support for Israel. The American-Israel Public Affairs

Committee (AIPAC) is the lobby's most powerful organization, and it openly touts its influence over U.S. Middle East policy. Prominent politicians from both parties acknowledge AIPAC's power and effectiveness. Former House Minority Leader Richard Gephardt once observed that if AIPAC were not "fighting on a daily basis to strengthen [the relationship], it would not be."

We also traced the lobby's impact on recent U.S. policies, including the March 2003 invasion of Iraq. Neoconservatives inside and outside the Bush administration, as well as leaders of a number of prominent pro-Israel organizations, played key roles in making the case for war. We believe the United States would not have attacked Iraq without their efforts. That said, these groups and individuals did not operate in a vacuum, and they did not lead the country to war by themselves. For instance, the war would probably not have occurred absent the Sept. 11, 2001, terrorist attacks, which helped convince President George W. Bush and Vice President Dick Cheney to support it.

With Saddam Hussein removed from power, the Israel lobby is now focusing on Iran, whose government seems determined to acquire nuclear weapons. Despite its own nuclear arsenal and conventional military might, Israel does not want a nuclear Iran. Yet neither diplomacy nor economic sanctions are likely to curb Tehran's nuclear ambitions. Few world leaders favor using force to deal with the problem, except in Israel and the United States. AIPAC and many of the same neoconservatives who advocated attacking Iraq are now among the chief proponents of using military force against Iran.

There is nothing improper about pro-Israel advocates trying to influence the Bush administration. But it is equally legitimate for others to point out that groups like AIPAC and many neoconservatives have a commitment to Israel that shapes their thinking about Iran and other Middle

East issues. More important, their perspective is not the last word on what is good for Israel or the United States. In fact, their prescriptions might actually be harmful to both countries.

THE MIND-SET MATTERS
Foreign policy is shaped by leaders and events, not lobbies.

by Dennis Ross

John Mearsheimer and Stephen Walt are troubled by the power and influence of the Israel lobby in Washington. The tone and argument of their essay in this magazine is more reasoned than their original working paper, but it suffers from the same flawed premise: U.S. foreign policy in the Middle East is distorted by this seemingly all-powerful lobby.

According to Mearsheimer and Walt, the Israel lobby is governed by its concern for Israel, not America. They say it drove the United States into a disastrous war in Iraq and is now pushing for a similarly dangerous war against Iran. Mearsheimer and Walt discuss other maladies caused by the lobby, but it's their concern about U.S. policies toward Iraq and Iran that have principally motivated them to "expose" the lobby.

No one questions the propriety of debating our policy choices in Iraq, Iran, or anywhere else. But such debates should be based on reality. To say that the Israel lobby is largely responsible for the U.S. invasion of Iraq presumes that elected leaders, their worldviews, and extraordinary events such as those on Sept. 11, 2001, don't matter. Mearsheimer and Walt should know better. Regardless of their position on the war in Iraq, do they seriously doubt that the mind-set of the man sitting in the Oval Office made a big difference? Al Gore was against going to war in 2002 and 2003. Yet, Al Gore was closer to leaders of the "Israel lobby" throughout his career than was President George W. Bush.

The reality is, neither the Israel lobby nor neoconservatives convinced Bush to go to war. September 11 did. Prior to 9/11, Bush's Iraq policy was one of "smart sanctions"—the containment of the Iraqi regime, not its overthrow. His worldview changed on 9/11. He came to believe that America could not wait to be hit again, and that the threat Saddam Hussein posed was all encompassing. This belief transformed his policies. Although Mearsheimer and Walt now acknowledge that "war would probably not have occurred absent the Sept. 11, 2001, terrorist attacks," they still persist in declaring that they "believe the United States would not have attacked Iraq without [the Israel lobby's] efforts." They may want to resolve this contradiction.

Mearsheimer and Walt's thinking on Iran is similarly confused. Do they really believe that only "the lobby" cares about Iran's acquiring nuclear weapons? They say that the United States need not be concerned about Iranian nukes because deterrence will work. This idea ignores the possibility that Iran's going nuclear will trigger others in the Middle East to do the same, and that the prospects of atomic miscalculation could make a nuclear war in the region a real possibility. A nuclear Iran could also fatally undercut the nonproliferation regime, which would make the world more dangerous. The British, French, and Germans—none of whom are anxious for war—understand these realities. That is why they introduced a U.N. Security Council resolution to prevent Iran from going nuclear. It isn't the Israel lobby that is pushing the British, French, and Germans to confront Iran any more than it is the Israel lobby that is driving U.S. policy.

Dennis Ross, "The Mind-Set Matters: Foreign Policy Is Shaped by Leaders and Events, Not Lobbies," *Foreign Policy* July/August 2006. Reprinted by permission of the author.

The truth is, the Israel lobby doesn't always get its way. It failed to prevent several major arms sales to Arab nations. It has failed to get the U.S. embassy in Israel moved from Tel Aviv to Jerusalem. It failed to prevent the Clinton administration from crafting a peace proposal that would have divided Jerusalem in two. In fact, never in the time that I led the American negotiations on the Middle East peace process did we take a step because "the lobby" wanted us to. Nor did we shy away from one because "the lobby" opposed it. That is not to say that AIPAC and others have no influence. They do. But they don't distort U.S. policy or undermine American interests. Republican and Democratic presidents alike have consistently believed in a special relationship with Israel because values matter in foreign policy. Policymakers know that, even if Mearsheimer and Walt do not.

A DANGEROUS EXEMPTION

Why should the Israel lobby be immune from criticism?

by Zbigniew Brzezinski

Given that the Middle East is currently the central challenge facing America, Professors John Mearsheimer and Stephen Walt have rendered a public service by initiating a much-needed public debate on the role of the "Israel lobby" in the shaping of U.S. foreign policy.

The participation of ethnic or foreign-supported lobbies in the American policy process is nothing new. In my public life, I have dealt with a number of them. I would rank the Israeli-American, Cuban-American, and Armenian-American lobbies as the most effective in their assertiveness. The Greek- and Taiwanese-American lobbies also rank highly in my book. The Polish-American lobby was at one time influential (Franklin Roosevelt complained about it to Joseph Stalin), and I daresay that before long we will be hearing a lot from the Mexican-, Hindu-, and Chinese-American lobbies as well.

Mearsheimer and Walt are critical of the pro-Israel lobby and of Israel's conduct in a number of historical instances. They are outspoken regarding Israel's prolonged mistreatment of the Palestinians. They are, in brief, generally critical of Israel's policy and, thus, could be labeled as being in some respects anti-Israel. But an anti-Israel bias is not the same as anti-Semitism. To argue as much is to claim an altogether unique immunity for Israel, untouchable by the kind of criticism that is normally directed at the conduct of states.

Anyone who recalls World War II knows that anti-Semitism is the unbridled and irrational hatred of Jews. The case made by Mearsheimer and Walt did not warrant the hysterical charges of anti-Semitism leveled at them by several academics in self-demeaning attacks published in leading U.S. newspapers. Sadly, some even stooped to McCarthyite accusations of guilt by association, triumphantly citing the endorsement of Mearsheimer and Walt's views by vile, fanatical racists as somehow constituting proof of the authors' anti-Semitism. In contrast, several of the Israeli reactions to the Mearsheimer and Walt article were quite measured and free of such mudslinging.

I do not feel qualified to judge the historical parts of their argument. But several of the current themes that emerge from their thinking strike me as quite pertinent. Mearsheimer and

Zbigniew Brzezinski, "A Dangerous Exemption: Why Should the Israel Lobby Be Immune from Criticism?" from *Foreign Policy* July/August 2006. Reprinted by permission of the author.

Walt adduce a great deal of factual evidence that over the years Israel has been the beneficiary of privileged—indeed, highly preferential—financial assistance, out of all proportion to what the United States extends to any other country. The massive aid to Israel is in effect a huge entitlement that enriches the relatively prosperous Israelis at the cost of the American taxpayer. Money being fungible, that aid also pays for the very settlements that America opposes and that impede the peace process.

The foregoing is related to the shift, over the past quarter of a century, of U.S. policy in the Middle East from relative impartiality (which produced the Camp David agreement), to increasing partiality in favor of Israel, to essentially the adoption of the Israeli perspective on the Israeli-Arab conflict. During the last decade, in fact, some U.S. officials recruited from AIPAC or from pro-Israel research institutions were influential in favoring the Israeli preference for vagueness regarding the final shape of any peace accord, thereby contributing to the protracted passivity of the United States regarding the Israeli-Palestinian conflict. In contrast, Arab Americans by and large have been excluded from serious participation in the U.S. policy process.

Finally, Mearsheimer and Walt also provide food for thought regarding the consequences of the growing role of lobbies in American foreign policy, given the increased inclination of the U.S. Congress to become engaged in legislating foreign policy. With members of congress involved in continuous electoral fundraising, the effect has been an increase in the influence of lobbies and, particularly, those that take part in targeted political fundraising. It is probably nor an accident that the most effective lobbies are also the ones that have been the most endowed. Whether that produces the best definition of the American national interest in the Middle East or elsewhere is open to question, and worthy of serious debate.

Of course, stifling such debate is in the interest of those who have done well in the absence of it. Hence the outraged reaction from some to Mearsheimer and Walt.

THE IRAQ SYNDROME

John Mueller

In this article, John Mueller examines the relationship between public opinion in the United States and the war in Iraq. As you read his article, ask yourself:

- What are the factors that he sees as shaping U.S. public opinion toward the war in Iraq?
- To what extent does public opinion have an impact on U.S. policy in Iraq?
- What is the "Iraq syndrome" and what is its potential for impact on U.S. foreign policy after Iraq?

John Mueller, "The Iraq Syndrome." Reprinted by permission of *Foreign Affairs* 84:6, November/December 2005. Copyright 2005 by the Council on Foreign Relations, Inc. www.ForeignAffairs.org.

THE WAR AND THE PUBLIC

American troops have been sent into harm's way many times since 1945, but in only three cases—Korea, Vietnam, and Iraq—have they been drawn into sustained ground combat and suffered more than 300 deaths in action. American public opinion became a key factor in all three wars, and in each one there has been a simple association: as casualties mount, support decreases. Broad enthusiasm at the outset invariably erodes.

The only thing remarkable about the current war in Iraq is how precipitously American public support has dropped off. Casualty for casualty, support has declined far more quickly than it did during either the Korean War or the Vietnam War. And if history is any indication, there is little the Bush administration can do to reverse this decline.

More important, the impact of deteriorating support will not end when the war does. In the wake of the wars in Korea and Vietnam, the American public developed a strong aversion to embarking on such ventures again. A similar sentiment—an "Iraq syndrome"—seems to be developing now, and it will have important consequences for U.S. foreign policy for years after the last American battalion leaves Iraqi soil.

DROWNING BY NUMBERS

The public gave substantial support to the military ventures in Korea, Vietnam, and Iraq as the troops were sent in. In all cases, support decreased as casualties—whether of draftees, volunteers, or reservists—mounted. In each case, the increase in the number of people who considered the venture to be a mistake was steep during the war's early stages, as reluctant supporters were rather quickly alienated; the erosion slowed as approval was reduced to the harder core. (The dramatic early drop in support for the war in Korea reflected the large number of casualties suffered in the opening phase of that war.)

The most striking thing about the comparison among the three wars is how much more quickly support has eroded in the case of Iraq. By early 2005, when combat deaths were around 1,500, the percentage of respondents who considered the Iraq war a mistake—over half—was about the same as the percentage who considered the war in Vietnam a mistake at the time of the 1968 Tet offensive, when nearly 20,000 soldiers had already died.

This lower tolerance for casualties is largely due to the fact that the American public places far less value on the stakes in Iraq than it did on those in Korea and Vietnam. The main threats Iraq was thought to present to the United States when troops went in—weapons of mass destruction and support for international terrorism—have been, to say the least, discounted. With those justifications gone, the Iraq war is left as something of a humanitarian venture, and, as Francis Fukuyama has put it, a request to spend "several hundred billion dollars and several thousand American lives in order to bring democracy to . . . Iraq" would "have been laughed out of court." Given the evaporation of the main reasons for going to war and the unexpectedly high level of American casualties, support for the war in Iraq is, if anything, higher than one might expect—a reflection of the fact that many people still connect the effort there to the "war" on terrorism, an enterprise that continues to enjoy huge support. In addition, the toppling of Saddam Hussein remains a singular accomplishment—something the American people had wanted since the 1991 Persian Gulf War.

When one shifts from questions about whether the war was a "mistake" or "worth it" to ones about whether the United States should get out, much the same pattern holds for Korea, Vietnam, and Iraq: relatively steep declines in support for continuing the war in the early stages, slower erosion later. However, it is close to impossible to judge how many people want to get out or stay the course at any given time because so much depends on how the question is worded. For example, there is far more support for "gradual withdrawal" or "beginning to withdraw" than for "withdrawing" or "immediate withdrawal." Thus in August 2005, *The Washington Post* found that 54 percent of respondents favored staying and 44 percent favored withdrawing when the options were posed this way: "Do you think the United States should keep its military forces in Iraq until civil order is restored there, even if that means continued U.S. military casualties, or, do you think the United States should withdraw its military forces from Iraq in order to avoid further U.S. military casualties, even if that means civil order is not restored there?" But in the same month, a Harris poll tallied only 36 percent in support of staying and 61 percent in support of withdrawing when it asked, "Do you favor keeping a large number of U.S. troops in Iraq until there is a stable government there or bringing most of our troops home in the next year?" Still, no matter how the questions are phrased, all the polls have logged increases in pro-withdrawal sentiment over the course of the war.

Many analysts have tried to link declining support to factors other than accumulating combat deaths. For example, the notion that public opinion sours as casualties increase has somehow turned into "support drops when they start seeing the body bags"—a vivid expression that some in the Bush administration have apparently taken literally. As a result, the military has worked enterprisingly to keep Americans from seeing pictures of body bags or flag-draped coffins in the hope that this will somehow arrest the decline in enthusiasm for the war effort. But such pictures are not necessary to drive home the basic reality of mounting casualties.

Growing opposition to the war effort also has little to do with whether or not there is an active antiwar movement at home. There has not been much of one in the case of the Iraq war, nor was there one during the war in Korea. Nonetheless, support for those ventures eroded as it did during the Vietnam War, when antiwar protest was frequent and visible. In fact, since the Vietnam protest movement became so strongly associated with anti-American values and activities, it may ultimately have been somewhat counterproductive.

Moreover, support for the war declines whether or not war opponents are able to come up with specific policy alternatives. Dwight Eisenhower never seemed to have much of a plan for getting out of the Korean War—although he did say that, if elected, he would visit the place—but discontent with the war still worked well for him in the 1952 election; Richard Nixon's proposals for fixing the Vietnam mess were distinctly unspecific, although he did from time to time mutter that he had a "secret plan." Wars hurt the war-initiating political party not because the opposition comes up with a coherent clashing vision—George McGovern tried that, with little success, against Nixon in 1972—but because discontent over the war translates into vague distrust of the capacities of the people running the country.

The impact of war discontent on congressional races is less clear. Democrats attempted to capitalize on the widespread outrage over Nixon's invasion of Cambodia in 1970 but were unable to change things much. And subsequent developments, including campaign reform legislation, have made incumbents increasingly less vulnerable.

DAMAGE CONTROL

President George W. Bush, like Lyndon Johnson before him, made countless speeches explaining what the effort in Iraq is about, urging patience, and asserting that progress is being made. But as was also evident during Woodrow Wilson's campaign to sell the League of Nations to the American public, the efficacy of the bully pulpit is much overrated. The prospects for reversing the erosion of support for the war in Iraq are thus limited. The run-ups to the two wars in Iraq are also instructive in this regard: even though both Presidents Bush labored mightily to sell the war effort, the only thing that succeeded in raising the level of enthusiasm was the sight of troops actually heading into action, which triggered a predictable "rally round the flag" effect.

Although the impact of official rhetoric is limited, favorable occurrences in the war itself can boost support from time to time. In the case of the war in Iraq, for example, there were notable upward shifts in many polls after Saddam was captured and elections were held. These increases, however, proved to be temporary, more bumps on the road than permanent changes in direction. Support soon fell back to where it had been before and then continued its generally downward course. The same is true of negative occurrences: a drop in support after the disclosure of abuses at Abu Ghraib in 2004 was in time mostly reversed.

Some scholars have argued that support for war is determined by the prospects for success rather than casualties. Americans are "defeat-phobic" rather than "casualty-phobic," the argument goes; they do not really care how many casualties are suffered so long as their side comes out the winner. For example, the political scientists Peter Feaver and Christopher Gelpi have calculated, rather remarkably, that Americans would on average be entirely willing to see 6,861 soldiers die in order to bring democracy to Congo.

There never were periods of continuous good news in the wars in Korea or Vietnam, so there is no clear precedent here. But should good news start coming in from Iraq—including, in particular, a decline in American casualty rates—it would more likely cause the erosion in public support to slow or even cease rather than trigger a large upsurge in support. For support to rise notably, many of those now disaffected by the war would need to reverse their position, and that seems rather unlikely: polls that seek to tap intensity of feeling find that more than 80 percent of those opposed to the war "strongly" feel that way. If you purchase a car for twice what it is worth, you will still consider the deal to have been a mistake even if you come to like the car.

Also relevant is the fact that despite the comparatively mild-mannered behavior of Democratic leaders in the run-up to the Iraq war, partisan differences regarding this war, and this president, are incredibly deep. Gary Jacobson, a political scientist at the University of California, San Diego, has documented that the partisan divide over the war in Iraq is considerably greater than for any military action over the last half century and that the partisan split on presidential approval ratings, despite a major narrowing after the attacks of September 11, 2001, is greater than for any president over that period— greater than for Clinton, Reagan, or Nixon. This means that Bush cannot look for increased Republican support because he already has practically all of it; meanwhile, Democrats are unlikely to budge much. There may be some hope for him among independents, but their war-support patterns more nearly track those of the almost completely disaffected Democrats than those of the steadfast Republicans.

Moreover, it is difficult to see what a spate of good news would look like at this point. A clear-cut victory, like the one scored by George H.W. Bush in the Gulf in 1991, is hugely unlikely—and the glow even of that one faded quickly as Saddam continued to hold forth in Iraq. From the start of the current Iraq war, the invading forces were too small to establish order, and some of the early administrative policies proved fatally misguided. In effect, the United States created an instant failed state, and clambering out of that condition would be difficult in the best of circumstances. If the worst violence diminishes, and Iraq thereby ceases to be quite so much of a bloody mess, the war will attract less attention. But there is still likely to be plenty of official and unofficial corruption, sporadic vigilantism, police misconduct, militia feuding, political backstabbing, economic travail, regional separatism, government incompetence, rampant criminality, religious conflict, and posturing by political entrepreneurs spouting anti-American and anti-Israeli rhetoric. Under such conditions, the American venture in Iraq is unlikely to be seen as a great victory by those now in opposition, over half of whom profess to be not merely dissatisfied with the war, but angry over it.

In all of this, what chiefly matters for American public opinion is American losses, not those of the people defended. By some estimates, the number of Iraqis who have died as a result of the invasion has reached six figures—vastly more than have been killed by all international terrorists in all of history. Sanctions on Iraq probably were a necessary cause of death for an even greater number of Iraqis, most of them children. Yet the only cumulative body count that truly matters in the realm of American public opinion, and the only one that is routinely reported, is the American one. There is nothing new about this: although there was considerable support for the wars in Korea and Vietnam, polls made clear that people backed the wars because they saw them as vital to confronting the communist threat; defending the South Koreans or the South Vietnamese per se was never thought of as an important goal.

THE POLITICS OF DEBACLE

In Iraq, as they did in Vietnam, U.S. troops face an armed opposition that is dedicated, resourceful, capable of replenishing its ranks, and seemingly determined to fight as long as necessary. In Vietnam, the hope was that after suffering enough punishment, the enemy would reach its "breaking point" and then either fade away or seek accommodation. Great punishment was inflicted, but the enemy never broke; instead, it was the United States that faded away after signing a face-saving agreement. Whether the insurgents in Iraq have the same determination and fortitude is yet to be seen. The signs thus far, however, are not very encouraging: the insurgency does not appear to be weakening.

Many people, including President Bush, argue that the United States must slog on because a precipitous exit from Iraq would energize Islamist militants, who would see it as an even greater victory than the expulsion of the Soviet Union from Afghanistan. A quick exit would confirm, the thinking goes, Osama bin Laden's basic theory: that terrorists can defeat the United States by continuously inflicting on it casualties that are small in number but still draining. A venture designed and sold as a blow against international terrorists would end up emboldening and energizing them.

The problem is that almost any exit from Iraq will have this effect. Bin Laden, as well as huge majorities in Muslim countries and in parts of Europe, believe that the United States invaded Iraq as part of its plan to control oil supplies in the Middle East. Although Washington has no intention of doing that, at least not in the direct sense that bin Laden and others mean, U.S. forces will inevitably leave Iraq without having accomplished what many consider to be Washington's real goals there—and the terrorist insurgents will claim credit for forcing the United States out before it fulfilled these key objectives. Iraq has also, of course, become something of a terrorist training—and inspiration—zone.

When the United States was preparing to withdraw from Vietnam, many Americans feared that there would be a bloodbath if the country fell to the North Vietnamese. And indeed, on taking control, the Communists executed tens of thousands of people, sent hundreds of thousands to "reeducation camps" for long periods, and so mismanaged the economy that hundreds of thousands fled the country out of desperation, often in barely floating boats. (What happened in neighboring Cambodia when the Khmer Rouge took over makes even the word "bloodbath" seem an understatement.)

There is a similar concern this time around: Iraq could devolve into a civil war after the Americans leave. Thus, U.S. officials have updated "Vietnamization" and applied it to Iraq. They are making strenuous efforts to fabricate a reasonably viable local government, police, and military that can take over the fight, allowing U.S. forces to withdraw judiciously. In Vietnam, of course, communist forces took over less than two years after the United States installed a sympathetic government. Although the consequences of a U.S. withdrawal from Iraq are likely to be messy, they may be less dire. The insurgency in Iraq, albeit deadly and dedicated, represents a much smaller, less popular, and less organized force than the Vietcong did, and it does not have the same kind of international backing. Moreover, many of the insurgents are fighting simply to get U.S. troops out of the country and can be expected to stop when the Americans

leave. The insurgency will likely become more manageable without the U.S. presence, even if there is a determined effort by at least some of the rebels to go after a government that, in their eyes, consists of quislings and collaborators. It is also impressive that efforts by the insurgents to stoke a civil war between the Shiites and the Sunnis have not been very successful thus far; most Shiites have refused to see the insurgents as truly representative of the Sunni population.

Even if Iraq does turn out to be a foreign policy debacle—by declining into a hopeless quagmire or collapsing into civil chaos—history suggests that withdrawing need not be politically devastating (unless, perhaps, failure in Iraq leads directly to terrorism in the United States). As it happens, the American people have proved quite capable of taking debacle in stride; they do not seem to be terribly "defeat-phobic." They supported the decision to withdraw U.S. troops from Lebanon in 1984 after a terrorist bomb killed 241 Americans in the civil war there; the man who presided over that debacle, Ronald Reagan, readily won reelection a few months later. Something similar happened to Bill Clinton when he withdrew troops from Somalia in 1994: by the time the next election rolled around, people had largely forgotten the whole episode.

The most remarkable, and relevant, precedent is the utter collapse of the U.S. position in Vietnam in 1975. The man who presided over that debacle, Gerald Ford, actually tried to use it to his advantage in his reelection campaign the next year. As he pointed out, when he came into office the United States was "still deeply involved in the problems of Vietnam, [but now] we are at peace. Not a single young American is fighting or dying on any foreign soil tonight." His challenger, Jimmy Carter, apparently did not think it good politics to point out the essential absurdity of Ford's declaration.

Moreover, even if disaster follows a U.S. withdrawal—as it did in Vietnam, Lebanon, and Somalia—the people dying will be Iraqis, not Americans. And the deaths of foreigners, as noted earlier, are not what move the public.

INDISPENSABLE NATION?

After the war in Vietnam, there was a strong desire among Americans never to do "that" again. And, in fact, there never was "another Vietnam" during the Cold War. Due to this "Vietnam syndrome," Congress hampered the White House's ability to pursue even rather modest anticommunist ventures in Africa and, to a lesser extent, Latin America (though there was bipartisan support for aiding the anti-Soviet jihad in Afghanistan). Meanwhile, the genocide in Cambodia was studiously ignored in part because of fears that paying attention might lead to the conclusion that American troops should be sent over to rectify the disaster; over most of the course of the genocide, the three major networks devoted a total of 29 minutes of their newscasts to a cataclysm in which millions died.

No matter how the war in Iraq turns out, an Iraq syndrome seems likely. A poll in relatively war-approving Alabama, for example, asked whether the United States should be prepared to send troops back to Iraq to establish order there in the event a full-scale civil war erupted after a U.S. withdrawal. Only a third of the respondents favored doing so.

Among the casualties of the Iraq syndrome could be the Bush doctrine, unilateralism, preemption, preventive war, and indispensable-nationhood. Indeed, these once-fashionable (and sometimes self-infatuated) concepts are already picking up a patina of quaintness. Specifically, there will likely be growing skepticism about various key notions: that the United States should take unilateral military action to correct situations or overthrow regimes it considers reprehensible but that present no immediate threat to it, that it can and should forcibly bring democracy to other nations not now so blessed, that it has the duty to rid the world of evil, that having by far the largest defense budget in the world is necessary and broadly beneficial, that international cooperation is of only very limited value, and that Europeans and other well-meaning foreigners are naive and decadent wimps. The United States may also become more inclined to seek international cooperation, sometimes even showing signs of humility.

In part because of the military and financial overextension in Iraq (and Afghanistan), the likelihood of any coherent application of military power or even of a focused military threat against the remaining entities on the Bush administration's once-extensive hit list has substantially diminished. In the meantime, any country that suspects it may be on the list has the strongest incentive to make the American experience in Iraq as miserable as possible. Some may also come to consider that deterring the world's last remaining superpower can be accomplished by preemptively and prominently recruiting and training a few thousand of their citizens to fight and die in dedicated irregular warfare against foreign occupiers.

Evidence of the Iraq syndrome is emerging. Already, Bush has toned down his language. When North Korea abruptly declared that it actually possessed nuclear weapons, the announcement was officially characterized as "unfortunate" and as "rhetoric we've heard before." Iran has already become defiant, and its newly elected president has actually had the temerity to suggest—surely the unkindest cut—that he does not consider the United States to be the least bit indispensable. Ultimately, the chief beneficiaries of the war in Iraq may be Iraq's fellow members of the "axis of evil."

THE IRAQ WAR OF 2003

Steve A. Yetiv

In this postscript to his book on the 1991 Persian Gulf War, Yetiv examines the factors that shaped the decision of the United States to go to war in Iraq in 2003. Written shortly after the war was initiated, he can provide only brief glimpses into how different approaches to understanding foreign policy making might be applied to this case. As you read this excerpt, ask yourself:

- What would the rational actor model applied to the Iraq decision look like?
- Where do we see the limits of the rational actor model in his discussion of this case?
- What new evidence accumulated since Yetiv's book was published in 2004 might be applied to understanding how the decision to go to war in Iraq came about?

THE IRAQ WAR OF 2003

In April 2003, dozens of statues of Iraq's ubiquitous dictator came crashing down at the hands of Iraqi civilians and U.S. military forces, forming an indelible image for the ages, unleashing a sense that a new dawn was perhaps at hand for Iraq. Saddam and his sons were either dead, hiding, or on the run. The Baathist regime was history.

The Persian Gulf War of 1991 and the Iraq War of 2003 etched the Persian Gulf region into the American mind with a firebrand, and, in their own strange way, reflected all things American at the outset of the twenty-first century. They were fast for a people that values alacrity, and not too overtly messy and inconvenient for a people that values convenience. And, of course, they were antiseptic to the point of being almost surreal. Both wars reflected American technological prowess in an age of great optimism in machines that few understood but that seemed to make enemies go away. The wars at once celebrated the destructive precision of smart bombs and the humanitarian dimension of their ability to not kill civilians. Americans could thus revel in their virtuous self-image, while also getting the job done.

But just as fast as the euphoria of military victory came, it went away, to be replaced by stark realities. In 1991, Operation Desert Storm was a success, but the patient lived—and proceeded to suppress brutally the Kurdish and Shia uprisings. And in the Iraq War, Washington faces the profound challenges of rebuilding a nation frozen in time by a cold, oppressive regime that had resisted change and hijacked a nation for its own narrow interests.

At the time of this writing, there is no telling how post-Saddam Iraq will unfold. It may take a year, or ten, or even a hundred to really answer that question. Nation-building does not occur overnight, nor does it presage its own direction. Historians may look back at the Iraq War and consider it to be the opening salvo of a "Golden Age of Democratization" in Iraq, or they may see it as a successful military victory that produced no broader changes of this kind. The truth is likely to lie somewhere in between, as it so often does.

Steve A. Yetiv, from *Explaining Foreign Policy: US Decision-Making and the Persian Gulf War*, pp. 222–234. © 2004 The Johns Hopkins University Press. Reprinted with permission of The Johns Hopkins University Press.

But while the future is hard to predict, we can continue to tell the ongoing story of wars in the Middle East. As that story goes, the Persian Gulf War left Saddam in power and able to continue to develop weapons of mass destruction (WMD) in defiance of U.N. Resolution 687, passed on April 2, 1991, shortly after the war's end. Referred to as the "mother of all resolutions" for its great length, it mandated full disclosure of all of Iraq's ballistic missile stocks and production facilities (over 150 kilometers in range), all nuclear materials, all chemical and biological weapons and facilities, and cooperation in their destruction. Paragraphs 10 through 12, furthermore, required Iraq to "unconditionally undertake not to use, develop, construct, or acquire" WMD. Resolution 687 also forced Iraq to accept the U.N. demarcated border with Kuwait, the inviolability of Kuwaiti territory, and the existence of U.N. peacekeepers on the Iraq-Kuwait border, and intrusive U.N. arms inspections aimed at ridding Iraq of its ability to produce WMD. Iraqi compliance with Resolution 687 was a prerequisite for lifting or reducing sanctions against it.[1]

All in all, seventeen U.N. resolutions, including Resolution 687, would be passed between 1991 and 2002 mandating Iraq's full compliance. In effect, the United States was in conflict with Iraq from the time it drove Iraq's army from Kuwait in 1991 and imposed no-fly zones over two-thirds of Iraq. Throughout the 1990s, it periodically attacked Iraq to punish its defiance of U.N. resolutions, and tried to overthrow the dictator outright using CIA-led operations. By 1998, regime change in Iraq had already become official U.S. policy, well before George W. Bush took office. But it was not until after the September 11, 2001, attacks by the terrorist group Al Qaeda that the Bush administration repeatedly expressed a strong and determined will to remove Saddam from power, by force if

necessary, as part of the global war on terrorism and as a way to rid Iraq of WMD. In his State of the Union address on January 29, 2002, President Bush identified Iraq, Iran, and North Korea as forming an "Axis of Evil." In a speech given at the U.S. Military Academy at West Point on June 1, he added that Washington would preempt threats from such rogue regimes and transnational terror groups before they could actually become imminent and massive dangers to the United States. Such statements eventually formed the core of a Bush doctrine of preemption which contrasted with the previous emphasis in American foreign policy on containing threats.[2]

On November 8, 2002, after two months of intense negotiation, all fifteen members of the U.N. Security Council signed Resolution 1441, the seventeenth U.N. resolution against Iraq.[3] It required Baghdad to admit U.N. inspectors from the U.N. Monitoring, Verification, and Inspection Commission (UNMOVIC) and the International Atomic Energy Agency and to comply fully with all U.N. resolutions. In Washington's view, Resolution 1441 also allowed for the use of force against Iraq because it indicated that "serious consequences" would follow if Baghdad failed to cooperate.

It is interesting, then, that as of early June 2003, Saddam's WMD had yet to be found. Two trailers were found that appeared to be equipped to produce WMD, but there was disagreement within the U.S. intelligence community about their exact purpose, and no "smoking gun" weapons were actually found in the trailers. In fact, after weeks of extensive searching, U.S. teams could find no actual WMD. This raised some interesting questions worldwide: did the Bush administration fabricate or exaggerate the WMD threat in order to gain support for a war that it thought was important for non-WMD reasons, such as reshaping the Middle East, liberating the Iraqi people, preempting any future WMD potential in Iraq, or, as the cynical view would have it, enhancing the president's re-election chances? Was the intelligence offered to the president inaccurate or selective? Were WMD simply hard to find in such a large country, offering the prospect that they would be discovered in due time, along with the understanding that perhaps Saddam's generals did not want to use these weapons for fear that they would be prosecuted for doing so, in a war they were sure to lose? Had Saddam or his generals spirited the key weapons out of the country before the war, possibly to use at a later time, to sell to terrorists, or to elude U.N. weapons inspectors?

In compliance with Resolution 1441, on December 7, 2002, Iraq gave the U.N. a report of more than 12,000 pages and several compact discs that purportedly described the country's arms program before and after 1990. In effect, the report asserted that Iraq had no WMD, raising suspicions in Washington and elsewhere in the world that Baghdad was obfuscating its capabilities. Serious doubts arose because Iraq itself had admitted to U.N. weapons inspectors that it had produced such weapons, including 8,500 liters of anthrax and a few tons of the nerve agent VX. U.N. inspectors, world leaders, and especially U.S. officials were thus curious as to what had happened to these weapons. Since Iraq refused to provide an acceptable answer—other than to say that they did not exist—many leaders around the world, not just in the United States, assumed the worst.

Subsequently, Iraq allowed U.N. inspectors to search the country for weapons; they found no "smoking gun" but were not satisfied with Iraq's cooperation. The United States, meanwhile, released intelligence information, including tape-recorded conversations among Iraqis, indicating that Iraq possessed WMD and was trying to hide it from U.N. inspectors. Up until the war, Iraq repeatedly denied that it had

WMD, as if the allegation were an outright fabrication by a war-hungry United States. It also treated U.S. accusations of its connection to Al Qaeda as nothing more than a pretext for war.

After weeks of strained negotiations among members of the U.N. Security Council, the United States and Britain moved to present the eighteenth U.N. resolution against Iraq. In contrast to the position of France, Russia, and China, who sought a period of months for continued U.N. inspections, the eighteenth resolution pushed openly for using force should Iraq not immediately comply. After France threatened to veto the resolution, a move that might have received support from Russia and China, and after Washington and London failed to secure the votes of the smaller countries on the Security Council, the two allies decided that Resolution 1441 provided sufficient basis for the use of force, even without the eighteenth resolution.

After providing Saddam, his sons, and key Iraqi leaders with an ultimatum to leave Iraq in forty-eight hours or face war, the United States proceeded to launch Operation Iraqi Freedom. It was supported by British forces and some Australian troops, and was backed by a broader "coalition of the willing," as the United States and Britain referred to it. However, unlike George H.W. Bush, the younger Bush faced harsh criticism that American foreign policy had become unilateral and arrogant, and that he had been much less successful in forming a highly engaged coalition.

On March 19, President Bush announced that the Iraq War had begun, with a precision strike on a bunker suspected of containing Iraq's leadership, a strike that some believed had killed Saddam Hussein and his top aides and could lead to Iraq's quick surrender. After Iraq did not surrender, the United States launched a massive air attack referred to as the "Shock and Awe" campaign, which was followed by a large ground attack mostly launched from Kuwait. Special forces worked within Iraq to undermine Saddam's regime using subversion and psychological operations, and the U.S. Air Force continued to bomb key Iraqi targets as American and British forces proceeded on the ground. At first, they faced unexpected resistance from Saddam's Fedayeen fighters, backed by some elements of Saddam's Republican Guards, in cities such as Basra and Nasiriyah.

Eventually, the Iraqi opposition was suppressed and U.S. forces marched toward Baghdad, in the process destroying Iraq's Republican Guard. The fall of Baghdad came much more quickly than most had expected, ending the main military phase of the war in about three weeks and revealing in stark relief that Saddam's rule was one of horror, gangsterism, and brutality. Iraq's regime appeared to scatter into thin air, but neither Saddam nor his sons were confirmed dead. In the following months, many Iraqi leaders either were killed or surrendered to American forces, and the United States faced the daunting task of rebuilding Iraq, providing internal security against looting and thievery, and laying down the roots of democratic government—tasks that many critics doubted could be accomplished effectively. . . .

Rational Acting

Through the lens of the rational actor model, we would re-create the decisions to attack Iraq as an effort to protect and advance U.S. national interests. On that score, we could say that the United States viewed Iraq as a threat even before September 11. This is because Iraq had not complied fully with U.N. resolutions requiring it to dismantle and forswear WMD. Were Iraq to provide terrorists with biological or chemical weapons, the destruction of September 11 would pale by comparison. If 9/11 taught the U.S. any lessons, it was that terrorists could not be allowed

to obtain WMD, because they would surely use them, thus altering the course of U.S. and possibly world history. The United States could not take the chance of letting such a scenario transpire.

Moreover, if Iraq obtained a nuclear weapon, Washington would have a hard time sending U.S. forces to the Persian Gulf to deal with Iraq's growing power. Such troops could, after all, be vaporized if Iraq were to use a nuclear weapon. In addition, all of the Middle East countries, but particularly Saudi Arabia and Kuwait, would be severely intimidated by Iraq. Thus, they would be much less likely to put more oil on the market to stabilize prices, if Iraq took a hawkish position on oil pricing. Iraq's influence over the global economy, which depends on reasonably priced oil, would rise, giving it the potential to cause a global recession and blackmail other nations to its own ends.

Rather than allowing such potential threats to develop, the United States could eliminate Iraq's regime, destroy its potential as a base of operations or support for terrorists, and free Iraqis from tyranny. Democratization in Iraq might spark more regional democratization, based on the notion that Middle Easterners, contrary to the warnings of critics, yearned for inalienable rights just as much as individuals anywhere else.

From the RAM perspective, we would re-create the decision to go to war as resulting from the calculation that the benefits minus the costs of war exceeded those of continued containment. Costly and prolonged containment would not have caused regime change, nor would it have eliminated Iraq's WMD, its connection to terrorism, or its oppression of its own people. War was also preferable to another option: continuing U.N. inspections of Iraq for many months, as France, Russia, Germany, and China wanted. Iraq could hide its weapons from inspectors indefinitely, while providing sporadic cooperation, thus delaying war for months, perhaps years. And

U.N. inspections would not achieve regime change, even if Iraq did cooperate fully. Quite the contrary, inspections could lead to greater international legitimacy for the regime, if Iraq indeed were somehow given a clean bill of health. The United States had to take a lead role, and was, in President Bush's words, in a "unique position" to act as a global leader, to lay out a vision, because the "vision thing matters."[4]

As an added benefit, regime change in Iraq would decrease U.S. dependence on Saudi Arabia as a site for military bases. A liberated Iraq would be less threatening, thus making such bases less important, and Washington might have access to military sites in Iraq itself. A U.S. withdrawal from Saudi Arabia—which was in fact announced in late April 2003—could decrease political internal pressures on the Saudi regime and deprive terrorists of a key reason to focus their hatred on the United States. Meanwhile, if Iraq became more friendly towards Washington than the Baathist regime had been, and began pumping more oil (once its oil infrastructure was rebuilt), U.S. and global dependence on the Saudi ability to pump extra oil in times of crisis or oil shortages might decrease. The overall decrease in U.S. dependence on Saudi Arabia would give it more freedom to pressure the royal family to crack down on potential terrorists and terrorist sympathizers in the kingdom.

A final benefit could arise for Israel. Saddam Hussein had paid Palestinian suicide bombers approximately 10 to 25 thousand dollars each for killing Israelis, and Iraq's WMD programs could have targeted Israel as well. With regime change, America's ally would feel more secure and be more willing to make concessions for peace, and the Arab parties would feel more pressure to do the same, now that a stalwart opponent of the peace process had been removed.

Of course, war carried the unknown costs of American and civilian casualties. However, the U.S. ability to use precision-guided and other weapons had increased so significantly since the 1991 war, and Iraq had become so weakened by wars and sanctions, that quick victory was likely, at a relatively low cost. Even if civilian casualties were high, the fact was that Iraqi civilians, according to the U.N., were dying each year by the thousands under the U.N. economic sanctions, due to the regime's brutality and neglect. Removing Saddam from power would also result in the lifting of U.N. economic sanctions.

War might have been avoided had Iraq fully complied with the U.S. demands, but, at some point, the United States preferred war to compliance, because if Iraq had complied, it could just come back another day to develop WMD, threaten the region, and possibly provide terrorists with the ability to attack the United States. For this reason, Washington's bargaining position with Iraq became quite tough.

Meanwhile, Iraq not only wanted to retain its weapons and its sense of national pride, it also did not trust Washington not to attack, even if it were to comply fully. This is because the United States talked about regime change at least as much as Iraqi compliance. If the regime was the real target, then war was coming anyway, which contributed to Iraq's reluctance to cooperate with U.N. inspectors. It did not want to be the sucker, in the terms of the Prisoner's Dilemma, that cooperated with an agreement to disarm, while the United States proceeded to attack or otherwise seek the regime's removal anyway. The probability of such an outcome made Iraq far less willing to seek a diplomatic outcome. In this sense, the nature of U.S.-Iraqi strategic interaction, as in the Persian Gulf War, contributed to war.

The Cognitive Dimension
While the rational actor model stresses the strategic context and careful decision-making, the

cognitive dimension takes us into the minds of decision makers. We might say that President Bush analogized back to the 1991 Persian Gulf War. He had learned from his father's experience that attacking Iraq can succeed quite well, despite the warnings of doomsayers. After all, Iraq's forces were not all that tough. After taking some serious air bombardment in 1991, they folded in a one-hundred-hour ground war. If anything, Iraq was far weaker in conventional military capability in 2003 than in 1991, due to twelve years of American containment and punishing air strikes, as well as U.N. sanctions and global isolation.

What failed to happen in 1991, however, was that Washington did not go far enough in eliminating the regime, and Saddam resurrected himself politically and reasserted his control over Iraq. Moreover, the vengeful dictator proceeded to try to assassinate George H.W. Bush in 1993, which prompted President Clinton to order a cruise-missile attack against his intelligence headquarters in Baghdad. George W. Bush remembered that well. As he pointed out to the press, Saddam was the guy that tried to kill his "daddy." No proud Texan of what was a growing political dynasty was willing to let a no-good dictator with a hearty appetite for nasty weapons take a potshot at his father and get away with it. Analogizing back to the 1991 war taught the lessons that beating Iraq was not difficult and that eliminating Saddam was necessary for ultimate victory, both for country and for family.

From Iraq's side, we might speculate that analogies were also at play. Indeed, Saddam may have believed that if he imposed many casualties on U.S. forces, Washington would retreat as it had in Somalia, Lebanon, or Vietnam, or sue for some type of peace that left Saddam effectively in power—a dictator's main goal. While the 1991 war did not allow for imposing large numbers of casualties, a war in 2003 very well could have, because the possibility of urban warfare, possibly in the heart of Baghdad for many weeks, was high.

Domestic Politics

The rational actor and cognitive models may provide some insights, but they ignore what all politicians think about: the home front and re-election.

Using the domestic politics model, we would thread together an explanation for war which emphasized domestic motives. Attacking Iraq could serve to divert attention from profound economic problems. Indeed, the Wall Street market bubble had burst, leaving Americans with a third of their 401(k) plans. Meanwhile, unemployment had hit nearly six percent, and the gross domestic product was barely inching along—problems that the Bush administration was trying to address with massive tax cuts. The only thing that appeared to be rising significantly was a lack of confidence on the part of consumers, whose spending accounts for two-thirds of the nation's economy. By February 2003, consumer confidence had dropped to a nine-year low.[5] A good war might do wonders in diverting attention from these domestic problems, which could threaten the president's re-election chances.

As conceived herein, painting Iraq as a grand threat and Saddam as evil incarnate in order to lay the groundwork for war, may very well have boxed President Bush into the path to war. So that when he faced unexpected global opposition, he still felt it necessary to go to war in lieu of pursuing U.N. inspections longer or switching to a containment strategy. Bush's war rhetoric, aimed primarily for domestic consumption, may have also convinced Saddam that he had nothing to lose by being more belligerent because the United States was resolved to attack Iraq and eliminate his regime. . . . There is evidence to suggest that this was partly at play in influencing Iraq's behavior prior to the 1991 Persian Gulf War, a war that

Washington saw as necessary in diminishing Iraq's military threat.

An even more cynical interpretation of the road to war features the notion that the president and vice president had strong contacts in the oil industry. War with Iraq would bring American firms big contracts to rebuild Iraq's oil industry and other basic functions. U.S. firms that were allotted such contracts would be more inclined to fund the administration's re-election campaign and that of other Republicans, and, in any event, such work would decrease the unemployment rate. The large contracts awarded to Vice President Cheney's former company Halliburton during the conflict added fuel to this line of thinking.

Groupthink Dynamics

The theory of groupthink would give us another take altogether. It would suggest that the dynamics in Bush's inner circle did not favor a serious evaluation of different options for dealing with Iraq. Quite the contrary, the group was driven partly by President Bush as a partial group leader who saw Saddam as an evil man atop a horrid regime that had to be removed by force. Other group members, facing stressful conditions and a determined position taken by the president and other key decision makers, were reluctant to voice serious objections to the course toward war, even if they thought that continued containment of Iraq or other options made better sense. Thus, early on, a concurrence-seeking tendency developed in which the road to war was not challenged within the decision-making group. War prevailed as an option because other options were not seriously considered and advanced in the inner circle.

Government Politics

In sharp contrast, the government politics model, in a nutshell, would explain the decision as a function of bargaining among individuals representing different bureaucracies. One possible explanation drawn from this perspective would be that Secretary of Defense Donald Rumsfeld viewed the removal of Saddam, possibly by a war with Iraq, as in line with the imperatives and interests of the Department of Defense (and possibly U.S. interests as well).

Rumsfeld prevailed at committee meetings in pushing this option because he is a good bargainer who understands the channels of power and effectively lobbies for his department and position. Moreover, the military success in removing the Taliban regime and dealing Al Qaeda a major blow in Afghanistan in response to the 9/11 attacks increased the influence of the Department of Defense in the bureaucratic sphere as well as Rumsfeld's influence in Bush's inner circle. His position on Iraq, then, gained greatest currency in an overall approach that was a collage of competing interests.

COMPARATIVE FOREIGN POLICY

The thumbnail sketch of each perspective offered above could be developed much further to offer competing, and possibly complementary, insights into the case. Additional perspectives could be added as well if there was evidence to suggest that generating them would be helpful. Using multiple perspectives could offer the basis for a more complete understanding of the decision, even without detailed information about it. However, they become even more useful once more is known about the case and the perspectives can be evaluated against the evidence.

It is, of course, far too early to evaluate the relative merits of the different perspectives, or even to sketch them more fully, but some speculation is worthwhile about decision-making in the two wars. Pending further research, three points at least seem promising to consider at this point. Naturally, myriad others may arise as we learn more about the Iraq War.

Decisions by Analogy

We can speculate fairly that, unlike in the Persian Gulf War, decision-making by analogy was either less important in the Iraq War, or quite different in nature. President George H.W. Bush repeatedly referred to Munich and to World War II, both in private and public discourse. By comparison, George W. Bush scarcely mentioned Munich, perhaps because the Iraq War was one of preemption, thus not fitting the 1930s analogy. After all, Saddam had not invaded another country in the recent past, nor did he threaten to create a domino-like effect of aggression through the region, as some thought he might in 1990. Nor was the Vietnam analogy prominent, though critics of the war did raise the specter of Vietnam. Perhaps this is because the ghost of Vietnam had already been dealt with in the 1991 war, not to mention in Kosovo and in Afghanistan after the 9/11 attacks.

Of course, we may find that decision makers did draw on other analogies, such as the experience in the 1991 war. But, that would represent a different analogy at work than in the 1991 case, with different lessons.

Government Politics and Groupthink: A Brief Comparison

Disagreements among decision makers about various courses of actions do not, in and of themselves, disconfirm the theory of groupthink. This is because the theory allows for discord outside the group context, even if it is muted within the group itself. However, it appears that greater disagreement existed, even within the group, in the Iraq War case than in the Persian Gulf War.[6] At a minimum, Rumsfeld was more hawkish about

going to war against Iraq and eschewing an effort to gain U.N. approval than was Secretary of State Colin Powell. While Secretary of State James Baker and Secretary of Defense Richard Cheney also preferred different routes in the Persian Gulf War, we may find that their level and intensity of disagreement, and the extent to which it permeated their bureaucracies, was much lower than that between Powell and Rumsfeld.

Moreover, we may also find that George W. Bush, unlike his father, was more likely to be swayed by discussions among group members than to shape group consensus, at least on key issues. For instance, George W. Bush asserted that it was his team of advisers who "convinced him" of the sensibility of the war plan, not vice versa.[7] If future work confirms that disagreement did occur among his advisers and that he did less to shape group dynamics than his father, groupthink will prove an unsuitable explanation. That will set up an interesting comparison to the Persian Gulf War case. Why did significant elements of groupthink arise in the Persian Gulf War case, but not in the Iraq War case? In particular, it would be profitable to explore if, in the Iraq War case, the level of camaraderie was lower; if George W. Bush pushed less for his own preferred approach than his father did; and if more attention was paid to evaluating options (norms for methodical procedures).

We may also find that the Iraq War case offers more evidence of bureaucratic politics than the Persian Gulf War case. Disagreements among inner circle members certainly do not confirm that government politics was at play. We would have to know much more about the case. What, for instance, drove the disagreements? Were the motivations bureaucratic or not? Did they occur in a committee setting or outside it? However, the existence of disagreements and, possibly, turf warfare at least creates the potential for bureaucratic politics to have been at play.

INDIVIDUALS MAKING HISTORY

While these two wars were different in important ways, they were similar in others. Above all, perhaps, President George W. Bush, like his father, played a vital role in defining the road to war. How, when, and to what extent his role was defining, as compared to other influences on foreign policy, will have to await future work. But it certainly seems possible that he fundamentally drove Washington towards war in lieu of continued containment of Iraq. Indeed, the Iraq War was more optional for Washington than was the Persian Gulf War. This is because it was preemptive rather than reactionary. And few would have criticized George W. Bush for continuing a strategy of containing Iraq.

Historians, like many in other disciplines, have struggled to understand the causal role of the individual versus non-individual forces. They have preferred in recent times to downplay the individual and play up systemic and deterministic forces, as well as such things as culture, geography, and even technology. However, the roles of George H.W. Bush and George W. Bush seem to support the "Great Man" theory of history. Contrary to its name, this theory or notion ascribes neither greatness nor heroism nor rightness to the individual. Rather, it posits that few individuals—in some cases, one individual—can be causally crucial.[8] By emphasizing free will, the hero-in-history theory downplays factors that limit or eliminate the ability of individuals to take bold, defining action.

. . . This "Great Man" notion . . . is too simplistic. It attributes variation in history chiefly to one source—the individual—and downgrades the importance of other factors. That is a problem because none of us can escape life's arrows; the day's challenge; the unpredictable combination of forces that can conspire to slow us down. It is within these limits, some laid out by the multiple perspectives, that individuals make their mark—or are marked. But, that said, the role of the two presidents in these two wars should give any determinist some pause. While a number of factors shape the behavior of individuals, they also differ quite significantly in how they respond to these factors, thus making it vital to understand those factors, the uniqueness of the individual, and the interaction between the two. . . .

NOTES

1. For the texts of major U.N. resolutions adopted in 1991, see *U.N. Security Resolutions on Iraq: Compliance and Implementation,* Report to the Committee on Foreign Affairs by the CRS (Washington, D.C.: GPO, March 1992).

2. This doctrine is encapsulated in chapter 5 of *The National Security Strategy of the United States of America* (Washington: The White House, September 2002).

3. For the text of U.N. Resolution 1441, see *Arms Control Today* 32 (December 2002), 28–32.

4. Bob Woodward, *Bush At War* (New York: Simon & Schuster), 341.

5. For details, see http://money.cnn.com/2003/02/25/news/economy/consumer/index.htm.

6. See Woodward, *Bush At War,* 344–49.

7. Interviewed by Tom Brokaw, "Commander-in-Chief: Inside the White House at War," aired on NBC 25 April 2003.

8. For classic analyses, see Sidney Hook, *The Hero In History*; Thomas Carlyle, *Sartor Resartus: On Heroes and Hero Worship* (1838; New York: E.P. Dutton, 1959); and Fred I. Greenstein, *Personality and Politics: Problems of Evidence, Inference and Conceptualization* (Princeton: Princeton University Press, 1969). . . .

CHAPTER 4

WAR AND VIOLENCE IN WORLD POLITICS
The Realist's World

For realists, war, the threat of war, and the preparation for war are at the core of international relations and must be central in the thinking of leaders of sovereign states. Since the end of the Cold War, the future of war has been a hotly debated topic, and many scholars have challenged long-held realist assumptions regarding the sources and nature of war in the international system. On this general topic, scholars can be divided into essentially three groups.

The first group focuses on the declining frequency of interstate war, and the most optimistic among them suggest that interstate war, at least among the great powers, may be obsolete. From a variety of perspectives, members of this group challenge essential realist assumptions about world politics. The second group argues that interstate war remains alive and well as a fact of international life and that a short-term cyclical downturn in the frequency of interstate war should not be mistaken for a permanent trend. This group is composed largely, though not exclusively, of realist thinkers. The third group accepts that the nature of war and the actors who engage in war have changed but stops short of embracing optimistic expectations of a more peaceful world. Indeed, some of the most pessimistic portraits of the future emerge from representatives of this group as they imagine a twenty-first–century world in which the use of violence by terrorists, including the possibility of use of weapons of mass destruction, undermines the traditional state monopoly on the use of violence in world politics.

In different ways, each of the selections in this chapter speaks to these larger perspectives on the role of war and violence in the twenty-first century. Robert Jervis provides a cautiously optimistic analysis of the peace that has prevailed among the great powers in recent decades and raises questions about the realist assumption that sustained peace among states requires the elimination of international anarchy. In contrast, Niall Ferguson's analysis of the sources of the violence that characterized the twentieth century leads him to suggest that world war in the twenty-first century remains a distinct possibility. Stephen Rosen's article considers the implications of nuclear proliferation on war and peace, and one of the concerns that he cites is the fear that proliferation might make it easier for terrorists to acquire such a weapon. However, John Mueller argues that fears of nuclear terrorism—and of terrorism in general—are exaggerated.

THEORIES OF WAR IN AN ERA OF LEADING-POWER PEACE

Robert Jervis

In this article, Robert Jervis, the former president of the American Political Science Association, describes the existence of a "security community" composed of the world's most developed nations in which the use of war to solve differences among them has become unthinkable. At the heart of the article is an attempt to explain this development from the perspectives of realism, liberalism, and constructivism. As you read his analysis, ask yourself:

⊛ According to Jervis how would realists, liberals, and constructivists explain this "security community"?

⊛ Is this "security community" likely to last and to expand in size?

⊛ How well do each of the three approaches (realism, liberalism, and constructivism) hold up in the face of the developments that Jervis discusses?

War and the possibility of war among the great powers have been the motor of international politics, not only strongly influencing the boundaries and distribution of values among them, but deeply affecting their internal arrangements and shaping the fates of smaller states. Being seen as an ever-present possibility produced by deeply rooted factors such as human nature and the lack of world government, these forces were expected to continue indefinitely. But I would argue that war among the leading great powers—the most developed states of the United States. West Europe, and Japan—will not occur in the future, and indeed is no longer a source of concern for them (Mueller 1989; also see Adler 1992; Duffield 2001; Goldgeier and McFaul 1992; Jervis 1991/1992; Mandelbaum 1998/1999; Shaw 1994; Singer and Wildavsky 1993; Ullman 1991; Van Evera 1990/1991). The absence of war among these states would itself be a development of enormous proportions, but the change goes even farther because war is not even contemplated. During the Cold War peace was maintained, but this was due to the fear that if the superpowers did not take care, they would indeed fight.

Now, however, the leading states form what Karl Deutsch called a pluralistic security community, a group among whom war is literally unthinkable—i.e., neither the publics nor the political elites nor even the military establishments expect war with each other (Deutsch et al. 1957; also see Adler and Barnett 1998; Melko 1973). No official in the Community would advocate a policy on the grounds that it would improve the state's position in the event of war with other members. Although no state can move away from the reliance on war by itself lest it become a victim, the collectivity can do so if each forsakes the resort to force.

Robert Jervis, excerpt from "Theories of War in an Era of Leading-Power Peace," *American Political Science Review,* 96:1, March 2002. Reprinted by permission of Cambridge University Press and the author.

Security communities are not unprecedented. But what is unprecedented is that the states that constitute this one are the leading members of the international system and so are natural rivals that in the past were central to the violent struggle for security, power, and contested values. Winston Churchill exaggerated only slightly when he declared that "people talked a lot of nonsense when they said nothing was ever settled by war. Nothing in history was ever settled *except* by wars" (quoted by Gilbert 1983, 860–1). Even cases of major change without war, such as Britain yielding hegemony in the Western Hemisphere to the United States at the turn of the 20th century, were strongly influenced by security calculations. Threatening war, preparing for it, and trying to avoid it have permeated all aspects of politics, and so a world in which war among the most developed states is unthinkable will be a new one. To paraphrase and extend a claim made by Evan Luard (1986, 77), given the scale and frequency of war among the great powers in the proceeding millennia, this is a change of spectacular proportions, perhaps the single most striking discontinuity that the history of international politics has anywhere provided.

Two major states, Russia and China, might fight each other or a member of the Community. But, as I discuss below, such a conflict would be different from traditional wars between great powers. Furthermore, these countries lack many of the attributes of great powers: their internal regimes are shaky, they are not at the forefront of any advanced forms of technology or economic organization, they can pose challenges only regionally, and they have no attraction as models for others. They are not among the most developed states and I think it would be fair to put them outside the ranks of the great powers as well. But their military potential, their possession of nuclear weapons, and the size of their economies renders that judgment easily debatable and so I will not press it but rather will argue that the set of states that form the Community are not all the great powers, but all the most developed ones.

Other states generally seen as Western also could fight, most obviously Greece and Turkey. Despite their common membership in NATO, the conflicts of interest are severe enough to lead each to contemplate war with the other. Neither is a leading power so this does not disturb my argument, although a thought-experiment that would transform them into such states without diminishing their animosity would.

CENTRAL QUESTIONS

Five questions arise. First, does the existence of the Community mean the end of security threats to its members and, more specifically, to the United States? Second, will the Community endure? Third, what are the causes of its construction and maintenance? Fourth, what are the implications of this transformation for the conduct of international affairs? Finally, what does this say about theories of the causes of war?

CONTINUED THREATS

The fact that the United States is not menaced by the most developed countries obviously does not mean that it does not face any military threats. Indeed, even before September 11 some analysts saw the United States as no more secure than it was during the Cold War, being imperiled by terrorists and "rogue" states, in addition to Russia and China. But even if I am wrong to believe that these claims are exaggerated, representing the political and psychological propensity for the "conservation of enemies" (Hartmann 1982; Mueller 1994); these conflicts do not have the potential to drive world politics the way that clashes among the leading powers did in the past. They do not permeate all facets of international politics and structure state–society relations; they do not represent a struggle for dominance in the international system or a direct challenge to American vital interests.

Even the fiercest foes of Russia, China, or the rogues do not see them as ready to launch unprovoked attacks against the United States or other members of the Community, let alone as out to control the world. Russia and China are not seeking to replace the United States; any clash will come out of these countries' desire for a sphere of influence and the American belief that such arrangements are inappropriate in today's world—at least for others. Thus while there are reasons why the United States might fight the PRC to protect Taiwan or Russia to protect the Baltic republics, these disputes are not like those that characterized great power conflicts over the past three centuries. The United States is defending not traditional national interests, let alone vital ones, but, in seeking what Wolfers (1962, 73–6) called "milieu goals," upholding values such as democracy, self-determination, and rejection of coercion as a means of changing the status quo. These may be deeply held both for their intrinsic value and for their role in maintaining America's worldwide reach, but they are more akin to the concerns of imperial powers than to sources of conflict between equal major powers.

WILL THE SECURITY COMMUNITY LAST?

Predictions about the maintenance of the Community are obviously disputable (indeed, limitations on people's ability to predict could undermine it), but nothing in the short period since the end of the Cold War points to an unraveling. The disputes within it do not seem to be increasing in number or severity and even analysts who stress the continuation of the struggle for world primacy and great power rivalries do not expect fighting [Huntington 1993; Kupchan 2002; Waltz 1993, 2000; however, Calleo (2001), Layne (2000), and Mearsheimer (1990, 2001) are ambiguous on this point]. If the United States is still concerned with maintaining its advantages over its allies, the reason is not that it believes that it may have to fight them but that it worries that rivalry could make managing world problems more difficult (Layne 2000; *New York Times,* March 8, 1992, 14; May 24, 1992, 1, 14). The Europeans' effort to establish an independent security force is aimed at permitting them to intervene when the United States chooses not to (or perhaps by threatening such action, to trigger American intervention), not at fighting the United States. Even if Europe were to unite and the world to become bipolar again, it is very unlikely that suspicions, fears for the future, and conflicts of interest would be severe enough to break the Community.

A greater threat would be the failure of Europe to unite coupled with an American withdrawal of forces, which could lead to "security competition" within Europe (Art 1996a; Mearsheimer 2001, 385–96). The fears would focus on Germany, but their magnitude is hard to gauge and it is difficult to estimate what external shocks or kinds of German behavior would activate them. The fact that Thatcher and Mitterrand opposed German unification is surely not forgotten in Germany and is an indication that concerns remain. But this danger is likely to constitute a self-denying prophecy in two ways. First, many Germans are aware of the need not only to reassure others by tying themselves to Europe, but also to make it unlikely that future generations of Germans would want to break these bonds even if they could. Second, Americans who worry about the residual danger will favor keeping some troops in Europe as the ultimate intra-European security guarantee.

Expectations of peace close off important routes to war. The main reason for Japanese aggression in the 1930s was the desire for a self-sufficient sphere that would permit Japan to fight the war with the Western powers that was seen as inevitable, not because of particular conflicts, but because it was believed that great powers always fight each other. In contrast, if states believe that a security community will last, they will not be hypersensitive to threats from within it and will not feel the need to undertake precautionary measures that could undermine the security of other members. Thus the United States is not disturbed that British and French nuclear missiles could destroy American cities, and while those two countries object to American plans for missile defense, they do not feel the need to increase their forces in response. As long as peace is believed to be very likely, the chance of inadvertent spirals of tension and threat is low.

Nevertheless, the point with which I began this section is unavoidable. World politics can change rapidly and saying that nothing foreseeable will dissolve the Community is not the same as saying that it will not dissolve (Betts 1992). To the extent that it rests on democracy and prosperity (see below), anything that would

undermine these would also undermine the Community. Drastic climate change could also shake the foundations of much that we have come to take for granted. But it is hard to see how dynamics at the international level (i.e., the normal trajectory of fears, disputes, and rivalries) could produce war among the leading states. In other words, the Community does not have within it the seeds of its own destruction.

Our faith in the continuation of this peace is increased to the extent that we think we understand its causes and have reason to believe that they will continue. This is our next topic.

EXPLANATIONS FOR THE SECURITY COMMUNITY

There are social constructivist, liberal, and realist explanations for the Community which, although preceding from different assumptions, invoke overlapping factors.

Constructivism

Constructivism points to the norms of nonviolence and shared identities that have led the advanced democracies to assume the role of each other's friend through the interaction of behavior and expectations. In contradistinction to the liberal and realist explanations, this downplays the importance of material factors and elevates ideas, images of oneself and others, and conceptions of appropriate conduct. The roots of the changes that have produced this enormous shift in international politics among some countries but not others are not specified in detail, but the process is a self-reinforcing one—a benign cycle of behavior, beliefs, and expectations.

People become socialized into attitudes, beliefs, and values that are conducive to peace. Individuals in the Community may see their own country as strong and good—and even better than others—but they do not espouse the virulent nationalism that was common in the past. Before World War I, one German figure could proclaim that the Germans were "the greatest civilized people known to history," while another declared that the Germans were "the chosen people of this century," which explains "why other people hate us. They do not understand us but they fear our tremendous spiritual superiority." Thomas Macaulay similarly wrote that the British were "the greatest and most highly civilized people that ever the world saw" and were "the acknowledged leaders of the human race in the causes of political improvement," while Senator Albert Beveridge proclaimed that "God has made us the master organizers of the world." These sentiments are shocking today because they are so at variance from what we have been taught to think about others and ourselves. We could not adopt these views without rejecting a broad set of beliefs and values. An understanding of the effects of such conceptions led the Europeans, and to an unfortunately lesser extent the Japanese, to denationalize and harmonize their textbooks after World War II and has similarly led countries with remaining enemies to follow a different path: the goals for the education of a 12-year-old child in Pakistan include the "ability to know all about India's evil designs about Pakistan; acknowledge and identify forces that may be working against Pakistan; understand the Kashmir problem" (quoted by Kumar 2001, 29).

For constructivists, the fact that all members of the Community are democracies is important not so much for the reasons given by liberals (see below) as for the sense of common identity that the similarity in regime has generated (Hampton 1998/1999, 240–4; Kahl 1998/1999; Risse-Kappen 1995; Wendt 1999, 353–7). The formation of common identities has been central to national integration (Cronin 1999; Deutsch 1953), and it stands to reason that it plays a major role not only in keeping states at peace, but in making war unthinkable. The evidence for shared identity within the Community is hard to find, however, or at least has not been produced (Cederman 2001). Moreover, constructivists say little about when and why shared identities disintegrate, as they do when a country lapses into civil war (Arfi 1998). Ironically, the spread of democracy might diminish the importance of democratic identity. The sense that being democratic is a vital part of one's self (as an individual or as a country) may diminish if it becomes less distinctive. Being democratic is highly salient when most others are not and when adversaries are hostile to democracy; in a world that is predominantly democratic, sources of identity may be different and more divisive.

The obvious objection to constructivism is that it mistakes effect for cause: its description is correct, but the identities, images, and self-images are superstructure, being the product of peace and of the material incentives discussed below. What is crucial is not people's thinking, but the factors that drive it. The validity of this claim is beyond the reach of current evidence, but what is clear is that the constructivist belief that the Community will last places great faith in the power of socialization and the ability of ideas to replicate and sustain themselves. This conception may betray an excessive faith in the validity of ideas that seem self-evident today but that our successors might reject. Constructivism may present us with actors who are "over-socialized" (Wrong 1976, Chap. 2) and leave too little role for agency in the form of people who think differently, perhaps because their material conditions are different.

Liberalism

The liberal explanation has received most attention. Although it comes in several variants, the central strands are the pacifying effects of democracy, economic interdependence, and joint membership in international organizations (Russett and Oneal 2001).

Democracy The members of the Community are democracies, and many scholars argue that democracies rarely if ever fight each other. Although the statistical evidence is, as usual, subject to debate, Jack Levy (1989, 88) is correct that this claim is "as close as anything we have to an empirical law in international politics."

Less secure, however, is our understanding of why this is the case. We have numerous explanations, which can be seen as competing or complementary. Democracies are systems of dispersed power, and dispersed power means multiple veto points and groups that could block war. (This seems true almost by definition, but if the accounts of former Soviet leaders are to be trusted, Brezhnev was more constrained by his colleagues than was Nixon, at least where arms control was concerned.) Related are the norms of these regimes: democracies function through compromise, nonviolence, and respect for law. To the extent that these values and habits govern foreign policy, they are conducive to peace, especially in relations with other democracies who reciprocate.

Other scholars have argued that the key element lies in the realm of information. By having a relatively free flow of intelligence and encouraging debate, democracies are less likely to make egregious errors in estimating what courses of action will maintain the peace (White 1990). The other side of the informational coin is that democracies can more effectively commit themselves and telegraph their intentions, and so avoid both unnecessary spirals of conflict and wars that stem from others' incorrect beliefs that the democracy is bluffing (although an obvious cost is an inability to bluff) (Fearon 1994; Schultz 2001; for qualifications and doubts, see Finel and Lord 2000).

The two parts of the informational argument can reinforce or be in tension with each other. If democratic processes make behavior highly predictable, then even dictatorships should be able to estimate what they will do, thereby reducing the distinctiveness of interactions among democracies. In fact, this does not seem to be the case, as the misjudgments of Hitler, Stalin and Saddam Hussein make clear. If democratic processes do not provide totally unambiguous evidence, however, one can conclude that predictability will be high only when each side both sends and receives information clearly, thereby explaining the advantages of democratic dyads.

Finally, in a recasting of the traditional argument that democracies are less likely to go to war because those who hold ultimate authority (i.e., the general public) will pay the price for conflict, some argue that the institutional and coalitional nature of democratic regimes requires their leaders to pursue successful policies if they are to stay in office (Bueno de Mesquita, Morrow, Siverson, and Smith 1999; Goemans 2000; a related argument is Snyder 1991). Thus democracies will put greater efforts into winning wars and be careful to choose to fight only wars they can win (Lake 1992; Reiter and Stam 1998). Autocracies have a narrower base and so can stay in power by buying off their supporters even if their foreign policies are unnecessarily costly. These arguments, while highly suggestive, share with earlier liberal thinking quite stylized assumptions about the preferences of societal actors and pay little attention to how each country anticipates the behavior of others and assesses how others expect it to behave.

The explanations for the democratic peace are thoughtful and often ingenious, but not conclusive. Many of them lead us to expect not only dyadic effects, but monadic ones as well—i.e., democracies should be generally peaceful, not just peaceful toward each other, a finding that most scholars deny (but not all: Rummel 1995). They also imply that one democracy would not seek to overthrow another, a proposition that is contradicted by American behavior during the Cold War. Furthermore, most of the arguments are built around dyads but it is not entirely clear that the posited causes would apply to multilateral groupings like the Community.

The more recent arguments implicitly dispute rather than fully engage older ones that focus on the obstacles to effective foreign policies in democracies: the fickleness of public opinion, the incentives that leaders have to seek short-run success at the cost of investing for the long run, the recruitment of inexperienced leaders, the parochialism that makes democracies prone to misunderstand others (Almond 1950; Lippmann 1955). Because extensive citizen participation can easily lead to emotional identification with the country, high levels of nationalism can be expected in democracies. Because public opinion has greater influence and pays only sporadic attention to foreign policy, consistency and commitments should be harder rather than easier for them. These once-familiar views may be incorrect, but they deserve careful attention.

The causal role of democracy is hard to establish because these regimes have been relatively rare until recently, much of the democratic peace can be explained by the Soviet threat, and the same factors that lead countries to become democratic are conducive to peace between them [e.g., being relatively rich and secure, resolving regional disputes (Thompson 1996)]. It is particularly important and difficult to control for the role of common interest, which loomed so large during the Cold War (Farber and Gowa 1995, 1997; also see Elman 1997; Layne 1994). But interests are not objective and may be strongly influenced by the country's internal regime. Thus the democracies may have

made common cause during the Cold War in part because they were democracies: common interest may be a mechanism by which the democratic peace is sustained as much as it is a competing explanation for it (for this and related issues, see Gartzke 1998, 2000; Maoz 1997; Oneal and Russett 1999; Schweller 2000). Moreover, if democracies are more likely to become economically interdependent with one another, additional common interest will be created. But to bring up the importance of interest is to highlight an ambiguity and raise a question. The ambiguity is whether the theory leads us to expect democracies *never* to fight each other or "merely" to fight *less* than do other dyads. The related hypothetical question is whether it impossible for two democracies to have a conflict of interest so severe that it leads to war. This troubles the stronger version of the argument because it is hard to answer in the affirmative.

But would democracies let such a potent conflict of interest develop? As striking as the statistical data is the fact—or rather the judgment—that the regimes that most disturbed the international order in the 20th century also devastated their own peoples—the USSR, Germany under the Nazis and, perhaps, under Kaiser Wilhelm. One reason for this connection may be the desire to remake the world (but because the international order was established by countries that were advanced democracies, it may not be surprising that those who opposed it were not). Not all murderous regimes are as ambitious (e.g., Idi Amin's Uganda), and others with both power and grand designs may remain restrained (e.g., Mao's China), but it is hard to understand the disruptive German and Soviet foreign policy without reference to their domestic regimes.

Interdependence The second leg of the liberal explanation for the Community is the high level of economic interdependence, which also could facilitate a common identity (Wendt 1994, 1999, 344–9), as earlier functional theorists of integration argued (Sterling-Folker 2000, 106–7). The basic argument was developed by Cobden, Bright, and the other 19th-century British liberals. As Cobden put it, "Free Trade is God's diplomacy and there is no other certain way of uniting people in bonds of peace." Although the evidence for this proposition remains in dispute, the causal story is straightforward. "If goods cannot cross borders, armies will" is the central claim, in the words of the 19th-century French economist Frederick Bastiat, which were often repeated by Secretary of State Cordell Hull. Extensive economic intercourse allows states to gain by trade the wealth that they would otherwise seek through fighting (Knorr 1966; Rosecrance 1986, 1999). Relatedly, individuals and groups develop a powerful stake in keeping the peace and maintaining good relations (but for evidence that bad relations do not necessarily impede trade, see Barbieri and Levy 1999). Thus it is particularly significant that in the contemporary world many firms have important ties abroad and that direct foreign investment holds the fates of important actors hostage to continued good relations (Milner 1988; Rosecrance 1986, Chap. 7). There can be a benign cycle here as increasing levels of trade strengthen the political power of actors who have a stake in deepening these ties (see, e.g., James and Lake 1989; Milner 1988). Furthermore, interdependence is more politically potent than it was in earlier eras because political leaders are now held accountable for the state of the economy and will be punished for a downturn.

The liberal view assumes that actors place a high priority on wealth, that trade is a better route to it than conquest, and that actors who gain economically from the exchange are politically powerful. These assumptions are often true, especially in the modern world, but are not without their vulnerabilities. At times honor and glory, in addition to more traditional forms of individual and national interest, can be more salient than economic gain. Thus as the Moroccan crisis of 1911 came to a head, General von Moltke wrote to his wife: "If we again slip away from this affair with our tail between our legs. . . . I shall despair of the future of the German Empire. I shall then retire. But before handing in my resignation I shall move to abolish the Army and to place ourselves under Japanese protectorate; we shall then be in a position to make money without interference and to develop into ninnies" (quoted by Berghahn 1973, 97). Traditional liberal thought understood this well and stressed that economic activity was so potent not only because it gave people an interest in maintaining peace, but because it reconstructed social values to downgrade status and glory and elevate material well-being (Hirschman 1977, 1986, Chaps. 3, 5; Schumpeter 1934). It follows that the stability of the Community rests in part upon people giving priority to consumption. Critics decry modern society's individualistic, material values, but one can easily imagine others that would generate greater international conflict.

Of course conquest can also bring wealth. The conventional wisdom that this is no longer true for modern economies, which depend less on agriculture and raw materials than on the intricate web of skilled tasks, has been challenged by Liberman's careful study of 20th-century conquests (1996a; also see Mearsheimer 2001, 148–52; for a partial rebuttal see Brooks 1999). But the net benefit from trade might have been even greater, especially when we consider the costs of arming and fighting. It also is not clear that conquered people will provide the innovation and ingenuity that produce wealth over the long run.

Here as elsewhere, expectations are crucial and this both strengthens and weakens the liberal argument. It strengthens it to the extent that most people believe that high levels of economic exchange strongly contribute to prosperity and expect tensions, let alone wars, to decrease trade and prosperity. But it is also important that people expect good economic relations to continue as long as their country does not disturb them. Since people set their policies by the predicted future benefits, even high levels of beneficial exchange will be ineffective if a deterioration is foreseen (Copeland 1996, 1999–2000).

Interdependence will have its pacifying effect only if actors who benefit from it are powerful. American social scientists often take for granted the model of contemporary American society in which this is the case and overlook the fact it is not universal. Thus Ripsman and Blanchard (1996/1997) note that while leading businessmen in Britain and Germany opposed World War I, just as liberalism leads us to expect, they were not powerful enough to force their preferences on their governments.

There are four general arguments against the pacific influence of interdependence. First, it is hard to go from the magnitude of economic flows to the costs that would be incurred if they were disrupted, and even more difficult to estimate how much political impact these costs will have, which depends on the other considerations at play and the political context. This means that we do not have a theory that tells us the magnitude of the effect. Second, even the sign of the effect can be disputed: interdependence can increase conflict as states gain bargaining leverage over each other, fear that others will exploit them, and face additional sources of disputes (Barbieri 1996; Keohane 2000, 2001; Waltz 1970, 1979, Chap. 7). These effects might not arise if states expect to remain at peace with each other, however. Third, it is clear that interdependence does not guarantee peace. High levels of economic integration did not prevent World War I, and nations that were much more unified than any security community have peacefully dissolved or fought civil wars. But this does not mean that interdependence is not conducive to peace.

Fourth, interdependence may be more an effect than a cause, more the product than a generator of expectations of peace and cooperation. Russett and Oneal (2001, 136) try to meet this objection by correlating the level of trade in one year, not with peace in that year, but with peace in the following one. But this does not get to the heart of the matter since trade the year before could be a product of expectations of future good relations.

Short of onerous and subjective coding of large numbers of cases to establish expectations about future relations, it may not be possible to ascertain which way the causal arrow runs. Indeed, it probably runs in both directions, with magnitudes that vary with other factors. But it is clear that the economic order in the current Community was premised on the belief that these countries could and had to remain at peace. One part of the reason was the lessons of the 1930s and the belief that economic rivalries led to political divisions and wars. Another part was the perceived threat from the Soviet Union, which, as Gowa (1994) has noted, meant that the fear of relative economic gains was eased if not reversed because partners' economic growth brought with it positive security externalities. This created a situation very different from that in the early 20th century when Britain and Germany, while heavily trading with each other, feared that the other's prosperity would endanger it. As one British observer put it after a trip to Germany in 1909: "every one of those new factory chimneys is a gun pointed at England" (quoted by Kennedy 1980, 315; but also see Liberman 1996b). Post-1945 European economic cooperation probably would not have occurred without American sponsorship, pressure, and security guarantees, and close American economic relations with Japan had similar political roots.

International Organizations Even those who argue for the pacifying effect of common memberships in international organizations aver that the magnitude of this effect is relatively slight, at least in the short run (Russett and Oneal 2001, Chap. 5), and so my discussion is brief. The causal mechanisms are believed to be several: enhanced information flows, greater ability to solve problems peacefully, an increased stake in cooperative behavior linked to the risk of being excluded from the organization if the state behaves badly, and possibly a heightened sense of common identity (Keohane 1984; much of the literature is summarized by Martin and Simmons 1998). Harder to pin down but perhaps most important are processes by which joint membership alters states' conceptions of their interest, leading them to see it not only as calling for cooperative reciprocations, but also as extending over a longer time-horizon and including benefits to others (Jervis 1999, 2001; March and Olsen 1998).

The obvious reasons to doubt the importance of shared institutional membership are that the incentives do not seem great enough to tame strong conflicts of interest and that membership may be endogenous to common interests and peaceful relations. States that expect war with each other are less likely to join the same international organizations and political conflicts that are the precursors to war may destroy the institutions or drive some members out, as Japan and Germany withdrew from the League of Nations during the 1930s. Even

with a strong correlation and reasonable control variables, the direction of causality is difficult to establish.

Realist Explanations

The crudest realist explanation for the Community would focus on the rise of the common threat from Russia and China. While not entirely implausible, this argument does not fit the views espoused by most elites in Japan and Europe, who are relatively unconcerned about these countries and believe that whatever dangers emanate from them would be magnified rather than decreased by a confrontational policy.

American Hegemony Two other realist accounts are stronger. The first argues that the Community is largely the product of the other enormous change in world politics—the American dominance of world politics. U.S. defense spending, to take the most easily quantifiable indicator, is now greater than that of the next eight countries combined (O'Hanlon 2001, 4–5). Furthermore, thanks to the Japanese constitution and the integration of armed forces within NATO, America's allies do not have to fear attacks from each other: their militaries—especially Germany's—are so truncated that they could not fight a major war without American assistance or attack each other without undertaking a military build-up that would give a great deal of warning. American dominance also leads us to expect that key outcomes, from the expansion of NATO, to the American-led wars in Kosovo and the Persian Gulf, to the IMF bailouts of Turkey and Argentina in the spring and summer of 2001 and the abandonment of the latter six months later, will conform to American preferences.

But closer examination reveals differences between current and past hegemonies. The U.S. usually gives considerable weight to its partners' views, and indeed its own preferences are often influenced by theirs, as was true in Kosovo. For their parts, the other members of the Community seek to harness and constrain American power, not displace it. The American hegemony will surely eventually decay but increased European and Japanese strength need not lead to war, contrary to the expectations of standard theories of hegemony and great power rivalry. Unlike previous eras of hegemony, the current peace seems uncoerced and accepted by most states, which does not fit entirely well with realism.

Nuclear Weapons The second realist argument was familiar during the Cold War but receives less attention now. This is the pacifying effect of nuclear weapons, which, if possessed in sufficient numbers and invulnerable configurations, make victory impossible and war a feckless option. An immediate objection is that not all the major states in the Community have nuclear weapons. But this is only technically correct: Germany and Japan could produce nuclear weapons if a threat loomed, as their partners fully understand. The other factors discussed in the previous pages may or may not be important; the nuclear revolution by itself would be sufficient to keep the great powers at peace.

While there is a great deal to this argument, it is not without its problems. First, because this kind of deterrence rests on the perceived possibility of war, it may explain peace, but not a security community. Second, mutual deterrence can be used as a platform for hostility, coercion, and even limited wars. In what Glenn Snyder (1965; also see Jervis 1989, 19–23, 74–106) calls the stability–instability paradox, the common realization that all-out war would be irrational provides a license for threats and lower levels of violence. In some circumstances a state could use the shared fear of nuclear war to exploit others. If the state thinks

that the other is preoccupied with the possibility of war and does not anticipate that the state will make the concessions needed to reduce this danger, it will expect the other to retreat and so can stand firm. In other words, the fact that war would be the worst possible outcome for both sides does not automatically lead to uncoerced peace, let alone to a security community. . . .

IMPLICATIONS

What are the implications of the existence of the security community for international politics in the rest of the world, for how the most developed states will carry out relations among themselves, and for general theories of war and peace?

International Politics in the Rest of the World

One obvious question is why the leading powers but not others have formed a security community. The preceeding discussion implies that the outcome is overdetermined. Compared to others, the states in the Community are richer, more democratic, more satisfied with the status quo, would lose more in a war, and have a more explicit American security guarantee. Furthermore, they were the core of the anti-Soviet coalition during the Cold War, which produced benefical path-dependent results. This does not mean that other security communities will not form, but only that they are not likely to fit the pattern discussed here.

Despite the fact that war is thinkable outside the Community, it is striking that several other regions appear to be peaceful, most obviously South America. The reasons remain unclear but may include the role of the superpowers in controlling dangerous conflicts during the Cold War, American hegemony more recently, and the example of peace among the developed countries. Although war remains possible, even a pessimist would have to note that there is little evidence that the countries outside the Community will recapitulate Europe's bloody history. For these countries, the main security danger stems from the civil wars and insurgencies, either of which can lead to interstate war (Herbst 2000; Holsti 1996). These developments are beyond the scope of this article, but the obvious challenge would be to bring them and the Community into a common theory.

International Politics Within the Community

In previous eras, no aspect of international politics and few aspects of domestic politics were untouched by the anticipation of future wars among the leading powers. As Charles Tilly (1990, 74) put it, "Over the millennium as a whole, war has been the dominant activity of European states." Much will then change in the Community. In the absence of these states amalgamating—a development that is out of the question outside of Europe and unlikely within it—they will neither consider using force against one another nor lose their sovereignty. There will then be significant conflicts of interest without clear means of resolving them. The states will continue to be rivals in some respects, and to bargain with each other. Indeed, the stability–instability paradox implies that the shared expectation that disputes will remain peaceful will remove some restraints on vituperation and competitive tactics. The dense network of institutions within the community should serve to provide multiple means for controlling conflicts but will also provide multiple ways for a dissatisfied country to show its displeasure and threaten disruption.

The fact that the situation is a new one poses challenges and opportunities for states. What goals will have highest priority? Will non-military alliances form? How important will

status be and what will give it? Bargaining will continue, and this means that varieties of power, including the ability to help and hurt others, will still be relevant. Threats, bluffs, warnings, the mobilization of resources for future conflicts, intense diplomatic negotiations, and shifting patterns of working with and against others all will remain. But the content of these forms will differ from those of traditional international politics.

Politics within the Community may come to resemble the relations among the United States and Canada and Australia, which Keohane and Nye (1977) described as complex interdependence: extensive transnational and transgovernmental relations, negotiations conducted across different issue areas, and bargaining power gained through asymmetric dependence but limited by overall common interests. Despite this path-breaking study, however, we know little about how this kind of politics will be carried out. As numerous commentators have noted, economic issues and economic resources will play large roles, but the changed context will matter. Relative economic advantage was sought in the past in part because it contributed to military security. This no longer being the case, the possibilities for cooperation are increased. States will still seek economic benefit, but will care about whether others are gaining more than they are only if they believe that this can produce political leverage or future economic benefits. The range of cases in which the latter is true is now thought to be fairly small, however (see, e.g., Busch 1999; Krugman 1991).

Even though force will not be threatened within the Community, it will remain important in relations among its members. During the Cold War the protection the United States afforded to its allies gave it an added moral claim and significant bargaining leverage. Despite the decreased level of threat, this will be true for the indefinite future because militarily

Japan and Europe need the United States more than the United States needs them. While the unique American ability to lead military operations such as those in the Persian Gulf and Kosovo causes resentments and frictions, it also provides a resource that is potent even—or especially—if it is never explicitly brought to the table.

Four Possible Futures Even within the contours of a Community, a significant range of patterns of relations is possible, four of which can be briefly sketched.

The greatest change would be a world in which national autonomy would be further diminished and the distinctions between domestic and foreign policy would continue to erode. Medieval Europe, with its overlapping forms of sovereignty rather than compartmentalized nation-states, which might dissolve because they are no longer needed to provided security and can no longer control their economies, is one model here (Bull 1977 264–76; Cerny 1993; Lipschutz 2000; Osiander 2001; Rosenau 1990; van Creveld 1999; for a discussion of how the changed environment will affect state structures and strength, see Desch 1996). Although most scholars see the reduction of sovereignty and the growth of the power of nongovernmental organizations as conducive to peace and harmony, one can readily imagine sharp conflicts, for example, among business interests, labor, and environmentalists; between those with different views of the good life; and between those calling for greater centralization to solve common problems and those advocating increased local control. But state power and interest would in any case greatly decrease and the notion of "national interest", always contested, would become even more problematic.

A second world, not completely incompatible with the first, would be one in which states in the Community play a large role, but with more extensive and intensive cooperation, presumably produced and accompanied by the internalization of the interests of others and stronger institutions (Keohane 2000). A possible model would be the United States before the Civil War (Deudney 1995). Relations would be increasingly governed by principles, laws, and persuasion rather than by more direct forms of power (Lukes 1974; Nye 1990), a change that could benignly spill over into relations outside the Community. Although bargaining would not disappear, there would be more joint efforts to solve common problems and the line between "high" and "low" politics would become even more blurred.

In this world, the United States would share more power and responsibility with the rest of the Community than is true today. While popular with scholars (e.g., Ikenberry 2001; Ruggie 1996), at least as likely is a continuation of the present trajectory in which the United States maintains hegemony and rejects significant limitations on its freedom of action. National interests would remain distinct and the United States would follow the familiar pattern in which ambitions and perceived interests expand as power does. Consistent with the continuing concern with competitive advantages (Mearsheimer 2001), both conflicts of interests and the belief that hegemony best produces collective goods would lead the United States to oppose the efforts of others to become a counterweight if not a rival to it (Art 1996a). In effect, the United States would lead an empire, albeit a relatively benign one. But doing so would be complicated by the American self-image that precludes it from seeing its role for what it is, in part because of the popularity of values of equality and supranationalism. Other members of the Community would resent having their interests overridden by the

United States on some occasions, but the exploitation would be limited by their bargaining power and the American realization that excessive discontent would have serious long-term consequences. So others might accept these costs in return for U.S. security guarantees and the ability to keep their own defense spending very low, especially because the alternative to American-dominated stability might be worse.

The fourth model also starts with the American attempt to maintain hegemony, but this time the burdens of American unilateralism become sufficient to produce a counter-balancing coalition, one that might include Russia and China as well (Waltz 1999, 2000; Layne 2000). Europe and Japan might also become more assertive because they fear not U.S. domination but the eventual withdrawal of the U.S. security guarantee. In this world, much that realism stresses—the clash of national interests, the weakness of international institutions, maneuvering for advantage, and the use of power and threats—would come to the fore, but with the vital difference that force would not be contemplated and the military balance would enter in only indirectly, as discussed above. This would be a strange mixture of the new and the familiar, and the central question is what *ultima ratio* will replace cannons. What will be the final arbiter of disputes? What kinds of threats will be most potent? How fungible will the relevant forms of power be?

Outlining these possibilities raises two broad questions that I cannot answer. First, is the future essentially determined, as many structural theories would imply, or does it depend on national choices strongly influenced by domestic politics, leaders, and accidents? Second, if the future is not determined, how much depends on choices the United States has yet to make, and what will most influence these choices?

IMPLICATIONS FOR THEORIES OF THE CAUSES OF WAR

Whatever its explanation, the very existence of a security community among the leading powers refutes many theories of the causes of war or, at least, indicates that they are not universally valid. Thus human nature and the drive for dominance, honor, and glory may exist and contribute to a wide variety of human behaviors, but they are not fated to lead to war.

The obvious rebuttal is that war still exists outside the Community and that civil wars continue unabated. But only wars fought by members of the Community have the potential to undermine the argument that, under some conditions, attributes of humans and societies that were seen as inevitably producing wars in fact do not do so. The cases that could be marshaled are the Gulf War and the operation in Kosovo, but they do not help these theories. These wars were provoked by others, gained little honor and glory for the Community, and were fought in a manner that minimized the loss of life on the other side. It would be hard to portray them as manifestations of brutal or evil human nature. Indeed, it is more plausible to see the Community's behavior as consistent with a general trend toward its becoming less violent generally: the abolition of official torture and the decreased appeal of capital punishment, to take the most salient examples (Mueller 1989).

The existence of the Community also casts doubt on theories that argue that the leading powers always are willing to use force in a struggle for material gain, status, and dominance. Traditional Marxism claims that capitalists could never cooperate; proponents of the law of uneven growth see changes in the relative power of major states as producing cycles of domination, stability, challenge, and war (Gilpin 1981; Kennedy 1987). Similarly, "power transitions" in which rising powers catch up with dominant ones are seen as very difficult to manage peacefully (Kugler and Lemke 1996; Organski and Kugler 1980; also see Modelski 1987; Thompson 1988). These theories, like the version of hegemonic stability discussed above, have yet to be tested because the United States has not yet declined. But if the arguments made here are correct, transitions will not have the same violent outcome that they had in the past, leading us to pay greater attention to the conditions under which these theories do and do not hold.

For most scholars, the fundamental cause of war is international anarchy, compounded by the security dilemma. These forces press hardest on the leading powers because while they may be able to guarantee the security of others, no one can provide this escape from the state of nature for them. As we have seen, different schools of thought propose different explanations for the rise of the Community and so lead to somewhat different propositions about the conditions under which anarchy can be compatible with peace. But what is most important is that the Community constitutes a proof by existence of the possibility of uncoerced peace without central authority. Because these countries are the most powerful ones and particularly war-prone, the Community poses a fundamental challenge to our understanding of world politics and our expectations of future possibilities.

REFERENCES

Adler, Emanuel. 1992. "Europe's New Security Order." In *The Future of European Security,* ed. Beverly Crawford. Berkeley: University of California Institute for International and Area Studies. Pp. 287–326.

Adler, Emanuel, and Michael Barnett, eds. 1998. *Security Communities.* Cambridge: Cambridge University Press.

Almond, Gabriel A. 1950. *The American People and Foreign Policy,* New York: Harcourt Brace.

Arfi, Badredine. 1998. "Ethnic Fear: The Social Construction of Insecurity." *Security Studies* 8 (Autumn): 151–203.

Aron, Raymond. 1966. *Peace and War.* Translated by Richard Howard and Annette B. Fox. Garden City, NY: Doubleday.

Art, Robert J. 1996a. "Why Western Europe Needs the United States and NATO." *Political Science Quarterly* 111 (Spring): 1–39.

Art, Robert J. 1996b. "American Foreign Policy and the Fungibility of Force." *Security Studies* 5 (Summer): 7–42.

Art, Robert J. 1999. "Force and Fungibility Reconsidered." *Security Studies* 8 (Summer): 183–189.

Baldwin, David A. 1999. "Force, Fungibility, and Influence." *Security Studies* 8 (Summer): 173–182.

Barbieri, Katherine. 1996. "Economic Interdependence: A Path to Peace or a Source of Interstate Conflict?" *Journal of Peace Research* 33 (February): 29–49.

Barbieri, Katherine, and Jack S. Levy. 1999. "Sleeping with the Enemy: The Impact of War on Trade." *Journal of Peace Research* 36 (July): 463–79.

Barkawi, Tarak, and Mark Laffey. 1999. "The Imperial Peace: Democracy, Force and Globalization." *European Journal of International Relations* 5 (December): 403–34.

Beck, Nathaniel, and Jonathan N. Katz. 2001. "Throwing the Baby Out With the Bath Water: A Comment on Green, Kim, and Yoon." *International Organization* 55 (Spring): 487–96.

Berghahn, V. R. 1973. *Germany and the Approach of War in 1914.* New York: St. Martin's Press.

Betts, Richard. 1992. "Systems of Peace or Causes of War? Collective Security, Arms Control, and the New Europe." *International Security* 17 (Summer): 5–43.

Bourne, Kenneth. 1970. *The Foreign Policy of Victorian England: 1830–1902.* Oxford: Clarendon Press.

Brooks, Stephen G. 1999. "The Globalization of Production and the Changing Benefits of Conquest." *Journal of Conflict Resolution* 43 (October): 646–70.

Bueno de Mesquita, Bruce, James Morrow, Randolph Siverson, and Alastair Smith. 1999. "An Institutional Explanation of the Democratic Peace." *American Political Science Review* 93 (December): 791–807.

Bull, Hedley. 1977. *The Anarchical Society: A Study of Order in World Politics.* New York: Columbia University Press.

Busch, Marc L. 1999. *Trade Warriors: States, Firms, and Strategic-Trade Policy in High-Technology Competition.* Cambridge: Cambridge University Press.

Cain, Peter. 1979. "Capitalism. War and Internationalism in the Thought of Richard Cobden." *British Journal of International Studies* 5 (October): 229–47.

Calleo, David. P. 2001. *Rethinking Europe's Future.* Princeton: Princeton University Press.

Cederman, Lars-Erik, ed. 2001. *Constructing Europe's Identity: The External Dimension.* Boulder, CO: Lynne Rienner.

Cerny, Philip G. 1992. "Plurilateralism: Structural Differentiation and Functional Conflict in the Post-Cold War World Order. *Millennium* 22 (Spring): 27–51.

Copeland, Dale C. 1996. "Economic Interdependence and War: A Theory of Trade Expectations." *International Security* 20 (Spring): 5–42.

Copeland, Dale C. 1999–2000. "Trade Expectations and the Outbreak of Peace: Détente 1970–74 and the End of the Cold War 1985–91." *Security Studies* 9 (Autumn-Winter): 15–59.

Cronin, Bruce. 1999. *Community Under Anarchy: Transnational Identity and the Evolution of Cooperation.* New York: Columbia University Press.

Desch, Michael C. 1996. "War and Strong States, Peace and Weak States?" *International Organization* 50 (Spring): 237–68.

Deudney, Daniel H. 1995. "The Philadelphia System: Sovereignty, Arms Control, and Balance of Power in the American States-Union Circa 1787–1861." *International Organization.* 49 (Spring): 191–228.

Deutsch, Karl W. 1953. *Nationalism and Social Communication.* New York: Wiley.

Deutsch, Karl W., et al. 1957. *Political Community and the North Atlantic Area: International Organizations in the Light of Historical Experience.* Princeton, NJ: Princeton University Press.

Deutsch, Morton. 1973. *The Resolution of Conflict: Constructive and Destructive Processes.* New Haven, CT: Yale University Press.

Diehl, Paul F., ed. 1999. *A Road Map to War: Territorial Dimensions on International Conflict.* Nashville: Vanderbilt University Press.

Duffield, John S. 2001. "Transatlantic Relations After the Cold War: Theory, Evidence, and the Future." *International Studies Perspectives* 2 (February): 93–115.

Elman, Miriam F., ed. 1997. *Paths to Peace: Is Democracy the Answer?* Cambridge, MA: MIT Press.

Farber, Henry, and Joanne Gowa. 1995. "Polities and Peace." *International Security* 20 (Fall): 123–46.

Farber, Henry, and Joanne Gowa. 1997. "Common Interests or Common Polities?" *Journal of Politics* 59 (May): 123–46.

Fearon, James D. 1994. "Domestic Political Audiences and the Escalation of International Disputes." *American Political Science Review* 88 (September): 577–92.

Finel, Bernard I., and Kristin M. Lord, eds. 2000. *Power and Conflict in the Age of Transparency.* New York: Palgrave.

Gartzke, Erik. 1998. "Kant We All Get Along? Motive, Opportunity, and the Origins of the Democratic Peace." *American Journal of Political Science* 42 (1): 1–27.

Gartzke, Erik. 2000. "Preferences and Democratic Peace." *International Studies Quarterly* 44 (June): 191–212.

Gartzke, Erik, Quan Li, and Charles Boehmer. 2001. "Investing in the Peace: Economic Interdependence and International Conflict." *International Organization* 55 (Spring): 391–438.

Gowa, Joanne. 1994. *Allies, Adversaries, and International Trade.* Princeton, NJ: Princeton University Press.

Gowa, Joanne. 1999. *Ballots and Bullets: The Elusive Democratic Peace.* Princeton, NJ: Princeton University Press.

Gilbert, Martin. 1983. *Winston S. Churchill, Vol. VI, Finest Hour 1939–1941.* London: Heinemann.

Gill, Stephen. 1990. *American Hegemony and the Trilateral Commission.* New York: Cambridge University Press.

Gilpin, Robert. 1981. *War and Change in World Politics.* Cambridge: Cambridge University Press.

Goemans, H. E. 2000. *War and Punishment: The Causes of War Termination and the First World War.* Princeton, NJ: Princeton University Press.

Goldgeier, James M., and Michael McFaul. 1992. "A Tale of Two Worlds: Core and Periphery in the Post-Cold War Era." *International Organization* 46 (Spring): 467–91.

Green, Donald P., Kim, Soo Yeon, and Yoon, David H. 2001. "Dirty Pool." *International Organization* 55 (Spring): 441–68.

Grieco, Joseph M. 1990. *Cooperation Among Nations: Europe, America, and Non-Tariff Barriers to Trade.* Ithaca, NY: Cornell University Press.

Halliday, Fred. 1994. *Rethinking International Relations.* Vancouver: University of British Columbia Press.

Hampton, Mary N. 1998/1999. "NATO, Germany, and the United States: Creating Positive Identity in Trans-Atlantia." *Security Studies* 8 (Winter–Spring): 235–69.

Harbaugh, William Henry. 1961. *The Life and Times of Theodore Roosevelt,* New York: Collier Books.

Hartmann, Frederick H. 1982. *The Conservation of Enemies: A Study in Enmity.* Westport, CT: Greenwood Press.

Hensel, Paul R. 2000. "Territory: Theory and Evidence on Geography and Conflict." In *What Do We Know About War?,* ed. John A. Vasquez, New York: Rowman and Littlefield. Pp. 57–84.

Herbst, Jeffrey. 2000. *States and Power in Africa: Comparative Lessons in Authority and Control.* Princeton NJ: Princeton University Press.

Hirschman, Albert O. 1945. *National Power and the Structure of Foreign Trade.* Berkeley and Los Angeles: University of California Press.

Hirschman, Albert O. 1977. *The Passions and the Interests: Political Arguments for Capitalism Before Its Triumph.* Princeton, NJ: Princeton University Press.

Hirschman, Albert O. 1986. *Rival Views of Market Societies and Other Recent Essays.* New York: Viking.

Hoffmann, Stanley. 1961. "International Systems and International Law." In *The International System,* eds. Klaus Knorr and Sidney Verba. Princeton, NJ: Princeton University Press. Pp. 205–37.

Holsti, K. J. 1996. *The State, War, and the State of War.* New York: Cambridge University Press.

Hull, Cordell. 1948. *The Memoirs of Cordell Hull,* Vol. 1. New York: Macmillan.

Huntington, Samuel P. 1993. "Why International Primacy Matters." *International Security* 17 (Spring): 68–83.

Hurrell, Andrew. 1998. "An Emerging Security Community in South America?" In *Security Communities,* eds. Emanuel Adler and Michael Barnett. Cambridge: Cambridge University Press. Pp. 228–64.

Huth, Paul K. 1996 *Standing Your Ground: Territorial Disputes and International Conflict.* Ann Arbor: University of Michigan Press.

Huth, Paul K. 2000. "Territory: Why are Territorial Disputes Between States a Central Cause of International Conflict?" In *What Do We Know About War?* ed. John A. Vasquez. New York: Rowman and Littlefield. Pp. 85–110.

Ikenberry, John G. 2001. *After Victory: Institutions. Strategic Restraint, and the Rebuilding of Order After Major Wars.* Princeton, NJ: Princeton University Press.

Inglehart, Ronald. 1977. *The Silent Revolution: Changing Values and Political Styles Among Western Publics.* Princeton, NJ: Princeton University Press.

Inglehart, Ronald. 1997. *Modernization and Postmodernization: Cultural. Economic, and Political Change in 43 Societies.* Princeton, NJ: Princeton University Press.

James, Scott, and David Lake. 1989. "The Second Face of Hegemony: Britain's Repeal of the Corn Laws and the American Walker Tariff of 1846." *International Organization* 43 (Winter): 1–30.

Jervis, Robert. 1989. *The Meaning of Nuclear Revolution: Statecraft and the Prospect of Armageddon.* Ithaca, NY: Cornell University Press.

Jervis, Robert. 1991/1992. "The Future of World Politics: Will It Resemble the Past?" *International Security* 16 (Winter): 39–73.

Jervis, Robert. 1997. *System Effects: Complexity in Political and Social Life.* Princeton, NJ: Princeton University Press.

Jervis, Robert. 1999. "Neorealism, Neoliberalism, and Cooperation: Understanding the Debate." *International Security* 24 (Summer): 42–63.

Jervis, Robert. 2002. "Comment on Schweller and Institutions." *International Security.*

Kacowicz, Arie M. 1998. *Zones of Peace in the Third World: South America and West Africa in Comparative Perspective.* Albany, NY: State University of New York Press.

Kahl, Colin H. 1998/1999. "Constructing a Separate Peace: Constructivism. Collective Liberal Identity, and Democratic Peace." *Security Studies* 8 (Winter-Spring): 94–144.

Kaufman, Stuart J. 2001. "The End of Anarchism: The Society of Nations, Institutions, and the Decline of War." Paper presented at the 2001 Annual Meeting of the International Studies Association, Chicago.

Keohane, Robert O. 1984. *After Hegemony: Cooperation and Discord in the World Political Economy.* Princeton, NJ: Princeton University Press.

Keohane, Robert O. 2001. "Governance in a Partially Globalized World." *American Political Science Review* 95 (March): 1–14.

Keohane, Robert O., and Joseph Nye, eds. 1977. *Power and Interdependence: World Politics in Transition.* Boston: Little, Brown.

Kennedy, Paul. 1980. *The Rise of Anglo-German Antagonism, 1860–1914.* Boston: George Allen and Unwin.

Kennedy, Paul. 1987. *The Rise and Fall of Great Powers: Economic Change and Military Conflict from 1500–2000.* New York: Random House.

King, Gary. 2001. "Proper Nouns and Methodological Propriety: Pooling Dyads in International Relations Data." *International Organization* 55 (Spring): 497–507.

Knorr, Klaus. 1966. *On the Uses of Military Power in the Nuclear Age.* Princeton, NJ: Princeton University Press.

Krugman, Paul. 1991. *Rethinking International Trade,* Cambridge, MA: MIT Press.

Kugler, Jacek, and Douglas Lemke, eds. 1996. *Parity and War: Evaluations and Extensions of The War Ledger.* Ann Arbor: University of Michigan Press.

Kumar, Amitava. 2001. "Bristling on the Subcontinent." *The Nation* April 23: 29–30.

Kupchan, Charles. 2002. *The End of the American Era.* New York: Knopf.

Lake, David. 1992. "Powerful Pacifists: Democratic States and War." *American Political Science Review* 86 (March): 24–37.

Layne, Christopher. 1994. "Kant or Cant: The Myth of the Democratic Peace." *International Security* 19 (Fall 1994): 5–49.

Layne, Christopher. 2000. "US Hegemony and the Perpetuation of NATO." *Journal of Strategic Studies* 23 (September): 59–91.

Levy, Jack S. 1989. "Domestic Politics and War." In *The Origins and Prevention of Major Wars,* eds. Robert I. Rotberg and Theodore K. Rabb. Cambridge: Cambridge University Press. Pp. 79–100.

Liberman, Peter. 1996a. *Does Conquest Pay? The Exploitation of Occupied Industrial Societies.* Princeton, NJ: Princeton University Press.

Liberman, Peter. 1996b. "Trading with the Enemy: Security and Relative Economic Gains." *International Security* 21 (Summer): 147–75.

Lippmann, Walter. 1955. *Essays in the Public Philosophy.* Boston: Little, Brown.

Lipschutz, Ronnie D. 2000. *After Authority: War, Peace, and Global Politics in the 21st Century.* Albany: SUNY Press.

Luard, Evan. 1986. *War in International Society: A Study in International Sociology.* London: I. B. Tauris.

Lukes, Steven. 1974. *Power: A Radical View.* London: Macmillan.

Mandelbaum, Michael. 1998/1999. "Is Major War Obsolete?" *Survival* 40 (Winter): 20–38.

Mansfield, Edward, and Jack Snyder. 1995. "Democratization and the Danger of War." *International Security* 20 (Summer): 5–38.

Maoz, Zeev. 1997. "The Controversy Over the Democratic Peace: Rearguard Action or Cracks in the Wall?" *International Security* 22 (Summer): 162–98.

March, James G., and Johan P. Olsen. 1998. "The Institutional Dynamics of International Political Orders." *International Organization* 52 (Autumn): 943–69.

Mares, David R. 2001. *Violent Peace: Militarized Interstate Bargaining in Latin America.* New York: Columbia University Press.

Martin, Lisa L., and Beth Simmons. 1998. "Theories and Empirical Studies of International Institutions." *International Organization* 52 (Autumn): 729–57.

Martin-Gonzalez, Felix. 1998. *The Longer Peace in South America, 1935–1995.* Unpublished Ph.D. dissertation. New York: Department of Political Science, Columbia University.

Mastanduno, Michael. 1991. "Do Relative Gains Matter? America's Response to Japanese Industrial Policy." *International Security* 16 (Summer): 73–113.

McMillan, Susan M. 1997. "Interdependence and Conflict." *Mershon International Studies Review* 41, Supplement 1 (May): 33–58.

Mearsheimer, John J. 1990. "Back to the Future: Instability in Europe After the Cold War." *International Security* 15 (Summer): 5–56.

Mearsheimer, John J. 2001. *The Tragedy of Great Power Politics.* New York: Norton.

Melko, Matthew, 1973. *52 Peaceful Societies.* Ontario: CPRI Press.

Milner, Helen V. 1988. *Resisting Protectionism: Global Industries and the Politics of International Trade.* Princeton, NJ: Princeton University Press.

Modelski, George. 1987. *Long Cycles in World Politics.* Seattle: University of Washington Press.

Morrow, James D. 1999. "How Could Trade Affect Conflict?" *Journal of Peace Research* 36 (4): 481–9.

Mueller, John. 1989. *Retreat from Doomsday: The Obsolescence of Major War.* New York: Basic Books.

Mueller, John. 1994. "The Catastrophe Quota: Trouble After the Civil War." *Journal of Conflict Resolution* 38 (September): 355–75.

Mueller, John. 1995. *Quiet Cataclysm: Reflections on the Recent Transformation of World Politics.* New York: HarperCollins.

Mueller, John. 2001. "The Remnants of War: Thugs as Residual Combatants." Unpublished paper. Columbus: Department of Political Science, Ohio State University.

Nye, Joseph S. 1990. *Bound to Lead: The Changing Nature of American Power.* New York: Basic Books.

O'Hanlon, Michael E. 2001. *Defense Policy Choices for the Bush Administration.* Washington, DC: Brookings Institution Press.

Oneal, John R., and Bruce Russett. 1999. "Is the Liberal Peace Just an Artifact of Cold War Interests? Assessing Recent Critiques." *International Interactions* 25 (3): 213–41.

Oneal, John R., and Bruce Russett. 2001. "Clear and Clean: The Fixed Effects of Liberal Peace." *International Organization* 55 (Spring): 469–86.

Organski, A. F. K., and Jacek Kugler, 1980. *The War Ledger.* Chicago: University of Chicago Press.

Owen, John, 1997. *Liberal Peace, Liberal War: American Politics and International Security.* Ithaca. NY: Cornell University Press.

Ray, James Lee. 1995. *Democracy and International Politics: An Evaluation of the Democratic Peace Proposition.* Columbia: University of South Carolina Press.

Ray, James Lee. 1998. "Does Democracy Cause Peace?" *Annual Review of Political Science, Vol. 1.* Palo Alto, CA: Annual Reviews.

Reiter, Dan, and Allan Stam III. 1998. "Democracy, War Initiation, and Victory." *American Political Science Review* 92 (June): 377–90.

Ripsman, Norrin M., and Jean-Marc F. Blanchard. 1996/1997. "Commercial Liberalism under Fire: Evidence from 1914 and 1936." *Security Studies* 6 (Winter): 4–51.

Risse-Kappen, Thomas. 1995. "Democratic Peace-Warlike Democracies? A Social Constructivist Interpretation of the Liberal Argument." *European Journal of International Relations* 1 (December): 491–517.

Rokeach, Milton, and Louis Mezei. 1966. "Race and Shared Belied as Factors in Social Choice." *Science* 151 (January 14): 167–72.

Rosecrance, Richard. 1986. *The Rise of the Trading State: Commerce and Conquest in the Modern World.* New York: Basic Books.

Rosecrance, Richard. 1999. *The Rise of the Virtual State: Wealth and Power in the Coming Century.* New York: Basic Books.

Rosenau. James N. 1990. *Turbulence in World Politics: A Theory of Change and Continuity.* Princeton, NJ: Princeton University Press.

Ruggie, John G. 1996. *Winning the Peace: American and World Order in the New Era.* New York: Columbia University Press.

Rummel, R. J. 1995. "Democracies ARE Less Warlike Than Other Regimes." *European Journal of International Relations* 1 (March): 457–79.

Russett, Bruce. 1993. *Grasping the Democratic Peace: Principles for a Post-Cold War World.* Princeton, NJ: Princeton University Press.

Russett, Bruce, and John R. Oneal. 2001. *Triangulating Peace: Democracy, Interdependence, and International Organizations.* New York: Norton.

Schultz, Kenneth A. 2001. *Democracy and Coercive Diplomacy.* New York: Cambridge University Press.

Schumpeter, Joseph. 1934. *The Theory of Economic Development.* Cambridge, MA: Harvard University Press.

Schweller, Randall L. 2000. "Democracy and the Post-Cold War Era." In *The New World Order,* eds. Birthe Hansen and Bertel Heurlin. New York: St. Martin's Press. Pp. 46–80.

Shaw, Martin. 1994. *Global Society and International Relations.* Cambridge: Polity Press.

Shaw, Martin. 2000. *Theory of the Global State.* New York: Cambridge University Press.

Sheetz, Mark. 1997/1998. "Debating the Unipolar Moment." *International Security* 22 (Winter): 168–72.

Singer, Max, and Aaron Wildavsky. 1993. *The Real World Order: Zones of Peace/Zones of Turmoil.* Chatham, NJ: Chatham House.

Snyder, Glenn. 1965. "The Balance of Power and the Balance of Terror." In *The Balance of Power,* ed. Paul Seabury. San Francisco: Chandler. Pp. 184–201.

Snyder, Jack. 1991. *Myths of Empire: Domestic Politics and International Ambition.* Ithaca, NY: Cornell University Press.

Sterling-Folker, Jennifer. 2000. "Competing Paradigms or Birds of a Feather? Constructivism and Neoliberal Institutionalism Compared." *International Studies Quarterly* 44 (March): 97–120.

Thompson, William R. 1988. *On Global War: Historical-Structural Approaches to World System Analysis.* Columbia: University of South Carolina Press.

Thompson, William R. 1996. "Democracy and Peace: Putting the Cart Before the Horse?" *International Organization* 50 (Winter): 141–74.

Tilly, Charles. 1990. *Coercion, Capital, and European States. AD 990–1990.* Cambridge, MA: Basil Blackwell.

Ullman, Richard H. 1991. *Securing Europe.* Princeton. NJ: Princeton University Press.

Van Creveld, Martin L. 1999. *The Rise and Decline of the State.* New York: Cambridge University Press.

Van der Pijl, Kees. 1998. *Transnational Classes and International Relations.* New York: Routledge.

Van Evera, Stephen. 1984. "The Cult of the Offensive and the Origins of the First World War." *International Security* 9 (Summer): 58–107.

Van Evera, Stephen. 1990/1991. "Primed for Peace: Europe after the Cold War." *International Security* 15 (Winter): 7–57.

Van Evera, Stephen. 1999. *Causes of War: Power and the Roots of Conflict.* Ithaca. NY: Cornell University Press.

Vasquez, Jonh A. 1993. *The War Puzzle.* New York: Cambridge University Press.

Waltz, Kenneth N. 1970. "The Myth of National Interdependence." In *The International Corporation,* ed. Charles P. Kindleberger. Cambridge, MA: MIT Press. Pp. 205–23.

Waltz, Kenneth N. 1993. "The Emerging Structure of International Politics." *International Security* 18 (Fall): 44–79.

Waltz, Kenneth N. 1999. "Globalization and Governance." *PS: Political Science & Politics* 32 (December): 693–700.

Waltz, Kenneth N. 2000. "Structural Realism after the Cold War." *International Security* 25 (Summer): 5–41.

Ward, Michael D., and Kristian Gleditsch. 1998. "Democratizing for Peace." *American Political Science Review* 92 (March): 51–62.

Wendt, Alexander. 1994. "Collective Identity Formation and the International State." *American Political Science Review* 88 (June): 384–96.

Wendt, Alexander. 1999. *Social Theory of International Politics.* Cambridge: Cambridge University Press.

White, Ralph. 1990. "Why Aggressors Lose." *Political Psychology* 11 (June): 227–42.

Wohlforth, William C. 1999. "The Stability of a Unipolar World." *International Security* 24 (Summer): 5–41.

Wolfers, Arnold. 1962. *Discord and Collaboration: Essays on International Politics.* Baltimore, MD: Johns Hopkins University Press.

Wrong, Dennis H. 1976. *Skeptical Sociology.* New York: Columbia University Press.

THE NEXT WAR OF THE WORLD

Niall Ferguson

Jervis's focus on peace among the great powers since World War II contrasts with Ferguson's characterization of the twentieth century as "the bloodiest era in history." As you read this selection, ask yourself:

- ❀ What are Ferguson's explanations of the violence of the twentieth century?
- ❀ What are the implications of his analysis for war, especially great power war, in the twenty-first century?
- ❀ What do you think are the prospects for great power war in your lifetime?

ONE HUNDRED YEARS OF BUTCHERY

In 1898, H. G. Wells wrote *The War of the Worlds,* a novel that imagined the destruction of a great city and the extermination of its inhabitants by ruthless invaders. The invaders in Wells' story were, of course, Martians. But no aliens were needed to make such devastation a reality. In the decades that followed the book's publication, human beings repeatedly played the part of the inhuman marauders, devastating city after city in what may justly be regarded as a single hundred-year "war of the world."

The twentieth century was the bloodiest era in history. World War I killed between 9 million and 10 million people, more if the influenza pandemic of 1918–19 is seen as a consequence of the war. Another 59 million died in World War II. And those conflicts were only two of the more deadly ones in the last hundred years. By one estimate, there were 16 conflicts throughout the last century that cost more than a million

Niall Ferguson, "The Next War of the World." First published in *Foreign Affairs,* 85:5, September/October 2006. Copyright © 2006 by Niall Ferguson. Reprinted with permission of the Wylie Agency.

lives, a further six that claimed between 500,000 and a million, and 14 that killed between 250,000 and 500,000. In all, between 167 million and 188 million people died because of organized violence in the twentieth century—as many as one in every 22 deaths in that period.

Other periods matched the twentieth century's rate of killing, if not its magnitude: consider the reigns of tyrants such as Genghis Khan and Tamerlane; some crises in imperial China, such as the An Lushan Rebellion in the eighth century and the Taiping Rebellion in the mid-nineteenth century; and some cases of Western imperial conquest, such as Belgian rule in the Congo and the German war against the Herero in German Southwest Africa. Yet the twentieth century differs from those earlier ages in one key way: it was supposed to be—and in a great many ways was—a time of unparalleled material progress.

In real terms, average per capita GDP roughly quadrupled between 1913 and 1998. By the end of the twentieth century, human beings in many parts of the world enjoyed longer and better lives than had been possible at any time before, thanks mainly to improved nutrition and health care. Rising wealth meant that more and more people were able to flee what Karl Marx and Friedrich Engels had called "the idiocy of rural life": between 1900 and 1980, the proportion of the world's population that lived in large cities more than doubled. And by working more productively, people had more time available for leisure. Some spent their free time successfully campaigning for political representation and the redistribution of income. As a result, governments ceased to confine themselves to providing only basic public goods, such as national defense and a fair judicial system, but instead became welfare states that sought nothing less than the elimination of poverty.

It might have been expected that such prosperity would eliminate the causes of war.

But much of the worst violence of the twentieth century involved the relatively wealthy countries at the opposite ends of Eurasia. The chief lesson of the twentieth century is that countries can provide their citizens with wealth, longevity, literacy, and even democracy but still descend into lethal conflict. Leon Trotsky nicely summed up the paradox when reflecting on the First Balkan War of 1912–13, which he covered as a reporter. The conflict, Trotsky wrote, "shows that we still haven't crawled out on all fours from the barbaric stage of our history. We have learned to wear suspenders, to write clever editorials, and to make chocolate milk, but when we have to decide seriously a question of the coexistence of a few tribes on a rich peninsula of Europe, we are helpless to find a way other than mutual mass slaughter." Trotsky later made his own contribution to the history of mass slaughter as the people's commissar for war and as the commander of the Red Army during the Russian Civil War.

Will the twenty-first century be as bloody as the twentieth? The answer depends partly on whether or not we can understand the causes of the last century's violence. Only if we can will we have a chance of avoiding a repetition of its horrors. If we cannot, there is a real possibility that we will relive the nightmare.

BLAME GAME

There are many unsatisfactory explanations for why the twentieth century was so destructive. One is the assertion that the availability of more powerful weapons caused bloodier conflicts. But there is no correlation between the sophistication of military technology and the lethality of conflict. Some of the worst violence of the century—the genocides in Cambodia in the 1970s and central Africa in the 1990s, for instance—was perpetrated with the crudest of weapons: rifles, axes, machetes, and knives.

Nor can economic crises explain the bloodshed. What may be the most familiar causal chain in modern historiography links the Great Depression to the rise of fascism and the outbreak of World War II. But that simple story leaves too much out. Nazi Germany started the war in Europe only after its economy had recovered. Not all the countries affected by the Great Depression were taken over by fascist regimes, nor did all such regimes start wars of aggression. In fact, no general relationship between economics and conflict is discernible for the century as a whole. Some wars came after periods of growth, others were the causes rather than the consequences of economic catastrophe, and some severe economic crises were not followed by wars.

Many trace responsibility for the butchery to extreme ideologies. The Marxist historian Eric Hobsbawm calls the years between 1914 and 1991 "an era of religious wars" but argues that "the most militant and bloodthirsty religions were secular ideologies." At the other end of the political spectrum, the conservative historian Paul Johnson blames the violence on "the rise of moral relativism, the decline of personal responsibility [and] the repudiation of Judeo-Christian values." But the rise of new ideologies or the decline of old values cannot be regarded as causes of violence in their own right. Extreme belief systems, such as anti-Semitism, have existed for most of modern history, but only at certain times and in certain places have they been widely embraced and translated into violence.

And as tempting as it is to blame tyrants such as Hitler, Stalin, and Mao for the century's bloodletting, to do so is to repeat the error on which Leo Tolstoy heaped so much scorn in *War and Peace*. Megalomaniacs may order men to invade Russia, but why do the men obey? Some historians have attempted to answer the novelist's question by indicting the modern nation-state.

The nation-state does indeed possess unprecedented capabilities for mobilizing masses of people, but those means could just as easily be harnessed, and have been, to peaceful ends.

Others seek the cause of conflict in the internal political arrangements of states. It has become fashionable among political scientists to posit a causal link between democracy and peace, extrapolating from the observation that democracies tend not to go to war with one another. The corollary, of course, is that dictatorships generally are more bellicose. By that logic, the rise of democracy during the twentieth century should have made the world more peaceful. Democratization may well have reduced the incidence of war between states. But waves of democratization in the 1920s, 1960s, and 1980s seem to have multiplied the number of civil wars. Some of those (such as the conflicts in Afghanistan, Burundi, China, Korea, Mexico, Mozambique, Nigeria, Russia, Rwanda, and Vietnam) were among the deadliest conflicts of the century. Horrendous numbers of fatalities were also caused by genocidal or "politicidal" campaigns waged against civilian populations, such as those carried out by the Young Turks against the Armenians and the Greeks during World War I, the Soviet government from the 1920s until the 1950s, and the Nazis between 1933 and 1945—to say nothing of those perpetrated by the communist tyrannies of Mao in China and Pol Pot in Cambodia. Indeed, such civil strife has been the most common form of conflict during the past 50 years. Of the 24 armed conflicts recorded as "ongoing" by the University of Maryland's Ted Robert Gurr and George Mason University's Monty Marshall in early 2005, nearly all were civil wars.

Conventional explanations for the violence of the twentieth century are inadequate for another important reason. None is able to explain convincingly why lethal conflict happened when and where it did. Ultimately, the interesting question is not, Why was the twentieth century more violent than the eighteenth or the nineteenth? but, Why did extreme violence happen in Poland and Serbia more than in Portugal and Sweden, and why was it more likely to happen between 1939 and 1945 than between 1959 and 1965?

In relative terms, Poland and Serbia were exceptionally prone to the ravages of warfare in the first half of the twentieth century. Polish Galicia was one of the killing fields of the eastern front between 1914 and 1917. Serbia had the highest mortality rate of any country during World War I; the war killed just under 6 percent of the country's prewar population. Far worse, the Polish mortality rate in World War II amounted to just under 19 percent; Polish Jews killed in the Holocaust accounted for a large share of that number. The Soviet rate was 11 percent, although the figure for Russians and Ukrainians, who dominated the ranks of the Red Army, was higher. Among other combatant countries, only Germany (including Austria) and Yugoslavia suffered war-induced mortality rates close to 10 percent. The next highest rates were for Hungary (8 percent) and Romania (6 percent). In no other country for which figures have been published did war mortality rise above 3 percent. Indeed, for four of the principal combatants—France, Italy, the United Kingdom, and the United States—total wartime mortality was less than 1 percent of the prewar population.

These figures give a good indication of the location and the timing of the worst twentieth-century violence. From around 1904 to 1953, the most dangerous place in the world was the triangle that lies between the Balkans, the Baltic Sea, and the Black Sea. Only slightly less dangerous over the same period was the region at the other end of Eurasia comprising Manchuria

and the neighboring Korean Peninsula. Indeed, it was there that the era of large-scale modern warfare began, when Japan attacked Russia in 1904. It was also there that the era came to a close 50 years later, with the end of the Korean War. Thereafter, the location and the type of violence changed. Despite its reputation as having been a "long peace," the Cold War sparked a series of bitter proxy wars around the world, particularly in Central America, sub-Saharan Africa, and Indochina. Those conflicts in effect constituted a Third World War—or, more aptly, the Third World's War.

THE THREE E'S

Three factors explain the timing and the location of the extreme violence of the twentieth century: ethnic disintegration, economic volatility, and empires in decline.

Patterns of migration combined with the persistence of religious and cultural traditions have always made some areas of human settlement more ethnically homogeneous than others. In 1900, in parts of the world such as England or France it was possible to travel hundreds of miles without encountering anyone who looked, spoke, dressed, or worshiped in significantly different ways from everyone else. But an ethnic and linguistic map of central and eastern Europe at that time would have resembled a patchwork quilt, reflecting the region's diversity. There, ethnic groups lived next door to one another— sometimes literally. The many-named town known variously as Czernowitz, Cernauti, and Chernivtsi is a case in point. Located in what is now Ukraine, Chernivtsi was once a multiethnic city inhabited by German professors, Austrian civil servants, Jewish merchants, and workers from many other ethnicities. To the nineteenth-century poet Karl Emil Franzos, Chernivtsi was Czernowitz, "the courtyard of the German paradise," an island of Kultur within "Half Asia." Yet the multiethnic balance on which such places rested tipped over disastrously in the three decades after 1914.

Conflict in multiethnic societies was not and is not inevitable. In fact, central and eastern Europe in the early 1900s saw remarkable advances in the integration and assimilation of ethnic minorities. People of different ethnicities not only lived near one another but also worked, played, and studied together. They even intermarried. For example, in cities such as Hamburg and Trieste, rates of intermarriage between Jews and non-Jews reached remarkable heights. The same trend was apparent after the 1917 revolution in what soon became the Soviet Union, particularly in big cities.

Assimilation, however, can be violently reversed. It is no accident that ethnic tensions increased in places such as the then Romanian city Cernauti in the interwar period. Before World War I, four dynasties—the Hapsburg, the Hohenzollern, the Ottoman, and the Romanov—had governed central and eastern Europe. Such regimes cared less about their subjects' nationality than about their subjects' loyalty. After 1918, the political map of the region was redrawn to create or re-create nation-states. Yet the region's ethnic diversity made it impossible to set up homogeneous polities. As a result, in Czechoslovakia, Poland, Romania, and Yugoslavia, the majority population in each accounted for less than 80 percent of the total population. Ethnic minorities in such countries suddenly found themselves treated as second-class citizens. As part of postwar Romania, for instance, Cernauti became the scene of escalating ethnic conflict because of systematic discrimination against German educational institutions and landowners by the Romanian authorities. This was how ethnic disintegration happened.

Economic volatility exacerbated political frictions. The frequency and the amplitude of changes in output and prices peaked between 1919 and 1939. During those years, measures of standard deviation for growth and inflation were nearly double what they were in the preceding and succeeding periods and roughly seven times what they have been since 1990. From the mid-1920s to the mid-1930s, stock markets also experienced their highest levels of volatility of the century. Although it is obvious that low growth or a recession contributes to social instability, rapid growth can also be destabilizing. This is especially true in multiethnic societies, where booms can appear to benefit market-dominant minorities disproportionately, such as the Armenians in Turkey in the early 1900s or the Jews in central and eastern Europe. When booms turn to busts, the prosperous minority can become the target of reprisals by the impoverished majority. As Gregor von Rezzori recalled of his youth in Cernauti during this period, all of the city's other ethnic groups "despised the Jews, notwithstanding that Jews played an economically decisive role." If they could agree on nothing else, Germans and Romanians could agree that Jews were "the natural target of their aggression," Rezzori wrote in his memoir *The Snows of Yesteryear*.

Of course, not all multiethnic societies that experienced economic volatility in those years descended into sectarian violence. In the still relatively segregated United States, for example, the number of violent acts of racial hatred, such as lynchings, declined between the world wars. The critical third factor determining both the location and the timing of twentieth-century violence was the decline and fall of empires.

The twentieth century was characterized by a remarkably high rate of imperial dissolution. In 1913, around 65 percent of the world's land and 82 percent of its population were under some kind of imperial rule. Those empires soon disintegrated. The Qing dynasty in China was overthrown before World War I, and in 1917 the Romanov dynasty fell from power. They were quickly followed by the Hapsburgs, the Hohenzollerns, and the Ottomans. Little more than two decades later, the British, Dutch, and French empires in Asia were dealt heavy blows by imperial Japan, leaving damage that not even the Allied victory in World War II could repair. The Portuguese empire limped on, but by the early 1970s it too had collapsed. The new empires that grew among the ruins of the old were shorter lived than their predecessors. Whereas some early modern empires lasted for centuries (Ottoman rule, for instance, endured for 469 years), the Soviet Union fell apart after only 69 years, the Japanese overseas empire crumbled after just 50 years, and Hitler's empire beyond Germany's borders hung on for barely six years.

Violence is most likely to occur as empires decline. The late Romans understood well the unpleasantness associated with imperial dissolution. Modern commentators, on the other hand, have generally been too eager to see empires end and too credulous about the benefits of "self-determination" to realize the potentially high costs of any transition from a multiethnic polity to a homogeneous one. As imperial authority crumbles, local elites compete for the perquisites of power. The stakes are particularly high in ethnically heterogeneous provinces. From the point of view of minorities, the prospect of a new political order can be deeply alarming; members of a minority group that has collaborated with the imperial power frequently find that the empire's disappearance leaves them vulnerable to reprisals.

Anyone who doubts whether imperial decline can foment conflict need only reflect on how rarely empires broke up peacefully in the twentieth century. One of the last acts of the Ottoman Empire was to attempt genocide against the Armenians. The Austrian, German, and Russian empires all met bloody ends as World War I drew to a close; indeed, the civil war and ethnic strife that followed the Russian Revolution in 1917 was as costly to the tsar's former subjects as the preceding war against Austria and Germany was. The most violent year in the entire history of British India was 1947, when partition led to the deaths of more than a million people in communal clashes between Hindus and Muslims. Even the relatively calm dissolution of the Soviet Union bred bitter conflict between Armenia and Azerbaijan over the mainly Armenian enclave of Nagorno-Karabakh, as well as the war between Chechen separatists and the Russian government.

THE ROCKY ROAD AHEAD

If the combination of ethnic disintegration, economic volatility, and empires in decline is the basic formula for twentieth-century conflict, then what are the implications for the twenty-first century?

The good news is that global economic volatility has been significantly lower in recent years than at almost any time in the last century. By widening and deepening international markets for goods, labor, and capital, globalization appears to have made the world economy less prone to crisis. At the same time, financial innovations have improved the pricing and the distribution of risk, and policy innovations such as inflation targeting have helped governments to limit rises in consumer price (if not asset price) inflation. International organizations such as the World Trade Organization and the International Monetary Fund have helped to avert trade disputes and other sources of economic instability.

A second obvious point is that the old zones of conflict are unlikely to be the new ones. Those who engaged in ethnic cleansing in the twentieth century, whether by forced migration or genocide, did their work too well, so that today central and eastern Europe (and Manchuria and Korea) are no longer ethnically heterogeneous. Chernivtsi today is overwhelmingly Ukrainian, for instance, with only a tiny remnant of its once-thriving Jewish community still living there. And third, the world of 2006 is supposed to be a world without empires; the danger of imperial decline should accordingly be much less than in the past century.

Unfortunately, these appearances are deceptive. Today, one region displays in abundance all of the characteristics of the worst conflict zones of the twentieth century. Economic volatility has remained pronounced there even as it has diminished in the rest of the world. An empire (albeit one that dares not speak its name) is losing its grip over the region. Worst of all, ethnic disintegration is already well under way, even though many commentators still conceive of what is currently the main conflict there as an insurgency against foreign invaders or a "clash of civilizations" between Islam and the West.

THAT PLACE IS THE MIDDLE EAST

Iraq has experienced severe economic volatility in recent years, first as a result of UN sanctions and then because of the U.S. invasion and the subsequent insecurity. Having declined by just under 8 percent in the last year of Saddam Hussein's reign, real GDP plummeted by more than 40 percent in 2003, the year the United States invaded. In 2004, output bounced back by an estimated 46 percent—but growth slowed last year to under 4 percent. That is about as extreme as volatility can get. Since oil production accounts for about two-thirds of Iraq's GDP, changes in the production and the price of oil have been the primary drivers of these economic

swings. Oil prices are now up, meaning Iraq's exports are worth more, but inflation is stuck between 20 and 30 percent, and oil production is running at just 16 percent of its prewar level because of sabotage and other problems.

Other indicators are only slightly less dire. Power generation remains 28 percent below the target that was supposed to have been achieved in 2004. And the unemployment rate is estimated to be between 25 and 40 percent. It is true that there has been some economic good news since the war. More Iraqis now have cars, and many more Iraqis now have telephones thanks to the creation of a cell-phone network. Iraqis today also have a free press. Yet these improvements in communications have also helped insurgents and militias to mobilize.

Iraq is not the only Middle Eastern country with a volatile economy. All six countries that border Iraq have seen their own share of ups and downs. In the past five years, per capita GDP growth in Iran has ranged between 0.3 and 7.3 percent; in Jordan, between 0.3 and 5.1 percent; in Kuwait, between −5.5 and 6.9 percent; in Saudi Arabia, between −6.0 and 3.3 percent; in Syria, between −0.4 and 3.3 percent; and in Turkey, between −9.0 and 7.4 percent. Over the past decade, Kuwait's average annual GDP performance was the lowest (−0.9 percent), while Iran's was the highest (3.0 percent). On the other hand, the average Kuwaiti is nearly ten times richer than the average Iranian. Inflation in the region in 2004 ranged from 0.3 percent in Saudi Arabia to nearly 15 percent in Iran. Unemployment rates are in the low double digits everywhere but in Saudi Arabia (where it is around 5 percent), but youth unemployment rates are generally twice as high—just under 20 percent in Turkey, for example, compared with an overall rate of 10 percent. Youth unemployment matters because these are relatively youthful societies. Roughly 20 percent of the population of Iraq and its neighbors is between 15 and 24 years old; the equivalent figure for Europe and the United States is about 14 percent.

The Middle East also has the misfortune to be a zone of imperial conflict. Most Americans will probably always reject the proposition that the United States is (or operates) a de facto empire. Such squeamishness may be an integral part of the U.S. empire's problem. To be an empire in denial means resenting the costs of intervening in the affairs of foreign peoples and underestimating the benefits of doing so. It is remarkable that in June 2004, just over a year after U.S. troops toppled Saddam, a majority of Americans already said they regarded the invasion of Iraq as a mistake. Although support for the war has vacillated since then, at no time since September 2004 have more than 55 percent of poll respondents said they approved of it. What makes the U.S. public's misgivings especially remarkable is that the number of U.S. military personnel who have died in this war has been very small by historical standards. The total as of mid-July 2006 was 2,544, of whom 525 had died as a result of non-combat-related causes.

The Islamic Republic of Iran, by contrast, is heir to an imperial tradition dating back to the time of the Safavid dynasty, which ruled Persia from 1501, and beyond. Although Iran's leaders prefer the rhetoric of religious revolution and national liberation, the historian cannot fail to detect in their long-held ambition to acquire nuclear weapons—and thereby dominate the Middle East—a legacy of Persia's imperial past. The Iranian president, Mahmoud Ahmadinejad, is not only a devotee of the Hidden, or Twelfth, Imam (who devout Shiites believe will return to the world as the Mahdi, or messiah, for a final confrontation with the forces of evil); he is also a war veteran at the head of a youthful nation. It is not wholly fanciful to see in him a potential Caesar or Bonaparte.

The third and most striking feature of the Middle East today is the acceleration of ethnic disintegration, which is most obvious in Iraq. In 1993, Harvard's Samuel Huntington predicted that in the post–Cold War world, "the principal conflicts of global politics [would] occur between nations and groups of different civilizations," particularly between a decadent "Judeo-Christian" West and a demographically ascendant Islamic civilization. For a time, events seemed to be fulfilling his prophecy. Many Americans interpreted the terrorist attacks of September 11, 2001, in Huntington's terms, while Islamists interpreted the U.S. invasions of Afghanistan and Iraq as wars by Christian "crusaders" against Muslims.

Yet a closer inspection of events since 1993 suggests a post–Cold War trend of clashes within, rather than between, civilizations. Of the 30 major armed conflicts that either are going on now or have recently ended, only nine can be regarded as being in any sense between civilizations. But 19 are in some measure ethnic conflicts, the worst being the wars that continue to bedevil central Africa. Moreover, most of those conflicts that have a religious dimension are also ethnic conflicts.

Events in Iraq suggest that there, too, what is unfolding is not a clash between the West and Islam but, increasingly, a clash within Islamic civilization itself. By some accounts, ethnic disintegration there is already well under way. In a June 6, 2006, cable to Secretary of State Condoleezza Rice, which was leaked to the press, Zalmay Khalilzad, the U.S. ambassador to Iraq, cataloged the evidence of mounting sectarian tension in and around the Green Zone in Baghdad. "Personal fears are reinforcing divisive or sectarian channels," Khalilzad wrote. "Ethnic and sectarian faultlines are becoming part of the daily media fare. One Shia employee told us she can no longer watch TV news with her mother, who is a Sunni, because her mother blamed all the government failings on the fact that the Shia are in charge." Even more worrisome, Khalilzad reported that U.S. embassy employees had "become adept in modifying [their] behavior to avoid Alasas, informants who keep an eye out for 'outsiders' in neighborhoods. The Alasa mentality is becoming entrenched as Iraqi security forces fail to gain public confidence."

Such news should come as no surprise. Baghdad and the provinces around it—Babil, Diyala, and Salahuddin—are precisely the regions of Iraq where ethnic conflict could have been predicted to occur given the current conditions of economic volatility and imperial crisis. They are the most ethnically mixed parts of the country, where Sunnis and Shiites or Sunnis and Kurds live cheek by jowl. Under Saddam's secular tyranny, these communities coexisted more or less peacefully. Anecdotal evidence even suggests that there was some intermarriage. Since Saddam's fall, however, integration has been reversed. Around 92 percent of the votes in the December 2005 election were cast for sectarian parties. In such a fractious atmosphere, the odds seem dangerously stacked against the once-dominant Sunni Arab minority. Not only do current constitutional arrangements raise the prospect that Iraq's oil revenue will flow largely to Shiite and Kurdish provinces, but the Sunnis are badly underrepresented in the Iraqi security forces. According to the Brookings Institution, Sunnis make up less than ten percent of the enlisted forces.

Although the atmosphere has cooled somewhat since the Askariya shrine bombing in February, the trend is clearly toward ethnic or sectarian conflict. The number of incidents of sectarian violence recorded in May 2006 was 250, compared with just 20 in the same month the year before and ten in May 2004. There has been a threefold increase in the homicide rate in Baghdad since February 2006, much of it the result of sectarian violence. The assassination of Abu Musab al-Zarqawi, the leader of al Qaeda in Iraq, in June was therefore less of a milestone than President George W. Bush had hoped. As insurgency has given way to civil war, Zarqawi had already ceased to be a key player.

THE FIRE NEXT TIME

What makes the escalating civil war in Iraq so disturbing is that it has the potential to spill over into neighboring countries. The Iranian government is already taking more than a casual interest in the politics of post-Saddam Iraq. And yet Iran, with its Sunni and Kurdish minorities, is no more homogeneous than Iraq. Jordan, Saudi Arabia, and Syria cannot be expected to look on insouciantly if the Sunni minority in central Iraq begins to lose out to what may seem to be an Iranian-backed tyranny of the majority. The recent history of Lebanon offers a reminder that in the Middle East there is no such thing as a contained civil war. Neighbors are always likely to take an unhealthy interest in any country with fissiparous tendencies.

The obvious conclusion is that a new "war of the world" may already be brewing in a region that, incredible though it may seem, has yet to sate its appetite for violence. And the ramifications of such a Middle Eastern conflagration would be truly global. Economically, the world would have to contend with oil at above $100 a barrel. Politically, those countries in western Europe with substantial Muslim populations might also find themselves affected as sectarian tensions radiated outward. Meanwhile, the ethnic war between Jews and Arabs in Israel, the Gaza Strip, and the West Bank shows no sign of abating. Is it credible that the United States will remain unscathed if the Middle East erupts?

Although such an outcome may seem to be a low-probability, nightmare scenario, it is already more likely than the scenario of endur-ing peace in the region. If the history of the twentieth century is any guide, only economic stabilization and a credible reassertion of U.S. authority are likely to halt the drift toward chaos. Neither is a likely prospect. On the con-trary, the speed with which responsibility for security in Iraq is being handed over to the pre-dominantly Shiite and Kurdish security forces may accelerate the descent into internecine strife. Significantly, the audio statement released by Osama bin Laden in June excoriated not only the American-led "occupiers" of Iraq but also "certain sectors of the Iraqi people—those who refused [neutrality] and stood to fight on the side of the crusaders." His allusions to "rejection-ists," "traitors," and "agents of the Americans" were clearly intended to justify al Qaeda's pol-icy of targeting Iraq's Shiites.

The war of the worlds that H. G. Wells imagined never came to pass. But a war of the world did. The sobering possibility we urgently need to confront is that another global conflict is brewing today—centered not on Poland or Manchuria, but more likely on Palestine and Mesopotamia.

AFTER PROLIFERATION: WHAT TO DO IF MORE STATES GO NUCLEAR

Stephen P. Rosen

In this article, Rosen discusses the consequences of nuclear proliferation and policy options that should be adopted in response to it. As you read this article, ask yourself:

- What is the basic difference between those Rosen calls optimists and pessimists regarding the conse-quences of proliferation?
- Where does Rosen fit into that debate between optimists and pessimists?
- What are his policy recommendations, and do they make sense to you?

Spurred by the progress of weapons programs in North Korea and Iran, nuclear prolifera-tion is once again at the top of the U.S. national security agenda. Practically all of the discussion about the issue has centered on how to prevent proliferation. Hawks have pushed for regime change or military strikes, whereas doves have favored arms control and negotiation. Even though none of these measures is likely to solve the problem, few observers have spent much time considering what a postproliferation world would look like.

Stephen P. Rosen, "After Proliferation: What to Do if More States Go Nuclear." Reprinted by permission of *Foreign Affairs* 85:5, September/October 2006. Copyright 2006 by the Council on Foreign Relations, Inc. www.ForeignAffairs.org.

Those who have done so can be divided into pessimists and optimists. The pessimists assume that the dangers of a nuclear confrontation will increase exponentially as the number of nuclear powers grows and that a future catastrophe is all but certain. Since little can be done to avert such a terrible outcome or mitigate its consequences, the argument goes, efforts to stop proliferation in the first place must be redoubled. The optimists, by contrast, assume that the stability that nuclear weapons seem to have brought to the superpowers' Cold War confrontation will be replicated. Far from being a sure disaster, they argue, the spread of nuclear weapons could be a relatively cheap and easy (albeit nerve-racking) solution to the age-old problem of war.

Actually, however, a postproliferation future is likely to be far more complex than either the pessimists or the optimists believe. In a multipolar nuclear world, international politics will continue but in an environment dominated by fear and uncertainty, with new dangers and new possibilities for miscommunication adding to and complicating familiar ones. As a result, many of the military plans, defense policies, and national security doctrines that officials in the United States and other countries now take for granted are likely to become obsolete and will need to be revised significantly.

WILL DETERRENCE WORK?

Assume, for the sake of argument, that within the next decade Iran manages to acquire a few crude nuclear weapons and that these can be delivered by ballistic missiles within the Middle East and by clandestine means to the United States and Europe. Assume also that Saudi Arabia and Turkey, out of fear or competitive emulation, also develop their own nuclear arsenals. How would strategic interactions in this new world play out?

During the Cold War, the small number of nuclear states meant that the identity of any nuclear attacker would be obvious. Preparations could thus be made for retaliation, and this helped deter first strikes. In a multipolar nuclear Middle East, however, such logic might not hold. For deterrence to work in such an environment, there would have to be detection systems that could unambiguously determine whether a nuclear-armed ballistic missile was launched from, say, Iran, Turkey, or Saudi Arabia. In earlier decades, the United States spent an enormous amount of resources on over-the-horizon radars and satellites that could detect the origin of missile launches in the Soviet Union. But those systems were optimized to monitor the Soviet Union and may not be as effective at identifying launches conducted from other countries. It may be technically simple for the United States (or Israel or Saudi Arabia) to deploy such systems, but until they exist and their effectiveness is demonstrated, deterrence might well be weak; it would be difficult to retaliate against a bomb that has no clear return address.

It gets worse. During the Cold War, most analysts considered it unlikely that nuclear weapons would be used during peacetime; they worried more about the possibility of a nuclear conflict somehow emerging out of a conventional war. That scenario would still be the most likely in a postproliferation future as well, but the frequency of conventional wars in the Middle East would make it a less comforting prospect. If a nuclear-armed ballistic missile were launched while conventional fighting involving non-nuclear-armed ballistic missiles was going on in the region, how confident would any government be that it could identify the party responsible? The difficulty would be greater still if an airplane or a cruise missile were used to deliver the nuclear weapon.

One of the greatest fears about Iran's possible acquisition of nuclear weapons, moreover, is that Tehran might give them to a terrorist group, which would dramatically increase the likelihood of their being used. Some argue that the Iranian government would never condone such a transfer; others that it would. There is no way of knowing for sure. What can be said, however, is that the likelihood of a clandestine transfer to radical Islamist terrorists will increase if the number of Islamic nuclear powers grows, if only because it would get more difficult to identify the state responsible for the transfer so as to punish it.

If an Islamist terrorist group acquired fissile material or a nuclear bomb today, it would be hard to determine with certainty which country had provided it. Attention would focus on Pakistan, the only Islamic state currently in possession of nuclear weapons. But uncertainty would grow if more Islamic states went nuclear, and retaliation would become all but impossible unless one were willing to strike back indiscriminately at all suspect states.

RACE MATTERS

During the Cold War, the United States and the Soviet Union engaged in an intense arms race and built up vast nuclear arsenals. Other binary nuclear competitions, however, such as that between India and Pakistan, have been free of such behavior. Those states' arsenals have remained fairly small and relatively unsophisticated.

Nuclear-armed countries in the Middle East would be unlikely to display such restraint. Iran and Iraq would be much too suspicious of each other, as would Saudi Arabia and Iran, Turkey and Iraq, and so forth. And then there is Israel. Wariness would create the classic conditions for a multipolar arms race, with Israel arming against all possible enemies and the Islamic states arming against Israel and one another.

Historical evidence suggests that arms races sometimes precipitate wars because governments come to see conflict as preferable to financial exhaustion or believe they can gain a temporary military advantage through war. Arguably, a nuclear war would be so destructive that its prospect might well dissuade states from escalating conflicts. But energetic arms races would still produce larger arsenals, making it harder to prevent the accidental or unauthorized use of nuclear weapons.

Nuclear arms races might emerge in regions other than the Middle East as well. Asia features many countries with major territorial or political disputes, including five with nuclear weapons (China, India, North Korea, Pakistan, and Russia). Japan and Taiwan could join the list. Most of these countries would have the resources to increase the size and quality of their nuclear arsenals indefinitely if they so chose. They also seem to be nationalist in a way that western European countries no longer are: they are particularly mindful of their sovereignty, relatively uninterested in international organizations, sensitive to slights, and wary about changes in the regional balance of military power. Were the United States to stop serving as guarantor of the current order, Asia might well be, in the words of the Princeton political science professor Aaron Friedberg, "ripe for rivalry"—including nuclear rivalry. In that case, the region would raise problems similar to those that would be posed by a nuclear Middle East.

The United States has not been strategically affected by the peacetime arms races of other countries since the global competition for naval power and the European bomber contests of the 1920s and 1930s. Were such rivalries to emerge now, it is unclear how Washington would, or should, respond. During the Cold War, U.S. and Soviet strategists worried not only about how to protect their own countries from nuclear attack but also about how to protect their allies. Questions about the credibility of such "extended deterrence" were never fully resolved, but their urgency was lessened, in the United States at least, by Washington's decision to bind itself tightly to its NATO partners (going so far as to station U.S. nuclear missiles in West Germany and Turkey). Similar questions will inevitably return if proliferation continues. In a future confrontation between Iran and Kuwait, for example, a nuclear-armed Tehran might well try to coerce its opponent while treating Washington's protests and threats as a bluff. Would heading off such challenges require the formation of a new set of tight alliances, explicit security guarantees, and integrated defense structures?

Another Cold War concept, known as the stability–instability paradox, posits that actors take advantage of the very fear of nuclear war to pursue lesser sorts of conflict with impunity. This, too, might play out in the future. A nuclear Iran, for example, might support increased terrorism against U.S. forces in the region on the theory that Washington would be reluctant to escalate the conflict.

TERMS OF USE

Nuclear weapons have not been used since 1945, and any further use would come as a profound shock. Yet some future nuclear actors might think that resorting to these weapons would serve their interests. It is not inconceivable, for example, that some state or group might want to show the rest of the world that it is willing and able to violate the most hallowed norms of the international system. Nazi Germany deliberately targeted civilian refugees in Poland in 1939 and in the Netherlands and France in 1940 as part of its strategy of Schrecklichkeit (instilling terror). A quasi-terrorist use of nuclear weapons, not by a small group but by a state that wanted to be recognized as fearsome, would be a contemporary analog.

What kind of state might attempt such a thing? If history is any guide, a state that openly rejects the existing international order, considers its opponents to be less than fully human, and seeks to intimidate others. Alternatively, internal conflicts could create hatreds so powerful that actors might resort to using nuclear weapons; consider, for example, how Moscow might respond if another Chechen attack killed hundreds of Russian children. Some states might also be tempted to use nuclear weapons in other ways. For example, before it started to abandon its nuclear weapons program, South Africa had planned to use its bombs if it was ever approaching military defeat, as a last-ditch effort to draw the superpowers into the conflict. If it were to cross the nuclear threshold, Taiwan might embrace a similar strategy.

By far, however, the most plausible use of nuclear weapons would involve a nuclear power that found itself on the losing side of a nonnuclear war. Such a state would be faced with a choice not between maintaining peace and initiating nuclear war but between accepting its impending defeat and gambling that escalation might suddenly end the fighting without defeat. Conflicts between Iran and Iraq or China and Taiwan are plausible candidates for such a nightmare.

THE DEFENSE SHOULD NOT REST

What, if anything, can be done to prepare intelligently for such contingencies? Pessimists say preparation is pointless, and optimists say it is unnecessary. But there are several steps prudent officials can and should take now.

To bolster the efficacy of deterrence in a world of small, closely located nuclear powers, it would be necessary to deploy surveillance systems that could identify and warn against aircraft movement and missile launches. These systems might be operated on a national or a multilateral basis; in fact, a number of states in exposed regions could contribute to collective efforts to detect airborne threats.

The construction of such a regional surveillance system, moreover, would put in place much of the infrastructure needed to support another useful tool: some form of missile defense. Skeptics of missile defense have often ridiculed, with some reason, the notion that such systems can be effective against nuclear weapons or large numbers of missiles. What they overlook, however, is that even leaky or somewhat ineffective defenses can play a constructive role in deterring an attack from a nuclear power with a small arsenal or lowering the odds that a full-scale nuclear conflict will erupt from a single use (of whatever origin).

Other kinds of defense could also help lower the odds of an attack or mitigate its terrible consequences. U.S. officials should develop the capacity to evacuate those cities at risk of a direct attack or of being in the path of nuclear fallout, as well as stockpile radiation meters, build fallout shelters, and implement other measures first devised in the 1950s. Civil defense came to be seen as a grotesque joke when the Soviet Union acquired tens of thousands of nuclear weapons. But, like missile defense, it could play an important role in a world of smaller nuclear powers.

Should a nuclear bomb get through nevertheless, it would be critical for the government of the targeted state to respond with policies other than doing nothing or ordering indiscriminate retaliation. One option would be to launch a massive nonnuclear military campaign against the responsible party to make sure that such an attack was never repeated. But even with all the will and money in the world, such a response simply could not be summoned up out of the blue; it would require careful planning and preparation.

The United States was able to launch an extraordinary mobilization effort in 1942 not simply because the attack on Pearl Harbor had galvanized the American public, but also because people such as Vannevar Bush (as head of the National Defense Research Committee) and Robert Lovett (as an aide to Secretary of War Henry Stimson) had spent years laying the groundwork for organizing civilian scientists and the automobile industry for military purposes. Unfortunately, no one has thought about planning for such mobilization in the United States in 50 years. And yet in the aftermath of a nuclear attack on the United States, the American people would demand that the government try to transform the world so that such an attack would never occur again. Starting to think through and plan such an effort now would be cheap and doable, and could dramatically expand the U.S. government's options later.

Meanwhile, controlling arms races in the Middle East and Asia would be difficult. Traditional arms control, which requires that parties allow mutual inventories of their weapons and submit to verification procedures, seems unlikely to be of much use, both because of deep-rooted mutual suspicions in these regions and because small nuclear powers have an incentive to hide their weapons and exaggerate the size and the effectiveness of their arsenals in order to discourage opponents from attacking them. Agreement on serious verification measures would thus be difficult to reach, and that in turn would undercut the prospects for effective agreements more generally.

Still, a peculiar form of nuclear transparency might be possible and helpful. But it would require that all states realize that nuclear war, even with limited arsenals, would result in their own deaths. How can the point be driven home? There is historical evidence that seeing nuclear weapons tested had a powerful effect on many people in the United States and the Soviet Union. Thus, paradoxically, nuclear proliferation might have to continue a while longer before it can be halted or slowed down: were nuclear tests to be conducted in full view again, the current generation of policymakers and their constituents might realize that the use of even a small number of nuclear weapons would lead to intolerable destruction.

In short, if nuclear proliferation continues, the world is likely to move into a new era with challenges significantly different from those of the Cold War. Several more small nuclear powers will likely coexist along with the large ones, and the problems of nuclear deterrence, arms races, offensive and defensive weaponry, and appropriate retaliation will need to be worked out again in new and more complex conditions. From the 1950s through the 1980s, nuclear strategy was a lively field of inquiry of great practical importance. It nearly died out with the end of the Cold War, as the prospects of a superpower nuclear confrontation receded. Unfortunately, it is now due for a revival.

TERRORPHOBIA: OUR FALSE SENSE OF INSECURITY

John Mueller

John Mueller has argued in many publications that war and violence in world politics are going out of fashion. But even many optimists who accept that great power war is becoming less likely have maintained that other forms of violence are increasing. Since the terror attacks of 9/11 the conventional wisdom is that the twenty-first century will see a sharp increase in terrorist violence. In this selection, Mueller challenges that conventional wisdom. As you read his article, ask yourself:

- Why does Mueller think we have exaggerated the threat of terrorism?
- How does he think we should respond to the threat of terrorism?
- Is Mueller's argument persuasive?

A few days after the 9/11 attacks, Vice President Dick Cheney warned that there might never be an "end date" in the "struggle" against terrorism, a point when it would be possible to say, "There, it's all over with." More than six and a half years later, his wisdom seems to have been vindicated, though perhaps not quite in the way he intended. At least in its domestic homeland security aspects, the so-called War on Terror shows clear signs of having developed into a popularly supported governmental perpetual-motion machine that could very well spin "till who laid the rails", as Mayor Shinn so eloquently, if opaquely, puts it

John Mueller, "Terrorphobia: Our False Sense of Insecurity." This article first appeared in *The American Interest* 3:5, May–June 2008, pp. 6–13. Reprinted by permission of The American Interest.

in *The Music Man*. Since none of the leading Democrats or Republicans running for president this year has managed to express any misgivings about this development, it is fair to assume that the "war" will amble on during whatever administration happens to follow the present one.

In some respects, ironically enough, the closest semblance to a notable opponent the enterprise has so far generated has been George W. Bush himself. The President has, of course, garnered great political benefit from the terrorism scare. He has consistently achieved his best ratings for handling the issue, and Karl Rove has been known to boast publicly about the political utility of fanning terrorist fears for the good of the Republican Party.[1] It is no accident that the President managed to use the t-word at least twenty and as many as 36 times in each of his post-9/11 State of the Union addresses (as opposed to only once in January 2001). However, for a while there he opposed slapping together all sorts of disparate government agencies into the hopelessly unwieldy Department of Homeland Security. He even allowed that letting a responsible Dubai company manage the occasional American port was not necessarily the end of the world. Eventually, he buckled on both issues, and he will probably buckle again when determined, outraged and likely bipartisan opposition rises up against his tentative proposal to halve the amount of Federal money ladled out each year to localities to fight terrorism.

But at least there were some transitory glimmers. We may not even get that much from his successor in the White House. The reason is that terrorism and the attendant "war" thereon have become fully embedded in the public consciousness, with the effect that politicians and bureaucrats have become as wary of appearing soft on terrorism as they are about appearing soft on drugs, or as they once were about appearing soft on Communism.

Key to this dynamic is that the public apparently continues to remain unimpressed by several inconvenient facts. One such fact is that there have been no al-Qaeda attacks whatsoever in the United States since 2001. A second is that no true al-Qaeda cell (or scarcely anybody who might even be deemed to have a "connection" to the diabolical group) has been unearthed in this country. A third is that the homegrown "plotters" who have been apprehended, while perhaps potentially somewhat dangerous at least in a few cases, have mostly been either flaky or almost absurdly incompetent.

Beyond these facts are a few comparisons that ought to arrest attention. One is that the total number of people killed worldwide by genuine al-Qaeda types and assorted wannabes outside of war zones since 9/11 averages about 300 per year. That is certainly 300 a year too many, but that number is smaller than the yearly number of bathtub drownings in the United States. Moreover, unless the terrorists are able somehow massively to increase their capacities, the likelihood that a person living outside a war zone will perish at the hands of an international terrorist over an eighty-year period is about one in 80,000. By comparison, an American's chance of dying in an auto accident over the same time interval is one in eighty.

Despite these facts, polls since 2001 do not demonstrate all that much of a decline in the percentage of the American public anticipating another terrorist attack, or expressing fear that they themselves might become a victim of it. The public has chosen to wallow in a false sense of insecurity, and it apparently plans to keep on doing so. Accordingly, it will presumably continue to demand that its leaders defer to its insecurities, and will uncritically approve as huge amounts of money are shelled out in a quixotic and mostly symbolic effort to assuage those insecurities.

This does not mean that most Americans spend a great deal of time obsessing over terrorism, or even paying all that much attention to it. Terrorism has for years now scored rather poorly on polls asking about the country's most important problem. Then again, people don't constantly think about motherhood either, but they would certainly not look kindly upon a politician or bureaucrat who was insufficiently sentimental about that venerable institution.

An apt comparison to this political-psychological circumstance would be the U.S. public's concern about the threat once presented by domestic Communists. Impelled by several spectacular espionage cases and by a seemingly risky international environment, fears about the dangers presented by "the enemy within" became fully internalized in the years after World War II. In a famous public-opinion study conducted at the height of the McCarthy period in the mid-1950s, sociologist Samuel Stouffer found Americans quite willing to support laws that would prevent Communists from speaking and teaching, and that would remove their books from public libraries. Some 43 percent professed to believe that domestic Communists presented a great or very great danger to the United States. At the same time, however, when Stouffer asked more broadly about what their primary worries were, most respondents voiced concerns about personal matters. Apprehensions about domestic Communism (or about restrictions on civil liberties) rarely came up without prompting. There was, Stouffer concluded, no "national anxiety neurosis" over the issue.

That conclusion probably holds for present concerns about domestic terrorism, too—at least outside of cable news shows. True enough, there was a lot of pseudo-rational evasive behavior after the 9/11 attacks. Indeed, several studies conclude that more than 1,000 Americans died between September 11, 2001 and the end of that year because, out of fear of terrorism, they avoided airplanes in favor of much more dangerous automobiles. However, things eventually settled down, and most Americans easily get through the day now without spending a lot of time thinking about domestic terrorism. There has been no great exodus from Washington or New York, and few have gone to the trouble of stocking up on emergency supplies despite the persistent, nanny-like urgings of the Department of Homeland Security to do so.

What this means, apparently, is that most Americans are sensible enough to take media alarmism in stride. On the fifth anniversary of 9/11, ABC's Charles Gibson somberly intoned, "Putting your child on a school bus or driving across a bridge or just going to the mall—each of these things is a small act of courage—and peril is a part of everyday life." Amazing then, isn't it, how without spending much time thinking about it, Americans seem somehow to have been able to summon the bravery to carry out those perilous tasks. (If shopping malls have now become jammed with heroes, that is a condition, too, I imagine most Americans will be able to live with. I, on the other hand, am determined to keep my distance.)

BURDENS OF POLITICAL COURAGE

Our problems do not arise, then, from a national anxiety neurosis, but more from other consequences of the fear of terrorism. One is that when a consensus about a threat becomes internalized, it becomes politically unwise, even disastrous, to oppose it—or even to lend only half-hearted support to it. Another is that the internalized consensus creates a political atmosphere in which government and assorted pork-barrelers can fritter away considerable money and effort on questionable enterprises, as long as they appear somehow to be focused on dealing with the threat. In the present context, the magic phrase, "We don't want to have another 9/11", tends to end the discussion.

Once again, the parallel with the post-World War II Red Scare is instructive. In that atmosphere politicians scurried to support spending billions upon billions of dollars to surveil, screen and protect, and to spy on an ever-expanding array of individuals who had aroused suspicion for one reason or another. Organizations were infiltrated, phones were tapped (each tap can require the full-time services of a dozen agents and support personnel), letters were intercepted, people were followed, loyalty oaths were required, endless leads (almost all to nowhere) were pursued, defense plants were hardened, concentration camps for prospective emergency use were established (an idea desperately proposed by Senate *liberals* in 1950), and garbage was meticulously sifted in the hope of unearthing scraps of incriminating information.

At the time, critics of this process focused almost entirely on the potential for civil liberties violations. This is a worthy concern, but hardly the only one. As far as I know, at no point during the Cold War did anyone say: "Yes, many domestic Communists adhere to a foreign ideology that ultimately has as its goal the destruction of capitalism and democracy by violence if necessary, but they're so pathetic they couldn't subvert their way out of a wet paper bag. So why are we expending so much time, effort and treasure over this issue?" It is astounding to me that this plausible, if admittedly debatable, point of view seems never to have been publicly expressed by any politician, pundit, professor or editorialist (although some may have believed it privately). On Stouffer's survey, only a lonely and obviously politically insignificant share of the population (about 2 percent) professed to believe that domestic Communists presented no danger at all.

Something similar is now happening in pursuit of the terrible, if vaporous, terrorist enemy within. Redirecting much of their effort from such unglamorous enterprises as dealing with organized crime and white-collar embezzlement (which, unlike domestic terrorism, have actually happened since 2001), agencies like the FBI have kept their primary focus on the terrorist threat. Like their predecessors during the quest to quash domestic Communism, they have dutifully and laboriously assembled masses of intelligence data and have pursued an endless array of leads. Almost all of this activity has led nowhere, but it will continue because, of course, no one wants to be the one whose neglect somehow led to "another 9/11."

Criticisms of the Patriot Act and of the Bush Administration's efforts to apprehend prospective terrorists focus almost entirely on concerns about civil liberties, worrying that the rights of innocent Americans might be trampled in the rush to pursue terrorists. This is a perfectly valid concern, but from time to time someone might wonder a bit in public about how much the quest to ferret out terrorists and to protect ourselves is costing, as well as about how meager the results have been. In their valuable recent book, *Less Safe, Less Free* (2007), David Cole and Jules Lobel ably detail and critique the process. As their title implies, they suggest that we are less safe in part because the FBI and other agencies have failed in their well-funded quest to uncover the enemy within. There's an alternative explanation, however: They have not failed, and we are not less safe; investigators haven't found much of anything because there isn't much of anything to find.

We can also expect continued efforts to reduce the country's "vulnerability" despite at least three confounding realities: There is an essentially infinite number of potential terrorist targets; the probability that any one of those targets will be hit by a terrorist attack is essentially zero; and inventive terrorists, should they ever actually show up, are free to redirect their attention from a target that might enjoy a degree of protection to one of many that don't. Nonetheless, hundreds of billions of dollars have been spent on this quixotic quest so far, and the process seems destined to continue or even accelerate, even though, as a senior economist at the Department of Homeland Security put it recently, "We really don't know a whole lot about the overall costs and benefits of homeland security."

To be sure, terrorist attacks certainly remain possible, and there is nothing wrong with trying to build resilience into our domestic security systems. But there are intelligent and reasonable ways to do this, ways that actually consider the risk vs. reward ratio of additional expenditures. And then there are the other paths that we seem to have been pursuing: No cost is too high! No risk is too small! Since when does it take political courage to defend a rational approach to public policy against an hysterical one?

PERPETUAL EMOTION

The experience with domestic Communism suggests another likely consequence of the War on Terror: Once a threat becomes internalized, concern can linger for decades even if there is no evidence to support it. The anxiety becomes self-perpetuating.

In the two decades following the Stouffer survey, news about domestic Communism declined until it essentially vanished all together. In the mid-1950s, there were hundreds of articles in the *Readers' Guide to Periodical Literature* listed under the categories "Communism-U.S." and "Communist Party-U.S." In the mid-1970s, in stark contrast, there were scarcely any. This, of course, reflected the fact that domestic Communism wasn't doing much of anything to

garner attention. The Cold War continued but there were no dramatic court cases like the one concerning the State Department's felonious document-transmitter, Alger Hiss, and his accuser Whittaker Chambers. There were no new atomic spy cases, like the ones involving Klaus Fuchs and Julius and Ethel Rosenberg, which had so mesmerized the public in the late 1940s and early 1950s.

In fact, despite huge anxieties about it at the time, there seem to have been *no* instances in which domestic Communists engaged in anything that could be considered espionage after 1950. Moreover, at no time did any domestic Communist ever commit anything that could be considered violence in support of the cause—this despite deep apprehensions at the time about that form of terrorism then dubbed "sabotage." And as all significant terrorist violence within the United States since 2001 has taken place on television—most notably and persistently on Fox's *24*—the same was true about domestic Communist violence during the Cold War. FBI informant Herbert Philbrick's 1952 confessional, *I Led Three Lives: Citizen, "Communist", Counterspy*, at no point documents a single instance of Communist violence or planned violence. Nonetheless, violence became a central focus when his story was transmuted into a popular television series that ran from 1953 to 1957 (reportedly one of Lee Harvey Oswald's favorites).

However, even though the domestic Communist "menace" had pretty much settled into well-deserved oblivion by the mid-1970s, surveys repeating the Stouffer questions at the time found that fully 30 percent of the public *still* considered domestic Communists a great or very great danger to the country. Those who found them to be of no danger had inched up only to about 10 percent.

Some have argued that unjustified fears (or "hysteria") about the Communist enemy within was created by the media, and some now say the same thing about apprehensions of the terrorist enemy within. But the fear of domestic Communism persisted long after the press had become thoroughly bored with the issue. This suggests that, while the media may exacerbate fears about perceived threats, they do not create them. That is, fears often have an independent source, and then take on a fictional life of their own.

Something similar may have happened with the "war on drugs." Over the last few decades, the drug evil has so impressed itself on the American public that the issue can scarcely be brought up for public discussion. Drug abuse used to be a big public concern—Ronald Reagan latched on to it, and George H.W. Bush pushed it further, particularly after it soared into public anxiety during the first year of his presidency. Somewhere along the line it became a politically untouchable issue. Certainly, neither Bill Clinton nor Bush the younger were tempted to tinker with the policy, much less re-examine it. In the meantime, the drug "war" has picked up its own political constituency: In California, for example, the powerful prison guard lobby takes the lead.

One could, of course, suggest that the long and costly drug "war" has pretty much been a failure. After all, drug use has hardly plummeted, and strenuous efforts to interdict supplies have not notably inflated street prices. But that discussion, considered by many to be political poison, never really happens, so the drug war and its attendant expenditures continue to ramble inexorably and consensually onward. This is true despite the fact that the so-called war is severely hampering efforts to rebuild war-torn Afghanistan by seeking to cut off that struggling country's only significant source of earned revenue.

Perspectives on terror, now thoroughly internalized, seem likely to take on a similarly unexamined, self-perpetuating trajectory. Moreover, Communism and the alleged threat presented by Japanese-Americans during World War II were capable of dying out entirely, but terrorism, like drugs, will always be with us. We could be in for a very long siege indeed.

This conclusion is suggested, as well, by the fact that routine fears and knee-jerk concerns continue despite a notable decline in the urgency of official warnings. Interested public officials have occasionally attempted to jigger things with various alarms, raising terror alerts from time to time, warning against "complacency", assuring all and sundry that the "war" must continue (and related budgets increase) because . . . well, because we have to do everything possible to prevent another 9/11. However, we have been subjected to only a few warnings lately.

Early last year, for example, former CIA Director George Tenet revealed on CBS's *60 Minutes* that his "operational intuition" was telling him that al-Qaeda had infiltrated a second or third wave into the United States, though he added with uncharacteristic modesty, "Can I prove it to you? No." And Secretary of Homeland Security Michael Chertoff informed us a few months later that his "gut" was telling him that there would be an attack during the summer. Apparently, it was only gas; nothing happened.

What Chertoff's gut is telling him these days, as far as I know, has gone unrecorded, even on the Homeland Security website, where the organization really might, as a public service, use some of its ever-escalating funds to publish routine updates—perhaps on a daily gut-o-meter. Homeland Security spokesmen might also explain why airport security, elevated to the "orange" level after an airline plot in another hemisphere was rolled up two years ago, remains at that level today when the extra security required by the higher rating can cost an individual airport, and therefore passengers, $100,000 per day.

But spooky misgivings inspired by guts and intuition are nothing compared to the colorful and unqualified fire-and-brimstone warnings issued by public officials in the past. In 2002, Tenet assured us without even a wisp of equivocation that al-Qaeda was "reconstituted", "planning in multi-theaters", and "coming after us." The next year, Chertoff's predecessor at Homeland Security, Tom Ridge, divined that "extremists abroad are anticipating near-term attacks that they believe will either rival or exceed" those of 2001. And in 2004, Attorney General John Ashcroft, with FBI Director Robert Mueller at his side, announced that "credible intelligence from multiple sources indicates that al-Qaeda plans to attempt an attack on the United States in the next few months", that its "specific intention" was to hit us "hard", and that the "arrangements" for that attack were already 90 percent complete. (Oddly enough, Ashcroft doesn't mention this memorable headline-grabbing episode in *Never Again*, his 2006 memoir of the period.)

Director Mueller himself has mellowed quite a bit over time. In 2003, he assured us that, although his agency had yet to actually identify even a single al-Qaeda cell in the United States, such unidentified (or imagined) entities nonetheless presented "the greatest threat", had "developed a support infrastructure" in the country, and had achieved "the ability and the intent to inflict significant casualties in the United States with little warning." At the time, intelligence reports were asserting—which is really to say guessing—that the number of trained al-Qaeda operatives in the United States was between 2,000 and 5,000, and FBI officials were informing rapt reporters that cells were "embedded in most U.S. cities with sizable Islamic communities", usually in the "run-down sections", that they were "up and active", and that electronic intercepts had found some to be "talking to each other." In 2005, at a time when the FBI admitted it still had been unable to unearth a single true al-Qaeda cell, Mueller continued his dire I-think-therefore-they-are projections: "I remain very concerned about what we are not seeing", he ominously ruminated. But in testimony last year, Mueller's chief rallying cry had been reduced to a comparatively bland, "We believe al-Qaeda is still seeking to infiltrate operatives into the U.S. from overseas."

Notably, even a specific (and lone) effort on the part of an official to dampen terrorism fears has had no noticeable impact on public perceptions. Last year, New York Mayor Michael Bloomberg actually went so far as to urge people to "get a life", pointing out that "you have a much greater danger of being hit by lightning than being struck by a terrorist." It is possible, however, that Bloomberg's glancing brush with reality (which, most interestingly, does not seem to have hurt him politically) was undercut by the fact that his city expends huge resources chasing after terrorists while routinely engaging in some of the most pointless security theater on the planet. For example, New York often extracts police officers from their duties to have them idle around at a sampling of the city's thousands of subway entrances, blandly watching as millions of people wearing backpacks or carrying parcels descend into the system throughout the city. It is also fond of trumpeting the fact that thousands of people each year call the city's counterterrorism hotline (8,999 in 2006 and more than 13,473 in 2007), while neglecting to mention that *not a single one* of these calls has yet led to a terrorism arrest.

IRONIES OF FEAR

H.L. Mencken once declared that "the whole aim of practical politics" is "to keep the populace alarmed (and hence clamorous to be led to safety) by menacing it with an endless series of hobgoblins, all of them imaginary." There is nothing imaginary about al-Qaeda, of course, though some of the proclaimed official sightings of the group in the United States do have an Elvis-like quality to them. But the American public has retained much of its sense of alarm about internal attacks despite the fact that the al-Qaeda hobgoblin hasn't actually carried any out for nearly seven years. And the public has retained its fear even when politicians and public officials, however belatedly, temper their scary and at times outright irresponsible bellowings.

All this may help to explain why there have been no al-Qaeda attacks in the United States for so many years, contrary to almost all anticipations. Perhaps the group's goal is not to destroy the United States with explosions, but to have the Americans destroy themselves by wallowing in fear and by engaging in counterproductive policy overreaction. Thus, shortly after 9/11, Osama bin Laden happily crowed that "America is full of fear, from its north to its south, from its west to its east. Thank God for that." And in 2004 he proclaimed his policy to be "bleeding America to the point of bankruptcy", noting with consummate glee that, "It is easy for us to provoke and bait. . . . All that we have to do is . . . raise a piece of cloth on which is written al-Qaeda in order to make the generals race there to cause America to suffer human, economic, and political losses." The 9/11 attacks, he calculated, cost only $500,000 to carry out, "while the attack and its aftermath inflicted a cost of more than $500 billion on the United States."

There may be some danger that the fear and policy overreaction al-Qaeda finds so gratifying may actually have the perverse effect of tempting them into further efforts within the country. If it is so easy to make the Americans go crazy and harm themselves economically, and at such bargain basement prices, why not do more of it? American defenses may have improved since 9/11, but no one would maintain they are so effective as to prevent a persistent, devoted and clever group of conspirators from being able to accomplish limited feats.

The ultimate nightmare of American scaremongers, setting off an atomic bomb, is well beyond al-Qaeda's capacities and very likely always will be, but to be impressive, terrorism doesn't have to be carried out at that level. Al-Qaeda or likeminded franchise affiliates need only infiltrate the country or locally recruit a handful of operatives to shoot up a few fast-food restaurants, set off a few forest fires, or explode a few small bombs in buses, shopping centers or highway overpasses. Look at what just two semi-sane "snipers" were able to do to the Washington, DC area in the summer of 2002.

If al-Qaeda remains capable of carrying out attacks of at least that magnitude, it must be that its leaders lack the intent to do so. There may be a number of reasons for this, but one might be that they see little need to stir the pot further because fear levels remain high and because the United States, no matter which party is in the White House and despite the Iraq experience, can probably be counted upon to lash out counterproductively in any case. It was the "experienced" and judicious Hillary Clinton, after all, who last year declared that Iran must be prevented from getting a nuclear weapon "at all costs." As Napoleon put it, "never interrupt your enemy when he is making a mistake."

Accordingly, since Americans and their policymakers continue to fear and overreact so predictably, al-Qaeda may continue to confine its pot-stirring to ominous verbal threats—all of which are readily embraced with rapt seriousness by its distant enemy. If this perspective is correct, such cheap talk would constitute tactically useful lies, but bin Laden clearly has had no reticence about fictions in the service of terror. As America invaded Afghanistan in 2001, for example, he told a visiting Pakistani journalist that al-Qaeda possessed nuclear weapons, a claim that was either a blatant lie or a self-gratifying fantasy. He may have been indulging that same proclivity when he spouted in 2002 that "the youth of Islam are preparing things that will fill your hearts with terror", or four years later that "operations are under preparation, and you will see them on your own ground once they are finished, God willing." (On the other hand, maybe there have been no attacks simply because God has been unwilling.)

An irony here, I suppose, is that if we were to come to our senses and calm down, al-Qaeda might conceivably come to feel obligated to attack again in order to restock the American reservoir of insecurity. But there isn't much danger of official calm. Even without further terrorist attacks (and for that matter, even without Osama bin Laden), the "war on terror" seems likely to continue to grind on for a long time. Seven years after Cheney's declaration, there is no foreseeable time when we will be able to bring ourselves to declare it "all over with."

NOTE

1. Note Senator Chuck Hagel's remark on this point in *The American Interest* (March/April 2008).

CHAPTER 5

INTERNATIONAL LAW
AND ORGANIZATION
The Promise of Liberal Institutionalism

In the 1970s and 1980s, the realist perspective on international relations was facing a growing intellectual challenge from scholars who called themselves neoliberals or liberal institutionalists. These neoliberals accepted certain realist premises such as the central role of the state in international relations. However, in noting the growing interdependence among states in the international system, especially in, but not limited to, the economic realm, neoliberals offered greater hope for cooperation among states than that offered by their realist counterparts. The proliferation of international organizations in the decades following World War II was one indication of this cooperative option.

For neoliberals, institutions included, but were not limited to, formal international organizations like the United Nations. They also included less formal sets of rules, norms, and expectations that provide a degree of order and predictability in relations among states. These more informal institutions, often referred to as *international regimes,* were seen as constraining the behavior of even the most powerful states and thereby limiting the impact of brute force in world politics. Thus, liberal institutionalists began to talk of such things as an international trade regime and a weapons proliferation regime that established expectations for acceptable state behavior. This emphasis on institutions inevitably led to a rediscovery of international law, a field that had been largely discarded in the era of realist dominance of international relations thinking after World War II.

The reading by Robert Keohane provides a statement and defense of liberal institutionalism by one of its leading proponents. That selection is followed by Anne-Marie Slaughter's discussion of the role and significance of international law. Slaughter makes the case that even a superpower such as the United States needs international law. In contrast, Michael Glennon argues that the U.S. invasion of Iraq in 2003 without UN approval and, arguably, in defiance of international law demonstrates the failures of both international law and of the UN Security Council to constrain the use of military force when a powerful state is determined to use it. The reading by Thomas Weiss examines the record of Security Council reform and the possibilities for increasing its credibility in the post-Iraq era. Your goal in reading the selections in this chapter should be to assess the extent to which institutions can and do play an important role in mitigating realist power politics.

INTERNATIONAL INSTITUTIONS: CAN INTERDEPENDENCE WORK?

Robert O. Keohane

Liberal institutionalism challenges the realist assumption that international cooperation is impossible under anarchy. Robert Keohane is one of the most prominent representatives of the liberal institutionalist approach. As you read this article, ask yourself:

* What does Keohane mean by "institutions"?
* Which assumptions of realism does he explicitly accept, and which does he reject?
* What are the common objections to liberal institutionalism, and how does Keohane respond to them?

To analyze world politics . . . is to discuss international institutions: the rules that govern elements of world politics and the organizations that help implement those rules. Should NATO expand? How can the United Nations Security Council assure UN inspectors access to sites where Iraq might be conducting banned weapons activity? Under what conditions should China be admitted to the World Trade Organization (WTO)? How many billions of dollars does the International Monetary Fund (IMF) need at its disposal to remain an effective "lender of last resort" for countries . . . threatened . . . with financial collapse? Will the tentative Kyoto Protocol on Climate Change be renegotiated, ratified, and implemented effectively? Can future United Nations peacekeeping practices—in contrast to the UN fiascoes in Bosnia and Somalia—be made more effective?

These questions help illustrate the growing importance of international institutions for maintaining world order. Twelve years ago in these pages, Joseph Nye and I gave "two cheers for multilateralism," pointing out that even the administration of President Ronald Reagan, which took office ill-disposed toward international institutions, had grudgingly come to accept their value in achieving American purposes. Superpowers need general rules because they seek to influence events around the world. Even an unchallenged superpower such as the United States would be unable to achieve its goals through the bilateral exercise of influence: the costs of such massive "arm-twisting" would be too great.

International institutions are increasingly important, but they are not always successful. Ineffective institutions such as the United Nations Industrial Development Organization or the Organization of African Unity exist alongside effectual ones such as the Montreal Protocol on Substances that Deplete the Ozone

Robert O. Keohane, "International Institutions: Can Interdependence Work?" *Foreign Policy* 110, Spring 1998. Copyright 1998 by Foreign Policy. Reproduced with permission of Foreign Policy in the format Textbook via Copyright Clearance Center. www.foreignpolicy.com.

Layer and the European Union. In recent years, we have gained insight into what makes some institutions more capable than others—how such institutions best promote cooperation among states and what mechanics of bargaining they use. But our knowledge is incomplete, and as the world moves toward new forms of global regulation and governance, the increasing impact of international institutions has raised new questions about how these institutions themselves are governed.

THEORY AND REALITY, 1919–89

Academic "scribblers" did not always have to pay much attention to international institutions. The 1919 Versailles Treaty constituted an attempt to construct an institution for multilateral diplomacy—the League of Nations. But the rejection of the League Covenant by the U.S. Senate ensured that until World War II the most important negotiations in world politics—from the secret German-Russian deals of the 1920s to the 1938 Munich conference—took place on an ad hoc basis. Only after the United Nations was founded in 1945, with strong support from the United States and a multiplicity of specialized agencies performing different tasks, did international institutions begin to command substantial international attention.

Until the late 1960s, American students of international relations equated international institutions with formal international organizations, especially the United Nations. *International Organization,* the leading academic journal on the subject, carried long summaries of UN meetings until 1971. However, most observers recognized long before 1972 that the United Nations did not play a central role in world politics. Except for occasional peace-keeping missions—of which the First UN Emergency Force in the Middle East between 1956 and 1967 was the most successful—its ability to resolve hostilities was paralyzed by conflicts of interest that resulted in frequent superpower vetoes in the Security Council. Moreover, the influx of new postcolonial states helped turn the General Assembly into an arena for North-South conflict after 1960 and ensured that the major Western powers, especially the United States, would view many General Assembly resolutions as hostile to their interests and values—for example, the New International Economic Order and the Zionism is Racism resolutions of the 1970s. Analysts and policy-makers in Europe, North America, and much of Asia concluded that international institutions were marginal to a game of world politics still driven by the traditional exercise of state power. The UN—called "a dangerous place" by former U.S. representative to the UN Daniel Patrick Moynihan—seemed more a forum for scoring points in the Cold War or North-South conflicts than an instrument for problem-solving cooperation.

In reality, however, even the most powerful states were relying increasingly on international institutions—not so much on the UN as other organizations and regimes that set rules and standards to govern specific sets of activities. From the late 1960s onward, the Treaty on the Non-Proliferation of Nuclear Weapons was the chief vehicle for efforts to prevent the dangerous spread of nuclear weapons. NATO was not only the most successful multilateral alliance in history but also the most highly institutionalized, with a secretary-general, a permanent staff, and elaborate rules governing relations among members. From its founding in 1947 through the Uruguay Round that concluded in 1993, the General Agreement on Tariffs and Trade

(GATT) presided over a series of trade rounds that have reduced import tariffs among industrialized countries by up to 90 percent, boosting international trade. After a shaky start in the 1940s, the IMF had—by the 1960s—become the centerpiece of efforts by the major capitalist democracies to regulate their monetary affairs. When that function atrophied with the onset of flexible exchange rates in the 1970s, it became their leading agent for financing and promoting economic development in Africa, Asia, and Latin America. The sheer number of intergovernmental organizations also rose dramatically—from about 30 in 1910 to 70 in 1940 to more than 1,000 by 1981.

The exchange rate and oil crises of the early 1970s helped bring perceptions in line with reality. Suddenly, both top policymakers and academic observers in the United States realized that global issues required systematic policy coordination and that such coordination required institutions. In 1974, then secretary of state Henry Kissinger, who had paid little attention to international institutions, helped establish the International Energy Agency to enable Western countries to deal cooperatively with the threat of future oil embargoes like the 1973 OPEC embargo of the Netherlands and United States. And the Ford administration sought to construct a new international monetary regime based on flexible rather than pegged exchange rates. Confronted with complex interdependence and the efforts of states to manage it, political scientists began to redefine the study of international institutions, broadening it to encompass what they called "international regimes"—structures of rules and norms that could be more or less informal. The international trade regime, for example, did not have strong formal rules or integrated, centralized management; rather, it provided

a set of interlocking institutions, including regular meetings of the GATT contracting parties, formal dispute settlement arrangements, and delegation of technical tasks to a secretariat, which gradually developed a body of case law and practice. Some international lawyers grumbled that the political scientists were merely using other terms to discuss international law. Nevertheless, political scientists were once again discussing how international rules and norms affect state behavior, even if they avoided the "L-word."

In the 1980s, research on international regimes moved from attempts to describe the phenomena of interdependence and international regimes to closer analysis of the conditions under which countries cooperate. How does cooperation occur among sovereign states and how do international institutions affect it? From the standpoint of political realism, both the reliance placed by states on certain international institutions and the explosion in their numbers were puzzling. Why should international institutions exist at all in a world dominated by sovereign states? This question seemed unanswerable if institutions were seen as opposed to, or above, the state but not if they were viewed as devices to help states accomplish their objectives.

The new research on international institutions broke decisively with legalism—the view that law can be effective regardless of political conditions—as well as with the idealism associated with the field's origins. Instead, scholars adopted the assumptions of realism, accepting that relative state power and competing interests were key factors in world politics, but at the same time drawing new conclusions about the influence of institutions on the process. Institutions create the capability for states to cooperate in mutually beneficial ways by reducing the costs of making and enforcing agreements—what economists refer to as "transaction costs." They rarely engage in centralized enforcement of agreements, but they do reinforce practices of reciprocity, which provide incentives for governments to keep their own commitments to ensure that others do so as well. Even powerful states have an interest, most of the time, in following the rules of well-established international institutions, since general conformity to rules makes the behavior of other states more predictable.

This scholarship drew heavily on the twin concepts of uncertainty and credibility. Theorists increasingly recognized that the preferences of states amount to "private information"—that absent full transparency, states are uncertain about what their partners and rivals value at any given time. They naturally respond to uncertainty by being less willing to enter into agreements, since they are unsure how their partners will later interpret the terms of such agreements. International institutions can reduce this uncertainty by promoting negotiations in which transparency is encouraged; by dealing with a series of issues over many years and under similar rules, thus encouraging honesty in order to preserve future reputation; and by systematically monitoring the compliance of governments with their commitments.

Even if a government genuinely desires an international agreement, it may be unable to persuade its partners that it will, in the future, be willing and able to implement it. Successful international negotiations may therefore require changes in domestic institutions. For instance, without "fast-track" authority on trade, the United States' negotiating partners have no assurance that Congress will refrain from adding new provisions to trade agreements as a condition for their ratification. Hence, other states are reluctant to enter into trade negotiations with the United States since they may be confronted, at the end of tortuous negotiations, with a redesigned agreement less favorable to them than the draft they initialed. By the same token, without fast-track authority, no promise by the U.S. government to abide by negotiated terms has much credibility, due to the president's lack of control over Congress.

In short, this new school of thought argued that, rather than imposing themselves on states, international institutions should respond to the demand by states for cooperative ways to fulfill their own purposes. By reducing uncertainty and the costs of making and enforcing agreements, international institutions help states achieve collective gains.

YESTERDAY'S CONTROVERSIES: 1989–95

This new institutionalism was not without its critics, who focused their attacks on three perceived shortcomings: First, they claimed that international institutions are fundamentally insignificant since states wield the only real power in world politics. They emphasized the weakness of efforts by the UN or League of Nations to achieve collective security against aggression by great powers, and they pointed to the dominant role of major contributors in international economic organizations. Hence, any effects of these international institutions were attributed more to the efforts of their great power backers than to the institutions themselves.

This argument was overstated. Of course, great powers such as the United States exercise enormous influence within international institutions. But the policies that emerge from these institutions are different from those that the United States would have adopted unilaterally. Whether toward Iraq or recipients of IMF loans, policies for specific situations cannot be entirely ad hoc but must conform to generally applicable rules and principles to be endorsed by multi-lateral institutions. Where agreement by many states is necessary for policy to be effective, even the United States finds it useful to compromise on substance to obtain the institutional seal of approval. Therefore, the decision-making procedures and general rules of international institutions matter. They affect both the substance of policy and the degree to which other states accept it.

The second counterargument focused on "anarchy": the absence of a world government or effective international legal system to which victims of injustice can appeal. As a result of anarchy, critics argued, states prefer relative gains (i.e., doing better than other states) to absolute gains. They seek to protect their power and status and will resist even mutually beneficial cooperation if their partners are likely to benefit more than they are. For instance, throughout the American-Soviet arms race, both sides focused on their relative positions—who was ahead or threatening to gain a decisive advantage—rather than on their own levels of armaments. Similar dynamics appear on certain economic issues, such as the fierce Euro-American competition (i.e., Airbus Industrie versus Boeing) in the production of large passenger jets.

Scholarly disputes about the "relative gains question" were intense but short-lived. It turned out that the question needed to be reframed: not, "do states seek relative or absolute gains?" but "under what conditions do they forego even mutually beneficial cooperation to preserve their relative power and status?" When there are only two major players, and one side's gains may decisively change power relationships, relative gains loom large: in arms races, for example, or monopolistic competition (as between Airbus and Boeing). Most issues of potential cooperation, however, from trade

liberalization to climate change, involve multi-lateral negotiations that make relative gains hard to calculate and entail little risk of decisive power shifts for one side over another. Therefore, states can be expected most of the time to seek to enhance their own welfare without being worried that others will also make advances. So the relative gains argument merely highlights the difficulties of cooperation where there is tough bilateral competition; it does not by any means undermine prospects for cooperation in general.

The third objection to theories of cooperation was less radical but more enduring. Theorists of cooperation had recognized that cooperation is not harmonious: it emerges out of discord and takes place through tough bargaining. Nevertheless, they claimed that the potential joint gains from such cooperation explained the dramatic increases in the number and scope of cooperative multilateral institutions. Critics pointed out, however, that bargaining problems could produce obstacles to achieving joint gains. For instance, whether the Kyoto Protocol will lead to a global agreement is questionable in part because developing countries refused to accept binding limits on their emissions and the U.S. Senate declared its unwillingness to ratify any agreement not containing such commitments by developing countries. Both sides staked out tough bargaining positions, hindering efforts at credible compromise. As a result of these bargaining problems, the fact that possible deals could produce joint gains does not assure that cooperative solutions will be reached. The tactics of political actors and the information they have available about one another are both key aspects of a process that does not necessarily lead to cooperation. Institutions may help provide "focal points," on which competing actors may agree, but new issues often lack such institutions. In this case, both the pace and the extent of cooperation become more problematic.

TODAY'S DEBATES

The general problem of bargaining raises specific issues about how institutions affect international negotiations, which always involve a mixture of discord and potential cooperation. Thinking about bargaining leads to concerns about subjectivity, since bargaining depends so heavily on the beliefs of the parties involved. And the most fundamental question scholars wish to answer concerns effectiveness: What structures, processes, and practices make international institutions more or less capable of affecting policies—and outcomes—in desired ways?

The impact of institutional arrangements on bargaining remains puzzling. We understand from observation, from game theory, and from explorations of bargaining in a variety of contexts that outcomes depend on more than the resources available to the actors or the payoffs they receive. Institutions affect bargaining patterns in complex and nuanced ways. Who, for example, has authority over the agenda? In the 1980s, Jacques Delors used his authority as head of the European Commission to structure the agenda of the European Community, thus leading to the Single European Act and the Maastricht Treaty. What voting or consensus arrangements are used and who interprets ambiguities? At the Kyoto Conference, agreement on a rule of "consensus" did not prevent the conference chair from ignoring objections as he gaveled through provision after provision in the final session. Can disgruntled participants block implementation of formally ratified agreements? In the GATT, until 1993, losers could prevent the findings of dispute resolution panels from being implemented; but in the WTO, panel

recommendations take effect unless there is a consensus not to implement them. Asking such questions systematically about international institutions may well yield significant new insights in future years.

Institutional maneuvers take place within a larger ideological context that helps define which purposes such institutions pursue and which practices they find acceptable. The Mandates System of the League of Nations depended in part on specific institutional arrangements, but more fundamental was the shared understanding that continued European rule over non-European peoples was acceptable. No system of rule by Europeans over non-Europeans could remain legitimate after the collapse of that consensus during the 15 years following World War II.

The end of the Cold War shattered a whole set of beliefs about world politics. Theories of international politics during the Cold War were overwhelmingly materialistic, reflecting a view of the world in which states pursued "national interests" shaped by geopolitical and economic realities. As Stalin once famously quipped about the pope: "How many divisions does he have?" Not only did an unarmed Pope John Paul II prevail in the contest for the allegiance of the Polish people, but after the failed 1991 coup against Gorbachev, the Soviet Union broke into its constituent parts on the basis of the norm of "self-determination," rather than along lines of military power or economic resources. State interests now depend in part on how people define their identities—as Serbs or Croats, Russians or Chechens. They also depend on the political and religious values to which their publics are committed.

Hence, the end of the Cold War made scholars increasingly aware of the importance of ideas, norms, and information—topics that some of them had already begun to explore.

Some years earlier, such a reorientation might have faced fierce criticism from adherents of game theory and other economics-based approaches, which had traditionally focused on material interests. However, since the mid-1980s, bargaining theory has shown more and more that the beliefs of actors are crucially important for outcomes. To adapt economist Thomas Schelling's famous example, suppose that you and I want to meet for lunch in New York City, but you work on Wall Street and I work on the Upper West Side. Where will we get together? We have a mutual interest in meeting, but each of us would prefer not to waste time traveling. If you leave a message on my answering machine suggesting a restaurant on Wall Street and are then unreachable, I have to choose between skipping lunch with you or showing up at your preferred location. Asymmetrical information and our mutual belief that I know where you will be waiting for me have structured the situation.

The procedures and rules of international institutions create informational structures. They determine what principles are acceptable as the basis for reducing conflicts and whether governmental actions are legitimate or illegitimate. Consequently, they help shape actors' expectations. For instance, trade conflicts are increasingly ritualized in a process of protesting in the WTO—promising tough action on behalf of one's own industries, engaging in quasi-judicial dispute resolution procedures, claiming victory if possible, or complaining about defeat when necessary. There is much sound and fury, but regularly institutionalized processes usually relegate conflict to the realm of dramatic expression. Institutions thereby create differentiated information. "Insiders" can interpret the language directed toward "outsiders" and use their own understandings to interpret, or manipulate, others' beliefs.

Finally, students of international institutions continue to try to understand why some institutions are so much more effective than others. Variation in the coherence of institutional policy or members' conformity with institutional rules is partially accounted for by the degree of common interests and the distribution of power among members. Institutions whose members share social values and have similar political systems—such as NATO or the European Union—are likely to be stronger than those such as the Organization for Security and Cooperation in Europe or the Association of South East Asian Nations, whose more diverse membership does not necessarily have the same kind of deep common interests. Additionally, the character of domestic politics has a substantial impact on international institutions. The distribution of power is also important. Institutions dominated by a small number of members—for example, the IMF, with its weighted voting system—can typically take more decisive action than those where influence is more widely diffused, such as the UN General Assembly.

OVERCOMING THE DEMOCRATIC DEFICIT

Even as scholars pursue these areas of inquiry, they are in danger of overlooking a major normative issue: the "democratic deficit" that exists in many of the world's most important international institutions. As illustrated most recently by far-reaching interventions of the IMF, the globalization of the world economy and the expanding role of international institutions are creating a powerful form of global regulation. Major international institutions are increasingly laying down rules and guidelines that governments, if they wish to attract foreign investment and generate growth, must follow. But these international institutions are managed by technocrats and supervised by high governmental officials. That is, they are run by élites. Only in the most attenuated sense is democratic control exercised over major international organizations. Key negotiations in the WTO are made in closed sessions. The IMF negotiates in secret with potential borrowers, and it has only begun in the last few months to provide the conditions it imposes on recipients.

The EU provides another case in point. Its most important decision-making body is its Council of Ministers, which is composed of government representatives who perform more important legislative functions than the members of the European Parliament. The council meets behind closed doors and does not publish its votes. It also appoints members to the European Commission, which acts as the EU executive, whose ties to the public are thus very indirect indeed. The European Parliament has narrowly defined powers and little status; most national parliaments do not closely scrutinize European-level actions. How much genuine influence do German or Italian voters therefore have over the council's decisions? Very little.

The issue here is not one of state sovereignty. Economic interdependence and its regulation have altered notions of sovereignty: Few states can still demand to be completely independent of external authority over legal practices within their territories. The best most states can hope for is to be able to use their sovereign authority as a bargaining tool to assure that others also have to abide by common rules and practices. Given these changes, the issue here is who has influence over the sorts of bargains that are struck? Democratic theory gives pride of place to the public role in deciding on the distributional and value tradeoffs inherent in legislation and regulation. But the practices of international institutions place that privilege in

the hands of the élites of national governments and of international organizations.

Admittedly, democracy does not always work well. American politicians regularly engage in diatribes against international institutions, playing on the dismay of a vocal segment of their electorates at the excessive number of foreigners in the United Nations. More seriously, an argument can be made that the IMF, like central banks, can only be effective if it is insulated from direct democratic control. Ever since 1787, however, practitioners and theorists have explored how authoritative decision making can be combined with accountability to publics and indirect democratic control. The U.S. Constitution is based on such a theory—the idea that popular sovereignty, though essential, is best exercised indirectly, through rather elaborate institutions. An issue that scholars should now explore is how to devise international institutions that are not only competent and effective but also accountable, at least ultimately, to democratic publics.

One possible response is to say that all is well, since international institutions are responsible to governments—which, in turn, are accountable in democracies to their own people. International regulation simply adds another link to the chain of delegation. But long chains of delegation, in which the public affects action only at several removes, reduce actual public authority. If the terms of multilateral cooperation are to reflect the interests of broader democratic publics rather than just those of narrow élites, traditional patterns of delegation will have to be supplemented by other means of ensuring greater accountability to public opinion.

One promising approach would be to seek to invigorate transnational society in the form of networks among individuals and nongovernmental organizations. The growth of such networks—of scientists, professionals in various fields, and human rights and environmental activists—has been aided greatly by the fax machine and the Internet and by institutional arrangements that incorporate these networks into decision making. For example, natural and social scientists developed the scientific consensus underlying the Kyoto Protocol through the Intergovernmental Panel on Climate Change (IPCC) whose scientific work was organized by scientists who did not have to answer to any governments. The Kyoto Protocol was negotiated, but governments opposed to effective action on climate change could not hope to renegotiate the scientific guidelines set by the IPCC.

The dramatic fall in the cost of long-distance communication will facilitate the development of many more such transnational networks. As a result, wealthy hierarchical organizations— multinational corporations as well as states—are likely to have more difficulty dominating transnational communications. Thirty years ago, engaging in prolonged intercontinental communication required considerable resources. Now individuals do so on the Internet, virtually free.

Therefore, the future accountability of international institutions to their publics may rest only partly on delegation through formal democratic institutions. Its other pillar may be voluntary pluralism under conditions of maximum transparency. International policies may increasingly be monitored by loose groupings of scientists or other professionals, or by issue advocacy networks such as Amnesty International and Greenpeace, whose members, scattered around the world, will be linked even more closely by modern information technology. Accountability will be enhanced not only by chains of official responsibility, but by the requirement of transparency. Official actions, negotiated among state representatives in inter-national organizations, will be subjected to scrutiny by transnational networks.

Such transparency, however, represents nongovernmental organizations and networks more than ordinary people, who may be as excluded from élite networks as they are from government circles. That is, transnational civil society may be a necessary but insufficient condition for democratic accountability. Democracies should insist that, wherever feasible, international organizations maintain sufficient transparency for transnational networks of advocacy groups, domestic legislators, and democratic publics to evaluate their actions. But proponents of democratic accountability should also seek counterparts to the mechanisms of control embedded in national democratic institutions. Governors of the Federal Reserve Board are, after all, nominated by the president and confirmed by the Senate, even if they exercise great authority during their terms of office. If Madison, Hamilton, and Jay could invent indirect mechanisms of popular control in the *Federalist Papers* two centuries ago, it should not be beyond our competence to devise comparable mechanisms at the global level in the twenty-first century.

As we continue to think about the normative implications of globalization, we should focus simultaneously on the maintenance of robust democratic institutions at home, the establishment of formal structures of international delegation, and the role of transnational networks. To be effective in the twenty-first century, modern democracy requires international institutions. And to be consistent with democratic values, these institutions must be accountable to domestic civil society. Combining global governance with effective democratic accountability will be a major challenge for scholars and policymakers alike in the years ahead.

LEADING THROUGH LAW

Anne-Marie Slaughter

A key premise of liberal institutionalism is increasing reliance on the institution of international law. In this selection, Slaughter suggests that the world as a whole and the United States in particular need international law. As you read the selection, ask yourself:

- Why does she think the United States needs international law?
- What is the larger point Slaughter attempts to make in focusing on the U.S. relationship to international law over the years?
- How similar or different are the international legal system and domestic legal systems?

Does the United States need international law? At times in recent years, it has acted as if it does not. Yet international law provides the foundation not only for momentous undertakings, such as the efforts to halt the spread of nuclear weapons and to protect the ozone layer, but also for more routine endeavors, such as defining the boundaries of territorial seas and guaranteeing the right of diplomats to move freely. The United States needs international law acutely now because it offers a way to preserve our power and pursue our most important interests while reassuring our friends and allies that they have no reason to fear us or to form alliances as a counterweight to our overwhelming might. And we will need the law more than ever in the future, to regulate the behavior not only of states but of the individuals within them.

International law is not some kind of abstract end in itself. It's a complex of treaties and customary practices that govern, for example, the use of force, the protection of human rights, global public health, and the regulation of the oceans, space, and all other global commons. Each of its specialized regimes is based in the consent of states to a specific set of rules that allow them to reap gains from cooper-ation and thereby serve their collective interests. Overall, the rule of law in the global arena serves America's interests and reflects its most fundamental values. But in many specific areas, existing rules are too weak, too old, or too limited to address current threats and challenges. The United States must recommit itself to pursuing its interests in concert with other nations, according to principles of action that have been agreed upon and that are backed by legal obligation, political will, and economic and military power. At the same time, it has every right to insist that other nations recognize the extent to which many rules must be revised, updated, and even replaced.

International law provides the indispensable framework for the conduct of stable and orderly international relations. It does not descend from on high. Rather, it's created by states to serve their collective interests. Consider, for instance, the concept of sovereignty itself, which is routinely described as the cornerstone of the international legal system. Sovereignty is not some mysterious essence of statehood. It is a deliberate construct, invented and perpetuated by states seeking to reduce war and violence in a particular set of historical circumstances.

Anne-Marie Slaughter, "Leading Through Law," *The Wilson Quarterly,* Autumn 2003, 27:4, pp. 37–44.
Reprinted by permission of the author.

The founding myth of modern international law is that the Treaty of Westphalia, which ended the Thirty Years' War in 1648, gave birth to the system of states and the concept of inviolable state sovereignty. The Thirty Years' War was the last of the great religious wars in Europe, which were fought not really between states as such but between Catholics and Protestants. As religious minorities in one territory appealed to the coreligionist monarch of another, the Continent burned for three decades, and its people bled in a series of battles among the Holy Roman Empire, France, Sweden, Denmark, Bohemia, and a host of smaller principalities. The Treaty of Westphalia restored the principle of *cuius regio eius religio*— that is, the prince of a particular region determines the religion of his people. In today's language, this means that one sovereign state cannot intervene in the internal affairs of another.

But in reality, it took centuries for the modern state system to develop, and absolute sovereignty has never existed in practice, as many states on the receiving end of great-power interventions would attest. The architects of the Treaty of Westphalia glimpsed a vision of a world of discrete states armored against one another by the possession of "sovereignty"—a doctrine of legal right against military meddling.

It's important to realize that the right of sovereignty did not mean the prohibition of war. States were still free to go to war, as a matter of international law, until the Kellogg-Briand Pact of 1928 formally outlawed war (to evidently little effect). Sovereignty was the foundation on which modern states were built, but as they matured, their attacks on one another rapidly became the principal threat to international peace and security. After the conflagrations of World War I and World War II, it was evident that if interstate war continued unchecked, states—and their peoples— might not survive into the 21st century. Hence, the innovation of the United Nations Charter:

Article 2(4) required all states to refrain from "the use of force in their international relations against the territorial integrity or political independence of any state." The right of sovereignty no longer included the right to make war.

Further, given the apparent link between Adolf Hitler's horrific depredations against the German people and his aggression toward other states, the right of sovereignty became increasingly encumbered with conditions on a sovereign state's treatment of its own people. Thus was born the international human rights movement, which today has turned traditional conceptions of sovereignty almost inside out. A distinguished commission appointed by the Canadian government at the suggestion of the UN secretary general released a report at the end of 2001 that defined a state's membership in the United Nations as including a responsibility to protect the lives and basic liberties of its people—and noting that if a member state failed in that responsibility, the international community had a right to intervene.

Why such a shift? Because the decade after the Cold War, much like the decades before the Treaty of Westphalia, revealed a seething mass of ugly conflicts within states. The dividing lines in those conflicts were drawn by ethnicity as much as religion, and the divisions were almost always fueled by opportunistic leaders of one faction or another. But unlike in the 16th and 17th centuries, the danger as the 20th century drew to a close was not so much from one sovereign's meddling in the affairs of another as in the failure of regional and international institutions to intervene early enough to prevent the conflicts from boiling into violence—producing streams of refugees and heartbreaking pictures broadcast into living rooms around the world.

The story of sovereignty, even highly simplified, illustrates a basic point about international law. It is an *instrumental* rather than an *essential* body of rules, instrumental to achieving the goals of peace, order, justice, human dignity, prosperity, and harmony between human beings and nature—in short, those ends that reflect the changing hopes and aspirations of humankind. It is a highly imperfect instrument, as indeed is domestic law. Because international law regulates a society of states with no central authority, it lacks even the hint of coercion that's implicit in every encounter with a domestic police officer. It can be enforced by the military might of one or more nations, but that sort of enforcement is the exception rather than the rule.

Yet for all its imperfections, international law survives because it is the only alternative for nations seeking to regularize their relations with one another and bind together credibly enough to achieve common gains. International law allows diplomats to escape parking tickets in New York City because without diplomatic immunity embassies would close. It allows a nation to set aside 12 miles of territorial waters for the use of its own fishing boats rather than just three or five or seven. And it allowed the first President Bush to assemble a UN coalition against Iraq quickly and easily in 1991 because Iraq had so flagrantly violated the UN Charter by invading Kuwait.

In the 1980s, political scientists such as Robert Keohane, Steve Krasner, and John Ruggie demonstrated more precisely what international lawyers had long believed: "Regimes," meaning everything from treaties to organizations to customary practices, allow nations to overcome a dilemma. The best solution to a problem can be achieved only through cooperation, but any individual state risks a "sucker's payoff" if it acts cooperatively and other states do not. Rules and settled practices overcome this dilemma by making it easier for states to negotiate credible commitments, to gather and share information, and to monitor one another and develop reputations for good or bad behavior.

America's Founding Fathers knew that the United States needed international law as a shield to protect a new and weak nation. They went to great pains to declare their new democracy a law-abiding member of the society of nations. The Declaration of Independence set forth the legal case for revolution out of "a decent respect to the opinions of mankind." The Constitution enshrined treaties as "the supreme law of the land," alongside the Constitution itself and federal law. The first Congress made it possible for aliens to sue in U.S. federal courts "for a tort only, in violation of the law of nations." The statute was originally intended to assure foreign citizens and their governments that they would find sure redress in U.S. courts for violations of the laws governing relations among countries, such as diplomatic immunity. Today, it allows foreign victims of grave human-rights violations to sue their torturers if they find them on U.S. soil.

Just over a century after its founding, the United States was an emerging power with a new prominence in world affairs. Yet its commitment to international law remained firm—much more so, in fact, than we generally recognize today. Though most accounts of the crucial period after World War I are dominated by the struggle between President Woodrow Wilson and the American isolationists who opposed his vision of world order, an important group of Republicans championed a view of international relations that rested on a commitment to international law more zealous than Wilson's. The leader of this group was Elihu Root (1845–1937), the most distinguished lawyer-statesman of his day, who served as secretary of war under William McKinley, secretary of state under Theodore Roosevelt, and as a U.S. senator from New York. As Jonathan Zasloff recalls in *New York University Law Review* (April 2003), more than a decade before

Wilson championed his great cause, Root was developing and implementing a distinctive vision of world order based solely on law. Using the kind of rhetoric that would later be associated with Wilson, Root scornfully declared that diplomacy in the past had "consisted chiefly of bargaining and largely cheating in the bargain." But unlike Wilson, who would propose a new international system based on the global spread of democracy and the political and military power of the League of Nations, Root argued for a system based strictly on law.

During the debate over the League, Root, though retired from the Senate, was the principal architect of Republican strategy. Leading Republican senators embraced U.S. engagement with the world, but only on the basis of law, not of binding military and political obligations. They supported legal institutions such as the Permanent Court of Arbitration (established in The Hague in 1899) and the new Permanent Court of International Justice (created by the League of Nations in 1921). But they rejected the collective security guarantee that lay at the core of the League Covenant. They would vote for the Covenant only with reservations attached. Root himself denounced the Covenant for abandoning "all effort to promote or maintain anything like a system of international law, or a system of arbitration, or of judicial settlement, through which a nation can assert its legal rights in lieu of war." Wilson, however, would accept no compromise, and the Covenant was defeated.

Root worked hard throughout his life to put his vision into effect (in 1912 he won the Nobel Peace Prize, in part for negotiating treaties of arbitration between the United States and more than 40 other nations). But the Japanese invasion of Manchuria in 1931 and the remilitarization of the Rhineland in 1936 made the shortcomings of both isolationism and pure legalism evident. In 1945, Republicans and Democrats finally came

together in strong support of a new international legal order in the United Nations, but one that melded law and power. The UN Charter was written, as *Time* put it, "for a world of power, tempered by a little reason." The provisions giving the Soviet Union, China, Britain, France, and the United States permanent seats on the Security Council, along with veto power over Council actions, were recognition that a law-based order has to accommodate the realities of great-power politics.

The interesting question is why the United States, the overwhelmingly dominant power at the end of World War II, would choose to embed itself in a web of international institutions—not just the United Nations but the World Bank, the International Monetary Fund, the General Agreement on Tariffs and Trade, and the North Atlantic Treaty Organization. In *After Victory* (2000), political scientist John Ikenberry argues compellingly that the United States pursued an institutional strategy as a way of entrenching a set of international rules favorable to its geopolitical and economic interests. Along the way, however, it was repeatedly compelled to accept real restraints on American power in order to assure weaker states in its orbit that it would neither abandon nor dominate them. For instance, U.S. officials had a sophisticated strategy for rebuilding Western Europe and integrating West Germany into a Western European order but sought to keep America aloof from the process. The Europeans, Ikenberry writes, "insisted that the binding together of Europe was only acceptable if the United States itself made binding commitments to them." The power of the United States to build a political order thus required the nation's willingness and ability to tie itself to a legal order.

Since the end of the Cold War, as Americans seem never to tire of repeating, America's power relative to that of other nations has only increased. But instead of hastening to reassure weaker nations by demonstrating our willingness to accept rules that further the common good, the United States is coupling its explicit drive for primacy with an equally explicit disdain for a whole range of treaties. Consider the current U.S. opposition to virtually all arms-control treaties—land mines, small arms, the Comprehensive Test Ban Treaty, the Anti-Ballistic Missile Treaty—and to efforts to strengthen existing treaties on biological and chemical warfare. The result? Nations around the world are arming themselves, if not directly against us, then at least, as in the case of the European Union, to ensure that they have an independent military capability.

The 1945 strategy was the right one, and it is now more essential than ever. We have an opportunity to lead *through* law, not against it, and to build a vastly strengthened international legal order that will protect and promote our interests. If we are willing to accept even minimal restraints, we can rally the rest of the world to adopt and enforce rules that will be effective in fighting scourges from terrorism to AIDS. The Bush administration, or rather some of its leading members, have constructed and promoted a simplistic dichotomy: international law versus national sovereignty. The ridiculousness of that position is evident the minute one turns to the international economic arena, where the World Trade Organization has the power to impose enormous constraints on U.S. sovereignty. A panel of three independent trade experts, for example, can rule on the legality or illegality of a federal statute under international trade law, and then enforce its judgment by authorizing trade sanctions against the United States by all WTO members. No human rights or arms control treaty has teeth nearly as sharp. Yet the Bush administration strongly supports an expansion of the WTO regime. Why? Because the free-trade system ensured by the WTO yields benefits that

greatly outweigh the costs of constraints on American freedom of action.

That is the right kind of calculus to make, rather than resorting to knee-jerk appeals to national sovereignty and fearmongering about world government. And by that sort of calculus, at a time when the United States is frightening and angering the rest of the world, the benefits—to ourselves and to other nations—of demonstrating once again that we are a super-power committed, at home and abroad, to the rule of law far outweigh the costs of self-imposed multilateralism.

International law today is undergoing profound changes that will make it far more effective than it has been in the past. By definition, international law is a body of rules that regulates relations among states, not individuals. Yet over the course of the 21st century, it will increasingly confer rights and responsibilities directly on individuals. The most obvious example of this shift can be seen in the explosive growth of international criminal law. Through new institutions such as the International Criminal Court, created in 2003 and based in The Hague, the international community is now holding individual leaders directly accountable for war crimes, crimes against humanity, and genocide. Most important, under a provision that was insisted on by the United States, all nations that are party to the treaty have committed themselves to domestic prosecutions of potential defendants before the court. Only if the states prove unable or unwilling to undertake these prosecutions will the court have jurisdiction. Under this arrangement, for example, Chile would have had primary responsibility to prosecute former dictator Augusto Pinochet as soon as he was out of office. If the Chilean prosecutors and courts had failed to act, he would have been remitted to The Hague. (Instead, Pinochet was arrested in Britain in 1998, under a warrant issued in Spain, and after being returned to Chile was ultimately spared prosecution because of ill health.) The political effect of this provision is a much-needed strengthening of those forces in every country that seek to bring to justice perpetrators of such crimes within their countries.

But criminal law is only one field of change. A similarly radical departure from the traditional model of state-to-state relations is reflected in the 1994 North American Free Trade Agreement. Under its terms, individual investors can sue NAFTA member states directly for failing to live up to their treaty obligations. In one celebrated case, a Canadian funeral home conglomerate is suing the United States for $725 million over a series of Mississippi state court decisions that it claims deliberately and unfairly forced it into bankruptcy; the decisions allegedly violated NAFTA guarantees that Canadian and Mexican investors will be granted equal treatment with domestic U.S. corporations. The WTO grows out of a more traditional form of law in which only states can bring suit against one another, but even in the WTO, evidence of the new trend can be seen in the knots of lawyers who congregate outside WTO hearing rooms to represent the interests of individual corporations directly affected by the rulings of the organization's dispute resolution panels. And now nongovernmental organizations such as Environmental Defense and Human Rights Watch are fighting for the right to submit briefs directly in cases that raise important environmental or human-rights issues.

As they come increasingly to apply directly to individuals, future international legal regimes will have more teeth than ever before—through links to domestic courts and by building up a direct constituency of important voters in important countries. The United States has long complained about the weaknesses of international treaty regimes, worrying that they bind states with strong domestic traditions of the rule of law but allow rampant cheating by states that lack such traditions or are without systems of domestic governance that check the power of leaders disinclined to follow the rules. Now is the moment to begin putting these international regimes on a new foundation, allowing them to penetrate the shell of state sovereignty in ways that will make the regimes much more enforceable.

If the United States participates in the formation of these new regimes and the reformation of the old, in areas that include foreign investment, anticorruption measures, environmental protection, and international labor rights, it can help shape a new generation of international legal rules that advance the interests of all law-abiding nations. If it does not participate, U.S. citizens will be directly affected by international rules that ignore U.S. interests. To take only one example, suppose the EU participated with other nations in drafting an international environmental treaty that imposed sanctions on corporations that didn't follow certain pollution regulations. The United States could stay out of the treaty, but any American corporation seeking to do business in the EU would be affected.

The United States needs international law, but not just any international law. We need a system of laws tailored to meet today's problems. The Bush administration is right to point out that the rules developed in 1945 to govern the use of force don't fit the security threats the world faces in 2003. But those aren't the only rules in need of revision. Well before September 11, politicians and public figures were calling for major changes in the rules governing the global economy (remember the cries for a "new global financial architecture"?), a redefinition of the doctrine of humanitarian intervention, and major UN reform, including expansion of the Security Council's membership. All those appeals proceeded from the premise that the rules and institutions created to address the economic, political, and security problems present after World War II were inadequate, and sometimes counterproductive, in the face of a new generation of threats to world order—to name but a few, AIDS and other new contagions, global warming, failed states, regional economic crises, sovereign bankruptcies, and the rise of global criminal networks trafficking in arms, money, women, workers, and drugs.

The mismatch between old rules and new threats is even more evident today. Two years after September 11, and one year after President Bush called on the Security Council to prove its strength and relevance in world affairs by enforcing a decade of resolutions against Saddam Hussein, the UN General Assembly convened this fall in a world that had changed radically yet again. Now both the United States and the UN are targets in a country and a region that seem to be spinning out of control. It's time to end the finger-pointing and get serious about generating new rules and updating old ones. Institutions, too, must be reinvigorated and reinvented. The UN Trusteeship Council, for example, could be used to spearhead the civilian rebuilding of countries devastated by war, disease, debt, and the despair of seemingly endless poverty.

The world needs international law. The United States needs the world. The dream of a just world under law may be no more than a dream. But the United States has never been stronger than when it has led the world in trying to make the dream a reality.

WHY THE SECURITY COUNCIL FAILED

Michael J. Glennon

As a key global institution of the post–World War II era, the contribution of the UN to global order provides an important test of the liberal institutionalist view of international relations. Glennon's critique of UN Security Council performance in the context of the U.S. decision to go to war against Iraq in 2003 is rooted in realist skepticism over the role of global institutions. As you read his article, ask yourself:

- What is it about his analysis that illustrates his status as a "realist"?
- What does he mean in suggesting that UN dysfunctionality is less a legal than a geopolitical problem?
- What is his view of America's stake in the United Nations?

SHOWDOWN AT TURTLE BAY

"The tents have been struck," declared South Africa's prime minister, Jan Christian Smuts, about the League of Nations' founding. "The great caravan of humanity is again on the march." A generation later, this mass movement toward the international rule of law still seemed very much in progress. In 1945, the League was replaced with a more robust United Nations, and no less a personage than U.S. Secretary of State

---

Michael J. Glennon, "Why the Security Council Failed." Reprinted by permission of *Foreign Affairs* 82:3, May/June 2003. Copyright 2003 by the Council on Foreign Relations, Inc. www.ForeignAffairs.com.

Cordell Hull hailed it as the key to "the fulfill-ment of humanity's highest aspirations." The world was once more on the move.

[In 2003], however, the caravan finally ground to a halt. With the dramatic rupture of the UN Security Council, it became clear that the grand attempt to subject the use of force to the rule of law had failed.

In truth, there had been no progress for years. The UN's rules governing the use of force, laid out in the charter and managed by the Security Council, had fallen victim to geopoliti-cal forces too strong for a legalist institution to withstand. By 2003, the main question facing countries considering whether to use force was not whether it was lawful. Instead, as in the nineteenth century, they simply questioned whether it was wise.

The beginning of the end of the inter-national security system had actually come slightly earlier, on September 12, 2002, when President George W. Bush, to the surprise of many, brought his case against Iraq to the General Assembly and challenged the UN to take action against Baghdad for failing to dis-arm. "We will work with the UN Security Council for the necessary resolutions," Bush said. But he warned that he would act alone if the UN failed to cooperate.

Washington's threat was reaffirmed a month later by Congress, when it gave Bush the authority to use force against Iraq without get-ting approval from the UN first. The American message seemed clear: as a senior administra-tion official put it at the time, "we don't need the Security Council."

Two weeks later, on October 25, the United States formally proposed a resolution that would have implicitly authorized war against Iraq. But Bush again warned that he would not be deterred if the Security Council rejected the measure. "If the United Nations doesn't have the will or the

courage to disarm Saddam Hussein and if Saddam Hussein will not disarm," he said, "the United States will lead a coalition to disarm [him]." After intensive, behind-the-scenes haggling, the council responded to Bush's challenge on November 7 by unanimously adopting Resolution 1441, which found Iraq in "material breach" of prior resolu-tions, set up a new inspections regime, and warned once again of "serious consequences" if Iraq again failed to disarm. The resolution did not explicitly authorize force, however, and Washington pledged to return to the council for another discussion before resorting to arms.

The vote for Resolution 1441 was a huge personal victory for Secretary of State Colin Powell, who had spent much political capital urging his government to go the UN route in the first place and had fought hard diplomatically to win international backing. Nonetheless, doubts soon emerged concerning the effectiveness of the new inspections regime and the extent of Iraq's cooperation. On January 21, 2003, Powell himself declared that the "inspections will not work." He returned to the UN on February 5 and made the case that Iraq was still hiding its weapons of mass destruction (WMD). France and Germany responded by pressing for more time. Tensions between the allies, already high, began to mount and divisions deepened still fur-ther when 18 European countries signed letters in support of the American position.

On February 14, the inspectors returned to the Security Council to report that, after 11 weeks of investigation in Iraq, they had discov-ered no evidence of WMD (although many items remained unaccounted for). Ten days later, on February 24, the United States, the United Kingdom, and Spain introduced a resolution that would have had the council simply declare, under Chapter VII of the UN Charter (the section dealing with threats to the peace), that "Iraq has failed to take the final opportunity afforded to it in Resolution 1441." France, Germany, and Russia once more proposed giving Iraq still more time. On February 28, the White House, increasingly frustrated, upped the ante: Press Secretary Ari Fleischer announced that the American goal was no longer simply Iraq's disarmament but now included "regime change."

A period of intense lobbying followed. Then, on March 5, France and Russia announced they would block any subsequent resolution authorizing the use of force against Saddam. The next day, China declared that it was taking the same position. The United Kingdom floated a compromise proposal, but the council's five permanent members could not agree. In the face of a serious threat to international peace and stability, the Security Council fatally deadlocked.

POWER POLITICS

At this point it was easy to conclude, as did President Bush, that the UN's failure to confront Iraq would cause the world body to "fade into history as an ineffective, irrelevant debating society." In reality, however, the council's fate had long since been sealed. The problem was not the second Persian Gulf War, but rather an earlier shift in world power toward a configuration that was simply incompatible with the way the UN was meant to function. It was the rise in American unipolarity—not the Iraq crisis—that, along with cultural clashes and different attitudes toward the use of force, gradually eroded the council's credibility. Although the body had managed to limp along and function adequately in more tranquil times, it proved incapable of performing under periods of great stress. The fault for this failure did not lie with any one country; rather, it was the largely inexorable upshot of the development and evolution of the international system.

Consider first the changes in power politics. Reactions to the United States' gradual ascent to towering preeminence have been predictable: coalitions of competitors have emerged. Since the end of the Cold War, the French, the Chinese, and the Russians have sought to return the world to a more balanced system. France's former foreign minister Hubert Vedrine openly confessed this goal in 1998: "We cannot accept . . . a politically unipolar world," he said, and "that is why we are fighting for a multipolar" one. French President Jacques Chirac has battled tirelessly to achieve this end. According to Pierre Lellouche, who was Chirac's foreign policy adviser in the early 1990s, his boss wants "a multipolar world in which Europe is the counterweight to American political and military power." Explained Chirac himself, "any community with only one dominant power is always a dangerous one and provokes reactions."

In recent years, Russia and China have displayed a similar preoccupation; indeed, this objective was formalized in a treaty the two countries signed in July 2001, explicitly confirming their commitment to "a multipolar world." President Vladimir Putin has declared that Russia will not tolerate a unipolar system, and China's former president Jiang Zemin has said the same. Germany, although it joined the cause late, has recently become a highly visible partner in the effort to confront American hegemony. Foreign Minister Joschka Fischer said in 2000 that the "core concept of Europe after 1945 was and still is a rejection of . . . the hegemonic ambitions of individual states." Even Germany's former chancellor Helmut Schmidt recently weighed in, opining that Germany and France "share a common interest in not delivering ourselves into the hegemony of our mighty ally, the United States."

In the face of such opposition, Washington has made it clear that it intends to do all it can to maintain its preeminence. The Bush administration released a paper detailing its national security strategy in September 2002 that left no doubt about its plans to ensure that no other nation could rival its military strength. More controversially, the now infamous document also proclaimed a doctrine of preemption— one that, incidentally, flatly contradicts the precepts of the UN Charter. Article 51 of the charter permits the use of force only in self-defense, and only "if an armed attack occurs against a Member of the United Nations." The American policy, on the other hand, proceeds from the premise that Americans "cannot let our enemies strike first." Therefore, "to forestall or prevent . . . hostile acts by our adversaries," the statement announced, "the United States will, if necessary, act preemptively"—that is, strike first.

Apart from the power divide, a second fault line, one deeper and longer, has also separated the United States from other countries at the un. This split is cultural. It divides nations of the North and West from those of the South and East on the most fundamental of issues: namely, when armed intervention is appropriate. On September 20,1999, Secretary-General Kofi Annan spoke in historic terms about the need to "forge unity behind the principle that massive and systematic violations of human rights— wherever they take place—should never be allowed to stand." This speech led to weeks of debate among UN members. Of the nations that spoke out in public, roughly a third appeared to favor humanitarian intervention under some circumstances. Another third opposed it across the board, and the remaining third were equivocal or noncommittal. The proponents, it is important to note, were primarily Western democracies. The opponents, meanwhile, were mostly Latin American, African, and Arab states.

The disagreement was not, it soon became clear, confined merely to humanitarian intervention. On February 22 of this year, foreign ministers from the Nonaligned Movement, meeting in Kuala Lumpur, signed a declaration opposing the use of force against Iraq. This faction, composed of 114 states (primarily from the developing world), represents 55 percent of the planet's population and nearly two-thirds of the UN's membership.

As all of this suggests, although the UN's rules purport to represent a single global view— indeed, universal law—on when and whether force can be justified, the UN's members (not to mention their populations) are clearly not in agreement.

Moreover, cultural divisions concerning the use of force do not merely separate the West from the rest. Increasingly, they also separate the United States from the rest of the West. On one key subject in particular, European and American attitudes diverge and are moving further apart by the day. That subject is the role of law in international relations. There are two sources for this disagreement. The first concerns who should make the rules: namely, should it be the states themselves, or supranational institutions?

Americans largely reject supranationalism. It is hard to imagine any circumstance in which Washington would permit an international regime to limit the size of the U.S. budget deficit, control its currency and coinage, or settle the issue of gays in the military. Yet these and a host of other similar questions are now regularly decided for European states by the supranational institutions (such as the European Union and the European Court of Human Rights) of which they are members. "Americans," Francis Fukuyama has written, "tend not to see any source of democratic legitimacy higher than the nation-state." But Europeans see democratic legitimacy as flowing from the will of the international community. Thus they comfortably submit to impingements on their sovereignty that Americans would find anathema. Security

Council decisions limiting the use of force are but one example.

DEATH OF A LAW

. . . More than anything else, however, it has been still another underlying difference in attitude—over the need to comply with the UN's rules on the use of force—that has proved most disabling to the UN system. Since 1945, so many states have used armed force on so many occasions, in flagrant violation of the charter, that the regime can only be said to have collapsed. In framing the charter, the international community failed to anticipate accurately when force would be deemed unacceptable. Nor did it apply sufficient disincentives to instances when it would be so deemed. Given that the UN is a voluntary system that depends for compliance on state consent, this short-sightedness proved fatal.

This conclusion can be expressed a number of different ways under traditional international legal doctrine. Massive violation of a treaty by numerous states over a prolonged period can be seen as casting that treaty into desuetude—that is, reducing it to a paper rule that is no longer binding. The violations can also be regarded as subsequent custom that creates new law, supplanting old treaty norms and permitting conduct that was once a violation. Finally, contrary state practice can also be considered to have created a non liquet, to have thrown the law into a state of confusion such that legal rules are no longer clear and no authoritative answer is possible. In effect, however, it makes no practical difference which analytic framework is applied. The default position of international law has long been that when no restriction can be authoritatively established, a country is considered free to act. Whatever doctrinal formula is chosen to describe the current crisis, therefore, the conclusion is the same. "If you want to know whether a man is religious," Wittgenstein said, "don't ask him, observe him." And so it is if you want to know what law a state accepts. If countries had ever truly intended to make the UN's use-of-force rules binding, they would have made the costs of violation greater than the costs of compliance.

But they did not. Anyone who doubts this observation might consider precisely why North Korea now so insistently seeks a nonaggression pact with the United States. Such a provision, after all, is supposedly the centerpiece of the UN Charter. But no one could seriously expect that assurance to comfort Pyongyang. The charter has gone the way of the Kellogg-Briand Pact, the 1928 treaty by which every major country that would go on to fight in World War II solemnly committed itself not to resort to war as an instrument of national policy. The pact, as the diplomatic historian Thomas Bailey has written, "proved a monument to illusion. It was not only delusive but dangerous, for it . . . lulled the public . . . into a false sense of security." These days, on the other hand, no rational state will be deluded into believing that the UN Charter protects its security.

Surprisingly, despite the manifest warning signs, some international lawyers have insisted in the face of the Iraq crisis that there is no reason for alarm about the state of the UN. On March 2, just days before France, Russia, and China declared their intention to cast a veto that the United States had announced it would ignore, Anne-Marie Slaughter (president of the American Society of International Law and dean of Princeton's Woodrow Wilson School) wrote, "What is happening today is exactly what the UN founders envisaged." Other experts contend that, because countries have not openly declared that the charter's use-of-force rules are no longer binding, those rules must still be regarded as obligatory. But state practice itself often provides the best evidence of what states regard as binding. The truth is that no state—surely not the United States—has ever accepted a rule saying, in effect, that rules can be changed only by openly declaring the old rules to be dead. States simply do not behave that way. They avoid needless confrontation. After all, states have not openly declared that the Kellogg-Briand Pact is no longer good law, but few would seriously contend that it is.

Still other analysts worry that admitting to the death of the UN's rules on the use of force would be tantamount to giving up completely on the international rule of law. The fact that public opinion forced President Bush to go to Congress and the UN, such experts further argue, shows that international law still shapes power politics. But distinguishing working rules from paper rules is not the same as giving up on the rule of law. Although the effort to subject the use of force to the rule of law was the monumental internationalist experiment of the twentieth century, the fact is that that experiment has failed. Refusing to recognize that failure will not enhance prospects for another such experiment in the future.

Indeed, it should have come as no surprise that, in September 2002, the United States felt free to announce in its national security document that it would no longer be bound by the charter's rules governing the use of force. Those rules have collapsed. "Lawful" and "unlawful" have ceased to be meaningful terms as applied to the use of force. As Powell said on October 20, "the president believes he now has the authority [to intervene in Iraq] . . . just as we did in Kosovo." There was, of course, no Security Council authorization for the use of force by NATO against Yugoslavia. That action blatantly violated the UN Charter, which does not permit humanitarian intervention any more than it does preventive war. But Powell was nonetheless right: the United States did indeed have all the authority it needed to attack Iraq—not because the Security Council authorized it, but because

there was no international law forbidding it. It was therefore impossible to act unlawfully.

HOT AIR

. . . Why did the winds of power, culture, and security overturn the legalist bulwarks that had been designed to weather the fiercest geopolitical gusts? To help answer this question, consider the following sentence: "We have to keep defending our vital interests just as before; we can say no, alone, to anything that may be unacceptable." It may come as a surprise that those were not the words of administration hawks such as Paul Wolfowitz, Donald Rumsfeld, or John Bolton. In fact, they were written in 2001 by Vedrine, then France's foreign minister. Similarly, critics of American "hyperpower" might guess that the statement, "I do not feel obliged to other governments," must surely have been uttered by an American. It was in fact made by German Chancellor Gerhard Schröder on February 10, 2003. The first and last geopolitical truth is that states pursue security by pursuing power. Legalist institutions that manage that pursuit maladroitly are ultimately swept away.

A corollary of this principle is that, in pursuing power, states use those institutional tools that are available to them. For France, Russia, and China, one of those tools is the Security Council and the veto that the charter affords them. It was therefore entirely predictable that these three countries would wield their veto to snub the United States and advance the project that they had undertaken: to return the world to a multipolar system. During the Security Council debate on Iraq, the French were candid about their objective. The goal was never to disarm Iraq. Instead, "the main and constant objective for France throughout the negotiations," according to its UN ambassador, was to "strengthen the role and authority of the Security Council" (and, he might have added, of France). France's interest lay in forcing the United States to back down, thus appearing to capitulate in the face of French diplomacy. The United States, similarly, could reasonably have been expected to use the council—or to ignore it—to advance Washington's own project: the maintenance of a unipolar system. "The course of this nation," President Bush said in his 2003 State of the Union speech, "does not depend on the decisions of others."

The likelihood is that had France, Russia, or China found itself in the position of the United States during the Iraq crisis, each of these countries would have used the council—or threatened to ignore it—just as the United States did. Similarly, had Washington found itself in the position of Paris, Moscow, or Beijing, it would likely have used its veto in the same way they did. States act to enhance their own power—not that of potential competitors. That is no novel insight; it traces at least to Thucydides, who had his Athenian generals tell the hapless Melians, "You and everybody else, having the same power as we have, would do the same as we do." This insight involves no normative judgment; it simply describes how nations behave.

The truth, therefore, is that the Security Council's fate never turned on what it did or did not do on Iraq. American unipolarity had already debilitated the council, just as bipolarity paralyzed it during the Cold War. The old power structure gave the Soviet Union an incentive to deadlock the council; the current power structure encourages the United States to bypass it. Meanwhile, the council itself had no good option. Approve an American attack, and it would have seemed to rubber-stamp what it could not stop. Express disapproval of a war, and the United States would have vetoed the attempt. Decline to take any action, and the council would again have been ignored. Disagreement over Iraq did not doom the council; geopolitical reality did. That was the

message of Powell's extraordinary, seemingly contradictory declaration on November 10, 2002, that the United States would not consider itself bound by the council's decision—even though it expected Iraq to be declared in "material breach."

It has been argued that Resolution 1441 and its acceptance by Iraq somehow represented a victory for the UN and a triumph of the rule of law. But it did not. Had the United States not threatened Iraq with the use of force, the Iraqis almost surely would have rejected the new inspections regime. Yet such threats of force violate the charter. The Security Council never authorized the United States to announce a policy of regime change in Iraq or to take military steps in that direction. Thus the council's "victory," such as it was, was a victory of diplomacy backed by force—or more accurately, of diplomacy backed by the threat of unilateral force in violation of the charter. The unlawful threat of unilateralism enabled the "legitimate" exercise of multilateralism. The Security Council reaped the benefit of the charter's violation.

As surely as Resolution 1441 represented a triumph of American diplomacy, it represented a defeat for the international rule of law. Once the measure was passed after eight weeks of debate, the French, Chinese, and Russian diplomats left the council chamber claiming that they had not authorized the United States to strike Iraq—that 1441 contained no element of "automaticity." American diplomats, meanwhile, claimed that the council had done precisely that. As for the language of the resolution itself, it can accurately be said to lend support to both claims. This is not the hallmark of great legislation. The first task of any lawgiver is to speak intelligibly, to lay down clear rules in words that all can understand and that have the same meaning for everyone. The UN's members have an obligation under the charter to comply with Security Council decisions. They therefore have a right to expect the council to render its decisions clearly. Shrinking from that task in the face of threats undermines the rule of law.

The second, February 24 resolution, whatever its diplomatic utility, confirmed this marginalization of the Security Council. Its vague terms were directed at attracting maximal support but at the price of juridical vapidity. The resolution's broad wording lent itself, as intended, to any possible interpretation. A legal instrument that means everything, however, also means nothing. In its death throes, it had become more important that the council say something than that it say something important. The proposed compromise would have allowed states to claim, once again, that private, collateral understandings gave meaning to the council's empty words, as they had when Resolution 1441 was adopted. Eighty-five years after Woodrow Wilson's Fourteen Points, international law's most solemn obligations had come to be memorialized in winks and nods, in secret covenants, secretly arrived at.

APOLOGIES FOR IMPOTENCE

States and commentators, intent on returning the world to a multipolar structure, have devised various strategies for responding to the council's decline. Some European countries, such as France, believed that the council could overcome power imbalances and disparities of culture and security by acting as a supranational check on American action. To be more precise, the French hoped to use the battering ram of the Security Council to check American power. Had it worked, this strategy would have returned the world to multipolarity through supranationalism. But this approach involved an inescapable dilemma: what would have constituted success for the European supranationalists?

The French could, of course, have vetoed America's Iraq project. But to succeed in this way would be to fail, because the declared American intent was to proceed anyway—and in the process break the only institutional chain with which France could hold the United States back. Their inability to resolve this dilemma reduced the French to diplomatic ankle-biting. France's foreign minister could wave his finger in the face of the American secretary of state as the cameras rolled, or ambush him by raising the subject of Iraq at a meeting called on another subject. But the inability of the Security Council to actually stop a war that France had clamorously opposed underscored French weakness as much as it did the impotence of the council.

Commentators, meanwhile, developed verbal strategies to forestall perceived American threats to the rule of law. Some argued in a communitarian spirit that countries should act in the common interest, rather than, in the words of Vedrine, "making decisions under [their] own interpretations and for [their] own interests." The United States should remain engaged in the United Nations, argued Slaughter, because other nations "need a forum . . . in which to . . . restrain the United States." "Whatever became," asked *The New Yorker*'s Hendrik Hertzberg, "of the conservative suspicion of untrammeled power . . . ? Where is the conservative belief in limited government, in checks and balances? Burke spins in his grave. Madison and Hamilton torque it up, too." Washington, Hertzberg argued, should voluntarily relinquish its power and forgo hegemony in favor of a multipolar world in which the United States would be equal with and balanced by other powers.

No one can doubt the utility of checks and balances, deployed domestically, to curb the exercise of arbitrary power. Setting ambition against ambition was the framers' formula for preserving liberty. The problem with applying this approach in the international arena, however, is that it would require the United States to act against its own interests, to advance the cause of its power competitors—and, indeed, of power competitors whose values are very different from its own. Hertzberg and others seem not to recognize that it simply is not realistic to expect the United States to permit itself to be checked by China or Russia. After all, would China, France, or Russia—or any other country— voluntarily abandon preeminent power if it found itself in the position of the United States? Remember too that France now aims to narrow the disparity between itself and the United States—but not the imbalance between itself and lesser powers (some of which Chirac has chided for acting as though "not well brought-up") that might check France's own strength.

There is, moreover, little reason to believe that some new and untried locus of power, possibly under the influence of states with a long history of repression, would be more trustworthy than would the exercise of hegemonic power by the United States. Those who would entrust the planet's destiny to some nebulous guardian of global pluralism seem strangely oblivious of the age-old question: Who guards that guardian? And how will that guardian preserve international peace—by asking dictators to legislate prohibitions against weapons of mass destruction (as the French did with Saddam)?

In one respect James Madison is on point, although the communitarians have failed to note it. In drafting the U.S. Constitution, Madison and the other founders confronted very much the same dilemma that the world community confronts today in dealing with American hegemony. The question, as the framers posed it, was why the powerful should have any incentive to obey the law. Madison's answer, in the Federalist Papers, was that the incentive lies in an assessment of future circumstances—in the unnerving possibility that the strong may one day become weak and then need the protection of the law. It is the "uncertainty of their condition," Madison wrote,

that prompts the strong to play by the rules today. But if the future were certain, or if the strong believed it to be certain, and if that future forecast a continued reign of power, then the incentive on the powerful to obey the law would fall away. Hegemony thus sits in tension with the principle of equality. Hegemons have ever resisted subjecting their power to legal constraint. When Britannia ruled the waves, Whitehall opposed limits on the use of force to execute its naval blockades—limits that were vigorously supported by the new United States and other weaker states. Any system dominated by a "hyperpower" will have great difficulty maintaining or establishing an authentic rule of law. That is the great Madisonian dilemma confronted by the international community today. . . .

BACK TO THE DRAWING BOARD

The high duty of the Security Council, assigned it by the charter, was the maintenance of international peace and security. The charter laid out a blueprint for managing this task under the council's auspices. The UN's founders constructed a Gothic edifice of multiple levels, with grand porticos, ponderous buttresses, and lofty spires—and with convincing façades and scary gargoyles to keep away evil spirits.

In the winter of 2003, that entire edifice came crashing down. It is tempting, in searching for reasons, to return to the blueprints and blame the architects. The fact is, however, that the fault for the council's collapse lies elsewhere: in the shifting ground beneath the construct. As became painfully clear this year, the terrain on which the UN's temple rested was shot through with fissures. The ground was unable to support humanity's lofty legalist shrine. Power disparities, cultural disparities, and differing views on the use of force toppled the temple. . . .

Some day policymakers will return to the drawing board. When they do, the first lesson of the Security Council's breakdown should become the first principle of institutional engineering: what the design should look like must be a function of what it can look like. A new international legal order, if it is to function effectively, must reflect the underlying dynamics of power, culture, and security. If it does not—if its norms are again unrealistic and do not reflect the way states actually behave and the real forces to which they respond—the community of nations will again end up with mere paper rules. The UN system's dysfunctionality was not, at bottom, a legal problem. It was a geopolitical one. The juridical distortions that proved debilitating were effects, not causes. "The UN was founded on the premise," Slaughter has observed in its defense, "that some truths transcend politics." Precisely—and therein lay the problem. If they are to comprise working rules rather than paper ones, legalist institutions—and the "truths" on which they act—must flow from political commitments, not vice versa.

A second, related lesson from the UN's failure is thus that rules must flow from the way states actually behave, not how they ought to behave. "The first requirement of a sound body of law," wrote Oliver Wendell Holmes, "is that it should correspond with the actual feelings and demands of the community, whether right or wrong." This insight will be anathema to continuing believers in natural law, the armchair philosophers who "know" what principles must control states, whether states accept those principles or not. But these idealists might remind themselves that the international legal system is, again, voluntarist. For better or worse, its rules are based on state consent. States are not bound by rules to which they do not agree. Like it or not, that is the Westphalian system, and it is still

very much with us. Pretending that the system can be based on idealists' own subjective notions of morality won't make it so. . . .

As the world moves into a new, transitional era, the old moralist vocabulary should be cleared away so that decision-makers can focus pragmatically on what is really at stake. The real questions for achieving international peace and security are clear-cut: What are our objectives? What means have we chosen to meet those objectives? Are those means working? If not, why not? Are better alternatives available? If so, what tradeoffs are required? Are we willing to make those tradeoffs? What are the costs and benefits of competing alternatives? What support would they command?

Answering those questions does not require an overarching legalist metaphysic. There is no need for grand theory and no place for self-righteousness. The life of the law, Holmes said, is not logic but experience. Humanity need not achieve an ultimate consensus on good and evil. The task before it is empirical, not theoretical. Getting to a consensus will be accelerated by dropping abstractions, moving beyond the polemical rhetoric of "right" and "wrong," and focusing pragmatically on the concrete needs and preferences of real people who endure suffering that may be unnecessary. Policymakers may not yet be able to answer these questions. The forces that brought down the Security Council—the "deeper sources of international instability," in George Kennan's words—will not go away. But at least policymakers can get the questions right.

One particularly pernicious outgrowth of natural law is the idea that states are sovereign equals. As Kennan pointed out, the notion of sovereign equality is a myth; disparities among states "make a mockery" of the concept. Applied to states, the proposition that all are equal is belied by evidence everywhere that they are not—neither in their power, nor in their wealth, nor in their respect for international order or for human rights.

Yet the principle of sovereign equality animates the entire structure of the United Nations—and disables it from effectively addressing emerging crises, such as access to WMD, that derive precisely from the presupposition of sovereign equality. Treating states as equals prevents treating individuals as equals: if Yugoslavia truly enjoyed a right to nonintervention equal to that of every other state, its citizens would have been denied human rights equal to those of individuals in other states, because their human rights could be vindicated only by intervention. This year, the irrationality of treating states as equals was brought home as never before when it emerged that the will of the Security Council could be determined by Angola, Guinea, or Cameroon—nations whose representatives sat side by side and exercised an equal voice and vote with those of Spain, Pakistan, and Germany. The equality principle permitted any rotating council member to cast a de facto veto (by denying a majority the critical ninth vote necessary for potential victory). Granting a de jure veto to the permanent five was, of course, the charter's intended antidote to unbridled egalitarianism. But it didn't work: the de jure veto simultaneously undercorrected and overcorrected for the problem, lowering the United States to the level of France and raising France above India, which did not even hold a rotating seat on the council during the Iraq debate. Yet the de jure veto did nothing to dilute the rotating members' de facto veto. The upshot was a Security Council that reflected the real world's power structure with the accuracy of a fun-house mirror—and performed accordingly. Hence the third great lesson of last winter: institutions cannot be expected to correct distortions that are embedded in their own structures.

STAYING ALIVE?

There is little reason to believe, then, that the Security Council will soon be resuscitated to tackle nerve-center security issues, however the war against Iraq turns out. If the war is swift and successful, if the United States uncovers Iraqi WMD that supposedly did not exist, and if nation-building in Iraq goes well, there likely will be little impulse to revive the council. In that event, the council will have gone the way of the League of Nations. American decision-makers will thereafter react to the council much as they did to NATO following Kosovo: Never again. Ad hoc coalitions of the willing will effectively succeed it.

If, on the other hand, the war is long and bloody, if the United States does not uncover Iraqi WMD, and if nation-building in Iraq falters, the war's opponents will benefit, claiming that the United States would not have run aground if only it had abided by the charter. But the Security Council will not profit from America's ill fortune. Coalitions of adversaries will emerge and harden, lying in wait in the council and making it, paradoxically, all the more difficult for the United States to participate dutifully in a forum in which an increasingly ready veto awaits it.

The Security Council will still on occasion prove useful for dealing with matters that do not bear directly on the upper hierarchy of world power. Every major country faces imminent danger from terrorism, for example, and from the new surge in WMD proliferation. None will gain by permitting these threats to reach fruition. Yet even when the required remedy is nonmilitary, enduring suspicions among the council's permanent members and the body's loss of credibility will impair its effectiveness in dealing with these issues.

However the war turns out, the United States will likely confront pressures to curb its use of force. These it must resist. Chirac's admonitions notwithstanding, war is not "always, always, the worst solution." The use of force was a better option than diplomacy in dealing with numerous tyrants, from Milosevic to Hitler. It may, regrettably, sometimes emerge as the only and therefore the best way to deal with WMD proliferation. If judged by the suffering of noncombatants, the use of force can often be more humane than economic sanctions, which starve more children than soldiers (as their application to Iraq demonstrated). The greater danger after the second Persian Gulf War is not that the United States will use force when it should not, but that, chastened by the war's horror, the public's opposition, and the economy's gyrations, it will not use force when it should. That the world is at risk of cascading disorder places a greater rather than a lesser responsibility on the United States to use its power assertively to halt or slow the pace of disintegration.

All who believe in the rule of law are eager to see the great caravan of humanity resume its march. In moving against the centers of disorder, the United States could profit from a beneficent sharing of its power to construct new international mechanisms directed at maintaining global peace and security. American hegemony will not last forever. Prudence therefore counsels creating realistically structured institutions capable of protecting or advancing U.S. national interests even when military power is unavailable or unsuitable. Such institutions could enhance American preeminence, potentially prolonging the period of unipolarity.

Yet legalists must be hard-headed about the possibility of devising a new institutional framework anytime soon to replace the battered structure of the Security Council. The forces that led to the council's undoing will not disappear. Neither a triumphant nor a chastened United States will have sufficient incentive to resubmit to old constraints in new contexts. Neither vindicated nor humbled competitors will have sufficient disincentives to forgo efforts to impose those constraints. Nations will continue to seek greater power and security at the expense of others. Nations will continue to disagree on when force should be used. Like it or not, that is the way of the world. In resuming humanity's march toward the rule of law, recognizing that reality will be the first step.

THE ILLUSION OF U.N. SECURITY COUNCIL REFORM

Thomas G. Weiss

In recent years, reform of UN Security Council membership and process has been the subject of much attention. Supporters of reform have argued that it is necessary to make the Council both more credible and more representative. In this piece, Weiss reviews and assesses the history and future prospects of Security Council reform. As you read his article, ask yourself:

⦿ Why has reform been so difficult to implement?

⦿ What reforms are likely and desirable?

⦿ On what points does Weiss agree or disagree with Glennon's analysis of the Security Council found in the previous reading in this volume?

Thomas G. Weiss, "The Illusion of U.N. Security Council Reform," *The Washington Quarterly,* 26:4, Autumn 2003, pp. 147–161. © 2003 by the Center for Strategic and International Studies (CSIS) and the Massachussetts Institute of Technology. Reprinted by permission of MIT Press Journals.

Can changing the membership or procedures of the United Nations Security Council improve its credibility? In the controversy surrounding a possible UN *imprimatur* for the use of force against Iraq, the debate over the council's credibility shifted from the question of adequate representation to whether the group can constrain U.S. power. Now, the obstacles to Security Council credibility go beyond issues of process—exclusive permanent membership and the right to veto—to include unparalleled U.S. military might. With the exception of the 1965 expansion from 11 to 15 members, efforts at Security Council reform since the organization's inception in 1945 have repeatedly proved implausible; today, uncontested U.S. power makes such efforts largely irrelevant.

At the same time, in choosing among available tactics and strategies, Washington should think twice about acting alone. Making better use of the Security Council in its current form—indeed, of the UN system more broadly—is usually in U.S. interests and should remain the preferred policy option.

THE HISTORICAL FAILURE OF REFORM

The principle of UN Charter reform, which includes altering everything from institutional purposes and structures to more mundane operating procedures, retains salience for diplomats in New York as a formal agenda item as well as an informal and enduring cocktail party pastime. In practice, however, substantive and substantial reform has proved virtually impossible. In fact, only three amendments have been made to the UN Charter in almost 60 years—and all dealing only with seat numbers in two of the six principal organs, once for the Security Council and twice for the United Nations Economic and Social Council. Use of the term "reform" is applied often

and far more broadly than constitutional changes to UN policy; for example, at the outset of their terms, UN secretaries general routinely initiate so-called reform measures that merely involve personnel changes and management shell games.[1]

The history of reform efforts geared toward making the Security Council more reflective of growing UN membership and of changing world politics since the organization's establishment conveys the slim prospects for meaningful change. UN founders deliberately divided member rights and roles by establishing a universal General Assembly with the most general functions and a restricted Security Council with executing authority for maintaining the peace—unanimity among the great powers was a prerequisite for action. This arrangement was designed to contrast with the Council of the League of Nations, a general executive committee for all of the organization's functions that failed miserably in the security arena because it required agreement from all states. Eternal seats for the era's great powers—the United States, the Soviet Union, France, the United Kingdom, and China—now known as the Permanent 5 (P-5) with the right to veto decisions of substance, was an essential component of the original 1945 deal.

At the San Francisco conference where the UN Charter was drafted, delegates who were dissatisfied with a revival of a kind of nineteenth-century Concert of Europe—with more powerful states given special roles—but also did not wish to impede the effective creation of the new world body expected that a review conference for all UN member states would be convened relatively quickly to discuss changes in the charter and organizational structures. Although Article 109 reserved the possibility of a General Conference "for the purposes of reviewing the present Charter," the P-5 preferred setting the bar high for any changes.[2] They not only resisted efforts to convene such a conference but also clearly communicated their intention to safeguard their veto rights. The increasing polarization of UN member countries during the Cold War in the 1950s prevented such a gathering then, and none has been convened since.

As originally defined in the UN Charter, the composition and decisionmaking procedures of the Security Council were increasingly challenged as membership steadily and dramatically grew following the acceleration of decolonization. Between the UN's establishment in 1945 and the end of the first wave of decolonization in 1963, the number of UN member states swelled from 51 to 114. Only six countries from Africa and Asia were UN members originally, while two decades later, more than half of the UN's membership were from these two developing continents. As a result, these newly decolonized countries demanded a better reflection of their numbers and priorities in the Security Council and throughout the UN system.

Most governments rhetorically support the mindless call for equity, specifically by increasing membership and eliminating the veto. Yet, no progress has been made on these numerical or procedural changes because absolutely no consensus exists about the exact shape of the Security Council or the elimination of the veto. True, the council does not reflect the actual distribution of twenty-first-century power, yet reform proposals emanating from diplomats and analysts have never addressed the true imbalance between seats at the table and actual military capacity outside of the Security Council chamber. They have sought to address, instead, the imbalance between the total number of countries in the world and Security Council membership as well as to dispute the absolute veto right held by five countries.

The only significant reform of the Security Council came to pass in 1965, after two-thirds of all UN member states ratified and all five permanent members of the Security Council approved Resolution 1990 (adopted by the General Assembly in December 1963) which proposed enlarging the Security Council from 11 to 15 members and the required majority from 7 to 9 votes. The veto power exclusively reserved for the P-5 was left intact.

The question of whether the Security Council should reflect the growing membership of the UN, let alone the lofty language of the UN Charter's Article 2, emphasizing "the principle of the sovereign equality of all its Members," resurfaced in the 1990s, paradoxically, as a by-product of the initial successes of the Security Council in the early post–Cold War era. The P-5 countries, increasingly on the same wavelength, reached consensus privately before going to the Security Council as a whole on a range of issues.[3] Yet, the logic of the axiom "if it ain't broken, don't fix it" gave way to grumblings about representation. Again, the argument for expansion was linked to equity, not to practical impact.

A series of decisions about beefed-up peacekeeping operations in areas that had formerly paralyzed the council, including several flash points of former East-West tensions (Afghanistan, Namibia, Kampuchea, and Nicaragua) and the end of the Iran-Iraq War, seemed to usher in a new era of Security Council activism and UN authority for decisionmaking about international peace and security. Such decisions set precedents for the council to take action against Iraq for its invasion of Kuwait in 1991 and then to override Iraqi sovereignty by providing succor to the Kurds and imposing intrusive measures on the regime in Baghdad.[4]

Suddenly, the Security Council was acting as had been originally intended. Sovereignty was no longer sacrosanct.[5] Excluded countries wanted a part of the action, to defend their own viewpoints from the risk of being ignored by a new sort of P-5 condominium. Moreover, consensus was the order of the day and casting vetoes appeared unseemly and anachronistic; only 12 substantive vetoes were invoked between January 1990 and June 2003 in contrast to the 193 over the preceding 45 years.[6]

In January 1992, newly elected Secretary General Boutros Boutros-Ghali began his term with the first-ever summit of the Security Council and shortly thereafter published his bullish *An Agenda for Peace,*[7] which spelled out an ambitious agenda for the UN's role in the maintenance of international peace and security. In looking ahead to the UN's half-century anniversary in 1995, a symbolically appropriate moment appeared on the international radar screen. "Was it not time to restructure the Security Council's composition and revise its anachronistic procedures so that matters of right would take precedence over matters of might," or so went the conventional wisdom and proposals from the 38th floor of 1 UN Plaza and from eminent individuals.[8]

TWO TIMELESS PROCEDURAL OBSTACLES

The logic behind the call in the early 1990s to recognize the changed world by setting aside the veto and doubling the number of permanent Security Council members—with Germany and Japan making particularly strong cases for membership, along with developing-country giants, such as India, Egypt, Brazil, and Nigeria—to reflect the new world order ran into two immediate problems.[9]

The Veto

Citing the need to avoid conditions that led to the downfall of the League of Nations, the P-5 insisted on having individual vetoes over UN Charter amendments. Article 108 effectively provides each permanent member with a trump card that can overrule any efforts to weaken its formal power, although virtually all of the other 186 member states criticize the veto as inequitable.[10] The veto has been and remains an obstacle to reform both because of the P-5's vested interests in preserving power and because no provision in the charter requires them to relinquish this right.

In their pursuit of *raisons d'état,* states use whatever institutions are available to serve their interests. Although arguably the United Kingdom and France as well as Russia are no longer considered major powers, their permanent status with vetoes gives them a substantial voice in international politics. As evidenced by the debate over Iraq, enhancing the Security Council's role is a primary objective of French and Russian foreign policies, giving these countries a say about where and how U.S. military power will be projected so long as Washington works through this framework. The P-5 countries, including the United States, are, in essence, guarding themselves; they will not give up their vetoes easily.

Membership

Political paralysis, when it comes to deciding on candidates for either permanently rotating or new permanent seats on the Security Council— the latter with or without vetoes—has further prevented successful Security Council reform. Increasing membership numbers beyond the current 15—5 permanent and 10 nonpermanent members serving rotating two-year terms—seems relatively unobjectionable to promote and reflect greater diversity. At the same time, those more interested in results than in process were quick to point out that a Security Council of 21 or 25 members would hardly improve effectiveness— a "rump" General Assembly certainly would have increased the chances for what one observer poetically called a *Sitzkrieg* over Iraq.[11]

Moreover, the group would be too large to conduct serious negotiations and still too small to represent the UN membership as a whole. Thus, the apparent agreement about some expansion to accommodate more seats at the table for the clearly underrepresented "global South" does not translate into consensus about which countries would be added.[12]

Even more difficult has been reaching agreement on new permanent members. If dominance by the industrialized countries was the problem, why were Germany and Japan obvious candidates? Would Italy not be more or less in the same league? Would it not make more sense for the European Union to be represented (rather than Paris, London, Berlin, and Rome individually)? How did Argentina feel about Brazil's candidacy? Pakistan about India's? South Africa about Nigeria's? How did such traditional UN stalwarts as Canada and the Nordic countries feel about a plan that would leave them on the sidelines but elevate larger developing countries, some of which represent threats to international peace and security? Moreover, if the veto was undemocratic and debilitating for the Security Council's work, should this privilege be given to new permanent members? Would that not make the lowest common denominator lower still?

Since its establishment in 1993, the entity with the lengthiest name in the annals of multilateral deliberations—the Open-Ended Working Group on the Question of Equitable Representation and Increase in the Membership of the Security Council and Other Matters Related to the Security Council—risks also setting a record for continuing to go nowhere for the longest period of time. This entity is a microcosm of a perpetual problem in the organization as a whole: the UN is so consumed with getting the process right that it often neglects the consequences.

BEYOND PROCESS: ADJUSTING TO A NEW WORLD

More recently, a third problem has arisen: Washington's emergence as what former French foreign minister Hubert Védrine aptly dubbed the *hyper-puissance*. Bipolarity has given way to what was supposed to be U.S. primacy, but the demonstrated military prowess in the war on Iraq made it crystal clear that primacy was a vast understatement. Scholars discuss the nuances of economic and cultural leverage resulting from U.S. soft power,[13] but the hard currency of international politics undoubtedly remains military might. Before the war on Iraq, Washington was already spending more on its military than the next 15–25 countries combined (depending on who was counting); with an opening additional appropriation of $79 billion for the war, the United States now spends more than the rest of the world's militaries combined.[14]

With a U.S. global presence as great as that of any empire in history,[15] Security Council efforts to control U.S. action are beginning to resemble the Roman Senate's efforts to control the emperor. Diplomats at UN headquarters have almost unanimously described the debate surrounding the withdrawn resolution before the war in Iraq as "a referendum not on the means of disarming Iraq but on the American use of power."[16] Complicating the picture further were splits among Europeans about the future design and leadership of the continent, with the EU's Common Security and Defense Policy and NATO joining the Security Council as victims.

Today, there are two world "organizations": the UN—global in membership—and the United States—global in reach and power. Jostling about UN Charter reform is a mere distraction. Critics of U.S. hegemony argue that the exercise of military power should be based on UN authority rather than capacity, but in reality, the two concepts are inseparable. As the UN's coercive capacity is always on loan, UN-led or UN-approved military operations take place only when Washington signs on. The value added by the participation of other militaries is mainly political; it is not meaningful in any operational way for enforcement (as opposed to traditional peacekeeping). This reality will not change until Europeans spend considerably more on defense so that they too have an independent military capacity. This argument will remain valid even if a new transatlantic bargain is struck about combining complementary U.S. military and European civilian instruments toward combating common security threats.[17]

If the Security Council is to enforce its collective decisions, U.S. participation is, at present and for the foreseeable future, a sine qua non. If its purpose is to prevent Washington from doing what it has decided is vital to U.S. interests, only a hopeless romantic would claim this is feasible. Although perhaps understandable as a visceral reaction, the idea that the remaining superpower will continue to participate—politically or financially—in an institution whose purpose has become to limit its power has no precedent.

If the Security Council continues to materially disagree with U.S. foreign policy on critical issues with any frequency, the UN could come to resemble its defunct predecessor, the League of Nations. In this, President George W. Bush was on target in his September 2002 address to the General Assembly: "We created the United Nations Security Council, so that, unlike the League of Nations, our deliberations would be more than talk, our resolutions would be more than wishes."[18] The Bush administration's *National Security Strategy of the United States of America* was published later that same month and could not be clearer: "[W]e will be prepared to act apart when our interests and unique responsibilities require."[19] In short, the Bush administration—and any U.S. administration—will never allow international institutions to limit actions that the United States deems necessary for its national security.

The future challenge for UN proponents is twofold: to determine when the Security Council will act as a multiplier for U.S. power and to persuade the United States that acting multilaterally will be in its interest. The trick is to determine in which situations Washington and the world organization will act in concert, that is, when will U.S. tactical multilateralism kick in?

EVOLUTIONARY, NOT REVOLUTIONARY, CHANGE

Although rhetorical fireworks over the last decade have not led to UN Charter reform, they undoubtedly have made possible pragmatic modifications in the Security Council's working methods.[20] New council procedures initiated by member states respond in concrete, if small, ways to the need for more openness and accountability as well as for more diverse inputs into decisionmaking.[21] Thus, they have taken steps to improve the democratic accountability of the Security Council.[22]

Over the last decade, the council president (a position that rotates each month) has adopted the practice of regularly briefing nonmembers and the press about private consultations, meaning that information rather than rumor circulates. Provisional agendas and draft resolutions also are now distributed rather than kept under lock and key. The council routinely holds consultations with senior UN staff and countries that contribute troops to UN efforts and has also convened several times at the level of foreign min3ister or head of state in an effort to increase the visibility of important deliberations and decisions.

When requested, the UN secretariat has in the last couple of years begun to organize missions by Security Council representatives to countries or regions in crisis to permit better exposure to a range of views and to provide firsthand experience on the ground. Under the so-called Arria formula, named after former Venezualan ambassador Diego Arria who in 1993 arranged an informal meeting with a visiting priest to discuss the conflict in the former Yugoslavia, an individual member of the Security Council can invite others for a candid exchange with independent experts and civil society. There have also been more formal meetings with heads of UN units or organizations as well as private retreats with the secretary general and his senior management team.

The reform debate has also led to other proposals that stop short of charter amendments and provide alternative formulas to finesse the issue of the veto. The P-5 could voluntarily exercise greater restraint, for example, by restricting the exercise of the veto only to matters that fall under the obligatory provisions of enforcement decisions taken under Chapter VII of the charter.[23] For cases of humanitarian intervention, the P-5 could abstain where vital interests are not involved.[24] Such restraint would offer no guarantees, of course, and would also set an unusual precedent of calling on selected states to give up rights acquired by treaties. Alternatively, coalitions of states might seek institutional moral stamps of approval outside the Security Council. The Kosovo Commission, an independent group of human rights proponents, made this point most distinctly by arguing that NATO's 1999 humanitarian war was "illegal" (because it had no Security Council authorization) but "legitimate" (because it was ethically justified).[25]

Another means of skirting the veto entails adopting "the General Assembly in Emergency Special Session under the 'Uniting for Peace' procedure."[26] Although this process has been used only three times to authorize military action—the last in the early 1960s for the Congo—it employs the idea of coalitions of the willing, which after all is one of the oldest aims of diplomats. Biting boycotts, for example, were set up against Italy by the League of Nations in the Abyssinian case of the late 1930s and by the UN against South Africa until the end of apartheid in the early 1990s. The original "Uniting for Peace" resolution even contained a clause referring to the voluntary creation of a UN force in cases where the Security Council was unable to act, that is, when it was paralyzed by the veto.

Acting through the General Assembly can be useful to circumvent a veto-wielding member of the Security Council in the clear international minority, but such a route has its limits. Once a security matter has been brought before the General Assembly, the main hurdle it faces is the requirement to have a two-thirds majority of members present and voting. Although the decision on the matter would only be a "recommendation" (whereas the Security Council's decisions are obligations), the necessary backing in the General Assembly might have a moral and political weight sufficient to categorize the use of force as "legal" even without the Security Council's endorsement. In such a case, the action would certainly be regarded as legitimate.[27]

Views are divided about the wisdom of raising the use of force outside the Security Council. Many countries, particularly some European and developing countries, are reluctant or even unwilling to acknowledge the legitimacy of military force that is not specifically sanctioned by the council, even for humanitarian purposes.[28] For these countries, the international political process in the Security Council, however flawed and even without reform, is at least regulated. Indeed, for a growing number of legislators in the

West, a bona fide Security Council authorization is essential to secure their consent to deploy national military forces. Setting aside this procedure, as NATO did in the case of Kosovo and the United States and United Kingdom did in the case of Iraq, threatens the fragile rules that underpin international society.[29]

In examining the legal gymnastics used to justify the use of force in Iraq, Duke University professor of law Michael Byers has recently made a case for "exceptional illegality." Rather than try to change long-standing and basically effective rules, he asks "whether, in truly exceptional circumstances where a serious threat exists, no invitation can be obtained, and the council is not prepared to act, states should simply violate international law without advancing strained and potentially destabilizing legal justifications."[30]

That is one possibility, but in any event, adaptations in actual Security Council behavior, rather than formal modifications or reforms to either its membership or procedures, are more likely to preserve and improve Security Council credibility. Attempts to formally reform the council are unlikely to make a dent in the way that states approach decisionmaking in it. The gains made in transparency in the past are not trivial, but more than 10 years of discussion have led to no reforms to the UN Charter. This time will be no different.

INITIATIVE STAYS IN WASHINGTON, NOT NEW YORK

In the contemporary world, the Security Council should retain, as specified in the UN Charter, the "primary responsibility for the maintenance of international peace and security." Yet, it will also retain the same permanent members with vetoes and, in all likelihood, the same number of nonpermanent members. "The key issue for the council," as the International Peace Academy's president David Malone tells us, "is whether it can engage the United States, modulate its exercise of power, and discipline its impulses."[31]

Will the inability to reform the UN Charter compromise the credibility of the Security Council, particularly regarding matters shaping the future use of force? The answer is "probably not" or at least "no more than in the past." Changing the composition of the Security Council would not, in any case, overcome its core weaknesses—the veto and almost total reliance upon U.S. military power. In short, the Security Council will remain the first port of call for authorizing the use of military force. The former foreign minister of Australia and president of the International Crisis Group, Gareth Evans, has pointed to the more difficult question: "whether it should be the last."[32]

Washington and the other permanent members would certainly answer "no." Major powers normally pursue their self-determined interests in their backyards without the UN's blessing— look no further than Côte d'Ivoire, Sierra Leone, Chechnya, or Xinjiang. The U.S. backyard, however, is considerably bigger than that of most other nations, and the ability of the United States to project military power worldwide is unparalleled. Friends and foes alike are uncomfortable with Washington's present gear: what the EU commissioner for external relations Chris Patten has dubbed "unilateralist overdrive."[33]

Washington should recall that the Security Council not only can enhance the legitimacy of U.S. actions but also can help share global risks and burdens, such as stabilizing postwar Iraq once sanctions were lifted by the Security Council. Recalling that the Somalia syndrome was a dominant domestic factor in the United States in the 1990s, it is likely that prospects for fiscal relief and limiting casualties will become more attractive to U.S. public opinion and limit U.S. enthusiasm for future unilateral operations. If the U.S.

economy remains sluggish and preemptive self-defense against rogue states expands, the UN will appear more and more appealing.[34]

In certain cases, U.S. interests can be best pursued through multilateral decisionmaking. The choice is not between the UN as a rubber stamp and a cipher—between the axis of subservience and the axis of irrelevance. Rather, depending on the issue, the stakes at hand, the positions of other potential allies, and the plausibility of collective military action, Washington, because of its power, has the historically rare opportunity to act either unilaterally or multilaterally.[35]

Acting through the Security Council is always a policy option but should not be a road that Washington always, or never, takes. Clearly, no U.S. administration will permit the council to stand in the way of pursuing the country's perceived interests in national security. Yet at the same time, the Security Council often may serve vital interests as well as give the United States cause to proceed cautiously and with international acquiescence, if not jubilant support.

The war on terrorism provides an evident example of overlapping U.S. and international security interests. Fighting this plague obviously requires cooperation across borders if policies are to be even modestly successful in stopping financial flows to terrorist organizations or improving intelligence. The Security Council, for example, responded instantly to the attacks on the World Trade Center and the Pentagon by passing an unequivocal condemnation of terrorism in Resolution 1368 on September 12, 2001. The text is remarkable for its brevity yet broad scope, with a clear recognition of "the inherent right of individual or collective self-defense in accordance with the Charter," which helped enhance the legitimacy of, and support for, operations in Afghanistan. It also improved the prospects for other types of international cooperation, such as sharing intelligence and halting money laundering. Only two weeks later, the Security Council adopted Resolution 1373, a landmark in uniformly obligating all member states under Chapter VII of the UN Charter to deny terrorists, regardless of their cause, location, or timing, the means to carry out their destructive tactics.[36]

Other examples of shared interests include confronting the global specter of infectious diseases (including the spread of HIV/AIDS, the Ebola virus, and SARS) as well as revived weapons inspections and postconflict reconstruction in Iraq. The UN's growing involvement in postwar Iraq has important symbolic benefits as well as real ones, as do international efforts to confront pandemics. Yet, more than lip service must be paid to the interests of other countries. Unless Washington is prepared to bend on occasion and to contribute to solutions in other regions and countries, these governments are unlikely to sign on when their helping hands are necessary for U.S. priorities.

Washington's multilateral record in the twentieth century conveys "mixed messages," as Columbia University's Edward Luck reminds us.[37] On the one hand, the United States has been the prime mover in creating virtually all of the current generation of intergovernmental organizations—from NATO to the Bretton Woods institutions to the UN family. On the other hand, the United States has often kept its distance and even withdrawn from the International Labor Organization and the UN Educational, Social, and Cultural Organization; and recently, of course, several new initiatives (including the Kyoto Protocol, the Statute on the International Criminal Court, and the ban on antipersonnel landmines) have been met with at best a cold shoulder or at worst outright hostility. This historical pattern of ambivalence is not about to change, given today's Security Council, especially because U.S. military predominance exists side by side with a growing presumption by officials and publics in other countries in favor of more inclusive decisionmaking in multilateral forums, especially about the deployment of military force.

Style is also of consequence. In debating the authorization of force in Iraq, determining whose behavior—that of Washington or Paris—was more churlish proved difficult. The United States nonetheless proceeded to carry out a very risky venture with little diplomatic and material support. Might a slightly more tolerant administration with a greater forbearance for working within the UN system have produced a viable Security Council resolution? When pursued creatively, the leverage of U.S. power can be employed to bring others on board, and diplomacy can succeed. For example, the unpopular proposal to reduce Washington's contribution to the UN budget was finally pushed through by consensus in December 2000 as a result of the agile leadership of Ambassador Richard Holbrooke and unusual financing provided by Ted Turner. Although the stakes were obviously lower in that case, resolving the problem was not a cakewalk either. Yet, in contrast to the fiasco over Iraq, U.S. diplomacy worked.[38]

The apparently growing U.S. appetite for unilateral action has caused painful indigestion among internationalists at home and allies abroad. The UN's menu offers more choices than the Bush administration realizes for "multilateralism à la carte," as proposed by former U.S. director of policy planning Richard Haass. Seats at the Security Council table have been the principal focus of reform discussions in New York, but their significance is largely illusory given the centralization of power in Washington. The country that actually orders from the menu and picks up the tab remains key. At the same time, a more gracious host would be desirable as the United States

should preserve the multilateral option of the Security Council, and of the UN more generally, which normally serve the United States' as well as broader international interests.

NOTES

1. See Kofi A. Annan, *Renewing the United Nations: A Programme for Reform,* A/51/ 1950, July 14, 1997. For a discussion of issues under debate, see Andy Knight, *A Changing United Nations: Multilateral Evolution and the Quest for Global Governance* (New York: Palgrave, 2000).
2. See Ruth B. Russell, *A History of the United Nations Charter: The Role of the United States, 1940–1945* (Washington, D.C.: Brookings Institution, 1958), pp. 742–749. For a recent view, see Rosemary Foot, S. Neil MacFarlane, and Michael Mastanduno, eds., *The United States and Multilateral Organizations* (Oxford and New York: Oxford University Press, 2003).
3. See Cameron Hume, *The United Nations, Iran and Iraq: How Peacemaking Changed* (Bloomington: Indiana University Press, 1994); C. S. R. Murthy, "Change and Continuity in the Functioning of the Security Council Since the End of the Cold War," *International Studies* 32, no. 4 (October–December 1995): 423–439.
4. For an overview, see Thomas G. Weiss, David R Forsythe, and Roger Coate, *The United Nations and Changing World Politics,* 4th ed. (Boulder, Colo.: Westview Press, 2007), chaps. 3 and 4.
5. Jarat Chopra and Thomas G. Weiss, "Sovereignty Is No Longer Sacrosanct: Codifying Humanitarian Intervention," *Ethics and International Affairs* 6 (1992): 95–118.
6. See David M. Malone, "Introduction," in *The Future of the UN Security Council,* ed. David M. Malone (Boulder, Colo.: Lynne Rienner, forthcoming).
7. Boutros Boutros-Ghali, *An Agenda for Peace,* 1995 (New York: United Nations, 1995) (includes the original 1992 report along with a humbler 1995 supplement).
8. See Commission on Global Governance, *Our Global Neighbourhood* (Oxford and New York: Oxford University Press, 1995); Independent Working Group on the Future of the United Nations, *The United Nations in Its Second Half-Century* (New York: Ford Foundation, 1995). For an analysis

of how experts have helped shape UN reform, see Edward C. Luck, "Blue Ribbon Power: Independent Commissions and UN Reform," *International Studies Perspectives* 1, no. 1 (2000): 89–104.

9. For an overview of the possible changes being discussed at the time, see Bruce Russett, Barry O'Neil, and James Sutterlin, "Breaking the Security Council Log-jam," *Global Governance 2,* no. 1 (January–April 1996): 65–79.

10. For discussions, see Russell, *History of the United Nations Charter,* pp. 713–719; Bruce Russett, ed., *The Once and Future Security Council* (New York: St. Martin's Press, 1997), pp. 2–5; Townsend Hoopes and Douglas Brinkley, *FDR and the Creation of the U.N.* (New Haven: Yale University Press, 1997), pp. 198–203.

11. David C. Hendrickson, "Preserving the Imbalance of Power," *Ethics and International Affairs* 17, no. 1 (2003): 160.

12. See James P. Muldoon Jr. et al., eds., *Multilateral Diplomacy and the United Nations Today* (Boulder, Colo.: Westview Press, 1999), pp. 7–77.

13. Joseph E. Nye Jr., *The Paradox of American Power: Why the World's Only Superpower Can't Go It Alone* (Oxford and New York: Oxford University Press, 2002). For a continuation of this argument after the war in Iraq, see Joseph E. Nye Jr., "U.S. Power and Strategy After Iraq," *Foreign Affairs* 82, no. 4 (July/August 2003): 60–73.

14. See Center for Defense Information, "Last of the Big Time Spenders: U.S. Military Budget Still the World's Largest, and Growing," www.cdi.org/budget/2004/world-military-spending.cfm (accessed June 19, 2003) (table based on data provided by the U.S. Department of Defense and the International Institute for Strategic Studies).

15. See Paul Kennedy, *The Rise and Fall of the Great Powers* (New York: Random House, 1987).

16. James Traub, "The *Next* Resolution," *New York Times Magazine,* April 13, 2003, p. 51.

17. See Andrew Moravcsik, "Striking a New Transatlantic Bargain," *Foreign Affairs* 82, no. 4 (July/August 2003): 74–89.

18. George W. Bush, remarks at the UN General Assembly, New York, September 12, 2002, www.whitehouse.gov/news/releases/2002/09/print/20020912-1.html (accessed June 19, 2003).

19. *The National Security Strategy of the United States of America,* September 2002, p. 31, www.whitehouse.gov/nsc/nss.pdf (accessed June 19, 2003).

20. See "Note by the President of the Security Council, Procedural Developments in the Security Council—2002," S/2002/603, May 30, 2002; for a discussion, see Malone, *The Future of the UN Security Council,* pt. 4.

21. The discussion of innovations draws on Edward C. Luck, "Reforming the United Nations: Lessons from a History in Progress," *International Relations Studies and the United Nations Occasional Papers* no. 1 (New Haven: Academic Council on the UN System, 2003), pp. 13–14, www.yale.edu/acuns/publications/UN_Reform/Luck_UN_Reform.pdf (accessed June 22, 2003).

22. See Charlotte Ku and Harold K. Jacobson, eds., *Democratic Accountability and the Use of Force in International Law* (Cambridge and New York: Cambridge University Press, 2003).

23. See Independent Working Group on the Future of the United Nations, *United Nations in Its Second Half-Century,* p. 16; Russett, O'Neill, and Sutterlin, "Breaking the Security Council Logjam," p. 77.

24. International Commission on Intervention and State Sovereignty (ICISS), *The Responsibility to Protect* (Ottawa: ICISS, 2001), p. xiii.

25. Independent International Commission on Kosovo, *Kosovo Report: Conflict, International Response, Lessons Learned* (Oxford and New York: Oxford University Press, 2000), p. 4.

26. ICISS, *Responsibility to Protect,* p. xiii.

27. For an extended argument related to humanitarian intervention, see Thomas G. Weiss and Don Hubert, *The Responsibility to Protect: Research, Bibliography, and Background* (Ottawa: ICISS, 2001), chaps. 6 and 7.

28. See Mohammed Ayoob, "Humanitarian Intervention and State Sovereignty," *International Journal of Human Rights* 6, no. 1 (spring 2002): 81–102.

29. Hedley Bull, *The Anarchical Society: A Study of Order in World Politics,* 3rd ed. (New York: Columbia University Press, 2002). For a contemporary argument related to Bull's original 1977 book, see Robert Jackson, *The Global Covenant: Human Conduct in a World of States* (Oxford and New York: Oxford University Press, 2000); Mohammed Ayoob, "Humanitarian Intervention and International Society," *Global Governance* 7, no. 3 (July–September 2001): 225—230.

30. Michael Byers, "Letting the Exception Prove the Rule," *Ethics and International Affairs* 17, no. 1 (2003): 15. Byers made a similar case about Kosovo

in Michael Byers and Simon Chesterman, "Changing the Rules about Rules? Unilateral Humanitarian Intervention and the Future of International Law," in *Humanitarian Intervention: Ethical, Legal and Political Dilemmas,* eds. J. F. Holzgrefe and Robert O. Keohane (Cambridge and New York: Cambridge University Press, 2003), pp. 177–203.

31. David M. Malone, "Conclusions," in *The Future of the UN Security Council.*

32. Gareth Evans, "The Responsibility to Protect and September 11" (speech sponsored by the Department of Foreign Affairs and International Trade, Ottawa, December 16, 2002).

33. Chris Patten, "Jaw-Jaw, not War-War," *Financial Times,* February 15, 2002, p. 16.

34. For details of this argument, see Mats Berdal, "The UN Security Council: Ineffective but Indispensable," *Survival* 45, no. 2 (summer 2003): 7–30.

35. See Stewart Patrick and Shepard Forman, eds., *Multilateralism and U.S. Foreign Policy: Ambivalent Engagement* (Boulder, Colo.: Lynne Rienner, 2002). A shorter version of the main argument, but with a moral dimension, is found in Stewart Patrick, "Beyond Coalitions of the Willing: Assessing U.S. Multilateralism," *Ethics and International Affairs* 17, no. 1 (2003): 37–54. For a companion volume that emphasizes international reactions to Washington's decisions to go it alone, see David M. Malone and Yuen Foong Khong, eds., *Unilateralism and U.S. Foreign Policy: International Perspectives* (Boulder, Colo.: Lynne Rienner, 2003).

36. For discussions, see Jane Boulden and Thomas G. Weiss, *Terrorism and the UN: Before and After September 11* (Bloomington: Indiana University Press, 2004); International Peace Academy, *Responding to Terrorism: What Role for the United Nations?* (New York: International Peace Academy, 2003).

37. Edward C. Luck, *Mixed Messages: American Politics and International Organization, 1919–1999* (Washington, D.C.: Brookings Institution, 1999).

38. See Gert Rosenthal, "The Scale of Assessments of the UN's Budget: A Case Study of How the U.S. Exercises Its Leverage in a Multilateral Setting," *Global Governance* (July–September 2004).

CHAPTER 6

THE HUMAN RIGHTS REVOLUTION

The Construction of International Norms

The insertion of issues of human rights into the agenda of international relations is a challenge to the nature of the international system as both realists and liberals have traditionally understood it. In seeking to limit the right of individual states to do what they like to their own citizens, this "human rights revolution," at least in theory, undercuts the idea of sovereignty that has been central to the international order since the 1648 Peace of Westphalia. As Kathryn Sikkink argues in the article included in this chapter, human rights norms are more than merely another issue in political science and international relations, but are, instead, "potent challenges to the central logic of the system of sovereign states."

Sikkink provides a constructivist analysis that explains the emergence and diffusion of human rights norms towards the end of the twentieth century. The rest of the readings in this chapter consider different dimensions in the record of this human rights revolution in practice. The selection from Julie Mertus focuses on the role that NGOs and other actors in civil society play in the development, diffusion, and monitoring of human rights norms, providing a more concrete look at the theoretical issues raised by Sikkink. Oona Hathaway's article examines the impact that human rights treaties have (or do not have) on the human rights practices of countries that sign and ratify them. Finally, the piece by James Kurth examines the record of humanitarian intervention to stop human rights abuses in progress.

In examining the record of the human rights revolution in practice, the central question is to what extent the international community not only "talks the talk" but also "walks the walk" of human rights enforcement. Realists, in particular, tend to be skeptical of the willingness and ability of the international community to do the latter. But keep in mind that the effectiveness of global human rights enforcement will not necessarily be an all or nothing proposition. It would be hard to find informed scholars who would argue that human rights norms in practice have either been completely ignored or comprehensively enforced in the practice of international relations. Instead, the debate is over the extent to which norms of human rights are enforced and taken seriously. After reading the selections in this chapter, you should be in a better position to assess both the achievements and shortcomings of the "human rights revolution" and to develop your own clear, but nuanced, understanding of the role of human rights in world politics.

TRANSNATIONAL POLITICS, INTERNATIONAL RELATIONS THEORY, AND HUMAN RIGHTS*

Kathryn Sikkink

In this selection, Sikkink explains the emergence and significance of human rights norms in the contemporary international system. In so doing she provides not only an interesting discussion of human rights norms, but also a useful illustration of the application of the "constructivist" approach to international relations theory. As you read this piece, ask yourself:

- What is the process by which human rights norms have emerged to influence international behavior?
- Why does the emergence of those norms pose a challenge to much established international relations theory?
- Why might one label Sikkink's analysis as "constructivist"?

The rise of human rights as an international issue in the later half of the 20th century presents a puzzle for students of comparative politics and international relations. Many of our dominant theories—realism, rational choice, and economic interest group theories—have trouble accounting for the rise of human rights politics except to dismiss them as marginal, insignificant, or an ideological cover beneath which economic groups or hegemonic countries pursue their interests. But as the . . . daily newspapers make abundantly clear, human rights issues are not marginal, and increasingly detailed policy and institutional mechanisms exist to ensure the implementation of international human rights standards. In some cases, these policies can have a direct impact on human rights practices, and have contributed to reduced repression and regime changes (see Sikkink 1993; Risse, Ropp, and Sikkink 1999).

As David Forsythe cogently argues . . . political scientists should be able to greatly facilitate the understanding of human rights in international perspective, and yet the discipline has, for the most part, ignored or marginalized human rights as a research topic. One reason may be that the dominant theories in the discipline do not give us the tools to understand the emergence of human rights as a crucial international issue area, nor the impact human rights ideas and policies can have upon state practices.

The emergence of human rights politics pushes us to explain why such policies emerge, and why these policies sometimes lead to significant domestic changes. Virtually any explanation of the rise of human rights must take into account the political power of norms and ideas and the increasingly transnational way in which those ideas are carried and diffused. In order to understand how human rights policies can lead to domestic change, in addition, we need to

Kathryn Sikkink, "Transnational Politics, International Relations Theory, and Human Rights," *PS: Political Science & Politics*, 31:3, September 1998. Reprinted by permission of Cambridge University Press and the author.

understand how those ideas get translated into political and economic pressures brought to bear on repressive countries and how such pressures contribute to opening space for domestic opposition, and often to redemocratization.

Understanding these changes are particularly important because human rights are not just another one among the many issue areas in political science today. Because international human rights norms question state rule over society and national sovereignty, human rights issues offer particularly potent challenges to the central logic of a system of sovereign states, as Hedley Bull recognized in his classic work, *The Anarchical Society*:

> Carried to its logical extreme, the doctrine of human rights and duties under international law is subversive of the whole principle that mankind should be organised as a society of sovereign states. For, if the rights of each man can be asserted on the world political stage over and against the claims of his state, and his duties proclaimed irrespective of his position as a servant or a citizen of that state, then the position of the state as a body sovereign over it citizens, and entitled to command their obedience, has been subject to challenge, and the structure of the society of sovereign states has been placed in jeopardy. The way is left open for the subversion of the society of sovereign states on behalf of the alternative organizing principle of a cosmopolitan community. (1977, 146)

I argue that at the end of the twentieth century, in a limited and imperfect sense, this scenario is now playing itself out. The new model is more similar to what Bull called "neo-medievalism," where non-state actors begin to undermine state sovereignty and a new system with "overlapping authority and multiple loyalty" emerges. Bull challenged researchers to document empirically the extent and nature of changes and to specify what kind of alternative vision of international politics might modify or supplant the centrality of interactions among sovereign states. International relations scholars and legal scholars . . . have made significant strides towards responding to these challenges, but much work still remains to be done (see Donnelly 1989; Forsythe 1991, 1983).

To understand the changes in the role of international human rights in international politics we must further develop our theories of the influences of norms and ideas on international politics. Normative and ideational concerns have always informed the study of international politics (Finnemore and Sikkink 1999). The dominance of realist and neo-realist models, however, partially displaced these normative and ideational concerns until the regimes scholarship of the early 1980s opened the way for the more extensive work on ideas, norms, and social construction processes in international relations scholarship in the late 1980s and the 1990s (see Krasner 1983; Kratochwil and Ruggie 1986; Wendt 1987; Goldstein and Keohane 1993; Katzenstein 1996; Finnemore 1996). These studies, however, do not yet add up to a more unified theory of norms and ideas in international relations. It is necessary to continue to build on previous research to generate more general propositions about the origins and effectiveness of norms.

Human rights presents a particularly promising case for exploring and extending a theory of norms in international relations. Research on human rights issues provides some insights into answers to the questions posed above. Political scientists are arriving at a consensus definition of norms as standards of appropriate behavior for actors with a given identity (Katzenstein 1996). How norms influence behavior may be understood as a two-stage process, involving a stage of "norm emergence" and a second stage of broad norm acceptance that legal theorist Cass Sunstein has called a "norm cascade." These two stages are divided by a threshold, or "tipping" point, at which a critical mass of relevant state actors adopt the norm (Sunstein 1997; Finnemore and Sikkink 1999). I would argue that many of the international human rights norms in the Universal Declaration have progressed through the period of norm emergence and that, since the late 1970s, we have been participating in an international human rights "norms cascade." Support for this claim can be found not only in the number of states that have ratified international human rights treaties, but also the degree to which states have incorporated international human rights into their foreign policies and domestic law.

Most will note that we are simultaneously in a period when human rights norms are increasingly important and human rights are increasingly imperilled globally. The prominence of major episodes of human rights violations, however, such as those in the former Yugoslavia and in Rwanda, should not detract from significant improvements in human rights in other regions—especially in Latin America and Eastern Europe. Indeed, the degree to which we are aware of human rights violations, and increasingly critical of the inadequate response of governments to these violations, is in part an indicator of the influence of human rights norms on expectations on foreign policy.

How do norms emerge in the first place? Some theorists have argued that international norms emerge when they are embraced and espoused by the hegemon (Krasner 1995; Ikenberry and Kupchan 1990). Krasner, for example, argues that "the content of human rights issues that were at the forefront in various historical periods reflected the concerns of those states which possessed a preponderance of economic and military power" (1995, 166). But these theorists don't provide a convincing explanation for why hegemonic states begin to pursue human rights policy. Realism cannot provide an explanation for the origins of the social purpose of hegemonic action on human rights (Ruggie 1983). Why did the British decide to use their naval power to end the slave trade, and eventually to end slavery? Why did the United States adopt a human rights policy? In the 1960s and 1970s, it was commonly assumed that U.S. economic and political interests required it to support anticommunist authoritarian regimes around the world. Why, in the mid-1970s, well before the end of the Cold War, did the United States change its perceptions of its interests and begin to initiate a human rights policy?

Norms research suggests that the origins of many international norms lie not in preexisting state interests but in strongly held principled ideas (ideas about right and wrong) and the desire to convert others to those ideas. Nadelmann (1990) has called this dimension "moral proselytizing" and the individuals who carry it out "transnational moral entrepreneurs." The emergence of this kind of moral proselytizing most often involves promoting norms governing the way states treat individuals, or how individuals treat each other. Research on the origins of international human rights norms reveals a key role played by individuals.

The Genocide Convention owed a singular debt to the work of Polish lawyer Raphael Lemkin, who coined the term "genocide" in 1944, helped promote the use of the term, and assisted in drafting and securing the passage of the anti-genocide treaty. Three jurists played a key role in originating norms for the international protection of human rights. Chilean Alejandro Alvarez, Russian Andre Mandelstam, and Greek Antoine Frangulis first drafted and publicized declarations on international rights of man in the inter-War period. The idea of human rights was almost single-handedly reinserted into the wartime debate over war aims by British author Herbert George Wells (Burgers 1992). Although nongovernmental actors have played a particularly important role in the origins of human rights norms, it is often the collaboration among norms entrepreneurs inside of governments, those within international organizations, and nongovernmental actors that leads to the emergence of human rights norms. The human rights language in the United Nations Charter and the text of the Universal Declaration for Human Rights are the result of the combined efforts of individuals associated with governments (like Eleanor and Franklin Roosevelt and Rene Cassin) NGO staffers, and private individuals. The Convention against Torture was crafted by government officials in consultation with Amnesty International in the aftermath of increased global awareness about torture created by Amnesty's Campaign Against Torture in 1973 (Burgers and Danelius 1988).

It is not enough for individuals to develop norms, they must promote them globally through intense campaigns. In many cases of emergent international norms, transnational coalitions (Risse-Kappen 1994) or networks of individuals in nongovernmental organizations conduct substantial transnational campaigns to persuade others of the importance and value of the new norms. This is the case with the anti-apartheid campaign (Klotz 1995), the anti-slavery campaign, the campaign for women's suffrage, campaigns for international human rights and the elimination of violence against women (Keck and Sikkink 1998), and recent campaigns against the use of landmines (Price 1998). Kowert and Legro (1996) refer to this process as "social diffusion," but that is all too passive a category for the very active work of norm advocacy carried out by networks. Norms (like ideas) don't float freely (Risse-Kappen 1994), nor are new collective understandings expected to seep across networks like inkblots (Kowert and Legro 1996). Networks are necessary but not sufficient conditions; not all international campaigns lead to the adoption of norms; there are numerous examples of extensive campaigns that failed.

These networks of nongovernmental organizations eventually need to secure the support of powerful state actors who endorse the norms and make normative socialization a part of their agenda. The process through which these early normative entrepreneurs bring the normative concerns to the attention of policymakers in powerful states is one of almost pure persuasion. These groups and individuals are generally not strong in any classic sense of the term, nor are they able to "coerce" agreement to a norm. They must persuade relying only upon the strength of their normative argument and the power of facts to support and dramatize their argument. Networks and moral entrepreneurs work to redefine an activity as wrong, often through the power of their language, information, and symbolic activity. But the emergence of human rights policy is not a simple victory of ideas over interests. Instead, it demonstrates the power of ideas to reshape understandings of national interest. The recent adoption of human rights policies did not represent the neglect of national interests but rather a fundamental shift in the perception of long-term national interests. Human rights policies emerged because policymakers began to question the principled idea that the internal human rights practices of a country are not a legitimate topic of foreign policy and the causal assumption that national interests are furthered by supporting repressive regimes that violate the human rights of their citizens. In order to understand the sources of this change in perception of interests, we need to look at the normative entrepreneurs both inside and outside of the state who began to push for changes in state policies.

Once norms have emerged, we still need an explanation for why particular norms become influential. We know that not all norms are equal, but we do not yet have clear theories that could explain why some norms "cascade" and other do not. In the case of human rights, how can we explain why they became "the single most magnetic political idea of the contemporary time," as Forsythe quotes Brzezinski saying.

There are a series of hypotheses in the literature about the conditions under which norms will be influential. The hegemonic socialization approach suggests that in order to explain which norms will be influential, we examine which norms are most forcefully espoused by hegemonic actors (Ikenberry and Kupchan 1990). This explanation, however, fails to account for how normative change occurs within the hegemon. Nor is it the case that all major human rights victories were the result of hegemonic pressures. There are crucial episodes of human rights changes, such as women's suffrage, or the global campaign against apartheid, where hegemons were followers, not leaders (Klotz 1995; Ramirez et al. 1997).

Another explanation for the spread of norms is that norms entrenched at the domestic level (not just in the hegemon but in a wide range of states) are projected internationally. Lumsdaine (1993) provides extensive documentation for the argument that norms about foreign aid have their roots in domestic antipoverty norms and are in many ways an international projection of the welfare state. While international human rights norms clearly resulted from the internationalization of domestic human rights norms, this explanation cannot explain why the internationalization of norms may follow the domestic normative process by centuries (in the sense that the Universal Declaration of Human Rights in 1948 extended to the international arena rights granted to French citizens in the French Declaration of the Rights of Man and the Citizen in 1789) while in other cases the internationalization follows much more directly. There is some evidence, however, of increasing simultaneity of domestic and international normative processes. For example, domestic and global campaigns for the elimination of domestic battery and violence against women are evolving together in many cases, with international normative developments used to spur domestic change and vice versa. This raises the issue of which domestic norms can be successfully internationalized. Many domestic norms do not lend themselves to easy internationalization, while others seem easier to project onto an international arena.

Forsythe (1993) discusses international legitimation as one part of an explanation of the increased importance of international human rights norms, and yet he recognizes that states have multiple sources of legitimacy. Why would states care about international legitimacy, and why and how have human rights increasingly become a yardstick of such legitimacy?

I believe there is something in the intrinsic quality of the human rights norms that gives them their force and influence. Human rights norms have a special status because they prescribe rules for appropriate behavior and they help define identities of liberal states. Human rights then become part of the yardstick used to define who is in and who is outside of the club of liberal states. Work by sociology's institutionalists suggests that Western cultural norms congruent with capitalism and liberalism will be particularly powerful (Thomas et al. 1987; also see Finnemore 1996). But there are many Western norms (some of them conflicting) that are congruent with liberalism and capitalism, but only a subset of such norms have powerful transnational effects. Boli and Thomas (1999) have refined this somewhat and argue that five principles are central to world culture: universalism, individualism, voluntaristic authority, rational progress, and world citizenship. Margaret Keck and I (1998) have advanced more specific claims. We argue that two broad categories of norms are particularly effective transnationally and cross-culturally: those involving bodily integrity and prevention of bodily harm for vulnerable or "innocent" groups, especially when there is a short causal chain between cause and effect; and norms for legal equality of opportunity. Norms entrepreneurs must speak to aspects of belief systems or life worlds that transcend a specific cultural or political context. Although notions of bodily harm are culturally interpreted, they also resonate with basic ideas of human dignity common to most cultures. If one basic motivation for espousing norms is empathy, then we would expect transcultural norms to be based on a basic human denominator that would provoke empathy. But issues involving bodily harm don't develop into international norms cascades in and of themselves. Bringing these issues to the fore requires the efforts of international norm entrepreneurs capable of drawing them to the attention of policymakers and the public. For example, transnational norms entrepreneurs, organized in advocacy networks, have successfully used graphic images of bodily harm as a means of mobilizing transnational campaigns against human rights violations in particular countries. What this argument about the intrinsic power of the issue suggests is that not all human rights norms are equal, and that we would expect some human rights norms to gain wide international acceptance more rapidly than others.

In summary, international relations theorists hoping to understand the politics of human rights will need a different model of international politics; one that sees the international system as an international society made up not only of states, but also of non-state actors that may have transnational identities and overlapping loyalties. While states continue to be the primary actors in this system, their actions need to be understood not as self-help behavior in anarchy, but as the actions of members of an international society of states and non-state actors. In such a society, states may make changes in their behavior not only because of the economic costs of sanctions, but because leaders of countries care about what leaders of other countries think of them. As James Fearon (1997) discussed, people sometimes follow norms because they want others to think well of them, and because they want to think well of themselves. People's ability to think well of themselves is influenced by norms held by a relevant community of actors. International law scholars have long recognized this inter-subjective nature of norms by referring to international law as relevant within a community of "civilized nations." Today, the idea of "civilized" nations has gone out of style, but international law and international organizations are still the primary vehicles for stating community norms and for conferring collective legitimation. Some legal scholars now discuss a community of "liberal states," seen as a sphere of peace, democracy, and human rights, and distinguish between relations among liberal states and those among liberal and nonliberal states (Slaughter 1995). Human rights norms have constitutive effects because good human rights performance is one crucial signal to others to identify a member of the community of liberal states. Political scientists need to be especially attentive to the politics of human rights not only because of their potential for promoting human dignity, but also because human rights issues are particularly useful cases for generating and exploring alternative models of international politics (Risse, Ropp, and Sikkink 1999).

NOTE

* I want particularly to recognize and thank three separate coauthors with whom I developed some of the ideas presented in this essay: Martha Finnemore. Margaret Keck and Thomas Risse. The stimulating exchanges and joint writing projects with each of these scholars have greatly contributed to my thinking on these issues, but (as always) they are not to blame for any of the mistakes.

REFERENCES

Bull, Hedley. 1997. *The Anarchical Society: A Study of Order in World Politics.* New York: Columbia University Press.

——— and Hans Danelius. 1988. *The United Nations Convention against Torture.* Dordrecht: Martinus Nijhoff.

Burgers. J. Herman. 1992. "The Road to San Franscisco: The Revival of the Human Rights Idea in the Twentieth Century." *Human Rights Quarterly* 14(4): 447.

Boli, John, and George Thomas. 1999. "INGOs and the Organization of World Culture." In *Constructing World Culture: International Nongovernmental Organizations since 1875.* ed. John Boli and George Thomas. Stanford CA: Stanford University Press.

Donnelly. Jack. 1989. *Universal Human Rights in Theory and Practice.* Ithaca: Cornell University Press.

Fearon, James. 1997. "What is Identity (As We Now Use the Word)?" University of Chicago. Manuscript.

Finnemore, Martha. 1996a. *National Interests in International Society.* Ithaca: Cornell University Press.

———. 1996b. "Norms. Culture, and World Politics: Insights from Sociology's Institutionalism." *International Organization* 50(2): 325–47.

———. and Kathryn Sikkink. 1998. "International Norm Dynamics and Political Change." *International Organization* 52(4).

Goldstein, Judith, and Robert O. Keohane, eds. 1993. *Ideas and American Foreign Policy.* Ithaca: Cornell University Press.

Ikenberry. G. John, and Charles Kupchan. 1990. "Socialization and Hegemonic Power." *International Organization* 44(3): 283–315.

Katzenstein, Peter J., ed. 1996. *The Culture of National Security.* New York: Columbia University Press.

Klotz, Audie. 1995. *Norms in International Relations: The Struggle against Apartheid.* Ithaca: Cornell University Press.

Kowert, Paul, and Jeffrey Legro. 1996. "Norms, Identity, and Their Limits: A Theoretical Reprise." In *The Culture of National Security,* ed. Peter Katzenstein. New York: Columbia University Press.

Krasner, Stephen D., ed. 1983. *International Regimes.* Ithaca: Cornell University Press.

———. 1993. "Sovereignty, Regimes. and Human Rights." In *Regime Theory and International Relations,* ed. Volker Rittberger. Oxford: Claredon Press.

Kratochwil, Friedrich. and John G. Ruggie. 1986. "International Organization: A State of the Art on an Art of the State." *International Organization* 40(4): 753–76.

Lumsdaine, David Halloran. 1993. *Moral Vision: The Foreign Aid Regime, 1949–1989.* Princeton: Princeton University Press.

Keck, Margaret, and Kathryn Sikkink. 1998. *Activists Beyond Borders: Advocacy Networks in International Politics.* Ithaca: Cornell University Press.

Nadelmann, Ethan. 1990. "Global Prohibition Regimes: The Evolution of Norms in International Society." *International Organization* 44(4): 479–526.

Price, Richard. 1998. "Reversing the Gun Sights: Transnational Civil Society Targets Land Mines." *International Organization* 52(3).

Ramirez, Francisco, Yasemin Soysal, and Suzanne Shanahan. 1997. "The Changing Logic of Political Citizenship: Cross-National Acquisition of Women's Suffrage Rights, 1890–1990." *American Sociological Review* 62:735–45.

Risse, Thomas, Stephen C. Ropp, and Kathryn Sikkink, eds. 1999. *The Power of Human Rights: International Norms and Domestic Change.* Cambridge: Cambridge University Press.

Risse-Kappen, Thomas. 1994. "Ideas Do Not Float Freely: Transnational Coalitions, Domestic Structure, and the End of the Cold War." *International Organization* 48(2): 185–214.

Ruggie, John G. 1983. "International Regimes, Transactions, and Change: Embedded Liberalism in the Postwar Economic Order." *International Organization* 36(2): 379–416.

Sikkink, Kathryn. "Human Rights, Principled Issue Networks, and Sovereignty in Latin America." *International Organization* 47(3): 411–41.

Slaughter, Ann-Marie. 1995. "International Law in a World of Liberal States." *The European Journal of International Law* 6:139–70.

Sunstein, Cass. 1997. "Social Norms and Social Roles." In *Free Markets and Social Justice,* ed. Cass Sunstein. New York: Oxford University Press.

Thomas, George M., John W. Meyer, Francisco O. Ramirez, and John Boli, eds. 1987. *Institutional Structure:* *Constituting State, Society and Individual.* Newbury Park, CA: Sage Publications.

Wendt, Alexander. 1987. "The Agent-Structure Problem in International Relations Theory." *International Organization* 41(3): 335–70.

RAISING EXPECTATIONS?: CIVIL SOCIETY'S INFLUENCE ON HUMAN RIGHTS AND U.S. FOREIGN POLICY

Julie A. Mertus

Constructivist scholars emphasize the role of norm emergence and diffusion in world politics and the role played in that regard by NGOs and other actors in civil society. In this article, Mertus provides brief case studies of both the impact and limits of the influence that these nonstate actors can have on the development and diffusion of human rights norms and practices. As you read this selection, ask yourself:

⬤ What is the role and strategy of NGOs and other actors from civil society in the human rights arena?

⬤ What impact have they had on human rights?

⬤ What are the limits and constraints on their influence?

INTRODUCTION

The strategic politics of non-governmental actors, as Margaret Keck and Kathryn Sikkink have observed, is 'rooted in values and aimed at changing values' (Klotz 1995, Keck and Sikkink 1998). . . . Advocacy groups frame our ways of understanding and presenting the world that 'underscore and embellish the seriousness and injustice of a social condition or redefine as unjust and immoral what was previously seen as unfortunate but perhaps tolerable' (Tarrow 1998: 110). By framing issues in human rights terms, NGOs and other actors seek to shape public opinion and influence policy options, ensuring that the human rights dimension of policy options is addressed. . . .

The most well-known tactic of human rights civil society has been that of 'naming, blaming and shaming', that is, naming human rights violations, publicly identifying the violator (traditionally a state, but increasingly a corporation or other actor), and shaming them into compliance by employing a public campaign (involving letter writing and other public acts of condemnation). This 'watch' role of civil society, popularized by Amnesty International's letter writing campaigns

Julie A. Mertus, excerpt from "Raising Expectations?: Civil Society's Influence on Human Rights and U.S. Foreign Policy," *Journal of Human Rights,* 3:1, March 2004. Reprinted by permission of the publisher Taylor & Francis Ltd, http://www.tandf.co.uk/journals.

and Human Rights Watch's various 'watch groups' for regions and topics, remains significant today. The efficacy of this tactic has improved as the technical expertise of the 'watchers' has been strengthened and as communication technology has advanced (Vandenberg 2001).

Even as the 'watch' campaigns have remained popular, civil society actors have engaged in policy analysis and advocacy activities in addition to atrocity reporting. Early on, human rights organizations focused on 'standard-setting', that is, the establishment of the human rights standards by which the conduct of states could be judged (Korey 2001). They also began serving as ombudsmen intervening on behalf of 'prisoners of conscience' and providing legal services and other support for victims and families of victims of gross human rights abuses (Korey 2001). They have advocated for the creation of systems and mechanisms to enforce human rights, at the international, national and regional levels, and have pressed for greater NGO access to the working of those systems (Korey 2001: 139, 229). All of these efforts have had an impact on US foreign policy, but it is the new strategies of more recent years that have targeted US foreign policy specifically. These efforts have moved beyond public shaming techniques focused singularly on human rights to advocacy approaches that integrate human rights into broader public policy agendas and suggest long-term solutions to the roots of human rights violations as well as addressing the impact of their ongoing manifestation.

The ability of civil society to influence US foreign policy has been advanced by the professionalization of the field and the increased mobility of individuals from the government sector to civil society. Today individuals working on human rights issues are likely to be former members of the Clinton administration and other previous administrations, former State Department employees who quit in protest over US policies, and former Ambassadors and military officers, as well as individuals who cut their teeth working on humanitarian projects in Afghanistan, election monitoring in Bosnia, or the founding of the Truth Commission in South Africa. And the organizations they join are more likely to be highly sophisticated, and staffed with lawyers, area experts, lobbyists, advocacy teams and recent graduates of new programs offering specific training in human rights. 'Before, human rights NGOs were a conglomerate of the elite, but with grassroots and idealism as their guide', says Martina Vandenberg (2001), a former Human Rights Watch researcher, 'Now they are a community of elite voyeurs with a few wild haired exceptions'. The age of email and Web pages makes it even more possible for individuals or a small cadre of folks hunched over computers to have an impact on a human rights issue (Wapner 2002a). But even these individuals are likely to have elite training, and over time even they are likely to either join larger organizations or collapse. . . .

Tapping this expertise, human rights organizations now reach deeper into the US foreign policy establishment and make new demands on the behavior of the US government and military. In contrast to the technique of public shaming, these new efforts often involve private meetings and cooperative information sharing, the provision of concrete policy proposals, and the offer of technical assistance. The new generation of human rights advocates target their advocacy more precisely and work deeper within government structures, turning to particularly sympathetic ears wherever they may be—as long as they have influence over policy makers (Wapner 2002a).

This essay highlights cases in which civil society actors have had an impact on a range of US foreign policy decision-making related to human rights. It presents . . . case studies which were chosen based on three criteria: (1) the issue profiled involves specific organizations who have some discernable impact on the application or formation of US foreign policy (in Martha Finnemore and Kathryn Sikkink's terminology; they are 'norm entrepreneurs'; 1998), despite the difficulties of gauging the exact impact of civil society organizations; (2) the examples are both ideologically liberal and conservative; (3) comparatively little has been written about these cases.

A TALE OF TWO TREATIES

Civil society organizations play vital roles in influencing the stance of the US toward international human rights treaties. As a recent white paper on 'The Role of an International Convention on the Human Rights of People with Disabilities' notes, the advantages of pursuing an international treaty include: (i) providing an immediate statement of international legal accountability; (ii) providing an authoritative and global reference point for domestic law and policy initiatives; (iii) providing mechanisms for more effective monitoring, including reporting on the enforcement of the convention by governments and nongovernmental organizations, supervision by a body of experts mandated by the convention, and possibly the consideration of individual or group complaints under a mechanism to be created by the convention; (iv) establishing a useful framework for international cooperation; and (v) providing transformative educative benefits for all participants engaged in the preparatory and formal negotiation phases (National Council on Disability 2002a).

The benefits of pursuing a treaty, however, must be weighed against competing arguments against multilateral treaty efforts. As the National Council on Disability White Paper (2002a) notes, treaty strategies are often blocked by 'well-worn and oddly unquestioned justifications for US non-participation in human rights treaties based on the complexities of our federal system, the notion that human rights are an exclusive concern of domestic jurisdiction and the US Constitution does not permit the use of the treaty power for regulation of such matters, the potential for conflict between treaty obligations and the Constitution, and the like'.

Nonetheless, despite the odds against them—or perhaps because of these odds—civil society continues to press for the adoption of new treaties. The following examples illustrate how in some cases, key individuals act as norm entrepreneurs by playing a persistent role in bringing certain concerns to the negotiating table and in shaping how they are discussed and ultimately reflected in the resulting treaty (Lumsdaine 1993). Throughout treaty negotiations, human rights advocates may be partners with or opponents of the US government and, as these examples suggest, the nature of the relationship between government and the NGO community is likely to change over time.

Mitigating Damage on Treaty Negotiations: Tobacco Control

The World Health Organization (WHO) had never negotiated an international treaty before, but the new WHO Director-General, Dr. Gro Harlem Brundtland, thought it was worth a try. The idea for an international treaty on tobacco control had been circulating ever since Professor Ruth Roemer at UCLA and her then student Allyn Taylor (who, by 1998, was a well established WHO legal consultant) wrote about the idea in the early 1980s and 1990s (Taylor and Roemer 1996). But it was not until Brundtland look the helm that WHO started the 'Tobacco-Free Initiative' and made international tobacco control a top priority for that organization (Brundtland 2000, Committee of Experts on

Tobacco Industry Documents 2000). In a move that surprised those who expected the WHO to maintain its non-activist tradition, the 191 member countries of WHO, meeting at the 1999 World Health Assembly, voted to support opening negotiations for the Framework Convention on Tobacco Control (FCTC) (Henderson 1999). Formal talks on the convention commenced in 2000 with the first session of the FCTC Intergovernmental Negotiating Body (INB) (World Health Organization 2003).

From the outset, WHO turned to non-governmental organizations for expertise and assistance. The London-based organization ASH (Action on Smoking and Health) was one of the NGOs working closely with WHO from the beginning, and a host of public health and human rights organizations soon joined on the effort. But they needed a strong US partner. ASH turned to the American-based Campaign for Tobacco-Free Kids, a privately-funded anti-smoking organization, to fill the void. While Tobacco-Free Kids had no experience with international standard-setting, it had a reputation for impeccable research, creative advocacy and unflagging energy. To spearhead the American side of the campaign, Tobacco-Free Kids hired attorney Judy Wilkenfeld as director of international programs. Having served as Special Advisor for Tobacco Policy in the US Food and Drug Administration (1994–1999) and Assistant Director of the Division of Advertising Practices in the US Federal Trade Commission (1980–1994), Wilkenfeld not only knew the issues, but also enjoyed congenial relations with many in the Clinton administration who would work on the proposed treaty.

Support for the treaty among NGOs grew rapidly. In March 2000, eight groups set out to 'inquire and induce and cajole more groups to join' (Wilkenfeld 2003). The coalition-building effort included groups from all over the spectrum of activism and issues pertaining to tobacco, including not only public health and human rights groups but also labor rights groups, women's organizations, and environmental groups. Within the course of three years, the coalition grew from the original eight to more than 120 partners.

For those from the US, the negotiation process involved a different cast of characters than that present in the usual treaty negotiation. Because the treaty was developed under the auspices of the World Health Organization, the State Department took a back seat to the Department of Health and Human Services, that is, they did not head the delegation. The NGOs enjoyed a cooperative partnership with the delegation under the Clinton administration headed by Thomas Novotny. 'The [Clinton] administration was in general supportive of the treaty and working against companies like Phillip Morris' (Wilkenfeld 2003). Wilkenfeld (2003) states, 'We didn't always agree with them, but we were able to deal with them and to tell them our disappointments. But then prior to the second session, there was a radical change in how the delegation behaved'.

The early work which the Campaign for Tobacco-Free Kids conducted was mostly as a collaborative partner of the US government. Initially there were 'major questions [of] whether the US and other tobacco-exporting nations will support a strong treaty' (Campaign for Tobacco-Free Kids 1999). Once the first round of negotiations was completed, however, there was a feeling of 'cautious optimism about the progress of the discussions' on the part of NGOs ('NGOs urge strong action on WHO tobacco treaty' 1999). On the fifth day of the first meeting, the US delegate gave a statement calling for 'a robust statement restricting advertising, sponsorship and promotion of tobacco, to the extent permitted under domestic law, with a special emphasis on eliminating those messages that have special appeal to children and adolescents' (Framework Convention on Tobacco Control 2000). With such strong support from the Clinton administration, the American NGOs focused less on the passage of a treaty, which appeared to be within grasp, and more on working with the government representatives to make the treaty a strong one.

The new presidential administration of George W. Bush brought an abrupt change in the relationship between NGOs and the US government. To ease the transition before the second international meeting on the convention, active NGO groups and the outgoing US delegates convened a meeting with the incoming US delegates. According to Judith Wilkenfeld (2003), who attended the meeting, 'prior to the second session, there was a radical change in how the delegation behaved . . . it became quite painful . . . they were backing away on second hand smoke— all of the provisions they had taken a decent stance on they were backing away from. Not to mention they were becoming more unilateral'. Other people in the US who were closely involved with the issue, such as Congressman Henry Waxman (Democrat, California), accused the US of taking cues from Phillip Morris in their international negotiations (Associated Press 2001). Even at this early stage of the new administration's involvement on the tobacco treaty issue, the lines were being drawn.

Throughout the rest of the negotiations, NGOs perceived the US government as 'no longer an ally, but an obstacle' (Wilkenfeld 2003). The lead official of the US delegation, Thomas Novotny, resigned after the second round of negotiations 'rather than argue the case of the new [Bush] administration on tobacco issues', including US proposals that would make certain mandatory steps voluntary and soften restrictions on advertising aimed at children and smoking in public places (Kaufman 2001: Al). Tensions mounted and by the fifth session of negotiations of the tobacco treaty, American NGOs attempting to influence foreign policy were at a point of collision with the delegation. 'As their behavior became worse and worse, more intransigent, more unilateral—so did our rhetoric', remembered Wilkenfeld (2003). The first press release on the US behavior came during the fifth meeting. Headlined 'U.S. Continues Obstructionist Behavior as Negotiations Resume on Proposed Tobacco Treaty', the statement accused the delegation of taking positions protecting industry interests rather than public health (Wilkenfeld 2002).

The leading American NGOs working on public health issues, many of whom have Republican reputations, were among those galvanized into taking the strongest stand yet on the negotiations. In a joint statement in February 2003, the American Cancer Society, American Heart Association, American Lung Association and Campaign for Tobacco-Free Kids called on the US to withdraw from the negotiations on the proposed international tobacco treaty ('Leading US public health groups tell US delegation to tobacco treaty negotiations: go home' 2003). They issued a statement that 'sent a message to the world community that US NGOs did not stand by the actions of their government' (Wilkenfeld 2003). The relationship of the NGOs toward the US delegation thus evolved from a cooperative partnership in the Clinton era, to being combative in the beginning of the Bush administration, to one of outright dismissal later in the Bush administration.

The openly confrontational tactics of the US representatives eventually gave way to a quieter 'poison pill' policy. On 1 March 2003, 171 nations reached agreement on a strong treaty. The US agreed to sign on to the treaty, but only if the convention were substantially changed. The US issued a new statement of position on the FCTC which was generally supportive, but which still complained that 'our ability to sign and ratify the Convention is undermined by the current prohibition on reservations'. The US proposal was essentially to allow any nation to opt out of any of the treaty's substantive provisions (Position of the United States of America: Framework Convention on Tobacco Control 2003). When the nongovernmental community received information regarding this development, it signaled a virtual call to arms in their activism and rhetoric. They launched a media blitz which yielded stories in all of the major US newspapers.

In another abrupt about-face, on 18 May 2003, Health and Human Services Secretary Tommy Thompson declared that the US would join the other members of the WHO in supporting the Framework Convention on Tobacco Control. 'This is an outstanding day when you can stand up and make a step forward for public health', Thompson said, adding, 'It is no exaggeration to state that the United States is a world leader in anti-smoking efforts'. Thompson did not specify whether the United States would sign the treaty, but said the US is 'carefully reviewing the text'.

Adoption of the treaty by the WHO assembly cleared the way for the FCTC to be opened for signature on 16 June 2003. The treaty commits nations to banning all tobacco advertising, promotion and sponsorship (with an exception for nations with constitutional constraints). It also commits them to requiring large warning labels covering at least 30 percent of the principal display areas of the cigarette pack. The treaty provides nations with a roadmap for enacting strong, science-based policies in other areas such as secondhand smoke protections, tobacco taxation, tobacco product regulation, combating cigarette smuggling, public education, and tobacco cessation treatment.

As of 11 November 2003, the treaty had been signed by 77 countries (Framework Convention Alliance 2003). The NGOs claimed an initial victory, but immediately began preparing for the hard work that lay ahead in urging nations to ratify and implement the treaty.

Initiating a Treaty: Disability Rights

'Nothing about us without us' (Charlton 1998): so goes the familiar refrain of the disability rights movement. When, in the last month of 2001, the US State Department began sizing up its position on a prospective international convention on disability rights, leaders in the disabled community wanted to make sure they had input from the outset. While the presidency of George W. Bush was unlikely to recommend that the US sign an international treaty on disability rights, the State Department had a variety of options, none of which the disability community considered constructive: it could use its powerful voice to obstruct the progress of a treaty desired by other countries; it could ignore the process; or it could indirectly support the process while still asserting its irrelevance to the United States. No matter how it acted, the State Department would leave its mark on the way disability issues are understood. Knowing this, the disability movement in the US geared up to try to work with government actors on framing the issues and initiating the treaty process.

The first step the disability movement took was to eliminate the chance that the US could ignore the growing momentum for an international treaty on disability rights and thus signal its irrelevance to the rest of the world. Once dead, a treaty process is hard to revive. The advocates needed to send a clear message to the US government that an international convention on disability rights was of great importance to disabled people in America and throughout the world. But disability rights advocates are an extremely diverse lot, and very few at that time were thinking in terms of international human rights. They had been a bit taken by surprise when Mexico raised the issue of an international disability rights convention as part of the Platform of Action adopted at the World Conference against Racism in Durban, South Africa. The speed with which the United Nations took up the issue was indeed breathtaking. On 28 November 2001, the UN General Assembly adopted by consensus a resolution calling for the establishment of an Ad Hoc Committee to elaborate 'a comprehensive and integral international convention to promote and protect the rights and dignity of persons with disabilities, based on the holistic approach in the work done in the field of social development, human rights and non-discrimination' (Comprehensive and Integral International Convention to Promote and Protect the Rights and Dignity of Persons with Disabilities 2001).

The establishment of the Ad Hoc Committee created a new focus and source of energy for disability activists. In planning their advocacy strategy, disability leaders tried to ensure that it was inclusive of the disability community as a whole and not dominated by European or North American members of the network, or by any particular sector of the disability community. . . .

To avoid privileging elites, the National Council on Disability embarked on an extensive capacity-building campaign. Significant publications included the National Council on Disability's *A Reference Tool: Understanding the Potential Content and Structure of an International Convention on the Human Rights of People with Disabilities* (2002b). Most significant was the White Paper publication entitled *Understanding the Role of an International Convention on the Rights of People with Disabilities* which was published by the

National Council of Disability (2002a) and around which two historical events took place. One event brought together leaders of the American disability community and leaders of the international human rights movement for the first time. Another brought together leaders of the American grassroots disability community for a day long conference on international disability rights, and the convention process in particular. To further enhance participation of people with disabilities in the decision-making process, a coalition of nine American-based disability organizations wrote a 'Rough Guide' to participation in the Ad Hoc Committee to help on-site participants influence the negotiations (Campaign Development Group 2002). Landmine Survivors Network followed up the first edition with revisions and five regional editions of the Rough Guide (Inter-American, African, European, Asia-Pacific and Middle Eastern) in anticipation of the meeting of the second Ad Hoc Committee at the UN in 2003.

In the months lending up to the first Ad Hoc Committee meeting, disability organizations lobbied hard to achieve access to the meeting at the United Nations. The participation of NGOs was far from decided. Only seven membership-based international disability groups comprising the International Disability Alliance (IDA) held ECOSOC consultative status, while many of the organizations taking leadership roles in the new treaty process were excluded from the IDA group, making coordination amongst NGOs a challenge. An additional obstacle was presented by the UN which kept disability organizations in limbo, refusing to commit on procedures for NGO participation. Just one week before the meeting was to commence, the UN General Assembly adopted a resolution which allowed all organizations enjoying consultative status with the Economic and Social Council to participate in ad hoc sessions and to speak in the general debate and provided that other, non-accredited organizations could apply for accreditation for the meeting (Accreditation and Participation of Non-governmental Organizations in the Ad Hoc Committee to Consider Proposals for a Comprehensive and Integral International Convention to Promote and Protect the Rights and Dignity of Persons with Disabilities 2002).

By the time of the first Ad Hoc meeting in July 2002, the State Department had come around from being apathetic to the treaty process, to being obstructionist. The State Department's original stance was classic American exceptionalism: the US did not need the treaty because it had the much stronger Americans with Disabilities Act (ADA). In so doing they implied that human rights treaties are for other people. At the 2002 Ad Hoc meeting, however, the US representatives stalled the process, poking technical holes in the document, asserting that the time was not ripe for a disability treaty.

Avraham Rabby, US Advisor for Economic and Social Affairs, told the UN delegates that the American experience (through the ADA) 'proves that, when crafted correctly, legislation can have real and lasting effects on the promotion of the rights of persons with disabilities and have a positive effect on the population as a whole' (2002). However, he warned that:

A new treaty, hurriedly conceived and formulated, will not necessarily change the practice of states. Indeed, experience has shown that the human rights instruments that have resulted in the most profound change in state practice have been those instruments which were carefully considered over a substantial period of time and which were adopted by consensus among states, after significant discussions and debate. (2002)

Disability advocates and human rights activists fought back by publicizing America's recalcitrant stance and by framing America's opposition in terms of hostility toward the disabled. Throughout the two weeks of the first Ad Hoc Committee meeting in 2002 in New York, meetings of a spontaneously created Disability Caucus were held adjacent to the Ad Hoc Committee conference room. This tactic was successful in terms of presenting, at various points, a unified voice of NGOs before the Ad Hoc Committee. The NGOs agreed to use the internet and other mechanisms to expose the United States' obstructionist behavior.

Before the close of the first Ad Hoc Committee, an urgent action alert was sent out to mobilize American disability activists to demand that the US withdraw its objection to the treaty (Light *et al.* 2002). Under intense pressure, the US delegation stepped aside and allowed the process to continue. While the end result of the meeting was only a decision to continue deliberations (Report of the Ad Hoc Committee on a Comprehensive and Integral International Convention on Protection and Promotion of the Rights and Dignity of Persons with Disabilities 2002) NGOs could claim victory (Meeting of the Ad Hoc Committee 2002).

The conclusion of the first Ad Hoc Committee meeting stepped up the domestic momentum for the disability community and its supporters. Four developments are particularly noteworthy (Lord 2003b). First, Senator Tom Harkin (Democrat, Iowa) established a working group after the first Ad Hoc Committee which, on a monthly basis, brought together disability activists and members of the National Council on Disability to discuss developments in relation to the convention. Activists worked with staffers from the officers of Senator Harkin, and Representatives James Langevin (Democrat, Rhode Island), and Tom Lantos (Democrat,

California) to develop a draft congressional resolution which would call on the United States to support the new convention effort. Activists also used the 'New Freedom Initiative' of President Bush to build an argument for support of the convention effort. Finally, the National Council on Disability's International Watch, a federal advisory group established to follow international disability issues, began to focus extensively on the new convention effort and discussed ways in which to build awareness of the effort in its monthly teleconferences.

At the next major United Nations meeting on the proposed convention, in June 2003, the US agreed to neither support nor obstruct the treaty process. The American representatives still insisted that American law was far superior and that, although some countries might need a treaty, the US did not (Boyd 2003). In marked contrast to the Tobacco Control Treaty negotiations, however, the US would take a stance which was very close to what NGOs were calling for from them, namely, a non-obstructionist position.

What explains the US adoption of a more congenial position? According to some human rights activists in Europe, the American UN Mission in Geneva was telling Washington to support this treaty effort, given the backlash about US action in Iraq and positions on other treaties (Anonymous 2003). Some activists in Washington DC assert that individual personalities in government were genuinely in support of the treaty; and others speculate that the US made a simple instrumental calculation that it had more to gain than to lose by a 'non-position position' (Lord 2003b). In any event, the American position paved the way for a remarkable outcome: the Ad Hoc Committee's decision to put the drafting of the initial treaty text in the hands of a Working Group consisting of 25 governments, 12 NGO representatives and one representative of a national human rights

institution. While this group is reminiscent of earlier treaty drafting processes, it is completely unprecedented in according 12 NGOs a formal place at the negotiating table via the drafting Working Group. In previous UN multilateral treaty negotiations in the human rights—and indeed other—sphere, the most that could be hoped for in the way of participation was informal observer status. . . .

SHAPING THE FOREIGN POLICY AGENDA

Civil society organizations have found creative ways to shape policy options far beyond participation in treaty processes. . . . While these activities may be described as 'lobbying', David Forsythe observes that 'in order to preserve their non-political and tax-free status . . . the groups tend to refer to these activities as education' (2000: 157). In recent years, examples of the civil society influencing the US foreign policy agenda can be claimed by both liberals and conservatives. For example, just as Ken Roth, the Executive Director of Human Rights Watch, convinced President Clinton to end his term by signing onto the treaty on the International Criminal Court (ICC), the conservative think tanks that provided President George W. Bush with his anti-ICC platform persuaded the new president to begin his term by 'unsigning' the treaty. . . .

As these examples illustrate, the members of civil society come from all political and ideological vantage points. In seeking to influence the philosophy and operation of US foreign policy, they forge unusual alliances and test new political strategies.

Mr. Smith Goes to Washington: The 'Lift and Strike' Campaign

On 23 August 1993 Stephen Walker became the third person that month to quit the US Foreign

Service in response to American policy in the Balkans. 'When I quit, I was under this delusion that no one outside the Beltway knew about or cared about Bosnia, and I would slink off and try to find a life doing something else', Walker recalled (2003). His work on Bosnia, however, had only just begun.

Walker, like many of his colleagues, believed that the war in Bosnia was resulting in wide scale atrocities that would likely continue to escalate unless a third party intervened or until the United Nations arms embargo, in place on all parts of former Yugoslavia, was lifted against Bosnia 'so that the [Bosnian] Muslims could defend themselves' (Walker 2003). President George H. Bush had supported the arms embargo in September 1991, when the Serb-controlled Yugoslav National Army was using its immense weapons stash against Croatia. A lot had changed 'on the ground in Bosnia' since 1991. The United Nations had recognized Bosnia as a separate state, war raged, and well documented reports of mass rape and massive forced expulsions of civilians had drawn public sympathy to the plight of the most victimized group, the Bosnian Muslims. Walker had had good reason for pinning his hopes on the newly-elected President Clinton turning US policy on Bosnia around. After all, throughout his campaign and his early presidency, Clinton had talked as if he would support the lifting of the arms embargo and the commencement of air strikes (Berdal 1994). Specifically, Clinton had declared that the United Nations, supported by the United States, must do 'whatever it takes to stop the slaughter of civilians and we may have to use military force. I would begin with air power against the Serbs' (Jennings 1994: 9). It was the Clinton administration's refusal to follow through with this pledge that led to Walker's resignation.

One of Walker's first speaking engagements as an ex-Foreign Service Officer was with Friends of Bosnia at Amherst College. 'I went out up there to find standing-room only, with all these people who knew about [Bosnia] and cared about it and felt frustrated with the policy and wanted to do something about it', remembers Walker (2003). The audience was united by its concern over Bosnia, not by any ideological platform. This is not to say that all views were represented. The 'left' remained 'fundamentally antagonistic to the idea of U.S. military intervention', and certain members of the 'right' opposed US military intervention in the absence of a direct threat to American security (Robbins 1994). But between right and left was a broad middle of both political conservatives and liberals, including many who had long activist careers opposing US intervention abroad, but who believed in the necessity of intervention in Bosnia.

Looking back at that time, Glenn Ruga, co-founder of the pro-intervention advocacy group Friends of Bosnia, sighs: 'Sometimes I feel it was a brief moment in human existence where people with a genuine commitment to human rights came together' (Ruga 2003). The diversity of the movement 'led to some strange bedfellows: Richard Perle, [Paul] Wolfowitz, Jeane Kilpatrick, Dick Cheney, Anthony Lewis and Susan Sontag' (Ruga 2003). This provoked some soul searching, particularly among the more left-leaning adherents to the cause. 'Generally; there was not much discomfort over the issue of human rights', remembered Ruga (2003). 'There was a general agreement on lifting the arms embargo. But some people had a very aggressive military agenda, talking about military hardware and strategy' and it took some of the activists a long time to 'understand that this is what we were calling for' (Ruga 2003).

'If Americans don't care about what is happening in Bosnia, what will they ever care about?' wondered Aryeh Neier, the former head of Human Rights Watch, now President of the Soros-funded Open Society Institute (Robbins 1994). The financier–philanthropist George Soros was already funneling a tremendous amount of money into humanitarian assistance, but this was not enough. Earlier that year, Soros had taken out a large newspaper ad urging the lifting of the arms embargo and the commencement of air strikes against Serbian targets. Soros had also begun funding a lobbyist group led by Marshall Harris, another former State Department officer who had quit over the US policy on Bosnia. The missing element in the campaign was a coordinated grassroots campaign. Thus, under the name American Committee to Save Bosnia, Walker began to organize grassroots support for a more aggressive US foreign policy in the Balkans ('Abdication' 1994).

The 'lift and strike' campaign garnered the support of Senators Bob Dole (Republican, Kansas) and Joe Lieberman (Democrat, Connecticut), who had sponsored a Senate resolution that called on Clinton to lift the arms embargo. But at that time there were few other allies for their proposal. 'We were told by one former member of Congress . . . you guys are crazy . . . they are never going to go for it' (Walker 2003). Walker had low expectations. 'We thought, we'll give it our best effort and a year from now, at least we'll be able to say, we tried.' So he set off to take the 'lift and strike' campaign 'to the people' (2003).

As it turned out, Walker had little difficulty getting his message across. The 'lift and strike' message resonated surprisingly well with both the general public and Congress. In testimony before the Senate, Lake would later contend that, in fact, the White House reached a compromise on the embargo which amounted to a *de facto* lifting. 'The United States would continue itself to implement the arms embargo, but we would no longer enforce it', Lake said. In other words, the US policy of 'no instructions' amounted to looking the other way when Bosnian Muslims did import arms. The only mistake with this approach, Lake asserted, was that Congress was 'not informed of the no-instructions policy'. On the other hand, 'Congress knew; as [the administration] did, that there were Iranian arms going in. . . . That had been briefed to the Congress in a variety of ways from the intelligence community. It was in the press. There was no secret about it' (CNN News 1997).

The 'no instructions' approach did not satisfy the activists who continued to push for an open endorsement of the lifting of the embargo. One of the greatest successes came on 27 July 1995, when in a 'stinging rebuke' to President Clinton's handling of the Bosnia crisis, the Senate voted 69–29 to lift unilaterally the arms embargo on Bosnia's government (Robbins 1995). The bill specified, however, that the embargo be lifted only after the United Nations peacekeeping force withdraws from Bosnia, or 12 weeks after the Bosnian government asks the UN to leave.

The bill still faced a fight in the House and a likely presidential veto, but the 'lift and strike' activists saw it as an enormous victory. 'It was like Civics 101 and *Mr. Smith Goes to Washington*', exclaimed Walker. 'I said, "My God, it worked! The system worked!" There were votes that we got because grassroots people faxed and called and lobbied and influenced their representatives to change their votes' (Walker 2003). Indeed, James O'Brien, a senior advisor to Madeline Albright, agrees that the activists were a major factor in the Congressional debate over Bosnia (O'Brien 2003). But according to O'Brien (2003), the activists' influence went far beyond these debates. 'Mostly they created issues and an agenda to which the Administration had to respond', he explained. 'They helped those of us [within the administration] arguing for U.S. engagement in Bosnia and certainly kept human rights issues front and center.'. . .

CONCLUSION

Human rights NGOs and other actors in civil society have changed considerably in the post-cold war era. Ideologically conservative or liberal, isolationist or interventionist, they leave a deep imprint on US foreign policy. Along with creating and interpreting issues in human rights terms, civil society actors are increasingly directly involved in domestic or international human rights litigation or in the drafting of legal instruments. Today, civil society is equally likely to act as a partner with the United States government as it is to take on an adversarial position with the government. Perhaps it is wise to conclude with a word of warning: civil society must remain strong enough to resist subordination by the state. At the same time, civil society must maintain open accountability and transparency in order to be considered legitimate in their roles as participants in the democratic processes of shaping of US foreign policy (Wapner 2002b).

REFERENCES

The Abdication (1994) *The New Republic*, 28 February, 7.

Accreditation and Participation of Non-Governmental Organizations in the Ad Hoc Committee to Consider Proposals for a Comprehensive and Integral International Convention to Promote and Protect the Rights and Dignity of Persons with Disabilities (2002) UN GA Res. A/RES/56/510 [available online at: http://www.un.org/csa/socdev/enable/rights/adhocngo82c.htm].

Anonymous (2003) Interview with author.

Associated Press (2001) White House is accused of deferring to big tobacco. *St. Louis Post Dispatch*, 20 November, A8.

Berdal, M. G. (1994) Fateful encounter: the United States and UN peacekeeping. *Survival*, 36(1), 30–50.

Boyd, R. F. (2003) Statement. Agenda item 5. Review of progress in the elaboration of a comprehensive and integral international convention on the protection and promotion of the rights and dignity of persons with disabilities. Second Session of the Ad Hoc Committee on a Comprehensive and Integral International Convention on Protection and Promotion of the Rights of Persons with Disabilities, 18 June, New York, 16–27 June [available online at: http://www.un.org/esa/socdev/enable/rights/contrib-us.htm].

Brundtland, G. H. (2000) Response of the Director General to the Report of the Committee of Experts on Tobacco Industry Documents, at 1, WHO Doc. WHO/DG/SP, 6 October [available online at: http://tobacco.who.int/repository/stp58/inquiryDGres1.pdf].

Campaign Development Group (2002) *Navigating the Ad Hoc Committee: A 'Rough' Guide to NGO Participation in the Development of a Treaty on the Rights of People with Disabilities* (Washington, DC: Campaign Development Group).

Campaign for Tobacco-Free Kids (1999) Memo on tobacco trends in the 21st century: domestic and global outlook. *US Newswire*, 16 December.

Charlton, J. I. (1998) *Nothing About Us Without Us: Disability, Oppression and Empowerment* (Berkeley, CA: University of California Press).

CNN News (1997) Senate Select Committee on Intelligence holds day two of hearings on the nomination of Anthony Lake as Director of Central Intelligence, CNN, 11 March [available online at: http://images.cnn.com/ALLPOLITICS/1997/03/12/fdch.lake].

Committee of Experts on Tobacco Industry Documents (2000) Tobacco industry strategies to undermine tobacco control activities at the World Health Organization, July [available online at: http://tobacco.who.int/repository/stp58/who_inquiry.pdf].

Comprehensive and Integral International Convention to Promote and Protect the Rights and Dignity of Persons with Disabilities (2001) Third Committee, 56 sess., Agenda Item 119(b), UN Doc. A/C.3/56/L.67/Rev.1, 28 November.

Dreyfuss, R. (2003) More missing intelligence. *The Nation*, 7 May.

Finnemore, M. and Sikkink, K. (1998) International norm dynamics and political change. *International Organization*, 52(4), 887, 909–912.

Forsythe, D. (2000) *Human Rights in International Relations* (Cambridge: Cambridge University Press).

Framework Convention Alliance (2003) FCA scorecard [available online at: http://fete.org/sign_rat/signed.shtml], accessed 13 November 2003].

Framework Convention on Tobacco Control (2000) *Alliance Bulletin* (Geneva), 5, 20 October [available online at: http://www.fctc.org/Issue_5.pdf].

Henderson, C. W. (1999) Health letter on CDC. World Health Assembly gives support to WHO technical programs, 26 July.

Jennings, P. with Danner, M. and Gelber, D. (1994) While America watched: the Bosnia tragedy, Peter Jennings Reporting, ABC News, ABC-51, 17 March, 9.

Kaufman, M. (2001) Negotiator in global tobacco talks quits, official said to Chafe at Softer U.S. Stands. *Washington Post,* 2 August, A1.

Keck, M. E. and Sikkink, K. (1998) *Activists Beyond Borders* (Ithaca, NY: Cornell University Press).

Klein, N. (2003) Bush to NGOs: watch your mouths. *The Globe and Mail,* 20 June.

Klotz, A. (1995) *Norms in International Relations: The Struggle Against Apartheid* (Ithaca, NY: Cornell University Press).

Korey, W. (2001) *NGOs and the Universal Declaration of Human Rights* (New York: St. Martin's Press).

Leading US public health groups tell US delegation to tobacco treaty-negotiations: go home (2003) Press release, 25 February [available online at: http://tobaccofreekids.org/Script/DisplayPressRelease.php3?Display=607].

Light, R. *et al.* (2002) Disability negotiations extra (8 August, 7:00 p.m. EDT) [available online at: http://www.worldenable.net/rights/adhoemeetsumm08a.htm].

Lord, J. E. (2003b) Interview with author (June).

Lumsdaine, D. (1993) *Moral Vision in International Politics* (Princeton, NJ: Princeton University Press).

Meeting of the Ad Hoc Committee (2002) NGO daily summaries: disability negotiations daily summary (29 July–9 August) 1(10), 9 August [available online at: http://www.worldenable.net/rights/adhoemeetsumm10.htm].

National Council on Disability (2002a). *Understanding the Role of an International Convention on the Human Rights of People with Disabilities: A White Paper* (Washington, DC: National Council on Disability) [available online at: http://www.ned.gov/newsroom/publications/unwhitepaper_05-23-02.html].

National Council on Disability (2002b) *A Reference Tool: Understanding the Potential Content and Structure of an International Convention on the Human Rights of people with Disabilities* (Washington, DC: National Council on Disability) [available online at: http://www.ned.gov/newsroom/publications/understanding_7-30-02.html].

NGOs urge strong action on WHO tobacco treaty (1999) *US Newswire,* 29 October.

O'Brien, J. (2003) Interview with author, June.

Position of the United States of America: Framework Convention on Tobacco Control (FCTC) (2003) [available online at: http://www.tobaccofreekids.org/pressoffice/release633/convention.pdf].

Rabby, A. (2002) US Advisor for Economic and Social Affairs. The Rights and Dignity of Persons with Disabilities. Statement at the Ad Hoc Committee on a Comprehensive and Integral International Convention on Protection and Promotion of the Rights and Dignity of Persons with Disabilities, New York, UN General Assembly, 30 July [available online at: http://www.state.gov/p/io/rls/rm/2002/12365.htm].

Report of the Ad Hoc Committee on a Comprehensive and Integral International Convention on Protection and Promotion of the Rights and Dignity of Persons with Disabilities (2002) United Nations, A/57/357 [available online at: http://www.un.org/csa/socdev/enable/rights/adhoca57357c.htm].

Robbins, C. A. (1994) A faraway war: inaction on Bosnia stirs critics to debate and despair. *The Wall Street Journal,* 18 March.

Robbins, C. A. (1995) Senate votes to allow arms for Bosnia. *The Wall Street Journal,* 27 July, A2.

Ruga, G. (2003) Interview with author, June.

Tarrow, S. (1998) *Power in Movement: Social Movements and Contentious Politics* (Cambridge: Cambridge University Press).

Taylor, A. L. and Roemer, R. (1996) International strategy for tobacco control. WHO Doc. WHO/PSA/96.6 [available online at: http://www5.who.int/tobacco/repository/stp4l/Taylor.pdf].

Vandenberg, M. (2001) Interview with author.

Walker, S. (2003) Interview with author, June.

Walzer, M. (1996) The civil society argument, in dimensions of radical democracy. In C. Mouffe (ed.) *Dimensions of Radical Democracy* (New York: Verso), 89.

Wapner, P. (2002a) Introductory essay: paradise lost? NGOs and global accountability, the democratic accountability of non-governmental organizations. *Chicago Journal of International Law,* 3(1), 155–160.

Wapner, P. (2002b) Defending accountability in NGOs. *Chicago Journal of International Law* 3(1), 197–205.

Wilkenfeld, J. (2002) U.S. continues obstructionist behavior as negotiations resume on proposed tobacco treaty. *Campaign for Tobacco-Free Kids,* 17 October [available online at: http://tobaccofreekids.org/Script/DisplayPressRelease.php3?Display=5539].

Wilkenfeld, J. (2003) Interview with author, June.

World Health Organization (2003) *Bulletin of the World Health Organization,* 81(4), 311 [available online at: http://www.who.int/bulletin/volumes/81/4/WHONews0403.pdf].

MAKING HUMAN RIGHTS TREATIES WORK: GLOBAL LEGAL INFORMATION AND HUMAN RIGHTS IN THE 21ST CENTURY

Oona A. Hathaway

Since the Universal Declaration of Human Rights in 1948, the world community has negotiated and adopted an extensive series of human rights treaties designed to set global standards for human rights. Oona Hathaway has conducted extensive research on the extent to which those treaties have had an impact on the human rights performance of countries that sign and ratify them. As you read this brief summary of her research, ask yourself:

- What is it that she finds to be "surprising" and "troubling"?
- What explains those troubling findings?
- What positive contributions does she see resulting from human rights treaties?

The adoption of the *Universal Declaration of Human Rights* in the wake of the horrors of the Second World War established human rights as a legitimate focus of international attention. In the half-century since, there have arisen nearly 100 universal and regional human rights agreements governing issues as diverse as discrimination against women, state-sponsored torture, and fair trials. Yet, as we embark on the twenty-first century, accompanied by the ongoing war on terrorism, there has been surprisingly little talk of these agreements. I want to take this opportunity to consider why, despite their ubiquity, human rights treaties have been largely ignored in current debates over how to address the myriad problems in the Middle East, and to suggest how we can make international agreements work more effectively to prevent abuses of human dignity.

International human rights treaties are premised on the assumption that such treaties will have some effect on countries' practices.

Oona A. Hathaway, "Making Human Rights Treaties Work: Global Legal Information & Human Rights in the 21st Century," *International Journal of Legal Information,* Vol. 31, 2003. Reprinted by permission of the author.

Indeed, this premise lies at the heart of international law. International lawyers have long assumed that, in the words of Louis Henkin, "almost all nations observe almost all principles of international law and almost all of their obligations almost all of the time." It has become increasingly obvious, however, that the reluctance of international lawyers to examine the efficacy of international law is particularly problematic in the area of international human rights. Unlike some areas of international law, in the area of human rights, countries have little to gain and much to lose from enforcing treaties against one another. Because of this and because human rights treaties tend to have weak built-in enforcement mechanisms, nations that join treaties can violate their commitments with relative impunity. And this is, of course, what many of them have done. Iraq, which ratified both the *Convention on the Prevention and Punishment of Genocide* and the *International Covenant on Civil and Political Rights* long before the United States did, has long engaged in what some consider to be genocidal action against its Kurdish population and shortly before the war held an election in which Saddam Hussein was re-elected in an uncontested election with 100% of the vote. And Afghanistan, which under the Taliban prohibited women's participation in political or civic life and condoned torture as a form of legitimate punishment, had long ago ratified the *Convention on the Political Rights of Women,* the *International Covenant on Civil and Political Rights,* and the *Convention Against Torture and Other Cruel, Inhuman or Degrading Treatment or Punishment.*

The enormous expansion in the number of human rights treaties since the creation of the landmark *Universal Declaration of Human Rights* more than 50 years ago is unquestionably a welcome symbol of the international community's deepening commitment to human rights. Yet, as the examples I cited above make clear, it is far less obvious that the burgeoning collection of treaties created to date has had the effects that its proponents intended. Indeed, despite the ongoing push to create and extend human rights treaties, strikingly little is known about their true effectiveness in achieving their central goals.

To begin to fill this gap, I undertook the first large-scale study of the effect of human rights treaties on the nations that ratify them.[1] I analyzed how 166 countries treated their citizens between 1960 and 1999, looking at five core areas of human rights: genocide, torture, civil freedom, fair trials, and women's political equality. Some of my findings were precisely what I had expected. Countries that ratified the human rights treaties that I examined usually had better human rights practices than countries that did not. For example, I found that nations that ratified the *Genocide Convention* were somewhat less likely to commit genocide than those that had not. I also found that regardless of whether they had ratified human rights treaties or not, democracies generally had better human rights practices than the group of nations as a whole.

Other of my findings, however, were more surprising. First, although countries that ratify treaties usually have better practices than those that do not, those differences are not as great as I had expected them to be, given the consensual nature of the human rights treaty regime. For example, the data show that countries that ratified the *Torture Convention* warranted a rating of 2.70 on a scale of 1 to 5 (where a 2.70 falls somewhere between "isolated instances of torture," and "some" or "occasional" allegations of torture), whereas those that had not ratified warranted a rating of 2.76—a relatively small difference.

Even more troubling, I found that countries with the worst human rights practices sometimes ratify human rights treaties as often as nations with the best practices do. To take a dramatic example, half of the countries responsible for the most widespread cases of genocide, including Rwanda in 1994 and Yugoslavia in the early 1990s, had ratified the *Convention on the Prevention and Punishment of the Crime of Genocide* at the time of the atrocities. This was essentially the same rate of ratification that I found among countries that had committed no genocide. Similarly, I found that roughly 40% of countries in which torture is reported to be widely practiced had signed the *Convention Against Torture and Other Cruel, Inhuman or Degrading Treatment or Punishment* at the time of the violations.

When I investigated whether these patterns could be traced to the treaties themselves or were due instead to other factors associated with ratification and practices, what I found was even more perplexing. My analysis suggests that treaties generally do not seem to have a direct, measurable positive effect on the human rights practices of countries that join them—and, in fact, might even have a negative effect in some cases. I looked at how treaties shaped countries' human rights practices in the context of a range of other factors that might be expected to influence countries' behavior—including the level of democratization, involvement in civil or international war, economic prosperity, global interdependence, aid dependency, and economic growth—and found no clear evidence of a positive effect, though ratification of treaties by fully democratic nations did sometimes appear to be associated with better practices. In fact, in the relatively few instances in which I saw clear links between treaty ratification and measures of country practices, ratification often appeared to be associated with *worse* practices than would otherwise be expected.

These findings do not necessarily mean that human rights treaties can actually make things worse. It is possible that countries with worse human rights practices are simply more inclined to ratify human rights treaties. Or perhaps we merely know more about the violations committed by countries who sign human rights treaties, making countries that do not sign treaties look better than they truly are. Nevertheless, I find not a single treaty for which ratification reliably seems to improve human rights practices and seven for which ratification seems to be associated with worse practices. At least this much is clear: There is little evidence that human rights treaties have a direct and immediate positive effect on the behavior of ratifying countries and some evidence of just the opposite.

This suggestion is not as outrageous as it might at first appear. Ratification of a human rights treaty, after all, allows a government to send a message to the world that it is committed to the principles outlined in the treaty. This message may be honest and sincere. But, as the examples I gave of Iraq and Afghanistan suggest, if the human rights treaty is poorly monitored and enforced, countries face little or no penalty for failure to match rhetoric with action. At the same time, countries that ratify human rights treaties may face less pressure to improve their human rights practices. Treaties, then, might allow some governments to, intentionally or unintentionally, substitute words (in the form of ratification) for deeds, thereby slowing, rather than hastening, improvements in human rights.

You may be wondering about now whether, given the news I've just shared with you, this paper really belongs under the heading given to this panel, "Doing Good: Human Rights in the

21st Century." Let me begin now to tell you why I think it does belong and why the situation is not as bleak as it may appear from what I have just said.

First, it is important to recognize that, in spite of the evidence I have presented, treaties probably do have important positive effects on state behavior. Even if human rights practices are worse than expected in the countries that ratify human rights treaties, the treaties may still foster gradual improvements in human rights practices in *all* countries through changing expectations for state behavior. Indeed, if there were changes in ratifying and nonratifying countries alike, this would not be detected by analysis, which can detect only treaty effects that are isolated to ratifying countries. Human rights treaties may have positive effects in ratifying countries over the very long term by creating public commitments to which human rights activists can point as they push nations to make gradual, if grudging, improvements down the road. For example, China's signature of the *International Covenant on Civil and Political Rights* in the late 1990s may have initially offset some pressure for real changes in China's practices, but it may also provide a tool that human rights groups can use to leverage more significant changes in China's practices down the road.

Second, the results of my study do not argue for abandoning the human rights treaty system but instead suggest ways in which it can be strengthened to better achieve its goals. It may be time to reexamine the current reliance on self-policing. A possible approach would be a stronger system of independent expert monitoring, which would be more likely to expose governments' failures to comply with their treaty commitments. A more radical approach might involve withdrawing membership from countries that flout the requirements of treaties

to which they have consented. Regardless of the precise method chosen to address the problem, my research suggests that guardians of human rights must remain vigilant, viewing ratification of treaties not as the end of the struggle for human dignity, but as a promising beginning in an evolving campaign.

Finally, and most relevant to this gathering, I believe that a central key to unlocking the potential of the international human rights treaty system is increasing global information about countries' human rights practices. The reason that some countries can use human rights treaties to offset pressure for improvements in their practices is not only because the treaties do not include strong enforcement mechanisms—mechanisms that, in truth, would likely be underutilized if they did exist. Rather, they are able to ignore their commitments because they can expect little information about their actions will be available to the world community. Nations that join human rights treaties and then fail to abide by them are often hiding behind a shield of ignorance. As the guardians of our global network of legal information, you can therefore play an important role in improving our human rights treaty system by helping to hold nations accountable for their actions in the court of world opinion. By gathering the information that exists about nations' human rights practices and helping to make it widely available and widely read, you can "do good" and help ensure a strong future for human rights in the 21st century.

NOTE

1. Much of what follows draws on research presented in Oona A. Hathaway, "Do Human Rights Treaties Make a Difference?," 111 *Yale Law Journal* 1935 (2002).

HUMANITARIAN INTERVENTION AFTER IRAQ: LEGAL IDEALS VS. MILITARY REALITIES

James Kurth

In this survey, Kurth examines the record of humanitarian intervention since the end of the Cold War. As you read this article, ask yourself:

- What, for Kurth, are the preconditions of genocide, and what are the implications for responding to it?
- What does he mean by the "legitimacy/efficacy tradeoff"?
- What, in his view, will be the impact of the Iraq war on humanitarian intervention?

. . . The 1990s were a decade of humanitarian intervention. The decade began with high hopes of ending massive human rights abuses, particularly large-scale massacres or genocides, through UN intervention. These hopes vanished after the UN's failures in Bosnia, Somalia, and Rwanda, but they were succeeded by new hopes for U.S. intervention, which hopes seemed to be validated by U.S. successes in Bosnia and Kosovo and even, to a degree, in Haiti. There were also the successful interventions carried out by Australia, with U.S. support, in East Timor in 1999 and by Britain in Sierra Leone in 2000.[1]

By the beginning of 2001, the hopes for a future in which humanitarian intervention would bring an end to the long and baleful history of genocides reached a sort of apotheosis in a major international document, *The Responsibility to Protect.*[2] Since then, a large contingent of international lawyers has continued to develop new doctrines of limited sovereignty that would give the "international community" or particular international organizations the right, indeed the obligation, to undertake military intervention against a national government that is engaging in massive human rights abuses of its citizens.[3]

Unfortunately, even as the theory and law of humanitarian intervention have ascended to unprecedented heights, the actual practice of humanitarian intervention has been in decline. So far, the 2000s have not seen effective humanitarian intervention by anyone, be it the international community and international organizations, the United States, or others. Instead of pursuing humanitarian interventions, the United States has engaged in two wars, one in Afghanistan and one in Iraq, that the Bush administration justified in human rights terms. This is especially true in the case of Iraq, but the real impact of that war has been to make humanitarian intervention by the United States elsewhere impossible. This radically reduces the prospects for successful humanitarian interventions in the future, while improving the prospects for undeterred and uninhibited ethnic massacres or genocides, such as has been occurring in the western Sudan.

ORGANIZED MASSACRES

Ethnic massacres or genocides are commonly thought to be the product of longstanding and widespread hatreds between opposing ethnic groups within a society. Certainly, these hatreds have been present to some extent in the most infamous ethnic massacres or genocides of recent years, and the ethnic-hatreds explanation for these conflicts has important policy implications for humanitarian interventions. If the ethnic hatreds are really longstanding and widespread, no outside intervention can get at the roots of the conflict. With the inevitable eventual departure of the intervention forces, the conflict is likely to erupt again, perhaps even attaining the scale of massacres or genocide again.

Ethnic hatreds among a population may be a necessary condition of massacres or genocide, but they are not a sufficient condition. There has always been a large organization, indeed usually a modern bureaucratic state, behind them.[4] In the prominent examples from the 1990s, this organization was the Milosevic regime and the Serbian state and para-state organizations (e.g., army and militias) that it controlled and deployed in Bosnia and Kosovo; the Hutu regime and its state and para-state organizations (again, army and militias) in Rwanda; and the Indonesian military and its auxiliary militias in East Timor. (In Sierra Leone, the organizations that directed the massacres were not part of the state, which had largely collapsed, but consisted of a number of warlords and their militias.)

When one adds to ethnic hatreds a state organization that can direct them, and indeed plan, order, and execute actions based on them, then one has the sufficient condition for genocide or massacre. This two-part explanation of ethnic conflict has important policy implications for intervention, and they are quite different from those of the ethnic-hatreds explanation. If massacres or genocides are really the product of a specific state or para-state military, then it will take another military from the outside to defeat them and to stop the killing. Once the murdering organizations are destroyed by the intervention forces, a peace of sorts can be established. The central question obviously then becomes, who

can and will provide the outside military force? Both the can (military capability) and the will (political will) are essential.

A humanitarian intervention therefore requires both a political authority, to decide upon and authorize it, and a military force, to carry it out. The possible political authorities have varied from the government of a particular nation-state, such as the United States or Britain; through regional organizations, such as NATO or the European Union; to the most universal organization of all, the UN. The possible military forces have varied from standing expeditionary forces (e.g., the military forces of, again, the United States or Britain), through temporary coalitions of similar military forces under the leadership of one of them (e.g., the NATO forces in Bosnia and Kosovo), to ad hoc multinational forces composed of disparate military units drawn from several different states (e.g., the UN peacekeeping forces in the initial phase of the interventions in Somalia, Bosnia, and Sierra Leone). In practice, therefore, there seems to be a correlation between the kind of political authority and the kind of military force.

THE TRADE-OFF BETWEEN LEGITIMACY AND EFFICACY

Judging by recent history, there may be something of a trade-off between the legitimacy and the efficacy of an intervention. The political authority with the greatest legitimacy among the widest number of states is the UN. However, almost any proposed humanitarian intervention is likely to be viewed by one of the five permanent members of the UN Security Council as a threat to its particular interests (as has recently been the case with China in regard to Sudan, where the Chinese have substantial oil concessions), and the proposed intervention will likely be vetoed. Thus, the most legitimate political authority is also likely to be the least efficacious one.

Conversely, the political authority with the greatest efficacy, in the sense of being able to decide upon and authorize an intervention quickly and coherently, is the government of a particular nation-state with modern, standing, expeditionary (overseas) military forces, probably the United States, Britain, France, Australia, or Canada. Interventions undertaken by either Britain or France have some legitimacy problems because of their colonial pasts (and because of France's recent interventions in Africa, which were clearly in pursuit of its particular interests). But interventions undertaken by the United States have their own legitimacy problems, because of the controversial record of past U.S. interventions and because of fears of a U.S. imperial future. Thus, the most efficacious political authority is also likely to be the least legitimate one.

Perhaps this trade-off between legitimacy and efficacy can be transcended by turning to the middle kind of political authority, that is, a regional organization composed of somewhat similar states. For example, the NATO interventions in Bosnia and Kosovo had a respectable degree of legitimacy and also a reasonable degree of efficacy. Unfortunately, most regional organizations are not yet organized to the point that they can decide upon and authorize something as difficult and demanding as a humanitarian intervention. This is the problem with such loose organizations as the Association of Southeast Asian Nations (ASEAN) and all the other regional groups in Asia and with the African Union (AU) and all the other regional groups in Africa.

THE DISMAL RECORD OF UN INTERVENTIONS

In the early 1990s, the answer to the question, "Who can and will intervene?" was the UN as the universal political authority, combined with ad hoc multinational forces assembled for each operation and composed of military units from several different nations. The UN had accumulated a relatively successful record of peacekeeping operations over the 1970s and 1980s this way. With the collapse of the Soviet Union, which had sometimes vetoed UN peacekeeping missions, it seemed that the UN could build upon its peacekeeping record and even expand its scope to peace-enforcing. Thus, when Somalia and Bosnia posed humanitarian problems in 1992, the major powers, including the United States, proposed this UN formula. It was also the answer initially applied to Sierra Leone when its state failed and the country fell into anarchy, murder, and mayhem.

As it turned out, each of these UN interventions in failed states became notorious failures themselves. In Somalia, the UN forces first had to be rescued by U.S. forces, and then both withdrew and left the Somalis in chaos, where the country remains even now. In Bosnia, the UN forces did not stop the ethnic massacres, which culminated in the murder of 7,000 men and boys in Srebrenica in 1995. In Sierra Leone, the UN forces had to be rescued by British forces, who then carried out an effective intervention. And in Rwanda, the UN forces were prevented by the UN leadership in New York from stopping the genocide of 800,000 Tutsi.[5]

There has been some slight improvement in UN interventions more recently. UN forces have been engaged in a continuing, though largely ineffective, intervention in the eastern region of the Democratic Republic of the Congo (formerly Zaire), where the anarchy and violence continue also. And since 2003, UN forces have maintained a tenuous and unstable peace in Liberia, a country that had been torn apart by a dozen years of warlord violence.

THE AMBIGUOUS RECORD OF OTHER INTERVENTIONS

The several cases in the 1990s where military intervention was clearly successful in stopping massacres were undertaken by U.S. and NATO forces (in Bosnia, in 1995, and Kosovo, in 1999); Australian forces, in East Timor in 1999; and the British, in Sierra Leone in 2000. U.S. military forces were also able to stop the human rights abuses by the military regime in Haiti in 1994.[6] However, the U.S.-installed successor government, the Aristide regime, perpetrated its own abuses in later years, until the United States intervened again in 2004 in order to depose it. This time, however, the U.S. military intervention was modest in scale and brief in duration. Upon the departure of American forces, a pervasive anarchy ensued.

These five cases largely complete the list of successful humanitarian interventions since 1991. They are balanced by some unsuccessful ones, such as that by U.S. and UN forces in Somalia (1992–93) and by West African forces in Liberia and in Sierra Leone (the mid-1990s). Moreover, the successful cases should be compared with, and perhaps are outweighed by, the many cases of non-intervention, when massacres or genocide persisted with no intervention by the UN, a regional organization, or a major power. The most notorious case was, of course, Rwanda, but the list also includes Sudan (in particular, the southern region until 2003 and the western region of Darfur since then), Burundi, and Angola. Overall, then, the historical record of humanitarian interventions is more one of failure than success.

THE SUCCESSFUL CASES OF HUMANITARIAN INTERVENTION

The above record might suggest ways humanitarian intervention could work in the future. In each of the five successful cases, the intervention was decided upon by the political authorities of a particular state—the United States (even if it operated within the framework of NATO), Britain, or Australia—and carried out by that state's professional military forces. These forces had expeditionary capabilities, and there was unity of command with respect to decision-making and decision-execution—that is, at both the political and the military levels. The interventions could therefore be undertaken decisively and quickly, and executed with focus, persistence, and effectiveness. This contrasts, for example, with the feckless UN intervention in Bosnia, where there was no unified political authority for its modern military forces, and the ineffective West African interventions in Liberia and Sierra Leone, where there was some unity of decision-making around the Nigerian government, but the intervening nations lacked modern military forces. Of course, even when the decision-making is unified and the military forces highly professional, the intervention will fail if political decision-makers are feckless, as was the case with the Clinton administration in Somalia.

THE NECESSARY ROLE OF A MODERN STATE

Under today's conditions, it would appear that a successful humanitarian intervention can only be undertaken when a modern state with modern military forces is willing to do so. Not only must the forces be highly professional, they must also be capable of expeditionary operations. The number of modern states is rather large, but of them, only the United States, Britain, France, Canada, and Australia possess modern, professional, and expeditionary military forces. It is no coincidence that the five successful humanitarian interventions were carried out by three of these countries (the United States, Britain, and Australia), that another (France) has a long history of (non-humanitarian) military interventions in Africa, and that Canada has a long history of participating in peacekeeping operations.

Among these five states, the United States obviously looms large. Indeed, in most cases, it is the only nation from which humanitarian intervention might come. The other four states capable of it can generally take the lead in deciding upon and carrying-out an intervention only in limited circumstances. Britain may take the lead in an intervention in one of the smaller of its former colonies, as in Sierra Leone; France on occasion may also take the lead in an intervention in one of its smaller former colonies, if the intervention directly serves its particular interests, as in the Ivory Coast in 2004. Australia may take the lead in an intervention in its immediate region, as in East Timor. As for Canada, which no longer has a substantial expeditionary capability, the only places where it might take the lead in an intervention are certain former British colonies in the Caribbean.

If one adds up all of the potential afflicted countries that might be rescued by Britain, France, Australia, or Canada, it is obvious that large numbers of countries (and especially large countries) are outside these countries' combined sphere of intervention. Excluded countries include such present and potential arenas of massacres or genocide as Sudan, Congo, Burundi, and, not too far in the future, other parts of Africa as well. Can we expect the United States to step into this African void?

THE UNITED STATES AND AFRICAN INTERVENTIONS

Even during the 1990s, when American willingness to undertake humanitarian intervention was at its peak, the United States evinced very little

interest in intervening in Africa. The failed intervention in Somalia was the exception that proves the rule. While Somalia is an African country, its location at the southern end of the Red Sea and just across from the Arabian Peninsula also puts it, for many geopolitical and economic purposes, in the Middle East. But even U.S. geopolitical and economic considerations were not enough to persuade the United States to remain in Somalia after its famous setback in Mogadishu. Somalia's humanitarian disaster has continued for more than a decade, right up until today.

Of course, the United States was at the center of the most notorious case of non-intervention in the last generation, Rwanda. As is well-known, the Clinton administration not only declined to have U.S. military forces intervene in Rwanda, but it actively prevented the UN from obtaining military forces from other countries. (This April 1994 decision for non-intervention was largely a reaction to the Mogadishu debacle six months earlier, in October 1993.)[7]

The United States did almost nothing even in the case of Liberia, the one African country where it had had a very long-standing and direct political and economic involvement, when that country collapsed into anarchy and massacres after 1989. It occasionally sent units of the Marines to protect or evacuate American citizens, but the murder and mayhem of Liberians continued for a dozen years.

Finally, in terms of sheer numbers of deaths caused by war, genocide, or anarchy, the two most massive human rights disasters of the past generation have been the Congo (more than 2 million deaths from war or from consequent famine and disease in the 1990s–2000s) and Sudan (more than 2 million deaths in southern Sudan in the 1980s–90s and now more than 200,000 deaths in Darfur since 2003). Washington has done nothing in the Congo, and the disaster continues. In regard to Sudan, the Bush administration did use extensive and focused diplomatic and political pressure to bring about a peace of sorts in southern Sudan in 2003–05. But this seems to be having the effect of displacing the human rights violations—indeed, the genocidal operations—of the Sudanese government into western Sudan. Washington has officially criticized these human rights violations as genocide, but has done nothing else, and the disaster continues.

Africa, therefore, presents a particularly tragic and paradoxical problem in regard to the prospects for humanitarian intervention. The continent presents the largest number of countries (and the largest countries) where massacres and genocides are now occurring and are likely to occur in the future. It is where the need for humanitarian intervention is greatest. For a small number of African countries (especially if they are small ones), either Britain or France might be able to undertake a successful intervention, not unlike their interventions in Sierra Leone or the Ivory Coast. However, for most African countries, only the United States will have the military capability to intervene successfully. But because of its lack of either deep historical connections or contemporary vital interests in Africa, it is not likely to have the political will to do so.

Washington's reluctance to undertake humanitarian interventions in Africa, or indeed any place else, in the near future is deepened by two other U.S. realities, one relating to the U.S. military and the other to the consequences of the Iraq War, that have recently come into being.

THE U.S. MILITARY'S PERSPECTIVE

Only a military force that can conduct land operations can carry out a true humanitarian intervention undertaken to defeat and destroy a local military or militia that is executing large-scale massacres or genocide. The U.S. Army and the U.S. Marines are both capable of this, but have very different specific capabilities.

The U.S. Army participated in successful interventions, or, more accurately, peacekeeping occupations, such as those in Haiti, Bosnia, and Kosovo in the 1990s. However, in each case the Army was initially reluctant to do so, and President Clinton had to exert considerable pressure on the Army leadership before they took up the task.[8] That is because the Army sees itself as the military service that fights other large armies in conventional ground-combat operations. Its classic historical opponents were the German and Soviet armies, and for decades the U.S. Army was designed to fight this kind of enemy. In the 1990s, the closest remaining equivalents were the Iraqi army and the North Korean army, and the Army was still organized to fight this kind of enemy. Although it would have been perfectly capable of fighting the regular army of the Milosevic regime, it was unprepared to fight irregular militias or to maintain a military occupation. The Army's reluctance to undertake this kind of military operation was powerfully reinforced by its experiences in Vietnam and Somalia. Thus it was reluctant to deploy to Haiti, Bosnia, and Kosovo. As it happened, the Army was able to withdraw quickly from Haiti, and even though it remained in Bosnia and Kosovo for a long period, it did not have to engage in significant combat there. This did not, however, make the Army any more eager to engage in these kinds of unconventional operations.

Indeed, the Iraq War has largely demonstrated the good sense of the Army's self-definition. The Army was extremely successful in defeating the regular Iraqi army in spring 2003. However, it has been very unsuccessful since then in dealing with the irregular Iraqi insurgents and in maintaining the military occupation. Its current ordeal in Iraq will make the Army extremely reluctant, even resistant, to undertake any such unconventional operations, including humanitarian interventions, in the future.

In contrast, the U.S. Marine Corps at one time emphasized its long role as an expeditionary force that could engage in unconventional or counter-insurgency operations against irregular forces.[9] But this tradition was eclipsed during World War II by a new one that focused on amphibious operations against another conventional force (e.g., the Japanese army on the islands of the Pacific), and during the Cold War, the Marines were even trained to fight the Soviet army in such places as northern Norway. However, in the 1990s, the Marines began to recover and reemphasize their earlier, expeditionary tradition. Although the experience of Iraq has been an ordeal for the Marines, as it has been for the Army, the Marines are more likely to view the experience as one to build upon, rather than one to avoid in the future. It is possible, therefore, that the U.S. Marine Corps will remain open to undertaking humanitarian interventions in the future.

For the most part, however, the Iraq War has had very damaging consequences for humanitarian intervention. The war has developed in a way that will make it almost impossible for the United States to undertake such an intervention over the next several years, and it has greatly impaired both the political will and the military capability necessary for such interventions.

THE CONSEQUENCES OF BOSNIA, KOSOVO, AND AFGHANISTAN

Had the Iraq War in 2003 followed the pattern of the Bosnian intervention of 1995, the Kosovo War of 1999, or the Afghan War of 2001, the prospects for more U.S. humanitarian interventions would have been greatly enhanced. In each of these cases, prior to the beginning of U.S. military operations, critics and skeptics—often with great professional expertise and reputation—had warned that U.S. forces would get bogged down in a long and difficult war. They pointed to Somalia, Lebanon, and especially Vietnam. As it happened, however, in Bosnia and Kosovo, U.S. air power, along with the ground forces of local allies, such as the Croatian Army and the Kosovo Liberation Army, was sufficient to win the war. In Afghanistan, the combination of U.S. air power and a small number of U.S. special forces—again, along with the more numerous ground forces of local allies, such as the Northern Alliance—was sufficient to win the war. The United States seemed to have perfected a new, American way of war, one that involved very little commitment of ground forces, that could achieve its objectives very quickly, and that would result in minimal American deaths. The critics and skeptics, it seemed, had been proven wrong. Most importantly, the United States could now look forward to similar quick and inexpensive successes in future military operations, including humanitarian interventions.

The human rights advocates in the Clinton administration drew this conclusion after Kosovo, and if Vice President Albert Gore had become president in 2001, the United States might have been ready to undertake another humanitarian intervention when an appropriate case arose. (In summer 2001, Macedonia seemed to be on the brink of an ethnic war.) In contrast, the Bush administration in its first months publicly and clearly expressed its view that humanitarian intervention was remote from U.S. vital interests. Human rights advocates, however, were still enthusiastic that humanitarian interventions with U.S. military forces could and should be a major pillar of the emerging order of universal human rights. They became even more enthusiastic after the apparent success of the Afghan War. Some, most notably Michael Ignatieff, director of the Carr Center for Human Rights Policy at Harvard University, even became advocates of an "American empire," which would impose and enforce human rights around the world.[10]

THE COURSE OF THE IRAQ WAR

When the Bush administration decided, after the 9/11 attacks but even before the conclusion of the Afghan War, that it would go to war with Iraq, it did so because of its own definition of U.S. vital interests. These included both security interests (the presumed threat of weapons of mass destruction under the control of Iraq or even Al Qaeda) and economic ones (the anticipated U.S. control of Iraqi oil production). But some prominent members of the administration— most obviously then Deputy Secretary of Defense Paul Wolfowitz, but also probably President Bush himself—saw a U.S. vital interest in bringing about the democratization of Iraq, and then using Iraq as a model to spread liberal democracy and free markets to other countries in the Middle East, most notably Syria and Iran.[11] And because the Saddam Hussein regime had engaged in massive human rights violations in the past (against the Kurds in 1988 and against both Kurds and Shiites in 1991), it was easy for the Bush administration to claim that its war against Iraq was actually a sort of humanitarian intervention. The fact that the massacres had occurred more than a decade before was unimportant. Michael Ignatieff and other prominent advocates of humanitarian intervention joined the Bush administration

and its supporters, neoconservative and other, in promoting and justifying the war against Saddam's regime.[12]

The first phase of the Iraq War (March–April 2003) followed the trajectory of the Bosnian, Kosovo, and Afghan wars and seemed to validate the new American way of war. Saddam's regime and the Iraqi army quickly collapsed, and the operation promised to go down as a great leap forward in the progress of democratization and humanitarian intervention. But then, in summer 2003, there began a persistent insurgency against the U.S.-led occupation forces. The continuing ordeal of U.S. military forces in Iraq may have totally demolished the confident predictions about the new American way of war and the grand speculations about a new American empire.

THE CONSEQUENCES OF THE IRAQ WAR

Among the casualties of the Iraq War has been the U.S. political will to undertake any new humanitarian interventions, let alone those that are remote from U.S. vital interests. Even with the reelection of President Bush in November 2004, the administration has no mandate to undertake a new intervention, in part because there is no credibility left in its justifications for undertaking its intervention in Iraq. Those political writers who only three years ago enthusiastically advocated the war, as well as interventions to impose democratization and human rights more generally, now devote themselves to criticizing the administration for its inept way of conducting the war and the occupation. Insofar as they contemplate any new military operations, it is only in regard to the growing nuclear capability of Iran. About humanitarian intervention, even with respect to the human rights disaster in Darfur, they have had nothing to say.

Even if by some oddity the American political will to undertake military interventions had survived the ordeal in Iraq and was ready to order a new intervention, the U.S. military capability to carry it out no longer exists. With the U.S. ground forces stretched to their limit in Iraq, there is no reserve of ground forces left to engage in sizable and extended operations anywhere else. It is telling to note that the U.S. Marine operation in Haiti in 2004 was much smaller and much briefer than the earlier, joint Army-Marine operation there in 1994; it was truly a case of too little, too late. The Haitian population has been left in anarchy and misery. In a sense, they too have become casualties of the Iraq War.

The Iraq War also diminished the United States' credibility in arguing for intervention before the UN, as with the Darfur genocide in Sudan. The way the United States treated the UN prior to the Iraq War—presenting evidence and arguments that were later discredited, then going to war despite UN opposition—gave it a bad reputation when the administration came to the UN again, in regard to Darfur, in fall 2004. Of course, the United States would have faced substantial opposition from, for example, China in the Security Council and the Arab and many African states in the General Assembly, because of their calculations of state interests. But the legacy of the Iraq War made it seem legitimate, and therefore made it easy, for these states to oppose the United States on Darfur.

By destroying the United States' political will, military capability, and diplomatic credibility, the Iraq War has made it almost impossible for the United States to undertake any humanitarian intervention in the foreseeable future. In particular, it has made it impossible for the United States to undertake any intervention against the greatest recent case of genocide, that by the Sudanese government and its auxiliaries

against the African population in Darfur. And so, they too in a sense have become casualties of the Iraq War.

The human rights advocates who supported going to war in Iraq have much to answer for. They did not themselves *cause* the war; the Bush administration had its own reasons and would have gone to war for these alone. However, the human rights advocates helped to *legitimate* the war; the administration used these advocates to confuse and divide liberals who were otherwise inclined to oppose the war. In a sense, these human rights advocates were accessories to the war and to its attendant deceptions. They contributed to the war and to the afflictions that it has brought to its victims, directly in Iraq and indirectly elsewhere, as in Darfur. They are guilty, in short, of a morally unconscionable recklessness.[13]

THE SPECTER OF AN IRAQ SYNDROME

The ghost of the Iraq War is likely to haunt America and to deter U.S. interventions for years, even after the war is over. For this is what happened in the aftermath of the Vietnam War. The U.S. debacle in Vietnam produced "the Vietnam syndrome." Its practical effect was a period of more than a decade in which both policymakers and the public were extremely reluctant to undertake any intervention with substantial numbers of ground forces. There were a couple of small and fitful uses of military force during this period (the Iranian rescue mission of 1980 and the Lebanese intervention of 1982–84), which failed in part because of insufficient forces. There was also the successful intervention in Grenada in 1983, a case of overwhelming force against a small and fitful opponent. That intervention was the first step in overcoming the Vietnam syndrome. But it was not until the United States employed military force to overthrow the Manuel Noriega regime in Panama in 1989 that it could be said that the United States was again willing to undertake military interventions on a substantial scale. The success in Panama laid the groundwork for the long series of U.S. wars and military interventions in the 1990s, beginning with the Gulf War.

It is worth observing that the Grenadian, Panamanian, and Haitian interventions were in America's traditional sphere of influence in the Caribbean basin. The United States has been intervening in this region for more than a century; it has extensive strategic and political interests there; and therefore it was a natural place to begin overcoming the Vietnam syndrome. As for the Bosnian and Kosovo interventions, the Clinton administration saw them as logical extensions of America's traditional interest in European stability, with the sphere of responsibility of the NATO alliance now being expanded from Western Europe into Eastern Europe.

Although it is to be hoped that the Iraq War will not reach the depths of the Vietnam debacle, it is very likely that it will produce its own "Iraq syndrome," an extreme reluctance in American policymakers and the public to undertake new military interventions, and this reluctance is likely to persist through the term of at least one presidential administration elected in the wake of the war. And if and when the United States again begins to undertake military interventions, it is likely to do so in defense of concrete and vital security, political, or economic interests, rather than in defense of human rights in countries that are remote from those interests. These interventions probably won't be in the Middle East or more broadly in the Muslim world. And given the lack of vital U.S. interests in Africa, they almost certainly won't be there, either. In short, the United States is unlikely to undertake military interventions in the very regions where, from a humanitarian view, they are most likely to be needed.

THE TWILIGHT OF HUMANITARIAN INTERVENTION?

With the only candidate states—United States, Britain, France, and perhaps Australia and Canada—unlikely to intervene or likely to intervene at most only in small countries that are former colonies or in their immediate region, there is not much hope for humanitarian intervention in the modern-state formula. And the other formula, that of ad hoc multinational military forces directed by the UN, has a dismal record and prospects. It will almost always be the case that one of the five permanent members of the Security Council will see the proposed intervention to be against its state interests and exercise its veto. It will also often be the case that a large number of countries in the General Assembly will oppose the intervention as a threat to their interests or as an outside intrusion into their particular region. Even if these political obstacles could be overcome for a particular humanitarian crisis, the ad hoc multinational military force will be assembled only after frustrating delays and only with poorly-organized forces, a classic case of too little, too late.

Between these two formulas there may lie a third: a regional organization directing a standing, modern military force whose units are drawn from the region. As an example, the EU, the organization with the greatest potential capability in this regard, could direct a standing force drawn from its member states that would be available to intervene in future ethnic conflicts in say, the Balkans. However, in this case, since NATO already possesses this capability, an EU force might be redundant.

The organization that could address the greater potential *need* would be the 53-member African Union, if it developed a standing force equipped and trained up to modern standards, which would require substantial financial and logistical support from the EU and the United States.[14] In the summer and fall of 2005, the EU and NATO undertook a tiny prototype of this kind of assistance, when they provided airlift and training support to several thousand AU soldiers charged with monitoring the situation (not with peacekeeping or peace-enforcing) in Darfur.

Of course, the AU's political will could be weak. Its decision-making process might recapitulate that of the UN, in that there may always be some members who would find it in their interest to veto an intervention. The military force could also be weak: before it would be able to undertake an effective humanitarian intervention, it would have to acquire many standards and skills, and the development of this force would take several years at least. The twin problems of weak political will and weak military force largely explain why the AU has not been very effective in Darfur.

Still, given the seeming inevitability of more ethnic conflicts and humanitarian crises in Africa for the foreseeable future, and given the seeming paucity of other options for effective humanitarian intervention, a standing AU intervention force may be the only plausible way to go. The EU and the United States can each provide material support to enable African states to move in that direction. And the time to move, already too late for Darfur and not too soon for the next humanitarian disaster, is now.

NOTES

1. See the Fall 2001 special issue of *Orbis* focusing on humanitarian intervention. A recent compilation of articles on humanitarian intervention forms the Winter/Spring 2005 issue of *Global Dialogue*, published by the Centre for World Dialogue, Nicosia, Cyprus. An earlier version of the present article was published in that volume.
2. International Commission on Intervention and State Sovereignty, *The Responsibility to Protect* (Ottawa, Ontario: International Development Research Centre, Dec. 2001).
3. See Amitai Etzioni, "Sovereignty as Responsibility," *Orbis*, 50:1, Winter 2006.
4. Samuel Totten, William S. Parsons, and Israel W. Charny, eds., *Century of Genocide: Eyewitness Accounts and Critical Views* (New York: Garland, 1997); Robert Melson, *Revolution and Genocide: On the Origins of the Armenian Genocide and the Holocaust* (Chicago: University of Chicago Press, 1996); Samantha Power, *'A Problem from Hell': America and the Age of Genocide* (New York: Basic Books, 2002).
5. Power, *A Problem from Hell*, chs. 9–11.
6. Even the U.S. interventions in Bosnia, Kosovo, and Haiti are seen as failures in the critical account by Gary T. Dempsey and Roger W. Fontaine, *Fool's Errands: America's Recent Encounters with Nation Building* (Washington, D.C.: Cato Institute, 2001). See also David Rieff, *A Bed for the Night: Humanitarianism in Crisis* (New York: Simon and Schuster, 2002), especially chs. 4 and 6.
7. Power, *"A Problem from Hell,"* pp. 340–4, 374–5, 510–11.
8. David Halberstam, *War in a Time of Peace: Bush, Clinton, and the Generals* (New York: Scribner, 2001).
9. Max Boot, *The Savage Wars of Peace: Small Wars and the Rise of American Power* (New York: Basic Books, 2002).
10. Michael Ignatieff, "The Burden," *New York Times Magazine*, Jan. 5, 2003 (the title given on the magazine's cover was "The American Empire (Get Used to It)"; see also his "The Challenges of American Imperial Power," *Naval War College Review*, Spring 2003.
11. James Kurth, "Ignoring History: U.S. Democratization in the Muslim World," *Orbis*, Spring 2005.
12. Michael Ignatieff, "I Am Iraq," *New York Times Magazine*, Mar. 23, 2003.
13. David Rieff, *At the Point of a Gun: Democratic Dreams and Armed Intervention* (New York: Simon and Schuster, 2004), especially pp. 157–72, "The Specter of Imperialism: The Marriage of the Human Rights Left and the New Imperialist Right."
14. On recent efforts at intervention by African international organizations, see Jeremy Levitt, "The Law on Intervention: Africa's Pathbreaking Model," *Global Dialogue*, Winter/Spring 2005.

CHAPTER 7

ECONOMIC GLOBALIZATION

The Consequences of Liberal Commercialism

In the last decades of the twentieth century, globalization became a phenomenon whose economic, political, and cultural implications were a source of much heated discussion and controversy. For some, globalization is a cause for celebration that represents the culmination of the liberal dream of a world without borders within which trade and prosperity would flourish, while nation-states and the political conflicts and wars they spawned would become obsolete. For "liberal commercialists," war is bad for business and in an increasingly interdependent world would become much more costly and, therefore, much less likely.

For others, globalization is a phenomenon whose costs and benefits are not distributed evenly. Thus, the interdependence of the globalization era could be as much a source of conflict as cooperation. For neo-Marxists, those conflicts are between rich and poor countries and among social classes within countries for whom the unequal distribution of the wealth produced in the globalization era is a source of tension. For realists, globalization has led to the growth and development of new contenders for power and influence in the world, including China and potentially India. In the realist view, these large, emerging nations present a challenge economically, politically, and, potentially, militarily, to the United States and others. Indeed, the tensions produced by globalization raise the possibility, for some like Niall Ferguson, that globalization itself might at some point be reversed.

The readings in this chapter begin with a selection by James Fallows in which he systematically compares what he calls the "Asian" (or neo-mercantilist) and "Anglo-American" (or liberal) perspectives on the global economy. The article by Daniel Drezner focuses on changing American perceptions of trade and globalization. As you read the Fallows and Drezner pieces, look for points of disagreement between them regarding the merits of the liberal and neo-mercantilist approaches. One of the major success stories of the globalization era is the tremendous growth experienced by China. The selection by C. Fred Bergsten provides a concise overview of both the accomplishments and challenges of the Chinese economic miracle. Some have suggested that the Chinese success story serves as a lesson for other developing countries that integration into the global economy is the ticket to economic development. But Dani Rodrik sees that view as utopian. Though Rodrik is not a neo-Marxist, his critique of liberals on this issue is one that many neo-Marxists share. The readings conclude with a selection by Niall Ferguson on the future of globalization.

HOW THE WORLD WORKS

James Fallows

In this article, Fallows systematically lays out the differences between the neo-mercantilist (what he calls the German or Asian) approach and the liberal (what he calls the Anglo-American) approach to the world economy. Though written in the early 1990s at a time when Japan seemed the looming economic threat to the United States, the analysis in his article could easily be applied to understanding U.S. and Chinese approaches to globalization today. (Just substitute the word *China* for *Japan* whenever the latter comes up in the article.) As you read this article, ask yourself:

* What are the key differences between the two approaches as Fallows lays them out for you?
* Which approach is most closely related to the realist perspective on world politics?
* How has the U.S. approach to the global economy varied over time and why?

In Japan in the springtime of 1992 a trip to Hitotsubashi University, famous for its economics and business faculties, brought me unexpected good luck. Like several other Japanese universities, Hitotsubashi is almost heartbreaking in its cuteness. The road from the station to the main campus is lined with cherry trees, and my feet stirred up little puffs of white petals. Students glided along on their bicycles, looking as if they were enjoying the one stress-free moment of their lives.

They probably were. In surveys huge majorities of students say that they study "never" or "hardly at all" during their university careers. They had enough of that in high school.

I had gone to Hitotsubashi to interview a professor who was making waves. Since the end of the Second World War, Japanese diplomats and businessmen have acted as if the American economy should be the model for Japan's own industrial growth. Not only should Japanese industries try to catch up with America's lead in technology and production but also the nation should evolve toward a standard of economic maturity set by the United States. Where Japan's economy differed

from the American model—for instance, in close alliances between corporations which U.S. antitrust laws would forbid—the difference should be considered temporary, until Japan caught up.

Through the 1980s a number of foreign observers challenged this assumption, saying that Japan's economy might not necessarily become more like America's with the passing years. Starting in 1990 a number of Japanese businessmen and scholars began publicly saying the same thing, suggesting that Japan's business system might be based on premises different from those that prevailed in the West. Professor Iwao Nakatani, the man I went to Hitotsubashi to meet, was one of the most respected members of this group, and I spent the afternoon listening to his argument while, through the window I watched petals drifting down.

On the way back to the station I saw a bookstore sign advertising Western-language books for sale. I walked to the back of the narrow store and for the thousandth time felt both intrigued and embarrassed by the consequences of the worldwide spread of the English language. In row upon row sat a jumble of books that had nothing in common except that they were published in English. Self-help manuals by Zig Ziglar. Bodice-rippers from the Harlequin series. A Betty Crocker cookbook. The complete works of Sigmund Freud. One book by, and another about, Friedrich List.

Friedrich List! For at least five years I'd been scanning used-book stores in Japan and America looking for just these books, having had no luck in English-language libraries. I'd scoured stores in Taiwan that specialized in pirated reprints of English-language books for about a tenth their original cost. I'd called the legendary Strand bookstore, in Manhattan, from my home in Kuala Lumpur, begging them to send me a note about the success of their search (it failed) rather than make me wait on hold. In all that time these were the first books by or about List I'd actually laid eyes on.

One was a biography, by a professor in the north of England. The other was a translation, by the same professor, of a short book List had written in German. Both were slim volumes, which, judging by the dust on their covers, had been on the shelf for years. I gasped when I opened the first book's cover and saw how high the price was—9,500 yen, about $75. For the set? I asked hopefully. No, apiece, the young woman running the store told me. Books are always expensive in Japan, but even so this seemed steep. No doubt the books had been priced in the era when one dollar was worth twice as many yen as it was by the time I walked into the store. I opened my wallet, pulled out a 10,000-yen note, took my change and the biography, and left the store. A few feet down the sidewalk I turned around, walked back to the store, and used the rest of my money to buy the other book. I would always have regretted passing it up.

Why Friedrich List? The more I had heard about List in the preceding five years, from economists in Seoul and Osaka and Tokyo, the more I had wondered why I had virtually never heard of him while studying economics in England and the United States. By the time I saw his books in the shop beneath the cherry trees, I had come to think of him as the dog that didn't bark. He illustrated the strange self-selectivity of Anglo-American thinking about economics.

I emphasize "Anglo-American" because in this area the United Kingdom and the United States are like each other and different from most of the rest of the world. The two countries have dominated world politics for more than a century, and the dominance of the English language lets them ignore what is being said and thought overseas—and just how isolated they have become. The difference shows up this way: The Anglo-American system of politics and economics, like any system, rests on certain principles and beliefs. But rather than acting as if these are the best principles, or the ones their societies prefer, Britons and Americans often act as if these were the only possible principles and no one, except in error, could choose any others. Political economics becomes an essentially religious question, subject to the standard drawback of any religion—the failure to understand why people outside the faith might act as they do.

To make this more specific: Today's Anglo-American world view rests on the shoulders of three men. One is Isaac Newton, the father of modern science. One is Jean-Jacques Rousseau, the father of liberal political theory. (If we want to keep this purely Anglo-American, John Locke can serve in his place.) And one is Adam Smith, the father of laissez-faire economics. From these founding titans come the principles by which advanced society, in the Anglo-American view, is supposed to work. A society is supposed to understand the laws of nature as Newton outlined them. It is supposed to recognize the paramount dignity of the individual, thanks to Rousseau, Locke, and their followers. And it is supposed to recognize that the most prosperous future for the greatest number of people comes from the free workings of the market. So Adam Smith taught, with axioms that were enriched by David Ricardo, Alfred Marshall, and the other giants of neoclassical economics.

The most important thing about this summary is the moral equivalence of the various principles. Isaac Newton worked in the realm of fundamental science. Without saying so explicitly, today's British and American economists act as if the economic principles they follow had a similar hard, provable, undebatable basis. If you don't believe in the laws of physics—actions create reactions, the universe tends toward greater entropy—you are by definition irrational. And so with economics. If you don't accept the views derived from Adam Smith—that free competition is ultimately best for all participants, that protection and interference are inherently wrong—then you are a flat-earther.

Outside the United States and Britain the matter looks quite different. About science there is no dispute. "Western" physics is the physics of the world. About politics there is more debate: with the rise of Asian economies some Asian political leaders, notably Lee Kuan Yew, of Singapore, and several cautious figures in Japan, have in effect been saying that Rousseau's political philosophy is not necessarily the world's philosophy. Societies may work best, Lee and others have said, if they pay less attention to the individual and more to the welfare of the group.

But the difference is largest when it comes to economics. In the non-Anglophone world Adam Smith is merely one of several theorists who had important ideas about organizing economies. In most of East Asia and continental Europe the study of economics is less theoretical than in England and America (which is why English-speakers monopolize Nobel Prizes) and more geared toward solving business problems.

In Japan economics has in effect been considered a branch of geopolitics—that is, as the key to the nation's strength or vulnerability in dealing with other powers. From this practical-minded perspective English-language theorists seem less useful than their challengers, such as Friedrich List.

TWO CLASHING WORLD VIEWS

Britons and Americans tend to see the past two centuries of economics as one long progression toward rationality and good sense. In 1776 Adam Smith's *The Wealth of Nations* made the case against old-style mercantilism, just as the Declaration of Independence made the case against old-style feudal and royal domination. Since then more and more of the world has come to the correct view—or so it seems in the Anglo-American countries. Along the way the world has met such impediments as neo-mercantilism, radical unionism, sweeping protectionism, socialism, and, of course, communism. One by one the worst threats have given way. Except for a few lamentable areas of backsliding, the world has seen the wisdom of Adam Smith's ways.

Yet during this whole time there has been an alternative school of thought. The Enlightenment philosophers were not the only ones to think about how the world should be organized. During the eighteenth and nineteenth centuries the Germans were also active—to say nothing of the theorists at work in Tokugawa Japan, late imperial China, czarist Russia, and elsewhere.

The Germans deserve emphasis—more than the Japanese, the Chinese, the Russians, and so on because many of their philosophies endure. These did not take root in England or America, but they were carefully studied, adapted, and applied in parts of Europe and Asia, notably Japan. In place of Rousseau and

Locke the Germans offered Hegel. In place of Adam Smith they had Friedrich List.

The German economic vision differs from the Anglo-American in many ways, but the crucial differences are these:

"Automatic" Growth versus Deliberate Development

The Anglo-American approach emphasizes the unpredictability and unplannability of economics. Technologies change. Tastes change. Political and human circumstances change. And because life is so fluid, attempts at central planning are virtually doomed to fail. The best way to "plan," therefore is to leave the adaptation to the people who have their own money at stake. These are the millions of entrepreneurs who make up any country's economy. No planning agency could have better information than they about the direction things are moving, and no one could have a stronger incentive than those who hope to make a profit and avoid a loss. By the logic of the Anglo-American system, if each individual does what is best for him or her, the result will be what is best for the nation as a whole.

Although List and others did not use exactly this term, the German school was more concerned with "market failures." In the language of modern economics these are the cases in which normal market forces produce a clearly undesirable result. The standard illustration involves pollution. If the law allows factories to dump pollutants into the air or water, then every factory will do so. Otherwise, their competitors will have lower costs and will squeeze them out. This "rational" behavior will leave everyone worse off. The answer to such a market failure is for the society—that is, the government—to set standards that all factories must obey.

Friedrich List and his best-known American counterpart, Alexander Hamilton, argued that industrial development entailed a more sweeping sort of market failure. Societies did not automatically move from farming to small crafts to major industries just because millions of small merchants were making decisions for themselves. If every person put his money where the return was greatest, the money might not automatically go where it would do the nation the most good. For it to do so required a plan, a push, an exercise of central power. List drew heavily on the history of his times—in which the British government deliberately encouraged British manufacturing and the fledgling American government deliberately discouraged foreign competitors. . . .

Consumers versus Producers

The Anglo-American approach assumes that the ultimate measure of a society is its level of consumption. Competition is good, because it kills off producers whose prices are too high. Killing them off is good, because more-efficient suppliers will give the consumer a better deal. Foreign trade is very good, because it means that the most efficient suppliers in the whole world will be able to compete. It doesn't even matter why competitors are willing to sell for less. They may really be more efficient; they may be determined to dump their goods for reasons of their own. In either case the consumer is better off. He has the ton of steel, the cask of wine, or—in today's terms—the car or computer that he might have bought from a domestic manufacturer, plus the money he saved by buying foreign goods.

In the Friedrich List view, this logic leads to false conclusions. In the long run, List argued, a society's well-being and its overall wealth are determined not by what the society can *buy* but by what it can *make*. This is the corollary of the familiar argument about foreign aid: Give a man a fish and you feed him for a day. Teach him how to fish and you feed him for his life.

List was not concerned here with the morality of consumption. Instead he was interested in both strategic and material well-being. In strategic terms nations ended up being dependent or independent according to their ability to make things for themselves. Why were Latin Americans, Africans, and Asians subservient to England and France in the nineteenth century? Because they could not make the machines and weapons Europeans could.

In material terms a society's wealth over the long run is greater if that society also controls advanced activities. That is, if you buy the ton of steel or cask of wine at bargain rates this year, you are better off, as a consumer, right away. But over ten years, or fifty, you and your children may be stronger as both consumers and producers if you learn how to make the steel and wine yourself. If you can make steel rather than just being able to buy it, you'll be better able to make machine tools. If you're able to make machine tools, you'll be better able to make engines, robots, airplanes. If you're able to make engines and robots and airplanes, your children and grandchildren will be more likely to make advanced products and earn high incomes in the decades ahead.

The German school argued that emphasizing consumption would eventually be self-defeating. It would bias the system away from wealth creation—and ultimately make it impossible to consume as much. To use a homely analogy: One effect of getting regular exercise is being able to eat more food, just as an effect of steadily rising production is being able to consume more. But if people believe that the reason to get exercise is to permit themselves to eat more, rather than for longer term benefits they will behave in a different way. List's argument was that developing productive power was in

itself a reward. "The forces of production are the tree on which wealth grows," List wrote in another book, called The *National System of Political Economy*.

> The tree which bears the fruit is of greater value than the fruit itself. . . . The prosperity of a nation is not . . . greater in the proportion in which it has amassed more wealth (ie, values of exchange), but in the proportion in which it has more *developed its powers of production*.

Process versus Result

In economics and politics alike the Anglo-American theory emphasizes how the game is played, not who wins or loses. If the rules are fair, then the best candidate will win. If you want better politics or a stronger economy, you should concentrate on reforming the rules by which political and economic struggles are waged. Make sure everyone can vote; make sure everyone can bring new products to market. Whatever people choose under those fair rules will by definition be the best result. Abraham Lincoln or Warren Harding, Shakespeare or *Penthouse*—in a fair system whatever people choose will be right.

The government's role, according to this outlook, is not to tell people how they should pursue happiness or grow rich. Rather, its role is that of referee—making sure no one cheats or bends the rules of "fair play," whether by voter fraud in the political realm or monopoly in the economic.

In the late twentieth century the clearest practical illustration of this policy has been the U.S. financial market. The government is actively involved—but only to guard the process, not to steer the results. It runs elaborate sting operations to try to prevent corporate officials from trading on inside information. It requires corporations to publish detailed financial reports every quarter, so that all investors will have the same information to work from. It takes companies to court—IBM, AT&T—whenever they seem to be growing too strong and stunting future competitors. It exposes pension-fund managers to punishment if they do not invest their assets where the dividends are greatest.

These are all ways of ensuring that the market will "get prices right," as economists say, so that investments will flow to the best possible uses. Beyond that it is up to the market to decide where the money goes. Short-term loans to cover the budget deficits in Mexico or the United States? Fine. Long-term investments in cold-fusion experimentation? Fine. The market will automatically assign each prospect the right price. If fusion engines really would revolutionize the world, then investors will voluntarily risk their money there.

The German view is more paternalistic. People might not automatically choose the best society or the best use of their money. The state, therefore, must be concerned with both the process and the result. Expressing an Asian variant of the German view, the sociologist Ronald Dore has written that the Japanese—"like all good Confucianists"—believe that "you cannot get a decent, moral society, not even an efficient society, simply out of the mechanisms of the market powered by the motivational fuel of self-interest." So, in different words, said Friedrich List.

Individuals versus the Nation

The Anglo-American view focuses on how individuals fare as consumers and on how the whole world fares as a trading system. But it does not really care about the intermediate levels between one specific human being and all five billion—that is, about communities and nations.

This criticism may seem strange, considering that Adam Smith called his mighty work *The Wealth of Nations*. It is true that Smith was more of a national-defense enthusiast than most people who now invoke his name. For example, he said that the art of war was the "noblest" of the arts, and he approved various tariffs that would keep defense-related industries strong—which in those days meant sailcloth making. He also said that since defense "is of much more importance than opulence, the act of navigation is, perhaps, the wisest of all the commercial regulations of England." This "act of navigation" was, of course, the blatantly protectionist legislation designed to restrict the shipment of goods going to and from England mostly to English ships.

Still, the assumption behind the Anglo-American model is that if you take care of the individuals, the communities and nations will take care of themselves. Some communities will suffer, as dying industries and inefficient producers go down, but other communities will rise. And as for nations as a whole, outside the narrow field of national defense they are not presumed to have economic interests. There is no general "American" or "British" economic interest beyond the welfare of the individual consumers who happen to live in America or Britain.

The German view is more concerned with the welfare, indeed sovereignty, of people in groups—in communities, in nations. This is its most obvious link with the Asian economic strategies of today. Friedrich List fulminated against the "cosmopolitan theorists," like Adam Smith, who ignored the fact that people lived in nations and that their welfare depended to some degree on how their neighbors fared. In the real world happiness depends on more than how much money you take home. If the people around you are also comfortable (though, ideally, not as comfortable as you), you are happier and safer than if they are desperate. This, in brief, is the case that today's Japanese make against the American economy: American managers and professionals live more opulently than their counterparts in Japan, but they have to guard themselves, physically and morally, against the down-and-out people with whom they share the country.

In the German view, the answer to this predicament is to pay explicit attention to the welfare of the nation. If a consumer has to pay 10 percent more for a product made by his neighbors than for one from overseas, it will be worse for him in the short run. But in the long run, and in the broadest definitions of well-being, he might be better off. . . .

Business as Peace versus Business as War

By far the most uplifting part of the Anglo-American view is the idea that everyone can prosper at once. Before Adam Smith, the Spanish and Portuguese mercantilists viewed world trade as a kind of battle. What I won, you lost. Adam Smith and David Ricardo demonstrated that you and I could win at the same time. If I bought your wine and you bought my wool, we would both have more of what we wanted, for the same amount of work. The result would be the economist's classic "positive sum" interaction. Your well-being and my well-being added together would be greater than they were before our trade.

The Germans had a more tragic, or "zero sum"-like, conception of how nations dealt with each other. Some won; others lost. Economic power often led to political power, which in turn let one nation tell others what to do. Since the Second World War, American politicians have often said that their trading goal is a "level playing field" for competition around the world. This very image implies a horizontal relationship among nations, in which they all good-naturedly joust as more or less equal rivals.

"These horizontal metaphors are fundamentally misleading," the American writer John Audis has written in the magazine *In These Times*.

Instead of being grouped horizontally on a flat field, nations have always been organized vertically in a hierarchical division of labor. The structure of the world economy more accurately resembles a pyramid or a cone rather than a plane. In the 17th century, the Dutch briefly stood atop the pyramid. Then, after a hundred year transition during which the British and French vied for supremacy, the British emerged in 1815 as the world's leading industrial and financial power, maintaining their place through the end of the century. Then, after about a forty-year transition, the U.S. came out of World War II on top of the pyramid. Now we are in a similar period of transition from which it is likely, after another two decades, that Japan will emerge as the leading industrial power.

The same spirit and logic run through List's arguments. Trade is not just a game. Over the long sweep of history some nations lose independence and control of their destiny if they fall behind in trade. Therefore nations must think about it strategically, not just as a matter of where they can buy the cheapest shirt this week.

In *The Natural System of Political Economy*, List included a chapter on this theme, "The Dominant Nation." Like many other things written about Britain in the nineteenth century, it makes bittersweet reading for twentieth-century Americans. "England's manufactures are based upon highly efficient political and social institutions, upon powerful machines, upon great capital resources, upon an output larger than that of all other countries, and upon a complete network of internal transport facilities," List said of the England of the 1830s, as many have said of the United States of the 1950s and 1960s.

> A nation which makes goods more cheaply than anyone else and possesses immeasurably more capital than anyone else is able to grant its customers more substantial and longer credits than anyone else. . . . By accepting or by excluding the import of their raw materials and other products, England—all powerful as a manufacturing and commercial country—can confer great benefits or inflict great injuries upon nations with relatively backward economies.

This is what England lost when it lost "dominance," and what Japan is gaining now.

Morality versus Power

By now the Anglo-American view has taken on a moral tone that was embryonic when Adam Smith wrote his book. If a country disagrees with the Anglo-American axioms, it doesn't just disagree: it is a "cheater." Japan "cheats" the world trading system by protecting its rice farmers. America "cheats" with its price supports for sugar-beet growers and its various other restrictions on trade. Malaysia "cheated" by requiring foreign investors to take on local partners. And on and on. If the rules of the trading system aren't protected from such cheating, the whole system might collapse and bring back the Great Depression.

In the German view, economics is not a matter of right or wrong, or cheating or playing fair. It is merely a matter of strong or weak. The gods of trade will help those who help themselves. No code of honor will defend the weak, as today's Latin Americans and Africans can attest. If a nation decides to help itself—by protecting its own industries, by discriminating against foreign products—then that is a decision, not a sin. . . .

WHEN WE ACTED THE WAY THEY DO

In 1991 the economic historian William Lazonick published an intriguing book, *Business Organization and the Myth of the Market Economy*. It examined the way industrial economies had behaved during the years when they became strongest—England in the eighteenth and nineteenth centuries, the United States in the nineteenth and twentieth centuries, and Japan from the late nineteenth century on.

These countries varied in countless ways, of course. The United Kingdom had a huge empire; the United States had a huge frontier; Japan had the advantage of applying technology the others had invented. Yet these success stories had one common theme, Lazonick showed. None of the countries conformed to today's model of "getting-prices right" and putting the consumer's welfare first. All had to "cheat" somehow to succeed.

Friedrich List had railed on about exactly this point in the 1840s, when England was the only industrial success story to observe. The British were just beginning to preach free-trade theory in earnest. They abolished the famous Corn Laws in 1846, exposing their inefficient domestic farmers to competition from overseas. Yet over the previous 150 years England had strong-armed its way to prosperity by violating every rule of free trade. It would be as if Japan, in the 1990s, finally opened its rice market to competition, in the name of free trade—and then persuaded itself that it had been taking a hands-off approach to industry for the previous 150 years. When England was building its technological lead over the rest of the world, Lazonick said, its leaders did not care just about the process of competition. They were determined to control the result, so that they would have the strongest manufacturers on earth.

British economists began talking about getting prices right only after they succeeded in promoting their own industries by getting prices wrong. Prices were wrong in that cheap competition from the colonies was forbidden. They were wrong in that the Crown subsidized and encouraged investment in factories and a fleet. They were right in that they made British industry strong.

By the time Adam Smith came on the scene, Lazonick said, the British could start lecturing other countries about the folly of tariffs and protection. Why should France (America, Prussia, China . . .) punish its consumers by denying them access to cheap, well-made English cloth? Yet the British theorists did not ask themselves why their products were so advanced, why "the world market . . . in the late eighteenth century was so *uniquely under British control*." The answer would involve nothing like laissez-faire.

The full answer would instead include the might of the British navy, which by driving out the French and Spanish had made it easier for British ships to dominate trade routes. It would involve political measures that prevented the Portuguese and Irish from developing textile industries that could compete with England's. It would include the Navigation Acts, which ensured a British monopoly in a number of the industries the country wanted most to develop. The answer involved land enclosure and a host of other measures that allowed British manufacturers to concentrate more capital than they could otherwise have obtained.

Lazonick summed up this process in a passage that exactly describes the predicament of the United States at the end of the twentieth century.

The nineteenth-century British advocated laissez-faire because, given the advanced economic development that their industries had already achieved, they thought that their firms could withstand open competition from foreigners. [They wanted] to convince other nations that they would be better off if they opened up their markets to British goods. . . . [They] accepted as a *natural fact of life* Britain's dominant position as the "workshop of the world" [emphasis added]. They did not bother to ask how Britain had attained that position. . . .

But the ultimate critique of nineteenth-century laissez-faire ideology is *not* that it ignored the role of national power in Britain's past and present. Rather, the ultimate critique is that laissez-faire failed to comprehend Britain's economic future— a future in which, confronted by far more powerful systems of national capitalism, the British economy would enter into a long-run relative decline from which it has yet to recover.

America's economic history follows the same pattern. While American industry was developing, the country had no time for laissez-faire. After it had grown strong, the United States began preaching laissez-faire to the rest of the world—and began to kid itself about its own history, believing its slogans about laissez-faire as the secret of its success.

The "traditional" American support for worldwide free trade is quite a recent phenomenon. It started only at the end of the Second World War. This period dominates the memory of most Americans now alive but does not cover the years of America's most rapid industrial expansion. As the business historian Thomas McCraw, of the Harvard Business School, has pointed out, the United States, which was born in the same year as *The Wealth of Nations,* never practiced an out-and-out mercantilist policy, as did Spain in the colonial days. But "it did exhibit for 150 years after the Revolution a pronounced tendency toward protectionism, mostly through the device of the tariff."

American schoolchildren now learn that their country had its own version of the Smith-List debate, when Thomas Jefferson and Alexander Hamilton squared off on what kind of economy the new nation should have. During George Washington's first term Hamilton produced his famous "Report on Manufactures," arguing that the country should deliberately encourage industries with tariffs and subsidies in order to compete with the mighty British. Jefferson and others set out a more pastoral, individualistic, yeoman-farmer vision of the country's future. As everyone learns in class, Hamilton lost. He was killed in a duel with Aaron Burr, he is not honored on Mount Rushmore or in the capital, as Jefferson is; he survives mainly through his portrait on the $10 bill. Yet it was a strange sort of defeat, in that for more than a century after Hamilton submitted his report, the United States essentially followed his advice.

In 1810 Albert Gallatin, a successor of Hamilton's as Secretary of the Treasury, said that British manufacturers enjoyed advantages that could keep Americans from ever catching up. A "powerful obstacle" to American industry,

he said, was "the vastly superior capital of Great Britain which enables her merchants to give very long term credits, to sell on small profits, and to make occasional sacrifices."

This, of course, is exactly what American manufacturers now say about Japan. Very little has changed in debates about free trade and protectionism in the past 200 years. If the antique language and references to out-of-date industries were removed from Hamilton's report of 1791, it could have been republished in 1991 and would have fit right into the industrial-policy debate. "There is no purpose to which public money can be more beneficially applied, than to the acquisition of a new and useful branch of industry" was the heart of Hamilton's argument—and, similarly, of many modern-day Democratic Party economic plans.

In the years before the American Revolution most leaders in the Colonies supported the concept of British protectionist measures. They were irritated by new taxes and levies in the 1760s and 1770s—but they had seen how effective Britain's approach was in developing industries. Through the nineteenth century the proper level of a national tariff was on a par with slavery as a chronically divisive issue. Northerners generally wanted a higher tariff, to protect their industries; farmers and southerners wanted a lower tariff, so that they could buy cheaper imported supplies. Many politicians were unashamed protectionists. "I don't know much about the tariff," Abraham Lincoln said, in what must have been an aw-shucks way. "But I know this much. When we buy manufactured goods abroad we get the goods and the foreigner gets the money. When we buy the manufactured goods at home, we get both the goods and the money." The United States had, just before Lincoln's term, forced the Japanese to accept treaties to "open" the Japanese market. These provided that Japan could impose a tariff of no more than five percent on most imported goods. America's average tariff on all imports was almost 30 percent at the time.

In the 1880s the University of Pennsylvania required that economics lecturers not subscribe to the theory of free trade. A decade later William McKinley was saying that the tariff had been the crux of the nation's wealth: "We lead all nations in agriculture; we lead all nations in mining; we lead all nations in manufacturing. These are the trophies which we bring after twenty-nine years of a protective tariff." The national tariff level on dutiable goods had varied, but it stayed above 30 percent through most of the nineteenth century. When the United States began to preach or practice free trade, after the Second World War, the average duty paid on imports fell from about nine percent in 1945 to about four percent in the late 1970s.

In addition to the tariff, nineteenth-century America went in heavily for industrial planning—occasionally under that name but more often in the name of national defense. The military was the excuse for what we would now call rebuilding infrastructure, picking winners, promoting research, and coordinating industrial growth. As Geoffrey Perret has pointed out in *A Country Made by War,* many evolutions about which people now say "That was good for the country" occurred only because someone could say at the time "This will be good for the military"—giving the government an excuse to step in.

In the mid-nineteenth century settlers moving west followed maps drawn by Army cartographers, along roads built by Army engineers and guarded by Army forts. At the end of the century the U.S. Navy searched for ways to build bigger, stronger warships and along the way helped foster the world's most advanced steel industry.

Just before Thomas Jefferson took office as President, the U.S. government began an ambitious project to pick winners. England surpassed America in virtually every category of manufacturing, and so, to a lesser degree, did France. Wheels turned and gears spun throughout Europe, but they barely did so in the new United States. In 1798 Congress authorized an extraordinary purchase of muskets from the inventor Eli Whitney, who was at the time struggling and in debt. Congress offered him an unprecedented contract to provide 10,000 muskets within twenty-eight months. This was at a time when the average production rate was one musket per worker per week. Getting the muskets was only part of what Congress accomplished: this was a way to induce, and to finance, a mass-production industry for the United States. Whitney worked round the clock, developed America's first mass-production equipment, and put on a show for the congressmen. He brought a set of disassembled musket locks to Washington and invited congressmen to fit the pieces together themselves—showing that the age of standardized parts had arrived.

"The nascent American arms industry led where the rest of manufacturing followed," Perret concluded. "Far from being left behind by the Industrial Revolution the United States, in a single decade and thanks largely to one man, had suddenly burst into the front rank." America took this step not by waiting for it to occur but by deliberately promoting the desired result.

For most of the next century and a half the U.S. government was less interested in improving the process of competition than in achieving a specific result. It cared less about getting prices right and more about getting ahead. This theme runs through the Agriculture Extension Service, which got information to farmers more rapidly than free-market forces might have; the shipbuilding programs of the late nineteenth century, which stimulated the machine-tool and metal-working industries; aircraft-building contracts; and medical research.

What America actually did while industrializing is not what we tell ourselves about industrialization today. Consumer welfare took second place; promoting production came first. A preference for domestic industries did cost consumers money. A heavy tariff on imported British rails made the expansion of the American railroads in the 1880s costlier than it would otherwise have been. But this protectionist policy coincided with, and arguably contributed to, the emergence of a productive, efficient American steel industry. The United

States trying to catch up with Britain behaved more or less like the leaders of Meiji (and postwar) Japan trying to catch up with the United States. Alexander Hamilton, dead and unmourned, won.

Thomas McCraw says that the American pattern was not some strange exception but in fact the norm. The great industrial successes of the past two centuries—America after its Revolution, Germany under Bismarck, Japan after the Second World War—all violated the rules of laissez-faire. Despite the obvious differences among these countries, he says, the underlying economic strategy was very much the same. . . .

TRADE TALK

Daniel Drezner

In this selection, political scientist Daniel Drezner examines changing American perceptions of international trade and the global economy. In it he explains why Americans have soured on trade and globalization and have adopted more mercantilist attitudes. As you read this selection, ask yourself:

- Why have Americans become more ambivalent about trade?
- How might changing attitudes in the U.S. impact globalization?
- How does Drezner's view of how the world works differ from that of James Fallows?

American perceptions about international trade have changed dramatically in the past two decades. Presidents can no longer craft positions on foreign economic policy in a vacuum. Trade now intersects with other highly politicized issues, ranging from the war on terror to environmental protection to bilateral relations with China. Old issues such as the

trade deficit and new issues such as offshore outsourcing have made a liberal trade policy one of the most difficult political sells inside the Beltway.

Indeed, shifts in domestic attitudes have created the least hospitable environment for trade liberalization in recent memory. Unfortunately, this inhospitable environment

Daniel Drezner, "Trade Talk." This article first appeared in *The American Interest* 1:2, Winter 2005, pp. 68–76. Reprinted by permission of The American Interest.

has arisen at a time when trade is more vital to the U.S. economy than ever. The challenge for this President and for those who succeed him will be to reinvigorate U.S. trade policies despite the current public mood. In short, it is the challenge to lead.

The first thing any president must do to lead effectively on economic issues is to persuade the country that trade matters. This should not be that hard, for trade manifestly does matter. In 1970 the sum of imports and exports accounted for less than 12 percent of U.S. GDP; by 2004 that figure had doubled to 24 percent. Approximately one out of every five factory jobs in the United States depends directly on trade. U.S. exports accounted for approximately 25 percent of economic growth during the 1990s, supporting an estimated 12 million jobs. U.S. farmers export the yield of one out of every three acres of their crops. In 2003 the United States exported $180 billion in high-tech goods and more than $280 billion in commercial services. From agriculture to manufacturing to technology to services, the U.S. economy needs international trade to thrive.

Researchers at the Institute for International Economics recently attempted to measure the cumulative payoff from trade liberalization since the end of World War II. Scott Bradford, Paul Grieco and Gary Hufbauer conservatively estimated that free trade generates economic benefits ranging from $800 billion to $1.45 trillion dollars per year in added output. This translates into an added per capita benefit of between $2,800 and $5,000—or, more concretely, an addition of between $7,100 and $12,900 per American household. The gains from future trade expansion have been estimated to range between $450 billion and $1.3 trillion per year in additional national income, which would increase per capita annual income between $1,500 and $2,000. There are few tools in the

U.S. government's policy arsenal that consistently yield rewards of this magnitude.

Trade expansion brings several benefits to the U.S. economy. It allows the United States to specialize in making the goods and services in which it is most productive. The bigger the market created by trade liberalization, the greater the benefits from specialization. Trade also increases competition within economic sectors. Over the past decades economists have repeatedly shown that industries exposed to trade are more productive than sectors in which cross-border exchange is limited or impossible. As available markets expand, the rate of return for technological and organizational innovations increases. With freer trade, firms and entrepreneurs have a greater incentive to take risks and to invest in new inventions and innovations.

These benefits also make it easier for the Federal Reserve to run a bullish monetary policy. An open market is a significant reason why the United States has been able in recent years to sustain robust economic growth, dramatic increases in labor productivity, low unemployment, modest inflation and historically low interest rates. The combination of these effects boosts the trajectory of feasible economic growth without triggering inflation, which in turn has allowed the Fed to pursue more expansionary monetary policies than would otherwise have been possible.

Trade is equally vital to American foreign policy. The regions of the world that have embraced trade liberalization—North America, Europe and East Asia—contain politically stable regimes and, despite some problems with radical Islamist minorities, make our best partners in the war on terror. The regions of the world with the most tenuous connection to global markets—the Middle East and Africa—are plagued by unstable regimes and remain hotbeds of terrorist and criminal activity. Trade is not a silver bullet for U.S. foreign policy; many other factors affect the rise of terrorism and political instability. Nevertheless, trade is a handmaiden to hope. It provides significant opportunity to individuals in poor countries, offering a chance for a better life for them and their children. Creating hope among people is a powerful long-term weapon in the war on terror.

Multiple economic analyses demonstrate that trade promotes economic freedom and economic development. Trade will be essential to advancing the Millennium Development Goals of halving global poverty by 2015. Exposure to the global economy correlates strongly with the spread of democracy, the rule of law and the reduction of violence.

Over the long term, trade liberalization is a win-win proposition among countries and therefore serves a useful purpose in promoting American interests and values. Most of the time, trade helps to reduce frictions between countries and serves as one of the most powerful tools of soft power at America's disposal. Bilateral relations have improved with every country that has signed a free-trade agreement (FTA) with the United States. If countries perceive that the rules of the global economic game benefit all participants—and not merely the United States—these countries will be more favorably disposed toward the United States on other foreign policy dimensions.

Over the very long term, U.S.-led trade expansion can cement favorable perceptions of the United States among rising powers. Both the CIA and private sector analysts project that China and India will have larger economies than most G-7 members by 2050. Decades from now, it would serve American interests if these countries looked upon the United States as a country that aided rather than impeded their economic ascent. Trade liberalization undertaken now serves as a down payment for good relations with rising great powers in the future.

OUR AMBIVALENT PUBLIC

Despite these significant economic and diplomatic benefits, the American public is increasingly hostile to freer trade. Between 1999 and 2004, public support for free trade dropped off a precipice. The most dramatic shift in opinion came from Americans making more than $100,000 a year: Support for promoting trade dropped from 57 percent to 28 percent in this group. According to a July 2004 poll jointly conducted by the Pew Research Center and the Council on Foreign Relations, 84 percent of Americans thought that protecting the jobs of American workers should be a top priority of American foreign policy. The same month, a poll conducted by the German Marshall Fund of the United States concluded that only 4 percent of Americans still supported NAFTA. Americans are also less enthusiastic about further international trade deals than are Europeans: 82 percent of the French and 83 percent of the British want more international trade agreements, compared to just 54 percent of Americans.

Hostile attitudes toward trade liberalization are even more concentrated when the focus turns to newer forms of trade, such as outsourcing. In 2004 at least ten different surveys asked Americans how they felt about the growing number of jobs being outsourced overseas. The results were consistently and strongly negative. Depending on the poll, between 61 and 85 percent of respondents agreed with the statement that outsourcing is bad for the American economy. Between 51 and 72 percent of Americans were even in favor of the government penalizing U.S. firms that engage in outsourcing. In a Harris poll taken in May and June of 2004, 53 percent of Americans said U.S. companies engaging in outsourcing were "unpatriotic." This hostility remains consistent regardless of how respondents are categorized. A 2004 *CFO Magazine* survey of chief financial officers revealed that 61 percent of them believed outsourcing was bad for the economy, while an April 2004 Gallup poll showed 66 percent of investors believed outsourcing was hurting the investment climate in the United States.

Free traders assert that greater liberalization will always benefit the economy. The polling data reveal that most Americans do not buy the "always", and instead believe in "fair trade." They believe that the expansion of trade leads to an increase in economic insecurity that outweighs any increase in national income. A fair-trade doctrine recommends the use of safeguards, escape clauses and other legal protections to slow down the economic and social effects of import competition. Such views have become dominant in the United States over the past two decades. But why?

THE IRON LAWS OF TRADE POLITICS

Three political facts of life have caused many Americans to shift their support from free trade to fair trade. First, during economic downturns or periods of slack job growth, public suspicion of free-trade policies explodes into hostility. Inevitably, foreign countries become the scapegoat for business cycle fluctuations that have little to do with trade. When presented with economic theories and statistical data on the one hand showing that trade is good for the economy, and anecdotes of job losses due to import competition on the other, most Americans are swayed by the anecdotes. There may be no discernible economic correlation between trade and overall employment, but many Americans believe there is one—a belief that policymakers ignore at their peril.

Combine this with a massive trade deficit and the perception problem becomes even more acute. Most Americans think a large trade deficit is bad for the economy, even though such deficits correlate *positively* with strong economic growth. Indeed, the growth in the trade deficit since 1998 has been accompanied by strong GDP growth and excellent productivity gains. Nevertheless, the U.S. trade deficit is projected to top $670 billion this year—in absolute dollar terms, the largest trade deficit in world economic history. In an uncertain economy, that number will lead to greater public skepticism about the merits of freer trade. To be sure, there are valid reasons to be concerned about the size of the current account deficit, but even those economists who voice such concerns do not recommend higher tariffs as the answer.

The second reason American support for free trade has dropped is that it is particularly difficult to make the case for trade expansion during election cycles. Trade generates large, diffuse benefits but concentrated—if smaller—costs. Those who bear the costs are more likely to vote on the issue—and make campaign contributions based on it—than those who reap the benefits. In this situation, politicians will always be tempted to engage in protectionist rhetoric. The latest example of this came when politicians on both sides of the aisle demanded government action to halt outsourcing. As election cycles continue to lengthen, this political temptation will only get stronger.

The third iron law of trade politics is that both advocates and opponents talk about trade in ways that simultaneously inflate its importance and frame the issue as a zero-sum proposition. Trade is both blamed and praised for America's various economic strengths and ills, even though domestic factors such as macroeconomic policy, stock market fluctuations and the pace of innovation are far more significant determinants of America's overall economic performance. Politicians routinely address trade issues by discussing how changes in policy will affect the trade deficit. The implicit understanding in their arguments is that it is better to run a trade surplus than a deficit, even though there is no economic data to support that view. Debates about trade inevitably revolve around the question of jobs, even though trade has a minimal effect on aggregate employment levels.

We should be used to this by now. A decade ago, the political debate over NAFTA was framed in terms of job creation and job destruction, despite the fact that every sober policy analysis concluded that NAFTA would not significantly affect the employment picture in the United States one way or the other. As a result, even politicians who advocate trade liberalization do so by focusing on increasing American exports and downplaying imports. If politicians talk about trade in a mercantilist, zero-sum way, Americans will be led to think about the issue this way as well.

NEW CONSTRAINTS ON TRADE POLITICS

. . . One new problem is that the percentage of the American economy exposed to international competition is on the rise. Over the next decade, technological innovation will convert what have been thought to be non-tradable sectors into tradable ones. Trade will start to affect professions that have not changed their practices all that much for decades—fields such as accounting, medicine, education and law. This will increase the number of Americans who perceive themselves to be vulnerable to international competition and economic insecurity. This insecurity is the driving force behind the growing hostility to free trade among the upper income brackets.

Another relatively new issue is the rise of China. Twenty years ago, there was a great deal of American hand-wringing at the prospect of Japan "overtaking" the U.S. economy. For *realpolitik* reasons, the current fear of China's economic rise will be worse. At least Japan was a stable democratic ally of the United States. China is neither democratic nor an ally, and the jury is still out with respect to its long-term stability.

Beijing has brought some of this enmity on itself. China's central bank has increasingly intervened in foreign exchange markets to maintain the dollar's strength against the yuan, even though China's currency has risen in value compared to other major currencies. In July 2005, China's central bank announced a slight devaluation against the dollar, with an intention to move to a managed float. However, Beijing has continued to purchase dollars at an extraordinary rate, ensuring that the yuan will not appreciate significantly anytime soon. China's interventions have exacerbated the U.S.-China trade deficit: In 2004 the bilateral deficit was a record $162 billion.

These practices—combined with China's high growth rate, the media firestorm over outsourcing and a recent flurry of Chinese corporate takeover efforts directed at U.S. firms—have created intense domestic pressures for some kind of retaliatory policy. In April 2005, a bill was introduced in the U.S. Senate that threatens a 27.5 percent tariff on Chinese goods unless Beijing revalues its currency; the bill garnered a veto-proof majority. In May, the House of Representatives proposed a different piece of legislation to widen the definition of exchange-rate manipulation to include China as an offender. Many congressmen reacted negatively to the proposed takeover of Unocal by the China National Offshore Oil Corporation, with the House passing a measure urging the President to block the purchase on national security grounds. This congressional hostility helped to scotch the proposed takeover.

China's economic growth and aggressive trade diplomacy also pose significant challenges to the United States from a security perspective. In 2004 China accounted for 31 percent of global growth in the demand for oil. China's energy diplomacy has led to ambitious deals with authoritarian regimes in Myanmar, Iran and Sudan, and has placed China's diplomacy in all three cases at loggerheads with that of the United States. China's growing interest in commercial relations with other Pacific Rim countries contrasts with U.S. regional policy, which prioritizes the war on terror. At a fundamental level, even if the United States benefits from the bilateral trading relationship, China appears to benefit more—and that could clash with the stated *National Security Strategy* objective of "dissuad[ing] potential adversaries from pursuing a military buildup in hopes of surpassing, or equaling, the power of the United States."

The content of current trade negotiations has also made trade a tougher sell. World Trade Organization negotiations have shifted much of their focus away from tariff reduction to ensuring that disparities in national regulations do not interfere with international trade. In large part this is due to the WTO's success at reducing border-level trade restrictions. For most areas of merchandise trade (agricultural, textile and clothing products excepted), tariffs and quotas have been at nominal levels since completion of the Uruguay Round in 1994. As for agriculture and textiles, liberalization of either sector will not be an easy sell. The end of the Multi-Fibre Agreement in January 2005 has led to "bra wars" between the developed world and China, with the Bush Administration using every tool at its disposal to staunch the flow of textile imports. As for agriculture, the lack of progress in those negotiations now threatens to derail the upcoming WTO's Ministerial Conference in Hong Kong.

Increasingly, trade negotiations inside and outside the WTO have revolved around the residual non-tariff barriers to trade—social and business regulations. The most obvious examples include labor standards, environmental protection, consumer health and safety, antitrust, intellectual property rights and immigration controls. Because most regulatory policies were originally devised as domestic policies, they are more politically difficult to change than tariffs or quotas.

Some of these new trade negotiations will touch third rails of American politics. For example, developing countries are pushing in the WTO for greater liberalization in the trade of "Mode 4" services, in which the person performing the service crosses a border to do his or her job. The benefits of such liberalization for the United States economy would be significant; Microsoft chairman Bill Gates warned early this year that visa restrictions were limiting U.S. access to highly trained computer engineers from other countries, undercutting America's ability to innovate. Despite the economic advantages, however, such a move raises politically sensitive questions. One obvious concern would be the effect this kind of liberalization would have on homeland security. Another prominent concern would be the effect on U.S. immigration policies: Opponents would claim that the liberalization of trade in services was back-door immigration.

The American public's growing hostility to freer trade has made congressional passage of trade agreements more difficult, and this in turn has worsened the public image of trade. The victory margins in congressional votes for trade legislation have narrowed over the years. In December 2001, the Bush Administration secured Trade Promotion Authority by a single vote in the House of Representatives. (Trade Promotion Authority—which used to be called "fast track"—allows the president to submit trade deals for congressional approval via a simple up-or-down vote, preventing any poison-pill amendments.) In July 2005, the Central American Free Trade Agreement passed by only two votes, and that was after significant White House lobbying of wavering representatives. The smaller the margin of victory, the more leverage wavering representatives have to extract district-specific spending or trade-distorting measures that undercut the original purpose of the trade deal. As a result, congressional negotiations over trade agreements have begun to give off the same whiff of pork that comes with transportation and agricultural bills.

WHAT CAN BE DONE?

Can the public's turn against free trade perhaps be ignored? Political analysts and trade experts alike argue that the political significance of this attitudinal shift remains an open question. Americans are skeptical about the benefits of trade, but they are not particularly passionate about it. Polling data, purchasing behavior and experimental evidence all suggest that American consumers talk like mercantilists but purchase goods like free traders. It is difficult to point to specific members of Congress who have lost their seats because they adopted an unpopular position on trade policy.

That said, international trade is viewed as increasingly salient by many Americans. Now is not the time for a policy of trade expansion to lose political legitimacy. This is particularly true given the . . . full plate of trade issues for the next several years. At the top of the list is the Doha Round of WTO talks. Thorny negotiations remain on the liberalization of trade in services and the reduction of internal price supports and market restrictions for agricultural producers. . . .

At the regional level, efforts to advance the Free Trade Area of the Americas and the Middle Eastern Free Trade Area Initiative are continuing, albeit at less than breakneck speed. At the

bilateral level, the [Bush] Administration . . . stepped up its use of free-trade agreements with favored allies. In the first term, FTAs were ratified with Singapore, Australia, Morocco and Chile. FTAs have been negotiated and signed with Bahrain and Oman. Negotiations with Panama, Peru, Ecuador, Colombia, Thailand and the United Arab Emirates are ongoing.

Can public attitudes be changed? The primary impediment to boosting public support for trade liberalization is not one of economics but of psychology. People *feel* that their jobs and wages are threatened. Even if the probability of losing one's job from import competition or outsourcing is small, the percentage of workers who know someone who has lost his or her job because of trade is much larger. In this sense, public perceptions about trade are akin to perceptions about crime: Knowing a victim of crime often makes the problem appear to be greater than it actually is. While these fears may be exaggerated, they are nonetheless real.

. . . The good news is that while the current political environment is challenging, it is not hopeless. Polling strongly suggests that a healthy majority of Americans—including skeptics of freer trade—supports policies that pair liberalization with policies that reduce the disruptions to groups that are negatively affected. These policies can take the form of expanded insurance opportunities, greater public investment in research and development, and retraining programs. The 2002 expansion of the Trade Adjustment Assistance program is a good first step, but more steps are needed: a wider use of wage insurance schemes, increased portability of health care coverage and including service-sector workers in assistance programs.

Another useful tactic would be to link trade to larger foreign policy priorities. One reason the United States was able to advance trade liberalization during the Cold War was the bipartisan consensus that a liberal trading system aided the cause of containment. Trade expansion can and should be presented as a critical element of the long-term grand strategy of the United States to spread democracy and defeat terrorism. Security arguments resonate with a broad majority of the American public. According to new polls, a large majority of Americans support promoting international trade with poor, democratic governments—a message consistent with President Bush's second Inaugural Address. As with the Cold War, a communications strategy that markets economic diplomacy as "America's first line of offense" would blunt the arguments of protectionists while promoting the virtues of trade liberalization. Greater presidential involvement in shifting public attitudes—including aggressive use of the bully pulpit—will be needed.

The alternative to blunting the shift in public opinion is to go with the flow. While politically expedient, adopting a more protectionist foreign economic policy will hurt the U.S. economy and ultimately undermine global stability. If barriers are placed on trade, the effect would be to preserve jobs in less competitive sectors of the economy and destroy current and future jobs in more competitive sectors. Trade protectionism would therefore lead to higher consumer prices, lower rates of return for investors and reduced incentives for innovation in the United States. The International Monetary Fund recently warned that trade protectionism in the United States would also magnify the negative effects of any global economic shock.

Ignoring public attitudes about trade is dangerous in the long run, and following the public mood on trade would be an unfortunate abdication of leadership by the Bush Administration in the short run. If the first step to recovery is recognizing that there is a problem, then responsible policymakers in Washington need to appreciate the extent to which the political terrain has shifted. The next step will be changing the American public's mind—a difficult but achievable task, if there is true leadership in the White House.

MEETING THE CHINA CHALLENGE

C. Fred Bergsten

The emergence of China is perhaps the big story of the globalization era. In this selection from a larger book on the subject, Bergsten provides a broad overview of the current status of China's growth and development. As you read his description, ask yourself:

⬡ What are the key questions that Bergsten identifies as central to assessing the future of China and its impact on the world?

⬡ What are the accomplishments and achievements of China in the globalization era?

⬡ What obstacles stand in the path to China's continued growth and stability?

C. Fred Bergsten, from *China: The Balance Sheet*. Copyright © 2006 by Center for Strategic and International Studies, and the Institute for International Economics. Reprinted by permission of Public Affairs, a member of Perseus Books Group.

THE STAKES FOR GETTING CHINA POLICY RIGHT

Complex. Contradictory. Confusing. For centuries, China has proven difficult for Americans to understand. Today, however, China is becoming one of the most powerful countries in the world. As the twenty-first century unfurls, the stakes have never been higher for getting U.S. policy toward China right.

The direction that China and U.S.-China relations take will define the strategic future of the world for years to come. No relationship matters more—for better or for worse—in resolving the enduring challenges of our time: maintaining stability among great powers, sustaining global economic growth, stemming dangerous weapons proliferation, countering terrorism, and confronting new transnational threats of infectious disease, environmental degradation, international crime, and failing states. And for the United States in particular, a rising China has an increasingly important impact on American prosperity and security, calling for some clear-eyed thinking and tough economic, political, and security choices.

Put simply, the U.S.-China relationship is too big to disregard and too critical to misread.

Unfortunately, in spite of the unmistakable importance of the China challenge, there is often far more heat than light in the U.S. debate about China. Most worrying are the pessimism and alarmism that too often cloud the public's perspective, and which do not account for the enduring strengths and comparative advantages the United States can bring to bear in successfully meeting the challenge of a rising China. . . .

ASKING THE RIGHT QUESTIONS

American strategy can—and must—respond to China's emergence in a way that assures regional security, realizes the greatest possible economic benefit, averts worst-case outcomes from China's socioeconomic convulsions, and increasingly integrates the country as a partner—or at least not an active opponent—in achieving a prosperous and stable world order for future generations.

All this can be done—if the United States asks the right questions, understands China's complexities, and reinforces America's strengths.

Broadly speaking, the critical questions to be addressed fall into four basic categories:

- *Continued growth or collapse?* What are the real sources of China's spectacular economic growth? What are its most troubling economic weaknesses? Will China continue to grow at such a pace, or overheat and collapse in the next spectacular case of failed development and financial mismanagement?
- *Democratization or disorder?* Will further rapid economic growth in China inevitably lead to more pluralistic and even democratic forms of government? Will China's sociopolitical transformation lead to widespread upheaval and unrest? Or will the Chinese leadership maintain political control while orchestrating ever greater prosperity? What are the implications of these different outcomes for U.S. interests?
- *Economic opportunity or threat?* Does China represent a major threat to American jobs, living standards, and access to energy and other vital commodities? Do its large holdings of U.S. financial assets endanger U.S. stability? Or is China predominantly a beneficial driver of global economic prosperity, offering opportunities that outweigh the risks, for businesses, workers, and consumers? What should the United States do to encourage the latter scenario?
- *Security partner or rival?* What are China's strategic intentions? Is China another pre-1914 or pre-1939 Germany? Imperial

Japan? Soviet Russia? Something more troubling—or less so? Are China and the United States destined to become enemies? Or can Beijing and Washington, as they have in the past, realize a new strategic and mutually beneficial *modus vivendi?*

CHINA'S DOMESTIC ECONOMY: CONTINUED GROWTH OR COLLAPSE?

. . . Many aspects of China's economic picture are impressive, even amazing. Already, China is the world's fourth largest economy and third largest trading nation. It has grown by about 10 percent per year for almost three decades, increasing its output by a factor of nine since launching its economic reforms in 1978. In the process, it has lifted more than 200 million people out of poverty.

Because China is so large and growing so rapidly, and also because it is extremely open to the world economy, in recent years it has accounted for about 12 percent of all growth in world trade—much more than the United States. China has nearly become the world's largest surplus country; in 2006, its foreign exchange reserves will likely reach $1 trillion, far more than any other country's. China is second only to the United States as a recipient of foreign direct investment. It has used its deep and rapid integration into the world economy, which has left it with among the lowest trade barriers of any developing country, to overcome internal resistance to continuing economic reform. And at a time when the global economy is increasingly technology-driven, China is graduating hundreds of thousands of engineering and science students each year.

It is also important, however, to also recognize the continuing weaknesses and downsides of China's domestic economy, especially in comparison to the United States. For example, despite its growth, China remains a poor country with per capita income averaging just one twenty-fifth that in America. China's average wage is one-thirtieth that of the United States and its average productivity level is equally lower (and wages, in any event, account for only 20 percent of the cost of producing textiles and 5 percent of the cost of producing semiconductors). China is seeking to advance to higher technology industries and greater value added, but it still spends only about 10 percent of what the United States devotes to research and development. Meanwhile, only about one-tenth of China's scientific graduates can compete internationally, and the great bulk of its "advanced technology" exports are commoditized products such as notebook computers, mobile phones, and DVD players.

Even over the next few years, let alone over further decades, China faces daunting challenges to sustaining its breathtaking growth. These include completing the reform of state-owned enterprises; improving the allocation of capital, in part through cleaning up the banking system; developing new economic policy tools to promote stability; lessening the income gaps that have opened up between the urban and rural areas and the coastal and inland regions; coping with urbanization and labor reallocation on a scale unprecedented in history; and meeting its enormous needs for energy, other raw materials, food, and water in an environmentally sound way.

It is difficult to know how China's future development will affect its approach to the global economy and international security. It is also difficult to know whether China's continued economic success, even if sustained for another decade or more, will produce a more democratic polity that would presumably be more congenial to U.S. interests—though most countries that reach middle-income status do become far more open politically as well as economically.

Still, it is hardly inconceivable that China could seek to take advantage of becoming the world's largest economy, as may well happen, to revise the international trade and finance rules to its own advantage. It may seek to impose its will in other ways on both its nearby and distant neighbors. It may devote a sizeable share of its growing economy to military purposes, and thus pose at least a potential threat in ever-widening theaters of possible conflict.

Regarding China's domestic economy, Americans should understand that there are limits to what the United States can do. Only if China were to blatantly attack Taiwan, or belligerently threaten other neighbors in a manner that triggered a new Cold War, would Europe and, especially, Japan and other Asian countries even consider joining the United States in applying the far-reaching sanctions that would be necessary to have any chance of limiting China's economic advance. However, properly managed, U.S. policy can—and already does— shape China's international economic aims and security policy in a positive direction.

On the other hand, even without direct U.S. pressures, China will be hard-pressed to ensure continued epochal change in the economy with a political system frozen in time. The political system that existed in 1978 when annual income per capita was $200 had to adapt to manage the $1,700 per capita Chinese economy of today. The $10,000 per capita China of tomorrow will likewise require dramatically different governance. And Beijing knows it.

CHINA'S DOMESTIC TRANSFORMATION: DEMOCRATIZATION OR DISORDER?

. . . The top priority for China's leadership is keeping a lid on the country's burgeoning polit-

ical, economic, and social challenges—and thus keeping the Party in power. Yet China's leaders face a conundrum: They recognize the imperative of "*gaige kaifang*" ("reform and opening") so the Chinese people can compete, innovate, and prosper in a globalizing world, but they also know these transformative forces will fuel domestic change and upheaval.

Consider just a few of the complex challenges on China's domestic agenda. Some 140 million persons, or about 15 percent of China's workforce, are economic migrants on the move. China boasts some 300,000 U.S. dollar millionaires, but also has more than 400 million persons living on the equivalent of less than $2 a day. Only about 15 percent of China's land is arable, and that amount is shrinking.

Sixteen of the world's twenty most air-polluted cities are in China. More than three-quarters of the surface water flowing through China's urban areas is considered unsuitable for drinking or fishing, and 90 percent of urban groundwater is contaminated. The gap between China's rich and poor rivals that of the United States, and the gulf is growing wider. Social unrest is on the rise, from some 8,700 major incidents reported in 1993 to 87,000 "public order disturbances" reported in 2005.

China's public health and demographic indicators also point to troubles ahead. China is "graying" at a fast pace, and will grow "old" before it grows "rich." While China's life expectancy of just over 71 years is near developed-world levels, premature deaths from heart disease, stroke, and diabetes will result in a loss of more than half a *trillion* U.S. dollars over the next ten years. Seventy thousand new HIV infections occur in China every year. The emergence of SARS, avian flu, tuberculosis, and other communicable diseases potentially threatens the health of millions of Chinese and millions more beyond China's borders.

But do all these problems add up to widespread chaos or significant political upheaval in the next five to ten years? For several important reasons, probably not. First, the Party leadership is intensely aware of these problems, and has become more adaptive: introducing piecemeal reforms, co-opting intellectual and business elites, imposing controls on information flows, and pronouncing policies aimed at alleviating the concerns of China's rural and urban poor.

Second, for the most part, the myriad challenges, while widespread, have not coalesced in a way that threatens either the political leadership or national stability. Currently, China's social unrest is highly localized, both geographically and in terms of specific grievances. On the other hand, when movements do appear to be well-organized and national in scope—such as the China Democracy Party or the Falun Gong—Beijing swiftly suppresses their activities.

Third, China continues to receive foreign technical assistance to help address its domestic challenges.

Finally, with China's foreign exchange reserves approaching $1 trillion in 2006, its leaders could bring considerable resources to bear on major problems if and as they choose.

Instead, it is more likely that the Chinese leadership will continue muddling through to deliver continued good economic prospects, maintain a hold on political power, and preserve basic order, despite a high incidence of unrest and growing socioeconomic ills.

But change is afoot. Today's China has over 390 million mobile phone subscribers, 111 million Internet users, 285,000 officially registered nongovernmental organizations, and some 140 million migrants on the move in search of economic opportunity. There are an estimated 70 million practicing Christians in China today—the equivalent of the total populations of Alabama, Florida, Kansas, Michigan, New York, Utah, Virginia, and Washington combined. Hundreds of millions of Chinese engage in traditional folk religions, worshipping local gods, heroes, and ancestors.

Meanwhile, though China is not a rule of law country, it now claims roughly 120,000 certified lawyers, 12,000 law firms, and more than 300 law schools—up from fewer than 2,000 lawyers and only two functioning law schools in 1979. China has incrementally improved the professionalism of its court system, strengthened procedural due process, opened up its legislative and regulatory processes, and introduced more consistent and predictable legal mechanisms, especially in administrative and economic law. While under single-party rule and far from a liberal democracy, Chinese society is more open today—economically, socially, and even politically—than it has been for the past half century or more.

Looking ahead over the near- to medium term, the United States should be prepared to deal with a China led by the Chinese Communist Party. This being the case, while calls for a more open, just, and democratic society in China must be an indispensable part of U.S. policy, they need to be tempered by informed and realistic expectations.

To begin, Americans should understand that Beijing's fixation on managing its domestic problems presents not only challenges but opportunities for the United States. It is true that Beijing's approach to managing its domestic challenges often translates into tight political controls on information and harsh crackdowns on dissent and unrest. On the other hand, with Chinese leaders focused predominantly inward, they are less inclined toward foreign adventurism. Moreover, China's real and growing domestic challenges offer enormous opportunities for the U.S. government and private sector to export ideas, expertise, and technologies, as well as the seeds for positive political, economic, and social development in China.

Doing what is possible to bring about positive outcomes in China clearly calls for intensified interaction by the U.S. public and private sectors with counterparts in China to address the country's domestic concerns. These activities will involve cooperation in a range of areas, including on energy and the environment, human rights, the rule of law, good government, anti-corruption, public health, social welfare, and the role of nongovernmental organizations.

The most compelling logic for such a course is that it is so clearly in the U.S. interest. An apprehensive, unstable, collapsing, or anarchic China could pose unacceptably high economic and security risks to the United States. Moreover, a weakening and wary China would probably also rein in the political and social progress of the past two decades. Even a relatively stable and growing China can spread problems across its borders, such as pollution, infectious diseases, organized crime, and trafficking in weapons, drugs, and people. Intensified interaction to help address China's domestic challenges would also improve the United States' ability to observe and accurately assess the country's circumstances and prospects going forward.

CHINA IN THE WORLD ECONOMY: OPPORTUNITY OR THREAT?

. . . Assuming current Chinese and U.S. growth rates continue, China will become the world's largest economy in thirty years. Its average income then would be about one-fourth of America's. China would also be by far the world's largest trading country. Its size alone would dominate Asia, and move it alongside the United States and the European Union as a global economic superpower. But it could also be the first economic superpower in history that is relatively poor in per capita income terms and guided by a non-democratic political system.

China's rise intensifies the pressures that technological change and globalization have already been bringing to bear for some time on less competitive portions of the American economy, and thus on domestic politics. In some low-skill and thus low-wage sectors, such as apparel and footwear, and in some low-technology industries that have become largely commoditized, such as color television sets, Chinese competition accelerates the decline already underway in U.S. domestic production and employment. Along with the growth of India and other rapidly developing countries, China's economic development places downward pressure on some U.S. wages and real incomes.

In addition, China's huge and rapidly growing bilateral trade surplus with the United States, which is far greater than Japan's ever reached in the past, generates strong U.S. political reactions. So will China's inevitable desire to buy major U.S. companies, as was seen in the emotional Congressional reaction to the China National Offshore Oil Company's bid for Unocal in 2005.

It is important, however, to place the impact of these changes in perspective. China is large enough and competitive enough to cause economic problems for the United States, but it has neither derailed our economy nor been the chief cause of our difficulties, any more than were Japan in the 1980s or other Asian countries in the early 1990s. All of these trends would be well underway with or without China. Indeed, China has seized much more of the U.S. market from other countries than from domestic U.S. production. None of China's gains have precluded the United States from achieving rapid economic growth, job creation, and indeed the attainment of virtually full employment, in the late 1990s and again today. Technology development and factors other than international competition have been much more important in limiting real wage gains and worsening U.S. income distribution in recent years.

China's adverse affects on the U.S. economy must also be set against the incontrovertible economic benefits China brings. Because of China's low-cost, high-quality products and its rapidly growing market for U.S. exports, the United States is on balance about $70 billion per year richer as a result of trade with China. China's exports to the United States and its investments in American financial assets help restrain U.S. inflation and interest rates, and thus permit faster economic growth and more job creation.

Different groups of Americans are affected differently by U.S. economic relations with China. Homeowners and workers in largely non-tradable industries, such as education and health care, which comprise much of the dominant services sector, benefit from lower product prices and interest rates. Low-wage apparel workers, though they gain relatively more than other Americans from the availability of low-cost Chinese products at Wal-Mart and elsewhere, may nevertheless be losers on balance as a result of the possible acceleration of their job dislocation. Companies that supply auto parts may lose market share to Chinese firms or to larger American companies that can source those products in China.

In response to the threats and opportunities China poses, the United States should pursue a three-part strategy. First, the United States must strive even more diligently to put its own house in order: correcting its budget and external imbalances; saving and investing more in its physical and especially human capital; strengthening its education system at both the K–12 level and at the high-skill end of the spectrum

to produce a labor force that will be able to compete with China and others; and providing transitional assistance for those Americans adversely affected by the accelerated pace of change globalization has wrought.

There is no need for any new China-specific legislation in the United States, such as across-the-board tariffs, or for Executive Branch standards and regulations uniquely targeting China. But maintaining sound and successful economic policies overall, including energy policies, will be crucial—both to shore up U.S. self-confidence and to diminish the temptation to scapegoat foreigners, as occurred vis-à-vis Japan during the prolonged period of poor U.S. economic performance in the 1970s and 1980s.

Second, the United States must insist that China accept and implement the international norms that apply to the strongest economies—and which are thus most responsible for maintaining global prosperity and stability. (In so doing, the United States will have to acknowledge that China had little role in creating those norms and will presumably have views on them as it increasingly engages in the process.) This would include meeting World Trade Organization commitments, reducing remaining trade barriers, respecting intellectual property rights, reducing its large global current account deficit, and permitting a sizeable increase in the value of its currency. Chinese failure to play a cooperative international role will inevitably produce strong protectionist reactions against it in other parts of the world, including the United States.

Third, the United States—along with the growing list of other major economic powers—must increasingly engage China in the institutional management of the world economy. The global economic community should avoid a situation in which China exercises its influence to push for some regional economic and trading alternatives in lieu of greater participation in global economic initiatives and decision-making. China is leading the effort to create an Asian Monetary Facility that could become an alternative to the International Monetary Fund for regional purposes. It is working on a free trade agreement with its neighbors in Southeast Asia. Its strong support for and participation in the "10+3" summits—bringing together the ten nations of Southeast Asia with Japan, South Korea, and China—could evolve into a broader "East Asian Community," including a region-wide preferential trade zone that would discriminate against the United States.

Rather, the goal should be twofold: not only to encourage China to play by the rules, but also to mobilize its leadership talents in promoting globally desirable economic and political outcomes. The alternative to effective global integration of China will be increasing international frictions, both between the United States and China itself and between the United States and its other chief economic partners, notably Europe and Japan, as they differ over how to respond to the China challenge.

CHINA'S FOREIGN AND SECURITY POLICY: PARTNER OR RIVAL?

. . . There is little evidence that China has developed and is pursuing a concrete and coherent long-term global strategy. Beijing's pattern of action suggests that its stated priorities—to "create a favorable international environment" to facilitate China's internal economic development, and to "preserve China's independence, sovereignty and territorial integrity"—indeed reflect the primary motivations behind China's current foreign and national security policy.

China's stated desire to develop its "comprehensive national power," whether economic, military, or otherwise, is connected to an ambition

to achieve great power status, and to ensure that its interests and freedom of action are protected in international affairs. Its priority attention to domestic development has resulted in a posture today that seeks to set aside areas of disagreement in relations with other nations, promote economic ties, and reassure others about the peaceful nature of China's rise. Beijing has placed increasing emphasis on relations with its immediate periphery.

The search for natural resources, particularly energy, to fuel its economic growth has become an increasingly important component of Chinese foreign policy in recent years. This has led to reinvigorated relations with the developing world, where many of these resources are located, and often led to support for unsavory regimes such as Burma, Sudan, Zimbabwe, and Iran. China's goals of unification with Taiwan also serve as a central animating component of Chinese foreign policy, in particular to isolate the island internationally and prevent its permanent separation.

China places enormous value on maintaining a positive relationship with the United States, whose vast market remains critical to China's successful development and growth. Beijing thus has been very careful in recent years not to challenge Washington directly or aggressively on international issues vital to U.S. interests, such as Iraq. That said, China is ambivalent at best about the United States' military presence and political influence in East Asia. Chinese leaders may privately acknowledge that China has benefited from the regional peace and stability the U.S. presence offers, but Beijing remains deeply suspicious about longer-term U.S. intentions toward China. From China's perspective, the U.S. military presence along its periphery, policy toward Taiwan, and promotion of democracy and human rights are potential threats.

Beijing calls openly for creation of a "multi-polar world"—a thinly veiled challenge to U.S. "uni-polar" leadership. China has led in developing multilateral bodies in the region that exclude the United States, such as the Shanghai Cooperation Organization, the 10+3 process, and the East Asia Summit.

Yet there does not seem to be a coherent Chinese strategy to openly challenge U.S. global leadership or construct an anti-U.S. bloc. Instead, in recent years, China has adroitly taken advantage of American preoccupations elsewhere around the world to exploit weak spots in U.S. relationships and strengthen its own international ties, especially in Asia. While today the apparent purpose of China's outreach is largely defensive and focused on economic interests, this posture over time could form the basis for more assertive leadership to counterbalance the United States or oppose U.S interests more actively.

Since the early 1990s, and accelerating in recent years, China has set out to comprehensively modernize its military: in doctrine, training, education, force structure, and overall operational capability. Beijing has implemented double-digit increases to its defense budget nearly every year since 1991; placed a growing emphasis on air, maritime, and strategic missile capabilities; streamlined the People's Liberation Army to create a more professional, efficient fighting force; attempted to improve joint interoperability; and upgraded its weapons platforms, primarily through foreign acquisitions.

Beijing's doctrine, training, procurement, and deployment strategy in recent years seems to be motivated particularly to address a Taiwan scenario. China also has closely observed U.S. military operations over the past decade, and its assessment of evolving U.S. capabilities has also informed its military modernization decisions, most notably Beijing's recognition of the increasing importance of information technology in modern warfare.

Chinese leaders have no illusions that the People's Liberation Army (PLA) is a match for the U.S. military. What China does seek are niche capabilities to exploit U.S. vulnerabilities in order to deter, complicate, and delay, if not defeat, U.S. (or other) intervention in a Taiwan scenario. Beijing also seeks more broadly to prevent the United States and its allies from containing China's economic and military development through military action or intimidation. While a Taiwan scenario may serve as a leading animating factor in China's military modernization strategy, operational capabilities developed in the process may have broader applications to assert Chinese territorial claims and other future interests beyond the Taiwan Strait.

There is little doubt that Beijing would take military action should it become clear that Taipei has foreclosed the possibility of future unification. However, at present, China seems to be taking a longer-term approach to the Taiwan question, to prevent independence rather than compel near-term unification. Such an approach is consistent with Beijing's focus on domestic development and on promoting a benign international image. It also reflects relative confidence in current trends in Taiwan politics, U.S. policy, and China's own military development to constrain Taiwan's options.

Longer-term trends are more troublesome, however. Even as cross-Strait economic ties continue to flourish, Taiwan national identity continues to grow, as will demands for greater international space. Meanwhile, China's deployment of missiles and other advanced military capabilities may create a decisive advantage for the mainland that could tempt Beijing toward a military solution or more aggressive attempts at coercion in the future. Populism and nationalism are also increasing on the mainland, which could put new pressure on the Chinese leadership to resolve the Taiwan issue. China's precise threshold for military action is unclear.

Looking ahead, nothing is preordained that the United States and China will become enemies. In fact, in political, economic, and national security terms, it is clearly in the interests of both sides to prevent such an outcome. China will need to increasingly recognize that as a rising power of 1.3 billion people, it cannot hide behind the notion that its impact on international affairs is minimal. Beijing will need to assume greater responsibility to act in ways that reinforce international norms above and beyond its immediate self-interest.

Washington will need to be prepared psychologically for the impact China's rise may have on the United States' relative power and influence in East Asia and beyond. While China is unlikely to challenge U.S. preeminence in political, economic, or military power for the foreseeable future, the rise in China's relative international power and influence may present economic challenges to the United States, and may alter U.S. strategic relationships with friends and even allies around the world as those nations accommodate China's rise.

The temptation for the United States to fall back on an actively hostile or antagonistic posture toward Beijing is a dangerous one for U.S. interests. Without serious provocation from Beijing, such a policy would isolate the United States and put Washington at odds with allies and friends around the world. The United States should remember that the international community is equally uncertain and concerned about the implications of China's rise for their interests, and will support, if sometimes only tacitly, reasonable U.S. moves to prevent the development of an irresponsible or dangerous China.

CONCLUSION: TOWARD A NEW UNITED STATES-CHINA RELATIONSHIP

China every day becomes all the more complex and contradictory. Gone is the bleak monolith of China's Maoist past. Today, in its place, there are many "Chinas"—rural and urban, wealthy and poor, educated and illiterate, international and isolated. Within this context of diversity and disparity, China's citizens and leadership are grappling with unprecedented domestic dynamism, coming to grips with globalization's challenges, and deliberating different political and economic futures.

U.S.-China relations are likewise complex and full of contradictions, all the more so as a result of deepening interdependence between the two powers. China stands as the United States' third largest trading partner and its second largest source of imports, shipping more than an eighth of what America buys from abroad. Sino-dollars get recycled to purchase American debt, helping finance the sizeable U.S. consumer and government spending deficits. Today, Chinese authorities are the second largest foreign official creditor to the United States, holding hundreds of billions of dollars of U.S. financial assets. Meanwhile, the United States is China's number one bilateral trade partner and export destination, and an important source of investment, technology, and expertise. On the international political and foreign policy scene, U.S. and Chinese interests are also increasingly complex and interwoven, even as they also diverge on several key issues.

The revival of China in the late twentieth and early twenty-first centuries may turn out to be one of the greatest transformations in modern history, surpassing even the stunning rise of Japan from the 1960s forward, and the ascendancies of the United States, Germany, and the Soviet Union in the twentieth century. By virtue of its size and the possibility of its continued run of economic expansion, as well as the uniqueness of its economic and political systems for such a major economic actor, China poses challenges that are literally unprecedented. . . .

TRADING IN ILLUSIONS

Dani Rodrik

Dani Rodrik criticizes as "utopian" the view of liberal, free traders that integration into the global economy will produce growth and poverty reduction in developing countries. As you read his article, ask yourself:

- What are the "admission requirements" to the global economy and why are they not always good for developing countries?
- What does Rodrik mean by the "Asian myths," and how does he explain the record of successful economic development in Asia?
- What does he mean by "growth begins at home"?

A senior U.S. Treasury official recently urged Mexico's government to work harder to reduce violent crime because "such high levels of crime and violence may drive away foreign investors." This admonition nicely illustrates how foreign trade and investment have become the ultimate yardstick for evaluating the social and economic policies of governments in developing countries. Forget the slum dwellers or *campesinos* who live amidst crime and poverty throughout the developing world. Just mention "investor sentiment" or "competitiveness in world markets" and policymakers will come to attention in a hurry.

Underlying this perversion of priorities is a remarkable consensus on the imperative of global economic integration. Openness to trade and investment flows is no longer viewed simply as a component of a country's development strategy; it has mutated into the most potent catalyst for economic growth known to humanity. Predictably, senior officials of the World Trade Organization (WTO), International Monetary Fund (IMF), and other international financial agencies incessantly repeat the openness mantra. In recent years, however, faith in integration has spread quickly to political leaders and policymakers around the world.

Joining the world economy is no longer a matter simply of dismantling barriers to trade and investment. Countries now must also comply with a long list of admission requirements, from new patent rules to more rigorous banking standards. The apostles of economic integration prescribe comprehensive institutional reforms that took today's advanced countries generations to accomplish, so that developing countries can, as the cliché goes, maximize the gains and minimize the risks of participation in the world economy. Global integration has become, for all practical purposes, a substitute for a development strategy.

This trend is bad news for the world's poor. The new agenda of global integration rests on shaky empirical ground and seriously distorts policymakers' priorities. By focusing on international integration, governments in poor nations divert human resources, administrative capabilities, and political capital away from more urgent development priorities such as education, public health, industrial capacity, and social cohesion. This emphasis also undermines nascent democratic institutions by removing the choice of development strategy from public debate.

World markets are a source of technology and capital; it would be silly for the developing world not to exploit these opportunities. But globalization is not a shortcut to development. Successful economic growth strategies have always required a judicious blend of imported practices with domestic institutional innovations. Policymakers need to forge a domestic growth strategy by relying on domestic investors and domestic institutions. The costliest downside of the integrationist faith is that it crowds out serious thinking and efforts along such lines.

EXCUSES, EXCUSES

Countries that have bought wholeheartedly into the integration orthodoxy are discovering that openness does not deliver on its promise. Despite sharply lowering their barriers to trade and investment since the 1980s, scores of countries in Latin America and Africa are stagnating or growing less rapidly than in the heyday of import substitution during the 1960s and 1970s.

By contrast, the fastest growing countries are China, India, and others in East and Southeast Asia. Policymakers in these countries have also espoused trade and investment liberalization, but they have done so in an unorthodox manner— gradually, sequentially, and only after an initial period of high growth—and as part of a broader policy package with many unconventional features.

The disappointing outcomes with deep liberalization have been absorbed into the faith with remarkable aplomb. Those who view global integration as the prerequisite for economic development now simply add the caveat that opening borders is insufficient. Reaping the gains from openness, they argue, also requires a full complement of institutional reforms.

Consider trade liberalization. Asking any World Bank economist what a successful trade-liberalization program requires will likely elicit a laundry list of measures beyond the simple reduction of tariff and nontariff barriers: tax reform to make up for lost tariff revenues; social safety nets to compensate displaced workers; administrative reform to bring trade practices into compliance with WTO rules; labor market reform to enhance worker mobility across industries; technological assistance to upgrade firms hurt by import competition; and training programs to ensure that export-oriented firms and investors have access to skilled workers. As the promise of trade liberalization fails to materialize, the prerequisites keep expanding. For example, Clare Short, Great Britain's secretary of state for international development, recently added universal provision of health and education to the list.

In the financial arena, integrationists have pushed complementary reforms with even greater fanfare and urgency. The prevailing view in Washington and other Group of Seven (G-7) capitals is that weaknesses in banking systems, prudential regulation, and corporate governance were at the heart of the Asian financial crisis of the late 1990s. Hence the ambitious efforts by the G-7 to establish international codes and standards covering fiscal transparency, monetary and financial policy, banking supervision, data dissemination, corporate governance, and accounting standards. The Financial Stability Forum (FSF)—a G-7 organization with minimal representation from developing nations—has designated 12 of these standards as essential for creating sound financial systems in developing countries. The full FSF compendium includes an additional 59 standards the agency considers "relevant for sound financial systems," bringing the total number of codes to 71. To fend off speculative capital movements, the IMF and the G-7 also typically urge developing countries to accumulate foreign reserves and avoid exchange-rate regimes that differ from a "hard peg" (tying the value of one's currency to that of a more stable currency, such as the U.S. dollar) or a "pure float" (letting the market determine the appropriate exchange rate).

A cynic might wonder whether the point of all these prerequisites is merely to provide easy cover for eventual failure. Integrationists can conveniently blame disappointing growth performance or a financial crisis on "slippage" in the implementation of complementary reforms rather than on a poorly designed liberalization. So if Bangladesh's freer trade policy does not produce a large enough spurt in growth, the World Bank concludes that the problem must involve lagging reforms in public administration or continued "political uncertainty" (always a favorite). And if Argentina gets caught up in a confidence crisis despite significant trade and financial liberalization, the IMF reasons that structural reforms have been inadequate and must be deepened.

FREE TRADE-OFFS

Most (but certainly not all) of the institutional reforms on the integrationist agenda are perfectly sensible, and in a world without financial, administrative, or political constraints, there would be little argument about the need to adopt them. But in the real world, governments face difficult choices over how to deploy their fiscal resources, administrative capabilities, and political capital. Setting institutional priorities to maximize integration into the global economy has real opportunity costs.

Consider some illustrative trade-offs. World Bank trade economist Michael Finger has estimated that a typical developing country must spend $150 million to implement requirements under just three WTO agreements (those on customs valuation, sanitary and phytosanitary measures, and trade-related intellectual property rights). As Finger notes, this sum equals a year's development budget for many least-developed countries. And while the budgetary burden of implementing financial codes and standards has never been fully estimated, it undoubtedly entails a substantial diversion of fiscal and human resources as well. Should governments in developing countries train more bank auditors and accountants, even if those investments mean fewer secondary-school teachers or reduced spending on primary education for girls?

In the area of legal reform, should governments focus their energies on "importing" legal codes and standards or on improving existing domestic legal institutions? In Turkey, a weak coalition government spent several months during 1999 gathering political support for a bill providing foreign investors the protection of international arbitration. But wouldn't a better long-run strategy have involved reforming the existing legal regime for the benefit of foreign and domestic investors alike?

In public health, should governments promote the reverse engineering of patented basic medicines and the importation of low-cost generic drugs from "unauthorized" suppliers, even if doing so means violating WTO rules against such practices? When South Africa passed legislation in 1997 allowing imports of patented AIDS drugs from cheaper sources, the country came under severe pressure from Western governments, which argued that the South African policy conflicted with WTO rules on intellectual property.

How much should politicians spend on social protection policies in view of the fiscal constraints imposed by market "discipline"? Peru's central bank holds foreign reserves equal to 15 months of imports as an insurance policy against the sudden capital outflows that financially open economies often experience. The opportunity cost of this policy amounts to almost 1 percent of gross domestic product annually—more than enough to fund a generous antipoverty program.

How should governments choose their exchange-rate regimes? During the last four decades, virtually every growth boom in the developing world has been accompanied by a controlled depreciation of the domestic currency. Yet financial openness makes it all but impossible to manage the exchange rate.

How should policymakers focus their anti-corruption strategies? Should they target the high-level corruption that foreign investors often decry or the petty corruption that affects the poor the most? Perhaps, as the proponents of permanent normal trade relations with China argued in the recent U.S. debate, a government that is forced to protect the rights of foreign investors will become more inclined to protect the rights of its own citizens as well. But this is, at best, a trickledown strategy of institutional reform. Shouldn't reforms target the desired ends directly—whether those ends are the rule of law, improved observance of human rights, or reduced corruption?

The rules for admission into the world economy not only reflect little awareness of development priorities, they are often completely unrelated to sensible economic principles. For instance, WTO agreements on anti-dumping, subsidies and countervailing measures, agriculture, textiles, and trade-related intellectual property rights lack any economic rationale beyond the mercantilist interests of a narrow set of powerful groups in advanced industrial countries. Bilateral and regional trade agreements are typically far worse, as they impose even tighter prerequisites on developing countries in return for crumbs of enhanced "market access." For example, the African Growth and Opportunity Act signed by U.S. President Clinton in May 2000 provides increased access to the U.S. market only if African apparel manufacturers use U.S.-produced fabric and yarns. This restriction severely limits the potential economic spillovers in African countries.

There are similar questions about the appropriateness of financial codes and standards. These codes rely heavily on an Anglo-American style of corporate governance and an arm's-length model of financial development. They close off alternative paths to financial development of the sort that have been followed by many of today's rich countries (for example, Germany, Japan, or South Korea).

In each of these areas, a strategy of "globalization above all" crowds out alternatives that are potentially more development-friendly. Many of the institutional reforms needed for insertion into the world economy can be independently desirable or produce broader economic benefits. But these priorities do not necessarily coincide with the priorities of a comprehensive development agenda.

ASIAN MYTHS

Even if the institutional reforms needed to join the international economic community are expensive and preclude investments in other crucial areas, pro-globalization advocates argue that the vast increases in economic growth that invariably result from insertion into the global marketplace will more than compensate for those costs. Take the East Asian tigers or China, the advocates say. Where would they be without international trade and foreign capital flows?

That these countries reaped enormous benefits from their progressive integration into the world economy is undeniable. But look closely at what policies produced those results, and you will find little that resembles today's rule book.

Countries like South Korea and Taiwan had to abide by few international constraints and pay few of the modern costs of integration during their formative growth experience in the 1960s and 1970s. At that time, global trade rules were sparse and economies faced almost none of today's common pressures to open their borders to capital flows. So these countries combined their outward orientation with unorthodox policies: high levels of tariff and non-tariff barriers, public ownership of large segments of banking and industry, export subsidies, domestic-content requirements, patent and copyright infringements, and restrictions on capital flows (including on foreign direct investment). Such policies are either precluded by today's trade rules or are highly frowned upon by organizations like the IMF and the World Bank.

China also followed a highly unorthodox two-track strategy, violating practically every rule in the guidebook (including, most notably, the requirement of private property rights). India, which significantly raised its economic growth rate in the early 1980s, remains one of the world's most highly protected economies.

All of these countries liberalized trade gradually, over a period of decades, not years. Significant import liberalization did not occur until after a transition to high economic growth had taken place. And far from wiping the institutional slate clean, all of these nations managed to eke growth out of their existing institutions, imperfect as they may have been. Indeed, when some of the more successful Asian economies gave in to Western pressure to liberalize capital flows rapidly, they were rewarded with the Asian financial crisis.

That is why these countries can hardly be considered poster children for today's global rules. South Korea, China, India, and the other Asian success cases had the freedom to do their own thing, and they used that freedom abundantly. Today's globalizers would be unable to replicate these experiences without running afoul of the IMF or the WTO.

The Asian experience highlights a deeper point: A sound overall development strategy that produces high economic growth is far more effective in achieving integration with the world economy than a purely integrationist strategy that relies on openness to work its magic. In other words, the globalizers have it exactly backwards. Integration is the result, not the cause, of economic and social development. A relatively protected economy like Vietnam is integrating with the world economy much more rapidly than an open economy like Haiti because Vietnam, unlike Haiti, has a reasonably functional economy and polity.

Integration into the global economy, unlike tariff rates or capital-account regulations, is not something that policymakers control directly. Telling finance ministers in developing nations that they should increase their "participation in world trade" is as meaningful as telling them that they need to improve technological capabilities—and just as helpful. Policy-makers need to know which strategies will produce these results, and whether the specific prescriptions that the current orthodoxy offers are up to the task.

TOO GOOD TO BE TRUE

Do lower trade barriers spur greater economic progress? The available studies reveal no systematic relationship between a country's average level of tariff and nontariff barriers and its subsequent economic growth rate. If anything, the evidence for the 1990s indicates a positive relationship between import tariffs and economic growth. . . . The only clear pattern is that countries dismantle their trade restrictions as they grow richer. This finding explains why today's rich countries, with few exceptions, embarked on modern economic growth behind protective barriers but now display low trade barriers.

The absence of a strong negative relationship between trade restrictions and economic growth may seem surprising in view of the ubiquitous claim that trade liberalization promotes higher growth. Indeed, the economics literature is replete with cross-national studies concluding that growth and economic dynamism are strongly linked to more open trade policies. A particularly influential study finds that economies that are "open," by the study's own definition, grew 2.45 percentage points faster annually than closed ones—an enormous difference.

Upon closer look, however, such studies turn out to be unreliable. In a detailed review of the empirical literature, University of Maryland economist Francisco Rodríguez and I have found a major gap between the results that economists have actually obtained and the policy conclusions they have typically drawn. For example, in many cases economists blame poor growth on the government's failure to liberalize trade policies, when the true culprits are ineffective institutions, geographic determinants (such as location in a tropical region), or inappropriate macroeconomic policies (such as an overvalued exchange rate). Once these misdiagnoses are corrected, any meaningful relationship across countries between the level of trade barriers and economic growth evaporates.

The evidence on the benefits of liberalizing capital flows is even weaker. In theory, the appeal of capital mobility seems obvious: If capital is free to enter (and leave) markets based on the potential return on investment, the result will be an efficient allocation of global resources. But in reality, financial markets are inherently unstable, subject to bubbles (rational or otherwise), panics, shortsightedness, and self-fulfilling prophecies. There is plenty of evidence that financial liberalization is often followed by financial crash—just ask Mexico, Thailand, or Turkey—while there is little convincing evidence to suggest that higher rates of economic growth follow capital-account liberalization.

Perhaps the most disingenuous argument in favor of liberalizing international financial flows is that the threat of massive and sudden capital movements serves to discipline policymakers in developing nations who might otherwise manage their economies irresponsibly. In other words, governments might be less inclined to squander their societies' resources if such actions would spook foreign lenders. In practice, however, the discipline argument falls apart. Behavior in international capital markets is dominated by mood swings unrelated to fundamentals. In good times, a government with a chronic fiscal deficit has an easier time financing its spending when it can borrow funds from investors abroad; witness Russia prior to 1998 or Argentina in the 1990s. And in bad times, governments may be forced to adopt inappropriate policies in order to conform to the biases of foreign investors; witness the excessively restrictive monetary and fiscal policies in much of East Asia in the immediate aftermath of the Asian financial crisis. A key reason why Malaysia was able to recover so quickly after the imposition of capital controls in September 1998 was that Prime Minister Mahathir Mohamad resisted the high interest rates and tight fiscal policies that South Korea, Thailand, and Indonesia adopted at the behest of the International Monetary Fund.

GROWTH BEGINS AT HOME

Well-trained economists are justifiably proud of the textbook case in favor of free trade. For all the theory's simplicity, it is one of our profession's most significant achievements. However, in their zeal to promote the virtues of trade, the most ardent proponents are peddling a cartoon version of the argument, vastly overstating the effectiveness of economic openness as a tool for fostering development. Such claims only endanger broad public acceptance of the real article because they unleash unrealistic expectations about the benefits of free trade. Neither economic theory nor empirical evidence guarantees that deep trade liberalization will deliver higher economic growth. Economic openness and all its accouterments do not deserve the priority they typically receive in the development strategies pushed by leading multilateral organizations.

Countries that have achieved long-term economic growth have usually combined the opportunities offered by world markets with a growth strategy that mobilizes the capabilities of domestic institutions and investors. Designing such a growth strategy is both harder and easier than implementing typical integration policies. It is harder because the binding constraints on growth are usually country specific and do not respond well to standardized recipes. But it is easier because once those constraints are targeted, relatively simple policy changes can yield enormous economic payoffs and start a virtuous cycle of growth and additional reform.

Unorthodox innovations that depart from the integration rule book are typically part and parcel of such strategies. Public enterprises during the Meiji restoration in Japan; township and village enterprises in China; an export processing zone in Mauritius; generous tax incentives for priority investments in Taiwan; extensive credit subsidies in South Korea; infant-industry protection in Brazil during the 1960s and 1970s—these are some of the innovations that have been instrumental in kick-starting investment and growth in the past. None came out of a Washington economist's tool kit.

Few of these experiments have worked as well when transplanted to other settings, only underscoring the decisive importance of local conditions. To be effective, development strategies need to be tailored to prevailing domestic institutional strengths. There is simply no alternative to a homegrown business plan. Policymakers who look to Washington and financial markets for the answers are condemning themselves to mimicking the conventional wisdom du jour, and to eventual disillusionment.

SINKING GLOBALIZATION

Niall Ferguson

In contrast to those observers who see globalization as a largely unrelenting force to which we must all adapt, Ferguson suggests that globalization could be reversed. As you read his piece, ask yourself:

- What are the lessons of the early twentieth-century experience with globalization?
- What are the factors that he suggests might "sink globalization" today?
- To what extent do the 2008 global financial crisis and its aftermath provide support for Ferguson's analysis?

TORPEDOED

Ninety years ago this May, the German submarine U-20 sank the Cunard liner Lusitania off the southern coast of Ireland. Nearly 1,200 people, including 128 Americans, lost their lives. Usually remembered for the damage it did to the image of imperial Germany in the United States, the sinking of the Lusitania also symbolized the end of the first age of globalization.

From around 1870 until World War I, the world economy thrived in ways that look familiar today. The mobility of commodities, capital, and labor reached record levels; the sea-lanes and telegraphs across the Atlantic had never been busier, as capital and migrants traveled west and raw materials and manufactures traveled east. In relation to output, exports of both merchandise and capital reached volumes not seen again until the 1980s. Total emigration from Europe between 1880 and 1910 was in excess of 25 million. People spoke euphorically of "the annihilation of distance."

Then, between 1914 and 1918, a horrendous war stopped all of this, sinking globalization. Nearly 13 million tons of shipping were sent to the bottom of the ocean by German submarine attacks. International trade, investment, and migration all collapsed. Moreover, the attempt to resuscitate the world economy after the war's end failed. The global economy effectively disintegrated with the onset of the Great Depression and, after that, with an even bigger world war, in which astonishingly high proportions of production went toward perpetrating destruction.

It may seem excessively pessimistic to worry that this scenario could somehow repeat itself—that our age of globalization could collapse just as our grandparents' did. But it is worth bearing in mind that, despite numerous warnings issued in the early twentieth century about the catastrophic consequences of a war among the European great powers, many people—not least investors, a generally well-informed class—were taken completely by surprise by the outbreak of World War I. The possibility is as real today as it was in 1915 that globalization, like the Lusitania, could be sunk.

BACK TO THE FUTURE

The last age of globalization resembled the current one in numerous ways. It was characterized by relatively free trade, limited restrictions on

Niall Ferguson, "Sinking Globalization." First published in *Foreign Affairs,* 84:2, March/April 2005.

migration, and hardly any regulation of capital flows. Inflation was low. A wave of technological innovation was revolutionizing the communications and energy sectors; the world first discovered the joys of the telephone, the radio, the internal combustion engine, and paved roads. The U.S. economy was the biggest in the world, and the development of its massive internal market had become the principal source of business innovation. China was opening up, raising all kinds of expectations in the West, and Russia was growing rapidly.

World War I wrecked all of this. Global markets were disrupted and disconnected, first by economic warfare, then by postwar protectionism. Prices went haywire: a number of major economies (Germany's among them) suffered from both hyperinflation and steep deflation in the space of a decade. The technological advances of the 1900s petered out: innovation hit a plateau, and stagnating consumption discouraged the development of even existing technologies such as the automobile. After faltering during the war, overheating in the 1920s, and languishing throughout the 1930s in the doldrums of depression, the U.S. economy ceased to be the most dynamic in the world. China succumbed to civil war and foreign invasion, defaulting on its debts and disappointing optimists in the West. Russia suffered revolution, civil war, tyranny, and foreign invasion. Both these giants responded to the crisis by donning the constricting armor of state socialism. They were not alone. By the end of the 1940s, most states in the world, including those that retained political freedoms, had imposed restrictions on trade, migration, and investment as a matter of course. Some achieved autarky, the ideal of a deglobalized society. Consciously or unconsciously, all governments applied in peacetime the economic restrictions that had first been imposed between 1914 and 1918.

The end of globalization after 1914 was not unforeseeable. There was no shortage of voices prophesying Armageddon in the prewar decades. Many popular writers earned a living by predicting a cataclysmic European war. Solemn Marxists had long foretold the collapse of capitalism and imperialism. And Social Darwinists had looked forward eagerly to a conflagration that would weed out the weak and fortify the strong.

Yet most investors were completely caught off guard when the crisis came. Not until the last week of July 1914 was there a desperate dash for liquidity; it happened so suddenly and on such a large scale that the world's major stock markets, New York's included, closed down for the rest of the year. As The Economist put it at the time, investors and financial institutions "saw in a flash the meaning of war." The Dow Jones Industrial Average fell by about 25 percent between January 1910 and December 1913 and remained flat through the first half of 1914. European bond markets, which had held up throughout the diplomatic crises of the 1900s, crashed only at the 11th hour, as the lights went out all over Europe.

Some economic historians detect the origins of the deglobalization that followed World War I in the prewar decades. They point, variously, to rising tariffs and restrictions on migration, a slight uptick in inflation starting around 1896, and the chronic vulnerability of the U.S. economy to banking crises. To this list, it might be added that the risk of further Russian and Chinese revolutions should have been fairly apparent after those of 1905 and 1911, respectively.

The trouble is that none of these problems can be said to have caused the great conflagration that was World War I. To be sure, the prewar world was marked by all kinds of economic rivalries—not least between British and German manufacturers—but these did not suffice to cause a disaster. On the contrary, businessmen on both sides agreed that a major war would be an economic calamity. The point seemed so obvious that war came to be seen by some optimistic commentators as all but impossible—a "great illusion," in the famous phrase of the author Norman Angell. Even when the war broke out, many people optimistically clung to the illusion that it would soon be over. Economist John Maynard Keynes said that it "could not last more than a year."

With the benefit of hindsight, however, five factors can be seen to have precipitated the global explosion of 1914–18. The first cause was imperial overstretch. By 1914, the British Empire was showing signs of being a "weary Titan," in the words of the poet Matthew Arnold. It lacked the will to build up an army capable of deterring Germany from staging a rival bid for European hegemony (if not world power). As the world's policeman, distracted by old and new commitments in Asia and Africa, the United Kingdom's beat had simply become too big.

Great-power rivalry was another principal cause of the catastrophe. The problem was not so much Anglo-German rivalry at sea as it was Russo-German rivalry on land. Fear of a Russian arms buildup convinced the German general staff to fight in 1914 rather than risk waiting any longer.

The third fatal factor was an unstable alliance system. Alliances existed in abundance, but they were shaky. The Germans did not trust the Austrians to stand by them in a crisis, and the Russians worried that the French might lose their nerve. The United Kingdom's actions were impossible to predict because its ententes with France and Russia made no explicit provisions for the eventuality of war in Europe. The associated insecurities encouraged risk-taking diplomacy. In 1908, for example, Austria-Hungary

brusquely annexed Bosnia. Three years later, the German government sent the gunboat Panther to Agadir to challenge French claims to predominance in Morocco.

The presence of a rogue regime sponsoring terror was a fourth source of instability. The chain of events leading to war, as every schoolchild used to know, began with the assassination of the Austrian Archduke Franz Ferdinand in Sarajevo by a Bosnian Serb, Gavrilo Princip. There were shady links between the assassin's organization and the Serbian government, which had itself come to power not long before in a bloody palace coup.

Finally, the rise of a revolutionary terrorist organization hostile to capitalism turned an international crisis into a backlash against the global free market. The Bolsheviks, who emerged from the 1903 split in the Russian Social Democratic Party, had already established their credentials as a fanatical organization committed to using violence to bring about world revolution. By straining the tsarist system to the breaking point, the war gave Lenin and his confederates their opportunity. They seized it and used the most ruthless terrorist tactics to win the ensuing civil war.

PARALLEL UNIVERSE

There are obvious economic parallels between the first age of globalization and the current one. Today, as in the period before 1914, protectionism periodically challenges the free-trade orthodoxy. By the standards of the pre-1914 United Kingdom, in fact, the major economies are already shamelessly protectionist when it comes to agriculture. Then, the United Kingdom imposed no tariffs on imported agricultural goods, whereas now the United States, the European Union, and Japan all use tariffs and subsidies to protect their farmers from foreign competition.

Today, no one can be sure how stable the international monetary system is, but one thing is certain: it is no more stable than the system that preceded World War I. Although gold is no longer the basis of the monetary system, there are pegged exchange rates, just as there were in 1914. In Europe, there is a monetary union—essentially a deutsche mark zone. In eastern Asia, there is a dollar standard. Both systems, however, are based on fiat currencies. Unlike before 1914, the core central banks in New York and Frankfurt determine the volume of currency produced, and they do so on the basis of an opaque mixture of rules and discretion.

Today, technological innovation shows no sign of slackening. From nanocomputers the size of a pinhead to scramjets that can cross the Atlantic in an hour, there seems no limit to human ingenuity, given sufficient funding of research and development. That is the good news. The bad news is that now technology also helps the enemies of globalization. Before 1914, terrorists had to pursue their bloody trade with Browning revolvers and primitive bombs. These days, an entire city could be obliterated with a single nuclear device.

Today, as before 1914, the U.S. economy is the world's biggest, but it is now much more important as a market for the rest of the world than it was then. Although the United States may enjoy great influence as the "consumer of first resort," this role depends on the willingness of foreigners to fund a widening current account deficit. A rising proportion of Americans may consider themselves to have been "saved" in the Evangelical sense, but they are less good at saving in the economic sense. The personal savings rate among Americans stood at just 0.2 percent of disposable personal income in September 2004, compared with 7.7 percent less than 15 years ago. Whether to finance domestic investment (in the late 1990s) or government borrowing (after 2000), the United States has come to rely increasingly on foreign lending. As the current account deficit has widened (it is now approaching 6 percent of GDP), U.S. net overseas liabilities have risen steeply to around 25 percent of GDP. Half of the publicly held federal debt is now in foreign hands; at the end of August 2004, the combined U.S. Treasury holdings of China, Hong Kong, Japan, Singapore, South Korea, and Taiwan were $1.1 trillion, up by 22 percent from the end of 2003. A large proportion of this increase is a result of immense purchases by eastern Asian monetary authorities, designed to prevent their currencies from appreciating relative to the dollar.

This deficit is the biggest difference between globalization past and globalization present. A hundred years ago, the global hegemon—the United Kingdom—was a net exporter of capital, channeling a high proportion of its savings overseas to finance the construction of infrastructure such as railways and ports in the Americas, Asia, Australasia, and Africa. Today, its successor as an Anglophone empire plays the diametrically opposite role—as the world's debtor rather than the world's creditor, absorbing around three-quarters of the rest of the world's surplus savings.

Does this departure matter? Some claim it does not—that it just reflects the rest of the world's desire to have a piece of the U.S. economic action, whether as owners of low-risk securities or sellers of underpriced exports. This is how Harvard economist Richard Cooper sees it. Assuming that the U.S. economy has a trend rate of growth of 5 percent a year, he argues that a sustained current account deficit of $500 billion per year would translate into external liabilities of 46 percent of GDP after 15 years, but that then U.S. foreign debt would "decline indefinitely."

Well, maybe. But what if those assumptions are wrong? According to the HSBC Group, the current account deficit could reach 8 percent of GDP by the end of the decade. That could push the United States' net external liabilities as high as 90 percent of GDP. When the United Kingdom accumulated net foreign debts of less than half this percentage, it was fighting World War II. In the war's aftermath, the resulting "sterling balances" owned by the rest of the world were one of the reasons the pound declined and lost its reserve currency status.

A sharp depreciation of the dollar relative to Asian currencies might not worry the majority of Americans, whose liabilities are all dollar-denominated. But its effect on Asia would be profound. Asian holders of dollar assets would suffer heavy capital losses in terms of their own currencies, and Asian exporters would lose some of their competitive advantage in the U.S. market. According to Michael Mussa of the Institute for International Economics, lowering the U.S. deficit to 2 percent of GDP over the next few years would require a further 20 percent decline in the dollar. The economists Maurice Obstfeld and Kenneth Rogoff estimate that the fall could be as much as 40 percent. And the University of California at Berkeley's Brad de Long has pointed out that,

> [i]f the private market—which knows that with high probability the dollar is going down someday—decides that that someday has come and that the dollar is going down *now,* then all the Asian central banks in the world cannot stop it [emphasis in original].

That day may be fast approaching. In the words of Federal Reserve Board Chairman Alan Greenspan last November, "the desire of investors to add dollar claims to their portfolios" must have a limit; a "continued financing even of today's current account deficits . . . doubtless will, at some future point, increase shares of dollar claims in investor portfolios to levels that imply an unacceptable amount of concentration risk."

The domestic effects of a dollar crash would be felt most sharply by the growing numbers of Americans with large mortgage debts who would suddenly face a rise in interest rates. The growth in the share of variable-rate mortgages in the volume of total household debt is seen by some as a sign that the U.S. mortgage market is growing more sophisticated. But it also increases the sensitivity of many American families to rises in the rates. The federal government has a pretty large variable-rate debt, too, given the very short maturities of a large proportion of federal bonds and notes. That fact means that higher rates could quickly affect the deficit itself, creating a dangerous feedback loop. And, of course, higher rates would be likely to lower growth and hence reduce tax revenues. In short, today's international fiat-money system is significantly, and dangerously, crisis-prone.

Another cause for concern is the fragility of China's financial system. This Asian miracle is unlikely to avoid the kind of crisis that marked the Asian miracles of the past. To get a sense of the dangers, consider China's Soviet-style domestic banking system and its puny domestic stock market: how can such rapid growth in manufacturing possibly be sustained with such inadequate financial institutions?

Pre-1914 globalization was remarkably susceptible to the international transmission of crises—what economists call "contagion." So is globalization nowadays. As Andrew Large of the Bank of England pointed out last November, the "search for yield" in an environment of low interest rates is encouraging investors, banks, and hedge funds to converge on similar trading strategies, raising "the prospect of one-way markets developing and market liquidity evaporating in response to a shock."

GHOSTS FROM THE PAST

As the economic parallels with 1914 suggest, today's globalization shows at least some signs of reversibility. The risks increase when one considers the present political situation, which has the same five flaws as the pre-1914 international order: imperial overstretch, great-power rivalry, an unstable alliance system, rogue regimes sponsoring terror, and the rise of a revolutionary terrorist organization hostile to capitalism.

The United States—an empire in all but name—is manifestly overstretched. Not only is its current account deficit large and growing larger, but the fiscal deficit that lurks behind it also is set to surge as the baby boomers retire and start to claim Social Security and Medicare benefits. The Congressional Budget Office (CBO) projects that over the next four decades, Social Security, Medicaid, and Medicare spending will rise to consume at least an additional 12 percent of GDP per year. The CBO also estimates that the transition costs of President George W. Bush's planned Social Security reform, if enacted, could create a budget shortfall of up to two percent of GDP a year for ten years. Add that to the fiscal consequences of making the president's first-term tax cuts permanent, and it becomes hard to imagine how the country will manage to stem the rising tide of red ink.

The U.S. empire also suffers from a personnel deficit: 500,000 troops is the maximum number that Washington can deploy overseas, and this number is simply not sufficient to win all the small wars the United States currently has (or might have) to wage. Of the 137,000 American troops currently in Iraq, 43 percent are drawn from the reserves or the National Guard. Even just to maintain the U.S. presence in Iraq, the Army is extending tours of duty and retaining personnel due to be discharged. Such measures seem certain to hurt re-enlistment rates.

Above all, the U.S. empire suffers from an attention deficit. Iraq is not a very big war. As one Marine told his parents in a letter home,

> compared to the wars of the past, this is nothing. We're not standing on line in the open—facing German machine guns like the Marines at Belleau Wood or trying to wade ashore in chest-deep water at Tarawa. We're not facing hordes of screaming men at the frozen Chosun Reservoir in Korea or the clever ambushes of Vietcong. We deal with potshots and I.E.D.'s [improvised explosive devices].

He was right; the Iraq war is more like the colonial warfare the British waged 100 years ago. It is dangerous—the author of that letter was killed three weeks after he wrote it—but it is not Vietnam or Korea, much less the Pacific theater in World War II. Yet the Iraq war has become very unpopular very quickly, after relatively few casualties. According to several polls, fewer than half of American voters now support it. And virtually no one seems to want to face the fact that the U.S. presence in Iraq—and the low-intensity conflict that goes with imperial policing—may have to endure for ten years or more if that country is to stand any chance of economic and political stabilization.

Then there is the second problem: great-power rivalry. It is true that the Chinese have no obvious incentive to pick a fight with the United States. But China's ambitions with respect to Taiwan are not about to disappear just because Beijing owns a stack of U.S. Treasury bonds. On the contrary, in the event of an economic crisis, China might be sorely tempted to play the nationalist card by threatening to take over its errant province. Would the United States really be willing to fight China over Taiwan, as it has pledged in the past to do? And what would happen if the Chinese authorities flexed their new financial muscles by dumping U.S. bonds on the world market? To the historian, Taiwan looks somewhat like the Belgium of old: a seemingly inconsequential country over which empires end up fighting to the death. And one should not forget Asia's most dangerous rogue regime, North Korea, which is a little like pre-1914 Serbia with nuclear weapons.

As for Europe, one must not underestimate the extent to which the recent diplomatic "widening of the Atlantic" reflects profound changes in Europe, rather than an alteration in U.S. foreign policy. The combination of economic sclerosis and social senescence means that Europe is bound to stagnate, if not decline. Meanwhile, Muslim immigration and the prospect of Turkey's accession to the European Union are changing the very character of Europe. And the division between Americans and Europeans on Middle Eastern questions is only going to get wider—for example, if the United States dismisses the European attempt to contain Iran's nuclear ambitions by diplomatic means and presses instead for military countermeasures.

These rivalries are one reason the world today also has an unstable alliance system (problem number three). NATO's purpose is no longer clear. Is it just an irrelevant club for the winners of the Cold War, which former Soviet satellites are encouraged to join for primarily symbolic reasons? Have divisions over Iraq rendered it obsolete? To say the least, "coalitions of the willing" are a poor substitute.

None of these problems would necessarily be fatal were it not for the fourth and fifth parallels between 1914 and today: the existence of rogue regimes sponsoring terror—Iran and Syria top the list—and of revolutionary terrorist organizations. It is a big mistake to think of al Qaeda as "Islamo-fascist" (as the journalist Christopher Hitchens and many others called the group after the September 11, 2001, attacks). Al Qaeda's members are much more like "Islamo-Bolshevists," committed to revolution and a reordering of the world along anticapitalist lines.

Like the Bolsheviks in 1914, these Islamist extremists are part of an underground sect, struggling to land more than the occasional big punch on the enemy. But what if they were to get control of a wealthy state, the way Lenin, Trotsky, and company did in 1917? How would the world look if there were an October Revolution in Saudi Arabia? True, some recent survey data suggest that ordinary Saudis are relatively moderate people by the standards of the Arab world. And high oil prices mean more shopping and fewer disgruntled youths. On the other hand, after what happened in Tehran in 1979, no one can rule out a second Islamist revolution. The Saudi royal family does not look like the kind of regime that will still be in business ten years from now. The only monarchies that survive in modern times are those that give power away.

But is Osama bin Laden really a modern-day Lenin? The comparison is less far-fetched than it seems ("Hereditary Nobleman Vladimir Ulyanov" also came from a wealthy family). In a proclamation to the world before the recent U.S. presidential election, bin Laden declared that his "policy [was] bleeding America to the point of bankruptcy." As he explained, "al Qaeda spent $500,000 on the [September 11 attacks], while America, in the incident and its aftermath, lost—according to the lowest estimate—more than $500 billion. Meaning that every dollar of al Qaeda defeated a million dollars, by the permission of Allah." Bin Laden went on to talk about the U.S. "economic deficit . . . estimated to total more than a trillion dollars" and to make a somewhat uncharacteristic joke:

> [T]hose who say that al Qaeda has won against the administration in the White House or that the administration has lost in this war have not been precise, because when one scrutinizes the results, one cannot say that al Qaeda is the sole factor in achieving those spectacular gains. Rather, the policy of the White House that demands the opening of war fronts to keep busy their various corporations—whether they be working in the field of arms or oil or reconstruction—has helped al Qaeda to achieve these enormous results.

Two things are noteworthy about bin Laden's quip: one, the classically Marxist assertion that the war in Iraq was motivated by capitalist economic interests; and two, the rather shrewd—and unfortunately accurate—argument that bin Laden has been getting help in "bleeding America to the point of bankruptcy" from the Bush administration's fiscal policy.

APOCALYPSE WHEN?

A doomsday scenario is plausible. But is it probable? The difficult thing—indeed the nearly impossible thing—is to predict a cataclysm. Doing so was the challenge investors faced in the first age of globalization. They knew there could be a world war. They knew such a war would have devastating financial consequences (although few anticipated how destructive it would be). But they had no way of knowing when exactly it would happen.

The same problem exists today. We all know that another, bigger September 11 is quite likely; it is, indeed, bin Laden's stated objective. We all know—or should know—that a crisis over Taiwan would send huge shockwaves through the international system; it could even lead to a great-power war. We all know that revolutionary regime change in Saudi Arabia would shake the world even more than the 1917 Bolshevik coup in Russia. We all know that the detonation of a nuclear device in London would dwarf the assassination of Archduke Ferdinand as an act of terrorism.

But what exactly can we do about such contingencies, if, as with the Asian tsunami, we cannot say even approximately when they might occur? The opportunity cost of liquidating our portfolios and inhabiting a subterranean bunker looks too high, even if Armageddon could come tomorrow. In that sense, we seem no better prepared for the worst-case scenario than were the beneficiaries of the last age of globalization, 90 years ago. Like the passengers who boarded the Lusitania, all we know is that we may conceivably sink. Still we sail.

CHAPTER 8

TRANSNATIONAL ACTORS AND ISSUES
The State System Under Stress

For realists, the primary responsibility of any state is to provide for the national security of its country and people from threats posed by the military capabilities of other sovereign states. In the early years of the twenty-first century, however, many critics of realism have pointed to a range of global challenges that: (a) do not emanate from foreign armies and (b) cannot be addressed by single states using traditional military instruments of power. Climate change, global disease, immigration flows, drug smuggling, and resource depletion are among the global challenges that many suggest are not only the greatest threats to human security, but also are inherently unsolvable by sovereign states acting on their own. If the sovereign state, moreover, can no longer provide for security from the greatest threats facing humankind, then it follows for some that the utility of the state and the entire Westphalian concept of the state system is in question.

The readings begin with an influential article by Jessica Mathews in which she argues that there is an inherent tension between "the fixed geography of states and the nonterritorial nature of today's problems and solutions" that is leading to a decline in state power. Mathews thus directly challenges the traditional realist understanding of how the world works. In contrast, the reading by Stephen Krasner is a realist reassertion and defense of the idea of state sovereignty. In Krasner's view, the demise of state sovereignty has been exaggerated.

The Mathews and Krasner articles are followed by a closer examination of two contemporary issues that in different ways help shed light on the larger debate over whether these global challenges undermine the system of state sovereignty. The David Victor article considers whether resource scarcity and climate change will provoke resource wars in which sovereign states employ military power to solve their resource and environmental challenges at the expense of other states. The James Fallows piece examines the Chinese state's efforts to control the flow of information over the Internet.

Your goals in reading the selections in this chapter should be both to learn more about the specific issues of resource scarcity and Chinese management of the Internet and to use those two issues as case studies that help you reflect on the merits of the larger theoretical arguments presented by Mathews and Krasner. To what extent, in other words, are these issues capable of being successfully addressed within the contours of the traditional state system? To what extent are they straining that state system and traditional realist notions of state sovereignty?

POWER SHIFT

Jessica T. Mathews

In this article, Jessica Mathews questions the ability of states and the state system to respond adequately to the global challenges facing the world today. She anticipates a post-Westphalian world in which states, though continuing to exist, will have to share more of their power with other actors. As you read this article, ask yourself:

- What is the main engine of change that she sees redistributing power in world politics?
- What nonstate actors are emerging as challengers to state power?
- Does she see this "power shift" as a positive or negative trend?

THE RISE OF GLOBAL CIVIL SOCIETY

The end of the Cold War has brought no mere adjustment among states but a novel redistribution of power among states, markets, and civil society. National governments are not simply losing autonomy in a globalizing economy. They are sharing powers—including political, social, and security roles at the core of sovereignty—with businesses, with international organizations, and with a multitude of citizens groups, known as nongovernmental organizations (NGOs). The steady concentration of power in the hands of states that began in 1648 with the Peace of Westphalia is over, at least for a while.[1]

The absolutes of the Westphalian system—territorially fixed states where everything of value lies within some state's borders; a single, secular authority governing each territory and representing it outside its borders; and no authority above states—are all dissolving. Increasingly, resources and threats that matter, including money, information, pollution, and popular culture, circulate and shape lives and economies with little regard for political boundaries. International standards of conduct are gradually beginning to override claims of national or regional singularity. Even

the most powerful states find the marketplace and international public opinion compelling them more often to follow a particular course.

The state's central task of assuring security is the least affected, but still not exempt. War will not disappear, but with the shrinkage of U.S. and Russian nuclear arsenals, the transformation of the Nuclear Nonproliferation Treaty into a permanent covenant in 1995, agreement on the long-sought Comprehensive Test Ban treaty in 1996, and the likely entry into force of the Chemical Weapons Convention in 1997, the security threat to states from other states is on a downward course. Nontraditional threats, however, are rising—terrorism, organized crime, drug trafficking, ethnic conflict, and the combination of rapid population growth, environmental decline, and poverty that breeds economic stagnation, political instability, and, sometimes, state collapse. . . .

These trends have fed a growing sense that individuals' security may not in fact reliably derive from their nation's security. A competing notion of "human security" is creeping around the edges of official thinking, suggesting that security be viewed as emerging from the conditions of daily life—food, shelter, employment,

Jessica T. Mathews, "Power Shift." Reprinted by permission of *Foreign Affairs* 76:1, January/February 1997. Copyright 1997 by the Council on Foreign Relations, Inc. www.ForeignAffairs.org.

health, public safety—rather than flowing downward from a country's foreign relations and military strength.

The most powerful engine of change in the relative decline of states and the rise of nonstate actors is the computer and telecommunications revolution, whose deep political and social consequences have been almost completely ignored. Widely accessible and affordable technology has broken governments' monopoly on the collection and management of large amounts of information and deprived governments of the deference they enjoyed because of it. In every sphere of activity, instantaneous access to information and the ability to put it to use multiplies the number of players who matter and reduces the number who command great authority. The effect on the loudest voice—which has been government's—has been the greatest.

By drastically reducing the importance of proximity, the new technologies change people's perceptions of community. Fax machines, satellite hookups, and the Internet connect people across borders with exponentially growing ease while separating them from natural and historical associations within nations. In this sense a powerful globalizing force, they can also have the opposite effect, amplifying political and social fragmentation by enabling more and more identities and interests scattered around the globe to coalesce and thrive.

These technologies have the potential to divide society along new lines, separating ordinary people from elites with the wealth and education to command technology's power. Those elites are not only the rich but also citizens groups with transnational interests and identities that frequently have more in common with counterparts in other countries, whether industrialized or developing, than with countrymen.

Above all, the information technologies disrupt hierarchies, spreading power among more people and groups. In drastically lowering the costs of communication, consultation, and coordination, they favor decentralized networks over other modes of organization. In a network, individuals or groups link for joint action without building a physical or formal institutional presence. Networks have no person at the top and no center. Instead, they have multiple nodes where collections of individuals or groups interact for different purposes. Businesses, citizens organizations, ethnic groups, and crime cartels have all readily adopted the network model. Governments, on the other hand, are quintessential hierarchies, wedded to an organizational form incompatible with all that the new technologies make possible. . . .

DIAL LOCALLY, ACT GLOBALLY

No one knows how many NGOs there are or how fast the tally is growing. Published figures are badly misleading. One widely cited estimate claims there are 35,000 NGOs in the developing countries; another points to 12,000 irrigation cooperatives in South Asia alone. In fact, it is impossible to measure a swiftly growing universe that includes neighborhood, professional, service, and advocacy groups, both secular and church-based, promoting every conceivable cause and funded by donations, fees, foundations, governments, international organizations, or the sale of products and services. The true number is certainly in the millions, from the tiniest village association to influential but modestly funded international groups like Amnesty International to larger global activist organizations like Greenpeace and giant service providers like CARE, which has an annual budget of nearly $400 million.

Except in China, Japan, the Middle East, and a few other places where culture or authoritarian governments severely limit civil society, NGOs' role and influence have exploded in the last half-decade. Their financial resources and—often more important—their expertise, approximate and sometimes exceed those of smaller governments and of international organizations. "We have less money and fewer resources than Amnesty International, and we are the arm of the U.N. for human rights," noted Ibrahima Fall, head of the U.N. Centre for Human Rights, in 1993. "This is clearly ridiculous." Today NGOs deliver more official development assistance than the entire U.N. system (excluding the World Bank and the International Monetary Fund). In many countries they are delivering the services—in urban and rural community development, education, and health care—that faltering governments can no longer manage.

The range of these groups' work is almost as broad as their interests. They breed new ideas; advocate, protest, and mobilize public support; do legal, scientific, technical, and policy analysis; provide services; shape, implement, monitor, and enforce national and international commitments; and change institutions and norms.

Increasingly, NGOs are able to push around even the largest governments. When the United States and Mexico set out to reach a trade agreement, the two governments planned on the usual narrowly defined negotiations behind closed doors. But NGOs had a very different vision. Groups from Canada, the United States, and Mexico wanted to see provisions in the North American Free Trade Agreement on health and safety, transboundary pollution, consumer protection, immigration, labor mobility, child labor, sustainable agriculture, social charters, and debt relief. Coalitions of NGOs formed in each country and across both borders. The opposition they generated in early 1991 endangered congressional approval of the crucial "fast track" negotiating authority for the U.S. government. After months of resistance, the Bush administration capitulated, opening the agreement to environmental and labor concerns. Although progress in other trade venues will be slow, the tightly closed world of trade negotiations has been changed forever.

Technology is fundamental to NGOs' new clout. The nonprofit Association for Progressive Communications provides 50,000 NGOs in 133 countries access to the tens of millions of Internet users for the price of a local call. The dramatically lower costs of international communication have altered NGOs' goals and changed international outcomes. Within hours of the first gunshots of the Chiapas rebellion in southern Mexico in January 1994, for example, the Internet swarmed with messages from human rights activists. The worldwide media attention they and their groups focused on Chiapas, along with the influx of rights activists to the area, sharply limited the Mexican government's response. What in other times would have been a bloody insurgency turned out to be a largely nonviolent conflict. "The shots lasted ten days," José Angel Gurría, Mexico's foreign minister, later remarked, "and ever since, the war has been . . . a war on the Internet."

NGOs' easy reach behind other states' borders forces governments to consider domestic public opinion in countries with which they are dealing, even on matters that governments have traditionally handled strictly between themselves. At the same time, cross-border NGO networks offer citizens groups unprecedented channels of influence. Women's and human rights groups in many developing countries have linked up with more experienced, better funded, and more powerful groups in Europe and the United States. The latter work the global media and lobby their own governments to pressure leaders in developing countries, creating a circle of influence that is accelerating change in many parts of the world.

OUT OF THE HALLWAY, AROUND THE TABLE

In international organizations, as with governments at home, NGOs were once largely relegated to the hallways. Even when they were able to shape governments' agendas, as the Helsinki Watch human rights groups did in the Conference on Security and Cooperation in Europe in the 1980s, their influence was largely determined by how receptive their own government's delegation happened to be. Their only option was to work through governments.

All that changed with the negotiation of the global climate treaty, culminating at the Earth Summit in Rio de Janeiro in 1992. With the broader independent base of public support that environmental groups command, NGOs set the original goal of negotiating an agreement to control greenhouse gases long before governments were ready to do so, proposed most of its structure and content, and lobbied and mobilized public pressure to force through a pact that virtually no one else thought possible when the talks began.

More members of NGOs served on government delegations than ever before, and they penetrated deeply into official decision-making. They were allowed to attend the small working group meetings where the real decisions in international negotiations are made. The tiny nation of Vanuatu turned its delegation over to an NGO with expertise in international law (a group based in London and funded by an American foundation), thereby making itself and the other sea-level island states major players in the fight to control global warming. *ECO*, an NGO-published daily newspaper, was negotiators' best source of information on the progress of the official talks and became the forum where governments tested ideas for breaking deadlocks.

Whether from developing or developed countries, NGOs were tightly organized in a global and half a dozen regional Climate Action Networks, which were able to bridge North-South differences among governments that many had expected would prevent an agreement. United in their passionate pursuit of a treaty, NGOs would fight out contentious issues among themselves, then take an agreed position to their respective delegations. When they could not agree, NGOs served as invaluable back channels, letting both sides know where the other's problems lay or where a compromise might be found. . . .

The influence of NGOs . . . has provoked a backlash among some governments. A handful of authoritarian regimes, most notably China, led the charge, but many others share their unease about the role NGOs are assuming. Nevertheless, NGOs have worked their way into the heart of international negotiations and into the day-to-day operations of international organizations, bringing new priorities, demands for procedures that give a voice to groups outside government, and new standards of accountability.

ONE WORLD BUSINESS

The multinational corporations of the 1960s were virtually all American, and prided themselves on their insularity. Foreigners might run subsidiaries, but they were never partners. A foreign posting was a setback for a rising executive.

Today, a global marketplace is developing for retail sales as well as manufacturing. Law, advertising, business consulting, and financial and other services are also marketed internationally. Firms of all nationalities attempt to look and act like locals wherever they operate. Foreign language skills and lengthy experience abroad are an asset, and increasingly a requirement, for top management. Sometimes corporate headquarters are not even in a company's home country.

Amid shifting alliances and joint ventures, made possible by computers and advanced communications, nationalities blur. Offshore banking encourages widespread evasion of national taxes. Whereas the fear in the 1970s was that multinationals would become an arm of government, the concern now is that they are disconnecting from their home countries' national interests, moving jobs, evading taxes, and eroding economic sovereignty in the process.

The even more rapid globalization of financial markets has left governments far behind. Where governments once set foreign exchange rates, private currency traders, accountable only to their bottom line, now trade $1.3 trillion a day, 100 times the volume of world trade. The amount exceeds the total foreign exchange reserves of all governments, and is more than even an alliance of strong states can buck. . . .

Again, technology has been a driving force, shifting financial clout from states to the market with its offer of unprecedented speed in transactions—states cannot match market reaction times measured in seconds—and its dissemination of financial information to a broad range of players. States could choose whether they would belong to rule-based economic systems like the gold standard, but, as former Citicorp chairman Walter Wriston has pointed out, they cannot withdraw from the technology-based marketplace, unless they seek autarky and poverty.

More and more frequently today, governments have only the appearance of free choice when they set economic rules. Markets are setting de facto rules enforced by their own power. States can flout them, but the penalties are severe—loss of vital foreign capital, foreign technology, and domestic jobs. Even the most powerful economy must pay heed. The U.S. government could choose to rescue the Mexican peso in 1994, for example, but it had to do so on terms designed to satisfy the bond markets, not the countries doing the rescuing.

The forces shaping the legitimate global economy are also nourishing globally integrated crime—which U.N. officials peg at a staggering $750 billion a year, $400 billion to $500 billion of that in narcotics, according to U.S. Drug Enforcement Agency estimates. Huge increases in the volume of goods and people crossing borders and competitive pressures to speed the flow of trade by easing inspections and reducing paperwork make it easier to hide contraband. Deregulation and privatization of government-owned businesses, modern communications, rapidly shifting commercial alliances, and the emergence of global financial systems have all helped transform local drug operations into global enterprises. The largely unregulated multi-trillion-dollar pool of money in supranational cyberspace, accessible by computer 24 hours a day, eases the drug trade's toughest problem: transforming huge sums of hot cash into investments in legitimate business.

Globalized crime is a security threat that neither police nor the military—the state's traditional responses—can meet. Controlling it will require states to pool their efforts and to establish unprecedented cooperation with the private sector, thereby compromising two cherished sovereign roles. If states fail, if criminal groups can continue to take advantage of porous borders and transnational financial spaces while governments are limited to acting within their own territory, crime will have the winning edge.

BORN-AGAIN INSTITUTIONS

Until recently, international organizations were institutions of, by, and for nation-states. Now they are building constituencies of their own and, through NGOs, establishing direct connections to the peoples of the world. The shift is infusing them with new life and influence, but it is also creating tensions.

States feel they need more capable international organizations to deal with a lengthening list of transnational challenges, but at the same time fear competitors. Thus they vote for new forms of international intervention while reasserting sovereignty's first principle: no interference in the domestic affairs of states. They hand international organizations sweeping new responsibilities and then rein them in with circumscribed mandates or inadequate funding. With states ambivalent about intervention, a host of new problems demanding attention, and NGOs bursting with energy, ideas, and calls for a larger role, international organizations are lurching toward an unpredictable, but certainly different, future.

International organizations are still coming to terms with unprecedented growth in the volume of international problem-solving. Between 1972 and 1992 the number of environmental treaties rocketed from a few dozen to more than 900. While collaboration in other fields is not growing at quite that rate, treaties, regimes, and intergovernmental institutions dealing with human rights, trade, narcotics, corruption, crime, refugees, antiterrorism measures, arms control, and democracy are multiplying. "Soft law" in the form of guidelines, recommended practices, nonbinding resolutions, and the like is also rapidly expanding. Behind each new agreement are scientists and lawyers who worked on it, diplomats who negotiated it, and NGOs that back it, most of them committed for the long haul. The new constituency also includes a burgeoning, influential class of international civil servants responsible for implementing, monitoring, and enforcing this enormous new body of law.

At the same time, governments, while ambivalent about the international community mixing in states' domestic affairs, have driven some gaping holes in the wall that has separated the two. In the triumphant months after the Berlin Wall came down, international accords, particularly ones agreed on by what is now the Organization for Security and Cooperation in Europe and by the Organization of American States (OAS), drew explicit links between democracy, human rights, and international security, establishing new legal bases for international interventions. In 1991 the U.N. General Assembly declared itself in favor of humanitarian intervention without the request or consent of the state involved. A year later the Security Council took the unprecedented step of authorizing the use of force "on behalf of civilian populations" in Somalia. Suddenly an interest in citizens began to compete with, and occasionally override, the formerly unquestioned primacy of state interests.

Since 1990 the Security Council has declared a formal threat to international peace and security 61 times, after having done so only six times in the preceding 45 years. It is not that security has been abruptly and terribly threatened; rather, the change reflects the broadened scope of what the international community now feels it should poke its nose into. As with Haiti in 1992, many of the so-called Chapter VII resolutions authorizing forceful intervention concerned domestic situations that involved awful human suffering or offended international norms but posed little if any danger to international peace.

Almost as intrusive as a Chapter VII intervention, though always invited, election monitoring has also become a growth industry. The United Nations monitored no election in a member state during the Cold War, only in colonies. But beginning in 1990 it responded to a deluge of requests from governments that felt compelled to prove their legitimacy by the new standards. In Latin America, where countries most jealously guard their sovereignty, the OAS monitored 11 national elections in four years.

And monitoring is no longer the passive observation it was in earlier decades. Carried out by a close-knit mix of international organizations and NGOs, it involves a large foreign presence dispensing advice and recommending standards for voter registration, campaign law, campaign practices, and the training of clerks and judiciaries. Observers even carry out parallel vote counts that can block fraud but at the same time second-guess the integrity of national counts.

International financial institutions, too, have inserted themselves more into states' domestic affairs. During the 1980s the World Bank attached conditions to loans concerning recipient governments' policies on poverty, the environment, and even, occasionally, military spending, a once sacrosanct domain of national prerogative. In 1991 a statement of bank policy holding that "efficient and accountable public sector management" is crucial to economic growth provided the rationale for subjecting to international oversight everything from official corruption to government competence.

Beyond involving them in an array of domestic economic and social decisions, the new policies force the World Bank, the International Monetary Fund, and other international financial institutions to forge alliances with business, NGOs, and civil society if they are to achieve broad changes in target countries. In the process, they have opened themselves to the same demands they are making of their clients: broader public participation and greater openness in decision-making. As a result, yet another set of doors behind which only officials sat has been thrown open to the private sector and to civil society.

LEAPS OF IMAGINATION

After three and a half centuries, it requires a mental leap to think of world politics in any terms other than occasionally cooperating but generally competing states, each defined by its territory and representing all the people therein. Nor is it easy to imagine political entities that could compete with the emotional attachment of a shared landscape, national history, language, flag, and currency.

Yet history proves that there are alternatives other than tribal anarchy. Empires, both tightly and loosely ruled, achieved success and won allegiance. In the Middle Ages, emperors, kings, dukes, knights, popes, archbishops, guilds, and cities exercised overlapping secular power over the same territory in a system that looks much more like a modern, three-dimensional network than the clean-lined, hierarchical state order that replaced it. The question now is whether there are new geographic or functional entities that might grow up alongside the state, taking over some of its powers and emotional resonance.

The kernels of several such entities already exist. The European Union is the most obvious example. Neither a union of states nor an international organization, the EU leaves experts groping for inadequate descriptions like "post-sovereign system" or "unprecedented hybrid." It respects members' borders for some purposes, particularly in foreign and defense policy, but ignores them for others. The union's judiciary can override national law, and its Council of Ministers can overrule certain domestic executive decisions. In its thousands of councils, committees, and working groups, national ministers increasingly find themselves working with their counterparts from other countries to oppose colleagues in their own government; agriculture ministers, for example, ally against finance ministers. In this sense the union penetrates and to some extent weakens the internal bonds of its member states. Whether Frenchmen, Danes, and Greeks will ever think of themselves first as Europeans remains to be seen, but the EU has already come much further than most Americans realize.

Meanwhile, units below the national level are taking on formal international roles. Nearly all 50 American states have trade offices abroad, up from four in 1970, and all have official standing in the World Trade Organization (WTO). German *Länder* and British local governments have offices at EU headquarters in Brussels. France's Rhône-Alpes region, centered in Lyon, maintains what it calls "embassies" abroad on behalf of a regional economy that includes Geneva, Switzerland, and Turin, Italy.

Emerging political identities not linked to territory pose a more direct challenge to the geographically fixed state system. The WTO is struggling to find a method of handling environmental disputes in the global commons, outside all states' boundaries, that the General Agreement on Tariffs and Trade, drafted 50 years ago, simply never envisioned. Proposals have been floated for a Parliamentary Assembly in the United Nations, parallel to the General Assembly, to represent the people rather than the states of the world. Ideas are under discussion that would give ethnic nations political and legal status, so that the Kurds, for example, could be legally represented as a people in addition to being Turkish, Iranian, or Iraqi citizens.

Further in the future is a proposed Global Environmental Authority with independent regulatory powers. This is not as far-fetched as it sounds. The burden of participating in several hundred international environmental bodies is heavy for the richest governments and is becoming prohibitive for others. As the number of international agreements mounts, the pressure to streamline the system—in environmental protection as in other areas—will grow.

The realm of most rapid change is hybrid authorities that include state and nonstate bodies such as the International Telecommunications Union, the International Union for the Conservation of Nature, and hundreds more. In many of these, businesses or NGOs take on formerly public roles. The Geneva-based International Standards Organization, essentially a business NGO, sets widely observed standards on everything from products to internal corporate procedures. The International Securities Markets Association, another private regulator, oversees international trade in private securities markets—the world's second-largest capital market after domestic government bond markets. In another crossover, markets become government enforcers when they adopt treaty standards as the basis for market judgments. States and NGOs are collaborating ad hoc in large-scale humanitarian relief operations that involve both military and civilian forces. Other NGOs have taken on standing operational roles for international organizations in refugee work and development assistance. Almost unnoticed, hybrids like these, in which states are often the junior partners, are becoming a new international norm.

FOR BETTER OR WORSE?

A world that is more adaptable and in which power is more diffused could mean more peace, justice, and capacity to manage the burgeoning list of humankind's interconnected problems. At a time of accelerating change, NGOs are quicker than governments to respond to new demands and opportunities. Internationally, in both the poorest and richest countries, NGOs, when adequately funded, can outperform government in the delivery of many public services. Their growth, along with that of the other elements of civil society, can strengthen the fabric of the many still-fragile democracies. And they are better than governments at dealing with problems that grow slowly and affect society through their cumulative effect on individuals—the "soft" threats of environmental degradation, denial of human rights, population growth, poverty, and lack of development that may already be causing more deaths in conflict than are traditional acts of aggression.

As the computer and telecommunications revolution continues, NGOs will become more capable of large-scale activity across national borders. Their loyalties and orientation, like those of international civil servants and citizens of non-national entities like the EU, are better matched than those of governments to problems that demand transnational solutions. International NGOs and cross-border networks of local groups have bridged North-South differences that in earlier years paralyzed cooperation among countries.

On the economic front, expanding private markets can avoid economically destructive but politically seductive policies, such as excessive borrowing or overly burdensome taxation, to which governments succumb. Unhindered by ideology, private capital flows to where it is best treated and thus can do the most good.

International organizations, given a longer rein by governments and connected to the grassroots by deepening ties with NGOs, could, with adequate funding, take on larger roles in global housekeeping (transportation, communications, environment, health), security (controlling weapons of mass destruction, preventive diplomacy, peacekeeping), human rights, and emergency relief. As various international panels have suggested, the funds could come from fees on international activities, such as currency transactions and air travel, independent of state appropriations. Finally, that new force on the global scene, international public opinion, informed by worldwide media coverage and mobilized by NGOs, can be extraordinarily potent in getting things done, and done quickly.

There are at least as many reasons, however, to believe that the continuing diffusion of power away from nation-states will mean more conflict and less problem-solving both within states and among them.

For all their strengths, NGOs are special interests, albeit not motivated by personal profit. The best of them, the ablest and most passionate, often suffer most from tunnel vision, judging every public act by how it affects their particular interest. Generally, they have limited capacity for large-scale endeavors, and as they grow, the need to sustain growing budgets can compromise the independence of mind and approach that is their greatest asset.

A society in which the piling up of special interests replaces a single strong voice for the common good is unlikely to fare well. Single-issue voters, as Americans know all too well, polarize and freeze public debate. In the longer run, a stronger civil society could also be more fragmented, producing a weakened sense of common identity and purpose and less willingness to invest in public goods, whether health and education or roads and ports. More and more groups promoting worthy but narrow causes could ultimately threaten democratic government.

Internationally, excessive pluralism could have similar consequences. Two hundred nation-states is a barely manageable number. Add hundreds of influential nonstate forces—businesses, NGOs, international organizations, ethnic and religious groups—and the international system may represent more voices but be unable to advance any of them.

Moreover, there are roles that only the state—at least among today's polities—can perform. States are the only nonvoluntary political unit, the one that can impose order and is invested with the power to tax. Severely weakened states will encourage conflict, as they have in Africa, Central America, and elsewhere. Moreover, it may be that only the nation-state can meet crucial social needs that markets do not value. Providing a modicum of job security, avoiding higher unemployment, preserving a livable environment and a stable climate, and protecting consumer health and safety are but a few of the tasks that could be left dangling in a world of expanding markets and retreating states.

More international decision-making will also exacerbate the so-called democratic deficit, as decisions that elected representatives once made shift to unelected international bodies; this is already a sore point for EU members. It also arises when legislatures are forced to make a single take-it-or-leave-it judgment on huge international agreements, like the several-thousand-page Uruguay Round trade accord. With citizens already feeling that their national governments do not hear individual voices, the trend could well provoke deeper and more dangerous alienation, which in turn could trigger new ethnic and even religious separatism. The end result could be a proliferation of states too weak for either individual economic success or effective international cooperation.

Finally, fearsome dislocations are bound to accompany the weakening of the central institution of modern society. The prophets of an internetted world in which national identities gradually fade, proclaim its revolutionary nature and yet believe the changes will be wholly benign. They won't be. The shift from national to some other political allegiance, if it comes, will be an emotional, cultural, and political earthquake.

DISSOLVING AND EVOLVING

Might the decline in state power prove transitory? Present disenchantment with national governments could dissipate as quickly as it arose. Continuing globalization may well spark a vigorous reassertion of economic or cultural nationalism. By helping solve problems governments cannot handle, business, NGOs, and international organizations may actually be strengthening the nation-state system.

These are all possibilities, but the clash between the fixed geography of states and the nonterritorial nature of today's problems and solutions, which is only likely to escalate, strongly suggests that the relative power of states will continue to decline. Nation-states may simply no longer be the natural problem-solving unit. Local government addresses citizens' growing desire for a role in decision-making, while transnational, regional, and even global entities better fit the dimensions of trends in economics, resources, and security.

The evolution of information and communications technology, which has only just begun, will probably heavily favor nonstate entities, including those not yet envisaged, over states. The new technologies encourage noninstitutional, shifting networks over the fixed bureaucratic hierarchies that are the hallmark of the single-voiced sovereign state. They dissolve issues' and institutions' ties to a fixed place. And by greatly empowering individuals, they weaken the relative attachment to community, of which the preeminent one in modern society is the nation-state.

If current trends continue, the international system 50 years hence will be profoundly different. During the transition, the Westphalian system and an evolving one will exist side by side. States will set the rules by which all other actors operate, but outside forces will increasingly make decisions for them. In using business, NGOs, and international organizations to address problems they cannot or do not want to take on, states will, more often than not, inadvertently weaken themselves further. Thus governments' unwillingness to adequately fund international organizations helped NGOs move from a peripheral to a central role in shaping multilateral agreements, since the NGOs provided expertise the international organizations lacked. At least for a time, the transition is likely to weaken rather than bolster the world's capacity to solve its problems. If states, with the overwhelming share of power, wealth, and capacity, can do less, less will get done.

Whether the rise of nonstate actors ultimately turns out to be good news or bad will depend on whether humanity can launch itself on a course of rapid social innovation, as it did after World War II. Needed adaptations include a business sector that can shoulder a broader policy role, NGOs that are less parochial and better able to operate on a large scale, international institutions that can efficiently serve the dual masters of states and citizenry, and, above all, new institutions and political entities that match the transnational scope of today's challenges while meeting citizens' demands for accountable democratic governance.

NOTE

1. The author would like to acknowledge the contributions of the authors of ten case studies for the Council on Foreign Relations study group, "Sovereignty, Nonstate Actors, and a New World Politics," on which this article is based.

SOVEREIGNTY

Stephen D. Krasner

In this piece, Stephen Krasner seeks to respond point by point to the most common arguments predicting the decline of the sovereign state. As you read his defense of the idea of state sovereignty, ask yourself:

* What points is he willing to concede to those who see state sovereignty under challenge?
* Why does he believe that assertions of the decline of the sovereign state are exaggerated?
* What misconceptions do many critics of sovereignty today have about the history of the idea of sovereignty?

THE SOVEREIGN STATE IS JUST ABOUT DEAD

Very wrong. Sovereignty was never quite as vibrant as many contemporary observers suggest. The conventional norms of sovereignty have always been challenged. A few states, most notably the United States, have had autonomy, control, and recognition for most of their existence, but most others have not. The polities of many weaker states have been persistently penetrated, and stronger nations have not been immune to external influence. China was occupied. The constitutional arrangements of Japan and Germany were directed by the United States after World War II. The United Kingdom, despite its rejection of the euro, is part of the European Union.

Even for weaker states—whose domestic structures have been influenced by outside actors, and whose leaders have very little control over transborder movements or even activities within their own country—sovereignty remains attractive. Although sovereignty might provide little more than international recognition, that recognition guarantees access to international organizations and sometimes to international finance. It offers status to individual leaders. While the great powers of Europe have eschewed many elements of sovereignty, the United States, China, and Japan have neither the interest nor the inclination to abandon their usually effective claims to domestic autonomy.

In various parts of the world, national borders still represent the fault lines of conflict, whether it is Israelis and Palestinians fighting over the status of Jerusalem, Indians and Pakistanis threatening to go nuclear over Kashmir, or Ethiopia and Eritrea clashing over disputed territories. Yet commentators nowadays are mostly concerned about the erosion of national borders as a consequence of globalization. Governments and activists alike complain that multilateral institutions such as the United Nations, the World Trade Organization, and the International Monetary Fund overstep their authority by promoting universal standards for everything from human rights and the environment to monetary policy and immigration. However, the most important impact of economic globalization and transnational norms will be to alter the scope of state authority rather than to generate some fundamentally new way to organize political life.

SOVEREIGNTY MEANS FINAL AUTHORITY

Not anymore, if ever. When philosophers Jean Bodin and Thomas Hobbes first elaborated the notion of sovereignty in the 16th and 17th centuries, they were concerned with establishing the legitimacy of a single hierarchy of domestic authority. Although Bodin and Hobbes accepted the existence of divine and natural law, they both (especially Hobbes) believed the word of the sovereign was law. Subjects had no right to revolt. Bodin and Hobbes realized that imbuing the sovereign with such overweening power invited tyranny, but they were predominately concerned with maintaining domestic order, without which they believed there could be no justice. Both were writing in a world riven by sectarian strife. Bodin was almost killed in religious riots in France in 1572. Hobbes published his seminal work, *Leviathan*, only a few years after parliament (composed of Britain's emerging wealthy middle class) had executed Charles I in a civil war that had sought to wrest state control from the monarchy.

This idea of supreme power was compelling, but irrelevant in practice. By the end of the 17th century, political authority in Britain was divided between king and parliament. In the United States, the Founding Fathers established a constitutional structure of checks and balances and multiple sovereignties distributed among local and national interests that were inconsistent with hierarchy and supremacy. The principles of justice, and especially order, so valued by Bodin and Hobbes, have best been provided by modern democratic states whose organizing principles are antithetical to the idea that sovereignty means uncontrolled domestic power.

If sovereignty does not mean a domestic order with a single hierarchy of authority, what does it mean? In the contemporary world, sovereignty primarily has been linked with the idea that states are autonomous and independent from each other. Within their own boundaries, the members of a polity are free to choose their own form of government. A necessary corollary of this claim is the principle of nonintervention: One state does not have a right to intervene in the internal affairs of another.

More recently, sovereignty has come to be associated with the idea of control over transborder movements. When contemporary observers assert that the sovereign state is just about dead, they do not mean that constitutional structures are about to disappear. Instead, they mean that technological change has made it very difficult, or perhaps impossible, for states to control movements across their borders of all kinds of material things (from coffee to cocaine) and not-so-material things (from Hollywood movies to capital flows).

Finally, sovereignty has meant that political authorities can enter into international agreements. They are free to endorse any contract they find attractive. Any treaty among states is legitimate provided that it has not been coerced.

THE PEACE OF WESTPHALIA PRODUCED THE MODERN SOVEREIGN STATE

No, it came later. Contemporary pundits often cite the 1648 Peace of Westphalia (actually two separate treaties, Münster and Osnabrück) as the political big bang that created the modern system of autonomous states. Westphalia—which ended the Thirty Years' War against the hegemonic power of the Holy Roman Empire—delegitimized the already waning transnational role of the Catholic Church and validated the idea that international relations should be driven by balance-of-power considerations rather than the ideals of Christendom. But Westphalia was first and foremost a new constitution for the Holy Roman Empire. The preexisting right of the principalities in the empire to make treaties was affirmed, but the Treaty of Münster stated that "such Alliances be not against the Emperor, and the Empire, nor against the Publick Peace, and this Treaty, and without prejudice to the Oath by which every one is bound to the

Emperor and the Empire." The domestic political structures of the principalities remained embedded in the Holy Roman Empire. The Duke of Saxony, the Margrave of Brandenburg, the Count of Palatine, and the Duke of Bavaria were affirmed as electors who (along with the archbishops of Mainz, Trier, and Cologne) chose the emperor. They did not become or claim to be kings in their own right.

Perhaps most important, Westphalia established rules for religious tolerance in Germany. The treaties gave lip service to the principle (*cuius regio, eius religio*) that the prince could set the religion of his territory—and then went on to violate this very principle through many specific provisions. The signatories agreed that the religious rules already in effect would stay in place. Catholics and Protestants in German cities with mixed populations would share offices. Religious issues had to be settled by a majority of both Catholics and Protestants in the diet and courts of the empire. None of the major political leaders in Europe endorsed religious toleration in principle, but they recognized that religious conflicts were so volatile that it was essential to contain rather than repress sectarian differences. All in all, Westphalia is a pretty medieval document, and its biggest explicit innovation—provisions that undermined the power of princes to control religious affairs within their territories—was antithetical to the ideas of national sovereignty that later became associated with the so-called Westphalian system.

UNIVERSAL HUMAN RIGHTS ARE AN UNPRECEDENTED CHALLENGE TO SOVEREIGNTY

Wrong. The struggle to establish international rules that compel leaders to treat their subjects in a certain way has been going on for a long time.

Over the centuries the emphasis has shifted from religious toleration, to minority rights (often focusing on specific ethnic groups in specific countries), to human rights (emphasizing rights enjoyed by all or broad classes of individuals). In a few instances states have voluntarily embraced international supervision, but generally the weak have acceded to the preferences of the strong: The Vienna settlement following the Napoleonic wars guaranteed religious toleration for Catholics in the Netherlands. All of the successor states of the Ottoman Empire, beginning with Greece in 1832 and ending with Albania in 1913, had to accept provisions for civic and political equality for religious minorities as a condition for international recognition. The peace settlements following World War I included extensive provisions for the protection of minorities. Poland, for instance, agreed to refrain from holding elections on Saturday because such balloting would have violated the Jewish Sabbath. Individuals could bring complaints against governments through a minority rights bureau established within the League of Nations.

But as the Holocaust tragically demonstrated, interwar efforts at international constraints on domestic practices failed dismally. After World War II, human, rather than minority, rights became the focus of attention. The United Nations Charter endorsed both human rights and the classic sovereignty principle of nonintervention. The 20-plus human rights accords that have been signed during the last half century cover a wide range of issues including genocide, torture, slavery, refugees, stateless persons, women's rights, racial discrimination, children's rights, and forced labor. These U.N. agreements, however, have few enforcement mechanisms, and even their provisions for reporting violations are often ineffective.

The tragic and bloody disintegration of Yugoslavia in the 1990s revived earlier concerns with ethnic rights. International recognition of the Yugoslav successor states was conditional upon their acceptance of constitutional provisions guaranteeing minority rights. The Dayton accords established externally controlled authority structures in Bosnia, including a Human Rights Commission (a majority of whose members were appointed by the Western European states). NATO created a de facto protectorate in Kosovo.

The motivations for such interventions—humanitarianism and security—have hardly changed. Indeed, the considerations that brought the great powers into the Balkans following the wars of the 1870s were hardly different from those that engaged NATO and Russia in the 1990s.

GLOBALIZATION UNDERMINES STATE CONTROL

No. State control could never be taken for granted. Technological changes over the last 200 years have increased the flow of people, goods, capital, and ideas—but the problems posed by such movements are not new. In many ways, states are better able to respond now than they were in the past.

The impact of the global media on political authority (the so-called CNN effect) pales in comparison to the havoc that followed the invention of the printing press. Within a decade after Martin Luther purportedly nailed his 95 theses to the Wittenberg church door, his ideas had circulated throughout Europe. Some political leaders seized upon the principles of the Protestant Reformation as a way to legitimize secular political authority. No sovereign monarch could contain the spread of these concepts, and some lost not only their lands but also their heads. The sectarian controversies of the 16th and 17th centuries were perhaps more politically consequential than any subsequent transnational flow of ideas.

In some ways, international capital movements were more significant in earlier periods than they are now. During the 19th century, Latin American states (and to a lesser extent Canada, the United States, and Europe) were beset by boom-and-bust cycles associated with global financial crises. The Great Depression, which had a powerful effect on the domestic politics of all major states, was precipitated by an international collapse of credit. The Asian financial crisis of the late 1990s was not nearly as devastating. Indeed, the speed with which countries recovered from the Asian flu reflects how a better working knowledge of economic theories and more effective central banks have made it easier for states to secure the advantages (while at the same time minimizing the risks) of being enmeshed in global financial markets.

In addition to attempting to control the flows of capital and ideas, states have long struggled to manage the impact of international trade. The opening of long-distance trade for bulk commodities in the 19th century created fundamental cleavages in all of the major states. Depression and plummeting grain prices made it possible for German Chancellor Otto von Bismarck to prod the landholding aristocracy into a protectionist alliance with urban heavy industry (this coalition of "iron and rye" dominated German politics for decades). The tariff question was a basic divide in U.S. politics for much of the last half of the 19th and first half of the 20th centuries. But, despite growing levels of imports and exports since 1950, the political salience of trade has receded because national governments have developed social welfare strategies that cushion the impact of international competition, and workers with higher skill levels are better able to adjust to changing international conditions. It has become easier, not harder, for states to manage the flow of goods and services.

GLOBALIZATION IS CHANGING THE SCOPE OF STATE CONTROL

Yes. The reach of the state has increased in some areas but contracted in others. Rulers have recognized that their effective control can be enhanced by walking away from issues they cannot resolve. For instance, beginning with the Peace of Westphalia, leaders chose to surrender their control over religion because it proved too volatile. Keeping religion within the scope of state authority undermined, rather than strengthened, political stability.

Monetary policy is an area where state control expanded and then ultimately contracted. Before the 20th century, states had neither the administrative competence nor the inclination to conduct independent monetary policies. The mid-20th-century effort to control monetary affairs, which was associated with Keynesian economics, has now been reversed due to the magnitude of short-term capital flows and the inability of some states to control inflation. With the exception of Great Britain, the major European states have established a single monetary authority. Confronting recurrent hyperinflation, Ecuador adopted the U.S. dollar as its currency in 2000.

Along with the erosion of national currencies, we now see the erosion of national citizenship—the notion that an individual should be a citizen of one and only one country, and that the state has exclusive claims to that person's loyalty. For many states, there is no longer a sharp distinction between citizens and noncitizens. Permanent residents, guest workers, refugees, and undocumented immigrants are entitled to some bundle of rights even if they cannot vote. The ease of travel and the desire of many countries to attract either capital or skilled workers have increased incentives to make citizenship a more flexible category.

Although government involvement in religion, monetary affairs, and claims to loyalty has declined, overall government activity, as reflected in taxation and government expenditures, has increased as a percentage of national income since the 1950s among the most economically advanced states. The extent of a country's social welfare programs tends to go hand in hand with its level of integration within the global economy. Crises of authority and control have been most pronounced in the states that have been the most isolated, with sub-Saharan Africa offering the largest number of unhappy examples.

NGOS ARE NIBBLING AT NATIONAL SOVEREIGNTY

To some extent. Transnational nongovernmental organizations (NGOs) have been around for quite awhile, especially if you include corporations. In the 18th century, the East India Company possessed political power (and even an expeditionary military force) that rivaled many national governments. Throughout the 19th century, there were transnational movements to abolish slavery, promote the rights of women, and improve conditions for workers.

The number of transnational NGOs, however, has grown tremendously, from around 200 in 1909 to over 17,000 today. The availability of inexpensive and very fast communications technology has made it easier for such groups to organize and make an impact on public policy and international law—the international agreement banning land mines being a recent case in point. Such groups prompt questions about sovereignty because they appear to threaten the integrity of domestic decision making. Activists who lose on

their home territory can pressure foreign governments, which may in turn influence decision makers in the activists' own nation.

But for all of the talk of growing NGO influence, their power to affect a country's domestic affairs has been limited when compared to governments, international organizations, and multinational corporations. The United Fruit Company had more influence in Central America in the early part of the 20th century than any NGO could hope to have anywhere in the contemporary world. The International Monetary Fund and other multilateral financial institutions now routinely negotiate conditionality agreements that involve not only specific economic targets but also domestic institutional changes, such as pledges to crack down on corruption and break up cartels.

Smaller, weaker states are the most frequent targets of external efforts to alter domestic institutions, but more powerful states are not immune. The openness of the U.S. political system means that not only NGOs, but also foreign governments, can play some role in political decisions. (The Mexican government, for instance, lobbied heavily for the passage of the North American Free Trade Agreement.) In fact, the permeability of the American polity makes the United States a less threatening partner; nations are more willing to sign on to U.S.-sponsored international arrangements because they have some confidence that they can play a role in U.S. decision making.

SOVEREIGNTY BLOCKS CONFLICT RESOLUTION

Yes, sometimes. Rulers as well as their constituents have some reasonably clear notion of what sovereignty means—exclusive control within a given territory—even if this norm has been challenged frequently by inconsistent principles (such as universal human rights) and violated in practice (the U.S.- and British-enforced no-fly zones over Iraq). In fact, the political importance of conventional sovereignty rules has made it harder to solve some problems. There is, for instance, no conventional sovereignty solution for Jerusalem, but it doesn't require much imagination to think of alternatives: Divide the city into small pieces; divide the Temple Mount vertically with the Palestinians controlling the top and the Israelis the bottom; establish some kind of international authority; divide control over different issues (religious practices versus taxation, for instance) among different authorities. Any one of these solutions would be better for most Israelis and Palestinians than an ongoing stalemate, but political leaders on both sides have had trouble delivering a settlement because they are subject to attacks by counterelites who can wave the sovereignty flag.

Conventional rules have also been problematic for Tibet. Both the Chinese and the Tibetans might be better off if Tibet could regain some of the autonomy it had as a tributary state within the traditional Chinese empire. Tibet had extensive local control, but symbolically (and sometimes through tribute payments) recognized the supremacy of the emperor. Today, few on either side would even know what a tributary state is, and even if the leaders of Tibet worked out some kind of settlement that would give their country more self-government, there would be no guarantee that they could gain the support of their own constituents.

If, however, leaders can reach mutual agreements, bring along their constituents, or are willing to use coercion, sovereignty rules can be violated in inventive ways. The Chinese, for instance, made Hong Kong a special administrative region after the transfer from British rule, allowed a foreign judge to sit on the Court of Final Appeal, and secured acceptance by other states not only for Hong Kong's participation in a number of international organizations but also for separate visa agreements and recognition of a distinct Hong Kong passport. All of these measures violate conventional sovereignty rules since Hong Kong does not have juridical independence. Only by inventing a unique status for Hong Kong, which involved the acquiescence of other states, could China claim sovereignty while simultaneously preserving the confidence of the business community.

THE EUROPEAN UNION IS A NEW MODEL FOR SUPRANATIONAL GOVERNANCE

Yes, but only for the Europeans. The European Union (EU) really is a new thing, far more interesting in terms of sovereignty than Hong Kong. It is not a conventional international organization because its member states are now so intimately linked with one another that withdrawal is not a viable option. It is not likely to become a "United States of Europe"—a large federal state that might look something like the United States of America—because the interests, cultures, economies, and domestic institutional arrangements of its members are too diverse. Widening the EU to include the former communist states of Central Europe would further complicate any efforts to move toward a political organization that looks like a conventional sovereign state.

The EU is inconsistent with conventional sovereignty rules. Its member states have created supranational institutions (the European Court of Justice, the European Commission, and the Council of Ministers) that can make decisions opposed by some member states. The rulings of the court have direct effect and supremacy within national judicial systems, even though these doctrines were never explicitly endorsed in any treaty. The European Monetary Union created a central bank that now controls monetary affairs for three of the union's four largest states. The Single European Act and the Maastricht Treaty provide for majority or qualified majority, but not unanimous, voting in some issue areas. In one sense, the European Union is a product of state sovereignty because it has been created through voluntary agreements among its member states. But, in another sense, it fundamentally contradicts conventional understandings of sovereignty because these same agreements have undermined the juridical autonomy of its individual members.

The European Union, however, is not a model that other parts of the world can imitate. The initial moves toward integration could not have taken place without the political and economic support of the United States, which was, in the early years of the Cold War, much more interested in creating a strong alliance that could effectively oppose the Soviet Union than it was in any potential European challenge to U.S. leadership. Germany, one of the largest states in the European Union, has been the most consistent supporter of an institutional structure that would limit Berlin's own freedom of action, a reflection of the lessons of two devastating wars and the attractiveness of a European identity for a country still grappling with the sins of the Nazi era. It is hard to imagine that other regional powers such as China, Japan, or Brazil, much less the United States, would have any interest in tying their own hands in similar ways. (Regional trading agreements such as Mercosur and NAFTA have very limited supranational provisions and show few signs of evolving into broader monetary or political unions.) The EU is a new and unique institutional structure, but it will coexist with, not displace, the sovereign-state model.

WHAT RESOURCE WARS?

David G. Victor

One possible result of global climate and resource challenges are efforts to meet those challenges through global cooperation that transcends the sovereign state. At the other extreme, those challenges could provoke sovereign states into competitive efforts to solve their climate and resource problems at the expense of other states. In the worst-case scenario, this could lead to resource wars. As you read the article by Victor, ask yourself:

- What are resource wars and what, specifically, according to pessimistic observers, will prompt them to break out?
- Why does Victor think the threat of resource wars is overstated?
- How do you think your government should act to meet global resource and climate challenges?

David G. Victor, "What Resource Wars?" from *The National Interest*, No. 92, November/December 2007. Reprinted by permission of The National Interest. Copyright 2007 The National Interest.

Rising energy prices and mounting concerns about environmental depletion have animated fears that the world may be headed for a spate of "resource wars"—hot conflicts triggered by a struggle to grab valuable resources. Such fears come in many stripes, but the threat industry has sounded the alarm bells especially loudly in three areas. First is the rise of China, which is poorly endowed with many of the resources it needs—such as oil, gas, timber and most minerals—and has already "gone out" to the world with the goal of securing what it wants. Violent conflicts may follow as the country shunts others aside. A second potential path down the road to resource wars starts with all the money now flowing into poorly governed but resource-rich countries. Money can fund civil wars and other hostilities, even leaking into the hands of terrorists. And third is global climate change, which could multiply stresses on natural resources and trigger water wars, catalyze the spread of disease or bring about mass migrations.

Most of this is bunk, and nearly all of it has focused on the wrong lessons for policy. Classic resource wars are good material for Hollywood screenwriters. They rarely occur in the real world. To be sure, resource money can magnify and prolong some conflicts, but the root causes of those hostilities usually lie elsewhere. Fixing them requires focusing on the underlying institutions that govern how resources are used and largely determine whether stress explodes into violence. When conflicts do arise, the weak link isn't a dearth in resources but a dearth in governance.

FEEDING THE DRAGON

Resource wars are largely back in vogue within the U.S. threat industry because of China's spectacular rise. Brazil, India, Malaysia and many others that used to sit on the periphery of the world economy are also arcing upward. This growth is fueling a surge in world demand for raw materials. Inevitably, these countries have looked overseas for what they need, which has animated fears of a coming clash with China and other growing powers over access to natural resources.

Within the next three years, China will be the world's largest consumer of energy. Yet, it's not just oil wells that are working harder to fuel China, so too are chainsaws. Chinese net imports of timber nearly doubled from 2000 to 2005. The country also uses about one-third of the world's steel (around 360 million tons), or three times its 2000 consumption. Even in coal resources, in which China is famously well-endowed, China became a net importer in 2007. Across the board, the combination of low efficiency, rapid growth and an emphasis on heavy industry—typical in the early stages of industrial growth—have combined to make the country a voracious consumer and polluter of natural resources. America, England and nearly every other industrialized country went through a similar pattern, though with a human population that was much smaller than today's resource-hungry developing world.

Among the needed resources, oil has been most visible. Indeed, Chinese state-owned oil companies are dotting Africa, Central Asia and the Persian Gulf with projects aimed to export oil back home. The overseas arm of India's state oil company has followed a similar strategy—unable to compete head-to-head with the major Western companies, it focuses instead on areas where human-rights abuses and bad governance keep the major oil companies at bay and where India's foreign policy can open doors. To a lesser extent, Malaysia engages in the same behavior. The American threat industry rarely sounds the alarm over Indian and Malaysian efforts, though, in part because those firms have less capital to splash around and mainly because their stories just don't compare with fear of the rising dragon.

These efforts to lock up resources by going out fit well with the standard narrative for resource wars—a zero-sum struggle for vital supplies. But will a struggle over resources actually lead to war and conflict?

To be sure, the struggle over resources has yielded a wide array of commercial conflicts as companies duel for contracts and ownership. State-owned China National Offshore Oil Corporation's (CNOOC) failed bid to acquire U.S.-based Unocal—and with it Unocal's valuable oil and gas supplies in Asia—is a recent example. But that is hardly unique to resources—similar conflicts with tinges of national security arise in the control over ports, aircraft engines, databases laden with private information and a growing array of advanced technologies for which civilian and military functions are hard to distinguish. These disputes win and lose some friendships and contracts, but they do not unleash violence.

Most importantly, China's going-out strategy is unlikely to spur resource wars because it simply does not work, a lesson the Chinese are learning. Oil is a fungible commodity, and when it is sourced far from China it is better to sell (and buy) the oil on the world market. The best estimates suggest that only about one-tenth of the oil produced overseas by Chinese investments (so-called "equity oil") actually makes it back to the country. So, thus far, the largest beneficiaries of China's strategy are the rest of the world's oil consumers—first and foremost the United States—who gain because China subsidizes production.

Until recently, the strategy of going out for oil looked like a good bet for China's interests. But, despite threat-industry fear-mongering, we need not worry that it will continue over the long term because Chinese enterprises are already poised to follow a new strategy that is less likely to engender conflict. The past strategy rested on a trifecta of passing fads. One fad was the special access that Chinese state enterprises had to cheap capital from the government and by retaining their earnings. The ability to direct that spigot to political projects is diminishing as China engages in reforms that expose state enterprises to the real cost of capital and as the Chinese state and its enterprises look for better commercial returns on the money they invest. Second, nearly all the equity-oil investments overseas have occurred since the late 1990s, as prices have been rising. Each has looked much smarter than the last because of the surging value of oil in the ground. But that trend is slowing in many places because the cost of discovering and developing oil resources is rising.

And the third passing fad in China's going-out strategy is the fiction that China can cut special deals—such as by channeling development assistance to pliable host governments—to confer a durable advantage for Chinese companies. While there is no question that the special deals are rampant—by some measures, most of China's foreign assistance is actually tied to natural-resources projects—the Chinese government and its overseas enterprises are learning that it is best to avoid these places for the long haul. Among the special havens where Chinese companies toil are Sudan, Nigeria, Chad, Iran and Zimbabwe—all countries where even Chinese firms find it hard to assure adequate stability to reliably extract natural resources.

As China grapples with these hard truths about going out, the strategy will come unstuck. It won't happen overnight, but evidence in this direction is encouraging. China already pursues the opposite strategy—seeking reliable hosts, multiple commercial partners and market-oriented contracts—when it secures natural resources that require technical sophistication. China's first supplies of imported natural gas, which started last year at a liquefied natural gas terminal in Shenzhen, came from blue-chip investments in Australia, governed by contracts and investments with major Western companies. With time, China will shift to such arrangements and away from the armpits of governance. At best, badly governed countries are mediocre hosts for projects that export bulk commodities, such as iron ore and raw crude oil. These projects, however, are least likely to engender zero-sum conflicts over resources because it is particularly difficult to corner the market for widely traded commodities, as China has learned with its equity-oil projects. Resources that require technical sophistication to develop tend to favor integration and stability, rather than a zero-sum struggle.

PERNICIOUS RENTS

The second surge in thinking about resource wars comes from all the money that is pulsing into resource-rich countries. There is no question that the revenues are huge. OPEC cashed $650 billion for 11.7 billion barrels of the oil it sold in 2006, compared with $110 billion in 1998, when it sold a similar quantity of oil at much lower prices. Russia's Central Bank reports that the country earned more than $300 billion selling oil and gas in 2006, about four times its annual haul in the late 1990s. But will this flood in rents cause conflict and war?

There is no question that large revenues—regardless of the source—can fund a lot of mischievous behavior. Iran is building a nuclear-weapons program with the revenues from its oil exports. Russia has funded trouble in Chechnya, Georgia and other places with oil and gas rents. Hugo Chávez opened Venezuela's bulging check-book to help populists in Bolivia and to poke America in ways that could rekindle smoldering conflicts. Islamic terrorists also have benefited, in part, from oil revenues that leak out of oil-rich societies or are channeled directly from sympathetic governments. But resource-related conflicts are multi-causal. In no case would simply cutting the resources avoid or halt conflict, even if the presence of natural resources can shift the odds. Certainly, oil revenues have advanced Iran's nuclear program, which is a potential source of hot conflict and could make future conflicts a lot more dangerous. But a steep decline in oil probably wouldn't strangle the program on its own. Indeed, while Iran still struggles to make a bomb, resource-poor North Korea has already arrived at that goal by starving itself and getting help from friends. Venezuela's checkbook allows Chávez to be a bigger thorn in the sides of those he dislikes, but there are other thorns that poke without oil money.

As we see, what matters is not just money but how it is used. While Al-Qaeda conjures images of an oil-funded network—because it hails from the resource-rich Middle East and its seed capital has oily origins—other lethal terror networks, such as Sri Lanka's Tamil Tigers and Ireland's Republican Army, arose with funding from diasporas rather than oil or other natural resources. Unlike modern state armies that require huge infusions of capital, terror networks are usually organized to make the most of scant funds. During the run-up in oil and gas prices, analysts have often claimed that these revenues will go to fund terror networks; yet it is sobering to remember that Al-Qaeda came out in the late 1990s, when oil earnings were at their lowest in recent history. Most of the tiny sums of money needed for the September 11 attacks came from that period. Al-Qaeda's daring attacks against the U.S. embassies in Kenya and Tanzania occurred when oil-rich patrons were fretting about the inability to make ends meet at home because revenues were so low. Ideology and organization trump money as driving forces for terrorism.

Most thinking about resource-lubed conflict has concentrated on the ways that windfalls from resources cause violence by empowering belligerent states or sub-state actors. But the chains of cause and effect are more varied. For states with weak governance and resources that are easy to grab, resources tend to make weak states even weaker and raise the odds of hot conflict. This was true for Angola's diamonds and Nigeria's oil, which in both cases have helped finance civil war. For states with stable authoritarian governments—such as Kuwait, Saudi Arabia, most of the rest in the western Gulf, and perhaps also Russia and Venezuela—the problem may be the opposite. A sharp decline in resource revenues can create dangerous vacuums where expectations are high and paltry distributions discredit the established authorities.

On balance, the windfall in oil revenues over recent years is probably breeding more conflict than would a crash in prices. However, while a few conflicts partly trace themselves to resources, it is the other pernicious effects of resource windfalls, such as the undermining of democratic transitions and the failure of most resource-reliant societies to organize their economies around investment and productivity, that matter much, much more. At best, resources have indirect and mixed effects on conflict.

CLIMATE DANGERS

The third avenue for concern about coming resource wars is through the dangers of global climate change. The litany is now familiar. Sea levels will rise, perhaps a lot; storms will probably become more intense; dry areas are prone to parch further and wet zones are likely to soak longer. And on top of those probable effects, unchecked climate change raises the odds of suffering nasty surprises if the world's climate and ecosystems respond in abrupt ways. Adding all that together, the scenarios are truly disturbing. Meaningful action to stem the dangers is long overdue.

In the United States over the last year, the traditional security community has become engaged on these issues. Politically, that conversion has been touted as good news because the odds of meaningful policy are higher if hawks also favor action. Their concerns are seen through the lens of resource wars, with fears such as: water shortages that amplify grievances and trigger conflict; migrations of "climate refugees", which could stress border controls and also cause strife if the displaced don't fit well in their new societies; and diseases such as malaria that could be harder to contain if tropical conditions are more prevalent, which in turn could stress healthcare systems and lead to hot wars.

While there are many reasons to fear global warming, the risk that such dangers could cause violent conflict ranks extremely low on the list because it is highly unlikely to materialize. Despite decades of warnings about water wars, what is striking is that water wars don't happen—usually because countries that share water resources have a lot more at stake and armed conflict rarely fixes the problem. Some analysts have pointed to conflicts over resources, including water and valuable land, as a cause in the Rwandan genocide, for example. Recently, the UN secretary-general suggested that climate change was already exacerbating the conflicts in Sudan. But none of these supposed causal chains stay linked under close scrutiny—the conflicts over resources are usually symptomatic of deeper failures in governance and other primal forces for conflicts, such as ethnic tensions, income inequalities and other unsettled grievances. Climate is just one of many factors that contribute to tension. The same is true for scenarios of climate refugees, where the moniker "climate" conveniently obscures the deeper causal forces.

The dangers of disease have caused particular alarm in the advanced industrialized world, partly because microbial threats are good fodder for the imagination. But none of these scenarios hold up because the scope of all climate-sensitive diseases is mainly determined by the prevalence of institutions to prevent and contain them rather than the raw climatic factors that determine where a disease might theoretically exist. For example, the threat industry has flagged the idea that a growing fraction of the United States will be malarial with the higher temperatures and increased moisture that are likely to come with global climate change. Yet much of the American South is already climatically inviting for malaria, and malaria was a serious problem as far north as Chicago until treatment and eradication programs started in the 19th century licked the disease. Today, malaria is rare in the industrialized world, regardless of climate, and whether it spreads again will hinge on whether governments stay vigilant, not so much on patterns in climate. If Western countries really cared about the spread of tropical diseases and the stresses they put on already fragile societies in the developing world, they would redouble their efforts to tame the diseases directly (as some are now doing) rather than imagining that efforts to lessen global warming will do the job. Eradication usually depends mainly on strong and responsive governments, not the bugs and their physical climate.

RETHINKING POLICY

If resource wars are actually rare—and when they do exist, they are part of a complex of causal factors—then much of the conventional wisdom about resource policies needs fresh scrutiny. A full-blown new strategy is beyond this modest essay, but here in the United States, at least three lines of new thinking are needed.

First, the United States needs to think differently about the demands that countries with exploding growth are making on the world's resources. It must keep their rise in perspective, as their need for resources is still, on a per capita basis, much smaller than typical Western appetites. And what matters most is that the United States must focus on how to accommodate these countries' peaceful rise and their inevitable need for resources. Applied to China, this means getting the Chinese government to view efficient markets as the best way to obtain resources—not only because such an approach leads to correct pricing (which encourages energy efficiency as resources become more dear), but also because it transforms all essential resources into commodities, which makes their particular physical location less important than the overall functioning of the commodity market. All that will, in turn, make resource wars even less likely because it will create common interests among all the countries with the greatest demand for resources. It will transform the resource problem from a zero-sum struggle to the common task of managing markets.

Most policymakers agree with such general statements, but the actual practice of U.S. policy has largely undercut this goal. Saber-rattling about CNOOC's attempt to buy Unocal—along with similar fear-mongering around foreign control of ports and new rules that seem designed to trigger reviews by the Committee on Foreign Investment in the United States when foreigners try to buy American-owned assets—sends the signal that going out will also be the American approach, rather than letting markets function freely. Likewise, one of the most important actions in the oil market is to engage China and other emerging countries fully in the International Energy Agency—which is the world's only institution for managing the oil commodity markets in times of crisis—yet despite wide bipartisan consensus on that goal, nearly nothing is ever done to execute such a policy. Getting China to source commodities through markets rather than mercantilism will be relatively easy because Chinese policymakers, as well as the leadership of state enterprises that invest in natural resource projects, already increasingly think that way.

The sweep of history points against classic resource wars. Whereas colonialism created long, oppressive and often war-prone supply chains for resources such as oil and rubber, most resources today are fungible commodities. That means it is almost always cheaper and more reliable to buy them in markets.

At the same time, much higher expectations must be placed on China to tame the pernicious effects of its recent efforts to secure special access to natural resources. Sudan, Chad and Zimbabwe are three particularly acute examples where Chinese (and in Sudan's case, Indian) government investments, sheltered under a foreign-policy umbrella, have caused harm by rewarding abusive governments. That list will grow the more insecure China feels about its ability to source vital energy and mineral supplies. Some of what is needed is patience because these troubles will abate as China itself realizes that going out is an expensive strategy that buys little in security. Chinese state oil companies are generally well-run organizations; as they are forced to pay the real costs of capital and to compete in the marketplace, they won't engage in these strategies. The best analog is Brazil's experience, where its state-controlled oil company has become ever smarter—and more market oriented—as the Brazilian government has forced it to operate at arm's length without special favors. That has not

only allowed Petrobras to perform better, but it has also made Brazil's energy markets function better and with higher security.

Beyond patience, the West can help by focusing the spotlight on dangerous practices—clearly branding them the problem. There's some evidence that the shaming already underway is having an effect—evident, for example, in China's recent decision to no longer use its veto in the UN Security Council to shield Sudan's government. At the same time, the West can work with its own companies to make payments to governments (and officials) much more transparent and to close havens for money siphoned from governments. Despite many initiatives in this area, such as the Extractive Industries Transparency Initiative and the now-stalled attempt by some oil companies to "Publish What You Pay", little has been accomplished. Actual support for such policies by the most influential governments is strikingly rare. America is notably quiet on this front.

With regard to the flow of resources to terrorists—who in turn cause conflicts and are often seen as a circuitous route to resource wars—policymakers must realize that this channel for oil money is good for speeches but perhaps the least important reason to stem the outflow of money for buying imported hydrocarbons. Much more consequential is that the U.S. call on world oil resources is not sustainable because a host of factors—such as nationalization of oil resources and insecurity in many oil-producing regions—make it hard for supply to keep pace with demand. This yields tight and jittery markets and still-higher prices. These problems will just get worse unless the United States and other big consumers temper their demand. The goal should not be "independence" from international markets but a sustainable path of consumption. When the left-leaning wings in American politics and the industry-centered National Petroleum Council both issue this same warning about energy supplies—as they have over the last year—then there is an urgent need for the United States to change course. Yet Congress and the administration have done little to alter the fundamental policy incentives for efficiency. At this writing, the House and Senate are attempting to reconcile two versions of energy bills, neither of which, strikingly, will cause much fundamental change to the situation.

Cutting the flow of revenues to resource-rich governments and societies can be a good policy goal, but success will require American policymakers to pursue strategies that they will find politically toxic at home. One is to get serious about taxation. The only durable way to rigorously cut the flow of resources is to keep prices high (and thus encourage efficiency as well as changes in behavior that reduce dependence on oil) while channeling the revenues into the U.S. government treasury rather than overseas. In short, that means a tax on imported oil and a complementary tax on all fuels sold in the United States so that a fuel import tax doesn't simply hand a windfall to domestic producers. And if the United States (and other resource consumers) made a serious effort to contain financial windfalls to natural-resources exporters, it would need—at the same time—to confront a more politically poisonous task: propping up regimes or easing the transition to new systems of governance in places where vacuums are worse than incumbents.

Given all the practical troubles for the midwives of regime change, serious policy in this area would need to deal with many voids.

Finally, serious thinking about climate change must recognize that the "hard" security threats that are supposedly lurking are mostly a ruse. They are good for the threat industry—which needs danger for survival—and they are good for the greens who find it easier to build a coalition for policy when hawks are supportive. Building a policy on this house of cards is no way to muster support for a problem that requires several decades of sustained effort. One of the greatest hurdles in the climate debate—one that is just now being cleared, but will reappear if policy advocates seize on false dangers—has been to contain the entrepreneurial skeptics who have sown public doubt about the integrity of the science on causes and effects of climate change.

The false logic now runs in both directions. Not only will climate change multiply threats by putting stress on societies, but a flood of articles warns of new territorial conflicts as warming opens the formerly ice-bound Arctic for exploration. Russia recently planted a flag on the seabed at the North Pole. In fact, the underlying causes of this exploration rush are ambiguous property rights and advances in undersea drilling that are unrelated to climate change. A similar pattern unfolded in the 1950s in Antarctica, which led to a standoff of territorial claims and no real harm to the region, no production of usable minerals and no resource wars.

The real dangers lie in the growing risk that climate change could be a lot worse than the likely scenarios, which could create severe and direct harm to societies that is much more worrisome than the indirect and remote risk of climate-induced resource wars. Yet politicians give more attention to imagined insecurities from climate change and rarely talk about climate as a game of odds and risk management. They talk even less about the resource war that nobody should want to win—mankind's domination of nature. For the real losers in unchecked climate change will be natural ecosystems unable, unlike humans, to look ahead and adapt.

THE CONNECTION HAS BEEN RESET

James Fallows

In this article, James Fallows examines the "Great Firewall" that the Chinese government has erected in order to try to control information available to Chinese citizens via the Internet. As you read this piece, ask yourself:

- What barriers to information has the Chinese government created to rein in the Internet?
- How effective are those barriers?
- What does the Chinese case imply for the larger question of the Internet's challenge to state sovereignty?

Many foreigners who come to China for the Olympics will use the Internet to tell people back home what they have seen and to check what else has happened in the world.

The first thing they'll probably notice is that China's Internet seems slow. Partly this is because of congestion in China's internal networks, which affects domestic and international transmissions alike. Partly it is because even electrons take a detectable period of time to travel beneath the Pacific Ocean to servers in America and back again; the trip to and from Europe is even longer, because that goes through America, too. And partly it is because of the delaying cycles imposed by China's system that monitors what people are looking for on the Internet, especially when they're looking overseas. That's what foreigners have heard about.

They'll likely be surprised, then, to notice that China's Internet seems surprisingly free and uncontrolled. Can they search for information about "Tibet independence" or "Tiananmen shooting" or other terms they have heard are taboo? Probably—and they'll be able to click right through to the controversial sites. Even if they enter the Chinese-language term for "democracy in China," they'll probably get results. What about Wikipedia, famously off-limits to users in China? They will probably be able to reach it. Naturally the visitors will wonder: What's all this I've heard about the "Great Firewall" and China's tight limits on the Internet?

In reality, what the Olympic-era visitors will be discovering is not the absence of China's electronic control but its new refinement—and a special Potemkin-style unfettered access that will be set up just for them, and just for the length of their stay. According to engineers I have spoken with at two tech organizations in China, the government bodies in charge of censoring the Internet have told them to get ready to unblock access from a list of specific Internet Protocol (IP) addresses—certain Internet cafés, access jacks in hotel rooms and conference centers where foreigners are expected to work or stay during the Olympic Games. (I am not giving names or identifying details of any Chinese citizens with whom I have discussed this topic, because they risk financial or criminal punishment for criticizing the system or even disclosing how it works. Also, I have not gone to Chinese government agencies for their side of the story, because the very existence of Internet controls is almost never discussed in public here, apart from vague statements about the importance of keeping online information "wholesome.")

Depending on how you look at it, the Chinese government's attempt to rein in the Internet is crude and slapdash or ingenious and well crafted. When American technologists write about the control system, they tend to emphasize its limits. When Chinese citizens discuss it—at least with me—they tend to emphasize its strength. All of them are right, which makes the government's approach to the Internet a nice proxy for its larger attempt to control people's daily lives.

Disappointingly, "Great Firewall" is not really the right term for the Chinese government's overall control strategy. China has indeed erected a firewall—a barrier to keep its Internet users from dealing easily with the outside world—but that is only one part of a larger, complex structure of monitoring and censorship. The official name for the entire approach, which is ostensibly a way to keep hackers and other rogue elements from harming Chinese Internet users, is the "Golden Shield Project." Since that term is too creepy to bear repeating, I'll use "the control system" for the overall strategy, which includes the "Great Firewall of China," or GFW, as the means of screening contact with other countries.

In America, the Internet was originally designed to be free of choke points, so that each packet of information could be routed quickly around any temporary obstruction. In China, the Internet came with choke points built in. Even now, virtually all Internet contact between China and the rest of the world is routed through a very small number of fiber-optic cables that enter the country at one of three points: the Beijing-Qingdao-Tianjin area in the north, where cables come in from Japan; Shanghai on the central coast, where they also come from Japan; and Guangzhou in the south, where they come from Hong Kong. (A few places in China have Internet service via satellite, but that is both expensive and slow. Other lines run across Central Asia to Russia but carry little traffic.) In late 2006, Internet users in China were reminded just how important these choke points are when a seabed earthquake near Taiwan cut some major cables serving the country. It took months before international transmissions to and from most of China regained even their pre-quake speed, such as it was.

Thus Chinese authorities can easily do something that would be harder in most developed countries: physically monitor all traffic into or out of the country. They do so by installing at each of these few "international gateways" a device called a "tapper" or "network sniffer," which can mirror every packet of data going in or out. This involves mirroring in both a figurative and a literal sense. "Mirroring" is the term for normal copying or backup operations, and in this case real though extremely small mirrors are employed. Information travels along fiber-optic cables as little pulses of light, and as these travel through the Chinese gateway routers, numerous tiny mirrors bounce reflections of them to a separate set of "Golden Shield" computers. Here the term's creepiness is appropriate. As the other routers and servers (short for file servers, which are essentially very large-capacity computers) that make up the Internet do their best to get the packet where it's supposed to go, China's own surveillance computers are looking over the same information to see whether it should be stopped.

The mirroring routers were first designed and supplied to the Chinese authorities by the U.S. tech firm Cisco, which is why Cisco took such heat from human-rights organizations. Cisco has always denied that it tailored its equipment to the authorities' surveillance needs, and said it merely sold them what it would sell anyone else. The issue is now moot, since similar routers are made by companies around the world, notably including China's own electronics giant, Huawei. The ongoing refinements are mainly in surveillance software, which the Chinese are developing themselves. Many of the surveillance engineers are thought to come from the military's own technology institutions. Their work is good and getting better, I was told by Chinese and foreign engineers who do "oppo research" on the evolving GFW so as to design better ways to get around it.

Andrew Lih, a former journalism professor and software engineer now based in Beijing (and author of the forthcoming book *The Wikipedia Story*), laid out for me the ways in which the GFW can keep a Chinese Internet user from finding desired material on a foreign site. In the few seconds after a user enters a request at the browser, and before something new shows up on the screen, at least four things can go wrong—or be made to go wrong.

The first and bluntest is the "DNS block." The DNS, or Domain Name System, is in effect the telephone directory of Internet sites. Each time you enter a Web address, or URL—www.yahoo.com, let's say—the DNS looks up the IP address where the site can be found. IP addresses are numbers separated by dots—for example, TheAtlantic.com's is 38.118.42.200. If the DNS is instructed to give back no address, or a bad address, the user can't reach the site in question—as a phone user could not make a call if given a bad number. Typing in the URL for the BBC's main news site often gets the no-address treatment: if you try news.bbc.co.uk, you may get a "Site not found" message on the screen. For two months in 2002, Google's Chinese site, Google.cn, got a different kind of bad-address treatment, which shunted users to its main competitor, the dominant Chinese search engine, Baidu. Chinese academics complained that this was hampering their work. The government, which does not have to stand for

reelection but still tries not to antagonize important groups needlessly, let Google.cn back online. During politically sensitive times, like last fall's 17th Communist Party Congress, many foreign sites have been temporarily shut down this way.

Next is the perilous "connect" phase. If the DNS has looked up and provided the right IP address, your computer sends a signal requesting a connection with that remote site. While your signal is going out, and as the other system is sending a reply, the surveillance computers within China are looking over your request, which has been mirrored to them. They quickly check a list of forbidden IP sites. If you're trying to reach one on that blacklist, the Chinese international-gateway servers will interrupt the transmission by sending an Internet "Reset" command both to your computer and to the one you're trying to reach. Reset is a perfectly routine Internet function, which is used to repair connections that have become unsynchronized. But in this case it's equivalent to forcing the phones on each end of a conversation to hang up. Instead of the site you want, you usually see an onscreen message beginning "The connection has been reset"; sometimes instead you get "Site not found." Annoyingly, blogs hosted by the popular system Blogspot are on this IP blacklist. For a typical Google-type search, many of the links shown on the results page are from Wikipedia or one of these main blog sites. You will see these links when you search from inside China, but if you click on them, you won't get what you want.

The third barrier comes with what Lih calls "URL keyword block." The numerical Internet address you are trying to reach might not be on the blacklist. But if the words in its URL include forbidden terms, the connection will also be reset. (The Uniform Resource Locator is a site's address in plain English—say, www.microsoft.com—rather than its all-numeric IP address.) The site

FalunGong.com appears to have no active content, but even if it did, Internet users in China would not be able to see it. The forbidden list contains words in English, Chinese, and other languages, and is frequently revised—"like, with the name of the latest town with a coal mine disaster," as Lih put it. Here the GFW's programming technique is not a reset command but a "black-hole loop," in which a request for a page is trapped in a sequence of delaying commands. These are the programming equivalent of the old saw about how to keep an idiot busy: you take a piece of paper and write "Please turn over" on each side. When the Firefox browser detects that it is in this kind of loop, it gives an error message saying: "The server is redirecting the request for this address in a way that will never complete."

The final step involves the newest and most sophisticated part of the GFW: scanning the actual contents of each page—which stories *The New York Times* is featuring, what a China-related blog carries in its latest update—to judge its page-by-page acceptability. This again is done with mirrors. When you reach a favorite blog or news site and ask to see particular items, the requested pages come to you—and to the surveillance system at the same time. The GFW scanner checks the content of each item against its list of forbidden terms. If it finds something it doesn't like, it breaks the connection to the offending site and won't let you download anything further from it. The GFW then imposes a temporary blackout on further "IP1 to IP2" attempts—that is, efforts to establish communications between the user and the offending site. Usually the first time-out is for two minutes. If the user tries to reach the site during that time, a five-minute time-out might begin. On a third try, the time-out might be 30 minutes or an hour—and so on through an escalating sequence of punishments.

Users who try hard enough or often enough to reach the wrong sites might attract the attention of the authorities. At least in principle, Chinese Internet users must sign in with their real names whenever they go online, even in Internet cafés. When the surveillance system flags an IP address from which a lot of "bad" searches originate, the authorities have a good chance of knowing who is sitting at that machine.

All of this adds a note of unpredictability to each attempt to get news from outside China. One day you go to the NPR site and cruise around with no problem. The next time, NPR happens to have done a feature on Tibet. The GFW immobilizes the site. If you try to refresh the page or click through to a new story, you'll get nothing—and the time-out clock will start.

This approach is considered a subtler and more refined form of censorship, since big foreign sites no longer need be blocked wholesale. In principle they're in trouble only when they cover the wrong things. Xiao Qiang, an expert on Chinese media at the University of California at Berkeley journalism school, told me that the authorities have recently begun applying this kind of filtering in reverse. As Chinese-speaking people outside the country, perhaps academics or exiled dissidents, look for data on Chinese sites—say, public-health figures or news about a local protest—the GFW computers can monitor what they're asking for and censor what they find.

Taken together, the components of the control system share several traits. They're constantly evolving and changing in their emphasis, as new surveillance techniques become practical and as words go on and off the sensitive list. They leave the Chinese Internet public unsure about where the off-limits line will be drawn on any given day. Andrew Lih points out that other countries that also censor Internet content—Singapore, for instance, or the United Arab Emirates—provide explanations whenever they do so. Someone who clicks on a pornographic or "anti-Islamic" site in the U.A.E. gets the following message, in Arabic and English: "We apologize the site you are attempting to visit has been blocked due to its content being inconsistent with the religious, cultural, political, and moral values of the United Arab Emirates." In China, the connection just times out. Is it your computer's problem? The firewall? Or maybe your local Internet provider, which has decided to do some filtering on its own? You don't know. "The unpredictability of the firewall actually makes it more effective," another Chinese software engineer told me. "It becomes much harder to know what the system is looking for, and you always have to be on guard."

There is one more similarity among the components of the firewall: they are all easy to thwart.

As a practical matter, anyone in China who wants to get around the firewall can choose between two well-known and dependable alternatives: the proxy server and the VPN. A proxy server is a way of connecting your computer inside China with another one somewhere else—or usually to a series of foreign computers, automatically passing signals along to conceal where they really came from. You initiate a Web request, and the proxy system takes over, sending it to a computer in America or Finland or Brazil. Eventually the system finds what you want and sends it back. The main drawback is that it makes Internet operations very, very slow. But because most proxies cost nothing to install and operate, this is the favorite of students and hackers in China.

A VPN, or virtual private network, is a faster, fancier, and more elegant way to achieve the same result. Essentially a VPN creates your own private, encrypted channel that runs alongside the normal Internet. From within China, a VPN connects you with an Internet server somewhere else. You pass your browsing and downloading requests to that American or Finnish or Japanese server, and it finds and sends back what you're looking for. The GFW doesn't stop you, because it can't read the encrypted messages you're sending. Every foreign business operating in China uses such a network. VPNs are freely advertised in China, so individuals can sign up, too. I use one that costs $40 per year. (An expat in China thinks: *that's a little over a dime a day.* A Chinese factory worker thinks: *it's a week's take-home pay.* Even for a young academic, it's a couple days' work.)

As a technical matter, China could crack down on the proxies and VPNs whenever it pleased. Today the policy is: if a message comes through that the surveillance system cannot read because it's encrypted, let's wave it on through! Obviously the system's behavior could be reversed. But everyone I spoke with said that China could simply not afford to crack down that way. "Every bank, every foreign manufacturing company, every retailer, every software vendor needs VPNs to exist," a Chinese professor told me. "They would have to shut down the next day if asked to send their commercial information through the regular Chinese Internet and the Great Firewall." Closing down the free, easy-to-use proxy servers would create a milder version of the same problem. Encrypted e-mail, too, passes through the GFW without scrutiny, and users of many Web-based mail systems can establish a secure session simply by typing "https:" rather than the usual "http:" in a site's address—for instance, https://mail.yahoo.com. To keep China in business, then, the government has to allow some exceptions to its control efforts—even knowing that many Chinese citizens will exploit the resulting loopholes.

Because the Chinese government can't plug every gap in the Great Firewall, many American observers have concluded that its larger efforts to control electronic discussion, and the democratization and grass-roots organizing it might nurture, are ultimately doomed. A recent item on an influential American tech Web site had the headline "Chinese National Firewall Isn't All That Effective." In October, *Wired* ran a story under the headline "The Great Firewall: China's Misguided—and Futile—Attempt to Control What Happens Online."

Let's not stop to discuss why the vision of democracy-through-communications-technology is so convincing to so many Americans. (Samizdat, fax machines, and the Voice of America eventually helped bring down the Soviet system. Therefore proxy servers and online chat rooms must erode the power of the Chinese state. Right?) Instead, let me emphasize how unconvincing this vision is to most people who deal with China's system of extensive, if imperfect, Internet controls.

Think again of the real importance of the Great Firewall. Does the Chinese government really care if a citizen can look up the Tiananmen Square entry on Wikipedia? Of course not. Anyone who wants that information will get it—by using a proxy server or VPN, by e-mailing to a friend overseas, even by looking at the surprisingly broad array of foreign magazines that arrive, uncensored, in Chinese public libraries.

What the government cares about is making the quest for information just enough of a nuisance that people generally won't bother. Most Chinese people, like most Americans, are interested mainly in their own country. All around them is more information about China and things Chinese than they could possibly take in. The newsstands are bulging with papers and countless glossy magazines. The bookstores are big, well stocked, and full of patrons, and so are the public libraries. Video stores, with pirated versions of anything. Lots of TV channels. And of course the Internet, where sites in

Chinese and about China constantly proliferate. When this much is available inside the Great Firewall, why go to the expense and bother, or incur the possible risk, of trying to look outside?

All the technology employed by the Golden Shield, all the marvelous mirrors that help build the Great Firewall—these and other modern achievements matter mainly for an old-fashioned and pre-technological reason. By making the search for external information a nuisance, they drive Chinese people back to an environment in which familiar tools of social control come into play.

Chinese bloggers have learned that if they want to be read in China, they must operate within China, on the same side of the firewall as their potential audience. Sure, they could put up exactly the same information outside the Chinese mainland. But according to Rebecca MacKinnon, a former Beijing correspondent for CNN now at the Journalism and Media Studies Center of the University of Hong Kong, their readers won't make the effort to cross the GFW and find them. "If you want to have traction in China, you have to *be* in China," she told me. And being inside China means operating under the sweeping rules that govern all forms of media here: guidance from the authorities; the threat of financial ruin or time in jail; the unavoidable self-censorship as the cost of defiance sinks in.

Most blogs in China are hosted by big Internet companies. Those companies know that the government will hold them responsible if a blogger says something bad. Thus the companies, for their own survival, are dragooned into service as auxiliary censors.

Large teams of paid government censors delete offensive comments and warn errant bloggers. (No official figures are available, but the censor workforce is widely assumed to number in the tens of thousands.) Members of the public at large are encouraged to speak up when they see subversive material. The propaganda ministries send out frequent instructions about what can and cannot be discussed. In October, the group Reporters Without Borders, based in Paris, released an astonishing report by a Chinese Internet technician writing under the pseudonym "Mr. Tao." He collected dozens of the messages he and other Internet operators had received from the central government. Here is just one, from the summer of 2006:

17 June 2006, 18:35

From: Chen Hua, deputy director of the Beijing Internet Information Administrative Bureau

Dear colleagues, the Internet has of late been full of articles and messages about the death of a Shenzhen engineer, Hu Xinyu, as a result of overwork. All sites must stop posting articles on this subject, those that have already been posted about it must be removed from the site and, finally, forums and blogs must withdraw all articles and messages about this case.

"Domestic censorship is the real issue, and it is about social control, human surveillance, peer pressure, and self-censorship," Xiao Qiang of Berkeley says. Last fall, a team of computer scientists from the University of California at Davis and the University of New Mexico published an exhaustive technical analysis of the GFW's operation and of the ways it could be foiled. But they stressed a nontechnical factor: "The presence of censorship, even if easy to evade, promotes self-censorship."

It would be wrong to portray China as a tightly buttoned mind-control state. It is too wide-open in too many ways for that. "Most people in China feel freer than any Chinese people have been in the country's history, ever," a Chinese software engineer who earned a doctorate in the United States told me. "There has never been a space for any kind of discussion before, and the government is clever about continuing to expand space for anything that doesn't threaten its survival." But it would also be wrong to ignore the cumulative effect of topics people are not allowed to discuss. "Whether or not Americans supported George W. Bush, they could not *avoid* learning about Abu Ghraib," Rebecca MacKinnon says. In China, "the controls mean that whole topics inconvenient for the regime simply don't exist in public discussion." Most Chinese people remain wholly unaware of internationally noticed issues like, for instance, the controversy over the Three Gorges Dam.

Countless questions about today's China boil down to: How long can this go on? How long can the industrial growth continue before the natural environment is destroyed? How long can the super-rich get richer, without the poor getting mad? And so on through a familiar list. The Great Firewall poses the question in another form: How long can the regime control what people are allowed to know, without the people caring enough to object? On current evidence, for quite a while.

CHAPTER | 9

GLOBAL FUTURES

For many observers of world politics, the passing of the Cold War era seemed to herald an era of global change that involved not just an alteration in the fortunes of individual states, but also a more fundamental transformation of the very nature of how the world of international relations works. Overall, the decade of the 1990s was an optimistic time that featured the end of the ideological clash between communism and capitalism, the diffusion of democracy on a global scale, and, in much of the world, a new prosperity produced by economic globalization. All those developments were not only inherently positive developments in their own right, but were also linked, by many, to the evolution of a new world politics in which war as an instrument of foreign policy was going out of fashion.

Along the way, more pessimistic notes were also sounded. Samuel Huntington's "clash of civilizations" thesis seemed to buy into the general argument that world politics was changing in a fundamental way, but his version of change was hardly of the optimistic variety. Likewise, realist scholars have attempted to hold their ground against the onslaught of criticism from those who argued that realism was an outmoded perspective that failed to explain the dramatic changes of the era. By the turn of the century, and especially following the terror attacks of September 11, 2001, and the U.S. invasion of Iraq in 2003, the pessimists seemed, in some quarters, to be reclaiming the upper hand.

The readings below sample some of this recent thinking on the question of change in world politics after the Cold War. As the title suggests, Robert Kagan's article tries to put to rest the optimistic expectations contained in Francis Fukuyama's "end of history" thesis by examining the resurgence and renewed confidence of autocratic governments in the early twenty-first century. Kagan's expectation of intensified conflict between democratic and autocratic states stands in sharp contrast not only to Fukuyama but also to Thomas Friedman's "Dell theory of conflict prevention" and its view of economic interdependence as the antidote to war and conflict in the new century.

Huntington's "clash of civilization" thesis echoes realist pessimism about the world, while the article by Kishore Mahbubani suggests that the domination of the world by what Huntington calls "Western civilization" is coming to an end and that the twenty-first century will be "the Asian century." Mahbubani (Dean of the Lee Kuan Yew School of Public Policy at the National University of Singapore and Singapore's former ambassador to the UN) suggests that a key question in assessing what the twenty-first century will look like is how the West handles and responds to its diminished power and status. The readings in this chapter conclude with Swanee Hunt's article, in which she suggests that whether the pessimists or the optimists are right about the future may depend on whether more women can be involved in the making of foreign policy.

HISTORY'S BACK: AMBITIOUS AUTOCRACIES, HESITANT DEMOCRACIES

Robert Kagan

Francis Fukuyama's optimistic declaration of the end of history back in 1989 was clearly stimulated by the global trend toward democracy underway at that time. In recent years, that optimism has been tempered by backsliding on democracy in Russia and by China's ability to resist democratization as its economic development continues to proceed at a rapid pace. The title of his article tells you where Kagan stands on this issue. As you read it, ask yourself:

- Is the resurgence of autocracy that Kagan discusses a temporary setback or a fundamental challenge to the "end of history" idea?
- How does Kagan see the impact of reinvigorated autocracies on international relations of the twenty-first century?
- In what respects is Kagan's analysis "realist"? In what respects is it not "realist"? Explain.

One wonders whether Russia's invasion of Georgia will finally end the dreamy complacency that took hold of the world's democracies after the close of the Cold War. The collapse of the Soviet Union offered for many the tantalizing prospect of a new kind of international order. The fall of the Communist empire and the apparent embrace of democracy by Russia seemed to augur a new era of global convergence. Great power conflict and competition were a thing of the past. Geo-economics had replaced geopolitics. Nations that traded with one another would be bound together by their interdependence and less likely to fight one another. Increasingly commercial societies would be more liberal both at home and abroad. Their citizens would seek prosperity and comfort and abandon the atavistic passions, the struggles for honor and glory, and the tribal hatreds that had produced conflict throughout history. Ideological conflict was also a thing of the past. As Francis Fukuyama famously put it,

"At the end of history, there are no serious ideological competitors left to liberal democracy." And if there were an autocracy or two lingering around at the end of history, this was no cause for concern. They, too, would eventually be transformed as their economies modernized.

Unfortunately, the core assumptions of the post-Cold War years have proved mistaken. The absence of great power competition, it turns out, was a brief aberration. Over the course of the 1990s, that competition reemerged as rising powers entered or reentered the field. First China, then India, set off on unprecedented bursts of economic growth, accompanied by incremental but substantial increases in military capacity, both conventional and nuclear. By the beginning of the 21st century, Japan had begun a slow economic recovery and was moving toward a more active international role both diplomatically and militarily. Then came Russia, rebounding from economic calamity to

Robert Kagan, "History's Back: Ambitious Autocracies, Hesitant Democracies," *The Weekly Standard,* August 25, 2008, Volume 013, Issue 46. Reprinted by permission of The Weekly Standard.

Robert Kagan, a contributing editor to *The Weekly Standard,* is the author most recently of *The Return of History and the End of Dreams.*

steady growth built on the export of its huge reserves of oil and natural gas.

Nor has the growth of the Chinese and Russian economies produced the political liberalization that was once thought inevitable. Growing national wealth and autocracy have proven compatible, after all. Autocrats learn and adjust. The autocracies of Russia and China have figured out how to permit open economic activity while suppressing political activity. They have seen that people making money will keep their noses out of politics, especially if they know their noses will be cut off. New wealth gives autocracies a greater ability to control information—to monopolize television stations and to keep a grip on Internet traffic, for instance—often with the assistance of foreign corporations eager to do business with them.

In the long run, rising prosperity may well produce political liberalism, but how long is the long run? It may be too long to have any strategic or geopolitical relevance. In the meantime, the new economic power of the autocracies has translated into real, usable geopolitical power on the world stage. In the 1990s the liberal democracies expected that a wealthier Russia would be a more liberal Russia, at home and abroad. But historically the spread of commerce and the acquisition of wealth by nations has not necessarily produced greater global harmony. Often it has only spurred greater global competition. The hope at the end of the Cold War was that nations would pursue economic integration as an alternative to geopolitical competition, that they would seek the "soft" power of commercial engagement and economic growth as an alternative to the "hard" power of military strength or geopolitical confrontation. But nations do not need to choose. There is another paradigm—call it "rich nation, strong army," the slogan of rising Meiji Japan at the end of the 19th century—in which nations seek economic integration and adaptation of Western institutions not in order to give up the geopolitical struggle but to wage it more successfully. The Chinese have their own phrase for this: "a prosperous country and a strong army."

The rise of these two great power autocracies is reshaping the international scene. Nationalism, and the nation itself, far from being weakened by globalization, has returned with a vengeance. There are the ethnic nationalisms that continue to bubble up in the Balkans and in the former republics of the Soviet Union. But more significant is the return of great power nationalism. Instead of an imagined new world order, there are new geopolitical fault lines where the ambitions of great powers overlap and conflict and where the seismic events of the future are most likely to erupt.

One of these fault lines runs along the western and southwestern frontiers of Russia. In Georgia, Ukraine, and Moldova, in the Baltic states of Estonia, Latvia, and Lithuania, in Poland, Hungary, and the Czech Republic, in the Caucasus and Central Asia, and even in the Balkans, a contest for influence is under way between a resurgent Russia, on one side, and the European Union and the United States on the other. Instead of an anticipated zone of peace, western Eurasia has once again become a zone of competition, in which military power—pooh-poohed by postmodern Europeans—once again plays a role.

Unfortunately, Europe is ill-equipped to respond to a problem that it never anticipated having to face. The European Union is deeply divided about Russia, with the nations on the frontline fearful and seeking reassurance, while others like France and Germany seek accommodation with Moscow. The fact is, Europe never expected to face this kind of challenge at the end of history. This great 21st-century entity, the EU, now confronts 19th-century power, and Europe's postmodern tools of foreign policy were not designed to address more traditional geopolitical challenges. There is a real question as to whether Europe is institutionally or temperamentally able to play the kind of geopolitical games in Russia's near-abroad that Russia is willing to play.

There is some question about the United States, as well. At least some portion of American elite opinion has shifted from post-Cold War complacency, from the conviction that the world was naturally moving toward greater harmony, to despair and resignation and the belief that the United States and the world's democracies are powerless to meet the challenge of the rising great powers. Fukuyama and others counsel accommodation to Russian ambitions, on the grounds that there is now no choice. It is the post-American world. Having failed to imagine that the return of great power autocracies was possible, they now argue there is nothing to be done and the wise policy is to accommodate to this new global reality. Yet again, however, their imagination fails them. They do not see what accommodation of the great power autocracies may look like. Georgia provides a glimpse of that future.

The world may not be about to embark on a new ideological struggle of the kind that dominated the Cold War. But the new era, rather than being a time of "universal values," will be one of growing tensions and sometimes confrontation between the forces of liberal democracy and the forces of autocracy.

In fact, a global competition is under way. According to Russia's foreign minister, "For the first time in many years, a real competitive environment has emerged on the market of ideas" between different "value systems and development models." And the good news, from the Russian point of view, is that "the West is losing its monopoly on the globalization process." Today when Russians speak of a multipolar world, they are not only talking about the redistribution of power. It is also the competition of value systems and ideas that will provide "the foundation for a multipolar world order."

International order does not rest on ideas and institutions alone. It is shaped by configurations of power. The spread of democracy in the last two decades of the 20th century was not merely the unfolding of certain ineluctable processes of economic and political development. The global shift toward liberal democracy coincided with the historical shift in the balance of power toward those nations and peoples who favored the liberal democratic idea, a shift that began with the triumph of the democratic powers over fascism in World War II and that was followed by a second triumph of the democracies over communism in the Cold War. The liberal international order that emerged after these two victories reflected the new overwhelming global balance in favor of liberal forces. But those victories were not inevitable, and they need not be lasting. Today, the reemergence of the great autocratic powers, along with the reactionary forces of Islamic radicalism, has weakened that order and threatens to weaken it further in the years and decades to come.

Does the United States have the strength and ability to lead the democracies again in strengthening and advancing a liberal democratic international order? Despite all the recent noise about America's relative decline, the answer is most assuredly yes. If it is true, as some claim, that the United States over the past decade suffered from excessive confidence in its power to shape the world, the pendulum has now swung too far in the opposite direction.

The apparent failure in Iraq convinced many people that the United States was weak, hated, and in a state of decline. Nor has anyone bothered to adjust that judgment now that the United States appears to be winning in Iraq. Yet by any of the usual measures of power, the United States is as strong today, even in relative terms, as it was in 2000. It remains the sole superpower, even as the other great powers get back on their feet. The military power of China and Russia has increased over the past decade, but American military power has increased more. America's share of the global economy has remained steady, 27 percent of global GDP in 2000 and 26 percent today. So where is the relative decline? So long as the United States remains at the center of the international economy, the predominant military power, and the leading apostle of the world's most popular political philosophy; so long as the American public continues to support American predominance, as it has consistently for six decades; and so long as potential challengers inspire more fear than sympathy among their neighbors, the structure of the international system should remain as the Chinese describe it: "one superpower and many great powers."

If American predominance is unlikely to fade any time soon, moreover, it is partly because much of the world does not really want it to. Despite the opinion polls, America's relations with both old and new allies have actually strengthened in recent years. Despite predictions that other powers would begin to join together in an effort to balance against the rogue superpower, especially after the Iraq war, the trend has gone in the opposite direction. The rise of the great power autocracies has been gradually pushing the great power democracies back in the direction of the United States. Russia's invasion of Georgia will accelerate this trend, but it was already underway, even if masked by the international uproar over the Iraq war.

On balance, traditional allies of the United States in East Asia and in Europe, while their publics may be more anti-American than in the past, are nevertheless pursuing policies that reflect more concern about the powerful, autocratic states in their midst than about the United States. The most remarkable change has occurred in India, a former ally of Moscow which today sees good relations with the United States as essential to achieving its broader strategic and economic goals, among them balancing China's rising power. Japanese leaders came to a similar conclusion a decade ago. In Europe there is also an unmistakable trend toward closer strategic relations with the United States, a trend that will be accelerated by Russian actions. A few years ago, Gerhard Schröder and Jacques Chirac flirted with drawing closer to Russia as a way of counterbalancing American power. But lately France, Germany, and the rest of Europe have been moving in the other direction. This is not out of renewed affection for the United States. It is a response to changing international circumstances and to lessons learned from the past. The Chirac-Schröder attempt to make Europe a counterweight to American power failed in part because the European Union's newest members from Central and Eastern Europe fear a resurgent Russia and insist on close strategic ties with Washington. That was true even before Russia invaded Georgia. Now their feeling of dependence on the United States will grow dramatically.

What remains is for the United States to translate this growing concern into concerted action by the world's democracies. This won't be easy, given the strong tendencies, especially in Europe, to seek accommodation with autocratic Russia. But this is nothing new—even during the Cold War, France and Germany sometimes sought to stand somewhere between the United States and the Soviet Union. Over time, France and Germany will have no choice but to join the majority of EU members who once again worry about Moscow's intentions.

So what to do? Instead of figuring out how to accommodate the powerful new autocracies, the United States and the world's other democracies need to begin thinking about how they can protect their interests and advance their principles in a world in which these are once again powerfully challenged. The world's democracies need to show solidarity with one another, and they need to support those trying to pry open a democratic space where it has been closing.

That includes in the great power autocracies themselves. It is easy to look at China and Russia today and believe they are impervious to outside influence. But one should not overlook their fragility and vulnerability. These autocratic regimes may be stronger than they were in the past in terms of wealth and global influence, but they still live in a predominantly liberal era. That means they face an unavoidable problem of legitimacy. Chinese leaders race forward with their economy in fear that any slowing will be their undoing. They fitfully stamp out even the tiniest hints of political opposition because they live in fear of repeating the Soviet collapse and their own near-death experience in 1989. They fear foreign support for any internal political opposition more than they fear foreign invasion. In Russia, Putin strains to obliterate his opponents, even though they appear weak, because he fears that any sign of life in the opposition could bring his regime down.

The world's democracies have an interest in keeping the hopes for democracy alive in Russia and China. The optimists in the early post–Cold War years were not wrong to believe that a liberalizing Russia and China would be better international partners. They were

just wrong to believe that this evolution was inevitable. Today, excessive optimism has been replaced by excessive pessimism. Many Europeans insist that outside influences will have no effect on Russia. Yet, looking back on the Cold War, many of these same Europeans believe that the Helsinki Accords of the 1970s had a subtle but eventually profound impact on the evolution of the Soviet Union and the eastern bloc. Is Putin's Russia more impervious to such methods than Brezhnev's Soviet Union? Putin himself does not think so, or he wouldn't be so nervous about the democratic states on his borders. Nor do China's rulers, or they wouldn't spend billions policing Internet chat rooms and waging a campaign of repression against the Falun Gong.

Whether or not China and Russia are susceptible to outside influence over time, for the moment their growing power and, in the case of Russia, the willingness to use it, pose a serious challenge that needs to be met with the same level-headed determination as previous such challenges. If Moscow is now bent on restoring its hegemony over its near neighbors, the United States and its European allies must provide those neighbors with support and protection. If China continues to expand its military capabilities, the United States must reassure China's neighbors of its own commitment to Asian security.

The future is not determined. It is up for grabs. The international order in the coming decades will be shaped by those who have the power and the collective will to shape it. The great fallacy of our era has been the belief that a liberal and democratic international order would come about by the triumph of ideas alone or by the natural unfolding of human progress. Many believe the Cold War ended the way it did simply because the better worldview triumphed, as it had to, and that the international order that exists today is but the next stage in humanity's forward march from strife and aggression toward a peaceful and prosperous coexistence. They forget the many battles fought, both strategic and ideological, that produced that remarkable triumph.

The illusion is just true enough to be dangerous. Of course there is strength in the liberal democratic idea and in the free market. But progress toward these ideals has never been inevitable. It is contingent on events and the actions of nations and peoples—battles won or lost, social movements successful or crushed, economic practices implemented or discarded.

After the Second World War, another moment in history when hopes for a new kind of international order were rampant, Hans Morgenthau warned idealists against imagining that at some point "the final curtain would fall and the game of power politics would no longer be played." The struggle continued then, and it continues today. Six decades ago American leaders believed the United States had the ability and responsibility to use its power to prevent a slide back to the circumstances that had produced two world wars and innumerable national calamities. Reinhold Niebuhr, who always warned against Americans' ambitions and excessive faith in their own power, also believed, with a faith and ambition of his own, that "the world problem cannot be solved if America does not accept its full share of responsibility in solving it." Today the United States shares that responsibility with the rest of the democratic world, which is infinitely stronger than it was when World War II ended. The only question is whether the democratic world will once again rise to the challenge.

THE DELL THEORY OF CONFLICT PREVENTION

Thomas L. Friedman

In this selection from his bestselling book, *The World Is Flat,* journalist Thomas Friedman articulates a popularized version of the liberal commercialist view of international relations. As you read this excerpt, ask yourself:

- What is the logic of his "Dell theory"?
- What "tests" of the theory does he discuss to provide evidence in support of the theory?
- How persuasive do you find his logic and evidence?

Free Trade is God's diplomacy. There is no other certain way of uniting people in the bonds of peace.

BRITISH POLITICIAN RICHARD COBDEN, 1857

Before I share with you the subject of this chapter, I have to tell you a little bit about the computer that I wrote this book on. It's related to the theme I am about to discuss. This book was largely written on a Dell Inspiron 600m notebook, service tag number 9ZRJP41. As part of the research for this book, I visited with the management team at Dell near Austin,

Texas. I shared with them the ideas in this book and in return I asked for one favor: I asked them to trace for me the entire global supply chain that produced my Dell notebook. Here is their report:

My computer was conceived when I phoned Dell's 800 number on April 2, 2004, and was connected to sales representative Mujteba Naqvi, who immediately entered my order into Dell's order management system. He typed in both the type of notebook I ordered as well as the special features I wanted, along with my personal information, shipping address, billing address, and credit card information. My credit card was verified by Dell through its work flow connection with Visa, and my order was then released to Dell's production system. Dell has six factories around the world—in Limerick, Ireland; Xiamen, China; Eldorado do Sul, Brazil; Nashville, Tennesee; Austin, Texas; and Penang, Malaysia. My order went out by e-mail to the Dell notebook factory in Malaysia, where the parts for the computer were immediately ordered from the supplier logistics centers (SLCs) next to the Penang factory. Surrounding every Dell factory in the world are these supplier logistics centers, owned by the different suppliers of Dell parts. These SLCs are like staging areas. If you are a Dell supplier anywhere in the world, your job is to keep your SLC full of your specific parts so they can constantly be trucked over to the Dell factory for just-in-time manufacturing.

"In an average day, we sell 140,000 to 150,000 computers," explained Dick Hunter, one of Dell's three global production managers. "Those orders come in over Dell.com or over the telephone. As soon these orders come in, our suppliers know about it. They get a signal based on every component in the machine you ordered, so the supplier knows just what he has to deliver. If you are supplying power cords for desktops, you can see minute by minute how many power cords you are going to have to deliver." Every two hours, the Dell factory in Penang sends an e-mail to the various SLCs nearby, telling each one what parts and what quantities of those parts it wants delivered within the next ninety minutes—and not one minute later. Within ninety minutes, trucks from the various SLCs around Penang pull up to the Dell manufacturing plant and unload the parts needed for all those notebooks ordered in the last two hours. This goes on all day, every two hours. As soon as those parts arrive at the factory, it takes thirty minutes for Dell employees to unload the parts, register their bar codes, and put them into the bins for assembly. "We know where every part in every SLC is in the Dell system at all times," said Hunter.

So where did the parts for my notebook come from? I asked Hunter. To begin with, he said, the notebook was codesigned in Austin, Texas, and in Taiwan by a team of Dell engineers and a team of Taiwanese notebook designers. "The customer's needs, required technologies, and Dell's design innovations were all determined by Dell through our direct relationship with customers," he explained. "The basic design of the motherboard and case—the basic functionality of your machine—was designed to those specifications by an ODM [original design manufacturer] in Taiwan. We put our engineers in their facilities and they come to Austin and we actually codesign these systems. This global teamwork brings an added benefit—a globally distributed virtually twenty-four-hour-per-day development cycle. Our partners do the basic electronics and we help them design customer and reliability features that we know our customers want. We know the customers better than our suppliers and our competition, because we are dealing directly with them every day." Dell notebooks are completely redesigned roughly every twelve months, but new features are constantly added during the year—through the supply chain—as the hardware and software components advance.

It happened that when my notebook order hit the Dell factory in Penang, one part was not available—the wireless card—due to a quality control issue, so the assembly of the notebook was delayed for a few days. Then the truck full of good wireless cards arrived. On April 13, at 10:15 a.m., a Dell Malaysia worker pulled the order slip that automatically popped up once all my parts had arrived from the SLCs to the Penang factory. Another Dell Malaysia employee then took out a "traveler"—a special carrying tote designed to hold and protect parts—and started plucking all the parts that went into my notebook.

Where did those parts come from? Dell uses multiple suppliers for most of the thirty key components that go into its notebooks. That way if one supplier breaks down or cannot meet a surge in demand, Dell is not left in the lurch. So here are the key suppliers for my Inspiron 600m notebook: The Intel microprocessor came from an Intel factory either in the Philippines, Costa Rica, Malaysia, or China. The memory came from a Korean-owned factory in Korea (Samsung), a Taiwanese-owned factory in Taiwan (Nanya), a German-owned factory in Germany (Infineon), or a Japanese-owned factory in Japan (Elpida). My graphics card was shipped from either a Taiwanese-owned factory in China (MSI) or a Chinese-run factory in China (Foxconn). The cooling fan came from a Taiwanese-owned factory in Taiwan (CCI or Auras). The motherboard came from either a Korean-owned factory in Shanghai (Samsung), a Taiwanese-owned factory in Shanghai (Quanta), or a Taiwanese-owned factory in Taiwan (Compal or Wistron). The keyboard came from either a Japanese-owned company in Tianjin, China (Alps), a Taiwanese-owned factory in Shenzen, China (Sunrex), or a Taiwanese-owned factory in Suzhou, China (Darfon). The LCD display was made in either South Korea (Samsung or LG.Philips LCD), Japan (Toshiba or Sharp), or Taiwan (Chi Mei Optoelectronics, Hannstar Display, or AU Optronics). The wireless card came from either an American-owned factory in China (Agere) or Malaysia (Arrow), or a Taiwanese-owned factory in Taiwan (Askey or Gemtek) or China (USI). The modem was made by either a Taiwanese-owned company in China (Asustek or Liteon) or a Chinese-run company in China (Foxconn). The battery came from an American-owned factory in Malaysia (Motorola), a Japanese-owned factory in Mexico or Malaysia or China (Sanyo), or a South Korean or Taiwanese factory in either of those two countries (SDI or Simplo). The hard disk drive was made by an American-owned factory in Singapore (Seagate), a Japanese-owned company in Thailand (Hitachi or Fujitsu), or a Japanese-owned factory in the Philippines (Toshiba). The CD/DVD drive came from a South Korean-owned company with factories in Indonesia and the Philippines (Samsung); a Japanese-owned factory in China or Malaysia (NEC); a Japanese-owned factory in Indonesia, China, or Malaysia (Teac); or a Japanese-owned factory in China (Sony). The notebook carrying bag was made by either an Irish-owned company in China (Tenba) or an American-owned company in China (Targus, Samsonite, or Pacific Design). The power adapter was made by either a Thai-owned factory in Thailand (Delta) or a Taiwanese, Korean, or American-owned factory in China (Liteon, Samsung, or Mobility). The power cord was made by a British-owned company with factories in China, Malaysia, and India (Volex). The removable memory stick was made by either an Israeli-owned company in Israel (M-System) or an American-owned company with a factory in Malaysia (Smart Modular).

This supply chain symphony—from my order over the phone to production to delivery to my house—is one of the wonders of the flat world.

"We have to do a lot of collaborating," said Hunter. "Michael [Dell] personally knows the CEOs of these companies, and we are constantly working with them on process improvements and real-time demand/supply balancing." Demand shaping goes on constantly, said Hunter, What is "demand shaping"? It works like this: At 10 a.m. Austin time, Dell discovers that so many customers have ordered notebooks with 40-gigabyte hard drives since the morning that its supply chain will run short in two hours. That signal is automatically relayed to Dell's marketing department and to Dell.com and to all the Dell phone operators taking orders. If you happen to call to place your Dell order at 10:30 a.m., the Dell representative will say to you, "Tom, it's your lucky day! For the next hour we are offering 60-gigabyte hard drives with the notebook you want—for only $10 more than the 40-gig drive. And if you act now, Dell will throw in a carrying case along with your purchase, because we so value you as a customer." In an hour or two, using such promotions, Dell can reshape the demand for any part of any notebook or desktop to correspond with the projected supply in its global supply chain. Today memory might be on sale, tomorrow it might be CD-ROMs.

Picking up the story of my notebook, on April 13, at 11:29 a.m., all the parts had been plucked from the just-in-time inventory bins in Penang, and the computer was assembled there by A. Sathini, a team member "who manually screwed together all of the parts from kitting as well as the labels needed for Tom's system," said Dell in their production report to me. "The system was then sent down the conveyor to go to burn, where Tom's specified software was downloaded." Dell has huge server banks stocked with the latest in Microsoft, Norton Utilities, and other popular software applications, which are downloaded into each new computer according to the specific tastes of the customer.

"By 2:45 p.m., Tom's software had been successfully downloaded, and [was] manually moved to the boxing line. By 4:05 p.m., Tom's system [was] placed in protective foam and a shuttle box, with a label, which contains his order number, tracking code, system type, and shipping code. By 6:04 p.m., Tom's system had been loaded on a pallet with a specified manifest, which gives the Merge facility visibility to when the system will arrive, what pallet it will be on (out of 75+ pallets with 152 systems per pallet), and to what address Tom's system will ship. By 6:26 p.m., Tom's system left [the Dell factory] to head to the Penang, Malaysia, airport."

Six days a week Dell charters a China Airlines 747 out of Taiwan and flies it from Penang to Nashville via Taipei. Each 747 leaves with twenty-five thousand Dell notebooks that weigh altogether 110,000 kilograms, or 242,500 pounds. It is the only 747 that ever lands in Nashville, except Air Force One, when the president visits. "By April 15, 2004, at 7:41 a.m., Tom's system arrived at [Nashville] with other Dell systems from Penang and Limerick. By 11:58 a.m., Tom's system [was] inserted into a larger box, which went down the boxing line to the specific external parts that Tom had ordered."

That was thirteen days after I'd ordered it. Had there not been a parts delay in Malaysia when my order first arrived, the time between when I phoned in my purchase, when the notebook was assembled in Penang, and its arrival in Nashville would have been only four days. Hunter said the total supply chain for my computer, including suppliers of suppliers, involved about four hundred companies in North America, Europe, and primarily Asia, but with thirty key players. Somehow, though, it all came together. As Dell reported: On April 15, 2004, at 12:59 p.m.,

"Tom's system had been shipped from [Nashville] and was tenured by UPS shipping LTL (3-5-day ground, specified by Tom), with UPS tracking number 1Z13WA374253514697. By April 19, 2004, at 6:41 p.m., Tom's system arrived in Bethesda, MD, and was signed for."

I am telling you the story of my notebook to tell a larger story of geopolitics in the flat world. To all the forces . . . that are still holding back the flattening of the world, or could actually reverse the process, one has to add a more traditional threat, and that is an outbreak of a good, old-fashioned, world-shaking, economy-destroying war. It could be China deciding once and for all to eliminate Taiwan as an independent state; or North Korea, out of fear or insanity, using one of its nuclear weapons against South Korea or Japan; or Israel and a soon-to-be-nuclear Iran going at each other; or India and Pakistan finally nuking it out. These and other classic geopolitical conflicts could erupt at any time and either slow the flattening of the world or seriously unflatten it.

The real subject of this chapter is how these classic geopolitical threats might be moderated or influenced by the new forms of collaboration fostered and demanded by the flat world—particularly supply-chaining. The flattening of the world is too young for us to draw any definitive conclusions. What is certain, though, is that as the world flattens, one of the most interesting dramas to watch in international relations will be the interplay between the traditional global threats and the newly emergent global supply chains. The interaction between old-time threats (like China *versus* Taiwan) and just-in-time supply chains (like China *plus* Taiwan) will be a rich source of study for the field of international relations in the early twenty-first century.

In *The Lexus and the Olive Tree* I argued that to the extent that countries tied their economies and futures to global integration and trade, it would act as a restraint on going to war with their neighbors. I first started thinking about this in the late 1990s, when, during my travels, I noticed that no two countries that both had McDonald's had ever fought a war against each other since each got its McDonald's. (Border skirmishes and civil wars don't count, because McDonald's usually served both sides.) After confirming this with McDonald's, I offered what I called the Golden Arches Theory of Conflict Prevention. The Golden Arches Theory stipulated that when a country reached the level of economic development where it had a middle class big enough to support a network of McDonald's, it became a McDonald's country. And people in McDonald's countries didn't like to fight wars anymore. They preferred to wait in line for burgers. While this was offered slightly tongue in cheek, the serious point I was trying to make was that as countries got woven into the fabric of global trade and rising living standards, which having a network of McDonald's franchises had come to symbolize, the cost of war for victor and vanquished became prohibitively high.

This McDonald's theory has held up pretty well, but now that almost every country has acquired a McDonald's, except the worst rogues like North Korea, Iran, and Iraq under Saddam Hussein, it seemed to me that this theory needed updating for the flat world. In that spirit, and again with tongue slightly in cheek, I offer the Dell Theory of Conflict Prevention, the essence of which is that the advent and spread of just-in-time global supply chains in the flat world are an even greater restraint in geopolitical adventurism than the more general rising standard of living that McDonald's symbolized.

The Dell Theory stipulates: No two countries that are both part of a major global supply chain, like Dell's, will ever fight a war against each other as long as they are both part of the same global supply chain. Because people embedded in major global supply chains don't want to fight old-time wars anymore. They want to make just-in-time deliveries of goods and services—and enjoy the rising standards of living that come with that. One of the people with the best feel for the logic behind this theory is Michael Dell, the founder and chairman of Dell.

"These countries understand the risk premium that they have," said Dell of the countries in his Asian supply chain. "They are pretty careful to protect the equity that they have built up or tell us why we should not worry [about their doing anything adventurous]. My belief after visiting China is that the change that has occurred there is in the best interest of the world and China. Once people get a taste for whatever you want to call it—economic independence, a better lifestyle, and a better life for their child or children—they grab on to that and don't want to give it up."

Any sort of war or prolonged political upheaval in East Asia or China "would have a massive chilling effect on the investment there and on all the progress that has been made there," said Dell, who added that he believes the governments in that part of the world understand this very clearly. "We certainly make clear to them that stability is important to us. [Right now] it is not a day-to-day worry for us . . . I believe that as time and progress go on there, the chance for a really disruptive event goes down exponentially. I don't think our industry gets enough credit for the good we are doing in these areas. If you are making money and being productive and raising your standard of living, you're not sitting around thinking, Who did this to us? or Why is our life so bad?"

There is a lot of truth to this. Countries whose workers and industries are woven into a major global supply chain know that they cannot take an hour, a week, or a month off for war without disrupting industries and economies around the world and thereby risking the loss of

their place in that supply chain for a long time, which could be extremely costly. For a country with no natural resources, being part of a global supply chain is like striking oil—oil that never runs out. And therefore, getting dropped from such a chain because you start a war is like having your oil wells go dry or having someone pour cement down them. They will not come back anytime soon.

"You are going to pay for it really dearly," said Glenn E. Neland, senior vice president for worldwide procurement at Dell, when I asked him what would happen to a major supply-chain member in Asia that decided to start fighting with its neighbor and disrupt the supply chain. "It will not only bring you to your knees [today], but you will pay for a long time—because you just won't have any credibility if you demonstrate you are going to go [off] the political deep end. And China is just now starting to develop a level of credibility in the business community that it is creating a business environment you can prosper in—with transparent and consistent rules." Neland said that suppliers regularly ask him whether he is worried about China and Taiwan, which have threatened to go to war at several points in the past half century, but his standard response is that he cannot imagine them "doing anything more than flexing muscles with each other." Neland said he can tell in his conversations and dealings with companies and governments in the Dell supply chain, particularly the Chinese, that "they recognize the opportunity and are really hungry to participate in the same things they have seen other countries in Asia do. They know there is a big economic pot at the end of the rainbow and they are really after it. We will spend about $35 billion producing parts this year, and 30 percent of that is [in] China."

If you follow the evolution of supply chains, added Neland, you see: the prosperity and stability they promoted first in Japan, and then in Korea and Taiwan, and now in Malaysia, Singapore, the Philippines, Thailand, and Indonesia. Once countries get embedded in these global supply chains, "they feel part of something much bigger than their own businesses," he said. Osamu Watanabe, the CEO of the Japan External Trade Organization (JETRO), was explaining to me one afternoon in Tokyo how Japanese companies were moving vast amounts of low- and middle-range technical work and manufacturing to China, doing the basic fabrication there, and then bringing it back to Japan for final assembly. Japan was doing this despite a bitter legacy of mistrust between the two countries, which was intensified by the Japanese invasion of China in the last century. Historically, he noted, a strong Japan and a strong China have had a hard time coexisting. But not today, at least not for the moment. Why not? I asked. The reason you can have a strong Japan and a strong China at the same time, he said, "is because of the supply chain." It is a win-win for both.

Obviously, since Iraq, Syria, south Lebanon, North Korea, Pakistan, Afghanistan, and Iran are not part of any major global supply chains, all of them remain hot spots that could explode at any time and slow or reverse the flattening of the world. As my own notebook story attests, the most important test case of the Dell Theory of Conflict Prevention is the situation between China and Taiwan—since both are deeply embedded in several of the world's most important computer, consumer electronics, and, increasingly, software supply chains. The vast majority of computer components for every major company comes from coastal China, Taiwan, and East Asia. In addition, Taiwan alone has more than $100 billion in investments in mainland China today, and Taiwanese experts run many of the cutting-edge Chinese high-tech manufacturing companies.

It is no wonder that Craig Addison, the former editor of *Electronic Business Asia* magazine, wrote an essay for the *International Herald Tribune* (September 29, 2000), headlined "A 'Silicon Shield' Protects Taiwan from China." He argued that "Silicon-based products, such as computers and networking systems, form the basis of the digital economies in the United States, Japan and other developed nations. In the past decade, Taiwan has become the third-largest information technology hardware producer after the United States and Japan. Military aggression by China against Taiwan would cut off a large portion of the world's supply of these products. . . . Such a development would wipe trillions of dollars off the market value of technology companies listed in the United States, Japan and Europe." Even if China's leaders, like former president Jiang Zemin, who was once minister of electronics, lose sight of how integrated China and Taiwan are in the world's computer supply chain, they need only ask their kids for an update. Jiang Zemin's son, Jiang Mianheng, wrote Addison, "is a partner in a wafer fabrication project in Shanghai with Winston Wang of Taiwan's Grace T.H.W. Group." And it is not just Taiwanese. Hundreds of big American tech companies now have R & D operations in China; a war that disrupted them could lead not only to the companies moving their plants elsewhere but also to a significant loss of R & D investment in China, which the Beijing government has been betting on to advance its development. Such a war could also, depending on how it started, trigger a widespread American boycott of Chinese goods— if China were to snuff out the Taiwanese democracy—which would lead to serious economic turmoil inside China.

The Dell Theory had its first real test in December 2004, when Taiwan held parliamentary elections. President Chen Shur-bian's pro-independence Democratic Progressive Party was expected to win the legislative runoff over the main opposition Nationalist Party, which favored closer ties with Beijing. Chen framed the election as a popular referendum on his proposal to write a new constitution that would formally enshrine Taiwan's independence, ending the purposely ambiguous status quo. Had Chen won and moved ahead on his agenda to make Taiwan its own motherland, as opposed to maintaining the status quo fiction that it is a province of the mainland, it could have led to a Chinese military assault on Taiwan. Everyone in the region was holding his or her breath. And what happened? *Motherboards won over motherland.* A majority of Taiwanese voted against the pro-independence governing party legislative candidates, ensuring that the DPP would not have a majority in parliament. I believe the message Taiwanese voters were sending was not that they never want Taiwan to be independent. It was that they do not want to upset the status quo right now, which has been so beneficial to so many Taiwanese. The voters seemed to understand clearly how interwoven they had become with the mainland, and they wisely opted to maintain their de facto independence rather than force de jure independence, which might have triggered a Chinese invasion and a very uncertain future.

Warning: What I said when I put forth the McDonald's theory, I would repeat even more strenuously with the Dell Theory: It does not make wars obsolete. And it does not guarantee that governments will not engage in wars of choice, even governments that are part of major supply chains. To suggest so would be naïve. It guarantees only that governments whose countries are enmeshed in global supply chains will have to think three times, not just twice, about engaging in anything but a war of self-defense. And if they choose to go to war anyway, the price they will pay will be ten times higher than

it was a decade ago and probably ten times higher than whatever the leaders of that country think. It is one thing to lose your McDonald's. It's quite another to fight a war that costs you your place in a twenty-first-century supply chain that may not come back around for a long time.

While the biggest test case of the Dell Theory is China versus Taiwan, the fact is that the Dell Theory has already proved itself to some degree in the case of India and Pakistan, the context in which I first started to think about it. I happened to be in India in 2002, when its just-in-time services supply chains ran into some very old-time geopolitics—and the supply chain won. In the case of India and Pakistan, the Dell Theory was working on only one party—India—but it still had a major impact. India is to the world's knowledge and service supply chain what China and Taiwan are to the manufacturing ones. By now readers . . . know all the highlights: General Electric's biggest research center outside the United States is in Bangalore, with seventeen hundred Indian engineers, designers, and scientists. The brain chips for many brandname cell phones are designed in Bangalore. Renting a car from Avis online? It's managed in Bangalore. Tracing your lost luggage on Delta or British Airways is done from Bangalore, and the backroom accounting and computer maintenance for scores of global firms are done from Bangalore, Mumbai, Chennai, and other major Indian cities.

Here's what happened: On May 31, 2002, State Department spokesman Richard Boucher issued a travel advisory saying, "We urge American citizens currently in India to depart the country," because the prospect of a nuclear exchange with Pakistan was becoming very real. Both nations were massing troops on their borders, intelligence reports were suggesting that they both might be dusting off their nuclear warheads, and CNN was flashing images of people flooding out of India. The global American firms that had moved their back rooms and R&D operations to Bangalore were deeply unnerved.

"I was actually surfing on the Web, and I saw a travel advisory come up on India on a Friday evening," said Vivek Paul, president of Wipro, which manages backroom operations from India of many American multinationals. "As soon as I saw that, I said, 'Oh my gosh, every customer that we have is going to have a million questions on this.' It was the Friday before a long weekend, so over the weekend we at Wipro developed a fail-safe business continuity plan for all of our customers." While Wipro's customers were pleased to see how on top of things the company was, many of them were nevertheless rattled. This was not in the plan when they decided to outsource mission-critical research and operations to India. Said Paul, "I had a CIO from one of our big American clients send me an e-mail saying, 'I am now spending a lot of time looking for alternative sources to India. I don't think you want me doing that, and I don't want to be doing it.' I immediately forwarded his message to the Indian ambassador in Washington and told him to get it to the right person." Paul would not tell me what company it was, but I have confirmed through diplomatic sources that it was United Technologies. And plenty of others, like American Express and General Electric, with back rooms in Bangalore, had to have been equally worried.

For many global companies, "the main heart of their business is now supported here," said N. Krishnakumar, president of MindTree, another leading Indian knowledge outsourcing firm based in Bangalore. "It can cause chaos if there is a disruption." While not trying to meddle in foreign affairs, he added, "What we explained to our government, through the Confederation of Indian Industry, is that providing a stable, predictable operating environment is now the key to India's development." This was a real education for India's elderly leaders in New Delhi, who had not fully absorbed how critical India had become to the world's knowledge supply chain. When you are managing vital backroom operations for American Express or General Electric or Avis, or are responsible for tracing all the lost luggage on British Airways or Delta, you cannot take a month, a week, or even a day off for war without causing major disruptions for those companies. Once those companies have made a commitment to outsource business operations or research to India, they expect it to stay there. That is a major commitment. And if geopolitics causes a serious disruption, they will leave, and they will not come back very easily. When you lose this kind of service trade, you can lose it for good.

"What ends up happening in the flat world you described," explained Paul, "is that you have only one opportunity to make it right if something [goes] wrong. Because the disadvantage of being in a flat world is that despite all the nice engagements and stuff and the exit barriers that you have, every customer has multiple options, and so the sense of responsibility you have is not just out of a desire to do good by your customers, but also a desire for self-preservation."

The Indian government got the message. Was India's central place in the world's services supply chain the only factor in getting Prime Minister Vajpayee to tone down his rhetoric and step back from the brink? Of course not. There were other factors, to be sure—most notably the deterrent effect of Pakistan's own nuclear arsenal. But clearly, India's role in global services was an important additional source of restraint on its behavior, and it was taken into account by New Delhi. "I think it sobered a lot of people," said Jerry Rao, who, as noted earlier, heads the

Indian high-tech trade association. "We engaged very seriously, and we tried to make the point that this was very bad for Indian business. It was very bad for the Indian economy. . . . [Many people] didn't realize till then how suddenly we had become integrated into the rest of the world. We are now partners in a twenty-four by seven by three-sixty-five supply chain."

Vivek Kulkarni, then information technology secretary for Bangalore's regional government, told me back in 2002, "We don't get involved in politics, but we did bring to the government's attention the problems the Indian IT industry might face if there were a war." And this was an altogether new factor for New Delhi to take into consideration. "Ten years ago, [a lobby of IT ministers from different Indian states] never existed," said Kulkarni. Now it is one of the most important business lobbies in India and a coalition that no Indian government can ignore.

"With all due respect, the McDonald's [shutting] down doesn't hurt anything," said Vivek Paul, "but if Wipro had to shut down we would affect the day-to-day operations of many, many companies." No one would answer the phones in call centers. Many e-commerce sites that are supported from Bangalore would shut down. Many major companies that rely on India to maintain their key computer applications or handle their human resources departments or billings would seize up. And these companies did not want to find alternatives, said Paul. Switching is very difficult, because taking over mission-critical day-to-day backroom operations of a global company takes a great deal of training and experience. It's not like opening a fast-food restaurant. That was why, said Paul, Wipro's clients were telling him, "'I have made an investment in you. I need you to be very responsible with the trust I have reposed in you.' And I think that created an enormous amount of back pressure on us that said

we have to act in a responsible fashion. . . . All of a sudden it became even clearer that there's more to gain by economic gains than by geopolitical gains. [We had more to gain from building] a vibrant, richer middle class able to create an export industry than we possibly could by having an ego-satisfying war with Pakistan." The Indian government also looked around and realized that the vast majority of India's billion people were saying, "I want a better future, not more territory." Over and over again, when I asked young Indians working at call centers how they felt about Kashmir or a war with Pakistan, they waved me off with the same answer: "We have better things to do." And they do. America needs to keep this in mind as it weighs its overall approach to outsourcing. I would never advocate shipping some American's job overseas just so it will keep Indians and Pakistanis at peace with each other. But I would say that to the extent that this process happens, driven by its own internal economic logic, it will have a net positive geopolitical effect. It will absolutely make the world safer for American kids.

Each of the Indian business leaders I interviewed noted that in the event of some outrageous act of terrorism or aggression from Pakistan, India would do whatever it takes to defend itself, and they would be the first to support that—the Dell Theory be damned. Sometimes war is unavoidable. It is imposed on you by the reckless behavior of others, and you have to just pay the price. But the more India and, one hopes, soon Pakistan get enmeshed in global service supply chains, the greater disincentive they have to fight anything but a border skirmish or a war of words.

The example of the 2002 India-Pakistan nuclear crisis at least gives us some hope. That cease-fire was brought to us not by General Powell but by General Electric.

We bring good things to life. . . .

THE CLASH OF CIVILIZATIONS?

Samuel P. Huntington

Huntington's 1993 "clash of civilizations" article quickly became identified as the pessimistic rejoinder to Fukuyama's "end of history" idea. As you read Huntington, ask yourself:

- What exactly does he mean by *civilizations* and why must they clash?
- Have events since 1993 supported or undermined his thesis?
- What are the points of similarity and difference between realism and Huntington's clash of civilizations idea?

THE NEXT PATTERN OF CONFLICT

World politics is entering a new phase, and intellectuals have not hesitated to proliferate visions of what it will be—the end of history, the return of traditional rivalries between nation states, and the decline of the nation state from the conflicting pulls of tribalism and globalism, among others. Each of these visions catches aspects of the emerging reality. Yet they all miss a crucial, indeed a central, aspect of what global politics is likely to be in the coming years.

It is my hypothesis that the fundamental source of conflict in this new world will not be primarily ideological or primarily economic. The great divisions among humankind and the dominating source of conflict will be cultural. Nation states will remain the most powerful actors in world affairs, but the principal conflicts of global politics will occur between nations and groups of different civilizations. The clash of civilizations will dominate global politics. The fault lines between civilizations will be the battle lines of the future.

Conflict between civilizations will be the latest phase in the evolution of conflict in the modern world. For a century and a half after the emergence of the modern international system with the Peace of Westphalia, the conflicts of the Western world were largely among princes—emperors, absolute monarchs and constitutional monarchs attempting to expand their bureaucracies, their armies, their mercantilist economic strength and, most important, the territory they ruled. In the process they created nation states, and beginning with the French Revolution the principal lines of conflict were between nations rather than princes. In 1793, as R. R. Palmer put it, "The wars of kings were over; the wars of peoples had begun." This nineteenth-century pattern lasted until the end of World War I. Then, as a result of the Russian Revolution and the reaction against it, the conflict of nations yielded to the conflict of ideologies, first among communism, fascism-Nazism and liberal democracy, and then between communism and liberal democracy. During the Cold War, this latter conflict became embodied in the struggle between the two superpowers, neither of which was a nation state in the classical European sense and each of which defined its identity in terms of its ideology.

These conflicts between princes, nation states and ideologies were primarily conflicts

Samuel P. Huntington, "The Clash of Civilizations?" Reprinted by permission of *Foreign Affairs*, 72:3, Summer 1993. Copyright 1993 by the Council on Foreign Relations, Inc. www.ForeignAffairs.org.

within Western civilization, "Western civil wars," as William Lind has labeled them. This was as true of the Cold War as it was of the world wars and the earlier wars of the seventeenth, eighteenth and nineteenth centuries. With the end of the Cold War, international politics moves out of its Western phase, and its centerpiece becomes the interaction between the West and non-Western civilizations and among non-Western civilizations. In the politics of civilizations, the peoples and governments of non-Western civilizations no longer remain the objects of history as targets of Western colonialism but join the West as movers and shapers of history.

THE NATURE OF CIVILIZATIONS

During the Cold War the world was divided into the First, Second and Third Worlds. Those divisions are no longer relevant. It is far more meaningful now to group countries not in terms of their political or economic systems or in terms of their level of economic development but rather in terms of their culture and civilization.

What do we mean when we talk of a civilization? A civilization is a cultural entity. Villages, regions, ethnic groups, nationalities, religious groups, all have distinct cultures at different levels of cultural heterogeneity. The culture of a village in southern Italy may be different from that of a village in northern Italy, but both will share in a common Italian culture that distinguishes them from German villages. European communities, in turn, will share cultural features that distinguish them from Arab or Chinese communities. Arabs, Chinese and Westerners, however, are not part of any broader cultural entity. They constitute civilizations. A civilization is thus the highest cultural grouping of people and the broadest level of cultural identity people have short of that which distinguishes humans from other species. It is defined both by common objective elements, such as language, history, religion, customs, institutions, and by the subjective self-identification of people. People have levels of identity: a resident of Rome may define himself with varying degrees of intensity as a Roman, an Italian, a Catholic, a Christian, a European, a Westerner. The civilization to which he belongs is the broadest level of identification with which he intensely identifies. . . .

WHY CIVILIZATIONS WILL CLASH

Civilization identity will be increasingly important in the future, and the world will be shaped in large measure by the interactions among seven or eight major civilizations. These include Western, Confucian, Japanese, Islamic, Hindu, Slavic-Orthodox, Latin American and possibly African civilization. The most important conflicts of the future will occur along the cultural fault lines separating these civilizations from one another.

Why will this be the case?

First, differences among civilizations are not only real; they are basic. Civilizations are differentiated from each other by history, language, culture, tradition and, most important, religion. The people of different civilizations have different views on the relations between God and man, the individual and the group, the citizen and the state, parents and children, husband and wife, as well as differing views of the relative importance of rights and responsibilities, liberty and authority, equality and hierarchy. These differences are the product of centuries. They will not soon disappear. They are far more fundamental than differences among political ideologies and political regimes. . . .

Second, the world is becoming a smaller place. The interactions between peoples of different civilizations are increasing; these increasing interactions intensify civilization consciousness and awareness of differences between civilizations and commonalities within civilizations. North African immigration to France generates hostility among Frenchmen and at the same time increased receptivity to immigration by "good" European Catholic Poles. Americans react far more negatively to Japanese investment than to larger investments from Canada and European countries. Similarly, as Donald Horowitz has pointed out, "An Ibo may be . . . an Owerri Ibo or an Onitsha Ibo in what was the Eastern region of Nigeria. In Lagos, he is simply an Ibo. In London, he is a Nigerian. In New York, he is an African." The interactions among peoples of different civilizations enhance the civilization-consciousness of people that, in turn, invigorates differences and animosities stretching or thought to stretch back deep into history.

Third, the processes of economic modernization and social change throughout the world are separating people from longstanding local identities. They also weaken the nation state as a source of identity. In much of the world religion has moved in to fill this gap, often in the form of movements that are labeled "fundamentalist." Such movements are found in Western Christianity, Judaism, Buddhism and Hinduism, as well as in Islam. In most countries and most religions the people active in fundamentalist movements are young, college-educated, middle-class technicians, professionals and business persons. The "unsecularization of the world," George Weigel has remarked, "is one of the dominant social facts of life in the late twentieth century." The revival of religion, "la revanche de Dieu," as Gilles Kepel labeled it, provides a basis for identity and commitment that transcends national boundaries and unites civilizations.

Fourth, the growth of civilization-consciousness is enhanced by the dual role of the West. On the one hand, the West is at a peak of power. At the same time, however, and perhaps as a result, a return to the roots phenomenon is occurring among non-Western civilizations. Increasingly one hears references to trends toward a turning inward and "Asianization" in Japan, the end of the Nehru legacy and the "Hinduization" of India, the failure of Western ideas of socialism and nationalism and hence "re-Islamization" of the Middle East, and now a debate over Westernization versus Russianization in Boris Yeltsin's country. A West at the peak of its power confronts non-Wests that increasingly have the desire, the will and the resources to shape the world in non-Western ways. . . .

Fifth, cultural characteristics and differences are less mutable and hence less easily compromised and resolved than political and economic ones. In the former Soviet Union, communists can become democrats, the rich can become poor and the poor rich, but Russians cannot become Estonians and Azeris cannot become Armenians. In class and ideological conflicts, the key question was "Which side are you on?" and people could and did choose sides and change sides. In conflicts between civilizations, the question is "What are you?" That is a given that cannot be changed. And as we know, from Bosnia to the Caucasus to the Sudan, the wrong answer to that question can mean a bullet in the head. Even more than ethnicity, religion discriminates sharply and exclusively among people. A person can be half-French and half-Arab and simultaneously even a citizen of two countries. It is more difficult to be half-Catholic and half-Muslim.

Finally, economic regionalism is increasing. . . . The importance of regional economic blocs is likely to continue to increase in the future. On the one hand, successful economic regionalism will reinforce civilization-consciousness. On the other hand, economic regionalism may succeed only when it is rooted in a common civilization. The European Community rests on the shared foundation of European culture and Western Christianity. The success of the North American Free Trade Area depends on the convergence now underway of Mexican, Canadian and American cultures. Japan, in contrast, faces difficulties in creating a comparable economic entity in East Asia because Japan is a society and civilization unique to itself. However strong the trade and investment links Japan may develop with other East Asian countries, its cultural differences with those countries inhibit and perhaps preclude its promoting regional economic integration like that in Europe and North America. . . .

As people define their identity in ethnic and religious terms, they are likely to see an "us" versus "them" relation existing between themselves and people of different ethnicity or religion. The end of ideologically defined states in Eastern Europe and the former Soviet Union permits traditional ethnic identities and animosities to come to the fore. Differences in culture and religion create differences over policy issues, ranging from human rights to immigration to trade and commerce to the environment. Geographical propinquity gives rise to conflicting territorial claims from Bosnia to Mindanao. Most important, the efforts of the West to promote its values of democracy and liberalism as universal values, to maintain its military predominance and to advance its economic interests engender countering responses from other civilizations. Decreasingly able to mobilize support and form coalitions on the basis of ideology, governments and groups will increasingly attempt to mobilize support by appealing to common religion and civilization identity.

The clash of civilizations thus occurs at two levels. At the micro-level, adjacent groups along the fault lines between civilizations struggle, often violently, over the control of territory and each other. At the macro-level, states from different civilizations compete for relative military and economic power, struggle over the control of international institutions and third parties, and competitively promote their particular political and religious values.

THE FAULT LINES BETWEEN CIVILIZATIONS

The fault lines between civilizations are replacing the political and ideological boundaries of the Cold War as the flash points for crisis and bloodshed. The Cold War began when the Iron Curtain divided Europe politically and ideologically. The Cold War ended with the end of the Iron Curtain. As the ideological division of Europe has disappeared, the cultural division of Europe between Western Christianity, on the one hand, and Orthodox Christianity and Islam, on the other, has reemerged. The most significant dividing line in Europe, as William Wallace has suggested, may well be the eastern boundary of Western Christianity in the year 1500. This line runs along what are now the boundaries between Finland and Russia and between the Baltic states and Russia, cuts through Belarus and Ukraine separating the more Catholic western Ukraine from Orthodox eastern Ukraine, swings westward separating Transylvania from the rest of Romania, and then goes through Yugoslavia almost exactly along the line now separating Croatia and Slovenia from the rest of Yugoslavia. In the Balkans this line, of course, coincides with the historic boundary between the Hapsburg and Ottoman empires. The peoples to the north and west of this line are Protestant or Catholic; they shared the common experiences of European history—feudalism, the Renaissance, the Reformation, the Enlightenment, the French Revolution, the Industrial Revolution; they are generally economically better off than the peoples to the east; and they may now look forward to increasing involvement in a common European economy and to the consolidation of democratic political systems. The peoples to the east and south of this line are Orthodox or Muslim; they historically belonged to the Ottoman or Tsarist empires and were only lightly touched by the shaping events in the rest of Europe; they are generally less advanced economically; they seem much less likely to develop stable democratic political systems. The Velvet Curtain of culture has replaced the Iron Curtain of ideology as the most significant dividing line in Europe. As the events in Yugoslavia show, it is not only a line of difference; it is also at times a line of bloody conflict.

Conflict along the fault line between Western and Islamic civilizations has been going on for 1,300 years. After the founding of Islam, the Arab and Moorish surge west and north only ended at Tours in 732. From the eleventh to the thirteenth century the Crusaders attempted with temporary success to bring Christianity and Christian rule to the Holy Land. From the fourteenth to the seventeenth century, the Ottoman Turks reversed the balance, extended their sway over the Middle East and the Balkans, captured Constantinople, and twice laid siege to Vienna. In the nineteenth and early twentieth centuries as Ottoman power declined Britain, France, and Italy established Western control over most of North Africa and the Middle East.

After World War II, the West, in turn, began to retreat; the colonial empires disappeared; first Arab nationalism and then Islamic fundamentalism manifested themselves; the West became heavily dependent on the Persian Gulf countries for its energy; the oil-rich Muslim countries became money-rich and, when they wished to, weapons-rich. Several wars occurred between Arabs and Israel (created by the West). France fought a bloody and ruthless war in Algeria for most of the 1950s; British and French forces invaded Egypt in 1956; American forces went into Lebanon in 1958; subsequently American forces returned to Lebanon, attacked Libya, and engaged in various military encounters with Iran; Arab and Islamic terrorists, supported by at least three Middle Eastern governments, employed the weapon of the weak and bombed Western planes and installations and seized Western hostages. This warfare between Arabs and the West culminated in 1990, when the United States sent a massive army to the Persian Gulf to defend some Arab countries against aggression by another. In its aftermath NATO planning is increasingly directed to potential threats and instability along its "southern tier."

This centuries-old military interaction between the West and Islam is unlikely to decline. It could become more virulent. The Gulf War left some Arabs feeling proud that Saddam Hussein had attacked Israel and stood up to the West. It also left many feeling humiliated and resentful of the West's military presence in the Persian Gulf, the West's overwhelming military dominance, and their apparent inability to shape their own destiny. Many Arab countries, in addition to the oil exporters, are reaching levels of economic and social development where autocratic forms of government become inappropriate and efforts to introduce democracy become stronger. Some openings in Arab political systems have already occurred. The principal beneficiaries of these openings have been Islamist movements. In the Arab world, in short, Western democracy strengthens anti-Western political forces. This may be a passing phenomenon, but it surely complicates relations between Islamic countries and the West.

Those relations are also complicated by demography. The spectacular population growth in Arab countries, particularly in North Africa, has led to increased migration to Western Europe. The movement within Western Europe toward minimizing internal boundaries has sharpened political sensitivities with respect to this development. In Italy, France and Germany, racism is increasingly open, and political reactions and violence against Arab and Turkish migrants have become more intense and more widespread since 1990. . . .

Historically, the other great antagonistic interaction of Arab Islamic civilization has been with the pagan, animist, and now increasingly Christian black peoples to the south. In the past, this antagonism was epitomized in the image of Arab slave dealers and black slaves. It has been reflected in the on-going civil war in the Sudan between Arabs and blacks, the fighting in Chad between Libyan-supported insurgents and the government, the tensions between Orthodox Christians and Muslims in the Horn of Africa, and the political conflicts, recurring riots and communal violence between Muslims and Christians in Nigeria. The modernization of Africa and the spread of Christianity are likely to enhance the probability of violence along this fault line. Symptomatic of the intensification of this conflict was the Pope John Paul II's speech in Khartoum in February 1993 attacking the actions of the Sudan's Islamist government against the Christian minority there.

On the northern border of Islam, conflict has increasingly erupted between Orthodox and Muslim peoples, including the carnage of Bosnia and Sarajevo, the simmering violence between Serb and Albanian, the tenuous relations between Bulgarians and their Turkish minority, the violence between Ossetians and Ingush, the unremitting slaughter of each other by Armenians and Azeris, the tense relations between Russians and Muslims in Central Asia, and the deployment of Russian troops to protect Russian interests in the Caucasus and Central Asia. . . .

The conflict of civilizations is deeply rooted elsewhere in Asia. The historic clash between Muslim and Hindu in the subcontinent manifests itself now not only in the rivalry between Pakistan and India but also in intensifying religious strife within India between increasingly militant Hindu groups and India's substantial Muslim minority. The destruction of the Ayodhya mosque in December 1992 brought to the fore the issue of whether India will remain a secular democratic state or become a Hindu one. In East Asia, China has outstanding territorial disputes with most of its neighbors. It has pursued a ruthless policy toward the Buddhist people of Tibet, and it is pursuing an increasingly ruthless policy toward its Turkic-Muslim minority. . . .

THE WEST VERSUS THE REST

The West is now at an extraordinary peak of power in relation to other civilizations. Its superpower opponent has disappeared from the map. Military conflict among Western states is unthinkable, and Western military power is unrivaled. Apart from Japan, the West faces no economic challenge. It dominates international political and security institutions and with Japan international economic institutions. Global political and security issues are effectively settled by a directorate of the United States, Britain and France, world economic issues by a directorate of the United States, Germany and Japan, all of which maintain extraordinarily close relations with each other to the exclusion of lesser and largely non-Western countries. Decisions made at the U.N. Security Council or in the International Monetary Fund that reflect the interests of the West are presented to the world as reflecting the desires of the world community.

The very phrase "the world community" has become the euphemistic collective noun (replacing "the Free World") to give global legitimacy to actions reflecting the interests of the United States and other Western powers.[1] Through the IMF and other international economic institutions, the West promotes its economic interests and imposes on other nations the economic policies it thinks appropriate. In any poll of non-Western peoples, the IMF undoubtedly would win the support of finance ministers and a few others, but get an overwhelmingly unfavorable rating from just about everyone else. . . .

Western domination of the U.N. Security Council and its decisions, tempered only by occasional abstention by China, produced U.N. legitimation of the West's use of force to drive Iraq out of Kuwait and its elimination of Iraq's sophisticated weapons and capacity to produce such weapons. It also produced the quite unprecedented action by the United States, Britain and France in getting the Security Council to demand that Libya hand over the Pan Am 103 bombing suspects and then to impose sanctions when Libya refused. After defeating the largest Arab army, the West did not hesitate to throw its weight around in the Arab world. The West in effect is using international institutions, military power and economic resources to run the world in ways that will maintain Western predominance, protect Western interests and promote Western political and economic values.

That at least is the way in which non-Westerners see the new world, and there is a significant element of truth in their view. Differences in power and struggles for military, economic and institutional power are thus one source of conflict between the West and other civilizations. Differences in culture, that is basic values and beliefs, are a second source of conflict. V. S. Naipaul has argued that Western civilization is the "universal civilization" that "fits all men." At a superficial level much of Western culture has indeed permeated the rest of the world. At a more basic level, however, Western concepts differ fundamentally from those prevalent in other civilizations. Western ideas of individualism, liberalism, constitutionalism, human rights, equality, liberty, the rule of law, democracy, free markets, the separation of church and state, often have little resonance in Islamic, Confucian, Japanese, Hindu, Buddhist or Orthodox cultures. Western efforts to propagate such ideas produce instead a reaction against "human rights imperialism" and a reaffirmation of indigenous values, as can be seen in the support for religious fundamentalism by the younger generation in non-Western cultures. The very notion that there could be a "universal civilization" is a Western idea, directly at odds with the particularism of most Asian societies and their emphasis on what distinguishes one people from another. Indeed, the author of a review of 100 comparative studies of values in different societies concluded that "the values that are most important in the West are least important worldwide."[2] In the political realm, of course, these differences are most manifest in the efforts of the United States and other Western powers to induce other peoples to adopt Western ideas concerning democracy and human rights. Modern democratic government originated in the West. When it has developed in non-Western societies it has usually been the product of Western colonialism or imposition.

The central axis of world politics in the future is likely to be, in Kishore Mahbubani's phrase, the conflict between "the West and the Rest" and the responses of non-Western civilizations to Western power and values.[3] Those responses generally take one or a combination of three forms. At one extreme, non-Western states can, like Burma and North Korea, attempt to pursue a course of isolation, to insulate their societies from penetration or "corruption" by the West, and, in effect, to opt out of participation in the Western-dominated global community. The costs of this course, however, are high, and few states have pursued it exclusively. A second alternative, the equivalent of "band-wagoning" in international relations theory, is to attempt to join the West and accept its values and institutions. The third alternative is to attempt to "balance" the West by developing economic and military power and cooperating with other non-Western societies against the West, while preserving indigenous values and institutions; in short, to modernize but not to Westernize. . . .

IMPLICATIONS FOR THE WEST

This article does not argue that civilization identities will replace all other identities, that nation states will disappear, that each civilization will become a single coherent political entity, that groups within a civilization will not conflict with and even fight each other. This paper does set forth the hypotheses that differences between civilizations are real and important; civilization-consciousness is increasing; conflict between civilizations will supplant ideological and other forms of conflict as the dominant global form of conflict; international relations, historically a game played out within Western civilization, will increasingly be de-Westernized and become a game in which non-Western civilizations are actors and not simply objects; successful political, security and economic international institutions are more likely to develop within civilizations than across civilizations; conflicts between groups in different civilizations will be more frequent, more sustained and more violent than conflicts between groups in the same civilization; violent conflicts between groups in different civilizations are the most likely and most dangerous source of escalation that could lead to global wars; the paramount axis of world politics

will be the relations between "the West and the Rest"; the elites in some torn non-Western countries will try to make their countries part of the West, but in most cases face major obstacles to accomplishing this; a central focus of conflict for the immediate future will be between the West and several Islamic-Confucian states.

This is not to advocate the desirability of conflicts between civilizations. It is to set forth descriptive hypotheses as to what the future may be like. If these are plausible hypotheses, however, it is necessary to consider their implications for Western policy. These implications should be divided between short-term advantage and long-term accommodation. In the short term it is clearly in the interest of the West to promote greater cooperation and unity within its own civilization, particularly between its European and North American components; to incorporate into the West societies in Eastern Europe and Latin America whose cultures are close to those of the West; to promote and maintain cooperative relations with Russia and Japan; to prevent escalation of local inter-civilization conflicts into major inter-civilization wars; to limit the expansion of the military strength of Confucian and Islamic states; to moderate the reduction of Western military capabilities and maintain military superiority in East and Southwest Asia; to exploit differences and conflicts among Confucian and Islamic states; to support in other civilizations groups sympathetic to Western values and interests; to strengthen international institutions that reflect and legitimate Western interests and values and to promote the involvement of non-Western states in those institutions.

In the longer term other measures would be called for. Western civilization is both Western and modern. Non-Western civilizations have attempted to become modern without becoming Western. To date only Japan has fully succeeded in this quest. Non-Western civilizations will continue to attempt to acquire the wealth, technology, skills, machines and weapons that are part of being modern. They will also attempt to reconcile this modernity with their traditional culture and values. Their economic and military strength relative to the West will increase. Hence the West will increasingly have to accommodate these non-Western modern civilizations whose power approaches that of the West but whose values and interests differ significantly from those of the West. This will require the West to maintain the economic and military power necessary to protect its interests in relation to these civilizations. It will also, however, require the West to develop a more profound understanding of the basic religious and philosophical assumptions underlying other civilizations and the ways in which people in those civilizations see their interests. It will require an effort to identify elements of commonality between Western and other civilizations. For the relevant future, there will be no universal civilization, but instead a world of different civilizations, each of which will have to learn to coexist with the others.

NOTES

1. Almost invariably Western leaders claim they are acting on behalf of "the world community." One minor lapse occurred during the run-up to the Gulf War. In an interview on "Good Morning America," Dec. 21, 1990, British Prime Minister John Major referred to the actions "the West" was taking against Saddam Hussein. He quickly corrected himself and subsequently referred to "the world community." He was, however, right when he erred.

2. Harry C. Triandis, *The New York Times*, Dec. 25, 1990, p. 41, and "Cross-Cultural Studies of Individualism and Collectivism," Nebraska Symposium on Motivation, vol. 37, 1989. pp. 41–133.

3. Kishore Mahbubani, "The West and the Rest," *The National Interest*, Summer 1992, pp. 3–13.

THE CASE AGAINST THE WEST: AMERICA AND EUROPE IN THE ASIAN CENTURY

Kishore Mahbubani

If Huntington is right about a clash of civilizations, Mahbubani suggests Western civilization is losing that clash. He argues, the West is not only facing the end of its global domination, but as it does so it is acting in ways that are exacerbating rather than solving global problems. As you read his article, ask yourself:

- In what ways does he see the West as exacerbating global problems?
- Is Mahbubani right that the era of Western dominance is over?
- If he is right, will the transition in power and influence from West to East occur peacefully over the course of the twenty-first century?

There is a fundamental flaw in the West's strategic thinking. In all its analyses of global challenges, the West assumes that it is the source of the solutions to the world's key problems. In fact, however, the West is also a major source of these problems. Unless key Western policymakers learn to understand and deal with this reality, the world is headed for an even more troubled phase.

The West is understandably reluctant to accept that the era of its domination is ending and that the Asian century has come. No civilization cedes power easily, and the West's resistance to giving up control of key global institutions and processes is natural. Yet the West is engaging in an extraordinary act of self-deception by believing that it is open to change. In fact, the West has become the most powerful force preventing the emergence of a new wave of history, clinging to its privileged position in key global forums, such as the UN Security Council, the International Monetary Fund, the World Bank, and the G-8 (the group of highly industrialized states), and refusing to contemplate how the West will have to adjust to the Asian century.

Partly as a result of its growing insecurity, the West has also become increasingly incompetent in its handling of key global problems. Many Western commentators can readily identify specific failures, such as the Bush administration's botched invasion and occupation of Iraq. But few can see that this reflects a deeper structural problem: the West's inability to see that the world has entered a new era.

Apart from representing a specific failure of policy execution, the war in Iraq has also highlighted the gap between the reality and what the West had expected would happen after the invasion. Arguably, the United States and the United Kingdom intended only to free the Iraqi people from a despotic ruler and to rid the world of a dangerous man, Saddam Hussein. Even if George W. Bush and Tony Blair had no malevolent intentions, however, their approaches were trapped in the Western mindset of believing that their interventions could lead only to good, not harm or disaster. This led them to believe that the invading U.S. troops would be welcomed with roses thrown at their feet by happy Iraqis. But the twentieth century showed that no country welcomes foreign invaders. The notion that any Islamic nation would approve of Western military boots on its soil was ridiculous. Even in the early twentieth century, the British invasion and occupation of Iraq was met with armed resistance. In 1920, Winston Churchill, then British secretary for war and air, quelled the rebellion of Kurds and Arabs in British-occupied Iraq by authorizing his troops to use chemical weapons. "I am strongly in favor of using poisoned gas against uncivilized tribes," Churchill said. The world has moved on from this era, but many Western officials have not abandoned the old assumption that an army of Christian soldiers can successfully invade, occupy, and transform an Islamic society.

Many Western leaders often begin their speeches by remarking on how perilous the world is becoming. Speaking after the August 2006 discovery of a plot to blow up transatlantic flights originating from London, President Bush said, "The American people need to know we live in a dangerous world." But even as Western leaders speak of such threats, they seem incapable of conceding that the West itself could be the fundamental source of these dangers. After all, the West includes the best-managed states in the world, the most economically developed, those with the strongest democratic institutions. But one cannot assume that a government that rules competently at home will be equally good at addressing challenges abroad. In fact, the converse is more likely to be true. Although the Western mind is obsessed with the Islamist terrorist threat, the West is mishandling the two immediate and pressing challenges of Afghanistan and Iraq. And despite the grave threat of nuclear terrorism, the Western custodians of the nonproliferation regime have allowed that regime to weaken significantly. The challenge posed by Iran's efforts to enrich uranium has been aggravated by the incompetence of the United States and the European Union. On the economic front, for the first time since World War II, the demise of a round of global trade negotiations, the Doha Round, seems imminent. Finally, the danger of global warming, too, is being mismanaged.

Yet Westerners seldom look inward to understand the deeper reasons these global problems are being mismanaged. Are there domestic structural reasons that explain this? Have Western democracies been hijacked by competitive populism and structural short-termism, preventing them from addressing long-term challenges from a broader global perspective?

Fortunately, some Asian states may now be capable of taking on more responsibilities, as they have been strengthened by implementing Western principles. In September 2005, Robert Zoellick, then U.S. deputy secretary of state, called on China to become a "responsible stakeholder" in the international system. China has responded positively, as have other Asian states. In recent decades, Asians have been among the greatest beneficiaries of the open multilateral order created by the United States and the other victors of World War II, and few today want to destabilize it. The number of Asians seeking a comfortable middle-class existence has never been higher. For centuries, the Chinese and the Indians could only dream of such an accomplishment; now it is within the reach of around half a billion people in China and India. Their ideal is to achieve what the United States and Europe did. They want to replicate, not dominate, the West. The universalization of the Western dream

represents a moment of triumph for the West. And so the West should welcome the fact that the Asian states are becoming competent at handling regional and global challenges.

THE MIDDLE EAST MESS

Western policies have been most harmful in the Middle East. The Middle East is also the most dangerous region in the world. Trouble there affects not just seven million Israelis, around four million Palestinians, and 200 million Arabs; it also affects more than a billion Muslims worldwide. Every time there is a major flare-up in the Middle East, such as the U.S. invasion of Iraq or the Israeli bombing of Lebanon, Islamic communities around the world become concerned, distressed, and angered. And few of them doubt the problem's origin: the West.

The invasion and occupation of Iraq, for example, was a multidimensional error. The theory and practice of international law legitimizes the use of force only when it is an act of self-defense or is authorized by the UN Security Council. The U.S.-led invasion of Iraq could not be justified on either count. The United States and the United Kingdom sought the Security Council's authorization to invade Iraq, but the council denied it. It was therefore clear to the international community that the subsequent war was illegal and that it would do huge damage to international law.

This has created an enormous problem, partly because until this point both the United States and the United Kingdom had been among the primary custodians of international law. American and British minds, such as James Brierly, Philip Jessup, Hersch Lauterpacht, and Hans Morgenthau, developed the conceptual infrastructure underlying international law, and American and British leaders provided the political will to have it accepted in practice. But neither the United States nor the United Kingdom will admit that the invasion and the occupation of Iraq were illegal or give up their historical roles as the chief caretakers of international law. Since 2003, both nations have frequently called for Iran and North Korea to implement UN Security Council resolutions. But how can the violators of UN principles also be their enforcers?

One rare benefit of the Iraq war may be that it has awakened a new fear of Iran among the Sunni Arab states. Egypt, Jordan, and Saudi Arabia, among others, do not want to deal with two adversaries and so are inclined to make peace with Israel. Saudi Arabia's King Abdullah used the opportunity of the special Arab League summit meeting in March 2007 to relaunch his long-standing proposal for a two-state solution to the Israeli-Palestinian conflict. Unfortunately, the Bush administration did not seize the opportunity—or revive the Taba accords that President Bill Clinton had worked out in January 2001, even though they could provide a basis for a lasting settlement and the Saudis were prepared to back them. In its early days, the Bush administration appeared ready to support a two-state solution. It was the first U.S. administration to vote in favor of a UN Security Council resolution calling for the creation of a Palestinian state, and it announced in March 2002 that it would try to achieve such a result by 2005. But here it is 2008, and little progress has been made.

The United States has made the already complicated Israeli-Palestinian conflict even more of a mess. Many extremist voices in Tel Aviv and Washington believe that time will always be on Israel's side. The pro-Israel lobby's stranglehold on the U.S. Congress, the political cowardice of U.S. politicians when it comes to creating a Palestinian state, and the sustained track record of U.S. aid to Israel support this view. But no great power forever sacrifices its larger national interests in favor of the interests of a small state. If Israel fails to accept the Taba accords, it will inevitably come to grief. If and when it does, Western incompetence will be seen as a major cause.

NEVER SAY NEVER

Nuclear nonproliferation is another area in which the West, especially the United States, has made matters worse. The West has long been obsessed with the danger of the proliferation of weapons of mass destruction, particularly nuclear weapons. It pushed successfully for the near-universal ratification of the Biological and Toxin Weapons Convention, the Chemical Weapons Convention, and the Nuclear Nonproliferation Treaty (NPT).

But the West has squandered many of those gains. Today, the NPT is legally alive but spiritually dead. The NPT was inherently problematic since it divided the world into nuclear haves (the states that had tested a nuclear device by 1967) and nuclear have-nots (those that had not). But for two decades it was reasonably effective in preventing horizontal proliferation (the spread of nuclear weapons to other states). Unfortunately, the NPT has done nothing to prevent vertical proliferation, namely, the increase in the numbers and sophistication of nuclear weapons among the existing nuclear weapons states. During the Cold War, the United States and the Soviet Union agreed to work together to limit proliferation. The governments of several countries that could have developed nuclear weapons, such as Argentina, Brazil, Germany, Japan, and South Korea, restrained themselves because they believed the NPT reflected a fair bargain between China, France, the Soviet Union, the United Kingdom, and the United States (the five official nuclear weapons states and five permanent members of the UN Security

Council) and the rest of the world. Both sides agreed that the world would be safer if the five nuclear states took steps to reduce their arsenals and worked toward the eventual goal of universal disarmament and the other states refrained from acquiring nuclear weapons at all.

So what went wrong? The first problem was that the NPT's principal progenitor, the United States, decided to walk away from the postwar rule-based order it had created, thus eroding the infrastructure on which the NPT's enforcement depends. During the time I was Singapore's ambassador to the UN, between 1984 and 1989, Jeane Kirkpatrick, the U.S. ambassador to the UN, treated the organization with contempt. She infamously said, "What takes place in the Security Council more closely resembles a mugging than either a political debate or an effort at problem-solving." She saw the postwar order as a set of constraints, not as a set of rules that the world should follow and the United States should help preserve. This undermined the NPT, because with no teeth of its own, no self-regulating or sanctioning mechanisms, and a clause allowing signatories to ignore obligations in the name of "supreme national interest," the treaty could only really be enforced by the UN Security Council. And once the United States began tearing holes in the fabric of the overall system, it created openings for violations of the NPT and its principles. Finally, by going to war with Iraq without UN authorization, the United States lost its moral authority to ask, for example, Iran to abide by Security Council resolutions.

Another problem has been the United States'—and other nuclear weapons states'— direct assault on the treaty. The NPT is fundamentally a social contract between the five nuclear weapons states and the rest of the world, based partly on the understanding that the nuclear powers will eventually give up their weapons. Instead, during the Cold War, the United States and the Soviet Union increased both the quantity and the sophistication of their nuclear weapons: the United States' nuclear stockpile peaked in 1966 at 31,700 warheads, and the Soviet Union's peaked in 1986 at 40,723. In fact, the United States and the Soviet Union developed their nuclear stockpiles so much that they actually ran out of militarily or economically significant targets. The numbers have declined dramatically since then, but even the current number of nuclear weapons held by the United States and Russia can wreak enormous damage on human civilization.

The nuclear states' decision to ignore Israel's nuclear weapons program was especially damaging to their authority. No nuclear weapons state has ever publicly acknowledged Israel's possession of nuclear weapons. Their silence has created a loophole in the NPT and delegitimized it in the eyes of Muslim nations. The consequences have been profound. When the West sermonizes that the world will become a more dangerous place when Iran acquires nuclear weapons, the Muslim world now shrugs.

India and Pakistan were already shrugging by 1998, when they tested their first nuclear weapons. When the international community responded by condemning the tests and applying sanctions on India, virtually all Indians saw through the hypocrisy and double standards of their critics. By not respecting their own obligations under the NPT, the five nuclear states had robbed their condemnations of any moral legitimacy; criticisms from Australia and Canada, which have also remained silent about Israel's bomb, similarly had no moral authority. The near-unanimous rejection of the NPT by the Indian establishment, which is otherwise very conscious of international opinion, showed how dead the treaty already was.

From time to time, common sense has entered discussions on nuclear weapons. President

Ronald Reagan said more categorically than any U.S. president that the world would be better off without nuclear weapons. Last year, with the NPT in its death throes and the growing threat of loose nuclear weapons falling into the hands of terrorists forefront in everyone's mind, former Secretary of State George Shultz, former Defense Secretary William Perry, former Secretary of State Henry Kissinger, and former Senator Sam Nunn warned in The Wall Street Journal that the world was "now on the precipice of a new and dangerous nuclear era." They argued, "Unless urgent new actions are taken, the U.S. soon will be compelled to enter a new nuclear era that will be more precarious, psychologically disorienting, and economically even more costly than was Cold War deterrence." But these calls may have come too late. The world has lost its trust in the five nuclear weapons states and now sees them as the NPT's primary violators rather than its custodians. Those states' private cynicism about their obligations to the NPT has become public knowledge.

Contrary to what the West wants the rest of the world to believe, the nuclear weapons states, especially the United States and Russia, which continue to maintain thousands of nuclear weapons, are the biggest source of nuclear proliferation. Mohamed ElBaradei, the director general of the International Atomic Energy Agency, warned in *The Economist* in 2003, "The very existence of nuclear weapons gives rise to the pursuit of them. They are seen as a source of global influence, and are valued for their perceived deterrent effect. And as long as some countries possess them (or are protected by them in alliances) and others do not, this asymmetry breeds chronic global insecurity." Despite the Cold War, the second half of the twentieth century seemed to be moving the world toward a more civilized order. As the twenty-first century unfurls, the world seems to be sliding backward.

IRRESPONSIBLE STAKEHOLDERS

After leading the world toward a period of spectacular economic growth in the second half of the twentieth century by promoting global free trade, the West has recently been faltering in its global economic leadership. Believing that low trade barriers and increasing trade interdependence would result in higher standards of living for all, European and U.S. economists and policymakers pushed for global economic liberalization. As a result, global trade grew from seven percent of the world's GDP in 1940 to 30 percent in 2005.

But a seismic shift has taken place in Western attitudes since the end of the Cold War. Suddenly, the United States and Europe no longer have a vested interest in the success of the East Asian economies, which they see less as allies and more as competitors. That change in Western interests was reflected in the fact that the West provided little real help to East Asia during the Asian financial crisis of 1997–98. The entry of China into the global marketplace, especially after its admission to the World Trade Organization, has made a huge difference in both economic and psychological terms. Many Europeans have lost confidence in their ability to compete with the Asians. And many Americans have lost confidence in the virtues of competition.

There are some knotty issues that need to be resolved in the current global trade talks, but fundamentally the negotiations are stalled because the conviction of the Western "champions" of free trade that free trade is good has begun to waver. When Americans and Europeans start to perceive themselves as losers in international trade, they also lose their drive to push for further trade liberalization. Unfortunately, on this front at least, neither China nor India (nor Brazil nor South Africa nor any other major developing country) is ready to take over the West's mantle. China, for example, is afraid that any effort to seek leadership in this area will stoke U.S. fears that it is striving for global hegemony. Hence, China is lying low. So, too, are the United States and Europe. Hence, the trade talks are stalled. The end of the West's promotion of global trade liberalization could well mean the end of the most spectacular economic growth the world has ever seen. Few in the West seem to be reflecting on the consequences of walking away from one of the West's most successful policies, which is what it will be doing if it allows the Doha Round to fail.

At the same time that the Western governments are relinquishing their stewardship of the global economy, they are also failing to take the lead on battling global warming. The awarding of the Nobel Peace Prize to former U.S. Vice President Al Gore, a longtime environmentalist, and the UN's Intergovernmental Panel on Climate Change confirms there is international consensus that global warming is a real threat. The most assertive advocates for tackling this problem come from the U.S. and European scientific communities, but the greatest resistance to any effective action is coming from the U.S. government. This has left the rest of the world confused and puzzled. Most people believe that the greenhouse effect is caused mostly by the flow of current emissions. Current emissions do aggravate the problem, but the fundamental cause is the stock of emissions that has accumulated since the Industrial Revolution. Finding a just and equitable solution to the problem of greenhouse gas emissions must begin with assigning responsibility both for the current flow and for the stock of greenhouse gases already accumulated. And on both counts the Western nations should bear a greater burden.

When it comes to addressing any problem pertaining to the global commons, such as the environment, it seems only fair that the wealthier members of the international community should shoulder more responsibility. This is a natural principle of justice. It is also fair in this particular case given the developed countries' primary role in releasing harmful gases into the atmosphere. R. K. Pachauri, chair of the Intergovernmental Panel on Climate Change, argued last year, "China and India are certainly increasing their share, but they are not increasing their per capita emissions anywhere close to the levels that you have in the developed world." Since 1850, China has contributed less than 8 percent of the world's total emissions of carbon dioxide, whereas the United States is responsible for 29 percent and western Europe is responsible for 27 percent. Today, India's per capita greenhouse gas emissions are equivalent to only 4 percent of those of the United States and 12 percent of those of the European Union. Still, the Western governments are not clearly acknowledging their responsibilities and are allowing many of their citizens to believe that China and India are the fundamental obstacles to any solution to global warming.

Washington might become more responsible on this front if a Democratic president replaces Bush in 2009. But people in the West will have to make some real concessions if they are to reduce significantly their per capita share of global emissions. A cap-and-trade program may do the trick. Western countries will probably have to make economic sacrifices. One option might be, as the journalist Thomas Friedman has suggested, to impose a dollar-per-gallon tax on Americans' gasoline consumption. Gore has proposed a carbon tax. So far, however, few U.S. politicians have dared to make such suggestions publicly.

TEMPTATIONS OF THE EAST

The Middle East, nuclear proliferation, stalled trade liberalization, and global warming are all challenges that the West is essentially failing to address. And this failure suggests that a systemic problem is emerging in the West's stewardship of the international order—one that Western minds are reluctant to analyze or confront openly. After having enjoyed centuries of global domination, the West has to learn to share power and responsibility for the management of global issues with the rest of the world. It has to forgo outdated organizations, such as the Organization for Economic Cooperation and Development, and outdated processes, such as the G-8, and deal with organizations and processes with a broader scope and broader representation. It was always unnatural for the 12 percent of the world population that lived in the West to enjoy so much global power. Understandably, the other 88 percent of the world population increasingly wants also to drive the bus of world history.

First and foremost, the West needs to acknowledge that sharing the power it has accumulated in global forums would serve its interests. Restructuring international institutions to reflect the current world order will be complicated by the absence of natural leaders to do the job. The West has become part of the problem, and the Asian countries are not yet ready to step in. On the other hand, the world does not need to invent any new principles to improve global governance; the concepts of domestic good governance can and should be applied to the international community. The Western principles of democracy, the rule of law, and social justice are among the world's best bets. The ancient virtues of partnership and pragmatism can complement them.

Democracy, the foundation of government in the West, is based on the premise that each human being in a society is an equal stakeholder in the domestic order. Thus, governments are selected on the basis of "one person, one vote." This has produced long-term stability and order in Western societies. In order to produce long-term stability and order worldwide, democracy should be the cornerstone of global society, and the planet's 6.6 billion inhabitants should become equal stakeholders. To inject the spirit of democracy into global governance and global decision-making, one must turn to institutions with universal representation, especially the UN. UN institutions such as the World Health Organization and the World Meteorological Organization enjoy widespread legitimacy because of their universal membership, which means their decisions are generally accepted by all the countries of the world.

The problem today is that although many Western actors are willing to work with specialized UN agencies, they are reluctant to strengthen the UN's core institution, the UN General Assembly, from which all these specialized agencies come. The UN General Assembly is the most representative body on the planet, and yet many Western countries are deeply skeptical of it. They are right to point out its imperfections. But they overlook the fact that this imperfect assembly enjoys legitimacy in the eyes of the people of this imperfect world. Moreover, the General Assembly has at times shown more common sense and prudence than some of the most sophisticated Western democracies. Of course, it takes time to persuade all of the UN's members to march in the same direction, but consensus building is precisely what gives legitimacy to the result. Most countries in the world respect and abide by most UN decisions because they believe in the authority of the UN. Used well, the body can be a powerful vehicle for making critical decisions on global governance.

The world today is run not through the General Assembly but through the Security Council, which is effectively run by the five permanent member states. If this model were adopted in the United States, the U.S. Congress would be replaced by a selective council comprised of only the representatives from the country's five most powerful states. Would the populations of the other 45 states not deem any such proposal absurd? The West must cease its efforts to prolong its undemocratic management of the global order and find ways to effectively engage the majority of the world's population in global decision-making.

Another fundamental principle that should underpin the global order is the rule of law. This hallowed Western principle insists that no person, regardless of his or her status, is above the law. Ironically, while being exemplary in implementing the rule of law at home, the United States is a leading international outlaw in its refusal to recognize the constraints of international law. Many Americans live comfortably with this contradiction while expecting other countries to abide by widely accepted treaties. Americans react with horror when Iran tries to walk away from the NPT. Yet they are surprised that the world is equally shocked when Washington abandons a universally accepted treaty such as the Comprehensive Test Ban Treaty.

The Bush administration's decision to exempt the United States from the provisions of international law on human rights is even more damaging. For over half a century, since Eleanor Roosevelt led the fight for the adoption of the Universal Declaration of Human Rights, the United States was the global champion of human rights. This was the result of a strong ideological conviction that it was the United States' God-given duty to create a more civilized world. It also made for a good ideological weapon during the Cold War: the free United States was fighting the unfree Soviet Union. But the Bush administration has stunned the world by walking away from universally accepted human rights conventions, especially those on torture. And much as the U.S. electorate could

not be expected to tolerate an attorney general who broke his own laws from time to time, how can the global body politic be expected to respect a custodian of international law that violates these very rules?

Finally, on social justice, Western nations have slackened. Social justice is the cornerstone of order and stability in modern Western societies and the rest of the world. People accept inequality as long as some kind of social safety net exists to help the dispossessed. Most western European governments took this principle to heart after World War II and introduced welfare provisions as a way to ward off Marxist revolutions seeking to create socialist societies. Today, many Westerners believe that they are spreading social justice globally with their massive foreign aid to the developing world. Indeed, each year, the members of the Organization for Economic Cooperation and Development, according to the organization's own estimates, give approximately $104 billion to the developing world. But the story of Western aid to the developing world is essentially a myth. Western countries have put significant amounts of money into their overseas development assistance budgets, but these funds' primary purpose is to serve the immediate and short-term security and national interests of the donors rather than the long-term interests of the recipients.

The experience of Asia shows that where Western aid has failed to do the job, domestic good governance can succeed. This is likely to be Asia's greatest contribution to world history. The success of Asia will inspire other societies on different continents to emulate it. In addition, Asia's march to modernity can help produce a more stable world order. Some Asian countries are now ready to join the West in becoming responsible custodians of the global order; as the biggest beneficiaries of the current system, they have powerful incentives to do so.

The West is not welcoming Asia's progress, and its short-term interests in preserving its privileged position in various global institutions are trumping its long-term interests in creating a more just and stable world order. Unfortunately, the West has gone from being the world's primary problem solver to being its single biggest liability.

LET WOMEN RULE

Swanee Hunt

In this piece, Swanee Hunt makes the case for more female involvement in the policy-making process. As you read her article, ask yourself:

- What evidence does she provide that more women in leadership positions would bring rewards in the conduct of world politics?
- Why are there not more female leaders today?
- Are you persuaded that "letting women rule" would make the world a more peaceful place?

MISSING OUT

Women have made significant strides in most societies over the last century, but the trend line has not been straight. In recent interviews with hundreds of female leaders in over 30 countries, I have discovered that where women have taken leadership roles, it has been as social reformers and entrepreneurs, not as politicians or government officials. This is unfortunate, because the world needs women's perspectives and particular talents in top positions. In 1998, Francis Fukuyama wrote in Foreign Affairs that women's political leadership would bring about a more cooperative and less conflict-prone world ("Women and the Evolution of World Politics," September/October 1998). That promise has yet to be fulfilled.

Granted, a few women are breaking through traditional barriers and becoming presidents, prime ministers, cabinet members, and legislators. But even as the media spotlight falls on the 11 female heads of government around the world, another significant fact goes unreported: most of the best and the brightest women eschew politics. Women are much more likely to wield influence from a nongovernmental organization (NGO) than from public office.

Women are still severely underrepresented in governments worldwide. A recent World Economic Forum report covering 115 countries notes that women have closed over 90 percent of the gender gap in education and in health but only 15 percent of it when it comes to political empowerment at the highest levels. Although 97 countries have some sort of gender quota system for government positions, according to the Inter-Parliamentary Union, an organization that fosters exchange among parliaments, women fill only 17 percent of parliamentary seats worldwide and 14 percent of ministerial-level positions—and most of those are related to family, youth, the disabled, and the elderly. At NGOs, the story is very different: women are consistently over-represented at the top levels.

This pattern also holds for the United States, where 16 of 100 members of the Senate and 71 of 435 members of the House of Representatives are women. The United States ranks 68 out of 189 countries, behind a dozen in Latin America, in terms of the number of women in the legislature. Those low numbers are consistent with Capitol Hill's historic antipathy toward females. Women were denied the vote for 133 years, refused an equal rights amendment, and shut out of government-funded health research for decades. At the same time, American women have gravitated en masse toward NGOs, where they have found fewer barriers to leadership. The 230 NGOs in the National Council of Women's Organizations represent ten million American women, and women lead many of the country's largest philanthropic organizations, including the Bill and Melinda Gates Foundation and the Ford Foundation. As for academia, Harvard, MIT, and Princeton currently have women at the helm.

Most other countries follow a similar pattern. The number of NGOs in the former Soviet republics grew exponentially after the fall of the Iron Curtain, and women formed the backbone of this new civil society, but the percentage of women in eastern European parliaments plummeted. In Lithuania, that percentage declined from approximately 33 percent during the communist era to 17.5 percent in 1997 and 10.6 percent in 2004. According to a group of journalists in Kyrgyzstan, women head 90 percent of NGOs but hold not a single seat in parliament, even though they made up 33 percent of the legislature at the end of the Soviet era. In China, the Communist Party-controlled All-China Women's Federation functions much as an NGO does, engaging women across the country on community issues, but despite the government's claims of equality, Chinese women have rarely held positions of political power. Likewise, in South Korea, women run some 80 percent of the country's NGOs but occupy less than 14 percent of the seats in the National Assembly. The story is the same in Africa. According to Robert Rotberg, director of the Program on Intrastate Conflict and Conflict Resolution at Harvard's Kennedy School of Government, "African women, who traditionally do the hard work of cultivation and all of the family rearing, also nurture NGOs and motivate civic initiatives. But they are widely expected to leave politics—and corruption and conflict—to men."

Women may thrive in NGOs. The world, however, needs them to take that experience into the political sphere. As the Sierra Leonean activist and former presidential candidate Zainab Bangura points out, "The real power isn't in civil society; it's in policymaking."

A WOMAN'S VIEW

Greater female political participation would bring significant rewards. Research sponsored by the World Bank has shown that countries with a high number of women in parliament enjoy lower levels of corruption. Another World Bank-sponsored study concludes that women are less likely to be involved in bribery and that corruption is less severe where women make up a large share of senior government officials as well as the labor force. A survey of research by Rachel Croson, of the Wharton School, and Uri Gneezy, of the University of California, San Diego, similarly concluded that women are more trustworthy than men. Consider Nigeria. The watchdog group Transparency International ranked it as the most corrupt country in the world in 2003. But that year, Ngozi Okonjo-Iweala left her job as a vice president at the World Bank to become the country's finance minister, and by 2005 Transparency International was hailing Nigeria as one of 21 most improved states. Change came thanks to the indictment of corrupt officials, as well as to reform in banking, insurance, the foreign exchange market, pensions, and income taxation. Similarly, in Liberia, international policymakers have been heartened to see President Ellen Johnson-Sirleaf prioritize the eradication of corruption. Knowing that foreign investment would flow only after a crackdown on the plundering culture of her predecessors, Johnson-Sirleaf fired the entire Finance Ministry staff and brought in women for the positions of finance minister, chief of police, commerce minister, and justice minister, among others.

Electing and appointing women to positions of political leadership turns out to be good for the broader economy as well. There is a correlation between women holding political office and the overall economic competitiveness of a nation. Augusto Lopez-Claros, chief economist and director of the World Economic Forum's Global Competitiveness Network, argues that "the Nordic countries seem to have understood the economic incentive behind empowering women: countries that do not fully capitalize on one-half of their human resources are clearly undermining their competitive potential." The high percentage of women in parliament in countries such as Rwanda (almost 49 percent of members in the lower house), Costa Rica (40 percent), and Mozambique (35 percent) suggests that it is not simply a nation's affluence that causes more women to assume leadership positions. If that were the case, the relatively prosperous United States should be in the top ranks of countries sending women to Congress instead of lagging behind countries such as El Salvador, Nepal, and Tajikistan.

In 2000, an Inter-Parliamentary Union poll of 187 female politicians in 65 countries found that 80 percent of the respondents believed that increased representation of women renews public trust in government, which in turn helps economic welfare. The politicians cited examples from countries as varied as El Salvador, Ethiopia, New Zealand, and Russia in which political activism by women led to "tangible improvements" in social services, the environment, the safety of women and children, and gender equality.

Worldwide, female legislators as a group tend to concentrate on helping marginalized citizens. In the United States, for example, Democratic and moderate Republican congresswomen are more likely than men to focus on socially conscious legislation. Perhaps female politicians take such concerns to heart because they have often honed their skills in the NGO arena. Chilean President Michelle Bachelet, for instance, returned from exile in 1979 to work with children of people who were tortured or who disappeared during the dictatorship of Augusto Pinochet. South Korean Prime Minister Han Myeong Sook was a social activist (and political prisoner) during her country's military dictatorship.

The lessons women learn while leading civil society may also explain why they have "higher moral or ethical standards than their male counterparts," according to the International NGO Training and Research Center. Hannah Riley Bowles, professor of public policy at Harvard's Kennedy School of Government, found that when negotiating for jobs, American women asked for 15 percent less than men did, but when negotiating on behalf of others, women's demands increased substantially. (No such difference was found among male negotiators.) Carrying that tendency into the political sphere, "women may hold back when promoting their own candidacy or securing the resources they need to rise to the fore," argues Bowles. But they can be "fabulous advocates for their constituents."

Given these qualities, it is no surprise that women's involvement in political negotiations tends to solidify conflict resolution. "If we put women in leadership, they have a degree of tolerance, an understanding that allows them to persist even when things seem to be very bad," notes Pumla Gobodo-Madikizela, a South African clinical psychologist who worked in grass-roots NGOs during apartheid and helped establish the Truth and Reconciliation Commission. Unlike men, she continues, "women have the power and emotional inclination to hold onto hope when it comes to negotiating with former enemies." As documented by the Initiative for Inclusive Security, in numerous settings, women have joined forces across party lines to shape peace agreements, sponsor legislation, and influence the drafting of constitutions.

They also come to the table with a different perspective on conflict resolution. Women are more likely to adopt a broad definition of security that includes key social and economic issues that would otherwise be ignored, such as safe food and clean water and protection from gender-based violence. This sentiment was expressed to me by South Korea's Song Young Sun, the National Assembly's military watchdog. Most of the men she serves with define security as protecting South Korea's territory against North Korea, she said; she believes that security considerations should also include "everything from economics to culture, environment, health, and food."

A MAN'S WORLD

If having women wield political power is so beneficial, why are there not more female leaders? A fundamental reason is that women themselves are not eager or willing to stand for political office. Women view politics as a dirty game, and their loftier standards may keep them away from the grit and grind of it. More than 200 public officials and NGO leaders throughout Kyrgyzstan responded to a 2004 United Nations Development Program poll by saying women would bring transparency, "a strong sense of responsibility," and "fair attitudes" to politics. But Nurgul Djanaeva, who heads a coalition of 88 Kyrgyz women's groups, bemoaned the situation: "The only way for me to feed my family, while working in government, is to be corrupt, so I'd rather work for an NGO and have a living wage."

It does not help that politics has traditionally been a man's world, and that many men—and some women—want to keep it that way. A woman may be considered "too soft" for political leadership—or "unfeminine" if she runs. Often, however, it is women themselves who doubt their own leadership abilities. According to the 2000 World Values Survey, women comprised 21 percent of respondents in Chile and 45 percent of respondents in Mexico who agreed strongly with the statement that men make better political leaders than women do. This distinct lack of self-assurance persists across cultures. According to research by the political scientists Richard Lawless and Jennifer Fox, authors of *It Takes a Candidate: Why Women Don't Run for Office*, American women were twice as likely as men to describe themselves as "not at all qualified to run for office," even when their credentials were equivalent. Only 25 percent of the women saw themselves as likely or very likely winners, compared with 37 percent of the men.

The traditional role society expects women to play does not spur them on to political leadership either. Reconciling political life with family commitments was the primary concern of the female politicians surveyed in 2000 by the

Inter-Parliamentary Union. Women usually believe that their obligations to family members—including parents and in-laws—as the primary caregiver are incompatible with holding public office. Rebeca Grynspan, former vice president of Costa Rica, voices the dilemma: "Society doesn't provide conditions under which we can do our jobs with tranquility and leave our children home with peace of mind, even if we can count on stable, supportive partners." The pressures for women to stay home and tend to their families are compounded by conservative religious doctrines. A fundamentalist interpretation of Islam threatens women's nascent political hopes in countries such as Kuwait, where women gained the right to vote and run for office in the 2006 elections but did not win any parliamentary seats. Similarly, Afghanistan and Iraq, where new constitutions reserve a quarter of parliamentary seats for women, are in danger of backsliding into a collision with resurgent extremism. In the West, the Catholic Church in such countries as Croatia urges women to focus on family rather than public life. Likewise, most women in U.S. politics find their views incompatible with the religious right: in 2004, only two of the 14 female senators, compared with 48 of the 86 male senators, voted consistently with the Christian Coalition.

Even when women want to run for political office, they encounter roadblocks. In most countries, male political party gatekeepers determine candidate lists, and the ordering of candidates on the lists is a fundamental factor in determining who goes to parliament. It takes more than affirmative-action measures, such as quotas or reserved seats, to ensure women's places on those lists; it takes parties' will. According to the Harvard political scientist Pippa Norris, who analyzed the 1997 British elections, the Labour Party showed rare resolve in setting aside for women half of the seats from which members of parliament were retiring and half of those considered "most winnable." That move doubled the total percentage of women in parliament from 9.2 to 18.2 percent of all seats. More typical, however, is the complaint of a Bosnian politician who told me wryly that her place on her party's candidate list dropped precipitously, thanks to backroom hacks and men muscling their way to the top.

Money constitutes another barrier for women. Coming up with fees to file as a candidate or run a campaign can be daunting. Few countries have emulated the creation of organizations such as EMILY's List ("EMILY" stands for "Early Money Is Like Yeast"), which raises contributions across the United States for Democratic pro-choice women.

The financial squeeze can be further compounded by the threat of physical harm. According to Phoebe Asiyo, a prominent Kenyan member of parliament for more than a quarter century, the greatest expense for women running for parliament in Kenya is around-the-clock security, which is necessary because of the danger of rape, a common intimidation tactic. Mary Okumu, a Stanford-educated Kenyan public health expert, was beaten up when she stood for election in 2002. Okumu says that she and other candidates routinely carried concealed knives and wore two sets of tights under their dresses in order to buy more time to scream during an attempted rape. Male opponents were also at risk of physical attack, but Okumu says that "for women political aspirants the violence also includes foul verbal abuse, beatings, abduction, and death threats."

Given prevailing social norms and the numerous barriers to entry to the political arena, as well as women's own perception of politics as a dirty game, it is unsurprising that many women turn away from elected office, believing that they have a better chance of achieving results in the NGO realm. In 1991, as a child, Ala Noori Talabani fled on foot from Saddam Hussein's army. Fourteen years later, she was elected to the interim Iraqi National Assembly. She seemed a model legislator—a well-educated, articulate former diplomat equally comfortable among villagers in Kirkuk, politicians in Baghdad, and policy analysts in Washington. Yet in 2006, she left politics in frustration to work with an NGO so that she could focus on the problems she cares about most: honor killings, domestic violence, and rape.

WHAT IS TO BE DONE?

The forces excluding women from political leadership are so strong that only a serious and comprehensive effort can bring about change. Fortunately, governments, foreign-aid organizations, think tanks, and academic institutions can stimulate both the supply of and the demand for women in the political arena.

At the most basic level, national governments should implement "family-friendly" policies, including straightforward measures such as easier access to daycare, flexible office hours, and limits to evening meetings. But in some countries, to be effective, policies will have to be designed according to more progressive interpretations of religious doctrine regarding gender roles. In 2004, Moroccan King Muhammad VI personally backed a new version of family law that was compatible with sharia and that gave women equal rights. His support of gender-sensitive legislation also increased women's political representation (from two in 2001 to 35 in 2002 of the 325 seats in parliament's lower house) and made Morocco one of the most socially progressive countries in the Muslim world. In May 2006, thanks to another of the king's initiatives, the first class of 50 female

imams graduated from an academy in Rabat. They are expected to do everything male imams do except lead Friday prayers in a mosque.

NGOs and governments have an important role to play in equipping women with the confidence and skills necessary to run for office. Grass-roots programs could help recruit and train women across the political spectrum. The Cambodian organization Women for Prosperity, for instance, has prepared more than 5,500 female candidates for elections in Cambodia. Embassies abroad could encourage established female officials to mentor new candidates, learning from the Forum of Rwandan Women Parliamentarians. In 2006, Rwanda's female parliamentarians returned to their districts to rally women to run for local office, increasing the proportion of female mayors and deputy mayors in the country from 24 to 44 percent in one election. Outsiders ought to boost the profile of Liberia's Johnson-Sirleaf, the only elected African female head of state, who recently urged female officeholders, "Don't stop with parliament. Join me. I'm lonely." The Initiative for Inclusive Security, which has brokered relationships between hundreds of female leaders in conflict regions and thousands of policymakers, is a creative and strong model of an external player working to encourage women's political participation. And governments should look to replicate innovative political party reforms that ensure gender equality, such as those promoted by Michal Yudin's group in Israel—WE (Women's Electoral) Power—which has pressured Knesset members to increase funding for parties that exceed the quota for women's participation.

Supporting transparent and equitable campaign-finance rules would also help women in the political arena. Women told me that when they have to choose between their children's school fees and their own campaign, their children win. Government campaign subsidies spread across political parties help level the field. Governments should go further by rewarding parties that boost the representation of women on their candidate lists and penalizing those that do not.

Female politicians also need to be protected. In Afghanistan, where women running for parliament in 2005 were attacked, local and international organizations asked governors, chiefs of police, tribal elders, and other community leaders to provide security details. At least one candidate who reported threats had police protection 24 hours a day. Security measures reassured women that state and community leaders backed their right to engage in politics.

Finally, and most important, governments ought to support quotas for women at all levels of government. In systems with proportional representation, "zippering," requiring that a woman be in every second or third slot on a ballot, has helped raise women's numbers; still, women rarely appear in the top two ballot slots. Although quotas may initially result in female members of parliament being taken less seriously, the upside far outweighs the downside, since quotas propel women into politics. Sixteen of the 19 countries—including Cuba, Iceland, South Africa, Spain, and Sweden—that have parliaments in which at least 30 percent of the members are women have implemented either legislative or party quotas.

LESS SWAGGER, MORE SWAY

Women's community-based wisdom, fresh ideas, and commitment to the social good may be the best news in domestic policy today. They have much to contribute to decisions regarding the environment, security, health care, finance, and education. In foreign policy as well, the world could use more sway and less swagger.

A critical mass of female leaders will change norms; that may be why President Bachelet appointed ten women alongside the ten men in her cabinet. Of course, there are exceptions, but generally speaking, stereotypical "feminine" qualities (such as the tendency to nurture, compromise, and collaborate) have been confirmed by social science research. The world needs those traits. With so many intractable conflicts, conventional strategies—economic sanctions, boycotts, or military intervention—have clearly proved inadequate. Women's voices would provide a call from arms.

None of these benefits to domestic and foreign policy, however, will be realized if just a few women reach positions of leadership. The few women who now make it to the top of a predominantly male hierarchy, and who do not come out of a women's movement, usually have attributes more similar to those of most men. Indira Gandhi, Margaret Thatcher, and Golda Meir had more "masculine" qualities than many of the men they bested, and they pushed little of the social agenda commonly of interest to women in politics. General wisdom about critical mass would predict that approximately 30 percent of officeholders have to be female for a significant effect to be felt on policy. As Anita Gradin remarked to me about her experience as a member of Sweden's parliament, the same group of women who were once in a small minority in the legislature talked, acted, and voted differently when their proportion increased significantly.

The more women shift from civil society into government, the more political culture will change for the better, and the more other women will follow. Advocates of women's leadership need to stop their handwringing over whether gender differences exist and appreciate the advantages women have over men's brawny style of governance, whether because of biology, social roles, or a cascading combination of the two. In the meantime, however, they will have to put up with some paternalistic responses, such as the one I received from a colonel at the Pentagon shortly after the United States' "shock and awe" attack on Iraq in 2003. When I urged him to broaden his search for the future leaders of Iraq, which had yielded hundreds of men and only seven women, he responded, "Ambassador Hunt, we'll address women's issues after we get the place secure." I wondered what "women's issues" he meant. I was talking about security.